This book encourages pupils to:
    use a wide range of mathematics
    discuss mathematical ideas
    undertake investigation
    participate in practical activities
    use reference material
    relate mathematics to everyday life
    select appropriate methods for a task
    analyse and communicate information
    discuss difficulties
    ask questions

KU-592-629

It is hoped that the pupil who uses this book will:
    develop a real interest in mathematics
    become well motivated
    gain much enjoyment from mathematics
    develop a fascination with mathematics
    develop an ability to use mathematics in other subjects
    become confident in the use of the calculator and computer
    gain a firm foundation for further study
    become proficient at applying mathematics to everyday life
    develop both independent and co-operative work habits
    become aware of the power and purpose of mathematics
    develop an ability to communicate mathematics
    develop an appreciation of the relevance of mathematics
    develop an ability to think precisely, logically and creatively
    become confident at mathematics
    gain a sense of satisfaction

Calculator keying sequences are for the Casio *fx–82LB*. Some slight variation may be needed for other models and makes.

The version of LOGO used is LOGOTRON—standard LOGO for the BBC. The version of BASIC used is BBC BASIC.

K.M. Vickers
1996

Acknowledgements

The author wishes to thank all those firms and enterprises who have so kindly given permission to reproduce tables and other material. A special thanks to S.M. Bennett, S.P.R. Coxon, J.A. Ogilvie and S. Napier for their valuable contributions; to F. Tunnicliffe for the illustrations and J. McClelland for the photographs. The author is grateful to the Examination Boards for allowing questions from past GCSE papers to be included.

The following examination boards have kindly granted permission for questions to be included: Edexcel Foundation, London Examinations; the Welsh Joint Education Committee; the Northern Examinations and Assessment Board; the Southern Examining Group; the Midland Examining Group; the Northern Ireland Council for the Curriculum Examinations and Assessment.

Every effort has been made to trace all the copyright holders. If any have been inadvertently overlooked the publishers will be pleased to make the necessary arrangement at the first opportunity.

Contents

NEW National Curriculum Mathematics

8

K. M. Vickers
M. J. Tipler
H. L. van Hiele

First published in 1993 by Canterbury Educational Ltd
Revised edition published in 1996 by:
Stanley Thornes (Publishers) Ltd
Ellenborough House, Wellington Street
CHELTENHAM Glos. GL50 1YW
England

99 00 01 02 / 10 9 8 7 6 5 4

A catalogue record for this book is available from the British Library

ISBN 0 7487 2793 0
ISBN 0 7487 2792 2 (with answers)

Printed and bound in Italy by STIGE, Turin

PREFACE

New National Curriculum Mathematics by K.M. Vickers and M.J. Tipler is a complete mathematics course, carefully designed and now updated to ensure full coverage of the revised 1995 National Curriculum.

This book completes the Intermediate Tier GCSE and covers all the material in Level 8 of the National Curriculum.

Throughout the book there is a variety of activities: skill developing exercises, investigations, practical work, problem solving activities, discussion exercises, puzzles and games. All the activities are related to the topic being studied. Whenever possible, activities and exercises have been written as open rather than closed tasks.

There is a good balance between tasks which develop knowledge, skills and understanding, and those which develop the ability to tackle and solve problems. Many activities do both. There is a thorough and careful development of each topic. Questions within each exercise or activity are carefully graded to build pupil confidence.

Throughout each topic, relevance to everyday life is emphasised. The acquisition of knowledge and skills is integrated with their use and application.

Each section begins with revision, printed on pink paper for ease of identification. Each section ends with a review chapter which contains revision questions on the material developed in this book. In each of the other chapters, every skill developing exercise finishes with review questions and there is a review at the end of these chapters.

Many questions from GCSE examinations are included: in the Revision Sections, in the Reviews at the end of each chapter and in the four Review Chapters.

This book does not replace the teacher. Rather, it is a resource for both the pupil and teacher. The teacher can be flexible about what is taught and when.

This book takes into consideration:
    pupil's needs
    pupil's interests
    pupil's experiences
    the need for pupils to explore mathematics
    the use of technology
    both independent and co-operative work habits

ALGEBRA

SHAPE, SPACE AND MEASURES

HANDLING DATA

Level Descriptions for Level 8

Attainment Target 1: Using and Applying Mathematics

■ Level 8

Pupils develop and follow alternative approaches. They reflect on their own lines of enquiry when exploring mathematical tasks; in doing so they introduce and use a range of mathematical techniques. Pupils convey mathematical meaning through consistent use of symbols. They examine generalisations or solutions reached in an activity, commenting constructively on the reasoning and logic employed, and make further progress in the activity as a result.

Attainment Target 2: Number and Algebra

■ Level 8

Pupils solve problems involving calculating with powers, roots and numbers expressed in standard form, checking for correct order of magnitude. They choose to use fractions or percentages to solve problems involving repeated proportional changes or the calculation of the original quantity given the result of a proportional change. They evaluate algebraic formulae, substituting fractions, decimals and negative numbers. They calculate one variable, given the others, in formulae such as $V = \pi r^2 h$. Pupils manipulate algebraic formulae, equations and expressions, finding common factors and multiplying two linear expressions. They solve inequalities in two variables. Pupils sketch and interpret graphs of linear, quadratic, cubic and reciprocal functions, and graphs that model real situations.

Attainment Target 3: Shape, Space and Measures

■ Level 8

Pupils understand and use mathematical similarity. They use sine, cosine and tangent in right-angled triangles when solving problems in two dimensions. They distinguish between formulae for perimeter, area and volume, by considering dimensions.

Attainment Target 4: Handling Data

■ Level 8

Pupils interpret and construct cumulative frequency tables and diagrams, using the upper boundary of the class interval. They estimate the median and interquartile range and use these to compare distributions and make inferences. They understand when to apply the methods for calculating the probability of a compound event, given the probabilities of either independent events or mutually exclusive events; they use these methods appropriately in solving problems.

NUMBER

Number Revision

ORDER of OPERATIONS

Calculation without the Calculator

If an expression such as $14 - 2(5 + 1)$ is worked out without the calculator we must
  work out the brackets first
  then do $\times$ and $\div$
  finally do $+$ and $-$
For instance,
$$14 - 2(5 + 1) = 14 - 2 \times 6$$
$$= 14 - 12$$
$$= 2$$

The word "of", used in calculation, means "multiply".
For instance, $\frac{5}{6}$ of 42 means $\frac{5}{6} \times 42$. That is, $\frac{5}{6}$ of $42 = 35$.

A fraction line acts as a bracket.
For instance, $\dfrac{3 + 4 \times 2}{7 + 3}$ means $(3 + 4 \times 2) \div (7 + 3)$.

Calculation with the Calculator

The scientific calculator does operations in the correct order. An expression such as
$14 - 2(5 + 1)$ is keyed in as $\boxed{14}\ \boxed{-}\ \boxed{2}\ \boxed{\times}\ \boxed{(}\ \boxed{5}\ \boxed{+}\ \boxed{1}\ \boxed{)}\ \boxed{=}$ to get the
correct answer of 2. (Some calculators do not need the $\times$ pressed before the $($ sign.

We sometimes need to **insert brackets** or **use the memory.**
For instance, $\dfrac{29 + 6}{4 + 3}$ can be worked out in one of the following ways.

  Either **Key** $\boxed{(}\ \boxed{29}\ \boxed{+}\ \boxed{6}\ \boxed{)}\ \boxed{\div}\ \boxed{(}\ \boxed{4}\ \boxed{+}\ \boxed{3}\ \boxed{)}\ \boxed{=}$
  or **Key** $\boxed{29}\ \boxed{+}\ \boxed{6}\ \boxed{=}\ \boxed{\text{Min}}\ \boxed{4}\ \boxed{+}\ \boxed{3}\ \boxed{=}\ \boxed{\text{SHIFT}}\ \boxed{\text{X}\leftarrow\!\rightarrow\!\text{M}}\ \boxed{\div}\ \boxed{\text{MR}}\ \boxed{=}$

PLACE VALUE

Place value is given by the following.

100000	10000	1000	100	10	1	•	$\frac{1}{10}$	$\frac{1}{100}$	$\frac{1}{1000}$

For instance, the number 4809·203 consists of four thousands
                    eight hundreds
                    nine ones (or units)
                    two tenths
           and   three thousandths

continued . . .

Place value may be used to multiply and divide numbers by 10, 100, 1000 etc.
For instance, $24 \times 1000 = 24000$, $2·4 \div 100 = 0·024$.
For instance to multiply 23×90, first multiply 23 by 10 to get 230,
then multiply 230×9 to get 2070.

LONG MULTIPLICATION and DIVISION

One method for long multiplication and one for long division is shown.
There are several others.

895×41

	800	90	5
40	32000	3600	200
1	800	90	5

$$895 \times 41 = 32000 + 3600 + 200$$
$$+ 800 + 90 + 5$$
$$= 36695$$

$895 \div 41$

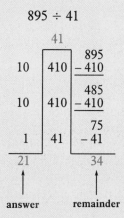

answer ← 21   remainder ← 34

INDEX NOTATION

3^4 is read as "three to the power of four" and means $3 \times 3 \times 3 \times 3$.

The square numbers are 1^2, 2^2, 3^2, 4^2,... That is 1, 4, 9, 16,...
The cube numbers are 1^3, 2^3, 3^3, 4^3,... That is 1, 8, 27, 64,...
The answer to "what number squared gives 9" is 3. 3 is called the square root of 9.
This is written as $\sqrt{9} = 3$.
The answer to "what number cubed gives 8" is 2. 2 is called the cube root of 8. This is
written as $\sqrt[3]{8} = 2$.

On a calculator 26^2 is keyed as $\boxed{26}$ $\boxed{\text{SHIFT}}$ $\boxed{x^2}$

$\sqrt{169}$ is keyed as $\boxed{169}$ $\boxed{\sqrt{}}$

$\sqrt[3]{216}$ is keyed as $\boxed{216}$ $\boxed{\text{SHIFT}}$ $\boxed{\sqrt[3]{}}$

Written as a product of prime numbers 24 is $2 \times 2 \times 2 \times 3$. That is, in index notation
$24 = 3 \times 2^3$.

INVERSE OPERATIONS

Inverse operations "undo" each other. Some inverse operations are adding and
subtracting, multiplying and dividing, squaring and finding a square root, cubing and
finding a cube root.

continued . . .

. . . from previous page

APPROXIMATION and ESTIMATION

To approximate (round) to d.p. (decimal places), decide how many figures are wanted after the decimal point. Omit all the following figures with the proviso that, if the first figure omitted is 5 or larger, increase the last figure kept by 1.
For instance, 34·548 rounded to 1 d.p. is 34·5; 34·548 rounded to 2 d.p. is 34·55.

To approximate to s.f. (significant figures), count from the first non-zero figure.
Zeros may need to be inserted so the size of the number is unchanged.
For instance, 34·548 rounded to 3 s.f. is 34·5, 345·48 rounded to 1 s.f. is 300; 0·03458 rounded to 2 s.f. is 0·035.

Finding a rough answer to a calculation is called estimating an answer. To estimate an answer proceed as follows.

Step 1　Round each number in the calculation to one (or perhaps two) significant figures.

Step 2　Use these rounded figures in the calculation to get an estimate of the answer.
For instance, an estimate of the answer to 212×48 is $200 \times 50 = 10000$.

Always estimate the answer when using the calculator for a calculation.

NUMBER LINES. NEGATIVE NUMBERS

< means "is less than"　　> means "is greater than".
On a number line, the smaller a number the further to the left it is placed.
For instance, since $2·1 < 2·8$, $2·1$ is to the left of $2·8$ on a number line;
since $\frac{4}{5} > \frac{2}{5}$, $\frac{4}{5}$ is to the right of $\frac{2}{5}$ on a number line.

The ⌞⁺⁄₋⌝ key on the calculator is pressed to display a negative number.
Positive numbers, such as +2, may be written without any sign.
Negative numbers, such as –2, are always written with the negative sign.
The negative numbers are shown on a number line, or scale, as numbers that are less than zero.

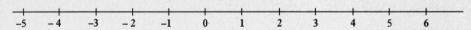

The integers include both the negative and positive whole numbers and also zero.
Zero is neither positive nor negative.

continued . . .

. . . from previous page

Negative numbers can be added or subtracted on a number line.
Negative numbers can be multiplied or divided as follows.
  Step 1   Multiply or divide the numbers, disregarding the signs.
  Step 2   Work out the sign for the answer using:
              two like signs (both $+$ or both $-$) gives a positive answer
              two unlike signs (one $+$, the other $-$) gives a negative answer.

DECIMALS

A decimal such as $0.166666\ldots$, in which the digit 6 repeats, is called a recurring decimal; it is written as $0.1\dot{6}$. Recurring decimals are sometimes called repeating decimals.

Multiplying a given number by a number greater than 1 will increase the given number. Multiplying by a number smaller than 1 will decrease the given number. For instance, 12.8×2.4 has an answer larger than 12.8; 12.8×0.4 has an answer smaller than 12.8.

Dividing a given number by a number larger than 1 will decrease the given number. Dividing by a number smaller than 1 will increase the given number. For instance, $12.8 \div 2.4$ has an answer smaller than 12.8; $12.8 \div 0.4$ has an answer larger than 12.8.

One method for multiplying decimals and one for dividing decimals is shown below.

74·6 × 0·28
$$
\begin{array}{r}
746 \\
\times\ \ 28 \\
\hline
5968 \\
1492\ \ \\
\hline
20888 \\
\hline
\end{array}
$$
So $74.6 \times 0.28 = 20.888$

74·6 ÷ 0·28
$$\frac{74.6}{0.28} = \frac{74.6}{0.28} \times \frac{100}{100}$$
$$= \frac{7460}{28}$$

$$
\begin{array}{r}
266.42 \\
28\overline{)7460.00\ldots} \\
\underline{56} \\
186 \\
\underline{168} \\
180 \\
\underline{168} \\
120 \\
\underline{112} \\
80 \\
\underline{56} \\
24
\end{array}
$$

So $74.6 \div 0.28 = 266.4$ to 1 d.p.

continued . . .

. . . *from previous page*

FRACTIONS and RATIO

In the fraction $\frac{4}{9}$, 4 is called the **numerator**; 9 is called the **denominator**.

The numerator is the number on top; the denominator is the number on the bottom.

$\frac{4}{9}$ is read as "four-ninths" and means 4 divided by 9. It also means 4 parts out of every 9.

$\frac{4}{9}$ may also be written as the **ratio** 4 : 9.

The ratio of two quantities x and y is written as x : y and is read as "the ratio of x to y".
A ratio compares quantities of the same kind.
For instance, if A = 3cm and B = 7mm then the ratio A : B is 3cm : 7mm which is 30mm : 7mm or simply 30 : 7.

Equivalent fractions (equal fractions) may be formed by multiplying (or dividing) both the numerator and denominator by the same number.

For instance, since $\frac{16}{24} = \frac{32}{48}$ (multiplying top and bottom by 2)

and $\frac{16}{24} = \frac{2}{3}$ (dividing top and bottom by 8)

then $\frac{2}{3}, \frac{16}{24}, \frac{32}{48}$ are equivalent fractions.

Equivalent ratios (equal ratios) may be formed by multiplying (or dividing) both parts of a ratio by the same number.
For instance, the ratios 2 : 3, 16 : 24 and 32 : 48 are equivalent ratios.

A fraction (or ratio) is written as the **simplest fraction** (or **simplest ratio**) if the numbers in the fraction (or ratio) are the smallest possible whole numbers. A fraction written in its simplest form is said to be written in its **lowest terms**.

For instance, since $\frac{16}{24} = \frac{2}{3}$ we say that, in its lowest terms the fraction $\frac{16}{24}$ is $\frac{2}{3}$.
For instance, since 1·2 : 3 = 12 : 30 = 2 : 5, we say that 1·2 : 3 written as the simplest ratio is 2 : 5.

All decimals may be written as fractions.
It is useful to remember the following: $0·1 = \frac{1}{10}$, $0·2 = \frac{1}{5}$, $0·3 = \frac{3}{10}$, $0·4 = \frac{2}{5}$, $0·5 = \frac{1}{2}$, $0·6 = \frac{3}{5}$, $0·7 = \frac{7}{10}$, $0·8 = \frac{4}{5}$, $0·9 = \frac{9}{10}$, $0·25 = \frac{1}{4}$, $0·75 = \frac{3}{4}$.

continued . . .

. . . from previous page

To **increase** (or decrease) a quantity **by a given fraction** firstly work out the actual increase (or decrease).

For instance, to decrease 720cm by $\frac{1}{3}$ proceed as follows:

Step 1 $\frac{1}{3}$ of 720cm = 240cm

Step 2 Decrease 720cm by 240cm to get the answer of 480cm.

To **increase** (or decrease) a quantity **in a given ratio** firstly rewrite the ratio as a fraction.
For instance, to increase 100g in the ratio 5 : 4 proceed as follows:

Step 1 Rewrite 5 : 4 as $\frac{5}{4}$.

Step 2 Find $\frac{5}{4} \times$ 100g = 125g.

To **share in a given ratio** proceed as shown in the following example.

Example To share £600 between two people in the ratio 2 : 3 take the following steps:

Step 1 For every £2 that the first person gets, the second person gets £3.
That is, from every £5, the first person gets £2 and the second person gets £3.

Hence the first person gets $\frac{2}{5}$ of the money; the second person gets $\frac{3}{5}$.

Step 2 $\frac{2}{5}$ of £600 = £240; $\frac{3}{5}$ of £600 = £360.
Hence one person gets £240 and the other gets £360.

PERCENTAGES

7% means 7 parts in every 100. That is, 7% means $\frac{7}{100}$.
Any percentage, decimal, fraction or ratio may be written in one of the other forms.

For instance, 7% may be rewritten as $\frac{7}{100}$ or 0·07 or 7 : 100.

For instance, $\frac{2}{5}$ may be rewritten as 0·4 or 40% or 2 : 5.

For instance, 0·61 may be rewritten as $\frac{61}{100}$ or 61% or 61 : 100.

For instance, 3 : 4 may be rewritten as $\frac{3}{4}$ or 0·75 or 75%.

In **percentage calculations** we usually rewrite the percentage as either a fraction or a decimal.

For instance, to find 15% of £5 we may begin with $\frac{15}{100} \times$ £5 or 0·15 × £5 to get answer of 75p.

continued . . .

. . . from previous page

For instance, to increase 860cm by 4% we can work out 4% of 860cm and add this to 860cm.

We can also increase 860cm by 4% as follows:

Increase = 4%   New length = 104% of 860
$$= 1 \cdot 04 \times 860$$
$$= 894 \cdot 4 \text{cm}$$

If we were decreasing 860cm by 4% we would have, New length = 96% of 860cm.

To **find a given quantity as a percentage of another quantity** proceed as follows:

Step 1   Write the given quantity as a fraction of the other quantity.

Step 2   Rewrite this fraction as a percentage.

For instance, to find £5 as a percentage of £8

we say £5 as a fraction of £8 is $\frac{5}{8}$ = $\frac{5}{8} \times 100\%$
$$= 62 \cdot 5\%$$

To find a **percentage increase (or decrease)** we compare the actual increase with the initial value.

$$\% \textbf{Increase} = \frac{\textbf{Actual Increase}}{\textbf{Initial Value}} \times \textbf{100\%}$$

$$\% \textbf{Decrease} = \frac{\textbf{Actual Decrease}}{\textbf{Initial Value}} \times \textbf{100\%}$$

For instance, to find the percentage decrease in a school roll which fell from 923 to 902, the calculation is:

% decrease $= \frac{21}{923} \times 100\%$
$$= 2 \cdot 3\% \text{ to 1 d.p.}$$

PROBLEM SOLVING

Four methods of problem solving are: making a list
  trial and improvement
  finding a pattern
  solving a simpler problem first

The **"trial and improvement"** method of finding an answer to a problem consists of the following steps:

Step 1   Guess a likely answer.

Step 2   Check to see if this answer fits the given facts (the trial).

Step 3   Make a better guess (the improvement).

Repeat from Step 2 until the actual answer is found.

REVISION EXERCISE

1. How much larger is the 9 than the 5 in (a) 6925 (b) 19·035?

2. Without doing any calculation, state which of these will have an answer greater than 269·7.

   (a) 269·7 × 0·34 (b) 269·7 ÷ 0·34 (c) 269·7 × 3·4 (d) 269·7 ÷ 3·4

3. Write the following as the simplest possible fraction.

   (a) $\frac{4}{50}$ (b) 0·24 (c) 5 : 30 (d) 30% (e) 0·007

4. (a) Estimate the answers to 437 × 82 and 416 ÷ 52.

   (b) Without using the calculator find the answers to 437 × 82 and 416 ÷ 52.

5.

   At both of these shops a CD usually costs £8·80.
   Shadia buys a CD in the sale at the Stereo Market. Lucy buys a CD in the sale at the Audio Discount Store.
   Who pays more, Shadia or Lucy? How much more?

6. Without using the calculator find

   (a) 11 + 3 × 7 (b) 27 − 2 (4 + 3) (c) 4 + (−6) (d) − 4 − (− 6)

   (e) 7^2 (f) 600 × 0·3 (g) $\frac{600}{0·3}$ (h) $\frac{5}{6}$ of 54

   (i) 0·64 × 0·2 (j) $\frac{0·64}{0·2}$ (k) −5 × (−2) (l) $\frac{-4 \times (-3)}{-2}$

7. (a) Write 24 and 45 as a product of prime numbers.

   (b) Hence find the smallest number that both 24 and 45 divide into.

   (c) Write 60 as a product of prime numbers.

   (d) Use your answer to (c) to find the smallest whole number 60 must be multiplied by to get a square number.

8. Before Paul got a 5% increase his salary was £12000. What was Paul's salary after the increase?

9. Elizabeth made a scale drawing of the floor plan of one of the school buildings. She used the scale 1 : 50.

    (a) On the drawing, one of the rooms was 160mm long. What was the actual length of this room?

    (b) The building was 12 metres wide. What was the width of the building on the drawing?

10. What is wrong with each of the following calculator keying sequences?

    (a) $\dfrac{18+24}{6}$ keyed as $\boxed{18}\ \boxed{+}\ \boxed{24}\ \boxed{\div}\ \boxed{6}\ \boxed{=}$

    (b) $\dfrac{13+3(4+7)}{15+8}$ keyed as

    $\boxed{(}\ \boxed{13}\ \boxed{+}\ \boxed{3}\ \boxed{\times}\ \boxed{(}\ \boxed{4}\ \boxed{+}\ \boxed{7}\ \boxed{)}\ \boxed{\div}\ \boxed{(}\ \boxed{15}\ \boxed{+}\ \boxed{8}\ \boxed{)}\ \boxed{=}$

    (c) $\dfrac{19+25}{15-4}$ keyed as $\boxed{19}\ \boxed{+}\ \boxed{25}\ \boxed{=}\ \boxed{\text{Min}}\ \boxed{15}\ \boxed{-}\ \boxed{4}\ \boxed{=}\ \boxed{\text{SHIFT}}\ \boxed{\text{X}\longleftrightarrow\text{M}}\ \boxed{\div}\ \boxed{\text{Min}}\ \boxed{=}$

11. A cycle manufacturer makes tricycles and bicycles. Last week, 101 wheels were used to make a total of 44 cycles (both tricycles and bicycles). Use "trial and improvement" to find the number of tricycles and the number of bicycles made by this manufacturer last week.

12. I am an integer.
    I am between –6 and –3.
    I am less than – 4
       Which integer am I?

13. $S = \frac{59}{2}\,[8+(-50)]$ can be used to work out the sum of all of the terms of the sequence 8, 7, 6, . . . –50.

    Find this sum, S.

14. Find the missing numbers.

    (a) 9 is the square root of . . .

    (b) the cube root of 8 is . . .

    (c) 9 is the square of . . .

15.

County	Primary Schools	Primary Pupils	Secondary Schools	Secondary Pupils
Cheshire	473	80037	72	65801
Durham	299	48929	45	36489
Devon	433	69529	73	55116
Gwent	229	39895	34	28359

This table gives the number of primary and secondary schools in four counties and the number of pupils in these schools.

(a) Estimate the total number of primary and secondary schools in these counties. Calculate this number.

(b) Find the average number of pupils in the secondary schools in these counties.

16. The speedometer of a car registers just 6 digits.
At the beginning of January, the reading on this speedometer was 98783·2km. At the end of January the reading was 01249·1km.
How far did this car travel during January?

17.

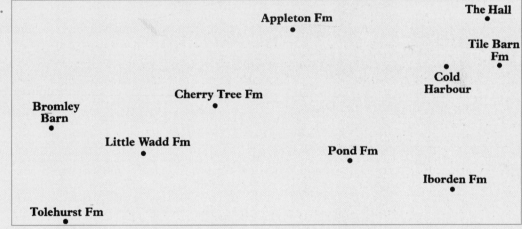

Scale 1 : 50 000

(a) Use the scale given on the map to find the missing numbers.
Map distance of 1mm represents actual distance of ⋯mm = ⋯m.

(b) To the nearest 50m, how far is it from Tolehurst Farm to Bromley Barn?

(c) To the nearest kilometre, how far is it from Appleton Farm to Iborden Farm?

(d) To the nearest kilometre, how far is it from Tile Barn Farm to Cherry Tree Farm?

(e) Shona's farm is approximately 5km from The Hall. What is the name of Shona's farm?

18. Evaluate the following, giving the answer to 1 d.p. when rounding is necessary.

(a) 4^2 (b) $\sqrt{4}$ (c) 4^3 (d) $\sqrt{72}$ (e) $(3{\cdot}17)^3$ (f) $\sqrt[3]{8}$

19.

Quality of popular coastal bathing waters : by Water Authority area
England, Wales and Northern Ireland   Numbers

Water Authority area	1986		1987	
	Number tested	Numbers failing to comply with EEC Bathing Water Directive coliform standards [2]	Number tested	Number failing to comply with EEC Bathing Water Directive coliform standards [2]
Northumbrian	19	10	19	10
Yorkshire	21	3	22	2
Anglian	28	8	28	10
Thames	2	1	2	2
Southern	65	24	65	27
Wessex (South Coast)	27	3	27	1
South West	103	25	109	13
Wessex (Bristol Channel)	11	4	11	5
Welsh	47	24	47	19
North West	30	26	30	20
England & Wales total	353	128	360	109
Northern Ireland	5	2	14	3

2 Failure to meet standards does not necessarily imply a danger to health.
Source: Water Authorities and Department of Environment (N)

Source: Key Data 1989/90   *From: Social Trends 1989, Table 9.20*

Where rounding is necessary give the answers to 1 decimal place.

(a) What total number of waters were tested in England, Wales and Northern Ireland in 1987?

(b) What percentage of waters tested in 1987 were in the South West area?

(c) What percentage of waters tested in the Southern area in 1987 failed to comply with the EEC Bathing Water Directive?

(d) How many more waters were tested in 1987 than in 1986?
What percentage increase was this?

(e) In the 10 areas in England and Wales, what was the average number of waters tested in 1986?

20. Write these ratios in their simplest form.

(a) £2 : 90p   (b) 1·6m : 480cm   (c) 45sec : 2min

21. (a) How much, in German money, will it cost Amanda to have one of these tape recorders sent to her?

(b) When Amanda bought marks, the exchange rate was
£1 = 2·73 marks.
How much British money does Amanda need to exchange to buy one of these tape recorders?

TAPE RECORDERS
TOP QUALITY
Special Price: 80 marks

Packing & Postage:
15 marks
(worldwide)

22. For a coursework task, Ben gained $\frac{5}{8}$ of the available marks while Natasha gained $\frac{2}{3}$.

    (a) Who got the better mark, Ben or Natasha?

    (b) If a : b gives the ratio of Ben's mark to Natasha's, find possible values for a and b.

23. $0.1\dot{6}$ Write this (a) as a decimal, rounded to 2 decimal places

    (b) as a percentage, rounded to 3 significant figures.

24.

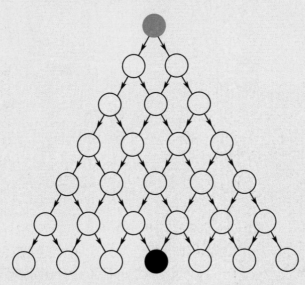

In how many different ways could you walk from the red circle to the black circle if you must always walk in the direction given by the arrows? (Begin with a simpler problem first.)

25. In manufacturing today, the average number of hours worked per week is 43·4. Fifty years ago, this average was 47·8 hours.
    What percentage decrease is this? (Answer to 1 decimal place.)

26. (a) The ratio of British coins to foreign coins in Samantha's coin collection is 2 : 5.
    Samantha has 28 British coins.
    How many foreign coins does she have?

    (b) The ratio of British coins to foreign coins in Bryant's coin collection is also 2 : 5.
    If Bryant has 70 coins, how many are foreign?

27. Use your calculator for the following. Give the answers to three significant figures.

    (a) $\dfrac{13\cdot7 - 8\cdot08}{5\cdot61 + 1\cdot35}$

    (b) $\dfrac{\sqrt{687}}{3(14\cdot7 + 7\cdot24)}$

28.

PRICES PER PERSON in £s Minimum two persons	THREE-NIGHT WEEKEND Friday–Monday		SEVEN-NIGHT HOLIDAY		EXTRA NIGHTS (Add to 7 night stays only)	
	BY CAR-FERRY SHORT SEA-CROSSING	FLY-DRIVE, BY AIR HEATHROW-PARIS	BY CAR-FERRY SHORT SEA-CROSSING	FLY-DRIVE, BY AIR HEATHROW-PARIS	BY CAR-FERRY	FLY-DRIVE
NORMANDY **HOTEL DE DIEPPE,** Rouen. Room & breakfast in twin/double	123	199	239	352	23	36
CHAMPAGNE **ALTEA,** Rheims Room & breakfast in twin/double	132	208	276	289	Fri/Sat/Sun 26 Mon-Thur 30	Fri/Sat/Sun 39 Mon-Thur 43
LOIRE VALLEY **DOMAINE DE SEILLAC,** Onzain HALFBOARD: in Chateaux: in twin/double	189	265	393	506	45	58
in 'Pavillon': each of two	162	238	330	443	36	49
each of three	133	215	278	377	31	40
each of four	120	201	256	348	29	36

HOTEL SUPPLEMENTS, Domaine de Seillac — per person per night.
Jul 6 – Aug 25; in Chateau, twin room £3.00; in 'Pavillon' — each of two £6.00; each of three £4.00; each of four £3.00

FERRY SUPPLEMENT, ON WEEKEND/3 NIGHT HOLIDAYS: £22.00 per car July 13 – Sep 2

SUPPLEMENTS FOR DEPARTURES FROM PROVINCIAL AIRPORTS ON DIRECT AIR FRANCE FLIGHTS TO PARIS:-
GATWICK deduct £23; STANSTED/SOUTHAMPTON deduct £7; BRISTOL add £8; BIRMINGHAM add £10 — Except Jul 14 – Sep 13 deduct £16: MANCHESTER add £24; NEWCASTLE add £2; EDINBURGH/GLASGOW add £44; ABERDEEN add £59; BELFAST add £36

(i) Find the cost of a holiday for 2 people for a three-night weekend

  (a) during April, staying in the Hotel de Dieppe, flying from Heathrow

  (b) during May, staying in the Chateaux, flying from Aberdeen

  (c) at the end of July, staying in the Pavillon, taking a car on the ferry.

(ii) Find the cost of a 12-day holiday for 2 people, beginning on a Thursday, staying at the Altea and flying from Gatwick.

29. (a)

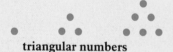

triangular numbers   **square numbers**

1 is both a square number and a triangular number. Find the next number that is both a square number and a triangular number.

(b)

Each of the pentagonal numbers is the sum of a triangular number and a square number. The pentagonal numbers 5 and 12 are shown here. Draw a similar diagram to show that 22 is also a pentagonal number.

(c) There is a relationship between the square numbers and the triangular numbers. Investigate to find this relationship.

30. Mariette's family were refunded the £26·25 VAT paid on photographic equipment they had bought while on holiday in England.

    What price (including $17\frac{1}{2}$% VAT) had they paid for this equipment?

Visitors
Claim back $17\frac{1}{2}$% VAT here.

31.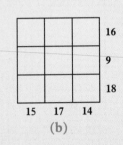

    (a)   (b)

    Is it possible to place numbers in the squares which add across and down to the given numbers? If so, find possible answers. If it is not possible, explain why not.

32. Before a meeting of the Governors of Nayworth School, each Governor had one telephone conversation with every other Governor. Altogether there were 45 telephone conversations. How many Governors did Nayworth School have?

33. $371 = 3^3 + 7^3 + 1^3$ Find another three-digit number that is equal to the sum of the cubes of its digits.

34.

    While on holiday, Edward wrote to 4 friends; Janine, Sarah, Emma and Debbie. His sister then put the letters in envelopes in such a way that not one of the letters was in the correct envelope.
    Janine's letter was put into Sarah's envelope. Debbie's letter was not in Emma's envelope. Whose letter was in Emma's envelope?

35. Fill in the missing numbers.

    (i) 7 __ × 100 = __ 2 __ 0   (ii) __ 0 × 30 = __ 8 0 __   **NEAB**

23

36. Do not use a calculator to answer this question.

(a) A travel company takes a party of people to a hockey match at Wembley.
17 coaches are used.
Each coach has seats for 46 passengers.
There are 12 empty seats altogether.
How many people are in the party?

(Write down all your working to show that you have not used a calculator.)

(b) 998 football supporters use another travel company to go to a football match at Wembley.
Each coach has seats for 53 passengers.

   (i) How many coaches are needed?

   (Write down all your working to show that you have not used a calculator.)

   (ii) How many empty seats are there?   **NEAB**

37. Miss Sondh drove 644 miles on her holiday.
She used 74 litres of petrol.
She wanted to estimate mentally how many miles she could drive on one litre.

(a) Write down suitable approximate values for the distance she drove and the petrol used.

(b) Use these figures to find mentally an estimate of how many miles she drove on one litre.   **MEG**

38. Rhianna measures her pencil and says

It is 13.6 cm long.

She knows that her measurement is correct to 1 decimal place.

Which two of the following lengths could **not** be the actual length of the pencil?

   13·649   13·7   13·61   13·55   13·66   **SEG**

39. Some students are using calculators to work out four questions.

Question 1. $\dfrac{2\cdot34 + 1\cdot76}{3\cdot22 + 1\cdot85}$

Question 2. $\dfrac{2\cdot34 + 1\cdot76}{3\cdot22} + 1\cdot85$

Question 3. $2\cdot34 + \dfrac{1\cdot76}{3\cdot22} + 1\cdot85$

Question 4. $2\cdot34 + \dfrac{1\cdot76}{3\cdot22 + 1\cdot85}$

(a) Tom presses keys as follows.

$$\boxed{2}\;\boxed{\cdot}\;\boxed{3}\;\boxed{4}\;\boxed{+}\;\boxed{1}\;\boxed{\cdot}\;\boxed{7}\;\boxed{6}\;\boxed{\div}\;\boxed{3}\;\boxed{\cdot}\;\boxed{2}\;\boxed{2}\;\boxed{+}\;\boxed{1}\;\boxed{\cdot}\;\boxed{8}\;\boxed{5}\;\boxed{=}$$

For which of the four questions is this the correct method?

(b) Jayne presses keys as follows.

$$\boxed{2}\;\boxed{\cdot}\;\boxed{3}\;\boxed{4}\;\boxed{+}\;\boxed{1}\;\boxed{\cdot}\;\boxed{7}\;\boxed{6}\;\boxed{=}\;\boxed{\div}\;\boxed{3}\;\boxed{\cdot}\;\boxed{2}\;\boxed{2}\;\boxed{+}\;\boxed{1}\;\boxed{\cdot}\;\boxed{8}\;\boxed{5}\;\boxed{=}$$

For which of the four questions is this the correct method?   **SEG**

40. (a) Leza bought a CD-player. She paid £28·00 deposit and 9 monthly payments of £8·40. How much did she pay altogether?

(b) Sandra also bought a CD-player. She paid 21 weekly payments of £5·20 but no deposit. How much more did she pay than Leza?

(c) Leza has 27 discs and Sandra has 21 discs. Write the ratio

   number of Leza's discs : number of Sandra's discs

in its simplest form.   **NICCEA**

41. A personal stereo was priced at £48. In a sale it was reduced to £42.

(a) By what fraction was the original price reduced?

(b) Write your fraction as a percentage.   **ULEAC**

42. The chart shows the percentage of letters that are delivered the day after posting in each of six European countries.

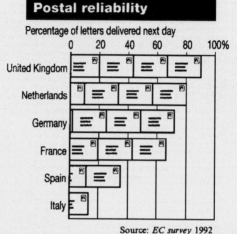

Source: *EC survey* 1992

(a) In Germany, 72% of all letters posted are delivered the next day.
Write 72% as a fraction in its simplest form.

(b) Which country has approximately $\frac{7}{20}$ of its letters delivered the next day?

(c) Forty million letters are posted every day in the United Kingdom.
Nine-tenths of these are delivered the next day.

In your head, calculate $\frac{9}{10}$ of 40 000 000.
Write down your answer.
Explain clearly how you worked out your answer.

NEAB

43. Anthea receives a telephone bill.
The bill shows the cost, in £, for 895 calls at 4·2 pence per call.

(a) What is the cost, in £, for the calls?

The total bill includes a rental charge of £19·54 which is added to the cost of the calls.
VAT at 17·5% is then added to this total.

Anthea writes down the following.

$$\text{Total bill (£)} = \frac{(\text{Cost of calls} + 19 \cdot 54) \times 117 \cdot 5}{100}$$

(b) Calculate Anthea's total bill giving your answer to an appropriate degree of accuracy.

SEG

44. You want to estimate the value of $21 \cdot 2 \times 31 \cdot 2$.
Each number must be written to 1 significant figure.

(a) Write down a suitable calculation which could be used.

(b) State the value of this estimate.

ULEAC

45. Day time temperatures in the desert can reach 35°C.

During the night temperatures may drop by 40°C.

Use these figures to find the temperature at night in the desert. **MEG**

46. The diagram below shows part of Durer's magic square.

When the magic square is complete, each of the numbers 1, 2, 3, ... 16, is placed in one of the sixteen small squares. Nine small squares have been filled in already.

The four numbers in each row of the completed square add up to 34.

The four numbers in each column add up to 34.

16			13
5	10		8
	6		
4	15		1

(a) Use this information to copy and complete the magic square.

(b) From your completed square, describe four groups of four numbers, other than rows and columns, which add up to 34. **MEG**

47. Janet invests £50 in a building society for one year.
The interest rate is 6% per year.

(a) How much interest, in pounds, does Janet get?

Nisha invests £60 in a different building society. She gets £3 interest after one year.

(b) Work out the percentage interest rate that Nisha gets. **ULEAC**

48.
$$\frac{10 \cdot 21 + 29 \cdot 75}{0 \cdot 2 \times 45}$$

(a) (i) Write down the sequence of keys you would press on your calculator to find the value of this expression.
(ii) Write down the calculator answer you would get.

(b) Show how you would estimate the answer to (a), without using a calculator. Write down your estimate. **ULEAC**

49. Yoshino is drawing a plan for her new garage.
The actual garage is going to be 5·80 metres long.

(a) How long is this in centimetres?

The measurements on the plan and the measurements on the actual garage are in the ratio 1 : 20.

(b) How long should the garage be on the plan? **MEG**

50. Here are the ingredients for making 18 rock cakes.

> 9 ounces of flour
> 6 ounces of sugar
> 6 ounces of margarine
> 8 ounces of mixed dried fruit
> 2 large eggs

Mark wants to make 12 rock cakes.

(a) **(i)** How much sugar does he need?

   (ii) How much mixed dried fruit does he need?
   Give your answer correct to the nearest ounce.

Mark only has 9 ounces of margarine. He has plenty of all the other ingredients.

(b) What is the greatest number of rock cakes he can make?   ULEAC

51. Jimmy tries to solve this problem using trial and improvement.

$$number \times 3 \cdot 1 = 5 \cdot 6$$

Continue Jimmy's working until you know the number correct to one decimal place.
Write down this number.

try 2·0	2·0 × 3·1 = 6·2	too large
try 1·5	1·5 × 3·1 = 4·65	too small
....	...... × 3·1 = ...	....
....	...... × 3·1 = ...	.... SEG

52.

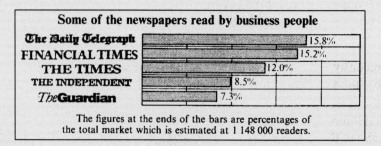

Some of the newspapers read by business people

The Daily Telegraph	15.8%
FINANCIAL TIMES	15.2%
THE TIMES	12.0%
THE INDEPENDENT	8.5%
The Guardian	7.3%

The figures at the ends of the bars are percentages of
the total market which is estimated at 1 148 000 readers.

(a) How many people are estimated to read the Financial Times? Give your answer to the
nearest thousand.

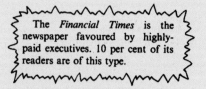

The *Financial Times* is the
newspaper favoured by highly-
paid executives. 10 per cent of its
readers are of this type.

(b) How many highly-paid executives are estimated to read the Financial Times? Give
your answer to the nearest thousand.

28 000 readers of *The Daily Telegraph* are chairmen or managing directors.

(c) What percentage of the Daily Telegraph's readers are chairmen or managing directors?

NICCEA

53. The floor in Fermats store is rectangular.
It measures 25m by 40m.
Draw a plan of the floor using a scale of 1 : 500.

SEG

54. The temperature during an Autumn morning went up from −3°C to 6°C.

(a) By how many degrees did the temperature rise?

During the afternoon the temperature then fell by 8 degrees from 6°C.

(b) What was the temperature at the end of the afternoon?

ULEAC

55. (a) Use your calculator to work out

(i) $\dfrac{59\cdot7}{3\cdot14\times2\cdot8}$

(ii) $\dfrac{57}{9\cdot8+7\cdot3}$

(iii) $\dfrac{1}{3\cdot9}+\dfrac{3\cdot1}{4\cdot3}$

(b) Explain how you could quickly check that your answer to (a) (iii) is of the right order of magnitude.

NEAB

56.

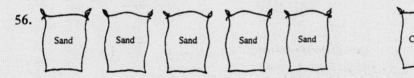

Mortar is made by mixing 5 parts by weight of sand with 1 part by weight of cement.
How much sand is needed to make 8400kg of mortar?

ULEAC

57. The London Police fitted cameras on traffic lights.
This table shows the number of accidents that occured before and after the cameras were fitted.

Type of accident	Number of accidents before cameras	Number of accidents after cameras
Minor	685	532
Serious	914	707
Very serious	146	103

(a) Calculate the total number of accidents which happened **before** the cameras were fitted.
Write this answer to the nearest hundred.

(b) Without using a calculator, estimate the number of accidents that occurred after the cameras had been fitted.
Show how you made your estimate.

(c) A spokesman for the police said:

> *"The total number of accidents
> has been reduced by almost 25%."*

Use the information in the table to decide if you agree with this statement.
Show all your working.
Give a clear reason for your decision.

NEAB

58. A 500ml can of English beer costs £1.

A 333ml bottle of Spanish Beer costs 150 pesetas.

Assume that £1 is about 200 pesetas.

English   Spanish

Which one gives you more beer for your money?
Show clearly how you worked out your answer.

NEAB

59. Three football players score 18, 15 and 12 goals respectively. Their club pays out £6000 in bonus money to these players. They share the bonus in the same ratio as the goals they score. Calculate the share of the bonus for each player.

WJEC

60.

Cost breakdown of an £11.49 compact disc

Record company profit — 23p
Design & packaging — 95p
Manufacture — £1.05
Distribution — £1.12
VAT — £1.50
Artists & other royalties — £1.91
Record company costs — £2.03
Dealer's margin — £2.70

(a) How much is the record company profit on each compact disc?

(b) What is the total of all the *other* parts of the cost breakdown?

(c) Calculate, to the nearest whole number, the record company's profit as a percentage of the total of all the other parts of the cost breakdown.

(d) The cost of manufacture rose by 8% and the cost of distribution rose by 5%.
By what percentage, calculated to 1 decimal place, should the dealer's margin fall to keep the cost of a compact disc at £11·49?   **NICCEA**

61. (a) **Without using a calculator,** write down an estimate of the square root of 40.
Give your estimate correct to one decimal place.

(b) Explain how you obtained your estimate to the square root of 40.

(c) Use a trial and improvement method to find the square root of 40 correct to two decimal places. Show your working clearly.   **NEAB**

62. Two sisters Jane and Sarah usually save £1 each per week. Jane suggests a new savings plan. She will save just 1p next week, 2p the week after, 4p the week after that, double again the next week, and so on.

Sarah continues to save £1 per week.

Investigate Jane's suggestion and compare the total amounts saved by the two sisters over various periods of time.   **WJEC**

Emilie du Châtelet

Emilie du Châtelet was born in Paris in 1706 and died in Lunéville, France in 1749.

Emilie was a mathematician, physicist and philosopher. She did not do any original mathematical work of note. Her important contribution to mathematics was translating and analysing the work of others. Emilie published an explanation of the ideas of the German mathematician, Gottfried Leibniz and of the English mathematician, Sir Isaac Newton.

She is best known for her translation of Sir Isaac Newton's book "Principia Mathematica". Many of Newton's ideas on geometry were not accepted by the French. Some of the changes that Emilie made in her translation made these ideas more easily understood. Many mathematicians believed that Emilie's translation made better sense than Newton's original.

She published works on religion and philosophy as well as on science.

As a young girl, Emilie was clumsy, plump and not at all attractive. Her parents, who were wealthy, gave her an excellent education as they thought it unlikely that she would ever marry. In fact, she grew into a tall, beautiful woman. She was educated firstly by governesses and tutors and then at private girls' schools in Paris. She was a brilliant student, excelling at mathematics, literature and languages. Her education also included music and science.

At the age of nineteen, she married the Marquis du Châtelet. Five years after they were married, Emilie's husband took up a military career. After this, they seldom saw each other.

In 1730 Emilie formed a lasting friendship with Voltaire, the famous French philosopher. She had an influence on his literary works. From 1734 until her death in 1749, Voltaire and Emilie lived at her chateau in the country. At this chateau, which had a well equipped laboratory, they continued their writing and scientific work.

In 1738, the Académie des Sciences offered a prize for an essay on the nature of fire. Both Emilie and Voltaire entered this competition which was won by the Swiss mathematician Leonhard Euler. Emilie's essay was considered to be worthy of publication and was published at the expense of the Académie.

Emilie became well known and students came to study with her. This was unusual in the 18th century when women were not well regarded as educators.

Emilie died at the age of 43, a few days after giving birth to her third child.

Based on an article from the book "Women Sum It Up" – Hazard Press

INTRODUCTION

INVESTIGATION 1:1

TOURNAMENT DRAWS

1. There are 8 groups in a maths. classroom.
    Each group is to compete in a maths. quiz with every other group.
    How many maths. quizzes will there be altogether?

    What if there were 10 groups?   What if there were 20 groups?

2. The 8 maths. groups compete in a game.
    The groups are paired off for the first round of the game.
    The winning groups from the first round are then paired off for the second round and so on.
    How many rounds need to be played to find the winning group?

    Make a table, or diagram, on which the names of the groups opposing each other, in each round, can be written.

    What if there were 10 groups?   What if there were 20 groups?

    You might like to investigate numbers of groups other than 8, 10 or 20.
    You might like to look for a pattern in the numbers of groups for which it is necessary to have a bye.

3. There are 8 teams entered in the local cricket competition.

    Each team must play every other team twice.
    How many games will there be altogether?

    What if there were 10 teams?
    What if there were 20 teams?   What if . . .

    Write up a draw for the 8-team competition showing the names of the opposing teams and the wicket on which they play if:
    *   each team plays every other team once on their own wicket and once on the opposing team's wicket i.e. once at home and once away
    *   the games are to be played on Saturdays
    *   each team plays just one game each Saturday
    *   the draw for this local cricket competition is to be arranged so that the competition will take as few Saturdays as possible

4. What is a "knock-out" competition?   What is a "round-robin" competition?
    Investigate the draws for these and for other types of competitions.

DISCUSSION EXERCISE 1:2

- In a team event the horses Flash, Ginger, Myrtle and Blacky were ridden by Anna, Meghan, Debbie and Siobhan. Debbie rode Blacky. Neither Anna nor Siobhan rode Flash. Anna did not ride Ginger. How could you work out who rode Ginger? Discuss. As part of your discussion work out who did ride Ginger.

- Rachel sailed her two-person yacht in 6 races. Sharon, Janine and Karen each sailed in two races with Rachel.
  Janine sailed in the 3rd race. Karen sailed in the 5th race but not in the 2nd. Neither Janine nor Karen sailed in the 1st or 6th race.
  How could you work out which girls sailed in which races? Discuss. As part of your discussion solve this problem.

Two techniques for problem solving are *"Making a Table"* and *"Drawing a Diagram"*. Worked examples, illustrating each, are given below. These are followed by a selection of problems, all of which may be solved by one or other of these techniques.

MAKING A TABLE

Worked Example When Jane, Emma and Hien went to the disco they decided to swap earrings and watches. Each of them wore someone else's earrings and the watch that belonged to yet another. If Hien wore Emma's earrings, whose watch did Emma wear?

Answer The following steps show how a table is completed from the given information.

Step 1

	Earrings	Watch
Hien	Emma	
Jane		
Emma		

We are told that Hien wore Emma's earrings.

Step 2

	Earrings	Watch
Hien	Emma	
Jane	Hien	
Emma		

Since Emma's earrings are worn by Hien and Jane doesn't wear her own, Jane must wear Hien's earrings.

Step 3

	Earrings	Watch
Hien	Emma	
Jane	Hien	
Emma	Jane	

Emma must wear Jane's earrings since these are the only ones left.

Step 4

	Earrings	Watch
Hien	Emma	Jane
Jane	Hien	Emma
Emma	Jane	Hien

The watch column can now be filled in since each girl must wear the watch of a friend whose earrings she doesn't wear.

Step 4 shows the completed table. From this table, we see that Emma wore Hien's watch.

Worked Example Shalome, Victoria, Elizabeth and Jenny each have one brother, Bryan or Ian or John or Neil.

Shalome is neither Ian's nor John's sister.
Victoria is neither Bryan's nor Neil's sister.
Elizabeth is neither Ian's nor Neil's sister.
Bryan is not Jenny's brother.
If John is Elizabeth's brother, whose brother is Neil?

Answer *Step 1* Place the given information on a table. Use a ✓ to show people are in the same family; use a ✕ to show they are not.

	Bryan	Ian	John	Neil
Shalome		✕	✕	
Victoria	✕			✕
Elizabeth		✕	✓	✕
Jenny	✕			

Step 2 Fill in the gaps in the table, using deduction, until Neil's sister is found. Each new entry is shown in red.

	Bryan	Ian	John	Neil
Shalome		✕	✕	
Victoria	✕			✕
Elizabeth	✕	✕	✓	✕
Jenny	✕			

Bryan cannot be Elizabeth's brother since John is.

	Bryan	Ian	John	Neil
Shalome	✓	✕	✕	
Victoria	✕			✕
Elizabeth	✕	✕	✓	✕
Jenny	✕			

Bryan must be Shalome's brother since he isn't Victoria's or Elizabeth's or Jenny's brother.

	Bryan	Ian	John	Neil
Shalome	✓	✕	✕	✕
Victoria	✕			✕
Elizabeth	✕	✕	✓	✕
Jenny	✕			

Neil cannot be Shalome's brother since Bryan is.

	Bryan	Ian	John	Neil
Shalome	✓	✗	✗	✗
Victoria	✗			✗
Elizabeth	✗	✗	✓	✗
Jenny	✗			✓

Neil is not Shalome's or Victoria's or Elizabeth's brother so he must be Jenny's brother.

Step 3   Write down the answer to the problem.
The answer is: Neil is Jenny's brother.

DRAWING A DIAGRAM

Worked Example   Jamie runs up the stairs, three at a time, starting with his right foot. Annie runs up, two at a time, starting with her left foot. If Annie begins on the second stair and Jamie begins on the first stair, which stair will be the first one on which both Annie and Jamie put their left foot?

Answer   Let J_R represent Jamie's right foot, J_L represent Jamie's left foot, A_R represent Annie's right foot and A_L represent Annie's left foot. Draw a diagram of a staircase. Place J_R on the 1st stair, J_L on the 4th stair, J_R on the 7th stair and so on. Place A_L on the 2nd stair, A_R on the 4th stair, A_L on the 6th stair and so on.

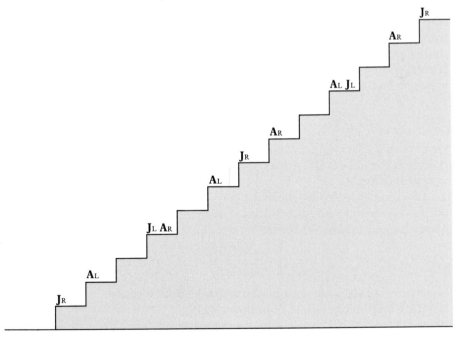

From the diagram, we see that the first stair on which both Jamie and Annie place their left foot is the 10th stair.

EXERCISE 1:3

Solve these problems, using one of the previous techniques or some other technique. If you make little progress using one technique, begin again using another.

1. Anna planted daffodil bulbs, 20cm apart, in a straight row. The row was 2m long. How many bulbs did Anna plant?

2. Circular bracelets are made by threading 3 red beads and 3 black beads onto nylon thread. How many different colour combinations could there be?

3. In Hurstfield, there are three sets of twins ; the Smiths, the Eades and the Holdens. In each of these sets of twins there is a boy and a girl. On a date, each of these twins dated another of these twins.
   If the Smith boy dated the Holden girl, who dated the Smith girl?

4. Sophie sets out in her boat to row to her friend's place, a distance of 6km by river. She is in no hurry to get there and takes a book to read. Sophie rows upstream for 2km, then reads. While she reads, she drifts back downstream 1km. Sophie continues her journey in this way, alternately rowing for 2km and drifting back 1km.
   If every kilometre she travels (either rowing upstream or drifting downstream) takes 15 minutes, find how long it takes Sophie to reach her friend's place.

5. One evening, Hari visited Mrs. Uren in hospital. On the way to the hospital, he bought flowers at the florists and grapes at the greengrocers. On the way home, he played squash at the gym.
   The florist is open during the evening on Tuesday, Friday and Saturday. The gym. is open every evening except Saturday. The greengrocers is open every evening except Thursday and Friday. What evening did Hari visit Mrs. Uren in hospital?

6. Square paving slabs are to be placed around a square garden to form a continuous border of uniform width.
   Show how exactly 84 paving slabs can be used.
   Is there more than one solution to this problem?

7. The Andersons, Coopers and Taylors are neighbours who live at 17, 19 and 21 Joyce Crescent.

   The Coopers live next door to the Andersons.
   Kate Cooper and Anna Taylor go to the same school.
   The labrador and terrier are not neighbours.
   There are no children at Number 19.
   Kate's labrador is very old.
   The terrier does not live at Number 17.
   Who lives at which address?

8.

   A   B   C   D   E

   Rebecca, Annabel, Megan, Lisa and Heather stand in a row to have their photo taken. No two of them are the same height. They stand with the tallest at one end and the rest of them arranged in order of their heights, as shown in the photo. Use the following clues to find who is who in the photo.

   Rebecca is taller than Annabel.
   Annabel is not the shortest.
   Rebecca is not the tallest.
   Only one girl is shorter than Heather.
   Megan is taller than Annabel.
   More than one girl is taller than Annabel.

9. A mountaineer sets out from base camp. He can carry a maximum of 5 days supplies. A number of porters go with him. Each porter can also carry a maximum of 5 days supplies. It will be 8 days before the mountaineer reaches the next camp where fresh supplies and more porters will be flown in.
   How many porters must go with the mountaineer to ensure that he reaches the next camp and that all the porters return safely to base camp?

Review 1 A rectangular garden, which measures 16m × 14m, is to have a fence built right around the perimeter. The fence posts are to be spaced one metre apart. If there must be a post at each of the four corners of the garden, how many posts will be needed altogether?

Review 2 In Avis Close there are four dogs, Churchill, Jake,
Millie and Paz. These dogs are all different breeds; one
is a collie, one is a terrier, one is a labrador and the
other is a spaniel.

Jake is neither a terrier nor a spaniel.
Paz is neither a spaniel nor a collie.
Churchill is neither a collie nor a terrier.
Millie is not a collie or a terrier or a labrador.

Which dog is which breed?

CHAPTER 1   REVIEW

1.   A sheet of stamps is 4 stamps long and 3 stamps wide. In how many ways could you cut
out four stamps which are all attached to each other?

2.   You and 6 friends want to go swimming.
You ask each of them which evening (Monday to Friday) is best.
These are their replies.

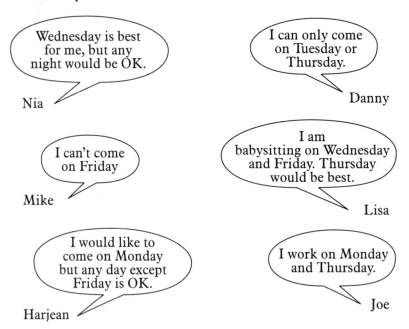

Wednesday is best
for me, but any
night would be OK.

Nia

I can only come
on Tuesday or
Thursday.

Danny

I can't come
on Friday

Mike

I am
babysitting on Wednesday
and Friday. Thursday
would be best.

Lisa

I would like to
come on Monday
but any day except
Friday is OK.

Harjean

I work on Monday
and Thursday.

Joe

You can go on any evening.
Which evening, or evenings, are possible for you all to go swimming together?
Explain how you got your answer.   **NEAB**

Charles Babbage

Charles Babbage was born at Teignmouth, Devon in 1792 and died at London in 1871. He is known as "The Father of Computers."

From 1828 until 1839 he was a professor of mathematics at Cambridge University. He resigned to concentrate on building elaborate calculating machines. He assisted in founding The Royal Astronomical Society, The British Association for the Advancement of Science, The Statistical Society of London and The Analytical Society. The aim of the Analytical Society was to introduce into England methods and notations then used in mathematics in Europe. He produced the first life insurance tables and wrote a book on analysing efficiency in manufacturing.

Babbage is usually best remembered not for these successes but for his failure to complete either his "Difference Engine" or his "Analytical Engine". It has been claimed that the technology at the time was the major cause of the failure but this has been disputed recently. The Difference Engine was to calculate and print, to 26 significant figures, various mathematical tables. Not only did he have government funding for this but he also invested, and lost, most of his own fortune. When this venture failed, he designed the "Analytical Engine" which was to perform many different calculations automatically. Babbage's Difference Engine was built in the 1980s and is in the Science Museum in London. Although Babbage's meticulous drawings for the machine were in existence, they had to be redrawn for modern manufacturing techniques.

It is said that Babbage wrote to the famous poet, Alfred Lord Tennyson, to complain about a couplet in the poem "The Vision of Sin." He is supposed to have written as follows:

Every minute dies a man
Every minute one is born.

Babbage's Difference Engine

I need hardly point out to you that this calculation would tend to keep the population of the world at a standstill, whereas it is a well-known fact that the said sum total is constantly on the increase. I would therefore take the liberty of suggesting that in the next edition of your excellent poem the erroneous calculation to which I refer should be corrected to have it read:

Every moment dies a man
And one and a sixteenth is born.

Strictly speaking this is not correct, the actual figure being so long that I cannot get it into a line, but something must, of course, be conceded to the laws of poetry.

INTRODUCTION

Discuss how to find the answers to the following problems. Find the answers.

1. Jamilah spent one third of her savings on her plane fare and one quarter of the remainder on her accommodation. She then had £120 left for spending money. What was Jamilah's plane fare?

2. To escape, a spy has to cross three borders.
   The spy agrees to pay one half of her money to someone at each border in order to be escorted to the next border.
   The spy needs to have at least £200 left after crossing the last border.
   What is the least amount of money this spy needs in order to escape?

PROPER and IMPROPER FRACTIONS. MIXED NUMBERS

A fraction such as $\frac{7}{8}$ is called a **proper fraction**. In a proper fraction the numerator (top) is smaller than the denominator (bottom).

A fraction such as $\frac{23}{4}$ is called an **improper fraction**. In an improper fraction the numerator is larger than the denominator. Improper fractions can be thought of as being "top heavy". Sometimes improper fractions are called **vulgar fractions.**

A number such as $3\frac{2}{5}$ is called a **mixed number.** A mixed number consists of a whole number and a fraction.

DISCUSSION EXERCISE 2:2

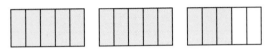

Each section of this diagram has been divided into fifths. The shading represents 13 fifths; that is $\frac{13}{5}$. Which mixed number does the shading represent?

Discuss how improper fractions can be rewritten as mixed numbers. Make and test statements as part of your discussion.

- **Discuss** how mixed numbers can be rewritten as improper fractions. Make and test statements as part of your discussion.

Worked Example (a) Rewrite $\frac{25}{6}$ as a mixed number.

(b) Rewrite $3\frac{4}{5}$ as an improper fraction.

Answer (a) $1 = \frac{6}{6}$, $2 = \frac{12}{6}$, $3 = \frac{18}{6}$, $4 = \frac{24}{6}$.   (b) 3 can be rewritten as $\frac{15}{5}$.

Hence $\frac{25}{6} = 4\frac{1}{6}$.   Hence $3\frac{4}{5} = \frac{19}{5}$.

EXERCISE 2:3

1.

| $\frac{7}{5}$ | $\frac{5}{7}$ | $\frac{2}{5}$ | $\frac{3}{4}$ | $\frac{4}{3}$ | $\frac{17}{4}$ | $\frac{8}{9}$ | $\frac{5}{6}$ | $\frac{6}{5}$ | $\frac{9}{8}$ | $\frac{10}{3}$ | $\frac{3}{10}$ |

(a) Which of these are proper fractions?   (b) Which are improper fractions?

2. Write these as mixed numbers.

(a) $\frac{13}{5}$ (b) $\frac{17}{4}$ (c) $\frac{5}{3}$ (d) $\frac{9}{2}$ (e) $\frac{11}{5}$

(f) $\frac{19}{6}$ (g) $\frac{25}{2}$ (h) $\frac{25}{3}$ (i) $\frac{36}{7}$ (j) $\frac{14}{9}$

3. Write these as improper fractions.

(a) $2\frac{3}{4}$ (b) $3\frac{1}{2}$ (c) $2\frac{2}{5}$ (d) $1\frac{5}{8}$ (e) $5\frac{1}{4}$

(f) $2\frac{5}{6}$ (g) $5\frac{3}{8}$ (h) $7\frac{1}{6}$ (i) $3\frac{4}{9}$ (j) $5\frac{3}{10}$

Review (i) Write as mixed numbers.   (a) $\frac{28}{5}$ (b) $\frac{19}{7}$

(ii) Write as improper fractions.   (a) $3\frac{1}{4}$ (b) $5\frac{2}{3}$

MULTIPLYING FRACTIONS

DISCUSSION EXERCISE 2:4

- Since $4 \times 5 = 4 + 4 + 4 + 4 + 4$, then $\frac{1}{2} \times 5 = \frac{1}{2} + \frac{1}{2} + \frac{1}{2} + \frac{1}{2} + \frac{1}{2}$.
  Discuss this statement. As part of your discussion, refer to the following diagrams.

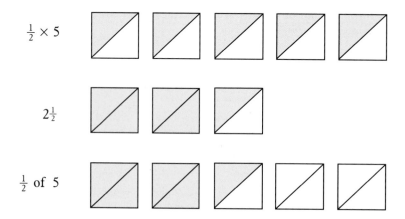

- Use diagrams to find the answers to $\frac{1}{4} \times 6$, $\frac{3}{5} \times 10$, $\frac{2}{3} \times 5$.
  Discuss how the answers could be found without using diagrams.

- This diagram can be used to find the answer to $\frac{1}{4} \times \frac{1}{3}$.
  Discuss.

- Draw diagrams to find the answers to $\frac{1}{2} \times \frac{1}{5}$, $\frac{3}{4} \times \frac{1}{3}$, $\frac{1}{4} \times \frac{2}{3}$, $\frac{5}{8} \times \frac{3}{4}$, $\frac{3}{8} \times \frac{4}{5}$, $\frac{3}{4} \times \frac{2}{3}$.
  Discuss how the answers could be found without using diagrams.

-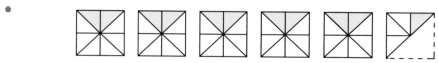

  This diagram shows that the answer to $\frac{1}{4} \times 5\frac{1}{2}$ is $\frac{11}{8}$ or $1\frac{3}{8}$.

  Discuss how to draw diagrams to find the answers to $\frac{1}{2} \times 3\frac{1}{4}$, $\frac{3}{4} \times 2\frac{1}{2}$, $\frac{2}{3} \times 3\frac{3}{4}$, $\frac{3}{5} \times 4\frac{1}{3}$.

  Discuss how to find the answers without drawing diagrams.

- Discuss how the following diagrams could be used to show that the answer to $2\frac{1}{2} \times 3\frac{2}{5}$ is $8\frac{1}{2}$.

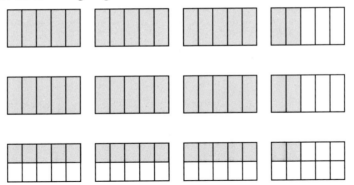

Discuss how the answer to $2\frac{1}{2} \times 3\frac{2}{5}$ could be found without using a diagram. As part of your discussion, you may like to find the answer to other multiplications involving mixed numbers.

- Make and test statements about how to multiply fractions. **Discuss.**

Fraction calculations can be simplified by **cancelling.**

Consider the calculation $\frac{3}{4} \times \frac{6}{5}$.

This may be written as $\frac{3 \times 6}{4 \times 5}$ or as $\frac{3 \times 6}{5 \times 4}$ or as $\frac{3}{5} \times \frac{6}{4}$.

$\frac{6}{4}$ may be replaced by the equivalent fraction $\frac{3}{2}$.

Then $\frac{3}{4} \times \frac{6}{5}$ $= \frac{3}{5} \times \frac{6}{4}$

$= \frac{3}{5} \times \frac{3}{2}$

$= \frac{9}{10}$

The working may be shortened as follows: $\frac{3}{{}_2\cancel{4}} \times \frac{\cancel{6}^3}{5} = \frac{9}{10}$

Rewriting $\frac{3}{4} \times \frac{6}{5}$ as $\frac{3}{{}_2\cancel{4}} \times \frac{\cancel{6}^3}{5}$ is called cancelling.

Example $\frac{{}^2\cancel{6}}{7} \times \frac{4}{\cancel{9}_3} = \frac{8}{21}$

To multiply fractions:

Step 1 Write any whole numbers or mixed numbers as improper fractions.
Step 2 Cancel if possible.
Step 3 Multiply the numerators; multiply the denominators.
Step 4 If the answer is an improper fraction, write it as a mixed number.

Example $\frac{1\cancel{2}}{3} \times \frac{7}{\cancel{10}_5} = \frac{7}{15}$

Example $4 \times \frac{3}{5} = \frac{4}{1} \times \frac{3}{5}$

$= \frac{12}{5}$

$= 2\frac{2}{5}$

Example $3\frac{3}{4} \times 1\frac{1}{5} = \frac{\cancel{15}^3}{\cancel{4}_2} \times \frac{\cancel{6}^3}{\cancel{5}_1}$

$= \frac{9}{2}$

$= 4\frac{1}{2}$

EXERCISE 2:5

1. Find the answer to these.

   (a) $\frac{2}{5} \times \frac{2}{7}$ (b) $\frac{2}{3} \times \frac{3}{5}$ (c) $\frac{5}{12} \times \frac{8}{9}$ (d) $\frac{2}{3} \times \frac{4}{5}$ (e) $\frac{5}{6} \times \frac{9}{11}$

   (f) $6 \times \frac{2}{5}$ (g) $3 \times \frac{4}{7}$ (h) $8 \times \frac{5}{6}$ (i) $\frac{2}{3}$ of $\frac{3}{4}$ (j) $\frac{3}{8}$ of 6

2. Calculate.

   (a) $2\frac{1}{4} \times 3\frac{1}{3}$ (b) $2\frac{3}{5} \times 1\frac{2}{3}$ (c) $3\frac{3}{4} \times 1\frac{3}{5}$ (d) $3\frac{1}{3} \times 1\frac{2}{5}$

   (e) $4\frac{1}{6} \times 2\frac{4}{5}$ (f) $4\frac{2}{7} \times 2\frac{1}{3}$ (g) $2 \times 1\frac{5}{8}$ (h) $4 \times 3\frac{1}{3}$

3. Find the answer to these.

   (a) $(1\frac{1}{2})^2$ (b) $(2\frac{2}{3})^2$ (c) $\frac{2}{3} \times 1\frac{2}{5} \times 2\frac{1}{7}$ (d) $2\frac{1}{2} \times 3\frac{3}{10} \times 1\frac{2}{3}$

4. Susan claims that three-fifths of one-quarter is the same as three-quarters of one-fifth. Is she correct?

5. Two-fifths of a garden is used to grow vegetables. One-quarter of this is planted in potatoes.
   What fraction of the garden is planted in potatoes?

6. A train travels at an average speed of 96mph.
   How far does it travel in $2\frac{1}{4}$ hours?

7. David's bedroom floor measures $3\frac{1}{4}$ metres by $3\frac{1}{2}$ metres.
   What is the area of this floor?

8. (a) Find three different pairs of fractions which multiply to $\frac{25}{32}$.

   (b) $\frac{a}{3} \times \frac{2}{b} = \frac{8}{15}$ What values could **a** and **b** have?

   Is there more than one answer?

Review 1 Find the answer to these.

   (a) $\frac{2}{3}$ of 8   (b) $\frac{5}{8} \times \frac{4}{15}$ (c) $6 \times 2\frac{2}{3}$ (d) $3\frac{1}{4} \times 1\frac{3}{5}$

Review 2 Find the area of the top of this square table.

DIVIDING FRACTIONS

DISCUSSION EXERCISE 2:6

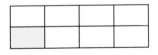

$\frac{1}{4}$ of $\frac{1}{2}$ shaded

or $\frac{1}{4} \times \frac{1}{2}$ shaded

$\frac{1}{8}$ shaded

$\frac{1}{4} \div 2$ shaded

or $\frac{1}{4} \div \frac{2}{1}$ shaded

Use these diagrams to compare $\frac{1}{4} \times \frac{1}{2}$ with $\frac{1}{4} \div \frac{2}{1}$. **Discuss.**

- Draw diagrams to compare   (a) $\frac{1}{2} \times \frac{1}{3}$ with $\frac{1}{2} \div \frac{3}{1}$ (b) $\frac{2}{5} \times \frac{1}{4}$ with $\frac{2}{5} \div \frac{4}{1}$.

  Discuss. As part of your discussion make and test statements about how to divide fractions.

To **divide by a fraction,** multiply by the reciprocal.
Remember: to find the reciprocal of a fraction, invert the fraction. That is, turn the fraction "upside down".

Example
$$\frac{3}{4} \div 6 = \frac{3}{4} \div \frac{6}{1}$$
$$= \frac{3}{4} \times \frac{1}{6}$$
$$= \frac{1}{8}$$

Example
$$6 \div \frac{3}{4} = \frac{6}{1} \div \frac{3}{4}$$
$$= \frac{6}{1} \times \frac{4}{3}$$
$$= 8$$

Example
$$\frac{3}{4} \div \frac{5}{12} = \frac{3}{4} \times \frac{12}{5}$$
$$= \frac{9}{5}$$
$$= 1\frac{4}{5}$$

Example
$$1\frac{2}{3} \div 4\frac{1}{6} = \frac{5}{3} \div \frac{25}{6}$$
$$= \frac{5}{3} \times \frac{6}{25}$$
$$= \frac{2}{5}$$

EXERCISE 2:7

1. Find the answer to these.

   (a) $\frac{3}{4} \div 3$ (b) $\frac{4}{5} \div 4$ (c) $\frac{9}{10} \div 5$ (d) $\frac{5}{8} \div 4$ (e) $\frac{7}{10} \div 3$

   (f) $3 \div \frac{3}{4}$ (g) $2 \div \frac{4}{5}$ (h) $9 \div \frac{3}{10}$ (i) $8 \div \frac{2}{3}$ (j) $4 \div \frac{1}{5}$

   (k) $\frac{2}{3} \div \frac{1}{2}$ (l) $\frac{7}{10} \div \frac{4}{5}$ (m) $\frac{9}{10} \div \frac{3}{4}$ (n) $\frac{5}{6} \div \frac{2}{3}$

2. Calculate.

   (a) $3\frac{1}{2} \div 2\frac{1}{2}$ (b) $2\frac{3}{4} \div 1\frac{1}{4}$ (c) $1\frac{2}{3} \div 2\frac{2}{3}$ (d) $1\frac{1}{3} \div 2\frac{2}{5}$ (e) $2\frac{3}{8} \div 1\frac{1}{4}$

   (f) $10 \div 1\frac{2}{3}$ (g) $8 \div 2\frac{2}{3}$ (h) $4\frac{1}{2} \div 3$ (i) $2\frac{1}{4} \div \frac{3}{8}$ (j) $3\frac{2}{5} \div \frac{3}{10}$

3. A recipe for a Christmas cake needs $\frac{1}{4}$ lb of flour.
   How many of these cakes can be made from a $2\frac{1}{2}$ lb bag of flour?

4. 1 gallon (8 pints) is about $4\frac{1}{2}$ litres.
   About how many pints is 1 litre?

5. A yacht is sailing at an average speed of $7\frac{1}{2}$ km/h.
   How long will this yacht take to travel 60km?

6. If $2\frac{1}{2}$ kg of fruit costs £3, what is the cost per kg?

7. A hovercraft completes one crossing in three-quarters of an hour.
   What is the greatest number of crossings that it could make in 18 hours?

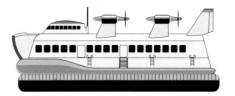

8. (a) Find three different pairs of fractions which give the answer $\frac{4}{9}$ when they are divided.

   (b) $\dfrac{4}{a} \div \dfrac{b}{3} = \dfrac{6}{7}$ What values could **a** and **b** have?
   Is there more than one answer?

Review 1 Calculate.   (a) $\frac{3}{5} \div \frac{9}{10}$ (b) $6 \div \frac{2}{3}$ (c) $3\frac{1}{8} \div 1\frac{2}{3}$

Review 2 It takes Saad $1\frac{1}{2}$ minutes to make a milkshake.
How many could he make in 12 minutes?

Review 3 A short skirt can be made from $\frac{3}{4}$ m of fabric.
How many of these skirts could be made from $10\frac{1}{2}$ m of this fabric?

INVESTIGATION 2:8

ALL THE DIGITS

$\frac{1}{5} = \frac{2697}{13485}$ Each of the digits 1, 2, 3, 4, 5, 6, 7, 8, 9 has been used once to form the fraction $\frac{1}{5}$.

Can other fractions such as $\frac{1}{2}$, $\frac{1}{3}$, $\frac{1}{4}$ etc. be formed in a similar way? **Investigate.**

$\frac{1}{9} = \frac{10638}{95742}$ Each of the ten digits 0 to 9 has been used once to form the fraction $\frac{1}{9}$.

Can these ten digits be rearranged in other ways to form the fraction $\frac{1}{9}$? **Investigate.**

ADDING and SUBTRACTING FRACTIONS

We can add 10 pence + 14 pence to get answer of 24 pence.
We can add 2a + 5a to get answer of 7a.

We cannot add 3x + 2a; neither can we add 5cm + 6kg.

To add two quantities they must be the same type of quantity.
This statement is also true for fractions.

To **add** (or **subtract**) **fractions** the fractions must be the same type.
Fifths may be added to fifths, quarters may be added to quarters but to add fifths to quarters
we must first rewrite as the same type. That is, we must find equivalent fractions which
have the same denominator.

Examples $\frac{2}{5} + \frac{1}{5} = \frac{3}{5}$ $\qquad\qquad\qquad$ $\frac{5}{8} - \frac{3}{8} = \frac{2}{8}$

$$= \frac{1}{4}$$

Example To find $\frac{4}{5} + \frac{3}{4}$ first find fractions equivalent to $\frac{4}{5}$ and $\frac{3}{4}$ which have the same
denominator.

$$\frac{4}{5} = \frac{8}{10} = \frac{12}{15} = \frac{16}{20} \qquad\qquad \frac{3}{4} = \frac{6}{8} = \frac{9}{12} = \frac{12}{16} = \frac{15}{20}$$

$$\text{Then } \frac{4}{5} + \frac{3}{4} = \frac{16}{20} + \frac{15}{20}$$

$$= \frac{31}{20}$$

$$= 1\frac{11}{20}$$

Worked Example In Baysdown, $\frac{3}{8}$ of the population is under 5 while $\frac{1}{3}$ is aged between
5 and 16. What fraction of the population is over 16?

Answer Fraction aged 16 or under $= \frac{3}{8} + \frac{1}{3}$

$$= \frac{9}{24} + \frac{8}{24}$$

$$= \frac{17}{24}$$

Fraction aged 16 or over $= 1 - \frac{17}{24}$

$$= \frac{24}{24} - \frac{17}{24}$$

$$= \frac{7}{24}$$

EXERCISE 2:9

1. Find the answer to these.
   (a) $\frac{1}{3} + \frac{1}{3}$ (b) $\frac{7}{12} + \frac{1}{12}$ (c) $\frac{7}{9} - \frac{2}{9}$ (d) $\frac{5}{9} - \frac{2}{9}$
   (e) $\frac{7}{10} + \frac{3}{10}$ (f) $\frac{5}{8} + \frac{7}{8}$ (g) $\frac{11}{12} + \frac{5}{12} - \frac{1}{12}$ (h) $\frac{7}{8} - \frac{1}{8} - \frac{3}{8}$

2. Calculate.
   (a) $\frac{3}{10} + \frac{2}{5}$ (b) $\frac{7}{8} - \frac{1}{4}$ (c) $\frac{5}{12} - \frac{1}{3}$ (d) $\frac{1}{4} + \frac{1}{3}$
   (e) $\frac{3}{4} + \frac{5}{6}$ (f) $\frac{5}{6} - \frac{1}{8}$ (g) $\frac{7}{10} - \frac{1}{12}$

3. Find the answer to these.
   (a) $\frac{1}{3} + \frac{3}{4} + \frac{5}{12}$ (b) $\frac{2}{3} + \frac{1}{8} + \frac{3}{4}$ (c) $\frac{7}{10} + \frac{1}{2} - \frac{2}{3}$ (d) $\frac{9}{10} - \frac{2}{5} - \frac{1}{4}$

4. In a horse race, there was $\frac{1}{3}$ of a length between the first and second horses and $\frac{1}{2}$ of a length between the first and third horses.
   What fraction of a length was there between the second and third horses?

5. The glass is filled from the thermos flask.
   Which now contains more, the glass or the thermos flask?

6. Three children share their parents' estate as follows: the eldest gets $\frac{1}{2}$, the youngest gets $\frac{1}{3}$. What fraction of the estate does the other child get?

7.

   Jenny estimated that her first golf shot reached $\frac{2}{5}$ of the way to the hole while her third (and last) shot covered $\frac{1}{8}$ of the distance.
   What fraction, of the distance to the hole, did Jenny's second shot cover?

8. Find the next term in the sequence $\frac{1}{2}, \frac{2}{3}, \frac{5}{6}, 1, \ldots$

Review 1   Find the answer to these.

(a) $\frac{5}{9} + \frac{3}{9}$ (b) $\frac{5}{6} - \frac{2}{3}$ (c) $\frac{2}{3} + \frac{3}{4}$ (d) $\frac{1}{4} + \frac{7}{12} - \frac{2}{3}$

Review 2   The earth consists of three main layers; crust, mantle and core. The mantle is about $\frac{4}{5}$ of the earth and the core is about $\frac{1}{6}$.
What fraction of the earth is crust?

To **add** (or **subtract**) **mixed numbers** we can begin by writing each mixed number as an improper fraction.

Examples
$$3\tfrac{2}{3} + 1\tfrac{3}{4} = \tfrac{11}{3} + \tfrac{7}{4}$$
$$= \tfrac{44}{12} + \tfrac{21}{12}$$
$$= \tfrac{65}{12}$$
$$= 5\tfrac{5}{12}$$

$$3\tfrac{1}{6} - 1\tfrac{1}{2} = \tfrac{19}{6} - \tfrac{3}{2}$$
$$= \tfrac{19}{6} - \tfrac{9}{6}$$
$$= \tfrac{10}{6}$$
$$= \tfrac{5}{3}$$
$$= 1\tfrac{2}{3}$$

Another method of adding (or subtracting) mixed numbers is to add (or subtract) the whole numbers, then add or subtract the fractions.

Example
$$3\tfrac{2}{3} + 1\tfrac{3}{4} = 3\tfrac{8}{12} + 1\tfrac{9}{12}$$
$$= 4\tfrac{17}{12}$$
$$= 5\tfrac{5}{12}$$

DISCUSSION EXERCISE 2:10

Discuss the advantages and disadvantages of both of the above methods. As part of your discussion use calculations such as: $3\tfrac{2}{3} + 1\tfrac{3}{4}$ $15\tfrac{1}{2} + 23\tfrac{3}{8}$ $14\tfrac{3}{5} - 7\tfrac{3}{10}$ $3\tfrac{1}{6} - 1\tfrac{1}{2}$

EXERCISE 2:11

1. Find the answer to these.

   (a) $1\frac{1}{2} + 2\frac{3}{4}$ (b) $3\frac{2}{3} + 1\frac{1}{4}$ (c) $2\frac{4}{5} - 1\frac{1}{2}$ (d) $5\frac{1}{2} + \frac{7}{10}$

   (e) $4\frac{5}{8} - 2\frac{3}{4}$ (f) $2\frac{1}{3} - \frac{4}{5}$ (g) $2\frac{1}{3} - 1\frac{1}{2}$

2. Sam works in a restaurant for $3\frac{1}{2}$ hours each Saturday and $2\frac{3}{4}$ hours each Sunday. How long does Sam work each weekend?

3. The last 8 pages of a magazine are for advertisements.

   Two days before publication, $6\frac{7}{8}$ pages of advertising had been sold, then $2\frac{1}{4}$ pages were cancelled. How much still has to be sold?

4. Find the next term in the sequence $\frac{2}{3}, 2\frac{1}{2}, 4\frac{1}{3}, 6\frac{1}{6}, \ldots$

5. What might ■ and ● be in each of the following?

   (a) ■ + ● $= 3\frac{5}{6}$ (b) ■ $- 2\frac{1}{2} =$ ●

6. Copy and complete these magic squares.
   Remember: the numbers on each row, column and diagonal must add to the same total.

$\frac{1}{2}$		
$1\frac{2}{3}$	1	
$\frac{5}{6}$		

   (a)

	$1\frac{2}{5}$	
$2\frac{1}{10}$	$2\frac{9}{20}$	$\frac{7}{10}$

   (b)

		$4\frac{3}{4}$
	$3\frac{23}{24}$	
$3\frac{1}{6}$		$6\frac{1}{3}$

   (c)

Review 1 Find the answer to these.

   (a) $3\frac{1}{4} + 1\frac{7}{10}$ (b) $2\frac{2}{3} - 1\frac{1}{4}$ (c) $2\frac{3}{8} - 1\frac{2}{3}$

Review 2 Beth made plum sauce. She filled these two bottles to the top.

   (a) How much plum sauce did Beth make altogether?

   (b) How much more did Beth pour into the large bottle than into the small bottle?

CALCULATIONS WITH ×, ÷, +, −

In the next exercise some questions involve just one of +, −, ×, ÷ and some involve more than one of these.

EXERCISE 2:12

---

1. Which operation, +, −, × or ÷, does the ⋆ stand for?

   (a) $4 \star \frac{1}{5} = 20$ (b) $4 \star \frac{1}{5} = 4\frac{1}{5}$ (c) $4 \star \frac{1}{5} = \frac{4}{5}$ (d) $4 \star \frac{1}{5} = 3\frac{4}{5}$

2. Andrea delivers papers 6 days a week. Each day her paper round takes $1\frac{3}{4}$ hours. How many hours a week does Andrea work on this paper round?

3. One-third of a cake has been eaten. Michael and his 3 friends share the rest of this cake. What fraction of the cake does each get, if they each get the same size piece?

4. Najma travels from Birmingham to Edinburgh, a distance of 485km. If $\frac{2}{5}$ of Najma's journey is by motorway, how many km does she travel on the other roads?

5. Copy these. Complete by finding the missing fractions.

   (a)

$\frac{2}{5}$	×		=	$\frac{3}{4}$
÷	■	÷	■	÷
	×	$\frac{3}{4}$	=	
=	■	=	■	=
$\frac{4}{5}$	×		=	

   (b)

$1\frac{1}{2}$	+	$\frac{2}{3}$	=	
−	■	■	■	×
		÷	=	$2\frac{2}{5}$
=	■	■	■	=
$\frac{3}{4}$	+		=	

6. Theatre tickets cost £5, £8 and £15. Of the 600 tickets sold for one performance, $\frac{1}{3}$ sold for £15 and $\frac{2}{5}$ sold for £8.

   (a) What fraction of the tickets sold for £5?

   (b) What total revenue from ticket sales did the theatre get for this performance?

7. Every $\frac{1}{4}$ of an hour a street cleaning machine cleans $1\frac{1}{3}$km of road. How many km does it clean in 3 hours?

8. This diagram is enlarged on a photocopier by a scale factor of $1\frac{1}{3}$.

    (a) How long is the enlarged design?

    (b) The enlarged design is then reduced back to its original size. What is the scale factor of this reduction?

9. Aaron spent $\frac{5}{8}$ of his savings, then half the remainder.
   What fraction of his savings did Aaron have left?

10. A tank, when three-quarters full, contains 45*l* of petrol.
    How much petrol does a full tank hold?

11. Three-fifths of a class are boys. Three-fifths of the girls play netball. Four girls do not play netball.
    How many boys are in this class?

Review 1   There were three candidates in an election; A.J. Beatie, T. Davison and I.M. Mahon.

Candidate	Fraction of Votes
A. J. Beatie	$\frac{1}{3}$
T. Davison	$\frac{1}{4}$
I. M. Mahon	

    (a) What fraction of the votes did I.M. Mahon poll?

    (b) Who won the election?

    (c) If 6756 people voted, how many votes did T. Davison get?

Review 2   On holiday, Beth spent one-third of her money on travel and two-fifths of the remainder on food and accommodation. She then had £60 for other expenses.
    How much did Beth spend on travel?

INVESTIGATION 2:13

FRACTION PATTERNS

$\frac{1}{2} + \frac{1}{4} + \frac{1}{8} + \frac{1}{16} + \frac{1}{32} + \ldots$ Investigate this fraction pattern.

You could begin by finding the sums $\frac{1}{2} + \frac{1}{4}$, $\frac{1}{2} + \frac{1}{4} + \frac{1}{8}$, $\frac{1}{2} + \frac{1}{4} + \frac{1}{8} + \frac{1}{16}$ etc.

You could use the fraction functions on a calculator to help in your investigation or you could use the following program. This will print the first 6 sums. To print more than 6 rewrite line 40.

```
10    MODE 3
20    DENOM = 2
30    SNUM = 1 : SDENOM = 2
40    FOR I = 1 TO 6
50    DENOM = 2 * DENOM
60    NEWSNUM = 2 * SNUM + 1
70    NEWSDENOM = 2 * SDENOM
80    PRINT SNUM , 1 , NEWSNUM
90    PRINT SPC (7) ; "_ _ _" ; SPC (3) ; " + " ; SPC (3) ; "_ _ _" ;
      SPC (3) ; " = " ; SPC (3) ; "_ _ _"
100   PRINT SDENOM , DENOM , NEWSDENOM
110   PRINT
120   SNUM = NEWSNUM : SDENOM = NEWSDENOM
130   NEXT
140   END
```

You could draw a sequence of diagrams such as the following.

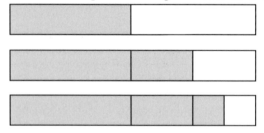

Investigate the fraction pattern: $\frac{1}{3} + \frac{1}{9} + \frac{1}{27} + \frac{1}{81} + \ldots$ You could use the above program. You will need to replace every 2 with 3.

Investigate other fraction patterns such as $\frac{1}{2} + \frac{1}{3} + \frac{1}{4} + \frac{1}{5} + \ldots$

$$\frac{1}{2} - \frac{1}{4} + \frac{1}{8} - \frac{1}{16} + \ldots$$

continued . . .

. . . from previous page

What fraction patterns occur in this diagram?
Investigate.

If more than one operation is involved in the same calculation, the operations must be done in the following order. Brackets, then $\times$ and $\div$, then $+$ and $-$.

Example $\quad 4\frac{1}{3} + 2\frac{2}{3} \div 2\frac{2}{5}$

$\quad = 4\frac{1}{3} + \frac{8}{3} \div \frac{12}{5}$

$\quad = 4\frac{1}{3} + \frac{\overset{2}{\cancel{8}}}{3} \times \frac{5}{\underset{3}{\cancel{12}}}$

$\quad = 4\frac{1}{3} + \frac{10}{9}$

$\quad = 4\frac{1}{3} + 1\frac{1}{9}$

$\quad = 5 + \frac{1}{3} + \frac{1}{9}$

$\quad = 5 + \frac{3}{9} + \frac{1}{9}$

$\quad = 5\frac{4}{9}$

Example $\quad 4\frac{1}{3} \div 2\frac{2}{3} + 2\frac{2}{5}$

$\quad = \frac{13}{3} \div \frac{8}{3} + 2\frac{2}{5}$

$\quad = \frac{13}{\underset{1}{\cancel{3}}} \times \frac{\overset{1}{\cancel{3}}}{8} + 2\frac{2}{5}$

$\quad = \frac{13}{8} + 2\frac{2}{5}$

$\quad = 1\frac{5}{8} + 2\frac{2}{5}$

$\quad = 3 + \frac{5}{8} + \frac{2}{5}$

$\quad = 3 + \frac{25}{40} + \frac{16}{40}$

$\quad = 3\frac{41}{40}$

$\quad = 4\frac{1}{40}$

Example $\quad (1\frac{3}{4} + 2\frac{1}{3}) \times 1\frac{3}{7}$

$\quad = (3 + \frac{3}{4} + \frac{1}{3}) \times 1\frac{3}{7}$

$\quad = (3 + \frac{9}{12} + \frac{4}{12}) \times 1\frac{3}{7}$

$\quad = 3\frac{13}{12} \times 1\frac{3}{7}$

$\quad = 4\frac{1}{12} \times 1\frac{3}{7}$

$\quad = \frac{\overset{7}{\cancel{49}}}{\underset{6}{\cancel{12}}} \times \frac{\overset{5}{\cancel{10}}}{\underset{1}{\cancel{7}}}$

$\quad = \frac{35}{6}$

$\quad = 5\frac{5}{6}$

EXERCISE 2:14

Find the answer to these.

1. $\quad 3\frac{1}{3} + \frac{2}{5} \times 4\frac{1}{6}$

2. $\quad \frac{3}{4} \div \frac{1}{2} + 3\frac{1}{2}$

3. $\quad 6 - 1\frac{7}{9} \times 3\frac{3}{8}$

4. $\quad \frac{3}{4}$ of $1\frac{1}{7} + 2\frac{1}{2}$

5. $\quad \frac{2}{3}$ of $(1\frac{1}{2} + \frac{3}{4})$

6. $\quad (2\frac{1}{2} - 1\frac{5}{8}) \div \frac{3}{4}$

7. $\quad \frac{4}{5}(1\frac{5}{12} + \frac{7}{8})$

8. $\quad \frac{5}{8} + \frac{7}{10} \div 1\frac{2}{5}$

9. $\quad 3\frac{2}{5} \div (8\frac{3}{7} - 7\frac{7}{10})$

10. $\quad (4\frac{1}{5} - \frac{3}{10}) \div 3\frac{1}{4}$

Review 1 $\quad 5\frac{1}{4} \times (\frac{3}{4} - \frac{2}{3})$

Review 2 $\quad 2\frac{7}{10} + 3\frac{1}{5} \div 1\frac{1}{3}$

PUZZLE 2:15

???

A coin collection was to be divided amongst three children so that the eldest was to get half of the coins, the youngest was to get a ninth of them and the other child was to get a third. There were 17 coins in this collection.
The oldest child decided the collection could be shared in this way as follows:

Borrow one coin from a friend to make a total of 18 coins.

The eldest takes $\frac{1}{2}$ of 18 = 9 coins.

The youngest takes $\frac{1}{9}$ of 18 = 2 coins.

The other child takes $\frac{1}{3}$ of 18 = 6 coins.

Now that the 17 coins have been taken, the borrowed coin is returned to the friend.
The youngest child saw that there was a catch and explained this catch to the other children. What explanation might the youngest child have given?

???

CHAPTER 2   REVIEW

1. Give the answer to these as a mixed number or a fraction in its simplest form.

    (a) $2\frac{1}{4} \times 3\frac{2}{3}$　　　**(b)** $3\frac{2}{3} \div 4\frac{2}{5}$　　　**(c)** $\frac{2}{5}$ of $3\frac{4}{7}$　　　**(d)** $\frac{3}{5}$ of $4 - 1\frac{2}{3}$

    (e) $6 + \frac{5}{6} \times \frac{3}{4}$　　　**(f)** $\dfrac{4\frac{1}{6} - 1\frac{5}{6}}{3\frac{1}{2}}$

2. Flyway Tours undertake short distance, medium distance and long distance flights. Last year $\frac{1}{4}$ of their flights were short distance and $\frac{2}{3}$ were medium distance.

    (a) What fraction of Flyway Tours' flights were long distance?
    Write your answer as a fraction in its simplest form.

58

Flyway Tours flew 630 long distance flights. The destination of $\frac{2}{5}$ of the long distance flights was Canada and $\frac{1}{3}$ of these were to the city of Vancouver in Canada.

(b) Calculate the number of flights to Vancouver last year.   **SEG**

3.

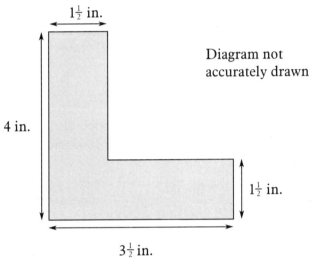

$1\frac{1}{2}$ in.

Diagram not accurately drawn

4 in.

$1\frac{1}{2}$ in.

$3\frac{1}{2}$ in.

The diagram shows the measurements, in inches, of the 'L' on an 'L' plate.
Work out the area of the 'L'.   **ULEAC**

4.   Two rods are fixed together to make a part for a motor.

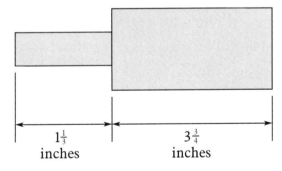

$1\frac{1}{3}$ inches

$3\frac{3}{4}$ inches

Work out the total length of the two rods.
Write your answer as a mixed number in its simplest form.   **ULEAC**

5.   Mustafa is paid £3·80 per hour as his basic rate of pay.

In one week he works 3 hours 40 minutes overtime at time and a half and $5\frac{1}{2}$ hours overtime at time and a quarter.
How much does Mustafa earn in overtime that week?   **SEG**

6. A child builds a tower from three similar cylindrical blocks. The smallest block, A, has radius 2·5cm and height 6cm.

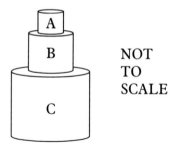

NOT
TO
SCALE

(a) Find the volume of the smallest block.

(b) Block B is an enlargement of A and block C is an enlargement of B, each with a scale factor of $1\frac{3}{4}$.
Find the total height of the tower.

MEG

Leopold Kronecker

Leopold Kronecker was born in 1823 at Liegnitz, in what was then Prussia. He died at Berlin in 1891.

He insisted that all mathematics be based on the positive integers. He used to say "God made the positive integers and all else is the work of man".

Kronecker had wealthy Jewish parents but from an early age he was interested in Protestant Christianity. However, he was 67 years old before he actually converted from Judaism.

His early education was with a private tutor. Later he attended a preparatory school and then the University of Berlin where he gained a doctorate in mathematics. As was usual with German university students at that time, he did part of his studies at other universities. While Kronecker was at Bonn University, the authorities were trying to stop the students drinking, duelling and brawling. By secretly siding with the students, Kronecker made many lasting friendships that were to later prove useful in the advancement of his ideas.

The custom at the time Kronecker completed his Ph.D. was for the successful student to give a party for his examiners. Kronecker's party was a wild affair. The memory of this party was one of the happiest of his life.

He got along easily with people and instinctively formed lasting friendships with people who were successful or were to become successful.

From university, Kronecker went into business. He managed the family mercantile and land business until the age of 30 when he was wealthy enough to retire. While in business, he continued his mathematics as a hobby.

From 1861, he gave lectures at the University of Berlin for no payment. These lectures were usually on his own personal work and research. In 1883 he was appointed Professor of Mathematics. He then travelled a great deal to attend scientific meetings. One of the countries he visited was Great Britain. Kronecker openly criticized other mathematicians in lectures and in conversation and it is claimed that his criticisms were a factor in the nervous breakdown of another of Germany's famous mathematicians.

Kronecker had a critical and questioning approach to everything, including mathematics. He was a short man, about five feet tall. He talked enthusiastically, with his whole body. A story is told of this excited short man, waving his arms and hands around in the midst of a group of spellbound students while the traffic all around came to a standstill.

As an old man, Kronecker claimed that music is the finest of all the fine arts with the possible exception of mathematics which he likened to poetry.

CALCULATING ORIGINAL QUANTITIES after PROPORTIONAL CHANGES

DISCUSSION EXERCISE 3:1

- Tilly told Jasmine she had sold her car for £1200 and made a 20% profit. Jasmine tried to work out how much Tilly had paid for the car. First she took 20% off £1200. Tilly said this was wrong. Why? Discuss. She then used trial and improvement.

Try   Tilly paid £900   20% of 900 $= \frac{20}{100} \times 900$

                                          $= 180$

      Sold for 900 + 180 = 1080   (too low)

Try   Tilly paid £1100   20% of 1100 $= \frac{20}{100} \times 1100$

                                           $= 220$

      Sold for 1100 + 220 = 1320   (too high)

Try   Tilly paid £1000   20% of 1000 $= \frac{20}{100} \times 1000$

                                           $= £200$

      Sold for 1000 + 200 = £1200   (correct)

Jasmine decided trial and improvement was the only way to work this out. Are there other ways? Discuss.

- Nick collects stamps. At Christmas time he increased his collection by $\frac{2}{5}$. He then had a total of 350 stamps.
  Julie said that Nick had $\frac{3}{5}$ of 350 before Christmas.
  Anna said that Nick had $\frac{5}{7}$ of 350 before Christmas.
  Sean said that Nick had $\frac{7}{5}$ of 350 before Christmas.
  Who is right, Julie, Anna or Sean? Discuss.

- Blake read that the town where he lived had increased in population by 10% this year to 8635. Blake wanted to know what the population was last year. He decided that to get the new population the old population must have been *multiplied* by 110%. To find the old population he *divided* the new population by 110%. Was Blake correct? Discuss.

  Blake read that the population of the next town had also increased by 10% to 8950. He worked out that the population the previous year was 8136·3̇6̇. In fact the population was 8136. Why are these figures different? Discuss.

Worked Example   This year Wolver Farm has 345 sheep. This is 15% more than last year. How many did they have last year?

Answer   Let n be the number of sheep Wolver Farm had last year.

Then $n + 15\%$ of $n = 345$

115% of $n = 345$

$\frac{115}{100} n = 345$

$n = 345 \div \frac{115}{100}$ (dividing both sides by $\frac{115}{100}$)

$n = 345 \times \frac{100}{115}$ (multiplying by the reciprocal)

$n = 300$

Note   115% could have been written as 1·15. The solution would then be

$n + 15\%$ of $n = 345$

115% of $n = 345$

$1{\cdot}15n = 345$

$n = \frac{345}{1{\cdot}15}$ (dividing both sides by 1·15)

$n = 300$

Worked Example   Bryce sold a stereo for £300. This was $\frac{1}{4}$ less than he paid for it. What did Bryce pay for this stereo?

Answer   Let x be the price Bryce paid for his stereo.

Then $x - \frac{1}{4}x = 300$

$\frac{3}{4}x = 300$

$x = 300 \div \frac{3}{4}$ (dividing both sides by $\frac{3}{4}$)

$x = 300 \times \frac{4}{3}$ (multiplying by the reciprocal)

$x = £400$

EXERCISE 3:2

1.   An antique was sold for £1400. This was a profit of 40%. What price was paid for the antique originally?

2.   Mrs Schmidt's salary was increased by 6% to £47,700. What was her salary before the increase?

3. Newfield College roll increased $\frac{1}{10}$ in the last year to 605. How many students went to Newfield College before the roll increased?

4. A school sold a set of workbooks for £1·35 at a profit of 25%. How much did the school pay for each set?

5. Hanrahan Gymnastics Club increased its membership by $\frac{3}{4}$ to 861. How many belonged to this club before the increase?

6. A plant increased its height by $\frac{2}{3}$ to 28cm. How high was the plant originally?

7. Find the original price of a painting sold for £1820 at a 4% profit.

8. When 9% interest was added to Julia's savings she had £163·50. How much did Julia have originally?

9. Ramon's height increased by $\frac{2}{7}$ in the last 5 years. He is now 171cm tall. How tall was Ramon 5 years ago?

10. When 15% discount was given, the price of a shirt was £13·60. What was the original price?

11. When $\frac{2}{5}$ of a packet of flour was used there was 900g left. How much was in the packet originally?

12. Denise surveyed the clubs at her school. She worked out the percentage increase or decrease in membership in the last year, giving the percentages to the nearest percent. What was the membership of each club last year?

Club	Current Membership	Increase or Decrease	
Drama	62	Increase	17%
Chess	18	Decrease	14%
Painting	67	Decrease	3%
Cricket	70	Increase	23%
Craft	101	Increase	1%
Athletics	45	Decrease	8%

13. If Oren sold his stereo for £179·55 he would make 5% profit. How much does Oren need to sell it for to make 10% profit? Give your answer to the nearest pound.

14. $\frac{3}{10}$ of the marks Giovanna lost in an examination were for one question. If she had got this question right she would have got $\frac{1}{3}$ more than her friend. Giovanna got 60%. What did her friend get?

Review 1 The number of telephone calls Tait Electronics made this month increased on last month by $\frac{1}{8}$. This month Tait Electronics made 765 calls. How many calls did the company make last month?

Review 2 A model was made of an antique chest so that a replica could be produced. The model was increased 75% in size to make the replica. If the height of the replica was 87·5cm, how high was the model?

Review 3 Accessories Unlimited had 25% off all belts and handbags. The new prices were rounded to the nearest penny. In the sale Julia bought a belt for £7·46 and a handbag for £26·25. What was the original price of these items?

REPEATED PROPORTIONAL CHANGES

DISCUSSION EXERCISE 3:3

---

* Bridget owns a boutique. She prices all the clothes so she makes a 40% profit. When her friend Anna bought a dress from her, she gave Anna a 40% discount. Did Bridget make any profit on this dress? **Discuss.**

* Neil claims that an increase of 10% followed by a decrease of 10% is less than an increase of 20% followed by a decrease of 20%. Is Neil correct? **Discuss.**

* Emalia sold her bike to Anna and made 25% profit. Anna sold the bike to Tara for a further 5% profit. Anna told Emalia that the bike had been sold to Tara for 30% more than Emalia had paid for it. Is Anna correct? **Discuss.**

When more than one calculation involving percentages or fractions takes place, each must be done separately.

For instance, if a manufacturer sells an article for 25% profit and it is sold again for a further 40% profit, we cannot add the 25% and 40% to find the total percentage profit.

Worked Example Donna is a buyer for "Fashion Warehouse". One line of dresses she buys cost £12·50. 30% mark up is put on these.

(a) What price does the Fashion Warehouse sell these dresses for?

(b) At the end of the summer these dresses are reduced by 25%. What profit or loss does the Fashion Warehouse make on them?

Answer (a) They sell for 130% of £12·50 $= \frac{130}{100} \times 12\cdot50$
$$= £16\cdot25$$

(b) Reduced Price $= 75\%$ of £16·25
$$= \frac{75}{100} \times 16\cdot25$$
$$= £12\cdot19 \text{ (to the nearest penny)}$$

This reduced price is less than the cost. Loss $= £12\cdot50 - £12\cdot19$
$$= 31\text{p}$$

Worked Example Mark is enlarging a 10cm drawing. He first enlarges it by setting the photocopier to 144%. He puts this enlarged drawing on the photocopier and sets it to 144%. How long is the final copy of the drawing?

Answer   1st enlargement $= 144\%$ of 10cm
2nd enlargement $= 144\%$ of 1st enlargement
$$= 144\% \text{ of } (144\% \text{ of } 10\text{cm})$$
$$= \frac{144}{100} \times \frac{144}{100} \times 10\text{cm}$$
$$= 20\cdot7\text{cm (to nearest mm)}$$

EXERCISE 3:4

1. Lengths of pipe which cost Steel Industries £2·50 each are sold to Homemakers for a 20% profit. Homemakers then sell these for $\frac{1}{3}$ more again. What price do Homemakers sell each length of pipe for?

2. A manufacturer adds 60% to the cost of materials to cover labour. She then adds a further 25% to get the selling price. At what price would she sell an article made from materials which cost 75p?

3. Kimberleys had a sale on all woollen jerseys. The marked price of all jerseys was reduced by $\frac{1}{4}$ and a cash customer was given a further 5% off. What price would a cash customer pay for a jersey originally marked at £26?

4. Claire sold a pony which cost her £360 for $\frac{1}{3}$ more than she paid for it. She missed the pony and bought it back for $\frac{1}{4}$ less than she sold it for. How much did Claire buy the pony back for?

5. Didier enlarged a drawing in a book by setting the photocopier to 130%. He decided this was too large. He put the enlarged drawing on the photocopier and set it to 90%. If the original drawing was 14cm by 18cm, what are the dimensions of the final copy?

6. Ashley embroidered tablecloths. She added $\frac{1}{2}$ to the cost of the tablecloths and sold them to Linen For Everyone. They sold them for 25% profit. If the tablecloths cost Ashley £15, how much did Linen For Everyone sell them for? Give your answer to the nearest pound.

7. A company's profit in 1995 was 12% higher than in 1994. In 1996 the profit decreased by $\frac{1}{4}$. If the profit in 1994 was £1,836,420 what was it in 1996? Give your answer to the nearest pound.

8. The number of lorries that used a particular route in 1992 was 9130. This increased by 10% in 1993. 1994's figures were about 5% lower than the 1993 figures. How many lorries used this route in 1994?

9. The rainfall in January was $\frac{2}{5}$ more than in December and December's rainfall was $\frac{1}{12}$ less than November's. If the rainfall in November was 6cm, what was it in January?

10. Craig Cycles ran a sales promotion. At 9a.m. on July 13 the price of all cycles dropped by 5%. At the beginning of each hour after this, until 5pm, the price dropped a further 5%. The price was rounded to the nearest pound each time it dropped. How much would a cycle priced at £299 at 8·30 a.m. cost at 4·30 p.m.?

11. Fitness House wanted to increase its membership by 15% each year for 5 years. In the first year membership increased by only 10% to 847.

   (a) If the 15% target is reached for the following 4 years, how many members will Fitness House have? (Round to the nearest person after each year's increase.)

   (b) If the 15% target had been reached for all 5 years, how many members would they have had?

12. A woman pays 5% of her salary on life insurance and saves 9% of the remainder. What percentage of her full salary is she saving?

13. Jonathan was given a salary of £15000 per annum. In addition he earned 5% commission on his sales and this commission was increased by $\frac{1}{2}$ if his sales in any one month were more than £20000. If sales in any month were more than £30000 then $\frac{1}{3}$ was added to the commission he had already earned. The following table gives the sales for one year. What was Jonathan's total salary that year?

Month	J	F	M	A	M	J	J	A	S	O	N	D
Sales (in thousands)	20·4	19·7	24·3	17·2	21·3	10·3	14·2	16·8	27·3	30·2	31·6	32·4

14. The weight of packets of Trent's icing sugar was increased by 25% for a sales promotion. William used $\frac{1}{5}$ of a packet to ice a cake. Victoria weighed the remainder and found there was 500g left. How many grams were in packets of Trent's icing sugar before the promotion?

    A. 1000g   B. 695g   C. 500g   D. 417g

15. After a 10% freight charge and then a 10% fee for insurance had been added, the price of a couch was £363. What was the original price?

Review 1   The population in a town increased 20% from 1985 to 1990 and a further 25% from 1990 to 1995. If the population in 1985 was 18420, what was it in 1995?

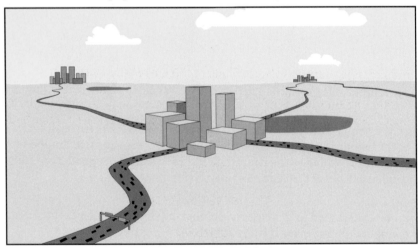

Review 2   A car worth £15000 is insured for $\frac{1}{5}$ more than its value. The car is stolen and the insurance company pays out the sum insured less $\frac{3}{20}$. What did the insurance company pay out?

PUZZLES 3:5

1. The original price is £15. After two mark ups the final price is £20·70. If one of the mark ups is 15%, what is the other?

2. The difference between decreasing a number by 7% and increasing it by 8% is 75. Find the number.

3. What percentage discount do the staff at Hats Galore get if they can buy at cost, hats that have been marked up 40%?

4. A sum of money is to be divided between three cousins. The first gets 20% of the money, the second gets 60% of what is left and the third gets £24. How much do the other two cousins get?

5. As sales increased, the Baby Factory reduced its prices. What percentage change in the amount of income would occur if sales increased by 40% but prices dropped by 5%?

CHAPTER 3   REVIEW

1. Tony bought a second-hand car for £7500. It decreased in value each year by 8% of its value at the beginning of that year. Calculate the value of the car 2 years after he bought it. **WJEC**

2.

> **BARGAINS!**
>
> **5% OFF ALL FARES!**
>
> **A BARGAIN
> FLIGHT TO MALAGA
> NOW COSTS
> ONLY £62.70**

What was the cost of a fare to Malaga before the reduction?   **NEAB**

3. Nesta invests £508 in a bank account at an interest rate of 8·5% per annum.

    (a) Calculate the interest on £508 after 1 year.

    At the end of the first year the interest is added to her bank account.
    The interest rate remains at 8·5%.

    (b) Calculate the total amount of money in Nesta's bank account at the end of the second
    year.   **ULEAC**

4. Valley Farm yoghurt is on special offer this month. Larger than normal tubs of yoghurt
    cost 24p and carry a label which reads

    (a) What should be the cost of one of these larger tubs of yoghurt at the normal price?

    (b) The larger than normal tub contains 150g of yoghurt. How much yoghurt is
    normally sold for 24p?   **NICCEA**

5. The National Currency Bank offered the following investment.

    > **INVEST WITH US FOR FIVE YEARS
    > AND WE WILL ADD 7% TO THE
    > VALUE OF YOUR INVESTMENT
    > EACH YEAR.**

    Alan invested £2000 with them.

    (a) How much was his investment worth after one year?

    (b) How much was his investment worth after five years?   **MEG**

6. In 1990, a charity sold $2\frac{1}{4}$ million lottery tickets at 25p each.
    80% of the money obtained was kept by the charity.

    (a) Calculate the amount of money kept by the charity.

In 1991, the price of a lottery ticket fell by 20%.
Sales of lottery tickets increased by 20%.
80% of the money obtained was kept by the charity.

(b) Calculate the percentage change in the amount of money kept by the charity.   ULEAC

7.   **Car prices: where the money goes**

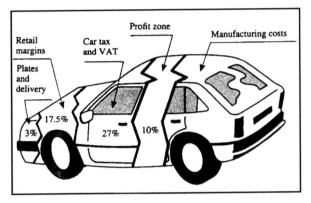

(a) What percentage of a car price are the manufacturing costs?

(b) The car price of an Esquire is £9,860.

Calculate

(i)   the car tax and VAT.

(ii) the retail margins.

(c) The retail margins of a Gala are £1,221.50. Calculate the car price.   **NICCEA**

Ada Lovelace

Ada Lovelace was born in England in 1815 and died at the age of 36 in 1852. She was the daughter of the famous poet, Lord Byron. A month after Ada was born, her father left England never to return. Neither Ada nor her mother saw him again. Lord Byron wrote about Ada in some of his poems.

Ada's mother was known for her mathematical ability. She had many influential friends, some of whom were mathematicians. Her friends nick-named her "The Princess of Parallelograms".

Ada did not attend school or any university. Her family was wealthy and she was taught by governesses and tutors. Ada's mother insisted that she receive instruction in mathematics which was not the custom for girls in those days. When Ada was five her daily lessons included grammar, spelling, reading, French, arithmetic, music, drawing and geography. Ada was tutored by mathematicians when she was older.

When she was 18, she met Charles Babbage. Some claim they met at a party; others claim they met when Ada went to his workshop. He tutored her for a time and they corresponded frequently. They became close friends.

Babbage was impressed with her understanding of his "Analytical Engine", an early computer. Ada wrote an analysis of the mathematics involved and described techniques which became important in computing. Her work was forgotten for many years. She is now viewed as the person who laid the groundwork for the development of computer language and computer programming. In the late 1970s she was honoured by the American Department of Defence who named the computer language ADA after her.

Ada did not publish her work using her own name as women mathematicians were not thought highly of in those times. She published using her initials A.A.L. Her husband, Lord Lovelace, whom she married when she was 19, encouraged her in her work. Although it was not the custom then, he took responsibility for running their household and bringing up their children.

Ada had a passion for horse racing. She and Charles Babbage worked out a betting system which Ada put into practice. It failed! It is claimed that she fell into debt and pawned the family jewels, creating a scandal.

Throughout her life Ada suffered from poor health and in later years lived in London to be close to her doctors. She was an asthmatic and was manic-depressive. It is believed that she suffered from anorexia. She died from cancer.

Based on an article from the book "Women Sum It Up" – Hazard Press

Estimating Answers to Calculations

ROUNDING ANSWERS SENSIBLY

72.083333

The calculator gives the answer to the calculation $\frac{17.3}{0.24}$ as 72·083333.
We would not give all of these 8 digits in the answer we write down.

We can choose whether to use decimal places (d.p.) or significant figures (s.f.) when we round an answer. The following guidelines can be used to decide how accurate an answer should be given.

1. Count how many d.p. (or s.f.) there are in the number with the fewest d.p. (or s.f.).
2. Round the answer to this many d.p. (or s.f.).

Using these guidelines, an acceptable answer to $\frac{17.3}{0.24}$ is 72 to 2 s.f. (17·3 has 3 s.f. while 0·24 has just 2 s.f.).

Using these guidelines, another acceptable answer to $\frac{17.3}{0.24}$ is 72·1 to 1 d.p. (17·3 has 1 d.p. while 0·24 has 2 d.p.).

These guidelines are not rules.
It sometimes seems sensible to give an answer to one more s.f. than these guidelines suggest.
For instance, it seems more sensible to give the answer to $\frac{1}{7}$ as 0·14 (2 s.f.) rather than 0·1 (1 s.f.).

These guidelines do not apply to a calculation, such as 6340×17, which has an exact answer. The calculator gives the answer to 6340×17 as 107780 and we usually write the answer as 107780. The calculator gives the answer to $\frac{3}{8}$ as 0·375 and we usually write the answer as 0·375.

DISCUSSION EXERCISE 4:1

● How would you write down the answers to the following calculations? **Discuss.**

Calculation	Calculator Display	Calculation	Calculator Display
$\frac{7}{11}$	0.6363636	48×1.34	64.32
$\frac{3}{16}$	0.1875	$\frac{8.14 \times 7.68}{0.89}$	70.241798
73×39	2847.	$\frac{0.005}{0.07}$	0.0714285
$\frac{73}{39}$	1.8717949	$\frac{0.08 \times 0.4}{0.6}$	0.0533333
$\frac{34000}{1500}$	22.666667	$\frac{63 \times 1.07}{0.3}$	224.7

● Never round until the final answer is found.

Suppose $A = \dfrac{3.4}{26.1}$ and $B = 5.9A$. We are to find the answer to B to 1 decimal place.

What answer do we get for B if we round the answer for A?

What answer do we get for B if we do not round the answer for A? **Discuss.**

ESTIMATING ANSWERS

When finding the answer to a calculation using the calculator, it is very easy to press an incorrect key. It is most important to have some idea of the size of the answer. You will then know if the answer shown on the calculator screen is reasonable.

Always **estimate** the answer when using the calculator for a calculation. The estimate does not have to be very accurate.

Each number in the calculation should be made as simple as possible so the estimate is easy to work out mentally. Some guidelines follow.

Guidelines: • Remember it is an estimate. The approximations don't need to be very accurate.
For instance, approximate $200 \div 5 \cdot 7$ as $20 \div 5$ rather than $20 \div 6$.

• Wherever possible, approximate to numbers such as $1, 2, 5, 10, 50, 100$ etc. that are easy to work with mentally.
For instance, $\dfrac{72 \cdot 6 \times 347 \cdot 05}{0 \cdot 89}$ may be approximated as $\dfrac{100 \times 350}{1}$ to give an estimate of 35000.

• Look for numbers that will cancel.
For instance, $\dfrac{12 \cdot 48 \times 487 \cdot 31}{3 \cdot 69}$ may be approximated as $\dfrac{\overset{3}{\cancel{12}} \times 500}{\underset{1}{\cancel{4}}}$ to give an estimate of 1500.

• Decimals, between 0 and 1, are often best approximated with fractions.
For instance, $\dfrac{82 \cdot 61}{0 \cdot 27}$ may be approximated as $80 \div \frac{1}{4}$ to give an estimate of 320.

• When multiplying or dividing, never approximate a number with 0. Rather, use $0 \cdot 1$ or $0 \cdot 01$ or $0 \cdot 001$ etc.
For instance, $205 \cdot 7 \times 0 \cdot 012$ should not be approximated as 200×0.
Rather, approximate as $200 \times 0 \cdot 01$ or $200 \times \frac{1}{100}$ to get an estimate of 2.

It is often convenient to use the symbol $\approx$ which means "is approximately equal to".

Worked Example   Estimate the answer to   (a) $8 \cdot 98 \times 24 \cdot 6$

(b) $(6 \cdot 35)^2$

(c) $\dfrac{198 \times 71 \cdot 6}{11 \cdot 3 \times 0 \cdot 83}$

(d) $0 \cdot 09 \times 59 \cdot 6$.

Answer   (a) $8 \cdot 89 \approx 10$, $24 \cdot 6 \approx 25$. An estimate is $10 \times 25 = 250$.

(b) $(6 \cdot 35)^2$ is more than 6^2 but less than 7^2.
An estimate for $(6 \cdot 35)^2$ is: between 36 and 49.

(c) $198 \approx 200$, $71 \cdot 6 \approx 70$, $11 \cdot 3 \approx 10, 0 \cdot 83 \approx 1$.
An estimate is $\dfrac{200 \times \overset{7}{\cancel{70}}}{\underset{1}{\cancel{10}} \times 1} = 1400$.

(d) $0 \cdot 09 \approx 0 \cdot 1 = \frac{1}{10}$, $59 \cdot 6 \approx 60$.
An estimate is $\frac{1}{10} \times 60 = 6$.

EXERCISE 4:2

1. Estimate the answer to these.

   (a) $7 \cdot 6 \times 4 \cdot 123$ (b) $67 \cdot 34 \div 9 \cdot 3$ (c) $7 \cdot 24 \times 18 \cdot 07$ (d) $(10 \cdot 14)^2$

   (e) $\dfrac{19 \cdot 6 \times 34 \cdot 7}{4 \cdot 35}$ (f) $\dfrac{7 \cdot 62 + 2 \cdot 21}{5 \cdot 23}$ (g) $81 \cdot 2 \times 0 \cdot 27$ (h) $\dfrac{27 \cdot 8 \times 3 \cdot 67}{7 \cdot 64}$

   (i) $\dfrac{28 \cdot 6 \times 24 \cdot 4}{5 \cdot 67 \times 4 \cdot 02}$ (j) $\dfrac{18 \cdot 3 + 11 \cdot 1}{57 \cdot 03}$ (k) $\dfrac{8 \cdot 34 \times 96 \cdot 7}{0 \cdot 26}$

2. Use the calculator to find the answer to these. Round the answers sensibly.
   Check that the answer is reasonable by making an estimate.

   (a) $37 \cdot 64 \times 23 \cdot 1$ (b) $44 \cdot 9 \div 8 \cdot 76$ (c) $0 \cdot 47 \times 19 \cdot 1$ (d) $\dfrac{38 \cdot 4 + 22 \cdot 5}{18 \cdot 4}$

   (e) $\dfrac{274 \times 31 \cdot 4}{49 \cdot 3}$ (f) $\dfrac{31 \cdot 2}{0 \cdot 24}$ (g) $(3 \cdot 24)^2$ (h) $\dfrac{(7 \cdot 05)^2}{4 \cdot 68}$

   (i) $\dfrac{87 \cdot 9}{1 \cdot 3 + 5 \cdot 01}$ (j) $\dfrac{4 \cdot 7 \times 49 \cdot 2}{0 \cdot 18}$ (k) $\dfrac{51 \cdot 6 \times 0 \cdot 12}{9 \cdot 8}$ (l) $\dfrac{24 \cdot 4 \times 8 \cdot 2}{3 \cdot 9 \times 2 \cdot 1}$

3. 1 nautical mile is approximately 1·853km.
   Estimate how many km are in 214 nautical miles.

4. 1 ounce is about 28·35 grams.
   Estimate the number of ounces in 600 grams.

5. Estimate, then use the calculator to find the answer to the following. If rounding is
   required, round your answers sensibly.

   (a) Find the cost of 9·7m of material at £8·19 a metre.

   (b) Find the perimeter of this triangle.

   7·9m   7·45m   7·08m

   (c) Shirts in a sale were priced at £8·85, £7·95, £11·15 and £5·45.
   During the first day of the sale, the following quantities were sold.
        27 at £8·85   15 at £7·95   24 at £11·15   47 at £5·45
   How much were all these shirts sold for?

   (d) Amanda has been visiting relatives in Australia.
   If the exchange rate is 1 Australian dollar for 37·02p, how much British money would
   Amanda get for the $48·65 she brought back to England with her?

(e) A formula for finding the area of a trapezium is
$A = \frac{1}{2}(a + b) \times h$.
a and **b** are the lengths of the parallel sides and **h** is the distance between these sides.
Find the area of this trapezium.

17·7cm

9·3cm

32·4cm

(f) A formula for finding the area of a circle is $A = \pi r^2$.
Using $\pi = 3\cdot142$, find the area of a circle with radius 26·7cm.

(g) A formula for the volume of a pyramid is $V = \frac{1}{3}$ (base area) × height.
Find the volume of a pyramid which has a rectangular base, measuring 81·2mm by 58·6mm, and height 19·7mm.

(h) Kareema is reading this book.
She takes an average of 2 min. 5 sec. to read a page.
How long will it take her to read the book?

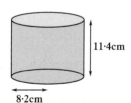

(i) Jim bought 213 feet of decking timber.
This was in planks, each 5′11″ long.
How many planks did Jim buy?

6. Write down 10 different calculations which could have an estimated answer of 15.
Use at least two of the operations $+, -, \times, \div$ and squaring in each calculation.
Use decimals in all of the calculations.

Review 1 Estimate the answer for these.

(a) $38\cdot2 \times 4\cdot67$

(b) $\dfrac{28\cdot7}{0\cdot44}$

(c) $\dfrac{21\cdot4 \times 38\cdot7}{3\cdot68 \times 4\cdot71}$

(d) $\dfrac{7\cdot204 + 2\cdot63}{1\cdot934}$

(e) $4\cdot9 \times (3\cdot14)^2$

Review 2 Estimate, then use the calculator to find the answer to the following. Round your answers sensibly.

(a) $\dfrac{36\cdot7 \times 72\cdot6}{6\cdot94}$

(b) $48\cdot6 \times 0\cdot098$

(c) $\dfrac{7\cdot64 + 14\cdot1}{3\cdot84}$

(d) $\dfrac{(9\cdot63)^2}{4\cdot78}$

Review 3 A formula for the volume of a cylinder is $V = \pi r^2 h$.
Using $\pi = 3\cdot142$, find the volume of this cylinder.
Give the answer to 2 s.f.

11·4cm

8·2cm

77

CHAPTER 4   REVIEW

1. David worked out that $\dfrac{40}{0\cdot08} = 50$. His teacher did a quick mental calculation and told
    David he had made a mistake.
    Show how David's teacher could have done this calculation mentally.   **NEAB**

2. A young couple want to set up their
    own business.
    They need to rent an office.
    They reply to this advertisement in the
    local paper.

    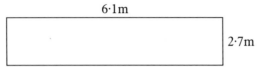

    OFFICES TO LET
    _____
    Good size

    *Most of our offices have floor space
    greater than 20 square metres.*

    (a) The first office they are shown has these floor measurements:

    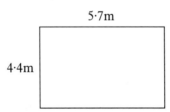

    6·1m

    2·7m

    Explain how to make a quick estimate of the floor area of this office **without using a
    calculator.**
    Is the floor space greater than 20 square metres?

    (b) The second office they look at has these floor measurements:

    5·7m

    4·4m

    (i)   Use your calculator to find the area of the floor space in this office.
          Give your answer to the nearest square metre.

    (ii) The height of the ceiling in this office is 3 metres.
          Calculate the volume of the office in cubic metres.   **NEAB**

3. Emma is using the formula $m = \dfrac{y-30}{x}$ to calculate the value of m when $y = 149\cdot136$
    and $x = 3\cdot961$. Her calculator is broken so she decides to estimate the value of m in her
    head.

    (a) Write down approximate values for y and x which Emma could use to estimate the
         value of m.

    (b) Write down the value of m she would get from using the approximate values
         in (a).   **ULEAC**

4. Sylvia worked for 35 hours at £3·10 per hour and also did 5 hours overtime at £4·10 per hour.
She calculated that she had earned £130·50.

   (a) Her friend Carl said "But £130·50 cannot be the exact answer".

     How could Carl work this out in his head without doing the complete calculation?

   (b) Sylvia then did a rough check and said to Carl "It's about right".

     What sort of rough check do you think Sylvia could have done?   **NEAB**

5. Show clearly how you would ESTIMATE for the following calculation.

$$(762 \times 0.385) \div (89 \times 1.13)$$ **WJEC**

6. The distance by road from Maidstone to Manchester is approximately 250 miles.
Work out an estimate for this distance in kilometres, given that 1 kilometre is about 0·62 miles.   **ULEAC**

7. Trudie uses the formula

$$a = \frac{v - u}{t}$$

She has to calculate the value of a, when $v = 118.07$, $u = 17.76$ and $t = 4.8$.

Trudie estimates the value of a **without using her calculator**.

   (a) **(i)** Write down numbers Trudie could use to estimate the value of a.

     (ii) Write down the estimate these numbers would give for the value of a.

Trudie then uses her calculator to find the value of a.

   (b) Here is the sequence of keys that she presses.

     [1] [1] [8] [·] [0] [7] [−] [1] [7] [·] [7] [6] [÷] [4] [·] [8] [=]

This gives an answer of 114·37 which is **not** correct.

Change the sequence above so that it will give the correct answer.   **ULEAC**

8. Flour costs 48p per kilogram. Brett bought 205kg and shared it equally among 14 people.
He calculated that each person should pay £0·72.

Without using a calculator, use a rough estimate to check whether this answer is about the right size. **You must show all your working.**   **SEG**

9. Last year I drove 12 071 miles in my car.
   I know that my car travels 30·4 miles on one gallon of petrol.
   One gallon of petrol cost £2·49.
   I estimate that I spent about £1000 on petrol in the year.

   Without using a calculator, do a rough calculation to check whether the estimate is about right.
   Show all the approximations you make.   **MEG**

10. Joan buys 37·6 litres of petrol for her car.

    Petrol costs 51·7p per litre.

    Her car can travel 238 miles on this amount of petrol.

    (a) Calculate the cost of the petrol per mile for her car.

       Give your answer to the nearest penny.

    (b) Joan buys 37·6 litres of petrol.

       Petrol is measured to the nearest tenth of a litre.

       Write down the minimum amount of petrol that she could have received.

    (c) (i) Calculate how many miles per gallon her car travels.

        Take 1 gallon to be 4·55 litres.

       (ii) Use approximations to show that your answer to part (i) is of the right order of magnitude.   **SEG**

11. Hannah does the following calculation.

    $$\frac{8\cdot7 \times 102}{(3\cdot1)^2}$$

    (a) **Without** using your calculator, work out an approximate answer to this calculation.

       You **must** show all your working.

    (b) Hannah's answer is 923·4.

       Explain whether Hannah's answer is of the right order of magnitude.   **SEG**

Robert Recorde

Robert Recorde was born in 1510 at Tenby, in Wales. He died in 1558 at London.

At the age of 15, Robert entered Oxford University. He studied and taught mathematics there, then went to Cambridge University where he gained a medical degree in 1545. He then went to London and served as physician to King Edward VI and Queen Mary.

In 1549, Recorde became Comptroller of His Majesty's Mint in Bristol. In 1551, he became Surveyor of the King's Mines and Monies in Ireland.

Robert Recorde was the most important mathematician in England in the 16th century. He introduced algebra into England. He wrote books on mathematics, astronomy and medicine. His mathematics text books were used in England for more than half a century.

His first book was "The Grounde of Artes", published in 1542. This book is often referred to as the first arithmetic book to be written in the English language. This is not true. Recorde himself said of this book "*I doubt not but some will like this my book aboue any other English Arithmetike hitherto written, & namely such as shal lacke instructers, for whose sake I haue plain-ly set forth the exāples, as no book (that I haue seene) hath hitherto.*"

"The Grounde of Artes", which was dedicated to King Edward VI, was a most popular arithmetic book. 28 editions were published, from 1542 to 1699. In this book, Recorde used the abacus to teach addition and subtraction. He also used the + and – signs. The book was well written with the theory carefully developed and hence easily understood. It contained many interesting practical applications. The following is an extract: "*Then what say you to this question? If I sold unto you an horse having 4 shoes, and in every shoe 6 nayles, with this condition, that you shall pay for the first nayle one ob : for the second nayle two ob : for the third nayle foure ob : and so forth, doubling untill the end of all the nayles, now I ask you, how much would the price of the horse come unto?*"

Recorde's most famous book was "The Whetstone of Witte", published in 1557. In this book he proposed and used the symbol =. He said the following: "*I will sette as I doe often in woorke use, a paire of paralleles, or Gemowe (twin) lines of one lengthe, this: $=\!=\!=\!=$, bicause noe 2. thynges, can be moare equalle.*"

The symbol = was not the only notation in use at that time for "equals". In fact, it was more than a century after Recorde used it in "The Whetstone of Witte" before it became the accepted notation. Both Sir Isaac Newton and Gottfried Leibniz helped to make it popular.

In his work on astronomy, Recorde agreed with the theory that the Earth revolves around the sun.

A year after the "Whetstone of Witte" was published, Robert Recorde died in prison. The reason for his imprisonment is not known. It is thought to have been for some dishonest transaction carried out in connection with his position as surveyor of the King's Mines and Monies in Ireland.

INTRODUCTION

? ?

Rewrite the numbers 1 to 10 using the following rules.

1. You must use as many digits as the number you are rewriting.
2. You must use a square root.
3. You are allowed to use the digits 1, 2, 4 only. These digits may be used more than once or not at all.
4. The operations $\times, \div, +, -$ may be used more than once or not at all.

For instance, the number 6 must be rewritten using 6 digits.
6 could be rewritten as $\sqrt{4} \times 2 + 2 - 1 \times 2 + 2$

? ?

CALCULATING with POWERS and ROOTS

When more than one operation is to be done work out the brackets, then work out the powers and roots, then do $\times$ and $\div$, then do $+$ and $-$.

Worked Example Calculate.

(a) $5 + 7^2$

(b) $1 - \sqrt{9}$

(c) $3\sqrt{16} + 17 \times (-2)$

(d) $4[2 + (-2)^3]$

(e) $-3(1 + 2\sqrt{16})$

(f) $\dfrac{13 + 4\sqrt{25}}{2}$

Answer (a) $5 + 7^2 = 5 + 49$
$= 54$

(b) $1 - \sqrt{9} = 1 - 3$
$= -2$

(c) $3\sqrt{16} + 17 \times (-2) = 3 \times 4 + 17 \times (-2)$
$= 12 - 34$
$= -22$

(d) $4[2 + (-2)^3] = 4[2 + (-8)]^3$
$= 4[-6]^3$
$= 4 \times (-216)$
$= -864$

(e) $-3(1 + 2\sqrt{16}) = -3(1 + 2 \times 4)$
$= -3(1 + 8)$
$= -3(9)$
$= -27$

(f) $\dfrac{13 + 4\sqrt{25}}{2} = \dfrac{13 + 4 \times 5}{2}$
$= \dfrac{13 + 20}{2}$
$= \dfrac{33}{2}$
$= 16 \cdot 5$

Note   In (f) the fraction line acts like a bracket since $\dfrac{13 + 4\sqrt{25}}{2}$ means $(13 + 4\sqrt{25}) \div 2$.

Remember on the calculator, $2\frac{5}{8}$ is found by keying $\boxed{2}$ $\boxed{a^{b/c}}$ $\boxed{5}$ $\boxed{a^{b/c}}$ $\boxed{8}$

$\sqrt{6\cdot4}$ is found by keying $\boxed{6\cdot4}$ $\boxed{\sqrt{}}$

$\sqrt[3]{6\cdot4}$ is found by keying $\boxed{6\cdot4}$ $\boxed{\text{SHIFT}}$ $\boxed{\sqrt[3]{}}$

$6\cdot4^2$ is found by keying $\boxed{6\cdot4}$ $\boxed{\text{SHIFT}}$ $\boxed{x^2}$

The $\boxed{x^y}$ key is used to find cubes such as 2^3, $6\cdot4^3$.

To find 2^3, key $\boxed{2}$ $\boxed{\text{SHIFT}}$ $\boxed{x^y}$ $\boxed{3}$ $\boxed{=}$ to get answer 8.

To find $6\cdot4^3$, key $\boxed{6\cdot4}$ $\boxed{\text{SHIFT}}$ $\boxed{x^y}$ $\boxed{3}$ $\boxed{=}$ to get answer $262\cdot1$ to 1 d.p.

Worked Example Use your calculator to evaluate these, giving the answers to one decimal place if rounding is necessary.

(a) $0\cdot3 \times 1\cdot6 + \sqrt{5}$

(b) $1\cdot2^2 + 3 \times 2\cdot4$

(c) $6\cdot7 + 2\cdot2\,(\sqrt{7\cdot8}\; - 12)$

(d) $\dfrac{(-2)^3 - (-3)^2}{-2 + (-3)}$

(e) $3\frac{5}{8} + (2\frac{3}{7})^2$

Answer (a) Key $\boxed{0\cdot3}$ $\boxed{\times}$ $\boxed{1\cdot6}$ $\boxed{+}$ $\boxed{5}$ $\boxed{\sqrt{}}$ $\boxed{=}$ to get $2\cdot7$ to 1 d.p.

(b) Key $\boxed{1\cdot2}$ $\boxed{\text{SHIFT}}$ $\boxed{x^2}$ $\boxed{+}$ $\boxed{3}$ $\boxed{\times}$ $\boxed{2\cdot4}$ $\boxed{=}$ to get $8\cdot64$.

(c) Key $\boxed{6\cdot7}$ $\boxed{+}$ $\boxed{2\cdot2}$ $\boxed{\times}$ $\boxed{(}$ $\boxed{7\cdot8}$ $\boxed{\sqrt{}}$ $\boxed{-}$ $\boxed{12}$ $\boxed{)}$ $\boxed{=}$ to get $-13\cdot6$ to 1 d.p.

(d) Key $\boxed{(}$ $\boxed{2}$ $\boxed{+/-}$ $\boxed{\text{SHIFT}}$ $\boxed{x^y}$ $\boxed{3}$ $\boxed{-}$ $\boxed{3}$ $\boxed{+/-}$ $\boxed{\text{SHIFT}}$ $\boxed{x^2}$ $\boxed{)}$ $\boxed{\div}$ $\boxed{(}$ $\boxed{2}$ $\boxed{+/-}$ $\boxed{+}$
$\boxed{3}$ $\boxed{+/-}$ $\boxed{)}$ $\boxed{=}$ to get $3\cdot4$.

(e) Key $\boxed{3}$ $\boxed{a^{b/c}}$ $\boxed{5}$ $\boxed{a^{b/c}}$ $\boxed{8}$ $\boxed{+}$ $\boxed{2}$ $\boxed{a^{b/c}}$ $\boxed{3}$ $\boxed{a^{b/c}}$ $\boxed{7}$ $\boxed{\text{SHIFT}}$ $\boxed{x^2}$ $\boxed{=}$
to get $9\cdot5$ to 1 d.p.

EXERCISE 5:2

1. Use the calculator to evaluate these. Round the answers to two decimal places.

   (a) $8{\cdot}2^3$ (b) $\sqrt{79}$ (c) $0{\cdot}79^2$ (d) $\sqrt[3]{79{\cdot}7}$

2. A stationery shop bought boxes of Christmas cards.
   Each box was a cube of volume $21952\,cm^3$.
   How high was each box?

3. Without using the calculator, find the answer to these.

   (a) $\sqrt{4}-5$

   (b) $2+5\sqrt{36}$

   (c) $5-3^2$

   (d) $3(1+4\sqrt{9}\,)$

   (e) $7-2(\sqrt{25}+1)$

   (f) $3\sqrt{4}-5\times(-3)$

   (g) $-2(4^2+1)$

   (h) $3[4-(-1)^3]$

   (i) $\dfrac{\sqrt{16}}{2}+\sqrt{9}$

   (j) $\dfrac{2^3}{4}-5$

   (k) $\dfrac{11+2\sqrt{9}}{5}$

   (l) $5\times(-3)+2(2^3+4)$

   (m) $\dfrac{2(15-3^3)}{-6}$

   (n) $\dfrac{5\sqrt{9}+6}{3-(-4)}$

   (o) $\dfrac{4-4^2}{-4}$

   (p) $4+\dfrac{4+\sqrt{4}}{4}$

4. Calculate. If rounding is necessary give the answer to 1 d.p.

   (a) $4-\sqrt{7}$

   (b) $2{\cdot}5-1{\cdot}2^2$

   (c) $3{\cdot}7+4{\cdot}6\sqrt{2}$

   (d) $5-3(\sqrt{10}-1)$

   (e) $2\sqrt{5}+3{\cdot}3^2$

   (f) $3{\cdot}5+5(1{\cdot}3^3-4)$

   (g) $\dfrac{3\sqrt{8}-2}{-6}$

   (h) $\dfrac{5{\cdot}2+3\sqrt{7}}{1{\cdot}3^2}$

   (i) $3\times(-2{\cdot}4)+\dfrac{1{\cdot}6}{2{\cdot}1^2}$

   (j) $\dfrac{(-5)^2+4^2}{-5+9}$

   (k) $\dfrac{\sqrt{8}+\sqrt{6}}{\sqrt{8}-\sqrt{6}}$

   (l) $4+(3\tfrac{2}{15})^2$

   (m) $6\tfrac{4}{5}-(1\tfrac{2}{5})^3$

   (n) $(2\tfrac{1}{3})^2+4(2\tfrac{2}{9}+\sqrt{2\tfrac{1}{2}}\,)$

Review Evaluate. If rounding is necessary give the answer to 1 d.p.

   (a) $6{\cdot}7^3$

   (b) $\sqrt[3]{2{\cdot}73}$

   (c) $3+\sqrt{3}$

   (d) $3[5-(-5)^2]$

   (e) $\dfrac{15+3\sqrt{4}}{-3}$

   (f) $5-2(4+\sqrt{6}\,)$

   (g) $-3{\cdot}4\times(-1{\cdot}6)^2$

   (h) $2\sqrt{5}-5\sqrt{2}$

   (i) $\dfrac{\sqrt{1{\cdot}8}+1{\cdot}8^2}{3-\sqrt{3}}$

   (j) $(8\tfrac{2}{7})^2+5\tfrac{3}{8}$

EVALUATING FORMULAE: using decimals, negative numbers, fractions.

To **evaluate a formula** we replace variables with the given values, then do the calculation. Evaluating a formula is the same as substituting in the formula. We may choose to use the calculator for the calculation.

Worked Example $a = 2bc - d^2$ Find the value of **a** if $b = 3, c = -4, d = -2$.

Answer Without using the calculator:

$$a = 2bc - d^2$$
$$= 2 \times 3 \times (-4) - (-2)^2$$
$$= -24 - 4$$
$$= -28$$

Using the calculator:

$$a = 2bc - d^2$$
$$= 2 \times 3 \times (-4) - (-2)^2$$
$$= -28$$

Keying $\boxed{2}\boxed{\times}\boxed{3}\boxed{\times}\boxed{4}\boxed{+/-}\boxed{-}\boxed{2}\boxed{+/-}\boxed{\text{SHIFT}}\boxed{x^2}\boxed{=}$

Worked Example $s = ut + \frac{1}{2}at^2$ Find s if $t = 0.2, u = -20, a = 10$.

Answer Without using the calculator:

$$s = ut + \tfrac{1}{2}at^2$$
$$= -20 \times 0.2 + \tfrac{1}{2} \times 10 \times (0.2)^2$$
$$= -4 + 5 \times 0.04$$
$$= -4 + 0.2$$
$$= -3.8$$

Using the calculator:

$$s = ut + \tfrac{1}{2}at^2$$
$$= -20 \times 0.2 + \tfrac{1}{2} \times 10 \times (0.2)^2$$
$$= -3.8$$

Keying $\boxed{20}\boxed{+/-}\boxed{\times}\boxed{0.2}\boxed{+}\boxed{0.5}\boxed{\times}\boxed{10}\boxed{\times}\boxed{0.2}\boxed{\text{SHIFT}}\boxed{x^2}\boxed{=}$

Worked Example

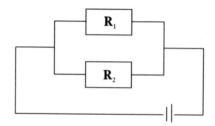

The total resistance R in this circuit is given by $R = \dfrac{R_1 R_2}{R_1 + R_2}$.

Find R if $R_1 = 7\frac{1}{2}$, $R_2 = 11\frac{1}{4}$.

Answer Without using the calculator:

$$R = \frac{7\frac{1}{2} \times 11\frac{1}{4}}{7\frac{1}{2} + 11\frac{1}{4}}$$

$$= \frac{\frac{15}{2} \times \frac{45}{4}}{18\frac{3}{4}}$$

$$= \frac{15}{2} \times \frac{45}{4} \div \frac{75}{4}$$

$$= \frac{\overset{1}{\cancel{15}}}{2} \times \frac{\overset{9}{\cancel{45}}}{\cancel{4}_1} \times \frac{\overset{1}{\cancel{4}}}{\cancel{75}_1}$$

$$= \frac{9}{2}$$

$$= 4\frac{1}{2}$$

Using the calculator:

$$R = \frac{7\frac{1}{2} \times 11\frac{1}{4}}{7\frac{1}{2} + 11\frac{1}{4}}$$

$$= 4\frac{1}{2}$$

Keying

EXERCISE 5:3

1. Area = length × width   Perimeter = 2 (length + width)

    These formulae can be used to find the area and perimeter of a rectangle.
    Find the area and perimeter of the following rectangles.

    (a) length = $2\frac{1}{4}$ m, width = $1\frac{1}{3}$ m   (b) length = $3\frac{1}{3}$ m, width = $2\frac{1}{4}$ m

2. The y-coordinate of any point on this graph can be calculated using the formula $y = -\frac{1}{2}x + 4$.

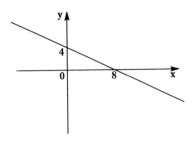

Use this formula to complete the following coordinates.

$(4, \ldots)$, $(-2, \ldots)$, $(2\frac{1}{2}, \ldots)$,

$(-3\frac{1}{2}, \ldots)$, $(9, \ldots)$

3. $y = mx + c$ Find the value of y if:

   (a) $m = -2$, $x = 3$, $c = -1$ (b) $m = -1$, $x = -2$, $c = 3$ (c) $m = \frac{1}{2}$, $x = -2$, $c = 5$

   (d) $m = -\frac{1}{2}$, $x = 3$, $c = -2$ (e) $m = 0\cdot5$, $x = -6$, $c = 2$.

4.   Area $= \frac{1}{2}bh$

   Find the area if (a) $b = 2\frac{1}{2}$, $h = 4\frac{2}{5}$

                      (b) $b = 13\frac{1}{3}$, $h = 8\frac{1}{4}$.

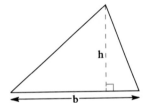

5. If $a = -4$, $b = 0\cdot5$, $c = 2$, $d = -\frac{1}{4}$ evaluate.

   (a) $3a - 5c$ (b) $a^2 - c^2$ (c) $8d + a - b$ (d) $cd + a$

   (e) $(a + c)(a - c)$ (f) $2a + 3c^2$ (g) $b - a^2$ (h) $\dfrac{c - a}{2b + a}$

   (i) $4(a + b - c)$ (j) $3 + a(b - d)$.

6. The mean of three numbers a, b, c is given by $m = \frac{1}{3}(a + b + c)$.

   Use this formula to find the mean of: (a) $2, 3, 6$

                                          (b) $2\frac{1}{2}, 3\frac{1}{4}, 5$.

7. $A = \frac{h}{2}(a + b)$ gives the area of a trapezium.

   Find the area of a trapezium for which:

   (a) $a = 4$, $b = 5\frac{1}{3}$, $h = 3$

   (b) $h = 4\frac{1}{6}$, $a = 5\frac{1}{2}$, $b = 4\frac{1}{10}$

8. To change a temperature from °C to °F we can use the formula $F = \frac{9}{5}C + 32$.
   Use this formula to write the following in °F.

   (a) 100°C   (b) 0°C   (c) –10°C   (d) –15°C   (e) – 40°C

9. $I = \frac{PRT}{100}$ Find I if   (a) P = 200, R = $6\frac{1}{4}$, T = 8

                             (b) P = 100, R = $8\frac{1}{2}$, T = $\frac{1}{2}$.

10. The volume of a pyramid is given by the formula
         $V = \frac{1}{3}$ (base area) × height.
    Use this formula to find the volume of the sketched pyramid.

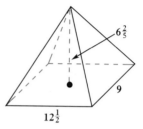

11. The marks from two tests are combined using the formula $M = \frac{2}{5}X + \frac{3}{5}Y$. M is the combined mark, X is the mark from the first test, Y is the mark from the second test.

    Use the formula to find M for the following students.

         Alison: 40 in Test 1, 55 in Test 2
         Brenda: 36 in Test 1, 60 in Test 2
         Ben: 42 in Test 1, 54 in Test 2

12. Overtime Wage = $\dfrac{\text{Basic Wage}}{37\frac{1}{2}}$ × $1\frac{1}{2}$ × h

    Find the overtime wage if:

    (a) h = 3, basic wage = £150

    (b) h = $2\frac{1}{2}$, basic wage = £120.

13. Use the formula $s = ut + \frac{1}{2}at^2$ to find s if:

    (a) u = 25, t = 3, a = –5   (b) u = –10, t = $\frac{1}{4}$, a = 8   (c) u = –5, t = 0·5, a = 10

    (d) u = –15, t = 0·5, a = –2

14. $s = \dfrac{v^2 - u^2}{2a}$ is a formula which gives the distance, s, travelled by a body moving with uniform acceleration, **a**. The initial velocity is **u** and the final velocity is **v**. Use this formula to find s (in metres) if:

    (a) a = 2m/s², v = 6m/s, u = 2m/s

    (b) a = 5m/s², v = 8·5m/s, u = 1·9m/s

    (c) a = 2·5m/s², v = 15m/s, u = 8·8m/s

15. Two particles are projected vertically upwards with velocity **u**. The second particle is projected **t** seconds after the first. These particles will meet at a height **h** (metres) where **h** is given by $h = \dfrac{4u^2 - g^2t^2}{8g}$ (g is the acceleration due to gravity.)

Find **h** to the nearest mm if (a) u = 25 m/s, t = 5 sec, g = 9·8 m/s²

(b) u = 25 m/s, t = 1 sec, g = 9·8 m/s²

16. The area of a triangle can be found by using the formula $A = \sqrt{s(s-a)(s-b)(s-c)}$ where s is half the perimeter and a, b, c are the lengths of the sides. Use this formula to find the area of this triangle.

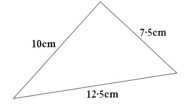

17. $\dfrac{1}{f} = \dfrac{1}{v} + \dfrac{1}{u}$. Find **f** if u = $7\frac{1}{2}$, v = 6.

Review 1 $C = \frac{5}{9}(F - 32)$ is a formula that can be used to change a temperature from °F to °C.
Write the following in °C.   (a) 14°F   (b) − 4°F

Review 2 y = m (x − 3) + 2.

Find y if (a) m = −3, x = 5   (b) m = 3, x = −5   (c) m = −1, x = −1

           (d) m = −2, x = $1\frac{1}{2}$ (e) m = $\frac{1}{2}$, x = −0·5.

Review 3 The sum of the first n terms of the sequence 1, $2\frac{1}{4}$, $3\frac{1}{2}$, ... can be found by using the formula $S = \dfrac{n}{2}[2 + (n - 1) \times 1\frac{1}{4}]$.

Use this formula to find the sum of

(a) the first 5 terms   (b) the first 17 terms.

Review 4 The formula $t = \dfrac{hc}{h + c}$ gives the time, **t** minutes, taken for a bath to fill if both the hot and cold taps are turned on. **h** minutes is the time it takes to fill the bath if just the hot tap is turned on, **c** minutes is the time taken if just the cold tap is turned on.

Find **t** if   (a) h = 5, c = $3\frac{1}{3}$ (b) h = $4\frac{4}{5}$, c = $2\frac{2}{5}$.

INDICES

3^4 is called a **power** of 3; 4 is called the **index**, 3 is called the **base**.

Indices is the plural of index. For instance, if we were speaking of the numbers 4 and 7 in 3^4 and 2^7 we would call 4 and 7 the indices.

The x^y key, on the calculator, may be used to find powers.

For instance, 2^7 is found by keying $\boxed{2}$ $\boxed{\text{SHIFT}}$ $\boxed{x^y}$ $\boxed{7}$ $\boxed{=}$

INVESTIGATION 5:4

PATTERNS with INDICES

1.
row 1 ⟶				1			
row 2 ⟶			1		1		
row 3 ⟶		1		2		1	
row 4 ⟶	1		3		3		1
row 5 ⟶	1	4		6		4	1
row 6 ⟶	1	5	10		10	5	1

The first 6 rows of Pascal's triangle are shown.
What is the sum of the numbers on each row?
What is the connection between these sums and indices?
Investigate.

2.
$$4^5 = 102\underline{4}$$
$$6^5 = 777\underline{6}$$
$$24^5 = 796262\underline{4}$$
$$37^5 = 6934395\underline{7}$$

What do you notice about the underlined digits?
Investigate other numbers to the power of 5. Look for patterns. As part of your investigation, make and test statements.

What if the index was 4 rather than 5?

What if . . .

DISCUSSION EXERCISE and INVESTIGATION 5:5

- $$2^3 = 2 \times 2 \times 2 \qquad\qquad 2^2 = 2 \times 2$$
$$= 8 \qquad\qquad\qquad\qquad = 4$$
$$8 \times 4 = 32$$

Write 32 as a power of 2. What do you notice about this power of 2 and the powers, 2^3 and 2^2, we began with? Discuss.

What if we began with different indices such as 4 and 5 instead of 3 and 2?
What if we began with the base 4 instead of 2?
What if we began with the base x?
What if we began with two different bases but the same index ; for instance, 2^3 and 5^3?
What if we began with two different bases and two different indices ; for instance, 2^3 and 4^2?

- $$2^6 = 2 \times 2 \times 2 \times 2 \times 2 \times 2 \qquad 2^2 = 2 \times 2$$
$$= 64 \qquad\qquad\qquad\qquad\qquad = 4$$
$$64 \div 4 = 16$$

Write 16 as a power of 2. What do you notice about this power of 2 and the powers 2^6 and 2^2? Discuss.
Make and test statements about division of powers.

- $$2^3 = 2 \times 2 \times 2 \qquad\qquad (2^3)^2 = 8^2$$
$$= 8 \qquad\qquad\qquad\qquad\quad = 64$$

Write 64 as a power of 2. Compare this with $(2^3)^2$. Discuss.

What if the indices were 5 and 2 rather than 3 and 2?
What if the indices were 2 and 4 rather than 3 and 2?
What if the base was 4 instead of 2?
What if ...

- *The answer is 2^6.* Write down many expressions that could be simplified to 2^6. Discuss.
The answer is x^4. Write down many expressions that could be simplified to x^4. Discuss.

- Use the results of your discussion and investigation to complete the following rules for indices.

$$a^m \times a^n = a^{\cdots}$$

$$a^m \div a^n = a^{\cdots}$$

$$(a^m)^n = a^{\cdots}$$

Worked Example Use the rules of indices to write the following as single powers of 7.

$$\text{(a)} \ 7^4 \times 7^9 \qquad \text{(b)} \ 7^8 \div 7^2 \qquad \text{(c)} \ (7^5)^3$$

Answer (a) $7^4 \times 7^9 = 7^{4+9}$ (b) $7^8 \div 7^2 = 7^{8-2}$ (c) $(7^5)^3 = 7^{5 \times 3}$
$$= 7^{13} \qquad\qquad\qquad\qquad = 7^6 \qquad\qquad\qquad\qquad = 7^{15}$$

Worked Example Simplify   (a) $x^y \times x^a$ (b) $a^x \times a^y \times a^z$ (c) $\dfrac{x^a}{x^y}$ (d) $(x^{3a})^b$

Answer (a) $x^y \times x^a = x^{y+a}$ (b) $a^x \times a^y \times a^z = a^{x+y+z}$ (c) $\dfrac{x^a}{x^y} = x^{a-y}$ (d) $(x^{3a})^b = x^{3ab}$

Worked Example Write the following without brackets.   (a) $(b^3h^2)^4$ (b) $(2a^2b)^3$

Answer (a) $(b^3h^2)^4 = b^3h^2 \times b^3h^2 \times b^3h^2 \times b^3h^2$
$$= b^{12}h^8$$

       (b) $(2a^2b)^3 = 2a^2b \times 2a^2b \times 2a^2b$
$$= 8a^6b^3$$

Worked Example Write $\dfrac{8^2 \times 2^5}{4^4}$ as a power of 2.

Answer Since $8 = 2^3$ and $4 = 2^2$, $\dfrac{8^2 \times 2^5}{4^4}$ may be written as $\dfrac{(2^3)^2 \times 2^5}{(2^2)^4}$
$$= \frac{2^6 \times 2^5}{2^8}$$
$$= 2^3$$

EXERCISE 5:6

1. Write these as a single power of 5.

   (a) $5^3 \times 5^6$ (b) $5^4 \times 5^3$ (c) $5^4 \times 5^4$ (d) $5^7 \times 5^{10}$

   (e) $5^6 \div 5^3$ (f) $5^5 \div 5^1$ (g) $5^{16} \div 5^4$ (h) $\dfrac{5^8}{5^4}$

   (i) $(5^2)^3$ (j) $(5^4)^4$ (k) $(5^3)^2$

2. Use the rules of indices to simplify these. Hence evaluate.

   (a) $2^4 \times 2^3$ (b) $3^2 \times 3^3$ (c) $\dfrac{5^7}{5^5}$ (d) $2^2 \times 2^3 \times 2^2$

   (e) $\dfrac{4^3 \times 4^6}{4^7}$ (f) $\dfrac{2^{13}}{2^4 \times 2^5}$ (g) $\dfrac{7^{11} \times 7^4}{7^9 \times 7^5}$ (h) $\dfrac{5^7 \times 5^3}{(5^4)^2}$

3. Which of the following statements are correct?
    (a) $4^3 \times 4^2 = 4^6$
    (b) $4^3 + 4^2 = 4^5$
    (c) $4^3 \times 2^2 = 8^5$
    (d) $(4^4)^2 = 16^6$
    (e) $4^8 \div 2^3 = 2^5$
    (f) $4^5 - 4^3 = 4^2$

4. Which of the following statements are correct?
    (a) $a^6 \div a^2 = a^3$
    (b) $a^6 \times a^2 = a^8$
    (c) $a \times a^4 = a^5$
    (d) $(x^2)^3 = x^6$
    (e) $x^3 \times x^4 \times x = x^8$
    (f) $(p^5)^3 = p^{15}$
    (g) $a^6 - a^2 = a^4$
    (h) $a^7 + a^2 = a^9$
    (i) $(2a^3)^2 = 2a^6$

5. Simplify these.
    (a) $x^4 \times x^5$
    (b) $a^3 \times a^9$
    (c) $p^{12} \div p^4$
    (d) $x^{16} \div x^2$

    (e) $b^a \times b^x$
    (f) $b^a \times b^c$
    (g) $a^x \div a^b$
    (h) $(a^x)^y$

    (i) $(x^{2a})^3$
    (j) $(p^{3x})^4$
    (k) $x^p \times x^p$
    (l) $b^a \times b^a$

    (m) $\dfrac{a^7 \times a^4}{a^3}$
    (n) $\dfrac{x^4 \times x^5}{(x^3)^2}$

6. Write these without brackets.
    (a) $(x^2y^3)^2$
    (b) $(a^3b)^4$
    (c) $(x^2yz^3)^5$
    (d) $(2a^2b^3)^4$

    (e) $(3p^3q^5)^3$
    (f) $(4a^5x^4)^2$
    (g) $(2xy^3z^3)^5$

7. (a) Write $\dfrac{9^2 \times 27}{3^5}$ as a power of 3.
    (b) Write $\dfrac{125 \times 5^{10}}{25^2}$ as a power of 5.

    (c) Write $\dfrac{16^3 \times 8^3}{2^9 \times 4^5}$ as a power of 2.

Review 1   Which of the following statements are correct?
    (a) $4^5 + 4^7 = 4^{12}$
    (b) $(3^2)^5 = 3^7$
    (c) $7^7 - 7^2 = 7^5$
    (d) $a^5 \times a^3 \times a^2 = a^{10}$
    (e) $(2a^3)^4 = 16a^7$
    (f) $x^8 \div x^2 = x^4$

Review 2   Use the rules of indices to simplify these.
    (a) $\dfrac{a^{14}}{a^7}$
    (b) $p^5 \times p^7$
    (c) $a^2 \times a^3 \times a$
    (d) $\dfrac{y^7 \times y^2}{y^5}$
    (e) $(x^3)^5$
    (f) $(3a^4)^2$
    (g) $(2x^3y^4)^3$

Review 3   Write $\dfrac{2^8 \times 4^3}{16 \times 8^2}$ as a power of 2.

INVESTIGATION 5:7

LAST DIGITS

$3^1 = 3$
$3^2 = 9$
$3^3 = 27$
$3^4 = 81$
$3^5 = 243$
$3^6 = 729$
$3^7 = 2187$
$3^8 = 6561$
$3^9 = 19683$

The last digits form the pattern:
$3, 9, 7, 1, 3, 9, 7, 1, 3, \ldots$
Can you predict what the last digit of 3^{24} is?
Can you predict what the last digit is of other powers of 3?
Investigate.

What if the base was a number other than 3?

Suppose we were asked to find the last two digits of 2^{250}. We could investigate to find a pattern or we could proceed as follows.

$2^5 = 32,$ $2^{10} = (2^5)^2$
                    $= 32 \times 32$
                    $= 1024$ The last two digits are 24.
$2^{20} = (2^{10})^2$

        $= 1024 \times 1024$ The last two digits are found by multiplying 24 by 24.

Proceeding in this manner, we could find the last two digits of $2^{40}, 2^{80}, 2^{160}$.

How could we use this method to find the last two digits of 2^{250}?
(Hint : Use $a^{m+n} = a^m \times a^n$.)

Investigate using this method and/or using a pattern to find the last two digits of any power of 2.

What if we were finding the last two digits of any power of 3?
What if . . .

RECIPROCALS

DISCUSSION EXERCISE 5:8

What is the relationship between the following pairs of numbers? **Discuss.**

$2, \frac{1}{2}$ $4, \frac{1}{4}$ $\frac{1}{7}, 7$ $\frac{2}{3}, \frac{3}{2}$ $\frac{5}{4}, \frac{4}{5}$ $2\frac{1}{2}, \frac{2}{5}$

Write down some other pairs of numbers with this relationship. **Discuss.**

The reciprocal of $\frac{3}{5}$ is $\frac{5}{3}$; the reciprocal of $\frac{a}{b}$ is $\frac{b}{a}$; the reciprocal of a is $\frac{1}{a}$.
To find the reciprocal of a number proceed as follows.

Step 1   Write down the number as a fraction, if it isn't already given as a fraction.
Step 2   Invert the fraction. That is, "tip the fraction upside down."

Worked Example Find the reciprocals of (a) $\frac{2}{5}$ (b) 5   (c) 0·8   (d) $\frac{3}{x}$ (e) 3x

Answer (a) The reciprocal of $\frac{2}{5}$ is $\frac{5}{2}$.

   (b) Since $5 = \frac{5}{1}$, the reciprocal of 5 is $\frac{1}{5}$.

   (c) $0·8 = \frac{8}{10}$ or $\frac{4}{5}$. The reciprocal of 0·8 is $\frac{5}{4}$ or 1·25.

   (d) The reciprocal of $\frac{3}{x}$ is $\frac{x}{3}$

   (e) Since $3x = \frac{3x}{1}$, the reciprocal of 3x is $\frac{1}{3x}$.

The $\frac{1}{x}$ key on the calculator is used to find the reciprocal of a number.
For instance, the reciprocal of 2 is found by keying $\boxed{2}$ $\boxed{\text{SHIFT}}$ $\boxed{\frac{1}{x}}$

EXERCISE 5:9

1.   Without using the calculator, find the reciprocal of these.

   (a) $\frac{2}{3}$ (b) $\frac{3}{4}$ (c) $\frac{3}{10}$ (d) $\frac{8}{7}$ (e) $\frac{5}{4}$ (f) $\frac{1}{6}$

   (g) 7   (h) 8   (i) 0·7   (j) 1·3

2.   Find the reciprocal of these.

   (a) $\frac{c}{a}$ (b) $\frac{a}{c}$ (c) $\frac{z}{x}$ (d) $\frac{x}{z}$ (e) $\frac{a}{x}$ (f) $\frac{x}{a}$

   (g) x   (h) d   (i) 2z   (j) 5x   (k) $\frac{x}{4}$ (l) $\frac{2}{x}$

3.   Use the calculator to find the reciprocal of these. Give the answer to 2 significant figures where rounding is necessary.

   (a) 0·14   (b) 7·2   (c) 0·3   (d) 10   (e) 25   (f) 54

Review 1   Give the reciprocal of these as a whole number or a fraction.

   (a) $\frac{3}{4}$ (b) 9   (c) 0·1   (d) k   (e) 3k   (f) $\frac{a}{3k}$

Review 2   Find the reciprocal of these, giving the answer to 2 d.p. where rounding is
   necessary.   (a) 0·6   (b) 20   (c) 1·16

DISCUSSION EXERCISE 5:10

- **Discuss** the following statements which may be true or false. For those that are false, make a similar correct statement.

  Statement 1 There is just one whole number that has no reciprocal.
  Statement 2 Dividing by a number is the same as multiplying by the reciprocal of that number.
  Statement 3 When a number is multiplied by its reciprocal the answer is 0.
  Statement 4 Negative numbers have no reciprocals.

- Adding and subtracting, multiplying and dividing, squaring and taking the square root are all inverse operations. What is the inverse operation for "taking the reciprocal"? **Discuss**.

USING RECIPROCALS to SOLVE EQUATIONS

The operation "take the reciprocal" is needed to solve some equations by the flowchart method. This operation is necessary if x is on the bottom line of the equation. Remember that the inverse for "taking the reciprocal" is also "taking the reciprocal".

Worked Example Find the value of x for which $\frac{3}{x} = 5$.

Answer Using the flowchart method:

Begin with x → $\boxed{\text{Take the reciprocal}}$ → $\frac{1}{x}$ → $\boxed{\times 3}$ → $\frac{3}{x}$

$\frac{3}{5}$ ← $\boxed{\text{Take the reciprocal}}$ ← $\frac{5}{3}$ ← $\boxed{\div 3}$ ← Begin with 5

The solution is x = $\frac{3}{5}$ or 0·6.

Worked Example Find the solution of the equation $\frac{2}{x+1} = 5$.

Answer

Begin with x → $\boxed{+1}$ → x + 1 → $\boxed{\text{Take the reciprocal}}$ → $\frac{1}{x+1}$ → $\boxed{\times 2}$ → $\frac{2}{x+1}$

$-0·6$ ← $\boxed{-1}$ ← $\frac{2}{5}$ ← $\boxed{\text{Take the reciprocal}}$ ← $\frac{5}{2}$ ← $\boxed{\div 2}$ ← Begin with 5

The solution is x = −0·6.

EXERCISE 5:11

1. Solve these equations.

   (a) $\dfrac{2}{x} = 9$ (b) $\dfrac{4}{x} = 10$ (c) $\dfrac{5}{x} = 1.8$

   (d) $\dfrac{2}{x-1} = 4$ (e) $\dfrac{5}{x+3} = 1$ (f) $\dfrac{1}{2x-1} = 3$

   (g) $\dfrac{4}{5x+2} = 5$ (h) $\dfrac{2}{1+3x} = 5$

2. $s = \dfrac{d}{t}$ is a formula which gives the average speed, **s**, if a distance, **d**, is covered in time **t**. Use this formula to find the time taken if:

   (a) s = 50km/h,   d = 240km   (b) s = 120km/h,   d = 500km

   (c) s = 10m/s,   d = 44m   (d) s = 20m/s,   d = 550m

3. $d = \dfrac{m}{v}$ gives the density, **d**, of an object of mass, **m**, and volume **v**. Find the volume of an object if: (a) d = 0·25g/cm³, m = 150g   (b) d = 1·5g/cm³, m = 60g

4. If just the hot tap is turned on, a bath can be filled in **h** minutes; if just the cold tap is turned on, a bath can be filled in **c** minutes. If both taps are turned on, a bath can be filled in **t** minutes where t is given by $\dfrac{1}{t} = \dfrac{1}{h} + \dfrac{1}{c}$. For Angela's bath, h = 8 minutes and c = 5 minutes. Find the time taken to fill Angela's bath if both taps are turned on. (Answer to the nearest minute.)

5.

   The total resistance R in this circuit, with resistors R_1 and R_2 in parallel, is given by $\dfrac{1}{R} = \dfrac{1}{R_1} + \dfrac{1}{R_2}$.

   Find the total resistance R if R_1 = 3·5 ohms and R_2 = 4·5 ohms.

Review 1 Solve these equations. (a) $\dfrac{3}{x} = 8$ (b) $\dfrac{5}{x+2} = 2$

Review 2 Ohm's Law, $\dfrac{V}{I} = R$, gives the relationship between voltage V, current I and resistance R. V is measured in volts, I is measured in amps and R is measured in ohms. Find the current if the voltage is 12 volts and the resistance is 2·4 ohms.

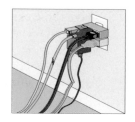

CHAPTER 5   REVIEW

1. **(i)** Use the rules of indices to write these as single powers of 3.

   (a) $3^4 \times 3^7$ **(b)** $3^7 \div 3^4$ **(c)** $(3^5)^2$ **(d)** $\dfrac{3^{13}}{3 \times 3^3}$

   (ii) Which of these statements are correct?

   (a) $a^9 \times a^2 = a^7$ **(b)** $a^8 \div a^4 = a^4$ **(c)** $(a^5)^3 = a^8$

   (iii) Write these without brackets.

   (a) $(x^2y)^3$ **(b)** $(x^{2p})^4$ **(c)** $(3xy^4)^2$

   (iv) Write $\dfrac{32 \times 4^4}{2^7}$ as a single power of 2.

   (v) Find the reciprocal of these, leaving your answer as a fraction.

   (a) $\dfrac{3}{11}$ **(b)** $\dfrac{7}{3}$ **(c)** $\dfrac{a}{4}$ **(d)** 3   **(e)** $\dfrac{a}{5x}$ **(f)** 2x

   (vi) Solve these equations.

   (a) $\dfrac{5}{2x} = 4$ **(b)** $\dfrac{6}{2x+1} = 2$

2. The total surface area, **S**, of a can is given by the formula
   $S = 2\pi r (r + h)$.

   (a) Calculate the value of S when r = 3·7cm and h = 10·4cm.
   Take π to be 3·14 or use the π key on your calculator.

   Bill uses the same formula to calculate the value of S when r = 2·6 and h = 9·4.

   (b) He presses keys as follows:

   $\boxed{2}\ \boxed{\cdot}\ \boxed{6}\ \boxed{+}\ \boxed{9}\ \boxed{\cdot}\ \boxed{4}\ \boxed{}\ \boxed{}\ \boxed{2}\ \boxed{\times}\ \boxed{\pi}\ \boxed{\times}\ \boxed{2}\ \boxed{\cdot}\ \boxed{6}\ \boxed{=}$

   Fill in the missing keys.

   SEG

3. The cost of hiring a car is £c.
    This cost is given by the formula

    $$c = 21\cdot50 + k\,(0\cdot27 + d),$$

    where k is the number of kilometres driven,
    d is a number which depends on the type of car.
    Jill hires a car and drives 90 kilometres.
    For this car the value of d is $0\cdot19$.
    How much will it cost her?   **SEG**

4. Use the formula $$p = \frac{q+r}{s}$$
    to find p when $q = \frac{2}{5}$, $r = \frac{5}{12}$ and $s = \frac{7}{30}$.   **MEG**

5. A rocket is fired from a cliff and its height h metres above sea level, after t seconds, is given by the formula

    $$h = 35t\,(83 - t) + 56\tfrac{1}{4}.$$

    Calculate the height of the rocket after $20\tfrac{1}{2}$ seconds.   **SEG**

6. Tony wanted to calculate $(13 \times 3)^2$.
    He pressed these buttons to get his answer.

    $$\boxed{1}\;\boxed{3}\;\boxed{\times}\;\boxed{3}\;\boxed{x^2}\;\boxed{=}$$

    He got the answer 117.

    (a) What is wrong with Tony's method?

    (b) What is the correct answer?   **SEG**

7. One answer to a question is

    $$x = \frac{-125 + \sqrt{125^2 + 4\times8\times187}}{16}$$

    Calculate this value of x.   **MEG**

8. Use the formula

    $$A = \tfrac{1}{4}\,c\,\sqrt{4a^2 - c^2}$$

    to calculate the value of A given that

    $c = 7\cdot23$ and $a = 8\cdot76$.

    Give your answer correct to 1 decimal place.   **ULEAC**

9.

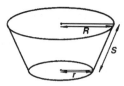

The area of sheet plastic needed to make the bucket shown in the diagram is given by the formula

$$\text{Area} = S\pi(R + r) + \pi r^2.$$

Use your calculator to find the area of plastic needed for a bucket with

$$r = 12{\cdot}5\text{cm}, \quad R = 14\text{cm} \quad \text{and} \quad S = 30\text{cm}.$$ **MEG**

10. The following formula gives distance, s, in terms of the acceleration a and speeds u and v.

$$s = \frac{v^2 - u^2}{2a}$$

(a) Find s when $a = 8$, $v = 1$ and $u = 15{\cdot}5$.

The formula above may be rearranged to give $u = \sqrt{v^2 - 2as}$

(b) Calculate the value of u when $a = 3\frac{1}{2}$, $s = 6\frac{2}{3}$ and $v = 18\frac{1}{2}$. **SEG**

11. In a geography project Tin Ling needed to find

$$\frac{(127 - 90)^2}{90} + \frac{(87 - 140)^2}{140} + \frac{(86 - 70)^2}{70}$$

Find this value. **MEG**

12. Use the formula $y = \dfrac{(x - c)}{\sqrt{(m^2 + 6)}}$ to calculate the value of y when $x = 20$, $c = 4{\cdot}7$ and $m = \frac{1}{2}$. **ULEAC**

13. Given that $a = \frac{1}{6}$, $b = \frac{1}{3}$, $c = \frac{3}{4}$, and $d = \frac{2}{3}$, calculate, in fractional form

(i) $bc + d$

(ii) $\dfrac{a}{(bc + d)}$. **WJEC**

14. The wind chill temperature, T°C, is given by the formula

$$T = 33 + (0\cdot45 + 0\cdot29\sqrt{v} - 0\cdot02v)\,(t - 35).$$

Here t°C is the air temperature and v mph is the wind speed.
Find T, to the nearest degree, when $t = -5$ and $v = 10$.   **SEG**

15. A formula for working out the area A of a triangle with sides x cm, y cm and z cm is given by

$$A = \sqrt{s(s - x)(s - y)(s - z)}$$

where $s = \dfrac{(x + y + z)}{2}$

Calculate the area of a triangle with $x = 2\frac{1}{2}$, $y = 3\frac{1}{4}$ and $z = 4\frac{3}{8}$.   **NEAB**

16. Scientists use the formula

$$\frac{1}{f} = \frac{1}{u} + \frac{1}{v}$$

to calculate the focal length, f, of a lens.
The lengths u, v and f are all measured in cm.
Calculate f when $u = 2\cdot4$ and $v = -3\cdot2$.   **NEAB**

Franciscus Vieta

Françios Viète, better known as Franciscus Vieta, was born in France in 1540 and died in 1603. He is known as "The Father of Modern Algebra". Interestingly, he disliked the Arabic name algebra.

Vieta was the most important mathematician of his time. He did not regard himself as a mathematician. Mathematics was what Vieta did as a leisure activity, not as a profession. He was a lawyer before becoming involved in politics. He became a member of a provincial government and later a King's adviser. He had important connections at the courts of Henry III and Henry IV.

Vieta is best known for using letters to represent numbers. He used consonants to represent known or given numbers and vowels to represent unknown numbers.

Vieta introduced a simplified notation for powers. For A, A^2, A^3 he used A, A quad., A cubus which clearly showed the relationship. His work on algebra established algebra as a separate study from arithmetic.

Apart from his work in algebra, he also made important contributions in other areas of mathematics.

He used decimal fractions and made a strong plea for these to be more widely used. In one of his books he wrote:

Sexagesimals and sixties are to be used sparingly or never in mathematics, and thousandths and thousands, hundredths and hundreds, tenths and tens, and similar progressions, ascending and descending, are to be used frequently or exclusively.

The notation he used for decimal fractions was to write the integer part of a number in bold-face type. He separated the integer part from the fractional part with either a comma or a stroke. That is, he wrote $21,305 \cdot 78$ as either **21,305**,78 or **21,305**|78. Although the decimal point was used by some mathematicians at this time, its use did not become common until shortly after Vieta's death when the scotsman, John Napier made it popular.

The work that Vieta did in geometry was further developed by the French mathematicians René Descartes and Pierre de Fermat. Sir Isaac Newton was later inspired by the work of these three.

Vieta was also interested in the reform of the calendar. He opposed Clavius' work on this. This lead to much criticism of him, mainly because of his unscientific approach.

It was for his work in deciphering codes that the French government valued Vieta. He deciphered a code used by the Spanish to send secret messages during a war between France and Spain. This gave the French a considerable advantage. The Spanish did not believe it was possible to decipher the code which contained more than 500 signs and symbols. They complained to the Pope that the French were using black magic and sorcery.

NEGATIVE INDICES

DISCUSSION EXERCISE 6:1

Since $2^3 = 2 \times 2 \times 2$ then $\frac{1}{2^3} = \frac{1}{2 \times 2 \times 2}$

$$= \frac{1}{8}$$

$$= 0 \cdot 125$$

Use the following calculator keying sequence to find the value of 2^{-3}.

[2] [SHIFT] [x^y] [3] [$+\!/\!-$] [=] . Compare the answers for $\frac{1}{2^3}$ and 2^{-3}.

What if 3 was replaced with 1?
What if 3 was replaced with 2?
What if 3 was replaced with 4?
What if 3 was replaced with 5?
What if . . .

Make a statement about the value of $\frac{1}{2^n}$ and 2^{-n}. **Discuss.**

Consider again $\frac{1}{2^3}$ and 2^{-3}. What if 2 was replaced by 4?

What if 2 was replaced by 5?

Make a statement about the value of a^{-n} and $\frac{1}{a^n}$. Test your statement for many values of
a and n.

EXERCISE 6:2

Find the missing index in each of the following.

1. $4^{-5} = \frac{1}{4^{\cdots}}$ 2. $7^{-2} = \frac{1}{7^{\cdots}}$ 3. $10^{-5} = \frac{1}{10^{\cdots}}$ 4. $1 \cdot 7^{-8} = \frac{1}{1 \cdot 7^{\cdots}}$

5. $\frac{1}{2^7} = 2^{\cdots}$ 6. $\frac{1}{3^6} = 3^{\cdots}$ 7. $\frac{1}{10^4} = 10^{\cdots}$ 8. $\frac{1}{3 \cdot 4^{10}} = 3 \cdot 4^{\cdots}$

9. $5^{-4} = \frac{1}{5^{\cdots}}$ 10. $\frac{1}{6^9} = 6^{\cdots}$ 11. $8^{-3} = \frac{1}{8^{\cdots}}$ 12. $\frac{1}{10^3} = 10^{\cdots}$

Review 1 $7^{-4} = \frac{1}{7^{\cdots}}$ **Review 2** $\frac{1}{10^9} = 10^{\cdots}$

DISCUSSION EXERCISE 6:3

- $254 \cdot 13 \times 10^3 = 254 \cdot 13 \times 1000$
  $= 254130$

  $254 \cdot 13 \times 10^{-3} = 254 \cdot 13 \times \frac{1}{10^3}$
  $= \frac{254 \cdot 13}{1000}$
  $= 0 \cdot 25413$

  Discuss the following statement in relation to these examples. "To multiply a decimal number by 10^n, where n is an integer, move the decimal point n places. If n is positive, move the decimal point in the positive direction; if n is negative, move the decimal point in the negative direction". As part of your discussion, rewrite other numbers such as $26 \cdot 2 \times 10^4$, $0 \cdot 7 \times 10^{-2}$, $7 \cdot 8 \times 10^2$, $8 \cdot 65 \times 10^{-1}$ etc. in decimal form.

- The answer to the calculation 50000×800000 is 40000000000.
  How is this answer displayed on a calculator screen? **Discuss.**

  The answer to the calculation 2600000×50000 is 130000000000.

  How is this displayed on the calculator screen? **Discuss.**

  The answer to a calculation is displayed on a calculator screen as $2.3^{\,05}$. What is the answer to this calculation? **Discuss.**

  Discuss the answers to the calculator displays for $\frac{5}{1000}$, $\frac{5}{10000}$, $\frac{5}{100000}$ etc.

STANDARD FORM

The numbers 10, 100, 1000, 10000, ... can be rewritten as $10^1, 10^2, 10^3, 10^4, ...$
The number 70000 can be rewritten as 7×10000 or as 7×10^4 or as $7 \cdot 0 \times 10^4$.
The number 736 can be rewritten as $7 \cdot 36 \times 100$ or as $7 \cdot 36 \times 10^2$.

The numbers $\frac{1}{10}, \frac{1}{100}, \frac{1}{1000}, \ldots$ can be rewritten as $\frac{1}{10^1}, \frac{1}{10^2}, \frac{1}{10^3}, \ldots$

or as $10^{-1}, 10^{-2}, 10^{-3}, \ldots$

The number $0 \cdot 086$ can be rewritten as $\frac{8 \cdot 6}{100}$ or $\frac{8 \cdot 6}{10^2}$ or $8 \cdot 6 \times 10^{-2}$.

The numbers $7 \cdot 0 \times 10^4$, $7 \cdot 36 \times 10^2$, $8 \cdot 6 \times 10^{-2}$ are written in a notation known as **Standard Index Notation**. Standard Index Notation is usually called **Standard Form**. It is also often called **Scientific Notation**.

Numbers written in **standard form** consist of two parts. They have a decimal number part in which there is always just one digit (not zero) before the decimal point and this part is multiplied by a power of 10.

For instance, the following numbers are in standard form: $6 \cdot 2 \times 10^{14}$, $7 \cdot 01 \times 10^{-1}$, $8 \cdot 3 \times 10^{0}$. The following numbers are *not* in standard form: $0 \cdot 6 \times 10^{6}$, $3 \cdot 4$, $78 \cdot 2 \times 10^{-3}$.

Another way of stating the standard form notation is:

Standard form is $a \times 10^{n}$ where $1 \leq a < 10$ and n is an integer.

Standard form is a very useful way of writing very large or very small numbers.
On a calculator screen, the standard form notation is not written in full; the $\times$ and 10 are omitted.
For instance, a calculator displays $7 \cdot 3 \times 10^{5}$ as 7.3 ^{05}. (Some of the older Casio scientific calculators and some other scientific calculators display $7 \cdot 3 \times 10^{5}$ as 7.3 05.)

Take the following steps to rewrite a number given in standard form as a number in decimal form.

Step 1   Move the decimal point. The index with the 10 gives the number of places and the direction in which the point is to be moved.

Step 2   Omit the multiplication sign and the power of 10.

Examples   1. $2 \cdot 47 \times 10^{4} = 24700$ (move the point 4 places in the positive direction)
2. $3 \cdot 0 \times 10^{-4} = 0 \cdot 0003$ (move the point 4 places in the negative direction)
3. $4 \cdot 5 \times 10^{0} = 4 \cdot 5$ (move the point 0 places)

Take the following steps to rewrite a number given in decimal form as a number in standard form.

Step 1   Write the decimal point after the first non-zero digit.

Step 2   Insert a multiplication sign and a power of 10. The index with the 10 is found by considering the number of places, and the direction, the point would need to be moved to get back to the original number.

Examples   1. $36 \cdot 2 = 3 \cdot 62 \times 10^{1}$ (the point in $3 \cdot 62$ needs to be moved 1 place in the positive direction to get $36 \cdot 2$)

2. $8957 = 8 \cdot 957 \times 10^{3}$ (the point in $8 \cdot 957$ needs to be moved 3 places in the positive direction to get 8957)

3. $5 = 5 \cdot 0 \times 10^{0}$ (the point in $5 \cdot 0$ needs to be moved zero places to get 5)

4. $0 \cdot 0903 = 9 \cdot 03 \times 10^{-2}$ (the point in $9 \cdot 03$ needs to be moved 2 places in the negative direction to get $0 \cdot 0903$)

5. $0 \cdot 004 = 4 \cdot 0 \times 10^{-3}$ (the point in $4 \cdot 0$ needs to be moved 3 places in the negative direction to get $0 \cdot 004$)

EXERCISE 6:4

1. Which of the following are in standard form?

   (a) $7 \cdot 3 \times 10^4$ (b) $62 \cdot 4 \times 10^2$ (c) $0 \cdot 3 \times 10^1$ (d) $2 \cdot 0 \times 10^0$

   (e) $3 \cdot 49$ (f) $8 \cdot 2 \times 10$ (g) $3 \cdot 05 \times 10^{-17}$ (h) $80 \cdot 1 \times 10^{-3}$

   (i) $7 \cdot 6824 \times 10^{92}$ (j) $0 \cdot 305 \times 10^4$

2. Write these in decimal form.

   (a) $3 \cdot 4 \times 10^2$ (b) $8 \cdot 12 \times 10^3$ (c) $6 \cdot 25 \times 10^{-2}$ (d) $8 \cdot 0 \times 10^{-3}$

   (e) $7 \cdot 03 \times 10^4$ (f) $2 \cdot 05 \times 10^0$ (g) $7 \cdot 8 \times 10^{-1}$ (h) $1 \cdot 01 \times 10^{-4}$

   (i) $3 \cdot 7 \times 10^5$ (j) $3 \cdot 7 \times 10^{-5}$ (k) $1 \cdot 52 \times 10^1$ (l) $3 \cdot 4 \times 10^0$

   (m) $4 \cdot 81 \times 10^{-3}$ (n) $8 \cdot 0 \times 10^1$ (o) $2 \cdot 61 \times 10^{-5}$ (p) $6 \cdot 0 \times 10^{10}$

   (q) $7 \cdot 05 \times 10^{-2}$ (r) $8 \cdot 154 \times 10^2$ (s) $8 \cdot 154 \times 10^{-3}$ (t) $9 \cdot 407 \times 10^1$

   (u) $9 \cdot 407 \times 10^{-1}$ (v) $6 \cdot 0 \times 10^4$ (w) $6 \cdot 0 \times 10^{-4}$

3. Find the missing index.

   (a) $36 \cdot 4 = 3 \cdot 64 \times 10^{\cdots}$ (b) $482 \cdot 5 = 4 \cdot 825 \times 10^{\cdots}$ (c) $7 = 7 \cdot 0 \times 10^{\cdots}$

   (d) $17 = 1 \cdot 7 \times 10^{\cdots}$ (e) $8478 = 8 \cdot 478 \times 10^{\cdots}$ (f) $0 \cdot 42 = 4 \cdot 2 \times 10^{\cdots}$

   (g) $0 \cdot 0591 = 5 \cdot 91 \times 10^{\cdots}$ (h) $0 \cdot 308 = 3 \cdot 08 \times 10^{\cdots}$ (i) $0 \cdot 008 = 8 \cdot 0 \times 10^{\cdots}$

   (j) $2 \cdot 6 = 2 \cdot 6 \times 10^{\cdots}$ (k) $89 = 8 \cdot 9 \times 10^{\cdots}$ (l) $0 \cdot 05 = 5 \cdot 0 \times 10^{\cdots}$

   (m) $0 \cdot 6 = 6 \cdot 0 \times 10^{\cdots}$ (n) $22 \cdot 71 = 2 \cdot 271 \times 10^{\cdots}$ (o) $0 \cdot 00092 = 9 \cdot 2 \times 10^{\cdots}$

4. Write these numbers in standard form.

   (a) 64   (b) 782   (c) 3640   (d) $55 \cdot 2$ (e) 7

   (f) 1000   (g) $34 \cdot 2$ (h) $555 \cdot 61$ (i) $72 \cdot 4$ (j) $0 \cdot 8$

   (k) $0 \cdot 91$ (l) $0 \cdot 0043$ (m) $0 \cdot 804$ (n) $0 \cdot 04$ (o) $2 \cdot 4$

   (p) $0 \cdot 24$ (q) 24   (r) $0 \cdot 0024$ (s) 240   (t) 9

   (u) 90   (v) $0 \cdot 09$ (w) $0 \cdot 9$

5. An estimate of the population in the UK in the year 2031 is $61 \cdot 2$ million. Write this in standard form.

6. In the early 1990s, the population of the South East of England was about $1 \cdot 8 \times 10^7$. Write this in decimal form.

7. About $1 \cdot 9 \times 10^6$ cars were registered in the UK in 1990. Write this in decimal form.

8. The velocity of light is $300\,000$ km/sec. Write this velocity in standard form.

9. In a year, light travels about 9.46×10^{12} km.
   Write this distance in decimal form.

10. The most distant objects yet observed are
    15 000 000 000 light-years distant from the earth.
    Write this in standard form.

11. The half-life of one of the polonium isotopes is about
    3.0×10^{-7} seconds.
    Write this in decimal form.

12. The wavelength of visible light is about 5.0×10^{-5} cm.
    Write this in decimal form.

13. The diameter of an atom is about $0.000\,000\,0001$ mm.
    Write this in standard form.

Review 1 Write these in decimal form.

  (a) 2.3×10^4 (b) 2.3×10^0 (c) 2.3×10^{-4} (d) 3.0504×10^{-1}

  (e) 9.01×10^6 (f) 6.4×10^{-3} (g) 3.465×10^2

Review 2 Write these in standard form.

  (a) 52.7   (b) 16 005   (c) 6   (d) 0.83

  (e) 0.1   (f) 0.000 2

Review 3 In mid 1991, there were about 2.2×10^6 people unemployed in the UK.
Write this in decimal form.

Review 4 The sun is about 0.000 016 light-years from the earth.
The centre of the Milky Way is about 26 000 light-years from the earth.
Write these distances in standard form.

MULTIPLYING and DIVIDING numbers written in STANDARD FORM

We use the laws of indices when we multiply or divide numbers written in standard form.

We use $a^x \times a^y = a^{x+y}$ and $a^x \div a^y = a^{x-y}$

107

Worked Example Calculate the following, giving the answers in standard form.

$$\text{(a)} \quad (2 \cdot 4 \times 10^{-4}) \times (3 \cdot 1 \times 10^{7}) \qquad \text{(b)} \quad (2 \cdot 4 \times 10^{-4}) \div (3 \cdot 0 \times 10^{7})$$

Answer (a) $(2 \cdot 4 \times 10^{-4}) \times (3 \cdot 1 \times 10^{7})$

$$= 2 \cdot 4 \times 10^{-4} \times 3 \cdot 1 \times 10^{7}$$
$$= 2 \cdot 4 \times 3 \cdot 1 \times 10^{-4} \times 10^{7}$$
$$= (2 \cdot 4 \times 3 \cdot 1) \times (10^{-4} \times 10^{7})$$
$$= 7 \cdot 44 \times 10^{3}$$

(b) $(2 \cdot 4 \times 10^{-4}) \div (3 \cdot 0 \times 10^{7})$

$$= \frac{2 \cdot 4 \times 10^{-4}}{3 \cdot 0 \times 10^{7}}$$
$$= \frac{2 \cdot 4}{3 \cdot 0} \times \frac{10^{-4}}{10^{7}}$$
$$= 0 \cdot 8 \times 10^{-11}$$
$$= 8 \cdot 0 \times 10^{-1} \times 10^{-11}$$
$$= 8 \cdot 0 \times 10^{-12}$$

EXERCISE 6:5

In this exercise, give all the answers in standard form.

1. Calculate.

(a) $(3 \cdot 7 \times 10^{5}) \times (2 \cdot 0 \times 10^{4})$

(b) $(5 \cdot 0 \times 10^{3}) \times (1 \cdot 7 \times 10^{6})$

(c) $(1 \cdot 82 \times 10^{5}) \times (4 \cdot 0 \times 10^{2})$

(d) $(2 \cdot 4 \times 10^{6}) \times (2 \cdot 0 \times 10^{-3})$

(e) $(4 \cdot 12 \times 10^{-5}) \times (2 \cdot 0 \times 10^{-3})$

(f) $(4 \cdot 24 \times 10^{7}) \div (2 \cdot 0 \times 10^{4})$

(g) $(6 \cdot 9 \times 10^{4}) \div (3 \cdot 0 \times 10^{7})$

(h) $\dfrac{8 \cdot 4 \times 10^{6}}{4 \cdot 0 \times 10^{-2}}$

(i) $\dfrac{7 \cdot 5 \times 10^{-3}}{5 \cdot 0 \times 10^{-5}}$

2. Calculate.

(a) $(4 \cdot 8 \times 10^{7}) \times (3 \cdot 0 \times 10^{5})$

(b) $(1 \cdot 5 \times 10^{4}) \div (5 \cdot 0 \times 10^{1})$

(c) $(4 \cdot 2 \times 10^{4}) \div (6 \cdot 0 \times 10^{-2})$

(d) $(3 \cdot 2 \times 10^{-2}) \times (4 \cdot 0 \times 10^{-4})$

(e) $(3 \cdot 2 \times 10^{-2}) \div (4 \cdot 0 \times 10^{-4})$

(f) $(6 \cdot 0 \times 10^{-3}) \times (8 \cdot 1 \times 10^{7})$

(g) $(1 \cdot 34 \times 10^{7}) \times (8 \cdot 76 \times 10^{3})$

(h) $(2 \cdot 681 \times 10^{3}) \times (3 \cdot 4 \times 10^{-4})$

(i) $(1 \cdot 44 \times 10^{7}) \div (1 \cdot 2 \times 10^{9})$

(j) $(8 \cdot 23 \times 10^{-2}) \times (7 \cdot 6 \times 10^{-3})$

(k) $(4 \cdot 75 \times 10^{-2}) \div (2 \cdot 5 \times 10^{3})$

3. A rectangle has length of $2 \cdot 6 \times 10^{3}$mm and width of $1 \cdot 8 \times 10^{2}$mm.
    What is the area of this rectangle?

4. One oxygen atom has a mass of about $2 \cdot 7 \times 10^{-23}$ grams.
    How heavy would 5000 oxygen atoms be?

5. The half-life of radium is about $1 \cdot 622 \times 10^3$ years.
   One year is about $8 \cdot 76 \times 10^3$ hours.
   How many hours is the half-life of radium?

6. The density of brass is $8 \cdot 5 \times 10^3$ kg/m³.
   What is the mass of $2 \cdot 4 \times 10^{-2}$ cubic metres of brass?

7. A large stone has a mass of $5 \cdot 5 \times 10^2$ kg. It is known that the density of this stone is $2 \cdot 2 \times 10^3$ kg/m³.
   What is the volume of this stone?

8. The mass of a hydrogen atom is about $1 \cdot 67 \times 10^{-24}$ g while that of a uranium atom is about $3 \cdot 95 \times 10^{-22}$ g.
   About how many times heavier is a uranium atom than a hydrogen atom? (Answer to 3 significant figures.)

9. The nearest star, Proxima Centauri, is about $4 \cdot 0 \times 10^{13}$ km from the earth.
   In a year, light travels about $9 \cdot 46 \times 10^{12}$ km.
   About how many light-years is Proxima Centauri from the earth?

10.

Planet	Diameter (km)
Mercury	$4 \cdot 9 \times 10^3$
Venus	$1 \cdot 2 \times 10^4$
Earth	$1 \cdot 3 \times 10^4$
Mars	$6 \cdot 8 \times 10^3$
Jupiter	$1 \cdot 4 \times 10^5$
Saturn	$1 \cdot 2 \times 10^5$
Uranus	$5 \cdot 2 \times 10^4$
Neptune	$4 \cdot 9 \times 10^4$
Pluto	$2 \cdot 4 \times 10^3$

(a) Which planet is the smallest?

(b) Which planet is the largest?

(c) Which planet has diameter about 10 times that of Venus?

(d) Which planet has diameter about half that of Mercury?

(e) One of the planets has diameter about 20 times larger than that of Pluto. Which planet?

(f) The diameter of Venus is larger than that of Pluto. About how many times larger?

(g) What is the ratio of the diameter of Pluto to the diameter of Saturn?

11. 'The mass of the earth is about $5 \cdot 97 \times 10^{24}$ kg. How many tonnes is this?

12. A billion is a million million. A trillion is a million billion. A quadrillion is a million trillion.
    Write, in standard form   (a) one trillion

    (b) one quadrillion.

13. 1 micron is 10^{-4} centimetres.

    (a) How many microns are there in 1mm?

    (b) 1 Angstrom is 10^{-8} centimetres. How many microns are there in 1 Angstrom?

Review 1   Calculate.

    (a) $(2 \cdot 4 \times 10^3) \times (4 \cdot 0 \times 10^2)$ (b) $(2 \cdot 0 \times 10^5) \times (5 \cdot 3 \times 10^0)$

    (c) $(8 \cdot 4 \times 10^3) \div (2 \cdot 0 \times 10^{-2})$ (d) $(6 \cdot 5 \times 10^{-1}) \times (7 \cdot 8 \times 10^{-3})$

    (e) $(2 \cdot 5 \times 10^{-3}) \div (5 \cdot 0 \times 10^{-2})$

Review 2   The U.K. value for one billion is $1 \cdot 0 \times 10^{12}$. The American value for one billion is $1 \cdot 0 \times 10^9$.

    How much larger is the U.K. value for one billion than the American value?

Review 3

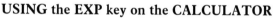

City	Bombay	Cape Town	Darwin	London	Paris	Rome	Tokyo
Distance (in km) from Berlin	$6 \cdot 3 \times 10^3$	$9 \cdot 6 \times 10^3$	$1 \cdot 3 \times 10^4$	$9 \cdot 2 \times 10^2$	$8 \cdot 7 \times 10^2$	$1 \cdot 2 \times 10^3$	$8 \cdot 9 \times 10^3$

    (i)   Which city is   (a) closest to Berlin

                        (b) the greatest distance from Berlin

                        (c) about twice as far from Berlin as Bombay

                        (d) about 10 times closer to Berlin as Tokyo?

    (ii) What is the ratio of the distance between Cape Town and Berlin to the distance between London and Berlin?

Review 4   1 hour $= 3 \cdot 6 \times 10^3$ seconds.

    (a) What is the velocity, in km/sec, of an object which is travelling at $7 \cdot 2 \times 10^2$ km/h?

    (b) The velocity of light is about $3 \cdot 0 \times 10^5$ km/sec. Give this velocity in km/h.

USING the EXP key on the CALCULATOR

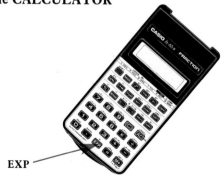

EXP

DISCUSSION EXERCISE 6:6

Look closely at what appears on the calculator screen after each of the following is keyed:

$\boxed{7\cdot82}$ then $\boxed{\text{EXP}}$ then $\boxed{3}$. **Discuss.**

Discuss how to use the EXP key to find the answer to a calculation such as
$$(7\cdot82 \times 10^3) \times (2\cdot0 \times 10^4).$$

What if the calculation was $(7\cdot82 \times 10^3) \times (2\cdot0 \times 10^{-4})$?

What if the calculation was $(7\cdot82 \times 10^{-3}) \times (2\cdot0 \times 10^{-4})$?

ADDING and SUBTRACTING NUMBERS written in STANDARD FORM

One way of calculating $3\cdot6 \times 10^6 + 2\cdot3 \times 10^4$ is by rewriting $3\cdot6 \times 10^6$ and $2\cdot3 \times 10^4$ in decimal form, then adding.

Another way is to use the EXP key on the calculator as follows.

Key $\boxed{3\cdot6}$ $\boxed{\text{EXP}}$ $\boxed{6}$ $\boxed{+}$ $\boxed{2\cdot3}$ $\boxed{\text{EXP}}$ $\boxed{4}$ $\boxed{=}$ to get a screen display of 3 623 000. If the answer is to be given in standard form, $3\cdot623 \times 10^6$ would be written down.

DISCUSSION EXERCISE 6:7

Another way of calculating $3\cdot6 \times 10^6 + 2\cdot3 \times 10^4$ is:
$$
\begin{aligned}
3\cdot6 \times 10^6 + 2\cdot3 \times 10^4 &= 3\cdot6 \times 10^4 \times 10^2 + 2\cdot3 \times 10^4 \\
&= 10^4 (3\cdot6 \times 10^2 + 2\cdot3) \\
&= 10^4 (360 + 2\cdot3) \\
&= 10^4 \times (362\cdot3) \\
&= 10^4 \times (3\cdot623 \times 10^2) \\
&= 3\cdot623 \times 10^6
\end{aligned}
$$

Discuss each step of this method. You may like to refer to **Chapter 8** for the step
$3\cdot6 \times 10^4 \times 10^2 + 2\cdot3 \times 10^4 = 10^4 (3\cdot6 \times 10^2 + 2\cdot3)$.

EXERCISE 6:8

Use a calculator or non-calculator method to find the answers to the questions in this exercise. Give all the answers in standard form.

1. Calculate.

    (a) $6\cdot8 \times 10^3 + 1\cdot5 \times 10^2$ (b) $2\cdot7 \times 10^5 - 8\cdot2 \times 10^4$ (c) $6\cdot07 \times 10^2 + 3\cdot4 \times 10^0$

(d) $4.152 \times 10^7 + 6.7 \times 10^3$ (e) $8.9 \times 10^2 - 2.81 \times 10^{-1}$ (f) $7.6 \times 10^2 + 8.541 \times 10^{-2}$

(g) $7.8 \times 10^{-3} - 4.6 \times 10^{-4}$ (h) $3.05 \times 10^{-2} + 1.62 \times 10^{-4}$ (i) $6.81 \times 10^9 - 3.04 \times 10^8$

2. In 1990, Central Government spent about £6.7×10^{10} while local authorities spent about £4.3×10^{10}. How much was spent by both?

3. There were about 1.459×10^5 males and 6.9×10^3 females in the army in 1990.

   About how many people were in the army?

4. In 1989, about 9.13×10^4 tonne of shell fish and 5.804×10^5 tonne of other fish was caught. What total weight of fish was caught in 1989?

5. In 1990, about 8.416×10^5 people were on the NHS hospital waiting lists. Of these, about 4.53×10^4 were waiting for plastic surgery.

   How many were waiting for surgery other than plastic surgery?

6. The cost of running NHS hospitals and community health services was about £1.6676×10^{10} in 1990 and £8.162×10^9 in 1980. What was the increase in running costs?

7. In April 1990, about 1.104×10^6 people flew on Domestic Services on UK airlines while in April 1989, about 9.802×10^5 people flew. How many more flew in April 1990 than in April 1989?

8. Q1 : 1.02×10^8 Q2 : 9.2×10^7 Q3 : 9.4×10^7 Q4 : 9.8×10^7

   These figures give the number of British Rail journeys on which passengers used season tickets in 1990. Q1 is the first quarter of 1990, Q2 is the second quarter etc. What total number of journeys in 1990 were season tickets used on?

Review 1   Calculate   (a) $6.1 \times 10^{-2} + 5.01 \times 10^{-3}$ (b) $8.7 \times 10^{-1} - 9.6 \times 10^0$.

Review 2   The Pacific Ocean covers an area of about 1.65×10^8 km^2 while the Atlantic Ocean covers about 8.22×10^7 km^2.

   (a) How much larger is the Pacific Ocean than the Atlantic Ocean?

   (b) What total area do these two oceans cover?

USING the SCIENTIFIC MODE on the CALCULATOR

To get the calculator operating in **scientific mode**, **Key** ‾MODE‾ followed by ‾8‾ . You do not need to remember that MODE 8 is the scientific mode as the 8 is printed beside SCI on the calculator.

To get the calculator out of scientific mode, **Key** ‾MODE‾ followed by ‾9‾ . You do not need to remember that MODE 9 is the normal mode as the 9 is printed beside NORM on the calculator.

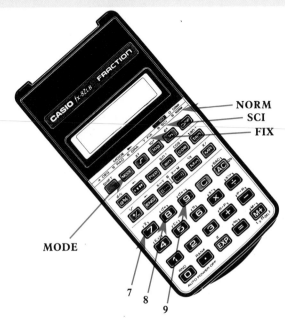

MODE

NORM
SCI
FIX

7   8   9

DISCUSSION EXERCISE 6:9

● Key the calculation 6.7821×3.488 as follows:

‾MODE‾ ‾8‾ ‾2‾ ‾6.7821‾ ‾×‾ ‾3.488‾ ‾=‾

What is the effect of keying the 2? **Discuss.** As part of your discussion first replace the 2 with 1, then with 3, then with 4, then with 5 etc.

When the calculator is operating in scientific mode, is the EXP key used in the normal way? **Discuss.** As part of your discussion key in some calculations such as

$$(3.4 \times 10^5) \times (1.05 \times 10^4)$$

● Key the calculation 6.7821×3.488 as follows:

‾MODE‾ ‾7‾ ‾2‾ ‾6.7821‾ ‾×‾ ‾3.488‾ ‾=‾

What is MODE FIX? **Discuss.** As part of your discussion replace the 2 with 1, 3, 4, 5 etc.

CALCULATIONS with LARGE or SMALL NUMBERS not written in standard form

Very large numbers, such as $753\,000\,000$, and very small numbers, such as $0{\cdot}000\,000\,000\,781$, cannot be keyed directly into an 8-digit calculator.
If numbers such as these are part of a calculation, they may be keyed into the calculator in standard form.

Worked Example   Calculate $34\,820\,000\,000 \times 734\,000\,000$.

Answer $34\,820\,000\,000 = 3{\cdot}482 \times 10^{10}$
          $734\,000\,000 = 7{\cdot}34 \times 10^{8}$
          Hence $34\,820\,000\,000 \times 734\,000\,000 = (3{\cdot}482 \times 10^{10}) \times (7{\cdot}34 \times 10^{8})$

Keying $\boxed{3{\cdot}482}$ $\boxed{\text{EXP}}$ $\boxed{10}$ $\boxed{\times}$ $\boxed{7{\cdot}34}$ $\boxed{\text{EXP}}$ $\boxed{8}$ $\boxed{=}$ gives a screen display of $2{\cdot}555788^{19}$.
We will give the answer to 3 significant figures since there were just 3 s.f. in one of the numbers being multiplied.
Hence $34\,820\,000\,000 \times 734\,000\,000 = 2{\cdot}56 \times 10^{19}$ to 3 s.f.

Note   An alternative keying sequence is:
$\boxed{\text{MODE}}$ $\boxed{8}$ $\boxed{3}$ $\boxed{3{\cdot}482}$ $\boxed{\text{EXP}}$ $\boxed{10}$ $\boxed{\times}$ $\boxed{7{\cdot}34}$ $\boxed{\text{EXP}}$ $\boxed{8}$ $\boxed{=}$
which gives a screen display of $2{\cdot}56^{19}$.

EXERCISE 6:10

Use the calculator to find the answer to these. Round your answers sensibly.

1. $253\,000\,000\,000 \times 3\,640\,000\,000$
2. $1\,300\,000\,000\,000 \times 28\,200\,000\,000$
3. $75\,000\,000\,000\,000 \times 824\,500\,000\,000$
4. $71\,598\,000\,000 \times 8\,143\,000\,000\,000$
5. $246\,000\,000 \div 134\,000\,000$
6. $897\,200\,000\,000 \div 9\,982\,000\,000$
7. $0{\cdot}000\,000\,000\,082 \times 0{\cdot}000\,000\,00\,37$
8. $0{\cdot}000\,00\,000\,789 \div 0{\cdot}000\,000\,000\,388$
9. $0{\cdot}000\,00\,000\,73 \times 0{\cdot}000\,000\,000\,834$
10. $0{\cdot}000\,000\,034\,82 \div 0{\cdot}000\,000\,078\,5$
11. $\dfrac{347\,000\,000\,000 \times 2\,440\,000\,000\,000}{2\,374\,000\,000}$
12. $\dfrac{458\,900\,000\,000}{361\,000\,000 \times 783\,000\,000}$

Review 1 $2\,480\,000\,000\,000 \div 17\,800\,000\,000$

Review 2 $0{\cdot}000\,000\,003\,281 \times 0{\cdot}0000\,000\,789$

PRACTICAL EXERCISE 6:11

Choose one branch of Science such as astronomy, chemistry, ecology etc.
Research a topic from your chosen branch of Science. Use reference books in this research.
Make a summary of your research. In your summary, include calculations done in standard form.

CHAPTER 6   REVIEW

1. (a) The approximate population of the United Kingdom is given in standard form as $5 \cdot 2 \times 10^7$.
    Write this as an ordinary number.

    (b) The thickness of grade A paper is $6 \cdot 0 \times 10^{-2}$ cm.
    Grade B paper is twice as thick as grade A.
    Calculate, in centimetres, the thickness of grade B paper.
    Write your answer in standard form.   **SEG**

2. The mass of an atom of oxygen is $0 \cdot 000\,000\,000\,000\,000\,000\,000\,027$ grams.

    (a) Write this number in standard form.

    (b) Calculate, in standard form, the mass of 5×10^8 atoms of oxygen.   **ULEAC**

3. A packet of paper contains 5×10^2 sheets.
    The packet is $4 \cdot 8$ cm thick.

4.8 cm

    (a) Work out the thickness of one sheet of paper in centimetres, giving your answer in standard form.

    (b) A magazine is made from 36 sheets of paper.

    The number of magazines printed is $3 \cdot 3 \times 10^6$.

    (i) Calculate how many sheets of paper are needed to print these magazines.

    Give your answer in **standard form**.

(ii) If all the magazines were piled on top of each other, how high would the pile be?

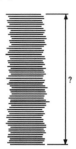

SEG

4. The mass of one hydrogen atom is

$$1.66 \times 10^{-27} \text{kg}.$$

In one litre of air there are 2.51×10^{22} atoms of hydrogen.

(a) What is the mass of the hydrogen in one litre of air?
Give your answer in standard form.

(b) Express your answer to (a) without using standard form. **SEG**

5. During 1987/8 there were 23 million telephone directories printed.

(a) Write this number in standard form.

One tonne is equal to 10^3 kg. The directories used 27 350 tonnes of paper.
(b) Write this in kilograms in standard form.

(c) What was the average mass of paper in one directory?

(d) Explain how you know whether your answer to part (c) is sensible. **MEG**

6. 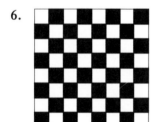 Centuries ago, a man promised to give his wife some grains of rice.
He took a chess board and placed
one grain on the first square,
two grains on the second square,
four grains on the third square,
eight grains on the fourth square,
and so on.

If he had completed all 64 squares on the chessboard he would have used approximately 1.845×10^{19} grains of rice.

One grain of rice weighs about 0.01 grams.

Calculate an estimate of the weight of rice used.

Give your answer in tonnes, correct to one significant figure.
[1 tonne = 1000 kg.] **MEG**

7. About 10^9 people live in China.
   About $2\cdot7 \times 10^8$ of them own bicycles.
   What percentage of people in China own bicycles?
   Show your working.   **NEAB**

8. The mean distance of the Earth from the Sun is 149·6 million kilometres.

   (a) Write the number 149·6 million in standard index form.

   The Earth travels a distance, D km, in one day.
   The value of D is given by the formula:-

   $$D = \frac{2\pi \times \text{mean distance of Earth from Sun}}{365}$$

   (b) Calculate the value of D, giving your answer in standard index form.   **ULEAC**

9. (a)

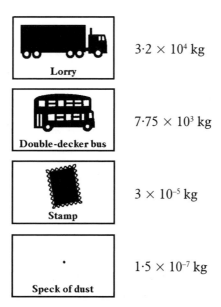

   Lorry — $3\cdot2 \times 10^4$ kg

   Double-decker bus — $7\cdot75 \times 10^3$ kg

   Stamp — 3×10^{-5} kg

   Speck of dust — $1\cdot5 \times 10^{-7}$ kg

   (i) How many buses weigh the same as a lorry?

   (ii) How many specks of dust weigh the same as a stamp?

   (b) The radius of the Earth is approximately $6\cdot4 \times 10^6$ m.
   Calculate the volume of the Earth given that

   $$\text{Volume of Earth} = \frac{4}{3}\pi \times (\text{radius})^3.$$

   Give your answer in standard form correct to two significant figures.   **SEG**

117

10. There are 0·35mg of Vitamin B$_6$ in one pint of milk.

    (a) **(i)** Express this quantity of Vitamin B$_6$ in grammes.

        (ii) Write this in standard form.

    (b) How many pints of milk will it take to provide 1g of Vitamin B$_6$? Give the answer in standard form.   **NICCEA**

11. The distance of the Earth from the Sun is approximately $1·496 \times 10^8$ **kilometres.**
The speed of light is approximately $2·998 \times 10^8$ **metres per second.**
Calculate the time that it takes light from the Sun to reach the Earth.
Give your answer in minutes and seconds to the nearest second.   **SEG**

12. The number 10^{100} is called a googol.

    (a) Write the number 50 googols in standard index form.

A nanometre is 10^{-9} metres.

    (b) Write 50 nanometres, in metres.
        Give your answer in standard index form.

    (c) How many nanometres are there in 10 metres?   **ULEAC**

13.

	Population (1990)	Area (km²)	Area (acres)
England	$4·7689 \times 10^7$	$1·3048 \times 10^5$	$3·2242 \times 10^7$
Wales	$2·881 \times 10^6$	$2·077 \times 10^4$	$5·132 \times 10^6$

    (a) Calculate the average population per square kilometre for England.

    (b) Find the total area of England and Wales in acres.

    (c) Use information from the table to express 1 acre in square kilometres.

        Show your working clearly and give your answer in standard form.   **MEG**

14. Between 1950 and 1985 the number of people living in towns and cities in developing countries increased from $2 \cdot 86 \times 10^8$ to $1 \cdot 14 \times 10^9$.

Calculate the increase in the number of people, giving your answer in standard form. **MEG**

15. The mass of the moon is $7 \cdot 343 \times 10^{19}$ tonnes.
The Earth has a mass 81 times bigger than that of the moon.

(a) Work out the mass of the Earth, giving your answer in standard form.

The mass of Mercury is $3 \cdot 250 \times 10^{20}$ tonnes.

(b) Calculate the difference between the mass of the moon and the mass of Mercury.

ULEAC

1. $y = \frac{1}{2}x - 3$ gives the equation of this line.
    Use this equation to complete the following coordinates.

    $(4, \ldots), (-2, \ldots), (-1, \ldots), (1\frac{1}{2}, \ldots), (-1\frac{1}{2}, \ldots)$

    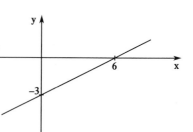

2. Find the missing index.

    (a) $3^{-8} = \frac{1}{3^{\cdots}}$

    (b) $\frac{1}{8^3} = 8^{\cdots}$

3. (a) Write $\frac{25}{6}$ as a mixed number.

    (b) Write $7\frac{3}{8}$ as an improper fraction.

4. In 1990, the population of Scotland was about 5·1 million.
    Write this in standard form.

5.

    Fence posts are to be placed 2m apart. How many fence posts are needed to build a fence of the length shown?

6. Estimate the answer to   (a) 0.25×83.4 (b) $\dfrac{7.8 \times 21.4}{0.23}$

7. Without using your calculator, find the answer to these.

    (a) $3 - 2\sqrt[3]{8}$ (b) $(-5)^3 - 4\sqrt{49}$ (c) $3 - 2[1 + (-4)^2]$ (d) $\dfrac{\sqrt{25} + 2^3}{-5}$

8. 1 hour is about 0·000 114 years. Write this in standard form.

9. In a survey, it was found that $\frac{1}{6}$ of families had 1 child, and $\frac{3}{10}$ had 2 children. What fraction of the families surveyed had 1 or 2 children?

10. In May, one of the ovens at "The Bread Bakehouse" was on for 1292 hours. This was a 5% decrease on the number of hours for April.
    How many hours was this oven on in April?

11. Write these in decimal form.

    (a) $4{\cdot}7 \times 10^4$ (b) $6{\cdot}0 \times 10^{-2}$ (c) $1{\cdot}8 \times 10^0$

12. Use the calculator to find the reciprocal of these. Give the answer to 2 significant figures if rounding is necessary.

    (a) $0{\cdot}34$ (b) $8{\cdot}2$ (c) 9   (d) 41

13. The surface area of a cube can be calculated from the formula:
    Surface Area $= 6x^2$ where x is the length of an edge.
    Use this formula to find the surface area of the sketched cube.

14. Mince is packed in trays, each weighing $\frac{3}{5}$ kg.
    How many lasagne meals could be made from 10 trays if each meal needs $\frac{3}{4}$ kg of mince?

15. Use the calculator to find these, rounding your answers sensibly. Estimate as a check.

    (a) $44{\cdot}7\,(5{\cdot}82 + 2{\cdot}15)$ (b) $\dfrac{0{\cdot}59 \times 135{\cdot}09}{6{\cdot}8 \times 1{\cdot}04}$

16. The diameter of an electron is about $4{\cdot}0 \times 10^{-13}$ cm.

    (a) How many mm is this?   (b) How many metres is this?

17. Write these as a single power of 3.

    (a) $3^4 \times 3^7$ (b) $\dfrac{3^9}{3^3}$ (c) $(3^2)^4$ (d) $\dfrac{9^4 \times 3^5}{27}$

18. The population of India is about 6.9×10^8 while that of France is about 5.47×10^7. The area of India is about 3.3×10^6 km^2 while that of France is about 5.5×10^5 km^2. Find (a) the population density (i.e. the number of people per square kilometre) of India

    (b) the population density of France.

19. A bracelet is made by threading four different coloured beads onto nylon thread.
    How many different colour combinations are possible?

20. James weighs 60 kg. $\frac{1}{3}$ of Simon's mass is the same as $\frac{2}{5}$ of James'. How heavy is Simon?

21. Use the formula $a = \dfrac{t^2 - s^2}{2d}$ to find **a** when $t = 0$, $s = 16.7$, $d = -7.5$.

22.

Distance from Earth	
Sun	1.5×10^6 km
Nearest Star	4.0×10^{13} km
Brightest Star	8.1×10^{13} km
Centre of Milky Way	2.5×10^{17} km
Nearest galaxies	1.6×10^{18} km
Andromeda Galaxy	1.4×10^{19} km
Galaxy in Virgo	7.1×10^{20} km
Galaxy in Gt. Bear	4.5×10^{22} km

(a) Is the Andromeda Galaxy closer to Earth than is the Centre of the Milky Way?

(b) How many times further from Earth is the Centre of the Milky Way than is the Brightest Star?

(c) What is about 50 times closer to the Earth than is the Galaxy in Virgo?

(d) Find the ratio of the distance of the Nearest Star from Earth to the distance of the Centre of the Milky Way from Earth.

(e) The velocity of light is about 3.0×10^5 km/sec. About how many kilometres will light travel in a year? (Give the answer to 2 s.f.)

(f) One light-year is the distance light will travel in one year. Using your answer for **(e)**, find the distance (in light-years) of the Nearest Star from Earth.

23. On their holiday, on the Norfolk Broads, the Petrie family travelled a total of 45 km on the canals.
    How many hours did they travel on these canals if they averaged $2\frac{1}{4}$ km per hour?

24. Use your calculator to evaluate these. If rounding is necessary, give the answers to one decimal place.

    (a) $3 \cdot 3 - 2\sqrt{7}$

    (b) $3 \times (-0 \cdot 8) - 2 + 3 \cdot 1^2$

    (c) $2 \cdot 6 - 1 \cdot 4 \, [3 \cdot 1 - (-2)^3]$

    (d) $\dfrac{4 \cdot 1^2 - 1 \cdot 4^2}{1 \cdot 4 - 4 \cdot 1}$

25. In 1993, there were 1080 pupils at Westcott High School. In 1994, the number of pupils increased by $\frac{1}{8}$. In 1995, there was a decrease of $\frac{2}{15}$.
    How many pupils were there at this school in 1995?

26. Jimmy, John, Jason and Justin each own a dog.
    The dogs are called Jess, Jasper, Julip and Jip.
    >John owns neither Jess nor Jip.
    >Jimmy does not own Julip.
    >Justin owns neither Julip nor Jess.
    If Jason owns Jasper, which dog is owned by each of the other three boys?

27. Give the reciprocal of these as a whole number or fraction.

    (a) $\frac{1}{15}$ (b) $\frac{4}{5}$ (c) 7   (d) $\dfrac{b}{x}$ (e) $2z$

28. Including VAT of $17\frac{1}{2}$ %, Valerie paid £213·85 for this TV.
    What price should be shown on this picture?

PRICE £ ▭▭
Excluding VAT

29. $s = \frac{1}{2}(u + v)\,t$. Find s if $t = 5\frac{3}{5}$, $u = 8\frac{1}{4}$, $v = 10\frac{1}{2}$.

30. Calculate.   (a) $\frac{3}{4} \times \frac{2}{15}$ (b) $8 \times 3\frac{3}{4}$ (c) $2\frac{2}{5} \times 3\frac{1}{8}$

    (d) $\frac{5}{9} \div \frac{2}{3}$ (e) $3\frac{3}{5} \div 2\frac{1}{10}$ (f) $\frac{5}{6} - \frac{1}{4}$ (g) $\frac{2}{5} + \frac{3}{4} + \frac{1}{2}$

    (h) $2\frac{2}{3} + 5\frac{3}{5}$ (i) $3\frac{1}{4} - 1\frac{5}{6}$ (j) $\frac{2}{5} + \frac{3}{4} \times 3\frac{1}{3}$ (k) $\frac{3}{5}(\frac{2}{3} + 2\frac{1}{4})$

31. (a) Estimate the area and perimeter
    of this triangle.

    (b) Calculate the area and perimeter,
    using your estimates as a check.

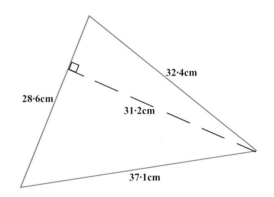

32·4cm
28·6cm
31·2cm
37·1cm

32. Use the rules of indices to simplify these.

    (a) $a^x \times a^b$ (b) $a^x \div a^b$ (c) $(a^x)^b$ (d) $\dfrac{a^x \times a^b}{a^z}$

    (e) $\dfrac{a^5 \times a^7}{(a^2)^3}$ (f) $(a^3b^4)^2$ (g) $(3a^4b)^2$

33. Of a group of friends, $\frac{2}{5}$ are aged 16 or over. $\frac{1}{4}$ of those under 16 are also under 15.
    What fraction of this group of friends is 15?

34. A publisher increased the price of maths. textbooks by 10% in each of two
    consecutive years.
    The total increase in price was   **A.** 20%   **B.** less than 20%   **C.** more than 20%.

35. Use the EXP key on the calculator to calculate:

    (a) $6·1 \times 10^3 + 2·7 \times 10^4$ (b) $2·71 \times 10^{-3} - 4·6 \times 10^{-4}$

    (c) $5\,230\,000\,000 \times 68\,000\,000$ (d) $\dfrac{0·000\,000\,000\,552}{0·000\,000\,028}$

36. Use the x^y key on your calculator to find these powers of 7.
    Continue finding answers for powers of 7.
    What pattern do you notice if you look at the last digits?
    Use this pattern to find the last digit of 7^{107}.

$7^2 =$
$7^3 =$
$7^4 =$
$7^5 =$
$7^6 =$
$7^7 =$

37. The earth's crust was formed about $4{\cdot}5 \times 10^9$ years ago.
    The first land plants occurred about $4{\cdot}5 \times 10^8$ years ago.
    The first flowering plants occurred about $1{\cdot}35 \times 10^8$ years ago.

    (a) How many years after the earth's crust was formed
    did the first land plants occur?

    (b) How long before the first flowering plants occurred
    did the first land plants occur?

38. The fraction $\frac{13}{42}$ is formed by using two of the digits 1, 2, 3, 4 in the numerator and
    the other two in the denominator. What is the largest proper fraction that can be
    formed in this way from the digits 1, 2, 3, 4?

39. An explorer, who can carry supplies for a maximum of 5 days, sets out from base camp.
    The next camp where supplies will be waiting is 8 days from base camp. The explorer
    can reach the next camp by building up supply depots along the way. For instance, at
    the end of the first day, 3 days supplies could be left at the first supply depot and the
    explorer could return to the base camp for more supplies.
    Find the minimum number of times the explorer needs to return to base camp for
    supplies.

40. Eric wanted to calculate $\left(\dfrac{4{\cdot}8 + 1{\cdot}27}{1{\cdot}2}\right)^2$

    He pressed these keys to get his answer.

    He got the answer 34·320069.

    This answer is wrong.

    (a) Explain clearly what is wrong with Eric's method.

    (b) Show a correct calculator sequence and calculate the correct answer.   **SEG**

125

41. The mass of a neutron is 1.675×10^{-24} grams.
Calculate the total mass of 1500 neutrons.
Give your answer in standard form. **ULEAC**

42. (a) Pauline paid £80 for a stamp for her collection. This stamp appreciated in value by 5% each year. What was its value 2 years after she bought it?

(b) Stephen bought a motor-cycle for £2500. It depreciated in value by 10% each year. What was its value 3 years after he bought it? **NICCEA**

43. Use a calculator to find the value of

(a) $\dfrac{3.86 + 17.59}{5}$ **(b)** $\dfrac{9.76 + 1.87}{18.3 - 15.8}$ **(c)** $\dfrac{330}{1.2 \times 5.5}$ **(d)** $\dfrac{1}{\sqrt{(0.16)}}$

NEAB

44. The masses of five planets are given in the table below.

Earth	5.98×10^{24} kg
Mars	6.57×10^{23} kg
Jupiter	1.25×10^{27} kg
Saturn	5.69×10^{26} kg
Venus	4.87×10^{24} kg

(a) (i) Which of these planets has a mass which is about 95 times that of the Earth?

(ii) How many times heavier than the Earth is the planet Jupiter?

(b) Find the ratio of the mass of the Earth to the mass of Mars in the form $1 : k$ where k is a number given correct to 2 significant figures. **SEG**

45. Given that $m = \frac{1}{2}$, $p = \frac{3}{4}$, $t = -2$,

calculate

(a) $mp + t$ **(b)** $\dfrac{(m + p)}{t}$ **NEAB**

126

46. Use the formula

$$y = \frac{x - t}{\sqrt{(1 - v^2)}}$$

to calculate the value of y given that

$x = 50$, $t = 2{\cdot}5$ and $v = 0{\cdot}6$.

Give your answer correct to 1 decimal place. Show all necessary working.   ULEAC

47.

NEAB CAR INSURANCE	
RENAULT 3	£570 per year
FORD FOXY	£360 per year

(a) Ahmed has a Renault 3 car.
He is given a reduction of 45% of his car insurance because he has not had a car accident.
This is called a 'No Claims' reduction.
Calculate the price Ahmed has to pay to insure his car.

(b) Barbara has a Ford Foxy car.
After taking her 'No Claims' reduction off she has to pay £234 to insure her car.
Calculate her 'No Claims' reduction as a percentage of £360.

(c) Christine has a Rover car.
She is given a 60% 'No Claims' reduction.
After taking her 'No Claims' reduction off she has to pay £82 to insure her car.
Calculate the original price of her car insurance.   NEAB

48. The Saddlethorpe Cricket Club give a trophy for the best player each season.

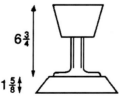

The trophy is $6\frac{3}{4}$ inches high.

It stands on a base $1\frac{5}{8}$ inches high.

What is the total height of the trophy and base?   MEG

49. The surface area of the Earth is approximately $1 \cdot 971 \times 10^8$ square miles. The surface area of the Earth covered by water is approximately $1 \cdot 395 \times 10^8$ square miles.

    (a) Calculate the surface area of the Earth not covered by water. Give your answer in standard form.

    (b) What percentage of the Earth's surface is not covered by water?   **NEAB**

50. **(a)** Calculate the value of

$$\sqrt{3 \cdot 1 + \frac{6}{3 \cdot 1} - \frac{9}{3 \cdot 1^2}}$$

    (b) Show how to check that your answer is of the right order of magnitude.   **NEAB**

51. **(a)** The population of Brazil is $1 \cdot 15 \times 10^8$.
The population of Peru is $1 \cdot 71 \times 10^7$.
How many more people live in Brazil than in Peru?
Give your answer in standard form.

    The population density of a country is calculated as

$$population\ density = \frac{population}{area}$$

    The area of Brazil is $3 \cdot 29 \times 10^6$ square miles.

    (b) Calculate the population density of Brazil.

    The population density of Peru is $34 \cdot 5$.
    (c) Calculate the area of Peru.
Give your answer in standard form.   **MEG**

52. **(a)** Use the formula $E = \frac{1}{2}v^2 + gh$

    to find E when $v = 4 \cdot 2$, $g = 9 \cdot 8$ and $h = -12 \cdot 9$.

    (b) Use the formula

$$\frac{1}{f} = \frac{1}{u} + \frac{1}{v}$$

    to find f when $u = 8$ and $v = -12$.   **MEG**

ALGEBRA

Algebra Revision

DIVISIBILITY

A number is divisible by 2 if it is an even number

divisible by 3 if the sum of its digits is divisible by 3

divisible by 4 if the number formed from the last two digits is divisible by 4

divisible by 5 if the last digit is 0 or 5

divisible by 6 if it is divisible by both 2 and 3

divisible by 8 if the number formed from the last three digits is divisible by 8

divisible by 9 if the sum of its digits is divisible by 9

divisible by 10 if the last digit is 0.

PRIME NUMBERS, FACTORS, MULTIPLES

A prime number is divisible by just two numbers, itself and 1.

The multiples of a number are found by multiplying the number by each of 1, 2, 3, . . .
For instance, the multiples of 10 are 10, 20, 30, . . .

A factor of a given number is a whole number that divides exactly into the given number. For instance, the factors of 10 are 1, 2, 5, 10.

A prime factor is a factor that is a prime number. For instance, the prime factors of 10 are 2 and 5.

EXPRESSIONS. FORMULAE. EQUATIONS

$x + 3$ is an expression.
$p = x + 3$ is a formula. The value of p depends on the value of x.
$2p - 4 = 1$ is an equation. Here p can have only one value; $x = 2 \cdot 5$.

ab means $a \times b$ 2a means $2 \times a$ a^2 means $a \times a$
3xa is usually written as 3ax. That is, the number is written first, then the letters are written in alphabetical order.

$5a + 2a$ can be simplified to $7a$
$5a + 3b - a + 2b$ can be simplified to $4a + 5b$
When we remove the brackets from $5(2a - 3)$ we get $10a - 15$.

continued . . .

. . . *from previous page*

Replacing variables, in a formula, with numbers is called **substituting in a formula**.

For instance, if $x = 3$ and $a = 2$ in $t = 4x - 5a$
then $t = 4 \times 3 - 5 \times 2$
$= 12 - 10$
$= 2$

Three methods of **solving equations** are : trial and improvement, flowchart method, balance method. The **trial and improvement** method is particularly useful for solving polynomial equations ; that is, equations which involve a square such as x^2 or a cube such as x^3.

The **flowchart method** for solving $2a - 4 = 1$ is shown below.

Begin with $a \longrightarrow \boxed{\times 2} \longrightarrow 2a \longrightarrow \boxed{-4} \longrightarrow 2a - 4$

$2 \cdot 5 \longleftarrow \boxed{\div 2} \longleftarrow 5 \longleftarrow \boxed{+4} \longleftarrow$ Begin with 1

Hence $a = 2 \cdot 5$.

The **balance method** for solving $2a - 4 = 1$ is shown below.
$$2a - 4 = 1$$
$$2a = 5 \text{ (adding 4 to both sides)}$$
$$a = 2 \cdot 5 \text{ (dividing both sides by 2)}$$

We would take these steps to solve $2a - 4 = 1$ using **trial and improvement**.
Guess a likely answer.
Check to see if this answer is correct.
Make another guess and so on.

The "**trial and improvement**" method for finding the solution (to 1 d.p.) for the equation $2x^3 - 1 = 9$ is shown below.
Try $x = 1$. If $x = 1, 2x^3 - 1 = 1$ which is less than 9.
Try $x = 2$. If $x = 2, 2x^3 - 1 = 15$ which is greater than 9.
Since 9 lies between 1 and 15, then the solution must be between 1 and 2.
Try $x = 1 \cdot 5$. If $x = 1 \cdot 5, 2x^3 - 1 = 5 \cdot 75$ which is less than 9.
Try $x = 1 \cdot 8$. If $x = 1 \cdot 8, 2x^3 - 1 = 10 \cdot 664$ which is greater than 9.
Try $x = 1 \cdot 7$. If $x = 1 \cdot 7, 2x^3 - 1 = 8 \cdot 826$ which is less than 9.
The solution lies between $1 \cdot 7$ and $1 \cdot 8$. Since $8 \cdot 826$ is closer to 9 than is $10 \cdot 664$, the solution to 1 d.p. is $x = 1 \cdot 7$.

When solving an equation always **check your solution** by substituting your solution back into the equation. For instance, to check that $p = 3 \cdot 5$ is a solution for $6p + 1 = 22$ proceed as follows:
If $p = 3 \cdot 5$ then $6p + 1 = 6 \times 3 \cdot 5 + 1$
$= 22$ Correct.

continued . . .

. . . *from previous page*

Take the following steps to **solve a problem** using equations.

Step 1   Choose a variable such as n or x for the unknown quantity.
Step 2   Rewrite the statements in mathematical symbols.
Step 3   Combine these statements into an equation.
Step 4   Solve the equation.
Step 5   Check the answer with the information in the problem.

COORDINATES. DRAWING a LINE

The **x-axis** is the horizontal axis.
The **y-axis** is the vertical axis.

The **coordinates** of a point are a pair of
numbers such as $(3, -2)$.
The first number is the **x-coordinate;** the
second number is the **y-coordinate.**

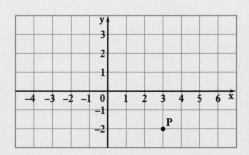

For the point $P(3, -2)$, the x-coordinate is 3 and the y-coordinate is -2.

The graph of a straight line may be drawn as follows.
   Step 1   Find the coordinates of three points on the line.
   Step 2   Plot these points.
   Step 3   Draw the line that passes through these points.
Note: The line could be drawn by plotting just two points but for greater accuracy it is
       wise to plot three points.

For instance, to draw the line $y = 2x + 1$ proceed as follows.
Choose three values for x, say $-1, 0, 1$. Substitute these values for x into $y = 2x + 1$ to
find the corresponding values of y; see the table below. Now plot the points $(-1, -1)$,
$(0, 1), (1, 3)$ and draw the line that goes through these points – see the graph below.

x	−1	0	1
y	−1	1	3

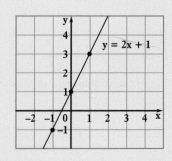

continued . . .

. . . *from previous page*

The lines $y = 2x$, $y = 2x + 1$, $y = 2x + 5$ are all parallel since the number multiplying the x is the same for all of them.

The lines $y = x + 4$, $y = 2x + 4$, $y = 5x + 4$ all meet the y-axis at the same place since the number added is the same for all of them.

SIMULTANEOUS EQUATIONS

Equations such as $\begin{cases} 3x - 4y = 23 \\ 4x + 3y = 14 \end{cases}$, which need to be solved together to find the value of x and y, are called **simultaneous equations**.

Some methods of solving these are: **trial and improvement, balance method** (also called the **elimination** method), **substitution method, graphical method.** In the graphical method, we draw the graphs of each equation on the same set of axes. The x and y-coordinates of the point where the graphs meet give the solution of the simultaneous equations.

The balance method depends on eliminating one of the unknowns.

$\left. \begin{array}{l} 3x - 4y = 23 \\ 4x + 3y = 14 \end{array} \right\}$ becomes $\begin{cases} 9x - 12y = 69 \quad \text{(multiplying both sides by 3)} \\ 16x + 12y = 56 \quad \text{(multiplying both sides by 4)} \end{cases}$

$\qquad\qquad\qquad\qquad\qquad 25x \qquad\; = 125 \quad \text{(adding the equations)}$

$\qquad\qquad\qquad\qquad\qquad\quad x = 5 \qquad \text{(dividing both sides by 25)}$

When $x = 5$, $4x + 3y = 14$ becomes $20 + 3y = 14$

$\qquad\qquad\qquad\qquad\qquad\qquad 3y = -6 \quad \text{(subtracting 20 from both sides)}$

$\qquad\qquad\qquad\qquad\qquad\qquad\; y = -2 \quad \text{(dividing both sides by 3)}$

Always check the solution by substituting the value of the unknowns into the original equation.

Problems which have two unknowns may be solved by using simultaneous equations if two equations can be written down. The following are the steps that need to be taken.

Step 1 Allocate a letter to each of the unknowns.

Step 2 From the given information, write down two equations that involve the unknowns.

Step 3 Solve these two simultaneous equations using a method of your choice.

Step 4 Check the solutions.

continued . . .

SEQUENCES

A **sequence** is a list of numbers such as $3, 7, 11, 15, \ldots$
t_1 means the first term, t_2 means the second term and so on. For instance, for the sequence $3, 7, 11, 15, \ldots$ $t_1 = 3$, $t_2 = 7$, $t_3 = 11$ etc.
t_n means the nth term. For instance, for the sequence $3, 7, 11, 15, \ldots$ $t_n = 4n - 1$.
Sometimes a letter other than t is used. For instance T_1, a_1, u_1, all mean the first term.

Sequences are sometimes based on the following special numbers : odd numbers, even numbers, squares, cubes, multiples.
The terms of a sequence are sometimes found by adding the same number to each previous term or by multiplying each previous term by the same number.

For instance $1, 4, 9, 16, \ldots$ is a sequence of square numbers.
$\qquad\qquad$ $2, 5, 8, 11, \ldots$ is a sequence in which each term is 3 more than the previous term.

The **Fibonacci Sequence** is $1, 1, 2, 3, 5, 8, 13, \ldots$ The first two terms are 1, 1. Each term after this is found by adding the two previous terms.

Many sequences can be found in **Pascal's Triangle.** The first few rows of this are :

```
            1

         1     1

      1     2     1

   1     3     3     1

1     4     6     4     1
```

In Pascal's triangle the numbers down the left and right-hand sides are always 1. That is, each row begins and ends with 1. All other numbers are the sum of the two numbers immediately above on the previous row.

Sometimes we can continue a sequence by using the **difference method.** For instance, the next term in the sequence $12, 14, 22, 36, 56, \ldots$ can be found as follows.

```
    12        14        22        36        56        82

         2         8        14        20        26

              6         6         6         6
```

$3, 7, 11, 15, \ldots$ and $5, 2, -1, -4, \ldots$ are examples of sequences which have **linear rules**.
The difference between any two consecutive terms is the same.
If we listed the differences as above, the numbers in the first row of differences would all be the same.

continued . . .

. . . from previous page

We can find the linear rule for a sequence such as $3, 7, 11, 15, \ldots$ as follows. The difference between any two consecutive terms is 4.

The rule is $\quad t_n = 4n + a$

$\quad\quad\quad t_1 = 4 \times 1 + a \;$ (replacing n with 1)

$\quad\quad\quad 3 = 4 + a \;$ (since $t_1 = 3$)

$\quad\quad\quad -1 = a \;$ (subtracting 4 from both sides)

The rule for the sequence $3, 7, 11, 15, \ldots$ is then $t_n = 4n - 1$.

$2, 5, 10, 17, \ldots$ and $3, 10, 21, 36$ are examples of sequences which have **quadratic rules**. If we listed the differences as at the bottom of the previous page, the numbers in the second row of differences would all be the same.

We can find the quadratic rule for a sequence such as $3, 10, 21, 36, \ldots$ as follows. Let the rule be $t_n = an^2 + bn + c$.

$$
\begin{array}{lcccc}
(a + b + c = 3) & \longleftarrow & 3 & 10 & 21 & 36 \\
\quad (3a + b = 7) & \longleftarrow & & 7 & 11 & 15 \\
\quad\quad (2a = 4) & \longleftarrow & & & 4 & 4 \\
\end{array}
$$

$2a = 4$	$3a + b = 7$	$a + b + c = 3$
$a = 2$	$3 \times 2 + b = 7$	$2 + 1 + c = 3$
	$6 + b = 7$	$3 + c = 3$
	$b = 1$	$c = 0$

The rule for the sequence $3, 10, 21, 36, \ldots$ is then $t_n = 2n^2 + n$.

INEQUALITIES

$n > -3$ is read as "n is greater than -3"

$n \geq -3$ is read as "n is greater than or equal to -3"

$n < -3$ is read as "n is less than -3"

$n \leq -3$ is read as "n is less than or equal to -3"

$-3 < n < 5$ is read as "n is greater than -3 but less than 5"

$\quad\quad\quad\quad$ or as "n is between -3 and 5"

$-3 < n \leq 5$ is read as "n is greater than -3 but less than or equal to 5"

Inequalities such as $n \leq -2$, $n > 1$, $2 \leq n < 5$ may be graphed on a number line. To display an inequality on the number line proceed as follows.

$\quad$*Step 1*$\quad$ Draw a line over all the values included.

$\quad$*Step 2*$\quad$ If the end point of the line is one of the values included, place the symbol $\bullet$ on this end point; if the end point is not one of the values included, place the symbol $\circ$ on this end point.

For instance,

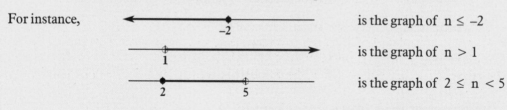

$\quad\quad\quad\quad\quad\quad\quad\quad\quad\quad\quad$ is the graph of $n \leq -2$

$\quad\quad\quad\quad\quad\quad\quad\quad\quad\quad\quad$ is the graph of $n > 1$

$\quad\quad\quad\quad\quad\quad\quad\quad\quad\quad\quad$ is the graph of $2 \leq n < 5$

continued . . .

. . . from previous page

Solutions for inequalities such as $3n - 4 \leq 1$, $3 - 2n > 5$ etc. may be found by first solving the equations $3n - 4 = 1$, $3 - 2n = 5$ etc. then finding the region of the number line for which the inequality is true.

For instance, to solve $3 - 2n > 5$, first solve $3 - 2n = 5$ to get $n = -1$.
Test a value of n, other than $n = -1$, in $3 - 2n > 5$.
Testing $n = 0$, we get $3 - 2 \times 0 > 5$
$$3 - 0 > 5$$
$$3 > 5 \text{ which is not true.}$$

Since $n = 0$ is not one of the solutions of $3 - 2n > 5$ the graph of $3 - 2n > 5$ is not to the right of -1. The graph must be to the left of -1. The solution of $3 - 2n > 5$ is then $n < -1$.

Solutions for inequalities may also be found using a method similar to the **balance method** used for equations. We must remember that
1. adding or subtracting a number from both sides leaves the sign of the inequality unchanged
2. multiplying or dividing both sides of an inequality by a positive number leaves the sign of the inequality unchanged
3. if both sides of an inequality are multiplied or divided by a negative number, the sign of the inequality changes.

For instance, $3 - 2n > 5$ may be solved as follows.

$$3 - 2n > 5$$
$$- 2n > 2 \quad \text{(subtracting 3 from both sides)}$$
$$n < \frac{2}{-2} \quad \text{(dividing both sides by } -2\text{)}$$
$$n < -1$$

REVISION EXERCISE

1.   1   2   3   4   6   8   11   14   19   20   25   30

(a) Which of these numbers are prime numbers?

(b) Which number is the cube of another number in the list?

(c) Which number is the square root of another number?

(d) Which numbers in the list are multiples of 4?

(e) Which numbers in the list are factors of 20?

2. Find three ways of continuing the sequence $1, 2, 4, \ldots$

3. I think of a number.
   I divide by 3, then add 3.
   This gives the same result as subtracting 1, then dividing by 2.
   What is the number?

4. Solve these equations.

   (a) $3x - 5 = 16$ (b) $2(3a + 2) = 7$ (c) $3n + 4 = n - 1$

   (d) $\dfrac{2x}{5} = -4$

5. Write down the inequalities displayed on the number lines. Use n for the variable.

   (i) (a) ◄———●———   (b) ———⊕——►   (c) ⊕———●———
                  3   -4 1   5

   (ii) (a) Display the inequality $-3 < x < 2$ on a number line.

         (b) Write down all the whole number solutions for x if $-3 < x < 2$.

6.

Speed in mph	0	30	60
Speed in km/h	0	48	96

   Use the values given in the table to draw a graph to change speeds in mph to speeds in km/h.
   Use your graph to answer the following questions.

   (a) Kate is cycling at a speed of 15mph. Jason is cycling at a speed of 25km/h. Who is cycling faster?

   (b) On Nick's journey, from Peterborough to Bedford, his car averaged 50mph. On the return journey, his average speed was 85km/h. Which journey was faster and by how much? (Answer in km/h.)

7. When Kate asked Nicholas what his house number was, Nicholas replied "Sixteen added to three times my house number is the same as two subtracted from five times my house number."

   (a) Write an equation for **h**, where **h** is Nicholas' house number.

   (b) Solve this equation to find Nicholas' house number.

8. Without doing any calculation, state the maximum number of solutions for the equation
   $x^3 + 2x^2 - x + 3 = 0$

137

9. Find the next three terms in the following sequences.

   (a) 1, 4, 9, 16, ...

   (b) 1, 2, 3, 5, 8, ...

   (c) 3, 4, 6, 9, ...

   (d) 1, 8, 27, 64, ...

   (e) 32, 16, 8, 4, ...

   (f) 1, 1, 2, 3, 5, 8, ...

   What name is given to the sequence in (f)?

10. Which inequality best describes the given statements.

    (a) The top speed of Jane's car is 140km/h.

    A. $s > 140$ B. $s \geq 140$ C. $s < 140$ D. $s \leq 140$

    (b) Class sizes in a school range from 15 to 31.

    A. $15 < s < 31$ B. $31 \leq s \leq 15$ C. $15 \leq s \leq 31$ D. $31 < s < 15$

11. A patio is 2 metres longer than it is wide.

    (i) Write an expression, involving x, for

       (a) the length of the patio

       (b) the perimeter of the patio

       (c) the area of the patio.

    (ii) How wide is the patio if the perimeter is 22 metres?

x metres

12. Two sides of a square are $(4n + 3)$cm and $(2n + 12)$cm.

    (a) Write down an equation for n. Solve this equation.

    (b) Find the perimeter of the square.

13.

  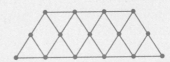

   "Garden Designs" are making screens by bolting short rods together. These diagrams represent their three smallest screens. In the smallest screen 14 rods and 9 bolts are used.

   (a) How many rods and how many bolts are used in the other two screens shown?

   (b) Selena wrote the relationship between r, the number of rods and b, the number of bolts as $r = b + 5$. She then realised this was not correct.
   What is the correct relationship between r and b?

14. Solve these simultaneous equations.

    (a) $2a + b = 8$
        $3a - b = 17$

    (b) $5m + 4n = 12$
        $5m - 2n = 9$

15. Simplify   (a) $3n - 4a - 5n + a$ (b) $2x + 3(4 - x)$

16. For what whole number values of n is the following true?
$$-6 \leq 4n < 12$$

17. Detectives from the "Snoopy" private detective agency charge an initial fee of £200 plus £75 for each day they are hired.
Detectives from the "Private Eye" agency charge no initial fee but their daily charge is £100 a day.

   (a) Write down an equation that would enable you to find the number of days for which the charge from both agencies would be the same. (Use d as the variable.)

   (b) Solve this equation.

18. A group of students designed a game based on divisibility.
The digits 0 to 9 were written on cards. Part of the play consisted of the following:

Four cards are dealt, face up, to a player.
The player arranges these in as many different ways as possible to make 4-digit numbers which are divisible by a number the player nominates.
The larger the number nominated, the more points the player scores.

| 2 | 3 | 8 | 5 |

During the play of this game, Kwan was dealt the cards shown. She decided to make numbers divisible by 8.

   (a) One arrangement she made was  . What other arrangements could she make?

   (b) How many arrangements could Kwan have made if she had decided to make numbers divisible by 6?

19.

t_1	t_2	t_3	t_4	...
2	5	8	11	...

t_1	t_2	t_3	t_4	...
6	18	54	162	...

The first 4 terms of two sequences are given in these tables.

   (a) A formula for the nth term of one of these sequences is $t_n = 2 \times 3^n$. Which sequence is this? What is the 7th term of this sequence?

   (b) The other sequence has a linear rule. Write this rule as $t_n = \ldots$

20. Two school parties went to the theatre.

(a) In the first party there were 2 adults and 26 students.
They paid a total of £103.
$2a + 26s = 103$ is an equation which describes this.
What does a stand for? What does s stand for?

(b) The second party paid £184 for 5 adults and 44 students.
Write an equation, using a and s, which describes this.

(c) Solve the two simultaneous equations from (a) and (b) to find the price paid by each adult and each student.

(d) What total saving did these 77 people make by going to this theatre in a school party?
What assumption did you have to make to be able to find this total saving?

21.

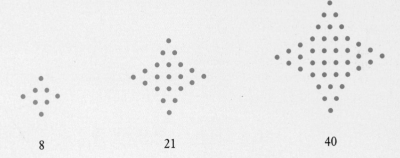

1   8   21   40

(a) Draw the next pattern in this sequence of octagonal numbers. How many dots are in this pattern?

(b) The following difference table can be formed from the numbers 1, 8, 21, 40.

$$1 \qquad 8 \qquad 21 \qquad 40$$
$$7 \qquad 13 \qquad 19$$
$$6 \qquad 6$$

Copy this difference table. Extend it to find the number of dots in the 8th pattern of octagonal numbers.

(c) Find a quadratic rule for the sequence 1, 8, 21, 40, . . .
Write the rule as $t_n = \ldots$

(d) Use the rule to find the number of dots in the 20th octagonal number.

22. Solve these inequalities.   (a) $2n - 3 \leq 8$ (b) $3 - 5n > 5$

23. A squash club charges £2·50 per game for non-members. Members pay a subscription of £20 per year and 50p per game.

(a) $C = 20 + 0.5n$ is a formula which gives the total cost for a member who plays n games in a year.
Draw the graph of $C = 20 + 0.5n$ using axes numbered as shown.

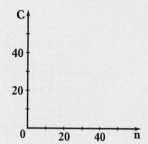

(b) Write a formula for the total cost for a non-member who plays n games.

(c) By drawing another graph on the same axes, find how many games could be played in a year before it becomes cheaper to be a member.

24. This diagram represents a rectangular garden. The shading represents the area in which an orchard is to be planted. The total area of the garden is 500m².

(a) Show that $x^2 + 8x + 12 = 500$ is an equation which describes this situation.

(b) Find the length of the orchard, to the nearest tenth of a metre. (*Hint*: use trial and improvement.)

25. (i) (a) Draw a set of axes, with the x-axis from 0 to 6 and the y-axis from 0 to 10.

(b) Copy and complete this table for $4x + 3y = 24$.
On your set of axes, draw the line $4x + 3y = 24$.

On the same set of axes, draw the line $2x + y = 10$.

x	0	3	6
y			

(ii) (a) A maths. test was in two sections. In the first section, each question was worth the same number of marks. More marks were given to the questions in the second section.
Let the questions in the first section be worth f marks and those in the second section each be worth s marks.
On this test, Aidi correctly answered 4 questions in the first section and 3 questions in the second section for a total of 24 marks.
Write down an equation, involving f and s, which describes this.

(b) $2f + s = 10$ is an equation which describes the number of questions Helen answered correctly and the marks she gained.
Use this equation and the equation from (a) to find how many marks were given to each question in the two sections.

(iii) Is there a connection between (i) and (ii) of this question? Explain your answer.

141

26.   1, 5, 9, 13, 17, 21, 25, 29, 33, 37, 41, 45, 49, 53, ,...

The 1st and 3rd terms of this sequence are square numbers. That is, t_1 and t_3 are square numbers.

(a) For the numbers that are written down, there are two other values of n for which t_n is a square number. What are these values of n?

(b) Use a difference table, or otherwise, to predict the next value of n for which t_n is a square number.

27. (i) Consider the sequence of odd numbers   1, 3, 5, 7, 9, 11, ...

    (a) Copy and complete
$$1 + 3 = 4$$
$$1 + 3 + 5 = 9$$
$$1 + 3 + 5 + 7 =$$
$$1 + 3 + 5 + 7 + 9 =$$

    (b) Write down a rule, in the form $S_n = \ldots$, which gives the sum of the first n terms of 1, 3, 5, 7, 9, 11, ...

    (c) Find the sum of the first 25 odd numbers.

    (d) The sum of the first n odd numbers is 361. What is n?

(ii) Darren and Julia were investigating odd numbers.

    (a) One of the statements Darren made was "If you add together two or more consecutive odd numbers, you always get a square number". He wrote down three examples which supported this statement. What might these have been?

    (b) Julia then wrote down an example which showed that Darren's statement wasn't correct. What might this example have been?

    (c) Rewrite Darren's statement so it is correct.

28. (a) Write down and simplify a formula for the total perimeter of this shape.

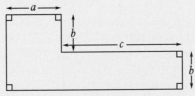

(b) Use your formula to work out the perimeter when $a = 3$, $b = 2$, $c = 4$.   **ULEAC**

29. Write down the next number and a rule for continuing each of the following number patterns.

(a) 2, 7, 12, 17,   (b) 1, 3, 9, 27,   **WJEC**

30. 　　　　　　　　3　4　9　13　15　23　25　28　64

Choosing numbers from the list above, fill in the blank spaces to make the following statements true.

(a) _____, _____ and _____ are prime numbers.

(b) _____ and _____ are factors of 200.

(c) _____ is a multiple of 7.

(d) _____ is a cube.

(e) $5 \div$ _____ $= \frac{1}{3}$.

NICCEA

31.

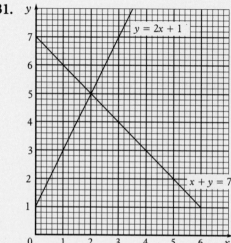

The diagram shows the graphs of the equations

$y = 2x + 1$ and $x + y = 7$.

Use the diagram to solve the simultaneous equations

$$y = 2x + 1,$$
$$x + y = 7.$$

ULEAC

32.

Row 1		1		Sum = 1
Row 2	3		5	Sum = 8 = 2^3
Row 3	7	9	11	Sum = 27 = 3^3

(a) Write down the numbers and the Sum which continue the pattern in Row 4.

(b) Which Row will have a Sum = 1000?

(c) What is the Sum of Row 20?

(d) The first number in a row is x.

What is the second number in this row? Give your answer in terms of x.

MEG

33. Write down all the whole number values of x, such that $-3 \leq x < 4$

SEG

34. Solve the equations

   (a) $x - 7 = -2$ **(b)** $4x - 8 = 17$ **(c)** $5(x - 3) = 20$ **MEG**

35.

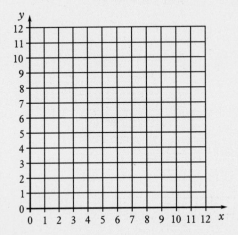

Using the above grid and drawing your path, complete the shape formed by using the following instructions.

START AT A (5, 8)

MOVE TO B (10, 7)

MOVE TO C (10, 4)

MOVE TO D (0, 4)

JOIN D TO A

Write down the coordinates of any point which lies inside your shape.   **WJEC**

36. (a) x is a whole number such that

$$-4 \leq x < 2.$$

   (i) Make a list of all the possible values of x.

   (ii) What is the largest possible value of x^2?

   (b) Every week Rucci has a test in Mathematics.
      It is marked out of 20.
      Rucci has always scored at least half the marks available.
      She has never quite managed to score full marks.

      Using x to represent Rucci's marks, write this information in the form of two inequalities.   **NEAB**

37. A long row of houses has been changed into flats.
Each house has three flats – basement, middle and top.

The flats are numbered in order – basement, then middle, then top, for each house in turn.
Flats numbered 1 to 5 are shown in the drawing.

(a) (i) Complete the table to show the flat numbers for the first five houses.

House	Basement Flat	Middle Flat	Top Flat
1			
2			
3			
4			
5			

(ii) Mrs Smith lives in the top flat in the tenth house.
What is the number of her flat?

(iii) Mr Patel and Mr Dobson are next door neighbours.
They both have basement flats.
Mr Dobson lives in flat 25.
What are the possible numbers of Mr Patel's flat?

(b) (i) Find a formula for the number of the middle flat for any house in the row.
(Remember to show that you have tested your formula.)

(ii) Miss Ling visits her friend.

I know it's a middle flat.
I think it's number 94.

Is Miss Ling correct?
Explain your answer.

NEAB

38. In this question an arrow means "is a factor of" (or 'divides exactly into').

The 'Factor Diagram' on the right shows that 3 is a factor of 6, 12 and 15; that 5 is a factor of 15; and that 6 is a factor of 12.

There is no line with an arrow connecting 6 and 15, and this means that 6 is not a factor of 15.

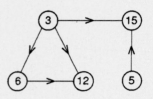

(a) Complete this Factor Diagram by putting in the arrows.

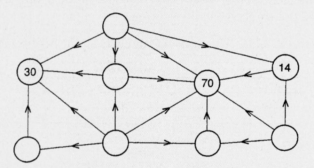

(b) In the empty circles in the Factor Diagram below, insert the six whole numbers (**all different and all greater than 1**) that are needed to complete this diagram correctly.

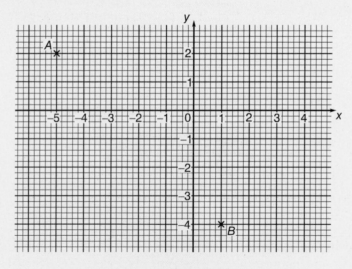

(c) Now make up your own Factor Diagram using 20 as the largest number. **MEG**

39. (a) Two points A and B are shown on the grid below.
Write down their coordinates.

(b) Complete the table of values below for

$$y = x - 2$$

x	-2	0	2	3	4
y		-2			2

(c) Draw the graph of $y = x - 2$ on the grid on the previous page.

(d) On the grid, draw the straight line AB.
Write down the coordinates of the point where the graph of $y = x - 2$ cuts the line AB.

MEG

40. This picture shows some packets of rice in the pans of a weighing machine.
Each packet of rice weighs x kg.

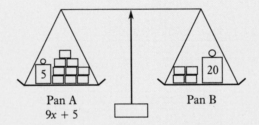

Pan A
$9x + 5$

Pan B

In Pan A there are 9 packets of rice and a weight of 5kg.
An expression for the total weight in kg in Pan A is $9x + 5$.
In Pan B there are 4 packets of rice and a weight of 20kg.

(a) Write down in terms of x an expression for the total weight in Pan B.

The total weight in each pan is the same.
(b) Write down an equation in terms of x to represent this information.

(c) Use your equation to calculate the weight, x kg, of one packet of rice.

ULEAC

41. Complete the Table for each sequence.

Sequence				next term	n^{th} term
1	4	9	16		
5	8	11	14		
$\frac{1}{5}$	$\frac{2}{6}$	$\frac{3}{7}$	$\frac{4}{8}$		

MEG

147

42. For off-peak electricity, customers can choose to pay by Method A or Method B.

Method A: £8 per quarter plus 4p per unit.
Method B: £12 per quarter plus 3p per unit.

A customer uses x units. The quarterly cost is £y.

The cost, £y, by *Method B* is $y = 0 \cdot 03x + 12$.

(a) **(i)** Complete the table of values for $y = 0 \cdot 03x + 12$.

x	100	200	300
y	15		

(ii) Draw the graph of $y = 0 \cdot 03x + 12$.

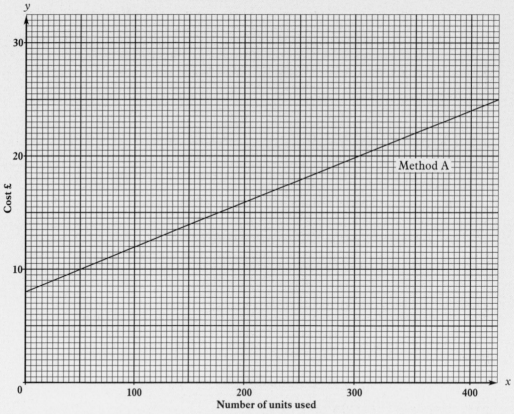

(b) For a certain number of units both methods give the same cost.
Use the graphs to find

(i) this number of units,

(ii) this cost.

(c) Complete the following statement

"Method . . . is always cheaper for customers who use more than . . . units".   **SEG**

43.

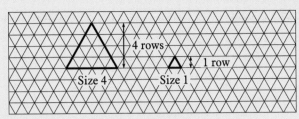

A triangle had been drawn on triangular grid paper.
The triangle is called a size 4 triangle because it is 4 rows deep.
The size 4 triangle contains 16 size 1 triangles.

(a) Investigate triangles of different sizes drawn on a triangular grid.

(b) From your investigation, try to answer the following.

    (i) Explain how to work out the number of size 1 triangles in a size 10 triangle.

    (ii) Write down an expression for the number of size 1 triangles in a size n triangle.

ULEAC

44. Fran, Jo and Tom share some money.
Jo gets 50p more than Tom.
Fran gets twice as much as Jo.
Let x be the number of pence Tom gets.

Write expressions in terms of x for the number of pence given to

(a) Jo.   (b) Fran.   (c) all three together.

The money shared is £6·70.
(d) Write down an equation in x and solve it to find x.

NICCEA

45.

> **LADDERS FOR HIRE**
>
> **We charge £3 delivery**
> **Plus £4.80 per day**

(a) How much will it cost to hire a ladder for 2 days?

(b) Mrs Hewitt hires a ladder.
The hire charge is £27.
For how many days did she hire the ladder?

SEG

46. Solve the equation $5(x - 2) = 3(x + 3)$ WJEC

47. Solve $3x + y = 4$
               $y = x + 2$ NEAB

48.

The air temperature, $T\,°C$, outside an aircraft flying at a height of h feet is given by the formula

$$T = 26 - \frac{h}{500}$$

An aircraft is flying at a height of 27 000 feet.

(a) Use the formula to calculate the air temperature outside the aircraft.

The air temperature outside an aircraft is –52°C.

(b) Calculate the height of the aircraft.   **ULEAC**

49. A computer program prints out the following numbers.

    1   2   4   8   11   16   22

When one of these numbers is changed, the numbers will form a pattern.
Circle the number which has to be changed and correct it.
Give a reason why your numbers now form a pattern.   **SEG**

50. Bunting is used to decorate the sports field.
It is made up of coloured flags attached to a rope.
Each flag is an equilateral triangle with sides 20cm long.

This diagram shows a piece of bunting.
It is 130cm long. There are gaps g cm long between the flags.

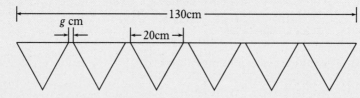

(a) (i) Complete this equation using g.

    .... $= 130$

    (ii) Solve this equation to find the value of g.

(b) A piece of bunting consists of p flags with the same gaps as before.

    (i) Write down an expression, using p, for the length of the piece of bunting.

    (ii) Find the value of p if the piece of bunting is 878cm long.   **NEAB**

51. A longlife battery and a standard life battery were both tested for their length of life.
The longlife battery lasted for x hours.
The standard life battery lasted for y hours.

(a) The combined length of life of the two batteries was 14 hours.
Explain why $x + y = 14$.

(b) The longlife battery lasted 3 hours longer than the standard life battery.
Write down another equation connecting x and y.

The graph of $x + y = 14$ has been drawn below.
(c) Complete the table of values for your equation in (b) and use it to draw the graph of
your equation.

Draw your graph on the axes below.

x	3	7	10
y			

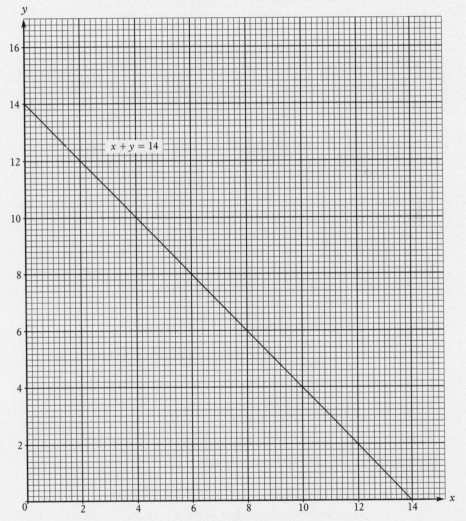

(d) Use your graphs to find the length of life of each type of battery.   **SEG**

151

52. Solve the following simultaneous equations by an algebraic (not graphical) method.

$$4x - 3y = 18$$
$$5x + 2y = 11$$

WJEC

53. (a) Complete the Table below for the given values of x and y.

x	y	$x + y$	$x - y$	$x^2 - y^2$
5	3	8	2	16
6	3			
9	2			

(b) Add two more sets of values for x and y of your own choosing, with x larger than y.

(c) What do you notice about the numbers in the last three columns?   **MEG**

54. Joe is making a pattern by surrounding black equilateral triangles with white equilateral triangles.

(a) Write down a general rule for the number of white triangles, w, in terms of the number of black triangles, b, in the pattern.

Joe has 92 white triangles.

(b) What is the greatest number of black triangles that he can surround in the pattern?

ULEAC

55. The rule for any term of a sequence is

$$\frac{n}{2n - 1}, \text{ where } n \text{ is the number of the term.}$$

(a) Use this rule to write down the first five terms of the sequence.

(b) The first five terms of a different sequence are

Term	1	2	3	4	5
Sequence	$\frac{1}{2}$	$\frac{2}{5}$	$\frac{3}{8}$	$\frac{4}{11}$	$\frac{5}{14}$

Write down the rule for the nth term of this sequence.   **SEG**

56. Solve the equation $\dfrac{3x - 5}{8} = 5$ **ULEAC**

57. Simone drew a graph to help her convert prices whilst on holiday in Spain.
The graph she drew converts between British money (£) and Spanish money (Pesetas).
The graph she drew is shown below.

At home, in Bradford, Simone had seen a pair of jeans for £14·99.
In Spain, some similar jeans cost 2700 Pesetas.

(a) How much, in £, will Simone save if she buys the jeans in Spain?

Later the exchange rate changes so that £1 is worth 180 Pesetas.

(b) Draw a new line on the graph to represent this exchange rate.

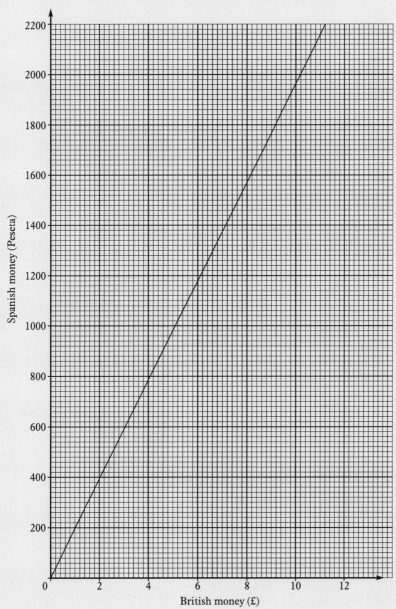

ULEAC

58. The "Durham" hotel charges £40 for a single room and £30 per person for a double room. One night 44 people stay in the hotel. The hotel receives £1500.

Let s represent the number of people staying in single rooms.

Let d represent the number of people staying in double rooms.

The equation for the number of people staying in the hotel is

$$s + d = 44.$$

(a) Write down an equation in terms of s and d for the amount of money received by the hotel.

(b) Solve these simultaneous equations. **SEG**

59. (a) (i) Complete the following number pattern:

$$
\begin{array}{ccc}
11 & = & 11 \\
11 \times 11 & = & 121 \\
11 \times 11 \times 11 & = & \boxed{} \\
\boxed{} & = & \boxed{}
\end{array}
$$

(ii) Look at the numbers in the right hand column. Write down what you notice about these numbers.

(b) Use your calculator to work out the next line of the pattern. What do you notice now? **NEAB**

60. The height, h metres, of a sky rocket t seconds after being launched is given by the formula

$$h = at^2 + bt + 2$$

where a and b are constants. The heights of the rocket above the ground at two different times are given in the table below.

t (seconds)	1	2
h (metres)	37	62

(a) At what height above the ground is the rocket launched?

(b) (i) Use the table of values to show that

$$
\begin{aligned}
a + b &= 35 \\
\text{and} \quad 4a + 2b &= 60
\end{aligned}
$$

(ii) Solve these simultaneous equations to find the value of a and the value of b.

(c) What was the height of the sky rocket $7\frac{1}{2}$ seconds after it was launched? **MEG**

61. Judy is using "trial and improvement" to solve the equation

$$x^2 + x = 11.$$

Complete her working and find a solution correct to one decimal place.

Try $x = 3.5$ $3.5^2 + 3.5 = 15.75$ too large

Try $x = 2.5$ $2.5^2 + 2.5 = 8.75$ too small

Try $x = 3.0$

Try $x =$ **SEG**

62. Mr Basset makes a vegetable garden.
It is a rectangular shape.
The length of the garden is 3 metres more than the width.

(a) The width of the garden is x metres.
Write down an algebraic expression for the length of the garden.

(b) Mr Basset wants his garden to have an area of 100m².

(i) Show that the width of the garden has to be between 8m and 9m.

(ii) By trial and improvement find the width of Mr Basset's vegetable garden.
(Give 1 decimal place in your answer.)   **NEAB**

Leonhard Euler

Leonhard Euler was born at Basel in Switzerland in 1707 and died at St. Petersburg (Leningrad) in Russia in 1783.

Leonhard's father was a clergyman who had studied mathematics. He passed his knowledge onto Leonhard and encouraged Leonhard in his studies of mathematics even though he had hoped his son would also become a clergyman.

Leonhard Euler became the most important mathematician of his time.

He studied theology, medicine, astronomy, physics, music and oriental languages as well as mathematics. At the age of 20, Euler went to the St. Petersburg Academy to teach medicine. This academy had been recently established by Catherine the Great. At the age of 26, Euler became the Academy's chief mathematician.

In 1741, he was invited by Frederick the Great to join the Berlin Academy. Euler spent 25 years there. His time in Germany was not altogether happy. Frederick was impressed with his mathematics but not with Euler as a person. Euler was not very sophisticated and Frederick called him "a mathematical cyclops". In 1766, Euler returned to the St. Petersburg Academy.

During his lifetime, Euler published more than 500 books on mathematics and many articles. His research averaged 800 pages a year. No mathematician has ever been such a prolific writer. He wrote on many aspects of mathematics, from elementary to advanced algebra, arithmetic and trigonometry. He wrote textbooks for use in Russian schools. He also wrote on mechanics, astronomy and music. Usually he wrote in Latin but sometimes in French, although his native tongue was German.

Euler was well known internationally. He frequently entered the competitions run by the Parisian Académie des Sciences and won 12 times. The essays he entered were on a variety of topics including the nature of fire, the masting of ships and tides.

Some of the notations we use today were developed by Euler. f(x) to mean "a function of x" is one such notation. He was not the first to use the symbol π for the ratio of a circle's circumference to its diameter but this symbol was not widely accepted until it appeared in one of Euler's books.

During Euler's time, attempts were made to find an expression that would give just prime numbers. An expression suggested by another mathematician was $2^{2^{n}} + 1$. Euler showed that although this expression gives prime numbers if n = 1, 2, 3 or 4 (we get the numbers 5, 17, 257 and 65537) it does not give a prime number if n = 5 (we then get 4 294 967 297).

It was said Euler could calculate without any apparent effort and was able to find the answers to complicated problems in his head.

Although Euler was blind for the last few years of his life he continued his work on mathematics until his death.

TRANSFORMING FORMULAE

Sometimes we need to rearrange a formula.

The formula $v = \frac{s}{t}$ can be rearranged as $s = vt$ or as $t = \frac{s}{v}$.

Written as $v = \frac{s}{t}$, v is said to be the subject of the formula.

Written as $s = vt$, s is the subject of the formula.

Written as $t = \frac{s}{v}$, t is the subject of the formula.

If a variable, such as s, is to be the **subject of a formula** then s must be written, on its own, on the left-hand side.

When we rearrange a formula, such as $v = \frac{s}{t}$, so that a variable other than v is the subject of the formula, we are said to have **transformed the formula**.

We can use a **flowchart** to transform formulae. On the flowchart, we make use of inverse operations. **Inverse operations** are operations which "undo" each other.

For instance, $4 \times 3 \div 3 = 4$ shows that multiplying and dividing are inverse operations.
For instance, $5 + 8 - 8 = 5$ shows that adding and subtracting are inverse operations.

Taking the reciprocal of 2 we get $\frac{1}{2}$. Now taking the reciprocal of $\frac{1}{2}$ we get $\frac{1}{\frac{1}{2}} = 1 \times \frac{2}{1} = 2$.

This shows that the inverse of "taking the reciprocal" is "taking the reciprocal".

Worked Example Make b the subject of the formula $A = bh$.

Answer Begin with b $\longrightarrow$ $\boxed{\times\, h}$ $\longrightarrow$ bh

$\dfrac{A}{h}$ $\longleftarrow$ $\boxed{\div\, h}$ $\longleftarrow$ Begin with A

Then $b = \dfrac{A}{h}$

Notes for using the flowchart method:
1. Always begin the first flowchart with the variable you want as the subject of the formula.
2. The first flowchart is completed once you have the expression that is on the right-hand side of the formula.
3. Always begin the second flowchart with the variable that is on the left-hand side of the formula.

Worked Example Make l the subject of the formula $S = \dfrac{n(a+l)}{2}$.

Answer Begin with $l \longrightarrow \boxed{+a} \longrightarrow a+l \longrightarrow \boxed{\times n} \longrightarrow n(a+l) \longrightarrow \boxed{\div 2} \longrightarrow \dfrac{n(a+l)}{2}$

$\dfrac{2S}{n} - a \longleftarrow \boxed{-a} \longleftarrow \dfrac{2S}{n} \longleftarrow \boxed{\div n} \longleftarrow 2S \longleftarrow \boxed{\times 2} \longleftarrow$ Begin with S

Then $l = \dfrac{2S}{n} - a$

Worked Example $x = \dfrac{a}{y}$. Express y in terms of x and a.

Answer Begin with y $\longrightarrow \boxed{\begin{array}{c}\text{Take the}\\\text{reciprocal}\end{array}} \longrightarrow \dfrac{1}{y} \longrightarrow \boxed{\times a} \longrightarrow \dfrac{a}{y}$

$\dfrac{a}{x} \longleftarrow \boxed{\begin{array}{c}\text{Take the}\\\text{reciprocal}\end{array}} \longleftarrow \dfrac{x}{a} \longleftarrow \boxed{\div a} \longleftarrow$ Begin with x

Then $y = \dfrac{a}{x}$

DISCUSSION EXERCISE 8:1

"Changing the subject of a formula is similar to solving an equation". **Discuss** this statement.

Discuss ways, other than using a flowchart, of making x the subject of the following formulae: $y = mx + c$, $a = c - x$, $y = \dfrac{a}{4x}$.

EXERCISE 8:2

1. Make h the subject of these formulae.

   (a) $A = \frac{1}{2}bh$ (b) $A = \frac{1}{2}(a+b)h$ (c) $V = lbh$ (d) $V = \frac{1}{3}Ah$

2. Make r the subject of   (a) $d = 2r$ (b) $C = 2\pi r$.

3. Make *l* the subject of   (a) $A = \pi rl$ (b) $P = 2(l + w)$.

4. Make m the subject of   (a) $y = mx + c$ (b) $d = \dfrac{m}{v}$ (c) $a = \dfrac{F}{m}$.

5. (a) $R = \dfrac{V}{I}$. Express I in terms of R and V.

    (b) Make x the subject of $y = m(x + 3) + 2$.

    (c) The interest I, earned by a sum of money P, invested for T years at an interest rate of R% is given by $I = \dfrac{PRT}{100}$. Express P in terms of I, R and T.

    (d) Make r the subject of the formula $D = \pi r + 5s$.

    (e) $v^2 = u^2 + 2as$. Express s in terms of v, u and a.

    (f) The area of a trapezium is given by the formula $A = \frac{1}{2}(a + b)h$ where a and b are the lengths of the parallel sides and h is the distance between these sides. Make b the subject of this formula.

    (g) Make R the subject of $A = P\left(\dfrac{100 + R}{100}\right)$.

    (h) The area of metal needed to make a cylindrical tin of radius r and height h is given by $A = 2\pi r(r + h)$. Express h in terms of A and r.

Review (a) $m = \dfrac{y}{x}$.   Make y the subject of this formula.

        (b) $m = \dfrac{y}{x}$.   Express x in terms of m and y.

        (c) $v = u + at$.   Express t in terms of v, u and a.

        (d) $F = \frac{9}{5}C + 32$ is a formula to convert temperatures given in degrees Celsius to degrees Fahrenheit. Make C the subject of this formula.

POWERS and ROOTS

$$4^2 = 4 \times 4 \qquad\qquad (-4)^2 = (-4) \times (-4)$$
$$= 16 \qquad\qquad\qquad\qquad = 16$$

That is, both 4^2 and $(-4)^2$ have answer of 16.

Squaring and taking the square root are inverse operations. Since both $4^2 = 16$ and $(-4)^2 = 16$, then both 4 and -4 are square roots of 16.

Since the symbol $\sqrt{}$ means the positive square root, then $\sqrt{16} = 4$. If we wish to use this symbol to refer to both the square roots of 16, we must use $\pm$ (read as "plus or minus") before $\sqrt{}$. For instance $\pm\sqrt{16} = 4$ or -4.

DISCUSSION EXERCISE 8:3

● Do all numbers have two square roots? **Discuss.**

$2^3 = 2 \times 2 \times 2$ That is, $2^3 = 8$. What is $(-2)^3$? What is $\sqrt[3]{8}$? Does 8 have more than one cube root? Do all numbers have a cube root? Does any number have more than one cube root? What is the inverse operation to cubing? **Discuss.**

● Suppose x is to be made the subject of the formula $a = x^2 + b$. Is $x = \sqrt{a - b}$ or $x = \pm \sqrt{a - b}$? **Discuss.**

Suppose x is to be made the subject of the formula $a = x^3 + b$. Is $x = \sqrt[3]{a - b}$ or $x = \pm \sqrt[3]{a - b}$? **Discuss.**

● Suppose x is to be made the subject of the formula $a = \sqrt{x} + b$. **Discuss** how this could be done.

TRANSFORMING FORMULAE involving POWERS and ROOTS

Worked Example $a = 5\sqrt{\frac{c}{b}}$. Express b in terms of a and c.

Answer Using a flowchart:

Begin with b $\longrightarrow$ [Take the reciprocal] $\longrightarrow$ $\frac{1}{b}$ $\longrightarrow$ [× c] $\longrightarrow$ $\frac{c}{b}$ $\longrightarrow$ [Take the positive square root] $\longrightarrow$ $\sqrt{\frac{c}{b}}$ $\longrightarrow$ [× 5] $\longrightarrow$ $5\sqrt{\frac{c}{b}}$

$\frac{25c}{a^2}$ $\longleftarrow$ [Take the reciprocal] $\longleftarrow$ $\frac{a^2}{25c}$ $\longleftarrow$ [÷ c] $\longleftarrow$ $\frac{a^2}{25}$ $\longleftarrow$ [Square] $\longleftarrow$ $\frac{a}{5}$ $\longleftarrow$ [÷ 5] $\longleftarrow$ Begin with a

Hence $b = \dfrac{25c}{a^2}$.

Worked Example Make c the subject of $a = b + c^2$.

Answer Using a flowchart:

Begin with c $\longrightarrow$ [Square] $\longrightarrow$ c^2 $\longrightarrow$ [Add b] $\longrightarrow$ $b + c^2$

$\pm \sqrt{a - b}$ $\longleftarrow$ [Take the square root] $\longleftarrow$ $a - b$ $\longleftarrow$ [Subtract b] $\longleftarrow$ Begin with a

Hence $c = \pm \sqrt{a - b}$.

Sometimes we know that the value of a variable cannot be negative. For instance, if we make r (the radius) the subject of the formula $A = \pi r^2$ (the formula for the area of a circle), we know that r must always be positive. In cases, such as this, when we take the square root we take just the positive square root.

Worked Example $V = \pi r^2 h$ is the formula for the volume of a cylinder of radius r and height h. Make r the subject of the formula.

Answer Using a flowchart:

Begin with r → | **Square** | → r^2 → | **Multiply by πh** | → $\pi r^2 h$

$\pm \sqrt{\dfrac{V}{\pi h}}$ ← | **Take the square root** | ← $\dfrac{V}{\pi h}$ ← | **Divide by πh** | ← Begin with V

Since r must be positive, $r = \sqrt{\dfrac{V}{\pi h}}$.

EXERCISE 8:4

1. Make r the subject of   (a) $A = \pi r^2$ (b) $V = \frac{1}{3}\pi r^2 h$ if in each case r must be positive.

2. Make x the subject of the following. (x may take negative or positive values.)

    (a) $a = x^2$ (b) $b = 5x^2$ (c) $c = \dfrac{2}{x^2}$ (d) $d = \dfrac{ax^2}{b}$

3. $I = \frac{1}{3}ml^2$. Express l in terms of I and m. (l can take positive values only.)

4. $E = \frac{1}{2}mv^2$. Express v in terms of E and m. (v may take positive or negative values.)

5. If a stone is dropped from the top of a lighthouse the distance, s, it falls in time, t, is given by $s = \frac{1}{2}gt^2$. Make t the subject of this formula.

6. $x = \dfrac{y^2}{4a}$. Express y in terms of x and a. (y may take positive or negative values.)

7. Make r the subject of   (a) $V = r^3$ (b) $V = \frac{4}{3}\pi r^3$.

8. Make l the subject of   (a) $n = \sqrt{l}$ (b) $n = \sqrt{l-2}$ (c) $n = \dfrac{a}{\sqrt{l}}$ (d) $n = \sqrt{\dfrac{a}{l}}$

9. $T = 2\pi \sqrt{\dfrac{l}{g}}$. Express l in terms of T and g.

Review (a) $I = \dfrac{c}{d^2}$. Express d in terms of I and c. (d may take positive values only.)

(b) The surface area of a sphere of radius r is given by the formula $A = 4\pi r^2$. Make r the subject of this formula.

(c) $y = \dfrac{x^2}{a^2}$. Express x in terms of y and a. (x may take positive or negative values.)

(d) Make n the subject of $a = b\sqrt{n+1}$.

USING FORMULAE

Worked Example $V = \frac{4}{3}\pi r^3$.   (a) Find V if $r = 2\cdot4$.   (b) Find r if $V = 20\cdot6$.

Take $\pi = 3\cdot142$. Give the answers to 3 significant figures.

Answer (a) If $r = 2\cdot4$, $V = \frac{4}{3} \times 3\cdot142 \times 2\cdot4^3$

$$= 57\cdot9 \text{ to 3 s.f.}$$

Keying | 4 | | ÷ | | 3 | | × | | 3·142 | | × | | 2·4 | | SHIFT | | x^y | | 3 | | = |

(b) If $V = 20\cdot6$, $20\cdot6 = \frac{4}{3} \times 3\cdot142 \times r^3$. To find r, we need to rearrange this as $r = \cdots$. This can be done using a flowchart as shown below.

Begin with r → **Cube** → r^3 → **Multiply by 4 × 3·142** → $4 \times 3\cdot142 \times r^3$ → **Divide by 3** → $\frac{4}{3} \times 3\cdot142 \times r^3$

$\sqrt[3]{\dfrac{3 \times 20\cdot6}{4 \times 3\cdot142}}$ ← **Take the cube root** ← $\dfrac{3 \times 20\cdot6}{4 \times 3\cdot142}$ ← **Divide by 4 × 3·142** ← $3 \times 20\cdot6$ ← **Multiply by 3** ← Begin with 20·6

i.e. $r = \sqrt[3]{\dfrac{3 \times 20\cdot6}{4 \times 3\cdot142}}$

$$= 1\cdot70 \text{ to 3 s.f.}$$

Keying | 3 | | × | | 20·6 | | ÷ | | (| | 4 | | × | | 3·142 | |) | | = | | SHIFT | | $\sqrt[3]{}$ |

Worked Example $v^2 = u^2 + 2as$. Find the two values for v if u = 25, a = 8·2, s = −20.

Answer $v^2 = u^2 + 2as$. $v = \pm \sqrt{u^2 + 2as}$

$$= \pm \sqrt{25^2 + 2 \times 8\cdot2 \times (-20)}$$

$$= 17\cdot2 \text{ or } -17\cdot2 \text{ to 3 s.f.}$$

Keying $\boxed{25}$ $\boxed{\text{SHIFT}}$ $\boxed{x^2}$ $\boxed{+}$ $\boxed{2}$ $\boxed{\times}$ $\boxed{8\cdot2}$ $\boxed{\times}$ $\boxed{20}$ $\boxed{\text{+/-}}$ $\boxed{=}$ $\boxed{\sqrt{}}$ gives the positive value 17·2.

DISCUSSION EXERCISE 8:5

Suppose we have to use the formula $V = \frac{4}{3}\pi r^3$ to find r for many different values of V. Instead of using a flowchart for each value of V we could rearrange $V = \frac{4}{3}\pi r^3$ to make r the

subject. **Check** that we get $r = \sqrt[3]{\dfrac{3V}{4\pi}}$. We could then use this rearranged formula to find

each value for r. Are there any disadvantages in doing this? Discuss.

What if just one value of r is to be found?

EXERCISE 8:6

Throughout this exercise take $\pi = 3\cdot142$ or use the π key on the calculator. Give answers to 3 significant figures if rounding is necessary.

1.   s = vt   Find the value of   (a) s when v = 45 and t = 0·2

(b) v when s = 120 and t = 3

(c) t when s = 75 and v = 20

(d) s when v = −15 and t = $\frac{1}{3}$.

2.   The sum of the interior angles of a polygon is given by
     S = 180 (n − 2)° where n is the number of sides.

(a) Find the sum of the interior angles of the
     sketched polygon.

(b) The sum of the interior angles of a polygon is
     2700°. How many sides has this polygon?

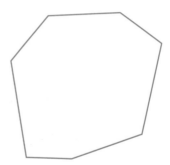

3. Use the formula $A = \pi r^2$ to find the radius of the circle which has an area of $7 \cdot 6 cm^2$.

4. The formula for the surface area, A, of a cone is $A = \pi r l$.

    Find (a) the surface area if $r = 7 \cdot 57$ and $l = 2 \cdot 46$

    (b) the slant height, l, if $A = 22$ and $r = 3 \cdot 18$

    (c) the radius if $A = 984$ and $l = 26$.

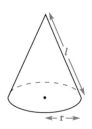

5. The sum of the first n odd numbers is given by $S = n^2$.

    (a) Find the sum of the first 20 odd numbers.

    (b) Find n if $S = 289$.

6. (a) Make x the subject of the formula $V = x^3$.

    (b) The volume of a cube is $80mm^3$. Find the length of an edge of this cube.

7. The surface area, A, of a sphere is given by the formula $A = 4\pi r^2$.

    (a) Find A if $r = 2 \cdot 36$.

    (b) Find r if $A = 18 \cdot 2$.

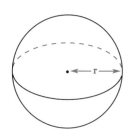

8. $s = \dfrac{v^2 - u^2}{2a}$ Find (a) s if $v = 6$, $u = 4 \cdot 2$, $a = 2$

    (b) the two values for v if $u = 24 \cdot 8$, $a = -2$, $s = 14$

    (c) a if $v = 40$, $u = 25$, $s = 120$.

9. $c^2 = a^2 + b^2$ Find (a) c if $a = 6 \cdot 1$, $b = 8 \cdot 5$

    (b) b if $c = 13$, $a = 5$

    (c) a if $b = 2 \cdot 71$, $c = 3 \cdot 84$.

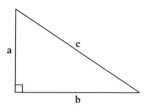

10. $T = 2\pi \sqrt{\dfrac{l}{g}}$ (a) Find T if $l = 10$ and $g = 9 \cdot 8$.

    (b) Find l if $T = 5 \cdot 2$ and $g = 9 \cdot 8$.

11. The formula for the surface area of a cylinder is $A = 2\pi r (r + h)$.

    Find (a) A if $r = 2 \cdot 7$ and $h = 5 \cdot 62$

    (b) h if $A = 226 \cdot 4$ and $r = 4 \cdot 25$.

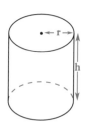

12. The formula $\frac{1}{R} = \frac{1}{R_1} + \frac{1}{R_2}$ is used in a Physics experiment.

   (a) Find the value of R if $R_1 = 6{\cdot}3$ and $R_2 = 7{\cdot}8$.

   (b) Find the value of R_1 if $R = 3{\cdot}6$ and $R_2 = 4$.

Review 1 $v = u + at$ Find the value of   (a) v when $u = 6{\cdot}8$, $a = 15$, $t = 25$

(b) u when $v = 70$, $a = -10$, $t = 2$

(c) a when $v = 8{\cdot}8$, $u = 6$, $t = 0{\cdot}4$

(d) t when $v = 85$, $u = 100$, $a = -5$.

Review 2 $y = \frac{4a}{x^2}$ is the equation of a curve.

   (a) Find the value of y when $x = 2$ and $a = 1{\cdot}6$.

   (b) Find the values of x when $y = 0{\cdot}4$ and $a = 3{\cdot}6$.

EXPRESSING ONE FORMULA in terms of ANOTHER

Worked Example $x = at^2$, $y = 2at$. Express x in terms of y and a. Give the answer in its simplest form.

Answer   Since x is to be expressed in terms of y and a but not in terms of t, we must eliminate t. We do this as follows.

Rearrange $y = 2at$ to get $t = \dfrac{y}{2a}$.

Substitute $t = \dfrac{y}{2a}$ into $x = at^2$ to get $x = a\left(\dfrac{y}{2a}\right)^2$

$$= a \times \frac{y^2}{4a^2}$$

$$= \frac{ay^2}{4a^2}$$

$$x = \frac{y^2}{4a}$$

EXERCISE 8:7

1. For this square, the area $A = x^2$ and the perimeter $P = 4x$.
   Express A in terms of P.

2. $x = t^2$, $y = \dfrac{1}{t}$.
   Express x in terms of y.

3. $v = at$, $s = \frac{1}{2}at^2$.
   Express s in terms of v and a. Give the answer in its simplest form.

4. $x = t + 1$, $y = 3t - 2$.
   Express y in terms of x. Give the answer in its simplest form.

Review For a circle $A = \pi r^2$, $C = 2\pi r$.
   Express A in terms of C and π. Give the answer in its simplest form.

USING FUNCTION NOTATION

f(x) means "a function of x". That is, an expression in which the variable is x.
f(4) means "the value of the function when x is replaced by 4."

Worked Example $f(x) = \dfrac{x+3}{x-2}$. Find the value of f(5).

Answer $f(x) = \dfrac{x+3}{x-2}$

$\qquad f(5) = \dfrac{5+3}{5-2}$

$\qquad\quad = \frac{8}{3}$

$\qquad\quad = 2\frac{2}{3}$

Worked Example h(a) = 2a − 3. For what value of **a** is h(a) = 5?

Answer h(a) = 2a − 3
$\qquad$ h(a) = 5
$\qquad$ Hence $\;$ 2a − 3 = 5
$\qquad\qquad\qquad$ 2a = 8 (adding 3 to both sides)
$\qquad\qquad\qquad$ a = 4 (dividing both sides by 2)

Worked Example $f(x) = (x + 3)^2$. Find the values of x for which $f(x) = 25$.

Answer $f(x) = (x + 3)^2$
            $f(x) = 25$
        Hence $(x + 3)^2 = 25$
            $x + 3 = \pm 5$ (taking the square root of both sides)

If $x + 3 = 5$ If $x + 3 = -5$
    $x = 2$ (subtracting 3 from both sides) $x = -8$ (subtracting 3 from both sides)

Hence $x = 2$ or -8.

DISCUSSION EXERCISE 8:8

- Suppose $g(x) = \dfrac{x + 4}{x - 1}$.

  To evaluate g(1) we begin as follows: $g(1) = \dfrac{1 + 4}{1 - 1}$

  Continue this evaluation. What is the answer to g(1)? **Discuss.**

- Suppose $f(a) = \dfrac{2a - 7}{1 + a}$.

  To find the value of **a** for which f(a) = 4 we begin as follows:

  $f(a) = \dfrac{2a - 7}{1 + a}$

  $f(a) = 4$

  Hence $\dfrac{2a - 7}{1 + a} = 4$

  $2a - 7 = 4(1 + a)$ [multiplying both sides by $(1 + a)$]

  Discuss how to continue to find the value of **a.**

EXERCISE 8:9

1. $f(x) = 2x + 1$. Find $f(1)$, $f(2)$, $f(-2)$, $f(-5)$, $f(\frac{1}{2})$, $f(-\frac{3}{4})$.

2. $f(x) = \dfrac{x + 3}{2}$. Find $f(5)$, $f(1)$, $f(-3)$, $f(-7)$, $f(0)$, $f(\frac{2}{3})$, $f(1\frac{1}{2})$.

3. $f(a) = 3a^2 - 5$. Find $f(3)$, $f(2)$, $f(-1)$, $f(-2)$, $f(\frac{1}{3})$, $f(-\frac{1}{2})$.

4. $g(a) = \frac{2a+3}{a}$. Find $g(4)$, $g(1)$, $g(0)$, $g(-2)$, $g(-\frac{1}{2})$.

5. $h(z) = \frac{z-1}{z+3}$. Find $h(1)$, $h(5)$, $h(0)$, $h(-1)$, $h(-3)$.

6. $g(x) = \frac{2x-5}{x+2}$. For what value of x does $g(x)$ have no answer?

7. (a) $h(x) = 3x - 4$. For what value of x is $h(x) = 11$?

   (b) $f(a) = 7 - 4a$. For what value of **a** is $f(a) = 3$?

   (c) $g(z) = 2(1 - 3z)$. For what value of z is $g(z) = -5$?

   (d) $f(x) = \frac{3x}{2} + 1$. For what value of x is $f(x) = \frac{1}{2}$?

   (e) $g(a) = 3(2a + 5)$. Find the value of **a** for which $g(a) = 12$.

   (f) $h(y) = 4 - \frac{y}{3}$. Find the value of y for which $h(y) = -1$.

   (g) $f(x) = 3 + 2(x - 1)$. Find the value of x for which $f(x) = \frac{3}{4}$.

8. (a) $f(x) = (x + 4)^2$. For what values of x is $f(x) = 36$?

   (b) $g(a) = (a - 1)^2$. For what values of **a** is $g(a) = 4$?

   (c) $h(b) = (b + 2)^2$. Find the values of b for which $h(b) = 9$.

   (d) $f(a) = (a + 5)^2$. For what values of **a** is $f(a) = 4$?

   (e) $g(x) = (x - 3)^2$. Find the values of x for which $g(x) = 1$.

9. (a) $g(a) = \frac{2+a}{3+a}$. For what value of **a** is $g(a) = 11$?

   (b) $h(z) = \frac{2z}{z+1}$. For what value of z is $h(z) = -3$?

   (c) $f(a) = \frac{4a-3}{1-2a}$. For what value of **a** is $f(a) = \frac{1}{2}$?

   (d) $g(x) = \frac{5(x-2)}{x}$. For what value of x is $g(x) = 2$?

Review 1 $g(a) = 7 - 4a^2$. Find $g(2)$, $g(-2)$, $g(\frac{1}{2})$.

Review 2 $f(y) = (y - 3)^2$. Find the values of y for which $f(y) = 4$.

Review 3 $f(x) = \frac{2-x}{3x}$. For what value of x is $f(x) = 5$?

Review 4 $h(z) = \frac{5z+2}{z+5}$. For what value of z has $h(z)$ no answer?

EXPANDING

To **expand** an expression such as $2(3a-4)$ we remove the brackets. We do this by multiplying everything inside the brackets by the number outside.
That is, $2(3a-4)$ is expanded as $6a-8$.

The "rectangle method" of expanding is developed in the next discussion exercise.

DISCUSSION EXERCISE 8:10

- $$5(2+7) = 5 \times 9$$
$$= 45$$
The expansion of $5(2+7)$ may be represented by this diagram.
Area of large rectangle $= 5(2+7)$.
Sum of areas of small rectangles $= 45$.

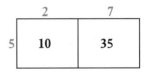

$3(n+2) = 3n+6$.
Discuss this statement, referring to the diagram.

-

How can this diagram be used to show that $n(n+3) = n^2 + 3n$? **Discuss**.

How can this diagram be used to show that $a(n+x) = an + ax$? **Discuss**.

How can this diagram be used to show that $3(n+4a) = 3n + 12a$? **Discuss**.

How can this diagram be used to show that $3x(2x+4a) = 6x^2 + 12ax$? **Discuss**.

- $8 (7 - 2) = 8 \times 5$
  $= 40$

Is the expansion of $8 (7 - 2)$ represented by this diagram?
Can we still talk about areas? **Discuss**.

	7	-2
8	56	-16

	n	-4
2n	$2n^2$	$-8n$

$2n (n - 4) = 2n^2 - 8n$.
Discuss this statement, referring to this diagram.

- **Discuss** diagrams which would show the following:

$$a (b - c) = ab - ac \qquad 2a (x - a) = 2ax - 2a^2$$

Worked Example Multiply out   (a) $3 (x + 2a)$ (b) $n (4 - 3n)$

(c) $\pi r (2h + r)$ (d) $-2 (x + 5)$

(e) $-3x (1 - 2x)$

Answer Using the "rectangle method" the answers are:

(a)

	x	2a
3	3x	6a

$3 (x + 2a) = 3x + 6a$

(b)

	4	$-3n$
n	4n	$-3n^2$

$n (4 - 3n) = 4n - 3n^2$

(c)

	2h	r
πr	$2\pi rh$	πr^2

$\pi r (2h + r) = 2\pi rh + \pi r^2$

(d)

	x	5
-2	$-2x$	-10

$-2 (x + 5) = -2x - 10$

(e)

	1	$-2x$
$-3x$	$-3x$	$6x^2$

$-3x (1 - 2x) = 6x^2 - 3x$

Worked Example Expand and simplify (a) $4 (n - 2) + 3n (4 + 5n)$
(b) $9x - 5 - 2 (3x - 2)$

Answer (a) $4 (n - 2) + 3n (4 + 5n) = 4n - 8 + 12n + 15n^2$
$= 16n - 8 + 15n^2$

(b) $9x - 5 - 2 (3x - 2) = 9x - 5 - 6x + 4$
$= 3x - 1$

EXERCISE 8:11

1. Multiply out   (a) $5(x + 3)$ (b) $3(n - 4)$ (c) $2(5 + 3n)$ (d) $4(3 - 2a)$

                 (e) $4(2x - 7)$ (f) $5(3p + 1)$ (g) $6(3 - 4n)$ (h) $2(1 - 3n)$

                 (i) $n(5 + 3n)$ (j) $x(2x + 3)$ (k) $x(3 - 2x)$ (l) $a(a - 5)$

                 (m) $2a(3 - a)$ (n) $4n(2n + 3)$.

2. Expand   (a) $-3(n + 2)$ (b) $-2(3 + 4a)$ (c) $-4(2n - 1)$ (d) $-5(3 - 4x)$

                 (e) $-6(3x + 5)$ (f) $-5(4 - 5x)$ (g) $-2p(p + 2)$ (h) $-3a(2a + 5)$

                 (i) $-3x(4 - x)$ (j) $-2n(3 + n)$ (k) $-3q(2q - 5)$.

3. Multiply out   (a) $4(x + b)$ (b) $3(x - a)$ (c) $x(n - 2a)$ (d) $n(4a + n)$

                 (e) $3a(4 - 5x)$ (f) $2n(3 - 4a)$ (g) $5n(3a - 2n)$ (h) $-2x(3a + x)$

                 (i) $-4x(x - a)$ (j) $-2a(3n - 4x)$ (k) $pq(p + q)$ (l) $\pi r(r + 2h)$

                 (m) $ab(h - a)$ (n) $rs(s - r)$.

4. Expand and simplify   (a) $4 + 3(2n + 3)$ (b) $n - 5 + 2(3 - 2n)$

                           (c) $3n^2 + n(3 + 2n)$ (d) $2n(3 - n) + 5n$

                           (e) $x(2x + 5) - x$ (f) $2a(4 - a) + 5 + 6a$

                           (g) $3(2n + 5) - 6 - n$ (h) $3(x + 4) + 2(3 + 2x)$

                           (i) $5(2a - 1) - 3(1 - 2a)$ (j) $5n(n - 2) + 2n(1 - 2n)$

                           (k) $x(3 + 4x) + 2x(x - 2)$ (l) $x(2 + x) - 2(2 - x)$

                           (m) $5(2 - n) + 2n(n + 3)$ (n) $2x(2x - 3) - 3(4 - x)$.

5. The answer is $6n - 3$. What expressions could be expanded and simplified to give this answer?

Review 1   Multiply out   (a) $2(l + w)$ (b) $-3(1 - 2a)$ (c) $x(x + 4)$

                          (d) $2n(a - 5n)$ (e) $-3n(4 + 3n)$ (f) $ab(b - a)$.

Review 2   Expand and simplify.

      (a) $3 + 2(3n - 4)$ (b) $2 - 3a - a(2 + 3a)$ (c) $4n^2 - 3n(1 - 2n)$

      (d) $2(3x + 5) + 3(2 - 5x)$

FACTORISING : COMMON FACTOR

To factorise an expression, we write the expression with brackets. That is, factorising is the reverse of expanding.
For instance, $2x + 6$ is the expanded form of $2(x + 3)$ while $2(x + 3)$ is the factorised form of $2x + 6$.

Notice that in $2x + 6$ both 2x and 6 have a factor of 2. That is, 2 is a common factor of 2x and 6.
When we factorise $2x + 6$ as $2(x + 3)$ the common factor is placed outside the bracket.

We can use the "rectangle method" to factorise as shown in the following example.

Example To use the "rectangle method" to factorise $12x - 8$ take the following steps.

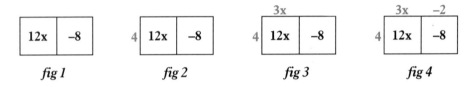

fig 1   fig 2   fig 3   fig 4

Step 1   Write the expression in a rectangle – *fig 1*.

Step 2   Write the common factor on the left-hand side – *fig 2*.

Step 3   Divide the common factor into each part of the expression in the rectangle – *fig 3* and *fig 4*.

Step 4   Use *fig 4* to write down the factorised expression.
This is $4(3x - 2)$.
$12x - 8$ is factorised as $4(3x - 2)$.

DISCUSSION EXERCISE 8:12

- Karim's method of factorising is shown here. $12x - 8$ **Step 1** $4(\quad)$
Step 2 $4(3x\quad)$
Step 3 $4(3x - 2)$

Discuss Karim's method.

- Gillian factorised $4x^2 + 6ax$ as $2(2x^2 + 3ax)$.
Hamish factorised $4x^2 + 6ax$ as $x(4x + 6a)$.
Although Gillian's and Hamish's factorising is not incorrect, neither has factorised $4x^2 + 6ax$ completely. How could $4x^2 + 6ax$ be factorised completely? **Discuss.**

Discuss how to completely factorise $6a^2 - 2a$ and $a^2b + ab^2$.

Always factorise completely. If the expression in the brackets has a common factor, then the factorising is not complete.

For instance, $24x + 30$ may be factorised as $2(12x + 15)$. Since $12x$ and 15 have a common factor of 3 the factorising is not complete. $24x + 30$ is completely factorised as $6(4x + 5)$.

For instance, $2\pi r^2 - \pi rh$ may be factorised as $\pi(2r^2 - rh)$. Since $2r^2$ and rh have a common factor of r, the factorising is not complete. $2\pi r^2 - \pi rh$ is completely factorised as $\pi r(2r - h)$.

It is a good idea to check your factorising by expanding. Suppose you have factorised $2n - 4$ as $2(n - 4)$. By expanding $2(n - 4)$ to $2n - 8$ you would see that you had factorised incorrectly.

EXERCISE 8:13

1. Copy and complete.

   (a) $3x + 6 = 3(\cdots + \cdots)$ (b) $5a - 10 = 5(\cdots - \cdots)$ (c) $14x + 4 = 2(\cdots + \cdots)$

   (d) $16n - 12 = 4(\cdots - \cdots)$ (e) $4x + 4 = 4(\cdots + \cdots)$ (f) $12n - 4 = \cdots(3n - 1)$

   (g) $15d - 25 = \cdots(3d - 5)$ (h) $18 + 3n = \cdots(6 + n)$ (i) $6 - 3a = \cdots(\cdots - a)$

   (j) $6 + 9x = \cdots(2 + \cdots)$ (k) $15x - 10 = \cdots(\cdots - 2)$.

2. Factorise (a) $2n + 2$.   (b) $3 - 3a$ (c) $4x + 12$ (d) $6 + 12a$

   (e) $14y - 7$ (f) $9x + 3$ (g) $8 - 12y$ (h) $10x + 25$

   (i) $8n + 4$ (j) $11 - 22n$ (k) $10 + 15n$ (l) $9 - 21x$

   (m) $12n + 8$ (n) $40 - 15n$ (o) $2x - 20$ (p) $20n + 16$

   (q) $18 - 6a$ (r) $12 + 16n$ (s) $6x - 20$ (t) $21 - 6n$

   (u) $32x - 24$ (v) $18n + 24$ (w) $16y - 24$ (x) $24 - 36n$

   (y) $40 + 24a$ (z) $18a - 45$.

3. Copy and complete

   (a) $2n^2 + n = n(\cdots + \cdots)$ (b) $ax - a = a(\cdots - \cdots)$ (c) $4x + 3x^2 = x(\cdots + \cdots)$

   (d) $6x - x^2 = \cdots(6 - \cdots)$ (e) $10n^2 + 4 = 2(\cdots + \cdots)$ (f) $30n + 12n^2 = \cdots(\cdots + 2n)$

   (g) $6p^2q + 3p = \cdots(\cdots + 1)$ (h) $\pi r - \pi h = \cdots(r - \cdots)$.

4. Factorise (a) $x^2 + 5x$ (b) $a^2 + 9a$ (c) $p^2 - 3p$ (d) $5y - y^2$

    (e) $x + x^2$ (f) $2y^2 - 5y$ (g) $a + 2a^2$ (h) $4n^2 - n$

    (i) $2p - 5p^2$ (j) $5a + 6a^2$ (k) $2a + a^2$ (l) $5a - a^2$

    (m) $5x^2 + 2x$ (n) $9n^2 + 4n$ (o) $2a^2 + 2$ (p) $5 + 5n^2$

    (q) $8x^2 + 4$ (r) $12 - 3y^2$.

5. Factorise completely (a) $4x^2 + 2x$ (b) $9a^2 - 3a$ (c) $6b + 3b^2$

    (d) $12n - 4n^2$ (e) $16a - 8a^2$ (f) $24n^2 + 32n$

    (g) $30x - 12x^2$ (h) $8a^2 - 4an^2$ (i) $p^2q + pq^2$

    (j) $ab^2 - a^2b$ (k) $6p^2q + 12q^2$ (l) $8p^2q - 4pq^2$

    (m) $3a^2b - 6ab^2$ (n) $n^3 + n^2$ (o) $6a^2 - 8a^3$.

Review Factorise (a) $5a - 15$ (b) $12n - 32$ (c) $3a^2 + 5a$

    (d) $15n - 20n^2$ (e) $\pi r^2 + \pi rh$ (f) $12ab^2 - 8a^2b$.

FURTHER EXPANDING

DISCUSSION EXERCISE 8:14

• $(2 + 6)(5 + 4) = 8 \times 9$
                    $= 72$
    This expansion can be represented on a diagram as shown below.

	5	4
2	10	8
6	30	24

Area of large rectangle $= (2 + 6)(5 + 4)$.
Sum of areas of small rectangles $= 72$.

$$(2 + 6)(5 - 4) = 8 \times 1$$
$$= 8$$

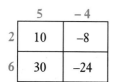

	5	−4
2	10	−8
6	30	−24

Is the expansion $(2 + 6)(5 - 4)$ represented by this diagram?
Can we still talk about areas? **Discuss.**
What if 6 was replaced by –6?
What if 5 was replaced by –5?

174

	x	4
a		
3		

The first step in expanding $(a + 3)(x + 4)$, using the "rectangle method", is to draw this diagram.
How might you continue? **Discuss.**
What if you were asked to expand $(a + b)(p + q)$?

	2n	5
3n	$6n^2$	15n
−4	−8n	−20

Could we use this diagram to expand $(3n − 4)(2n + 5)$? **Discuss.** As part of your discussion, you may like to replace n with a number.
What if 5 was replaced by −5?
What if 2n was replaced by −2n?

• Jennifer's method for expanding $(3n − 4)(2n + 5)$ was:
$$(3n − 4)(2n + 5) = 3n(2n + 5) − 4(2n + 5)$$
$$= 6n^2 + 15n − 8n − 20$$
Jennifer simplified her expansion to $6n^2 + 7n − 20$. **Discuss** Jennifer's method.

Worked Example Expand and simplify   (a) $(3x − 2)(x − 5)$

(b) $(a + 2b)(3a − b)$.

Answer Using the "rectangle method", the expansions can be found from the following diagrams.

(a)

	x	−5
3x	$3x^2$	−15x
−2	−2x	10

(b)

	3a	−b
a	$3a^2$	−ab
2b	6ab	$−2b^2$

$$(3x − 2)(x − 5) = 3x^2 − 2x − 15x + 10$$
$$= 3x^2 − 17x + 10$$

$$(a + 2b)(3a − b) = 3a^2 + 6ab − ab − 2b^2$$
$$= 3a^2 + 5ab − 2b^2$$

EXERCISE 8:15

1. Expand and simplify.

   (a) $(2n + 3)(3n + 2)$ (b) $(2x + 1)(3x + 5)$ (c) $(4a + 3)(3a + 1)$

   (d) $(4n - 5)(3n + 1)$ (e) $(2a - 3)(a + 7)$ (f) $(2x + 3)(x - 4)$

   (g) $(5x - 1)(2x - 3)$ (h) $(n - 7)(n + 4)$ (i) $(x + 3)(2x - 5)$

   (j) $(5n - 1)(n - 4)$ (k) $(3x - 1)(x + 5)$ (l) $(3a + 2)(3a - 1)$

   (m) $(2x - 3)(3x + 2)$ (n) $(n - 3)(2n - 3)$ (o) $(5y - 2)(y + 2)$

   (p) $(3x - 2)(2 + x)$ (q) $(5a + 2)(5 + 2a)$ (r) $(2 - 3d)(d + 3)$

   (s) $(3 + 2x)(2 - 3x)$ (t) $(3 - n)(2n + 1)$ (u) $(3x + 2)(3x - 2)$

   (v) $(2 + n)(2 - n)$ (w) $(5x - 4)(5x + 4)$

2. Multiply out. Simplify if possible.

   (a) $(a + 2n)(a + 3n)$ (b) $(x + a)(3x + a)$ (c) $(2a + n)(3a + 5n)$

   (d) $(c - 3x)(2c + x)$ (e) $(2x - a)(5x + a)$ (f) $(3x - y)(2x - y)$

   (g) $(3a + 2n)(2a + 5n)$ (h) $(3x - 2n)(2x + n)$ (i) $(5a + 2n)(3a - 4n)$

   (j) $(2n - 3y)(5n - y)$ (k) $(3a + 2n)(5a - 3n)$ (l) $(4n - x)(3n - 2x)$

   (m) $(2x + n)(2x - n)$ (n) $(3n - 2a)(3n + 2a)$ (o) $(5x + 2y)(5x - 2y)$

   (p) $(ax + d)(x + c)$ (q) $(n + a)(bn + c)$ (r) $(an - x)(bn + y)$

   (s) $(ax + c)(bx - d)$ (t) $(q + px)(s - x)$ (u) $(p + q)(a + b)$

   (v) $(2p - a)(s + 3t)$ (w) $(5x + 2n)(a - 3b)$

3. Rectangular paving tiles come in different sizes.
   If the length of a tile is $3x - 1$ the width is $2x + 1$.

   (a) Write an expression for the area of a tile.

   (b) Multiply out and simplify your expression.

   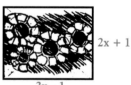

   $2x + 1$

   $3x - 1$

Review 1 Multiply out and simplify.

   (a) $(x + 5)(x + 2)$ (b) $(2n - 3)(3n - 1)$ (c) $(1 - 3a)(5 + 2a)$

   (d) $(2y - 3)(2 + 3y)$ (e) $(5x - 2)(5x + 2)$

Review 2 Expand. Simplify if possible.

   (a) $(a + 3b)(2a + b)$ (b) $(4x - n)(3x + 2n)$ (c) $(rx + s)(tx - u)$

   (d) $(3n + a)(p - 2q)$

FACTORISING QUADRATIC EXPRESSIONS

DISCUSSION EXERCISE 8:16

- Angela expanded $(x + 5)(x + 4)$, $(x + 4)(x + 2)$, $(x + 1)(x + 3)$, $(x + 2)(x + 6)$ using the "rectangle method".

	x	4
x	x^2	4x
5	5x	20

$$(x + 5)(x + 4) = x^2 + 5x + 4x + 20$$
$$= x^2 + 9x + 20$$

	x	3
x	x^2	3x
1	x	3

$$(x + 1)(x + 3) = x^2 + x + 3x + 3$$
$$= x^2 + 4x + 3$$

	x	2
x	x^2	2x
4	4x	8

$$(x + 4)(x + 2) = x^2 + 4x + 2x + 8$$
$$= x^2 + 6x + 8$$

	x	6
x	x^2	6x
2	2x	12

$$(x + 2)(x + 6) = x^2 + 2x + 6x + 12$$
$$= x^2 + 8x + 12$$

Brett found a quicker way of expanding these.

He wrote $(x + 5)(x + 4)$

$5 \times 4 = 20$
$5 + 4 = 9$ So $(x + 5)(x + 4) = x^2 + 9x + 20$

Check Brett's method with $(x + 4)(x + 2)$, $(x + 1)(x + 3)$, $(x + 2)(x + 6)$.
Discuss why Brett's method works.

Brett said his method worked even when the signs in the brackets weren't both +. He gave these examples.

$(x + 3)(x - 5)$

$3 \times (-5) = -15$
$3 + (-5) = -2$ So $(x + 3)(x - 5) = x^2 - 2x - 15$

$(x - 2)(x - 1)$

$-2 \times (-1) = 2$
$-2 + (-1) = -3$ So $(x - 2)(x - 1) = x^2 - 3x + 2$

Is Brett correct? **Discuss.** As part of your discussion expand the following using both the "rectangle method" and Brett's method.

$(x - 5)(x + 2)$ $(x + 4)(x - 3)$ $(x - 3)(x - 2)$ $(x + 6)(x - 3)$ $(x - 1)(x - 4)$

- Brett was asked to factorise $x^2 + 7x + 10$; that is, to write $x^2 + 7x + 10$ as $(....)(....)$. He said the numbers in the brackets must multiply to 10 and add to 7. Is Brett correct? **Discuss.**

To factorise $x^2 + 2x - 15$ Brett said he had to find two numbers which multiply to -15 and add to 2.
He said these numbers were 5 and -3.
He then factorised $x^2 + 2x - 15$ as $(x + 5)(x - 3)$.
How could you check that Brett factorised correctly? **Discuss.**

How might Brett factorise $x^2 - 8x + 15$ and $x^2 - 2x - 15$? **Discuss.**

To expand, we write without brackets. For instance, $(x + 5)(x - 3)$ is expanded as $x^2 + 2x - 15$.

To **factorise** we write with brackets. For instance, $x^2 + 2x - 15$ is factorised as $(x + 5)(x - 3)$.

Worked Example Factorise   (a) $x^2 + 9x + 14$ (b) $x^2 - x - 30$ (c) $p^2 + p - 30$

(d) $a^2 - 25a + 100$.

Answer (a) $x^2 + 9x + 14 = (x + 2)(x + 7)$ since $7 \times 2 = 14$ and $7 + 2 = 9$

(b) $x^2 - x - 30 = (x + 5)(x - 6)$ since $5 \times (-6) = -30$ and $5 + (-6) = -1$

(c) $p^2 + p - 30 = (p - 5)(p + 6)$ since $-5 \times 6 = -30$ and $-5 + 6 = 1$

(d) $a^2 - 25a + 100 = (a - 20)(a - 5)$ since $-20 \times (-5) = 100$ and $-20 + (-5) = -25$

EXERCISE 8:17

1. Which two numbers   (a) multiply to 7 and add to 8
   (b) multiply to –5 and add to 4
   (c) multiply to 15 and add to –8
   (d) multiply to –35 and add to –2
   (e) multiply to 45 and add to 14
   (f) multiply to 12 and add to –8
   (g) multiply to –24 and add to 2
   (h) multiply to 200 and add to –30?

2. Copy and complete these.
   (a) $x^2 + 5x + 4 = (x + 4)(x + \ldots)$ (b) $p^2 + 8p + 12 = (p + \ldots)(p + 2)$
   (c) $a^2 - 8a + 15 = (a - 5)(a - \ldots)$ (d) $x^2 - x - 20 = (x + \ldots)(x - 5)$
   (e) $x^2 + 8x + 15 = (\ldots\ldots)(x + 5)$ (f) $y^2 - 5y + 4 = (y - 1)(\ldots\ldots)$
   (g) $p^2 - 2p - 3 = (p + 1)(\ldots\ldots)$ (h) $x^2 - 7x + 12 = (\ldots\ldots)(x - 3)$
   (i) $x^2 - 5x - 14 = (x + \ldots)(x - \ldots)$ (j) $p^2 + 2p - 3 = (p + \ldots)(p - \ldots)$
   (k) $a^2 - 4a - 5 = (a - \ldots)(a + \ldots)$ (l) $a^2 + 3a - 28 = (a - \ldots)(a + \ldots)$
   (m) $y^2 + 105y + 500 = (y + \ldots)(y + \ldots)$ (n) $x^2 + 5x - 50 = (x + \ldots)(x - \ldots)$
   (o) $x^2 - 50x + 600 = (x - \ldots)(x - \ldots)$ (p) $a^2 - 12a - 160 = (a + \ldots)(a - \ldots)$

3. Factorise these.
   (a) $x^2 + 7x + 10$ (b) $a^2 + 8a + 7$ (c) $y^2 + 6y + 5$ (d) $p^2 + 4p + 3$
   (e) $x^2 - 12x + 11$ (f) $a^2 - 4a + 3$ (g) $x^2 - 7x + 10$ (h) $p^2 + 4p - 21$
   (i) $x^2 - 3x - 10$ (j) $a^2 + 2a - 15$ (k) $x^2 + 7x + 12$ (l) $x^2 - 8x + 12$
   (m) $x^2 - x - 12$ (n) $a^2 + a - 12$ (o) $p^2 + 9p - 10$ (p) $p^2 - 10p + 16$
   (q) $x^2 - 2x - 24$ (r) $a^2 + 11a + 24$ (s) $a^2 - 25a + 24$ (t) $p^2 + 5p - 24$

(u) $x^2 - 13x + 30$ (v) $x^2 + x - 30$ (w) $a^2 - 5a - 36$ (x) $x^2 - 20x + 36$

(y) $x^2 - 6x + 9$

4. Write these as a product. That is, factorise.

(a) $a^2 - 4a - 21$ (b) $x^2 + 15x + 50$ (c) $p^2 - 10p + 25$ (d) $x^2 - 12x + 27$

(e) $a^2 + a - 42$ (f) $x^2 - 12x + 35$ (g) $a^2 + 8a - 48$ (h) $p^2 - 3p - 70$

(i) $p^2 - 14p - 120$ (j) $x^2 + 19x + 60$ (k) $x^2 + 8x - 240$

Review   Factorise these.

(a) $a^2 + 10a + 9$ (b) $x^2 - x - 2$ (c) $p^2 - 12p + 11$

(d) $x^2 + x - 20$ (e) $a^2 - 6a + 8$ (f) $y^2 + 2y - 15$

(g) $p^2 - 5p - 36$ (h) $x^2 - 9x - 36$ (i) $a^2 - 7a + 12$

(j) $y^2 + 5y - 6$ (k) $a^2 + 2a - 15$ (l) $x^2 + 17x + 42$

(m) $a^2 - 14a + 48$ (n) $x^2 + 11x - 60$ (o) $p^2 + 98p - 200$

(p) $n^2 + 24n + 144$ (q) $x^2 - 39x + 360$

QUADRATIC EQUATIONS

DISCUSSION EXERCISE 8:18

- What numbers go in the gaps?

  $3 \times 0 = \underline{\hphantom{xx}}$ $4 \times 0 = \underline{\hphantom{xx}}$ $0 \times 7 = \underline{\hphantom{xx}}$ $-8 \times 0 = \underline{\hphantom{xx}}$ $0 \times (-2) = \underline{\hphantom{xx}}$

  $5 \times \underline{\hphantom{xx}} = 0$ $-8 \times \underline{\hphantom{xx}} = 0$ $\underline{\hphantom{xx}} \times 6 = 0$ $\underline{\hphantom{xx}} \times (-3) = 0$ $15 \times \underline{\hphantom{xx}} = 0$

  If n is any number, what is the answer to $n \times 0$?
  What goes in the gaps? $n \times \underline{\hphantom{xx}} = 0$, $\underline{\hphantom{xx}} \times n = 0$

  Gael said that if $a \times b = 0$ then one of the numbers **a** or **b** must be 0. Is Gael right?
  Discuss.

- Ibrahim was finding values of x which made the product $(x + 2)(x - 3)$ equal to 0.
  He said that $x = -2$ was one of the values. Was he right?
  He said another value was $x = 3$. Was he right?
  Can you find other values of x which make $(x + 2)(x - 3) = 0$?

  Ibrahim explained why $x = 4$ and $x = -1$ are the only two values of x which make
  $(x - 4)(x + 1)$ equal to 0. How might he have explained? Discuss.

Worked Example Find the values of n for which $(n + 3)(n - 7) = 0$.

Answer $(n + 3)(n - 7) = 0$.

Either $n + 3 = 0$

$n = 0 - 3$ (subtracting 3 from both sides)

n = –3

or $n - 7 = 0$

$n = 0 + 7$ (adding 7 to both sides)

n = 7

Worked Example Solve the quadratic equation $x^2 - 5x + 6 = 0$.

Answer $x^2 - 5x + 6 = 0$

$(x - 2)(x - 3) = 0$

Either $x - 2 = 0$

$x = 0 + 2$ (adding 2 to both sides)

x = 2

or $x - 3 = 0$

$x = 0 + 3$ (adding 3 to both sides)

x = 3

Worked Example Solve the equation $a(a + 8) = 0$.

Answer $a(a + 8) = 0$

Either **a = 0**

or $a + 8 = 0$

$a = 0 - 8$ (subtracting 8 from both sides)

a = –8

Worked Example Find the values of x which satisfy $x^2 + 3x = 4$.

Answer $x^2 + 3x = 4$

$x^2 + 3x - 4 = 0$ (rearranging to get 0 on the right-hand side)

$(x + 4)(x - 1) = 0$

Either $x + 4 = 0$

$x = 0 - 4$ (subtracting 4 from both sides)

x = – 4

or $x - 1 = 0$

$x = 0 + 1$ (adding 1 to both sides)

x = 1

EXERCISE 8:19

1. Solve these quadratic equations.
   (a) $(x-2)(x-7)=0$ (b) $(n-1)(n-3)=0$ (c) $(p+3)(p-2)=0$
   (d) $(a+4)(a+5)=0$ (e) $(n-2)(n+1)=0$ (f) $(y+5)(y-2)=0$
   (g) $(x-3)(x-8)=0$ (h) $(x-4)(x+5)=0$ (i) $(x-6)(x-7)=0$
   (j) $(n+3)(n-5)=0$ (k) $(n+5)(n+9)=0$ (l) $(a-15)(a+1)=0$
   (m) $(x+17)(x-7)=0$ (n) $(a-5)(a+12)=0$ (o) $(x+24)(x+30)=0$
   (p) $(n+18)(n+50)=0$ (q) $(x+20)(x-100)=0$ (r) $(a+28)(a+34)=0$
   (s) $(p-78)(p+78)=0$ (t) $(n-8)(n-8)=0$

2. Find the two values of n which satisfy these equations.
   (a) $n^2+5n+4=0$ (b) $n^2+10n+16=0$ (c) $n^2+n-6=0$
   (d) $n^2-n-6=0$ (e) $n^2-6n+5=0$ (f) $n^2-8n+15=0$
   (g) $n^2+7n+10=0$ (h) $n^2+11n-12=0$ (i) $n^2+2n-15=0$
   (j) $n^2+n-12=0$ (k) $n^2-5n-6=0$ (l) $n^2-7n+12=0$
   (m) $n^2-5n-24=0$ (n) $n^2-11n+24=0$ (o) $n^2+5n-24=0$
   (p) $n^2+11n+24=0$ (q) $n^2+2n-24=0$ (r) $n^2-10n+24=0$
   (s) $n^2-14n+24=0$ (t) $n^2+23n-24=0$ (u) $n^2-2n-24=0$
   (v) $n^2-23n-24=0$

3. Solve.
   (a) $x(x-5)=0$ (b) $n(n+3)=0$ (c) $a^2+5a=0$
   (d) $p^2-6p=0$ (e) $x^2+24x=0$

4. Rearrange these equations so they have 0 on the right-hand side. Hence solve them.
   (a) $a^2+4a=12$ (b) $x^2+x=12$ (c) $n^2-3n=10$ (d) $x^2-7x=8$
   (e) $n^2-2n=8$ (f) $n^2+11n=-24$ (g) $a^2+5a=14$ (h) $a^2-4a=5$
   (i) $y^2=7y-6$ (j) $x^2-3x+3=1$

Review 1   Find the two values of n for which these equations are true.
   (a) $(n+8)(n-7)=0$ (b) $(n+5)(n+3)=0$ (c) $(n-3)(n+5)=0$
   (d) $(n+8)(n-3)=0$ (e) $n(n+10)=0$

Review 2   Solve these quadratic equations.
   (a) $x^2-4x+3=0$ (b) $n^2+14n+13=0$ (c) $a^2-3a-40=0$
   (d) $p^2+5p-6=0$ (e) $x^2-10x+9=0$ (f) $x^2-7x-18=0$
   (g) $x^2+10x+25=0$ (h) $n^2-9n+18=0$ (i) $p^2-9p=0$
   (j) $x^2-10x-24=0$ (k) $n^2+12n=0$ (l) $n^2+3n-40=0$

Review 3   Find the two values of x for which these are true.
   (a) $x^2-5x=6$ (b) $x^2-7x=-10$ (c) $x^2+4x=21$
   (d) $x^2+5x+4=10$

PROBLEMS INVOLVING QUADRATIC EQUATIONS

To **solve problems involving quadratic equations** take the following steps.

Step 1 Write an equation.
Step 2 Rewrite the equation so 0 is on the right-hand side.
Step 3 Solve the equation.
Step 4 Check to see if the answers fit the question. Sometimes one of the answers will not be possible.

Worked Example   A river in flood carries a tree $t^2 - 23t$ metres downstream in t seconds. How long does it take for the tree to be carried 50 metres downstream?

Answer We need to solve the equation $t^2 - 23t = 50$.

$$t^2 - 23t = 50$$
$$t^2 - 23t - 50 = 0$$
$$(t - 25)(t + 2) = 0$$
$$\text{Either } t - 25 = 0 \qquad \text{or} \qquad t + 2 = 0$$
$$t = 25 \qquad\qquad\qquad t = -2$$

Since time cannot take negative values the solution $t = -2$ is not possible. Hence, the required answer is 25 seconds.

Worked Example   The product of two consecutive integers is 72.
   (a) Let n be the smaller integer. Write an expression for the other integer.
   (b) Write an equation for the given information.
   (c) Show that the equation can be rewritten as $n^2 + n - 72 = 0$.
   (d) Solve $n^2 + n - 72 = 0$. Hence find the consecutive integers.

Answer (a) $n + 1$
   (b) $n(n + 1) = 72$
   (c) $n(n + 1) = 72$
$$n^2 + n = 72$$
$$n^2 + n - 72 = 0$$
   (d) $n^2 + n - 72 = 0$
$$(n + 9)(n - 8) = 0$$
$$\text{Either } n + 9 = 0 \qquad \text{or} \qquad n - 8 = 0$$
$$n = -9 \qquad\qquad\qquad n = 8$$

If $n = -9$, then $n + 1 = -8$.
If $n = 8$, then $n + 1 = 9$.
Hence the consecutive integers are -9 and -8 or 8 and 9.

EXERCISE 8:20

1. A ball rolls down a 6 metre long groove. In t seconds it travels a distance of $t(t - 5)$ metres. How long does this ball take to travel from the top to the bottom of the groove?

2. Amanda's distance from the top of a ski-tow is given by the formula
$s = t^2 + 3t$. s is in metres, t is in seconds.
Tony solved a quadratic equation to find the time it took Amanda to
be 130m from the top.
Write and solve this equation to find this time.

3. The sum of a number and its square is 42. Let n be the number.

   (a) Write a quadratic equation for n. Rearrange so 0 is on the right-hand side.

   (b) Solve this equation to find the number.

4. The area of this rectangle is 48cm².

   (a) Write an equation for this information.

   (b) Show that the equation can be rearranged
   as $n^2 + 2n - 63 = 0$.

   (c) Solve $n^2 + 2n - 63 = 0$.

   (d) Use your answer to (c) to find the length and width of the rectangle.

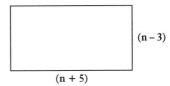

5. When a swimming pool is filled, the depth d is given by $d = t^2 + 35t$. d is in
centimetres, t is in hours.
How long does it take to fill this pool to a depth of 200cm?

6.

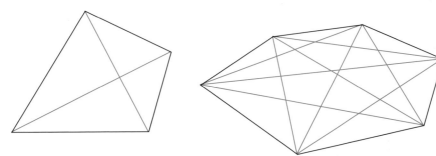

n (n – 3) = 2d is the relationship between the number, n, of sides and the number, d, of
diagonals of a polygon.

   (a) Show that $n^2 - 3n - 88 = 0$ is an equation for n, the number of sides of a polygon
   which has 44 diagonals.

   (b) Solve $n^2 - 3n - 88 = 0$ to find how many sides this polygon has.

7. The difference between the square of Ajaz's house number and the number itself is 90.
Write and solve an equation to find this house number.
Is there more than one answer?

8. The square of Jill's age is 210 more than her age. If **a** is Jill's age, an equation for this is $a^2 = a + 210$.

   (a) Rewrite this equation with 0 on the right-hand side.

   (b) Solve this equation to find Jill's age.

9. (a) An expression for any even number is $2n$, where n is a whole number. Write an expression for the next even number.

   (b) Show that $4n^2 + 4n$ is an expression for the product of two consecutive even numbers.

   (c) The product of two consecutive even numbers is 224.
   Show that the equation $4n^2 + 4n = 224$ can be rewritten as $n^2 + n - 56 = 0$.

   (d) Solve the equation $n^2 + n - 56 = 0$.

   (e) Use your answer to (d) to find the two consecutive even numbers which multiply to 224.

Review 1 The difference between the square of a number and the number itself is 30.
Write and solve an equation to find the two possible values of the number.

Review 2 A lorry, with faulty brakes, is parked on a hill. The lorry rolls down the hill for a distance of 48 metres and collides with a parked car. If the lorry rolls a distance of $t^2 + 2t$ metres in t seconds, find the time for which it rolled.

Review 3 The area of the triangle is 28cm².
$\frac{1}{2} \times 2n \times (n + 3) = 28$ is an equation for n.

   (a) Show that this equation can be rewritten as $n^2 + 3n - 28 = 0$.

   (b) Solve $n^2 + 3n - 28 = 0$.

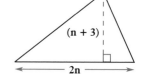

   (c) Only one of the answers found in (b) gives the value of n for this triangle. Explain why the other does not.

CHAPTER 8   REVIEW

1. Factorise   (a) $4x^2 + 5x$ (b) $x^2 + 5x + 6$ (c) $x^2 - x - 20$.

2. Solve the quadratic equation $x^2 + 5x - 66 = 0$.

3. Eurowide Travel Company offers car insurance to people taking their car to Europe.
The insurance cost, £C, to be paid is calculated from the formula
$$C = 22 + 3d$$
where d is the number of days.

   (a) Ron Jones insured his car for 18 days. How much did he have to pay?

   (b) Make d the subject of the formula.   **NICCEA**

4. Multiply out the brackets and simplify your answer.

$$(2x - 3)(x + 4)$$ **SEG**

5. Factorise completely

$$6x^2 + 9x$$ **ULEAC**

6. **(a)** Factorise completely $36x + 6x^2$

(b) Given that $y = 3 + 5x$,
express x in terms of y.   **NEAB**

7. **(a)** Multiply out and simplify $(3x - 2)(2x + 3)$

(b) Factorise $3x^2 - 15x$ **MEG**

8.

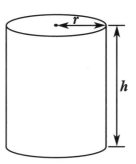

The formula for finding the total surface area of a cylinder is

$$A = 2\pi r^2 + \pi rh.$$

(a) Factorise the expression $2\pi r^2 + \pi rh$.

(b) Rearrange A $= 2\pi r^2 + \pi rh$ to make h the subject of the formula.   **SEG**

9. **(a)** Expand and simplify $(2x + 3)(x - 4)$.

(b) Factorise completely $10x^2 - 5x$.   **ULEAC**

10. **(a)** Simplify $6(x - 3) + 9(4 - x)$.

(b) Factorise $6x^2 + 3xy$.   **NICCEA**

11. (a) Factorise completely $12p^2q - 15pq^2$.

(b) Expand and simplify $(2x - 3)(x + 5)$.

(c) The cost, C pence, of printing n party invitations is given by

$$C = 120 + 40n.$$

Find a formula for n in terms of C.   **MEG**

12. Make L the subject of the formula $T = 2\pi\sqrt{\dfrac{L}{10}}$ **MEG**

13.

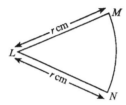

The area of the sector MLN of a circle, centre L, is 600cm².

The total perimeter of the sector is 100cm.

It can be shown that the radius, r cm, of the sector satisfies the equation

$$r^2 - 50r + 600 = 0.$$

Find the values of r which satisfy this equation.   **NEAB**

14. (a) Your teacher asks you to work out 0.7×600 in your head.
You are not allowed to write anything down and you cannot use a calculator.
Explain clearly the method you would use.

(b) Factorise $ax + ay$.

(c) Use your answers to both **(a)** and **(b)** to work out, without using a calculator,

$$(0.7 \times 470) + (0.7 \times 130).$$ **NEAB**

15. Some pieces of scientific equipment are packed into cylinders of radius r and height h.
For added protection, the cylinders fit neatly into thick metal shells. The weight W of a
cylinder is given by the formula,

$$W = \tfrac{1}{40}\{(r + 1)^2 + 2rh\}.$$

(a) Find the value of W when $r = 6$ and $h = 7$.

(b) Express h in terms of W and r.

(c) Find the value of h when $r = 7$ and $W = 4.6$.   NICCEA

16. (a) (i) Multiply out $4x(x + 3)$.

   (ii) Multiply out and simplify $(2x + 3)(2x + 3)$.

(b)

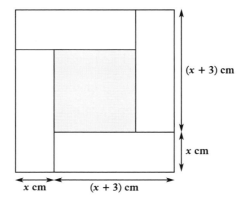

Four identical rectangular tiles are placed around a square tile as shown in the diagram.

Using your answers to **(a)**, or otherwise, find the area of the square tile.   NEAB

17. The three-digit numbers in the following table are all divisible by 11.
They also have the property that the middle digit is the sum of the other two.

242	363	495
253	374	550
264	385	561
275	396	572

The value of the first digit is 100x.
The value of the third digit is y.

(a) Write down an expression in x and y for the value of the middle digit.

(b) Write down an expression in x and y for the value of the three-digit number and show that it may be simplified to give

$$110x + 11y$$

(c) Factorise the expression in **(b)** and use your answer to explain why any three-digit number whose middle digit is the sum of the other two is divisible by 11.   SEG

18. In the formula $R^3 = KT^2$,

T is the time, in years, that it takes a planet to make one orbit round the Sun,
R is the distance, in miles, of the planet from the Sun,
K is a constant number.

(a) The planet Earth is $9{\cdot}3 \times 10^7$ miles from the Sun.

It takes one year to make one orbit round the Sun.

Use the formula to calculate the value of K.

Give your answer in standard form.

(b) Rearrange the formula to express T in terms of R and K.

(c) The planet Venus is $6{\cdot}7 \times 10^7$ miles from the Sun.

Using your answers for **(a)** and **(b)**, or otherwise, calculate the time it takes Venus
to make one orbit round the Sun. **NEAB**

19. (a) $f(x) = \dfrac{x}{2x - 3}$

(i) Find the value of $f(3)$.

(ii) For what value of x is $f(x) = 3$?

(iii) For what value of x has $f(x)$ no value?

(b) $x = 2t \quad y = 2t^2 + 1$ Express y in terms of x.

William Oughtred

William Oughtred was born at Eton in 1574 and died at Albury in Surrey in 1660.
He made popular the use of the $\times$ sign for multiplication. In fact he experimented with many new notations, including :: for ratio. Apart from the $\times$ sign, none of his notations became popular. His best known publication was his "Clavis mathematicae" (Key to mathematics) which he wrote for the purpose of teaching the Earl of Arundel. In this book he included Hindu-Arabic notation, decimals and algebra. His writings had a great influence on English mathematics at that time.

William was a student at Cambridge University and became a teacher there. In 1603 he left Cambridge and the following year he was appointed vicar of Shalford in Surrey. Later, he became rector of Albury. His time as a minister included the years of the Commonwealth when more than 8000 ministers were removed from their parishes. Oughtred was not removed from his. He continued to devote much of his time to mathematics and gave free lessons. One of his pupils was Christopher Wren, who designed and built St. Paul's Cathedral.

It is said that Oughtred was a much better mathematician than a preacher. Someone described his preaching as pitiful. He knew more mathematics than most professors.

William Oughtred is best known as the inventor of the slide rule which was widely used until quite recently. Most of the calculations we use the calculator for were able to be performed on the slide rule. Because hand-held calculators are now reasonably priced, students buy calculators rather than slide rules.

In a biography of William Oughtred the following is written.

He was a little man, had black haire, and blacke eies (with a great deal of spirit). His head was always working. He would drawe lines and diagrams on the dust . . . did use to lye a bed till eleaven or twelve a clock . . . Studyed late at night; went not to bed till 11 a clock; had his tinder box by him; and on the top of his bed-staffe, he had his inkehorne fix't. He slept but little. Sometimes he went not to bed in two or three nights.

Straight-Line Graphs: $y = mx + c$

INTRODUCTION

INVESTIGATION 9:1

LINE GRAPHS

Throughout this investigation either   1.   *use a graphics calculator*

                       or   2.   *use a computer graphics package*

                       or   3.   *if neither a graphics calculator nor a computer with suitable software is available then draw the lines on graph paper. Do this by finding the coordinates of 3 points and drawing the line that goes through these 3 points.*

continued . . .

. . . *from previous page*

- Graph the lines $y = x + 2$
  $$y = 2x + 2$$
  $$y = 3x + 2$$
  $$y = -x + 2$$
  $$y = -2x + 2$$
  $$y = -3x + 2$$

What do you notice about these 6 line equations?
What do you notice about the 6 graphs?

Make and test a statement about the position of the line $y = 4x + 2$.

What if the lines were $y = 3x - 3$
$$y = 2x - 3$$
$$y = x - 3$$
$$y = -x - 3$$
$$y = -2x - 3?$$

What if the lines were $y = 3x - 1$
$$y = 2x - 1$$
$$y = x - 1$$
$$y = -x - 1$$
$$y = -2x - 1?$$

What if the lines were $y = 3x$
$$y = 2x$$
$$y = x$$
$$y = -x$$
$$y = -2x$$
$$y = -3x?$$

- Graph the lines $y = 2x + 2$
  $$y = 2x + 1$$
  $$y = 2x$$
  $$y = 2x - 1$$
  $$y = 2x - 2$$

What do you notice about these 5 line equations?
What do you notice about the 5 graphs?

Make and test a statement about the position of the lines $y = 2x + 3$ and $y = 2x - 3$.

What if the lines were $y = 3x + 2$, $y = 3x + 1$, $y = 3x$, $y = 3x - 1$, $y = 3x - 2$?

What if the lines were $y = x + 2$, $y = x + 1$, $y = x$, $y = x - 1$, $y = x - 2$?

What if the lines were $y = -2x + 2$, $y = -2x + 1$, $y = -2x$, $y = -2x - 1$, $y = -2x - 2$?

What if . . .

GRADIENT

The **gradient** of a line is a measure of the slope, or the steepness of a line.
The steeper the line the greater the gradient.

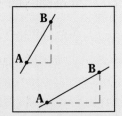

> $$\text{Gradient} = \frac{\text{vertical distance between two points on the line}}{\text{horizontal distance between these two points}}$$

To find the gradient of a line take the following steps.

Step 1   Mark two points on the line as A and B. It is sensible to mark these points where grid lines meet.

Step 2   Find the vertical distance between A and B. Find the horizontal distance between A and B.

Step 3   Calculate the gradient by dividing the vertical distance by the horizontal distance.

DISCUSSION EXERCISE 9:2

The line in *fig 1* has a **positive gradient**.

The line in *fig 2* has a **negative gradient**.

         fig 1   *fig 2*

One way of telling whether a line has a positive or negative gradient is as follows.

We "read" the line from left to right, the way we read a line of words. If we move up the line, the gradient is positive. If we move down the line the gradient is negative. **Discuss** this method.

Think of other ways of remembering which lines have a positive gradient and which have a negative gradient. **Discuss.**

Worked Example   Find the gradient of these lines.

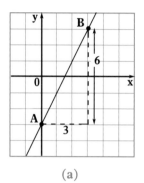
(a)

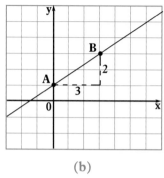
(b)

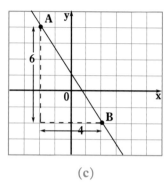
(c)

Answer (a) Vertical distance between A and B is 6; horizontal distance is 3.

Hence gradient $= \frac{6}{3}$. That is, gradient $= 2$.

(b) Vertical distance between A and B is 2; horizontal distance is 3.

Hence gradient $= \frac{2}{3}$.

(c) This line has a negative gradient. Vertical distance between A and B is 6;

horizontal distance is 4. Hence gradient $= -\frac{6}{4}$. That is, gradient $= -\frac{3}{2}$.

Note   In mathematics, a gradient is usually given as a whole number or a fraction.

EXERCISE 9:3

1.

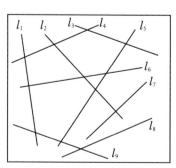

(a) Name the lines which have a positive gradient.

(b) Name the lines which have a negative gradient.

(c) There are two pairs of lines which have the same gradient. Name these pairs of lines.

2.

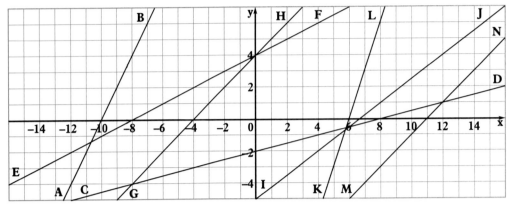

Find the gradient of these lines.

3.

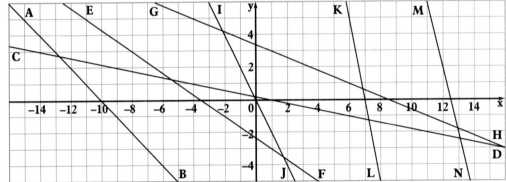

Find the gradient of these lines.

4.

Find the gradient of these lines.

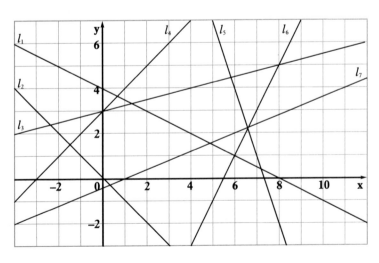

5. The three vertices of a triangle are P(2, 1), Q(4, –3), R(7, 0). Find the gradient of each side of this triangle.

6.  The gradient of a road is shown.

   (a) What is the gradient as a fraction?

   (b) Complete this statement "For every 100 metres horizontally, the road rises . . . metres".

7.

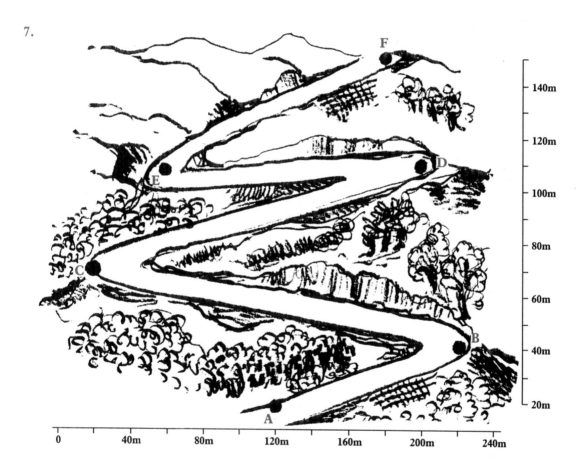

This diagram represents a road winding up a hill.
The scale, on the right, gives the distance above sea level.

Write the gradient, of each section of this road, as a percentage. Round your answers to the nearest 5%.

195

8.

The gradient of the roof on this shed is 1 : 12.

(a) Write this gradient as a fraction.

(b) At its highest point the shed is 5m high, as shown. How high is the shed at its lowest point?

Review 1

Find the gradient of each
line on this graph.

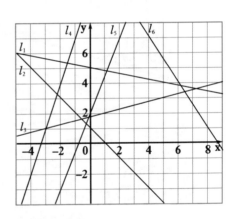

Review 2   The gradient of a ski-tow is 2 : 5.
Complete this statement "For every 10m horizontally, the ski-tow rises . . .m".

Review 3   The vertices of a quadrilateral are $(-3, 2)$, $(1, 5)$, $(7, 4)$, $(3, -1)$.
Find the gradient of the diagonals of this quadrilateral.

The LINE EQUATION y = mx + c

INVESTIGATION 9:4

LINE EQUATIONS

●

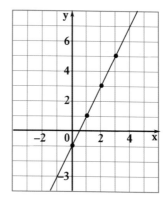

The coordinates of four points on this graph are $(0,-1)$, $(1,1)$, $(2,3)$, $(3,5)$.

Linda found the equation of this line.

She drew this mapping diagram, then wrote the difference table below.

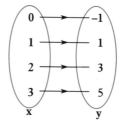

-1   1   3   5

    2   2   2

She then said the relation between x and y was $y = 2x + a$.
She found **a** as follows:

since $y = -1$ when $x = 0$ then $-1 = 2 \times 0 + a$
$$-1 = a$$

The relation is then $y = 2x - 1$. Linda concluded that the equation of the line is $y = 2x - 1$.

Would Linda's method have worked if she had begun with the coordinates of the points $(0,-1)$, $(1,1)$, $(3,5)$ on a mapping diagram as shown?

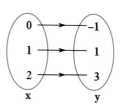

What if she had begun with the coordinates
$(0,-1)$, $(1,1)$, $(2,3)$?

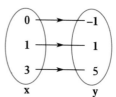

continued . . .

. . . from previous page

What if she had begun with the coordinates (1, 1), (2, 3), (3, 5)?

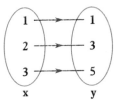

What if she had begun with the coordinates (0 –1), (2, 3), (3, 5)?

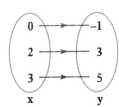

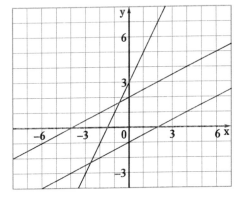

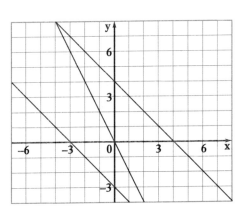

For each line shown on these graphs, find the equation by drawing a mapping diagram and finding the relation between x and y.

What is the connection between the numbers in each line equation and the graph of the line? **Investigate.**
You may wish to draw some more lines as part of your investigation.

- Suppose you were to write a report on how to draw line graphs. What would you include in your report? Would you include examples? If so, which examples would you choose?

In the line equation **y = mx + c, c** gives the point where the line crosses the y-axis and **m** is the gradient.
We can use this to draw a line, instead of plotting points.

Worked Example Draw the line y = 3x − 4.

Answer The gradient of this line is 3, which may be written as $\frac{3}{1}$.

The line crosses the y-axis at − 4.
The diagrams below show the steps to be taken to draw this line.

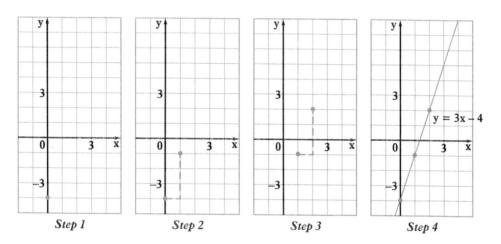

| *Step 1* | *Step 2* | *Step 3* | *Step 4* |

Step 1   Mark a point at − 4 on the y-axis.
Step 2   Go along 1 and up 3 to mark the next point.
Step 3   Repeat Step 2 to mark the third point.
Step 4   Draw the line that goes through the marked points. Label the line.

Worked Example Draw the line y = 2 − x.

Answer y = 2 − x may be rewritten as y = −1x + 2.
The gradient is −1 which may be rewritten as $\frac{-1}{1}$.
The line crosses the y-axis at 2.

To draw the line: Begin at 2 on the y-axis; go along 1
and down 1 (up −1 is the same as down 1) to get
another point; from this point go along 1 and
down 1 to get another point. Draw the line through
all 3 points. Label the line.

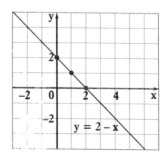

Worked Example Draw the line $y = 1\frac{1}{2}x$.

Answer $y = 1\frac{1}{2}x$ may be rewritten as $y = \frac{3}{2}x + 0$.

The gradient is $\frac{3}{2}$. The line crosses the y-axis at 0.

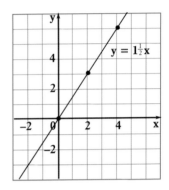

To draw the line: Begin at 0 on the y-axis; go along 2 and up 3 to get another point; from this point go along 2 and up 3 to get another point. Draw the line through all three points. Label the line.

EXERCISE 9:5

1. Write down the gradient of each of these lines.

    (a) $y = 2x + 5$　　　(b) $y = \frac{1}{3}x$　　　(c) $y = x - 2$　　　(d) $y = -3x + 2$

    (e) $y = -\frac{1}{2}x + 6$　　(f) $y = 2 + 3x$　　(g) $y = 4 - x$　　(h) $y = 3 + 5x$

    (i) $y = 3 - 5x$　　　(j) $y = \frac{2}{3}x - 7$　　(k) $y = -\frac{3}{5}x$

2. Where do the lines, given in **question 1**, cross the y-axis?

3. Draw a pair of axes with values for both x and y from –5 to 8. On these axes, draw and clearly label the following lines.

    $y = 2x + 3$　　$y = 3x - 4$　　$y = x - 1$　　$y = \frac{1}{2}x$

4. Draw a set of axes. Number both the x and y-axes from – 4 to 10. On this set of axes, draw and label the following lines.

    $y = -3x + 5$　　$y = -\frac{3}{2}x + 8$　　$y = -x - 2$　　$y = -2x$

5. Draw a pair of axes with values for both x and y from – 6 to 6. On these axes, draw and label the following lines.

    $y = -x - 2$　　$y = \frac{2}{3}x$　　$y = 4 - \frac{1}{2}x$　　$y = 2x - 5$　　$y = 3 + \frac{1}{2}x$

6. Draw the following pairs of lines. (In each case, decide how large the axes should be.)
   Write down the coordinates of the point where the lines meet.

   (a) $y = 2x - 1$; $y = -x + 5$

   (b) $y = 3 - x$; $y = x - 3$

   (c) $y = \frac{1}{2}x + 2$; $y = x + 3$

   (d) $y = 3x$; $y = -2x - 5$

   (e) $y = x - 2$; $y = 5x - 2$

   (f) $y = 3 - 2x$; $y = 4x$

   (g) $y = \frac{5}{4}x + 3$; $y = 1 + \frac{1}{4}x$

7.

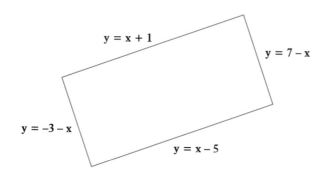

y = x + 1   y = 7 − x   y = −3 − x   y = x − 5

The equations of the four sides of a rectangle are shown.
Find the coordinates of the vertices of this rectangle.

Review 1 Write down the gradient of each of these lines.

   (a) $y = -2x + 7$ (b) $y = \frac{2}{3}x$ (c) $y = -8 + 3x$ (d) $y = 4 - x$

Review 2 Where do the lines, given in **question 1**, cross the y-axis?

Review 3 Draw the following pairs of lines. Write down the coordinates of the point where the lines meet. (On each graph, number both the x and y axes from − 6 to 6.)

   (a) $y = x - 4$; $y = -x$

   (b) $y = 2x + 5$; $y = -\frac{2}{3}x - 3$

   (c) $y = \frac{1}{2}x + 1$; $y = 6 - 2x$

REARRANGING LINE EQUATIONS into the form $y = mx + c$

$2y = 5x - 4$, $x + y = 3$, $2x - 3y = 12$, $y = \frac{1}{2}x + 3$ are all equations of straight lines. The last equation, $y = \frac{1}{2}x + 3$, is in the form $y = mx + c$. The other three equations may all be rearranged into the form $y = mx + c$ by using the technique of "changing the subject of a formula".

Worked Example Rearrange each of the following into the form $y = mx + c$.

(a) $2y = 5x - 4$ (b) $x + y = 3$ (c) $2x - 3y = 12$

Answer We need to make y the subject of each. One method of doing this is to use a flowchart as follows.

(a) Begin with y $\longrightarrow$ | Multiply by 2 | $\longrightarrow$ 2y

$\dfrac{5x - 4}{2}$ $\longleftarrow$ | Divide by 2 | $\longleftarrow$ Begin with $5x - 4$

Hence $y = \dfrac{5x - 4}{2}$

$y = \dfrac{5x}{2} - \dfrac{4}{2}$

$y = \frac{5}{2}x - 2$

(b) Begin with y $\longrightarrow$ | Add x | $\longrightarrow$ x + y

$3 - x$ $\longleftarrow$ | Subtract x | $\longleftarrow$ Begin with 3

Hence $y = 3 - x$
$y = -x + 3$

(c) Begin with y $\longrightarrow$ | Multiply by –3 | $\longrightarrow$ –3y $\longrightarrow$ | Add 2x | $\longrightarrow$ 2x – 3y

$\dfrac{12 - 2x}{-3}$ $\longleftarrow$ | Divide by –3 | $\longleftarrow$ $12 - 2x$ $\longleftarrow$ | Subtract 2x | $\longleftarrow$ Begin with 12

Hence $y = \dfrac{12 - 2x}{-3}$

$y = \dfrac{12}{-3} - \dfrac{2x}{-3}$

$y = -4 + \frac{2}{3}x$

$y = \frac{2}{3}x - 4$

DISCUSSION EXERCISE 9:6

$$2y = 5x - 4$$

$$y = \frac{5x - 4}{2} \qquad \text{(dividing both sides by 2)}$$

$$y = \frac{5x}{2} - \frac{4}{2}$$

$$y = \tfrac{5}{2}x - 2$$

Compare this "balance" method of rewriting $2y = 5x - 4$ in the form $y = mx + c$ with the "flowchart" method.

Discuss the advantages and disadvantages of each method. As part of your discussion, use the "balance" method to rewrite both $x + y = 3$ and $2x - 3y = 12$ in the form $y = mx + c$.

EXERCISE 9:7

1. Write each of the following line equations in the form $y = mx + c$.

   (a) $x + y = 3$　　　　(b) $x + y = 6$　　　　(c) $x + y = -7$

   (d) $3y = 2x + 6$　　　(e) $2y = x - 4$　　　　(f) $4y = 6x + 8$

   (g) $x + 2y = 2$　　　　(h) $x + 3y = -3$　　　(i) $2x + 2y = 1$

   (j) $3x + 2y = -4$　　　(k) $x + 2y - 1 = 0$　　(l) $2x + y + 1 = 0$

2. Rearrange these line equations into the form $y = mx + c$.

   (a) $x - y = 4$　　　　(b) $x - y = -1$　　　　(c) $3x - y = 6$

   (d) $2x - y = -2$　　　(e) $2x - 3y = 12$　　　(f) $3x - 2y = -6$

   (g) $x - 4y = 4$　　　　(h) $2x - 5y = 10$　　　(i) $x - y - 6 = 0$

   (j) $4x - 2y + 1 = 0$　　(k) $3x - 4y - 12 = 0$

3. Draw a pair of axes with both x and y values from -6 to 6. On these axes draw and clearly label the following lines.

   $$2x + y = 5 \qquad 3y = 2x \qquad y = 3x - 2 \qquad x + 2y = 8$$

4. Draw a set of axes. Number both the x and y axes from -5 to 8. On this set of axes, draw and label the following lines.

   $$2x - y = 0 \qquad x - y = 4 \qquad 2x - 5y = 10 \qquad 3x - 4y + 8 = 0$$

5. Find the coordinates of the points of intersection of the following pairs of lines.

   (a) $y = x + 5$; $x + y = -1$ (b) $x + y = 1$; $x - y = 5$

   (c) $x + 2y = 3$; $x - y = 0$ (d) $2x + y = 1$; $x + y + 2 = 0$

   (e) $2x + y + 3 = 0$; $x + 2y = 0$

6.

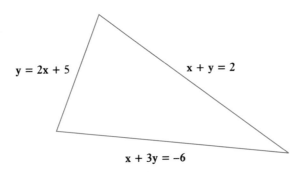

   y = 2x + 5   x + y = 2

   x + 3y = −6

   The equations of the three sides of a triangle are shown.
   Find the coordinates of the vertices of this triangle.

Review 1   Write these line equations in the form $y = mx + c$.

   (a) $x + y = -2$ (b) $3y = x - 6$ (c) $x + 2y = 8$

   (d) $6x + 3y = 2$ (e) $x - y = 7$ (f) $2x - 3y = -18$

   (g) $x + y - 4 = 0$

Review 2   (a) Draw a set of axes. Number both the x and y axes from −6 to 8. On these axes,
              draw and label the following lines.
                   $2x + y = 4$ $x - 2y = 6$ $2x + 5y = 10$ $2x - y = 0$

           (b) What are the coordinates of the point where the lines $x - 2y = 6$ and
                $2x - y = 0$ meet?

DISCUSSION EXERCISE 9:8

Compare the plotting points method of drawing a line with the $y = mx + c$ method.
Discuss.
As part of your discussion, compare these methods for line equations written in different ways.

HORIZONTAL and VERTICAL LINES

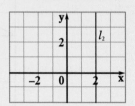

The coordinates of some points on the line l_1 are $(-4, 2)$, $(-1, 2)$, $(0, 2)$, $(3, 2)$. Regardless of the value of x, the value of y is always 2. The equation of this line is $y = 2$.

The coordinates of some points on the line l_2 are $(2, -1)$, $(2, 0)$, $(2, 2)$, $(2, 4)$. Regardless of the value of y, the value of x is always 2. The equation of this line is $x = 2$.

DISCUSSION EXERCISE 9:9

- Do all horizontal lines have equation $y = a$, where **a** is some number? Do all vertical lines have equation $x = a$, where **a** is some number? **Discuss.** As part of your discussion, draw many horizontal and vertical lines.

- Can you find the equation of a horizontal line, such as $y = 2$ shown above, by using $y = mx + c$? **Discuss.**
  Can you find the equation of a vertical line, such as $x = 2$ shown above, by using $y = mx + c$? **Discuss.**

FINDING EQUATIONS of GIVEN LINES

Take the following steps to write down the equation of a line drawn on a graph.
  Step 1 From the graph, find the values of c and m.
  Step 2 In the equation $y = mx + c$, replace c and m with these values.
  Step 3 Tidy up the equation. Use the guidelines that follow.

Guidelines for tidying up an equation.
  1. Do not leave fractions in the equation.
  2. Do not leave a negative at the beginning of either side of the equation.
  3. If both the x and y terms are on the left-hand side of the equation, begin with the x term.

Worked Example   Find the equations of the lines l_1, l_2, l_3, l_4 and l_5.

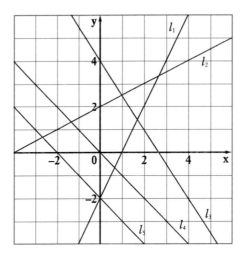

Answer   For l_1 $c = -2$, $m = \frac{2}{1}$ or 2.

The equation is $y = 2x - 2$

For l_2 $c = 2$, $m = \frac{1}{2}$.

The equation is $y = \frac{1}{2}x + 2$

$2y = x + 4$ (multiplying both sides by 2)

For l_3 $c = 4$, $m = -\frac{3}{2}$.

The equation is $y = -\frac{3}{2}x + 4$

$2y = -3x + 8$ (multiplying both sides by 2)

$3x + 2y = 8$ (adding 3x to both sides)

Note   An alternative way of tidying up the equation $2y = -3x + 8$ is to write it as $2y = 8 - 3x$.

For l_4 $c = 0$, $m = -1$.

The equation is $y = -x + 0$

$x + y = 0$ (adding x to both sides)

For l_5 $c = -2$, $m = -1$.

The equation is $y = -x - 2$

$x + y = -2$ (adding x to both sides)

$x + y + 2 = 0$ (adding 2 to both sides)

Note   We do not leave the equation as $x + y = -2$ since the right-hand side begins with a negative.

EXERCISE 9:10

1. Tidy up these line equations.

(a) $y = -x$

(b) $2y = -x + 3$

(c) $y = -3x + 1$

(d) $y = -4$

(e) $x = -3$

(f) $2y = -x - 3$

(g) $y = -2x - 3$

(h) $y = \frac{1}{2}x + 1$

(i) $y = -\frac{2}{3}x + 4$

(j) $y = \frac{2}{5}x$

(k) $y = 3x - \frac{1}{2}$

(l) $y = -x + \frac{2}{5}$

(m) $y = 3 - \frac{1}{2}x$

2. Write down the equations of these lines.

(a)

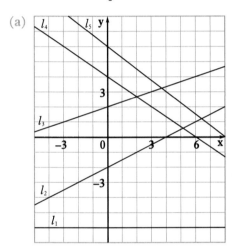

(b)

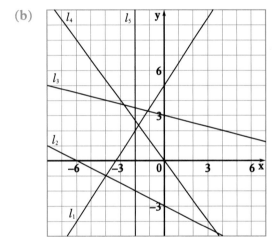

3. A(−2, 5), B(4, 2), C(6, 3) are the vertices of a triangle. Draw this triangle on a set of axes. (Number both the x and y axes from −10 to 10). Hence write down the equations of the sides of the triangle.

4. The scale on the x-axis is different from the scale on the y-axis.
The gradient of the line is *not* 1.

(a) The gradient of the line is

A. 2　　B. 10　　C. 5　　D. 0·2

(b) Find the equation of the line.

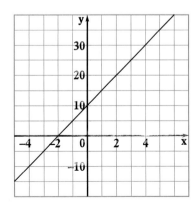

5.

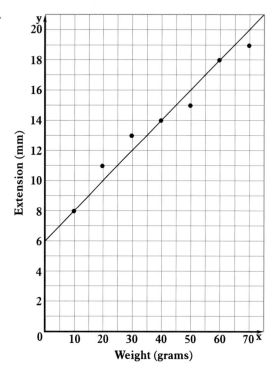

Helen gathered data on the extension of a spring for different weights hung from it. She plotted the scatter diagram, then drew on this line of best fit.

Find the equation of this line of best fit.

Review 1 Tidy up these line equations.

(a) $3y = -2x$

(b) $y = \frac{3}{4}x - 2$

(c) $2y = -x - 1$

(d) $x = -4$

Review 2   Write down the equation of these lines.

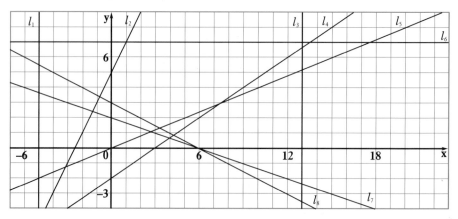

CHAPTER 9   REVIEW

1.

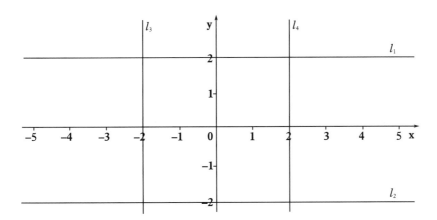

(a) l_1 has equation   **A.** $x = 2$ **B.** $y = 2$ **C.** $x = -2$ **D.** $y = -2$

(b) l_2 has equation   **A.** $x = 2$ **B.** $y = 2$ **C.** $x = -2$ **D.** $y = -2$

(c) l_3 has equation   **A.** $x = 2$ **B.** $y = 2$ **C.** $x = -2$ **D.** $y = -2$

(d) l_4 has equation   **A.** $x = 2$ **B.** $y = 2$ **C.** $x = -2$ **D.** $y = -2$

2. **(a)** Helen entered the equation $y = 1\frac{1}{2}x + 3$ into the computer and obtained this graph.

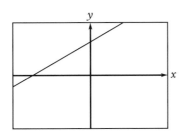

Roy then entered the equation $2y - 3x = 6$ and got the same graph.
Rearrange Roy's equation to show that it is equivalent to Helen's.

(b) (i) What is the gradient of the graph of $2x + y = 10$?

(ii) On the axes below, draw a sketch of the graph of $2x + y = 10$.

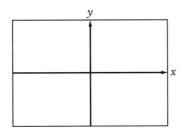

SEG

3. A set of rectangular tiles is made.
The length l cm, of each tile is equal to its width, w cm, plus two centimetres so $l = w + 2$.

(a) Draw the graph of $l = w + 2$ to show this rule.
Label this Line **A**.

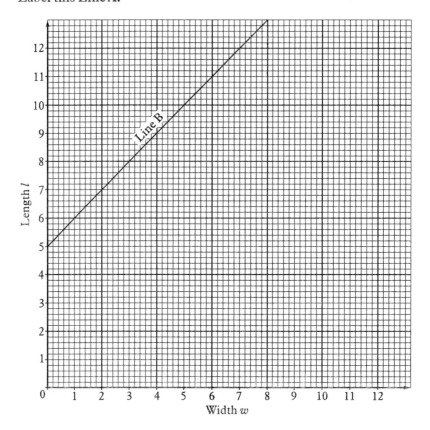

(b) Line **B** shows the rule connecting the length and the width of a different set of tiles. What is this rule?   **SEG**

4. The equations of five straight lines are

$$y = x - 2,$$
$$y = 2x + 3,$$
$$y = 3x + 2,$$
$$y = 5x + 2,$$
$$y = 3x - 3.$$

Two of the lines go through the point $(0, 2)$.
(a) Write down the equations of these two lines.

Two of the lines are parallel.
(b) Write down the equations of these two lines.   ULEAC

5. The television repair charges made by "Household Services" depend on the length of time taken for the repair as shown on the graph.

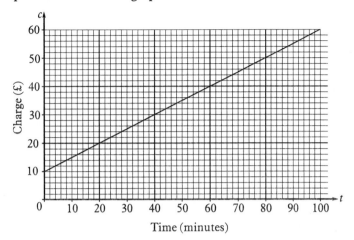

Time (minutes)

(a) (i) Calculate the gradient of the line.

(ii) What does this gradient represent?

(b) Write down the equation of the line.

(c) Mr Bank's repair will cost £84 or less.
Calculate the maximum time that can be spent on the repair. **SEG**

6. The table shows the largest quantity of salt, w grams, which can be dissolved in a beaker of water at temperature $t°C$.

$t°C$	10	20	25	30	40	50	60
w grams	54	58	60	62	66	70	74

(a) On the grid on the next page plot the points and draw a graph to illustrate this information.

(b) Use your graph to find

(i) the lowest temperature at which 63g of salt will dissolve in the water.

(ii) the largest amount of salt that will dissolve in the water at 44°C.

(c) (i) The equation of the graph is of the form

$$w = at + b$$

Use your graph to estimate the values of the constants a and b.

(ii) Use the equation to calculate the largest amount of salt which will dissolve in the water at 95°C.

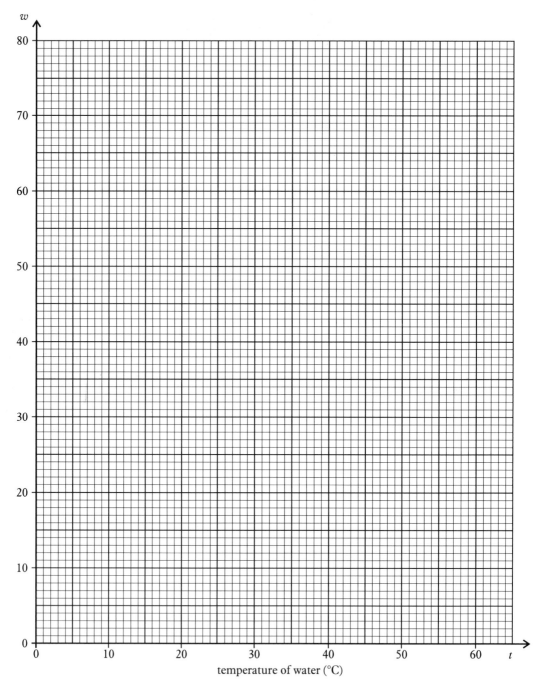

temperature of water (°C)

NEAB

Sir Isaac Newton

Sir Isaac Newton was born at Woolsthorpe, Lincoln on Christmas Day in 1642 and died in 1727.

His father died shortly before Isaac was born. His mother remarried when he was two. Isaac then went to live with his grandmother. He went to a local school where it was reported that he paid little attention to his studies and was ranked among the lowest in the school. It is said that his main interests were carpentry, mechanics, writing poetry and drawing.

When Isaac was 14 his stepfather died. His mother then took Isaac from school to help on the farm. He showed no interest in farming. At the suggestion of an uncle, he returned to school when he was 18. The following year, 1661, he entered Trinity College at Cambridge.

In his first years at Trinity College he was not an outstanding student. It was not until about his fourth year that his genius became apparent. At first, chemistry was what interested Isaac most. Throughout his life he maintained this interest although he did his most famous work in mathematics and physics. During his early years at Trinity College he read books by Oughtred and Viète and other mathematicians.

In 1669 he became a Professor of Mathematics at Cambridge, a position he held until 1696. During the Black Plague of London he returned to Woolsthorpe where he had months of uninterrupted study. This time was the most creative of his career. By the time he was 25 he had invented calculus (a most important branch of mathematics), discovered the law of universal gravitation and proved that white light is a mixture of colours.

His research on light was published in 1672. His revolutionary ideas were criticized by many and Newton vowed to publish nothing further. Many of his other discoveries were not published for many years.

Newton's chief contribution to mathematics was the development of calculus. His laws of motion formed the basis for scientific development for centuries.

One of the most famous quarrels between mathematicians was between Newton and Gottfried Leibniz, a German mathematician. The argument was about who had invented calculus. Supporters of Newton accused Leibniz of stealing Newton's ideas. The quarrel developed into one of great bitterness. As a result of this, British mathematicians for generations afterwards were virtually ignored by those on the continent and the development of mathematics in Britain suffered as a consequence.

Newton was a famous man in his own lifetime. While at Cambridge he was a Member of Parliament. After he left Cambridge he was Warden of the Mint and later Master of the Mint, positions which involved him living in the Tower of London. He was a foreign associate of the Académie des Sciences and President of the Royal Society for many years. In 1705 he was knighted by Queen Anne.

Newton was a modest man. He once wrote *"If I have seen further than most men, it is because I have stood on the shoulders of giants"*.

He was also reported to be absent-minded. A story is told that while entertaining guests at dinner he left the room to get some wine. While out of the room he became distracted and didn't return to his guests. Another story is told that he dismounted his horse to lead it up a hill; when he attempted to remount the horse he found he had only the bridle in his hand and the horse was nowhere to be seen.

Newton was buried in Westminster Abbey, a great honour for one who began life as a farm boy. Voltaire, the French philosopher attended the funeral and said later *"I have seen a professor of mathematics, only because he was great in his vocation, buried like a king who had done good to his subjects"*.

GRAPHING LINEAR INEQUALITIES in 2 VARIABLES

2x + 3 ≥ 1 is a linear inequality in one variable, x. A linear inequality in one variable can be graphed on a number line.

2x + y ≥ 1 is a linear inequality in two variables, x and y. A linear inequality in two variables can be graphed on a plane; that is, on a set of axes.

DISCUSSION EXERCISE 10:1

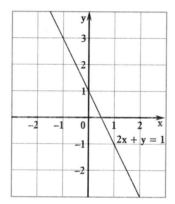

x = 2, y = –1. Is the inequality 2x + y > 1 true for these values of x and y? Where, in relation to the line 2x + y = 1, is the point (2, –1)? Discuss.

What if x = 2, y = 3?

What if x = 1, y = 2?

What if x = 0, y = –2?

What if x = –2, y = 3?

What if x = $\frac{1}{2}$, y = –1?

What if x = 1, y = –1?

What if x = 0, y = 1?

What if . . .

Where, on the graph, are all the points for which the inequality 2x + y > 1 is true?
Where are all the points for which 2x + y < 1 is true?
Where are all the points for which 2x + y = 1 is true?
Discuss.

• Draw the line $x - y = 2$.

Choose points; write down the x and y-coordinates of these points. Test these values of x and y in the inequality $x - y < 2$.

Make and test a statement about regions of the plane for which the following are true: $x - y < 2$, $x - y = 2$, $x - y > 2$, $x - y \leq 2$, $x - y \geq 2$. Discuss.

You may like to repeat this for other lines such as $x + 2y = 4$, $x + 2y = -4$, $2x - y = 2$.

A line divides a plane into two regions; a region on one side of the line and a region on the other side of the line.

For instance, the line $3x - 2y = 6$ divides the plane into a region above the line and a region below the line. In one of these regions $3x - 2y < 6$ and in the other $3x - 2y > 6$.

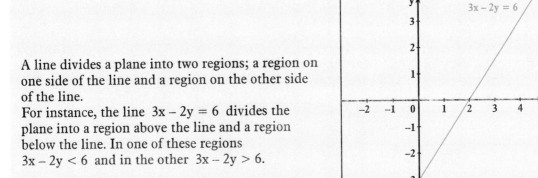

We take the following steps to shade the region given by an inequality.

Step 1   Draw the boundary line. The equation of this line is found by replacing the inequality sign with an = sign.

If the inequality sign is ≥ or ≤ the boundary line is solid since the inequality is true for points on this line.

If the inequality sign is > or < the boundary line is dotted since the inequality is not true for points on this line.

Step 2   Choose a point on the plane. (Don't choose a point on the boundary line.) Test the coordinates of this point in the inequality.

If the inequality is true for these values of x and y shade this side of the boundary line.

If the inequality is not true for these values of x and y shade the other side of the boundary line.

Note   We can draw the boundary line by plotting points or we can draw it by finding the gradient and where it crosses the y-axis.

In the following worked examples the first method is used.

Worked Example Shade the region for which x + 2y ≥ 4.

Answer The boundary line has equation x + 2y = 4.

x	-2	0	2
y	3	2	1

The line goes through the points (–2, 3), (0, 2), (2, 1). Since the inequality sign is ≥ this boundary line is a solid line.

Testing the coordinates of P (3, 2) in the inequality x + 2y ≥ 4 we get:
$$3 + 2 \times 2 \geq 4$$
$$7 \geq 4 \text{ True}$$

Since the inequality is true for these values of x and y, the point P is in the region where the inequality is true. Hence we shade the region which includes P.

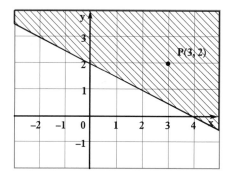

Worked Example Shade the region for which 2x – y < –1.

Answer The boundary line is the line 2x – y = –1.

x	-1	0	1
y	-1	1	3

The line goes through the points (–1, –1), (0, 1), (1, 3). Since the inequality sign is < this line is dotted.

Testing the coordinates of P (1, 1) in the inequality 2x – y < –1 we get 2 × 1 – 1 < –1 i.e. 1 < –1. False. Hence P is not a point in the required region. We shade the region which does not include P.

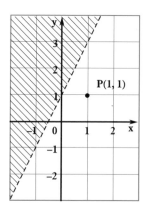

216

EXERCISE 10:2

1. Shade the region in which the following inequalities are true. Draw a separate graph for each. Number both the x and y-axes from –5 to 5.

    (a) $y \geq 2x + 1$ (b) $y \leq x - 4$ (c) $y > -x + 3$ (d) $x + y < 1$

    (e) $2x + y \geq -1$ (f) $x + 2y \leq 4$ (g) $x - y > 1$ (h) $x + 2y \geq 2$

    (i) $3x - 2y < 4$ (j) $4x - 2y \geq -1$ (k) $2x - 3y > 0$

2. The shaded area is given by

    (a)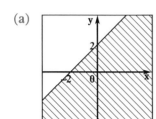

          A. $y \leq x + 2$

          B. $y < x + 2$

          C. $y \geq x + 2$

          D. $y > x + 2$

    (b)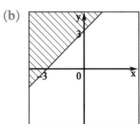

          A. $x - y \geq -3$

          B. $x - y > -3$

          C. $x - y \leq -3$

          D. $x - y < -3$

    (c)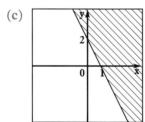

          A. $2x + y > 2$

          B. $2x + y \geq 2$

          C. $2x + y < 2$

          D. $2x + y \leq 2$

Review   Draw graphs to show the region for which these inequalities are true.

      (a) $y < 2x - 4$ (b) $x + 2y \geq 4$ (c) $x - y \leq 3$ (d) $3x - 2y > 6$

FINDING REGIONS where a NUMBER of INEQUALITIES are TRUE

DISCUSSION EXERCISE 10:3

- The line $y = -1$ is shown on this graph.
  In which region of this graph are the following
  inequalities true: $y > -1$, $y \geq -1$, $y < -1$, $y \leq -1$?
  Discuss. Test points as part of your discussion.

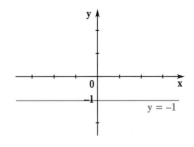

The line x = 2 is shown on this graph.
In which region of this graph are the following
inequalities true: x > 2, x ≥ 2, x < 2, x ≤ 2? Discuss.

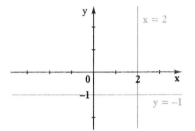

In which region of this graph are both x ≥ 2 *and*
y ≤ –1 true? Discuss.

- To shade the region in which both y ≥ 2x + 1 and x + 2y ≤ 4 we could begin by
  drawing the lines y = 2x + 1 and x + 2y = 4 on the same set of axes.
  How might we continue? Discuss.

Worked Example Draw a diagram to show where both of the inequalities x < 3 and
x + 2y ≥ – 4 are true.

Answer The two diagrams below show the steps to be taken.

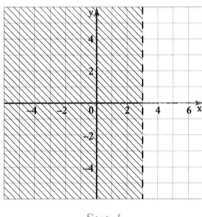

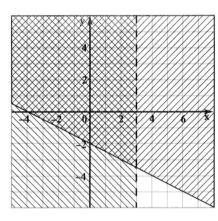

Step 1   *Step 2*

Step 1 shows the region where x < 3 shaded as

Step 2 shows the region where x + 2y ≥ – 4 shaded as   on the same
graph as the region for x < 3.

The region that is shaded with both types of shading i.e. as   is the region
where both the inequalities x < 3 and x + 2y ≥ – 4 are true.

Worked Example The region R is defined by the three inequalities $x < 3, y \le 2x$,
$x - y < 2$. Shade the region R.

Answer

Begin by shading $x < 3$ as

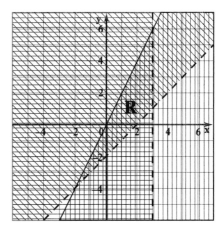

Then shade $y \le 2x$ as

Finally shade $x - y < 2$ as

R is the region shaded as
Label this region as R.

Note   To make the required region more distinct it is a good idea to go over the shading,
and the boundaries, with a coloured pencil.

EXERCISE 10:4

In this exercise, number both the x and y-axes from – 4 to 6.

1.   Shade the region in which both of the inequalities are true.

   (a) $x < -1$ and $y \le 3$ (b) $x \ge 2$ and $y \ge 3$

   (c) $x > 3$ and $y < x$ (d) $y < 3$ and $y \ge x + 1$

   (e) $y \ge 2x - 1$ and $x \ge 1$ (f) $y > 3$ and $x - y > -3$

   (g) $x + y \le 0$ and $x \ge -3$

2.   Draw a diagram to show where both inequalities are true.

   (a) $y \ge x - 2$ and $y < x + 4$ (b) $y < 2x$ and $y \ge x + 1$

   (c) $x + y > 2$ and $y > x - 3$ (d) $2x + y \ge 4$ and $2y \le x + 2$

   (e) $x - 2y < 4$ and $y \le x$ (f) $2x - 3y \le 6$ and $3x + 2y < 0$

3.   The region A is defined by four inequalities. Shade this region A if the inequalities are

   (a) $y \le 4, y \ge -3, x \le 5, x \ge 0$ (b) $y \ge 0, x \ge -3, y \le 3, x \le 1$.

Inequalities

4. The region R is defined by three inequalities. Shade R in the following cases.

(a) $x \geq 0$, $y \geq 0$, $y \geq x + 3$　　　　(b) $y \leq x$, $x < 3$, $y \geq -3$

(c) $y \geq -3$, $x \geq -1$, $y < 2x + 1$　　(d) $x + y \leq 3$, $x \geq 0$, $y \geq 0$

(e) $x > -3$, $y \geq -1$, $x + y < 2$.

Review 1　The region S is defined by two inequalities. Shade this region S if the inequalities are　　(a) $x \leq 5$, $y \geq 1$

(b) $y \geq x - 1$, $y < 3$

(c) $2x - y > 1$, $x + y < 0$.

Review 2　Draw a diagram to show where all three inequalities are true.

(a) $x \geq -2$ and $y \leq 4$ and $y > 2x - 3$

(b) $x \geq 0$ and $4y \leq x - 4$ and $x - y \leq 4$

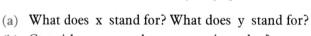

EXERCISE 10:5

1. Amanda bought a number of phone cards. Some cost £5 each and some cost £10 each. She spent less than £50. The inequality $5x + 10y < 50$ describes this.

(a) What does x stand for? What does y stand for?

(b) Can x or y have negative values?

(c) Draw a graph to show the region that contains all possible values of x and y for which the inequalities are true.

2. Books in a sale are priced as shown.

Kay went to this book sale prepared to spend up to £12. $2x + y \leq 12$ is an inequality which could be used to describe the amount of money Kay spent.

(a) What does x stand for? What does y stand for?

(b) Can either x or y have a negative value?

(c) Draw a graph to show the region that contains all the possible numbers of books Kay bought.

3. Jon wants to get a total of more than 10 marks for his history and science projects. $h + s > 10$ is an inequality which describes this.

The history project is marked out of 12 and the science project out of 15. That is, $h \leq 12$ and $s \leq 15$.

(a) Can either h or s have a negative value?

(b) Draw a diagram to show the region that contains all the possible marks which satisfy all the inequalities. (Have h on the vertical axis and s on the horizontal axis.)

4. Jon has two projects to do, one for history and the other for science. The inequality h + s ≤ 4 defines the total time (in hours) he plans to spend on these projects.

   (a) Could either h or s be negative? Write down two more inequalities.

   (b) Jon plans to spend not more than 3 hours on either project. Use this information to write down another two inequalities.

   (c) Draw a diagram to show the region that contains all possible values of h and s that satisfy all the inequalities. (Have h on the vertical axis and s on the horizontal axis.)

Review   A committee is to have a maximum of 10 members.
At least 3 members are to be men. No more than 6 members may be women.
If w stands for the number of women on the committee and m stands for the number of men, m + w ≤ 10 is one of the inequalities which define the members of this committee.

   (a) Can m or w be negative?

   (b) Write down 3 more inequalities which define the members of this committee.

   (c) Draw a graph to show the region which gives all the possible numbers of men and women on the committee. (Have m on the vertical axis and w on the horizontal axis.)

WRITING INEQUALITIES for GIVEN REGIONS

Worked Example

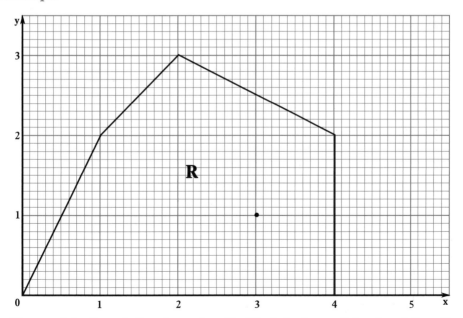

Five straight lines define the region R. Find the inequalities that define R.

Answer Write down the equation of each of the five boundary lines.

These are $y = 0$, $y = 2x$, $y = x + 1$, $y = -\frac{1}{2}x + 4$ (which can be rearranged as $x + 2y = 8$), $x = 4$.

Choose a point within the region R, say P $(3, 1)$. Now test the coordinates of this point in an inequality formed from the equation of each boundary line. This is shown below.

Suppose $y \geq 0$. Testing P $(3, 1)$ in $y \geq 0$ we get $1 \geq 0$ which is true. Hence $y \geq 0$ is one of the inequalities.

Suppose $y \geq 2x$. Testing P $(3, 1)$ in $y \geq 2x$ we get $1 \geq 2 \times 3$ or $1 \geq 6$ which is not true. Hence $y \geq 2x$ is not one of the inequalities. The correct inequality must be $y \leq 2x$.

Suppose $y \geq x + 1$. Testing P $(3, 1)$ in $y \geq x + 1$ we get $1 \geq 3 + 1$ or $1 \geq 4$ which is not true. The correct inequality must be $y \leq x + 1$.

Suppose $x + 2y \geq 8$. Testing P $(3, 1)$ in $x + 2y \geq 8$ we get $3 + 2 \times 1 \geq 8$ or $5 \geq 8$ which is not true. The correct inequality must be $x + 2y \leq 8$.

Suppose $x \geq 4$. Testing P $(3, 1)$ in $x \geq 4$ we get $3 \geq 4$ which is not true. The correct inequality must be $x \leq 4$.

Hence R is defined by the inequalities $y \geq 0$, $y \leq 2x$, $y \leq x + 1$, $x + 2y \leq 8$, $x \leq 4$.

EXERCISE 10:6

1.

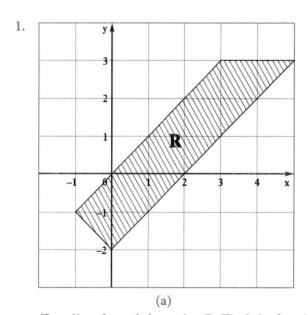

(a)

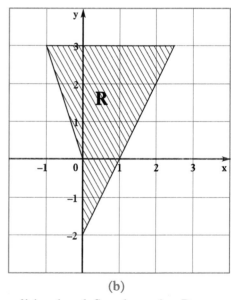

(b)

Four lines bound the region R. Find the four inequalities that define the region R.

2. The region R is defined by 3 inequalities.
Find these inequalities.

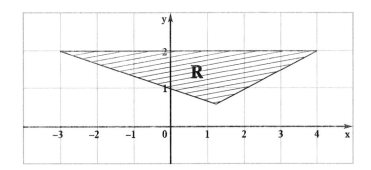

3.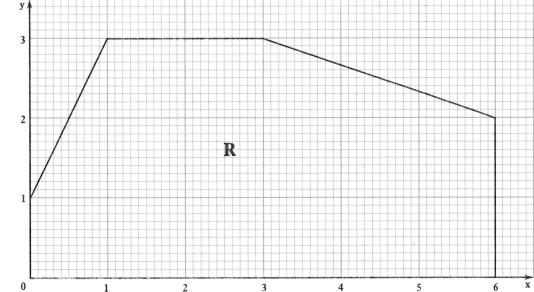

Write down the 6 inequalities that define the region R.

4.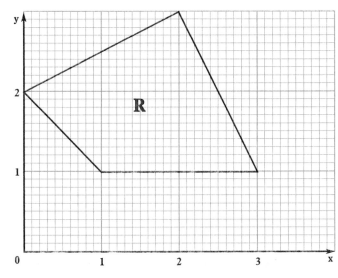

The region R is defined by four inequalities, one of which is $2x + y \leq 7$.

Find the other three inequalities.

5.

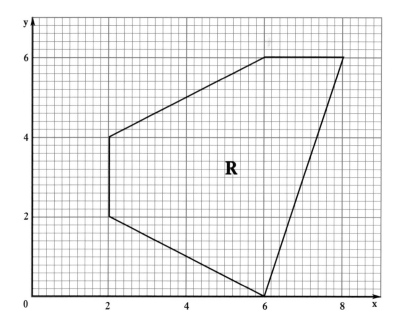

The region R is defined by five inequalities, two of which are $3x - y \leq 18$, $x - 2y \geq -6$.

Find the other three inequalities.

Review

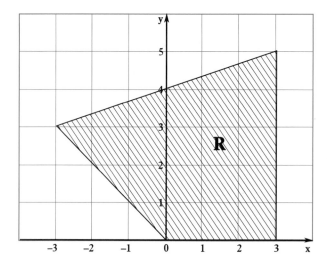

The region R is defined by four inequalities.

Find these inequalities.

SOLVING QUADRATIC INEQUALITIES

The linear equation $2x = 6$ has just one solution; $x = 3$.
The point 3 divides the number line into two regions; a
region to the right of 3 and a region to the left of 3. In one of
these regions, the inequality $2x > 6$ is true; in the other
region, $2x < 6$ is true.

The quadratic equation $x^2 = 16$ has two solutions; $x = -4$ and $x = 4$.
The points -4 and 4 divide the number line into three
regions; a region to the left of -4, a region between -4 and 4
and a region to the right of 4. The inequality $x^2 > 16$ is true
in two of these regions while the inequality $x^2 < 16$ is true for the other region.
We may test a point in each of the three regions to find whether $x^2 > 16$ or $x^2 < 16$.

Worked Example Solve the inequality $x^2 > 16$.

Answer Find the end points of the regions by solving $x^2 = 16$.
If $x^2 = 16$, then $x = 4$ and $x = -4$.

Since the inequality sign is $>$, the symbol $\circ$
is placed on these end points.

Now test a point in each of the three regions.

Choose a point to the left of -4, say -5. In $x^2 > 16$, replace x with -5.
Is $(-5)^2 > 16$? That is, is $25 > 16$? Since the answer to this question is Yes,
solutions for the inequality are in the region to the left of -4.
So far we have

Choose a point between -4 and 4, say 3. In $x^2 > 16$, replace x with 3.
Is $(3)^2 > 16$? That is, is $9 > 16$? Since the answer to this question is No,
solutions for the inequality are not in the region between -4 and 4.

Choose a point to the right of 4, say $x = 6$. In $x^2 > 16$, replace x with 6.
Is $6^2 > 16$? That is, is $36 > 16$? Since the answer to this question is Yes,
solutions for the inequality are in the region to the right of 4.
We now have

From this number line graph we see that the solutions for $x^2 > 16$ are $x < -4$
and $x > 4$.

The previous worked example illustrates the steps to take when **using a number line graph to solve a quadratic inequality.**

Step 1   Replace the inequality sign with an = sign.
Solve the equation formed to find the end points of the regions into which the number line is divided.

Step 2   Place the symbol ○ or the symbol ● on these end points.
○   is used if the sign of the inequality is > or <.
●   is used if the sign of the inequality is ≥ or ≤.

Step 3   Test a point in each region to find the region (or regions) for which the inequality is true.
Build up the number line graph as you test the points.

Step 4   Use the number line graph to write down the solution.

Worked Example   Solve the inequality $2x^2 - 5 \leq 13$.

Answer   If $2x^2 - 5 = 13$
then $2x^2 = 18$ (adding 5 to both sides)
$x^2 = 9$ (dividing both sides by 2)
$x = 3$ or $x = -3$

Since the inequality sign is ≤, place the symbol ● on the –3 and 3.

Replace x with – 4. $2(-4)^2 - 5 \leq 13$, i.e. $27 \leq 13$. Not true.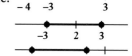

Replace x with 2. $2(2)^2 - 5 \leq 13$, i.e. $3 \leq 13$. True.

Replace x with 5. $2(5)^2 - 5 \leq 13$, i.e. $45 \leq 13$. Not true.

The completed number line graph is _____.

The solution for $2x^2 - 5 \leq 13$ is $-3 \leq x \leq 3$.

EXERCISE 10:7

1.   Solve these inequalities.

(a) $x^2 \geq 9$ (b) $x^2 > 4$ (c) $n^2 > 36$ (d) $n^2 \geq 100$

(e) $a^2 < 25$ (f) $a^2 < 100$ (g) $x^2 \leq 49$ (h) $x^2 > 64$

(i) $x^2 > 81$ (j) $n^2 \leq 4$

2. Solve these inequalities.

(a) $2x^2 \geq 8$ (b) $3x^2 \geq 48$ (c) $3x^2 < 12$ (d) $x^2 - 2 < 47$

(e) $x^2 + 5 > 30$ (f) $x^2 - 4 \leq 60$ (g) $2x^2 - 5 < 13$ (h) $\dfrac{x^2}{4} \leq 9$

(i) $3x^2 + 2 < 77$ (j) $7 + 2x^2 > 9$

3. Write down all the whole number values of n for which

(a) $n^2 \leq 25$ (b) $5n^2 < 45$ (c) $\dfrac{n^2}{2} < 8$ (d) $2n^2 + 11 \leq 13$

(e) $n^2 \geq 4$ (f) $3n^2 + 4 > 7$.

4. What can you say about p if (a) $p^2 + 3 > 19$ (b) $2p^2 - 25 < 73$?

Review Solve (a) $n^2 > 25$ (b) $\dfrac{a^2}{4} \geq 16$ (c) $3x^2 - 1 \leq 11$.

CHAPTER 10   REVIEW

1. The diagram shows part of the graph of $x + 2y = 8$.

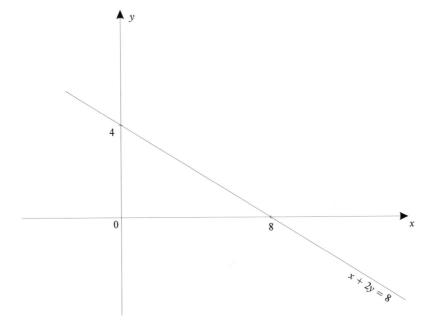

Shade in the region on the diagram which satisfies **all** the following three inequalities:

$$x + 2y \leq 8$$
$$x \geq 0$$
$$y \geq 0$$

ULEAC

2. **(a)** Complete this table of values for $y = 2x - 1$.

x	-2	-1	0	1	2	3
y			-1			

(b) On the grid plot the points represented by the values in your table. Join the points with a straight line.

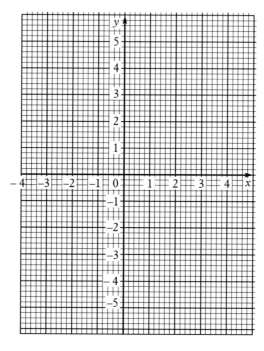

(c) Use your graph to find the value of x when $y = \frac{1}{2}$.

(d) Shade the region of your graph which represents $y \geq 2x - 1$ **ULEAC**

3. Label with the letter R the single region which satisfies all of the inequalities

$$x \geq 0, \quad y \geq x, \quad y \leq 2x + 1, \quad y \leq 8 - x.$$

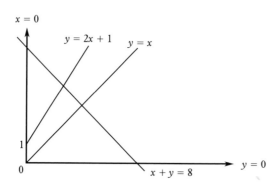

SEG

4. The line $x = 5$ is drawn on the axes below.

On the same axes draw the appropriate boundary lines and carefully shade the area that contains all the points satisfying the inequalities

$$x > 5, \ y > 8 \ \text{and} \ y < 30 - 2x.$$

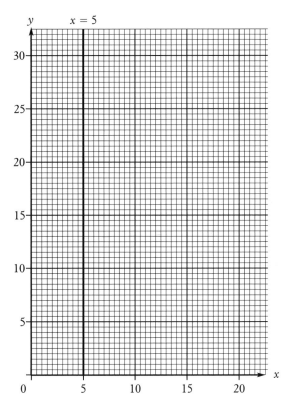

SEG

5. Solve the following inequalities for x.

(a) $1 + 3x < 7$

(b) $x^2 < 1$ NEAB

6. (a) Write down (i) the smallest and (ii) the largest whole numbers which satisfy

$$-6 < x < 2.$$

(b) Solve the inequalities:

(i) $\frac{1}{2}x \geq 1$,

(ii) $3x - 2 > 7$,

(iii) $x^2 < 25$.   MEG

7. (a) Solve the following inequalities for x.

    (i) $4x + 10 < 19 + 2x$.

    (ii) $x^2 \geq 19$.

  (b) The graph of $y = 10$ and $x = 3$ are drawn on the axes below.

    (i) Draw the line $y = 2x + 10$ on the same axes.

    (ii) Shade the region satisfied by the inequalities

$$y \leq 2x + 10, \quad y \geq 10 \quad \text{and} \quad x \leq 3.$$

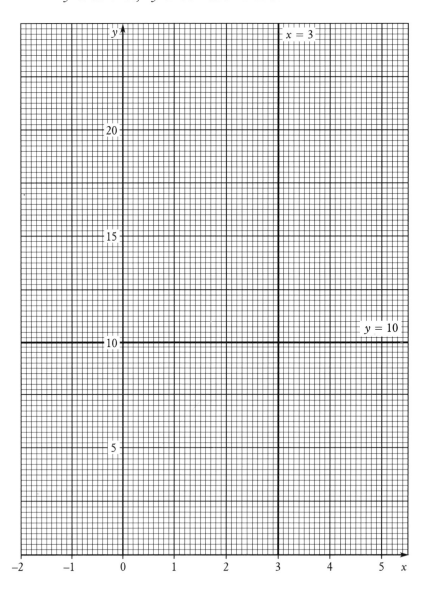

8. A café makes pizzas and quiches every morning. The total cost of making a pizza is 35p and the total cost of making a quiche is 25p. The cooking time for a pizza is 15 minutes and for a quiche is 45 minutes. They are cooked at the same temperature and can be moved into and out of the oven without disturbance.

The total amount of money available for making the pizzas and quiches is £38 per day. The pizzas and quiches take up the same amount of space in the oven, which can hold a maximum of 25 items at a time. The oven is available for cooking the pizzas and quiches for a maximum of two hours each morning.

Let the number of pizzas and quiches made each morning be x and y respectively.

(a) Show that x and y satisfy the inequalities

$$7x + 5y \leq 760$$
and
$$x + 3y \leq 200.$$

(b) The lines $7x + 5y = 760$ and $x + 3y = 200$ are drawn on the graph paper below. Shade the region on your graph which satisfies all the conditions above.

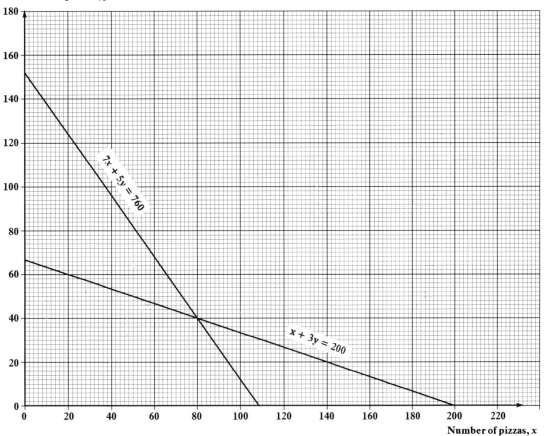

WJEC

9. Solve the inequalities

   (a) $2x - 9 < 3$ (b) $2x^2 \geq 32$.   **MEG**

10. A haulage firm has to remove 200 tonnes of gravel.
    It uses x lorries which can each carry 8 tonnes, and y lorries which can each carry 10 tonnes.

    (a) Show that $4x + 5y \geq 100$

         Each 8-tonne lorry costs £25 per load and each 10-tonne lorry costs £40 per load.

         The total cost of carrying the gravel must not be more than £750.

         The firm has only twenty 8-tonne lorries.

         Two inequalities relating to x and y are $x \geq 0$ and $y \geq 0$.

    (b) Write down two more inequalities relating to x and y.

    (c) On the grid below show clearly the region which satisfies all the inequalities involved.

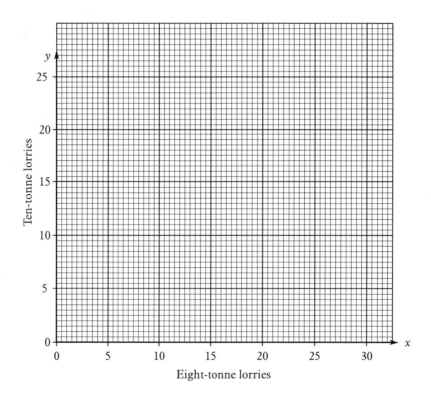

Eight-tonne lorries   **NEAB**

232

11.

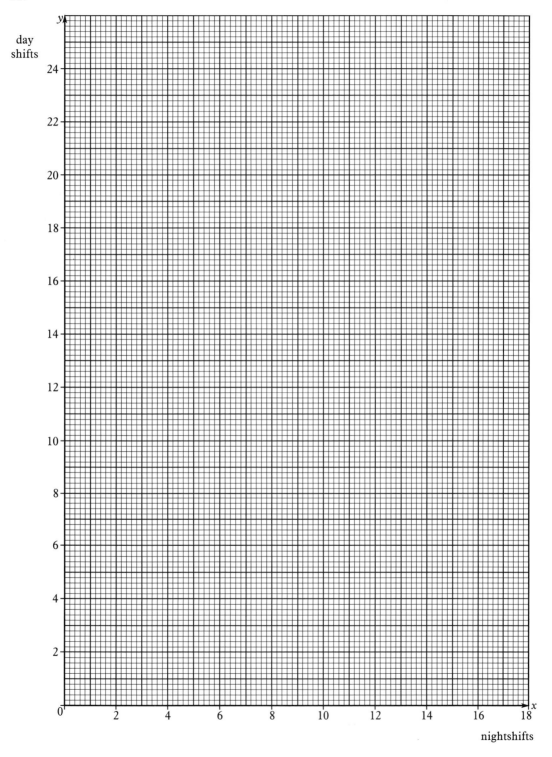

day
shifts

nightshifts

Eve is employed by a Nursing Home and is required to work both night-shifts and day-shifts.

Eve earns £48 for a night-shift lasting 10 hours and earns £36 for a day-shift lasting 8 hours.

During each month, Eve works x night-shifts and y day-shifts.

(a) Her employment pattern is subject to four restrictions.

    (i) She must work at least 6 night-shifts per month.
Express this condition as an inequality.

    (ii) She must not work more than 176 hours per month.
Show that $5x + 4y \leq 88$.

    (iii) Eve is guaranteed earnings of at least £720 per month.
Show that $4x + 3y \geq 60$.

    (iv) The number of night-shifts worked must not exceed twice the number of day-shifts worked.
This can be expressed as $x \leq 2y$.

(b) Illustrate the above four inequalities by a suitable diagram on the graph paper on the previous page. Identify the region containing the set of points satisfying all four inequalities.   **NICCEA**

12.

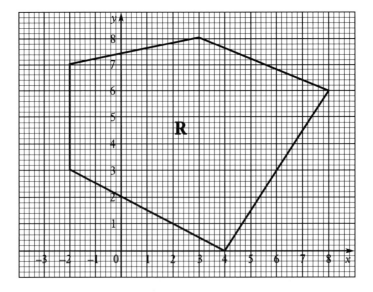

The region R is defined by 5 inequalities. One of these is $x - 5y + 37 \geq 0$.

Write down the other 4 inequalities.

Blaise Pascal

Blaise Pascal was born at Clermont in France in 1623 and died in 1662.

As a baby, he became ill with tuberculosis. At that time, many illnesses were blamed on witches. Some claim that an old lady said she had put a spell on Blaise when he was born and this spell could be lifted if an animal was killed. A cat was chosen to be sacrificed but it took fright and jumped out of a window — it hit the road below and died; Blaise recovered.

Blaise's father was interested in mathematics but he was reluctant to allow his son to begin studying mathematics when he was young. Some say this was because he wanted his son to develop other interests; others say it was because it was thought at that time that the study of mathematics overstretched the brain of children. Blaise showed such considerable mathematical talent by the age of 12 that his father relented and began to teach him.

At 14, Blaise joined his father in weekly meetings with other mathematicians at what was to become the Académie des Sciences.

At 16, Pascal published his first work. This was what is known as Pascal's Theorem which dealt with properties of a hexagon inscribed in a conic. (The circle, hyperbola and parabola are conics.)

At 18, Pascal began work on a calculating machine and within a few years had built and sold 50 of these. He presented one to the king and one to the royal chancellor. At the time Pascal invented this calculating machine, his father was a collector of taxes. Some claim that Pascal invented the machine because his father needed a quick way of adding and subtracting.

At 23, Pascal and his brother-in-law performed a famous scientific experiment. They took a barometer to the top of a high hill and observed that the level of mercury in the barometer decreased as they climbed higher and higher.

At 31, while trying to solve a famous gambling problem, Pascal connected the study of probability to the "Arithmetic Triangle", later to become known as Pascal's Triangle (see Books 6 and 7). This triangle had been known for about 600 years. It had been written about by an Arab mathematician in 1425 and by a Chinese scholar in 1261.

Pascal was a religious man. In 1646, with the encouragement of one of his sisters, he joined a very strict religious sect. A few years later he left the sect. He rejoined in 1654 after an accident. Some say he took the fact that he survived the accident as a sign that he should turn his back on the world. After this, he did little further mathematical work. Four years later he died, at the age of 39.

Mechanical Calculator made by Pascal in 1642

11   Graphs of some Special Functions and Real-Life Situations   11

EXPLORING CALCULATOR and COMPUTER GENERATED GRAPHS

INVESTIGATION 11:1

EXPLORING GRAPHS

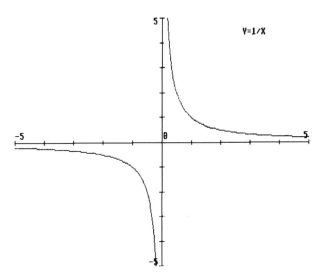

Y=1/X

Use a graphics calculator or a computer graphics package to get this graph of $y = \frac{1}{x}$ on the screen. **Discuss** the following questions in relation to this graph.

Can x take all values?
Can y take all values?
Between which values of x does y increase as x increases?
Between which values of x does y decrease as x increases?

On the same screen, display the following graphs. $y = \frac{1}{x}$, $y = \frac{2}{x}$, $y = \frac{3}{x}$, $y = \frac{4}{x}$
Explore relationships between these graphs.

What if 1, 2, 3 and 4 were replaced with $-1, -2, -3, -4$?
What if 1, 2, 3 and 4 were replaced with $0·1, 0·2, 0·3, 0·4$?
What if x was replaced with $x - 1$?
What if x was replaced with $x + 1$?
What if ...

INVESTIGATION AND DISCUSSION EXERCISE 11:2

● Use a graphics calculator or a computer graphics package to **investigate** each of the groups of graphs given below.

If you do not have a graphics calculator or a computer graphics package available, draw the graphs by plotting points.

For instance; for $y = x^2 - 9$, taking the whole number values of x from -4 to 4 and using the calculator to find the y-values we get:

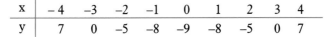

x	-4	-3	-2	-1	0	1	2	3	4
y	7	0	-5	-8	-9	-8	-5	0	7

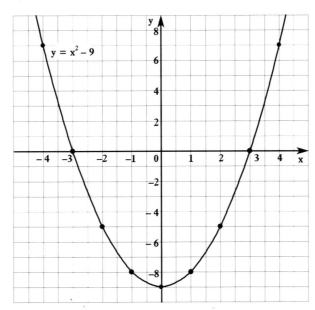

As part of your investigation and discussion, consider questions such as those in the previous investigation as well as:

Where does the graph cross the x-axis?
Where does the graph cross the y-axis?
Is there a maximum value that y can take?
Is there a minimum value that y can take?
Is there a relationship between the graphs; if so, what is this relationship?

Look closely at the graphs in each of the groups. **Discuss** what the graphs have in common. For instance, you should notice that the graph of $y = x^2 - 9$ and the other graphs in this group all have one turning point and an axis of symmetry.

Group 1 $y = x^2$, $y = x^2 + 2$, $y = x^2 - 2$, $y = (x + 2)^2$, $y = (x - 2)^2$, $y = x^2 + 9$, $y = x^2 - 9$, $y = (x + 9)^2$, $y = (x - 9)^2$

Group 2 $y = x^2$, $y = 2x^2$, $y = 4x^2$, $y = \frac{1}{2}x^2$, $y = \frac{1}{4}x^2$

Group 3 $y = x^2$, $y = -x^2$, $y = (x + 3)^2$, $y = -(x + 3)^2$, $y = 3x^2$, $y = -3x^2$

Group 4 $y = x^2$, $y = x^2 + 3$, $y = x^2 + 3x$, $y = x^2 + 3x - 4$, $y = x^2 + 4x + 3$

- **Investigate** the relationship between the graphs $y = x^2 + 4x$, $y = x^2 - 3$, $y = x^2 + 4x + 3$ and the solutions of the polynomial equations $x^2 + 4x = 0$, $x^2 - 3 = 0$, $x^2 + 4x + 3 = 0$. (Use "trial and improvement" to solve the equations.)

  What if $y = x^2 + 3$?

- **Investigate** each of the groups of graphs given below. Use a graphics calculator or a computer graphics package. If you have neither of these available, draw the graphs by plotting points.

  For instance; for $y = -x^3 - 2x^2 + 5x + 6$, taking whole number values of x from -4 to 4 and using the calculator to find the y-values we get:

x	-4	-3	-2	-1	0	1	2	3	4
y	18	0	-4	0	6	8	0	-24	-70

  Since the y-value corresponding to $x = 4$ is very large we will not include the point $(4, -70)$ on our graph.

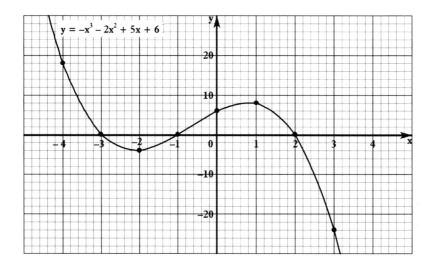

Group 1 $y = x^3$, $y = 2x^3$, $y = 4x^3$, $y = \frac{1}{2}x^3$, $y = \frac{1}{4}x^3$

Group 2 $y = x^3$, $y = -x^3$, $y = 3x^3$, $y = -3x^3$

Group 3 $y = x^3$, $y = x^3 + 2$, $y = x^3 - 4$, $y = -x^3 + 3$, $y = -x^3 - 3$

Group 4 $y = x^3$, $y = (x - 2)^3$, $y = (x + 2)^3$, $y = (4 - x)^3$, $y = (3 - x)^3$

Group 5 $y = (x + 1)(x - 2)(x - 3)$, $y = (x - 2)(x + 2)(x + 4)$, $y = (x + 2)^2(x - 3)$, $y = (x - 3)^2(x + 2)$

Group 6 $y = x^3 + x^2 - 6x + 3$, $y = x^3 - x^2 - 2x$, $y = 8 - 12x + 6x^2 - x^3$, $y = -x^3 - 2x^2 + 5x + 6$

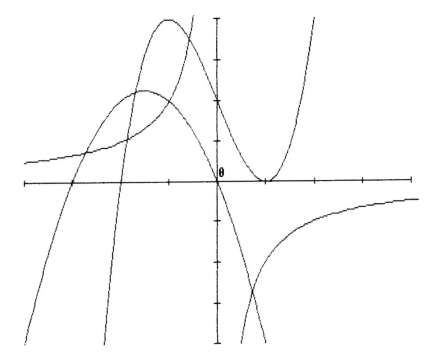

What might the equations of these calculator drawn graphs be? Discuss.

● Make a report on what you have learned in **Investigation 11:1** and **Investigation and Discussion Exercise 11:2.**

INVESTIGATION 11:3

SHADOWS

Shine a torch beam on a dark wall. Hold the torch at different angles to get different shapes for the spot of light on the wall.
Investigate.

RECOGNISING GRAPHS of LINEAR, QUADRATIC, CUBIC and RECIPROCAL FUNCTIONS

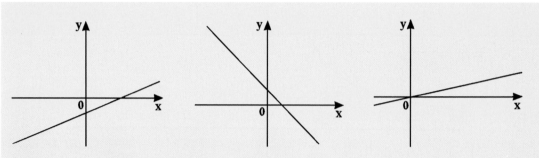

x, $2x$, $3x + 4$, $-2x$, $4 - \frac{1}{2}x$ are all **linear functions** of x. The graphs $y = x$, $y = 2x$, $y = 3x + 4$, $y = -2x$, $y = 4 - \frac{1}{2}x$ are all **straight-line graphs**.
In a linear function of x, the highest power of x is x^1.

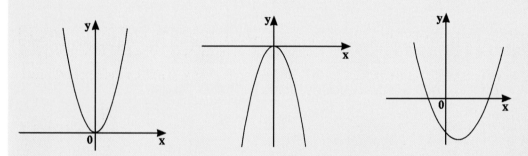

x^2, $2x^2 - 3$, $-5x^2$, $x^2 + 6x$, $2x^2 + 5x - 1$ are all **quadratic functions** of x. The graphs $y = x^2$, $y = 2x^2 - 3$, $y = -5x^2$, $y = x^2 + 6x$, $y = 2x^2 + 5x - 1$ are all **parabolas**. These graphs all have an axis of symmetry and one turning point.
In a quadratic function, the highest power of x is x^2.

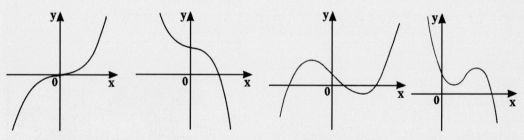

x^3, $-4x^3$, $2x^3 - 4x^2$, $2 - x^3$, $x^3 + 2x^2 - x + 1$ are all **cubic functions** of x. The graphs of $y = x^3$, $y = -4x^3$, $y = 2x^3 - 4x^2$, $y = 2 - x^3$, $y = x^3 + 2x^2 - x + 1$ are called **cubic graphs**.
Some cubic graphs have two turning points, others have none.
In a cubic function, the highest power of x is x^3.

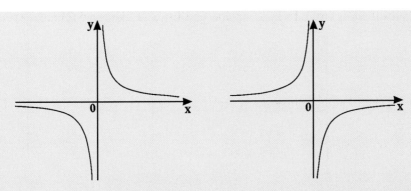

$\frac{1}{x}$, $\frac{3}{2x}$, $\frac{-4}{x}$ are all **reciprocal functions** of x. The graphs of $y = \frac{1}{x}$, $y = \frac{3}{2x}$, $y = \frac{-4}{x}$ are called **hyperbolas**. These graphs have two axes of symmetry. These graphs always consist of two separate congruent curves.

In a reciprocal function, the x is on the denominator.

EXERCISE 11:4

1. (a) Which of the following could be the graph of $y = x^2 - 7x + 10$? Explain your choice.

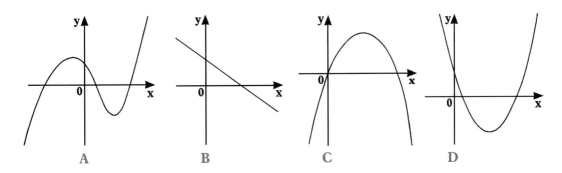

(b) Which of the following could be the graph of $y = -2x^3$? Give reasons for your choice.

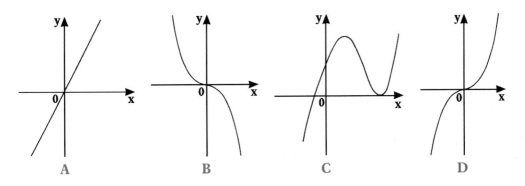

(c) Which of the following could be the graph of $y = 4x - x^2$? Explain your choice.

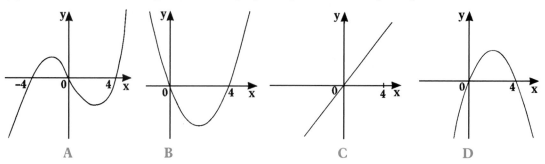

(d) Which of the following could be the graph of $y = \frac{3}{x}$? Explain your choice.

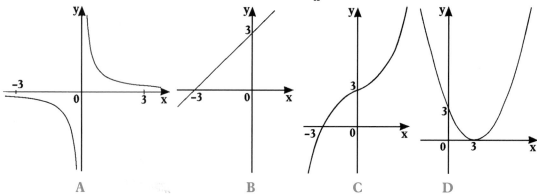

2. Choose sensible scales on the axes when you plot the graphs in this question. You should use different scales on the x and y-axes.

(a) Copy and complete the table for $y = \frac{x^3}{2}$.

Plot the graph of $y = \frac{x^3}{2}$.

x	−3	−2	−1	0	1	2	3
y	−13·5	− 4					

(b)

x	− 4	−3	−2	−1	0	1	2	3	4
y				− 4					11

Copy and complete the table for $y = x^2 - 5$.
Draw the graph of $y = x^2 - 5$.

(c)

x	−3	−2	−1	0	1	2	3
y		4			−5		

Copy and complete the table for $y = x^3 - 6x$.

Plot the graph of $y = x^3 - 6x$. You may like to plot a few more points around the turning points.

242

(d)

x	−5	−4	−3	−2	−1	$-\frac{1}{2}$	0	$\frac{1}{2}$	1	2	3	4	5
y			$3\frac{1}{3}$	5			no value						

Copy and complete the table for $y = \dfrac{-10}{x}$.

Plot the graph of $y = \dfrac{-10}{x}$.

3. Match the graphs with the equations.

(a)

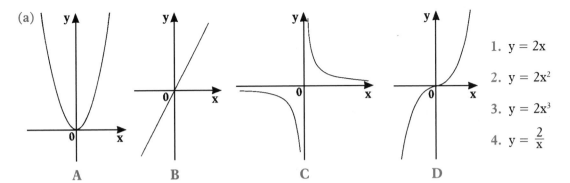

1. $y = 2x$

2. $y = 2x^2$

3. $y = 2x^3$

4. $y = \dfrac{2}{x}$

A   B   C   D

(b)

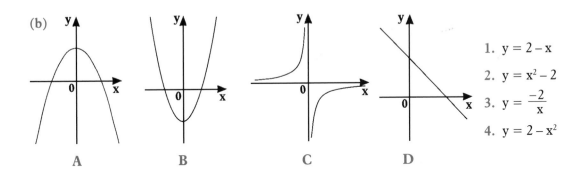

1. $y = 2 - x$

2. $y = x^2 - 2$

3. $y = \dfrac{-2}{x}$

4. $y = 2 - x^2$

A   B   C   D

(c)

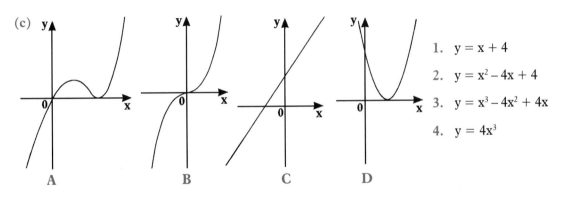

1. $y = x + 4$

2. $y = x^2 - 4x + 4$

3. $y = x^3 - 4x^2 + 4x$

4. $y = 4x^3$

A   B   C   D

4. For an exhibition of posters, the miniature posters were to have an area of 60cm².
   If the width of one of these miniature posters is x cm and the height is y cm:

   (a) Show that $y = \dfrac{60}{x}$.

   (b) Copy and complete the table for $y = \dfrac{60}{x}$.

x	5	10	15	20	25	30
y					2·4	

   (c) Draw the graph of $y = \dfrac{60}{x}$ for values of x from 5 to 30.

   (d) One of the miniature posters in the exhibition had a width of 7·5cm. Use your graph to find the height of this poster.

5. (i) Berryfields Orchard pack their cherries into wooden boxes which have square ends, as shown. These boxes are twice as long as they are wide.

   (a) If the width of one of these boxes is x centimetres, show that the volume is given by $V = 2x^3$ cubic centimetres.

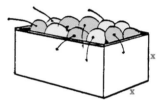

   (b) Copy and complete the table for $V = 2x^3$.

x	5	10	15	20	25
V	250				31250

   (c) Draw the graph of $V = 2x^3$ for values of x from 5 to 25.

   (d) One of these cherry boxes has a volume of 20,000 cubic centimetres. Use your graph to find the approximate width of this box.

   (ii) The cherry boxes do not have lids.

   (a) Show that the area of wood used in one of these boxes is $8x^2$ square centimetres.

   (b) Copy and complete the table for $A = 8x^2$.

x	5	10	15	20	25
A			1800		

   (c) Draw the graph of $A = 8x^2$ for values of x from 5 to 25.

   (d) 2500cm² of wood is needed to make one of these boxes. Use your graph to find the approximate width of this box.

Review 1 Which of the following could be the graph of $y = x^3 - 2x^2 - x + 2$? Explain your choice.

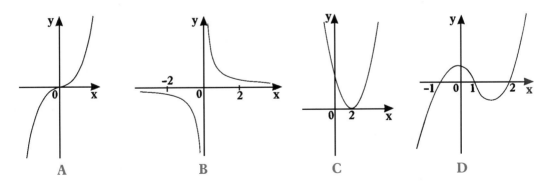

A   B   C   D

Review 2 Which of the graphs drawn in the previous question could have the equation

(a) $y = \dfrac{2}{x}$

(b) $y = x^2 - 4x + 4$

(c) $y = x^3$?

Review 3 Plastic trays, on which rings are displayed in a jewellers', have square bases. The dimensions of these trays are shown in the diagram.

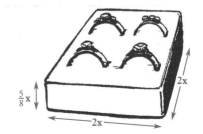

(a) Show that the area of plastic needed to make one of these trays is $A = 9x^2$.

(b) Copy and complete the table for $A = 9x^2$.

x	4	8	12	16	20
A	144			2304	

(c) Draw the graph of $A = 9x^2$ for values of x from 4 to 20. (Choose sensible scales for the x and A-axes.)

(d) Use the graph to find the approximate area of plastic needed to make a tray which is 15cm long.

(e) 3000 square centimetres of plastic is needed to make a tray. Use your graph to find the approximate length of this tray.

DISCUSSION EXERCISE 11:5

Imagine you are throwing a ball to someone.
Does the ball travel in a straight line?
Does the ball rise and then fall?
Discuss.

The path of a thrown ball that rises and then falls has something in common with each of the pictures shown below. What?
Discuss.

What other things could have been in the series of pictures above?
Discuss.

PRACTICAL EXERCISE 11:6

Make a parabolic reflector as follows:

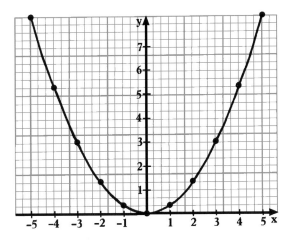

Step 1   Draw a grid of 1 cm squares on a sheet of A3 paper.
Plot the parabola $y = \frac{1}{3}x^2$, using the whole sheet (or nearly the whole sheet).

Step 2   Bend a piece of wire (or other strong but flexible material) to the shape of this parabola. Do this with 5 pieces of wire. (Each piece of wire will need to be about 60 cm long.)

Step 3   Use these 5 pieces of bent wire to make a skeleton shape as shown.

Have the wires placed symmetrically. To keep the shape rigid, tie the wire together at A.

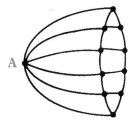

Step 4   Line the inside of the shape with foil. Make this lining as smooth as possible.

What do you think will happen if you take your parabolic reflector outside and point the opening towards the sun? Talk about precautions you should take *before* you take the reflector outside.

What if your reflector had been made using the parabola $y = x^2$?
What if your reflector had been made using the parabola $y = 4x^2$?
What if . . .

SKETCHING GRAPHS

One way of quickly **sketching a line graph** such as $2x + y = 6$ is to find where the line crosses the x and y-axes. We can do this as follows.

$2x + y = 6$ When x = 0, $2 \times 0 + y = 6$ When y = 0, $2x + 0 = 6$
$0 + y = 6$ $2x = 6$
$y = 6$ $x = 3$

We now have the two points $(0, 6)$ and $(3, 0)$. The graph is now sketched as shown.

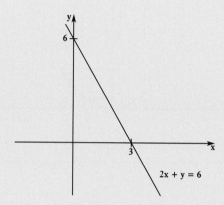

We can quickly sketch graphs such as $y = 3x^2$, $y = \dfrac{-3}{x}$, $y = \frac{1}{4}x^3$ from knowing the shape of the graphs of $y = x^2$, $y = \dfrac{-1}{x}$, $y = x^3$. We use this knowledge along with the coordinates of just one point. This is shown in the examples which follow.

Example   To sketch the graph of $y = 3x^2$ take these steps.

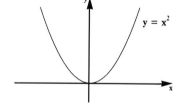

Step 1   The shape is similar
to $y = x^2$, which is shown.

Step 2 $y = 3x^2$. When $x = 1$, $y = 3$. One point on the
graph of $y = 3x^2$ is $(1, 3)$.

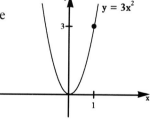

Step 3   Sketch the graph.

248

Example   To sketch the graph of $y = \dfrac{-3}{x}$ take these steps.

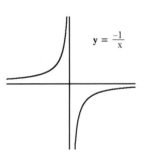

Step 1   The shape is similar to $y = \dfrac{-1}{x}$, which is shown.

Step 2 $y = \dfrac{-3}{x}$. When $x = 1$, $y = \dfrac{-3}{1}$

$$= -3$$

One point on the graph is $(1, -3)$.

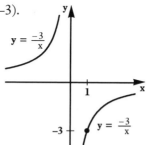

Step 3   Sketch the graph.

Example   To sketch the graph of $y = \frac{1}{4}x^3$ take these steps.

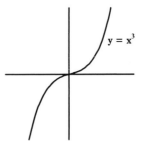

Step 1   The shape is similar to that shown.

Step 2 $y = \frac{1}{4}x^3$.   When $x = 1$, $y = \frac{1}{4} \times 1^3$

$$= \tfrac{1}{4} \times 1$$

$$= \tfrac{1}{4}$$

One point on the graph is $(1, \frac{1}{4})$

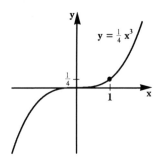

Step 3 Sketch the graph.

EXERCISE 11:7

Do not use graph paper in this exercise.

1. Sketch these graphs, showing the coordinates of just one point.

   (a) $y = \dfrac{2}{x}$ (b) $y = 2x^3$ (c) $y = 2x^2$

   (d) $y = 4x^2$ (e) $y = \dfrac{-1}{x}$ (f) $y = \tfrac{1}{3}x^2$

   (g) $y = \dfrac{-4}{x}$ (h) $y = -2x^2$ (i) $y = -4x^3$

   (j) $y = \tfrac{1}{4}x^2$ (k) $y = \tfrac{1}{2}x^3$ (l) $y = \dfrac{1}{2x}$

2. Sketch these lines, showing where they meet the x and y axes.

   (a) $y = x + 4$ (b) $y = 3x - 6$ (c) $y = 2 - x$

   (d) $3x + y = 3$ (e) $2x + 3y = 6$ (f) $x - 2y = 4$

   (g) $2x - 5y = 10$ (h) $4x + 3y = 24$ (i) $5x + 2y = 5$

   (j) $4x - 2y = 6$ (k) $x + 2y - 6 = 0$ (l) $3x - y + 1 = 0$

   (m) $x + 4y + 5 = 0$

Review 1 Sketch these graphs.

   (a) $y = 3x^3$ (b) $y = \dfrac{-2}{x}$ (c) $y = \tfrac{1}{2}x^2$

Review 2 Sketch these lines.

   (a) $y = 5 - 2x$ (b) $3x + 2y = 12$ (c) $3x - 2y - 6 = 0$

   (d) $2x + y + 3 = 0$

INVESTIGATION 11:8

EXPONENTIAL GRAPHS

Use a graphics calculator or a computer graphics package. If neither is available, draw the graphs by plotting points as shown below.

Table for $y = 2^x$

x	−3	−2	−1	0	1	2	3
y	0·125	0·25	0·5	1	2	4	8

Remember   The value of 2^{-3} is found by keying as follows.

$\boxed{2}$ $\boxed{\text{SHIFT}}$ $\boxed{x^y}$ $\boxed{3}$ $\boxed{+/-}$ $\boxed{=}$

Graph of $y = 2^x$

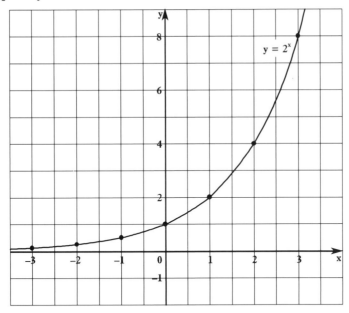

What do the graphs $y = 2^x$, $y = 3^x$, $y = 4^x$, $y = 5^x$ have in common? Investigate.

Investigate to find the relationship between the graphs of $y = 2^x$ and $y = 2^{-x}$.

What if the graphs were $y = 2^x$ and $y = (\frac{1}{2})^x$?
What if the graphs were $y = 2^{-x}$ and $y = (\frac{1}{2})^x$?
What if . . .

GRAPHS of REAL-LIFE SITUATIONS

DISCUSSION EXERCISE 11:9

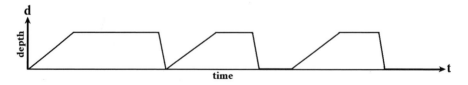

This graph shows the depth of water in a washing machine during one complete cycle. Which parts of this graph show the machine filling, rinsing, spinning and draining? Discuss.

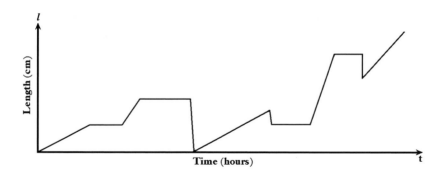

This graph shows the length of a scarf that Anna is knitting.
Discuss each section of this graph.

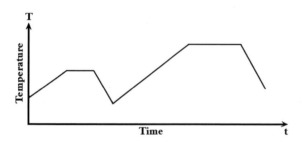

What might this graph represent? Discuss.
What if temperature was replaced with distance?

EXERCISE 11:10

1. This graph shows the cost of four different cuts of beef.

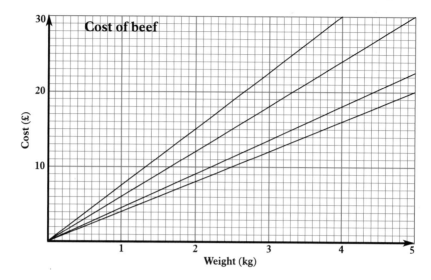

(a) What is the cost of 2·5kg of the cheapest cut?

(b) Sam paid £13·50 for 3kg. Which cut did Sam buy?

(c) Aaron and Ann each bought 2kg of beef. Ann paid £1 more than Aaron. Which cuts did Aaron and Ann buy?

2.

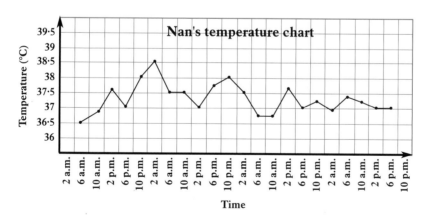

Nan's temperature was taken at four-hourly intervals, during her stay in hospital.

(a) If Nan was admitted to hospital on March 4th, on what date was she discharged?

(b) How many times did Nan's temperature rise?

(c) "During Nan's stay in hospital, her average temperature reading was about 37·3°C." Is this statement true?

3.

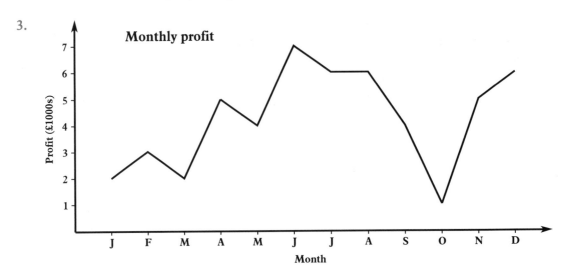

This graph shows the monthly profit (to the nearest £1000) of a car sales firm.

(a) Which month, or months, had the greatest profit?

(b) Which two consecutive months had the same profit?

(c) What was the increase in profit between the end of May and the end of June?

(d) How much profit was made during the whole year?

(e) What reasons can you think of for the rapid decrease in profit during September and October?

(f) Find the average monthly profit for this year. (Answer to the nearest £1000.)

4.

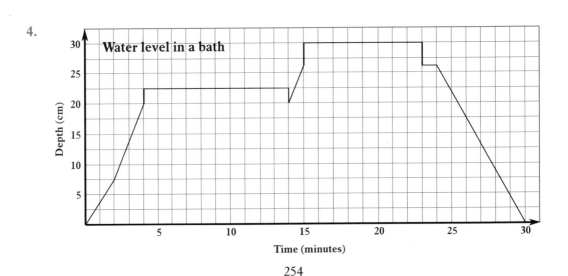

254

Ramon baths his two dogs, Jasper and Jess. He baths Jess first, then Jasper. The graph shows the water level in the bath.

(a) Does it appear as if Ramon filled the bath with both the hot and cold taps turned on together?

(b) Which dog is bathed for the longer time?

(c) Which dog is larger, Jess or Jasper?

(d) How long after Jasper is taken out of the bath, does Ramon begin to empty it?

(e) Is Ramon more likely to add hot or cold water after Jess is taken out of the bath?

(f) Use your answers to (a) and (e) to decide if Ramon initially put cold water or hot water into the bath.

Review

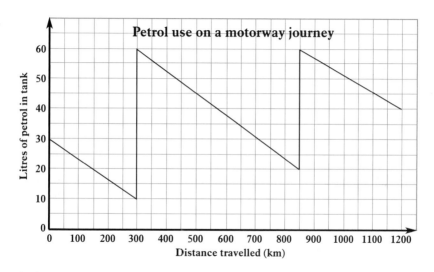

This graph shows the amount of petrol in the fuel tank of Tamara's car during a journey on a motorway in Europe.

(a) How much petrol was in the tank at the beginning of the journey?

(b) What total distance did Tamara travel?

(c) How many times did she stop for petrol?

(d) Assuming that Tamara filled the tank up each time she stopped, what was the capacity of the tank?

(e) Did the fuel gauge read "$\frac{1}{2}$" or "$\frac{1}{4}$" or "$\frac{3}{4}$" at the beginning of the journey?

(f) How much petrol was used altogether on this journey?

(g) Could Tamara have completed the journey if she had only filled the tank up once?

(h) What was the petrol consumption rate, in km/l, on this journey?

(i) Find the petrol consumption rate in litres per 100km. (Answer to 1d.p.)

255

DISCUSSION EXERCISE 11:11

● What questions could be asked and answered from the following graph? **Discuss.**

Radio and television audiences[1] throughout the day, 1989[2]
United Kingdom

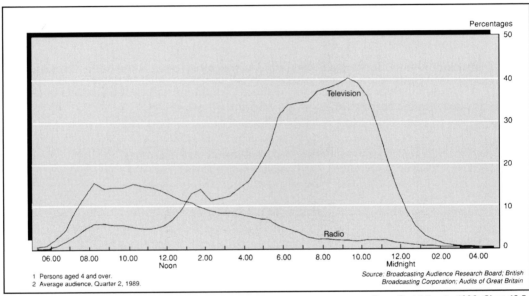

1 Persons aged 4 and over.
2 Average audience, Quarter 2, 1989.

Source: Broadcasting Audience Research Board; British Broadcasting Corporation; Audits of Great Britain

Source: Key Data 1990/91

From: Social Trends, 1990, Chart 10.5

● Collect other line graphs from newspapers or magazines. **Discuss** these graphs.

INVESTIGATION 11:12

LEAKING WATER

Water is leaking from a hole in the bottom of a cylindrical container. A graph could be plotted to show the depth of water in the container every minute. Would you expect this to be a straight line graph? **Investigate.**

What if water is leaking from a bucket such as that shown?

You may like to investigate water leaking from containers of other shapes. As part of your investigation carry out some experiments.

MATCHING GRAPHS to REAL-LIFE SITUATIONS

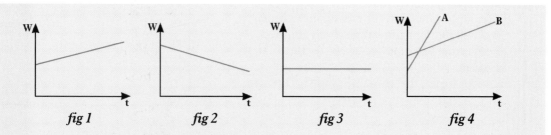

fig 1   *fig 2*   *fig 3*   *fig 4*

fig 1 shows w increasing as t increases.

fig 2 shows w decreasing as t increases.

fig 3 shows w stays the same as t increases.

fig 4 shows that for both graphs w is increasing as t increases. For graph A, w is increasing at a faster rate than for graph B.

DISCUSSION EXERCISE 11:13

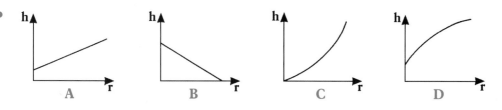

A   B   C   D

Graph D shows that as r increases, h at first increases quickly and then more slowly. What happens to h, as r increases, in the other graphs? Discuss.

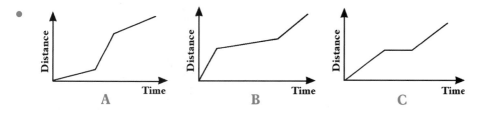

A   B   C

These are the graphs of three cycle journeys.

Graph A shows that at first the speed was quite slow, then the speed was quite fast, then the cyclist slowed down. The speed in the last section of the journey was not as slow as in the first part.

Describe the cycle journeys represented by graphs B and C. Discuss.

● At the beginning of an experiment, Josiah
filled a measuring cylinder with water.
This graph shows that the measuring cylinder
remained full for a time, then it was emptied.
The cylinder was emptied at a faster rate than it
was filled.
How can we tell this from the graph? Discuss.

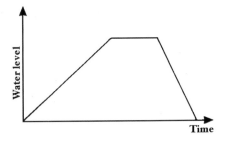

●

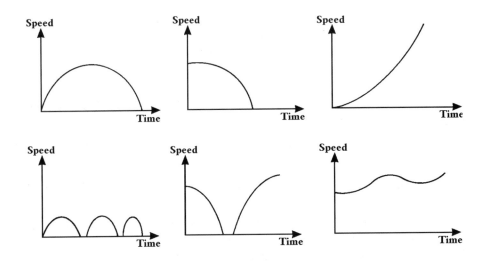

One of these graphs could represent a car in a traffic jam. Which one?
What might the other graphs represent? Discuss.

●

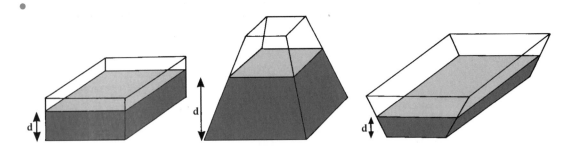

Suppose the above containers are being filled with a liquid at the
rate of 200m*l* per second. In each case the depth, d, of the liquid is
increasing as time increases.
The graph, at the right, could represent how the depth changes
with time for one of these containers. Which one? Discuss.
Discuss possible graphs for the other two containers.

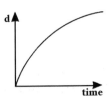

258

Worked Example   Match the graphs with the situations.

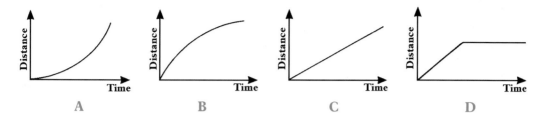

A   B   C   D

1.   A car slowing down going up a hill.
2.   A car cruising on the M4.
3.   A car hitting a concrete wall.
4.   A car rolling down a hill.

Answer   **Graph A** shows distance increasing slowly at first, then more quickly. Situation **4.** could have this description.

Graph B shows distance increasing quickly at first, then more slowly. Situation **1.** could have this description.

Graph C shows distance increasing at the same rate. Situation **2.** could have this description.

Graph D shows distance increasing at the same rate at first, then the distance is unchanged. Situation **3.** could have this description.

That is, A matches 4, B matches 1, C matches 2, D matches 3.

EXERCISE 11:14

1.

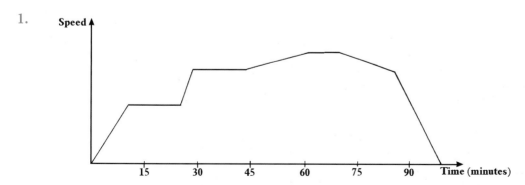

Beatrice took part in a charity run. This graph shows her speed during this run.
Describe Beatrice's run.

2.

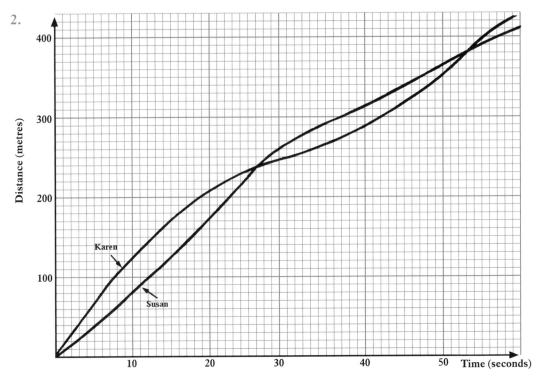

Karen and Susan were two of the runners in a 400m race.

(a) At what times were Karen and Susan level with each other?

(b) Did Karen finish before Susan or Susan before Karen?

(c) Who had the faster speed during the first 10 seconds?

(d) Who was leading after 50 seconds? About how far ahead was she?

(e) How might an announcer have spoken about Karen's and Susan's progress during this race? Write a short report on this.

3.

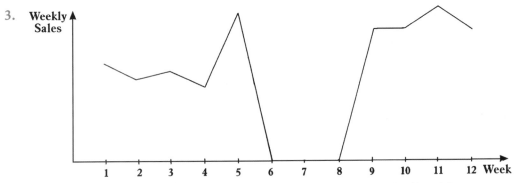

This graph shows the sales by "Best Bookshop" of a newly published book by a best-selling author.

What do you think happened in   (a) the 6th week   (b) the 9th week

(c) the 5th week?

4.

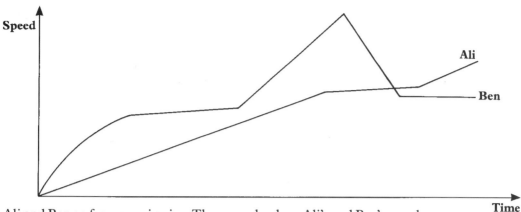

Ali and Ben go for a morning jog. These graphs show Ali's and Ben's speeds on one morning.

Compare the times, distances and speeds. Write a short report.

5.

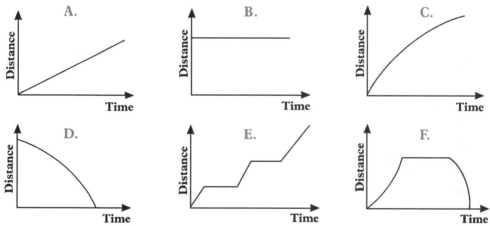

One of these graphs could represent a cricket ball thrown from one player to another. Which graph might this be?

What might the other graphs represent?

6. A beaker of liquid was used as part of an experiment. This graph shows the level of the liquid during this experiment.

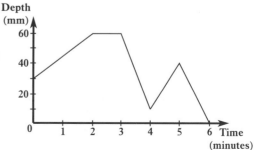

(a) What was the depth of liquid at the beginning of this 6-minute experiment?

(b) How much liquid was in the container at the end of this time?

(c) Describe what was happening to the depth of liquid during the 6 minutes.

7.

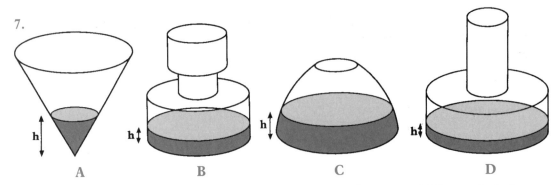

Water is poured into these containers at the rate of 150ml per second. The graphs below show how the height of the water changes with time.
Match the containers with the graphs.

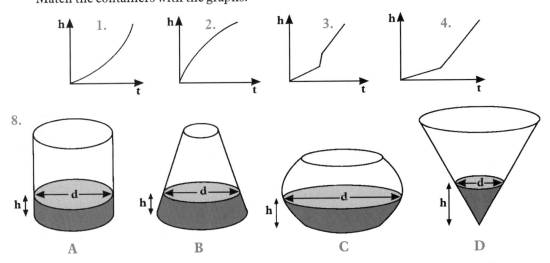

8.

These containers are being filled with a liquid. The graphs below show how the diameter of the surface of the liquid changes as the height of the liquid increases.
Which graph belongs to which container?

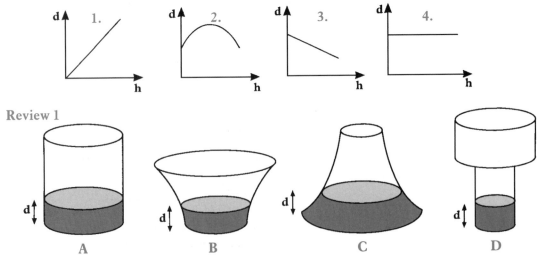

Review 1

Water is poured at the rate of 100m*l* per second into these containers. The graphs below show how the depth of water changes with time.
Match the containers with the graphs.

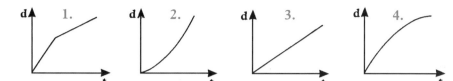

Review 2

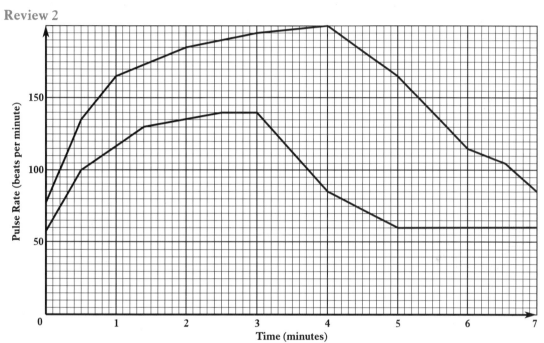

Before Felicity began an aerobics exercise programme, she did a 3-minute fitness test. The top graph shows her pulse rate during this test and for 4 minutes afterwards. After six months on the aerobics programme, she did the same fitness test again. The bottom graph shows her pulse rate during and immediately after this test. The gym. that Felicity was going to wrote a report based on these graphs. What might have been written in this report?

DISCUSSION EXERCISE 11:15

• Consider the following sequence of events: a cricket ball leaves the bowler's hand
                                          the ball is hit by the batsman
                                          the ball comes to rest against a fence
                                          the ball is picked up
                                          the ball is thrown to the bowler

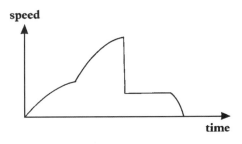

Does this graph show the change in speed of the cricket ball in the sequence of events on the previous page? **Discuss**.

- Can you think of sports which could produce graphs similar to those shown below? **Discuss**.

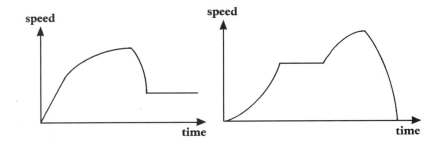

- Choose a sport. (Some suggestions follow.)
  Draw a distance/time graph or a speed/time graph for a person or a ball or some other equipment that is involved in this sport. **Discuss** your graph.
  Suggestions: rowing, abseiling, football, netball, horse riding, car racing, gymnastics.

PRACTICAL EXERCISE 11:16

Work in groups to produce a well researched and well presented project on the actual use of graphs.
The project could be presented in booklet form or as an illustrated talk or as a wall mural or in some other way.

Some suggestions for the project are: use in hospitals
                                        use in factories and/or businesses
                                        use in local Councils

Each group should initially discuss and make decisions on the following:
    what is to be included in the project
    how information is to be gathered
    how the project is to be presented
    what tasks are to be done by each student in the group
    what date each task is to be completed by

CHAPTER 11 REVIEW

1. The annual cost of the heat lost through a wall depends on the length of the wall. When the wall is a square of length x m the annual cost, £y, is given by the equation $y = 5x^2$.

   (a) Calculate the cost, £y, when x is 8m.

   (b) The table shows the cost, £y, for different values of x m.

Length, x (m)	3	4	5	6	7
Cost, y (£)	45	80	125	180	245

   Use the table of values to draw the graph of $y = 5x^2$.

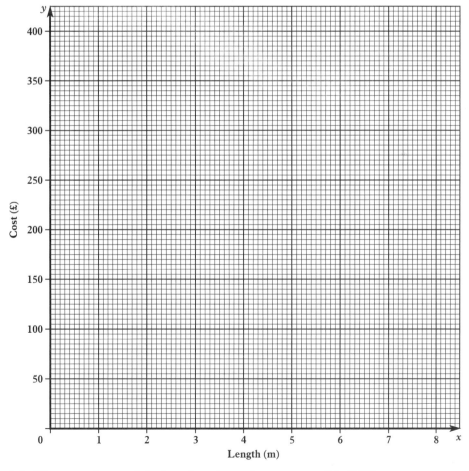

   (c) The annual cost of the heat lost through a square wall is £150. Use your graph to estimate the length of the wall.

   SEG

2. This diagram shows Jane's path when she completed a high dive.

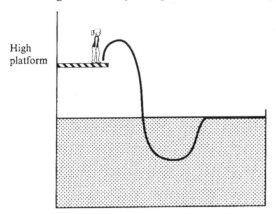

High
platform

The graph below shows how her speed varied with time after she dived from the high platform.

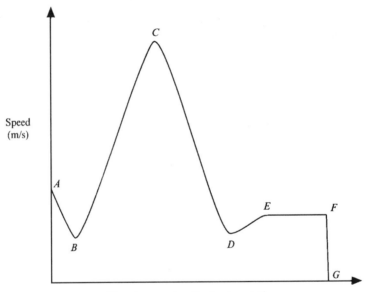

Time, in seconds, after leaving platform

Write a sentence to describe what happened to Jane's speed between each of the points listed below.
You should link her speed with where she is on her dive and suggest reasons for any sudden changes in speed.

(a) A to B (b) B to C (c) C to D

(d) D to E (e) E to F (f) F to G **NEAB**

266

3. The sketch shows the graph of $y = 2x + 1$.

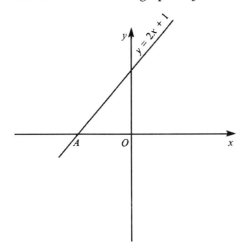

(i) Give the co-ordinates of the point A.

(ii) On the grid above, sketch the graph of $y = 2x - 1$.

(iii) From your graphs explain why the equations $y = 2x + 1$ and $y = 2x - 1$ cannot be solved simultaneously. **NEAB**

4. **(a)** Complete this mapping diagram for $x \longrightarrow x^2$ (or $y = x^2$).

$$x \longrightarrow x^2$$
$$3 \longrightarrow .....$$
$$2 \longrightarrow .....$$
$$1 \longrightarrow 1$$
$$0 \longrightarrow 0$$
$$-1 \longrightarrow 1$$
$$-2 \longrightarrow .....$$
$$-3 \longrightarrow .....$$

(b) On the graph paper on the next page, plot the points and draw the graph representing the mapping $x \longrightarrow x^2$ (or $y = x^2$).

(c) From your graph, **estimate** the value of

(i) $1 \cdot 6^2$

(ii) $\sqrt{5}$

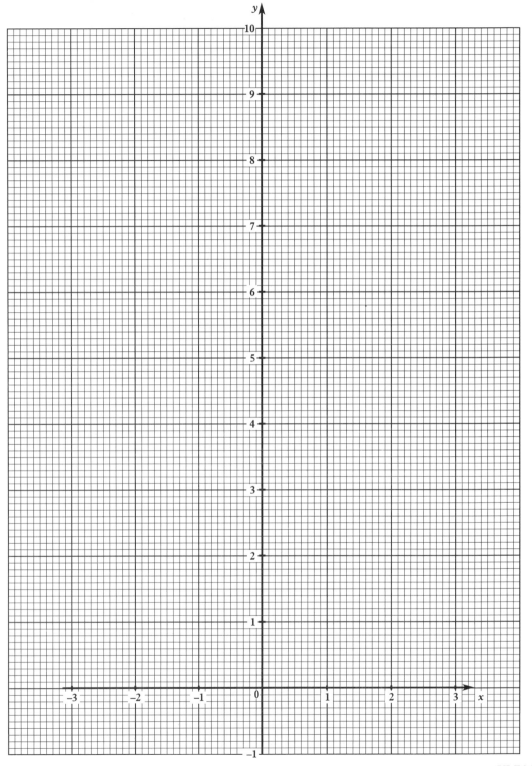

ULEAC

5.

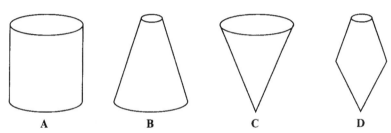

A   **B**   **C**   **D**

Water is leaking at a steady rate from one of these four containers labelled A to D. The graph below shows how the height, h, of the water in the container changes with time.

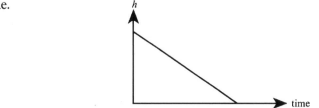

Write down the letter of the container which matches the graph.   **ULEAC**

6. (a) Complete the table below and draw the graph of the mapping $y = x^2 - 3$.

x	-3	-2	-1	0	1	2	3
$y = x^2 - 3$							

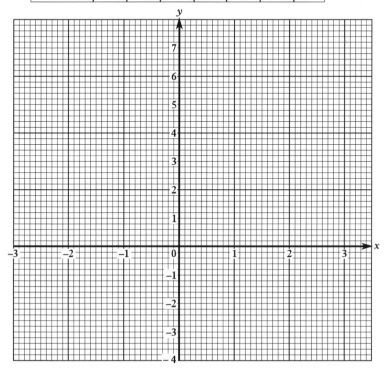

(b) Use your graph to write down the two values of x for which $y = 3$.   **SEG**

7.

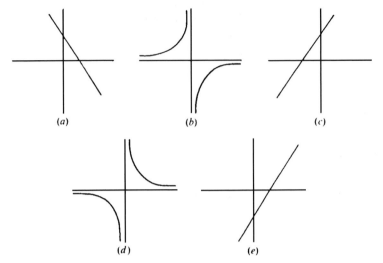

(a)   (b)   (c)

(d)   (e)

Which of the above graphs could represent the function

(i) $y = 2x + 3$.   **(ii)** $y = \dfrac{6}{x}$.   **NICCEA**

8.

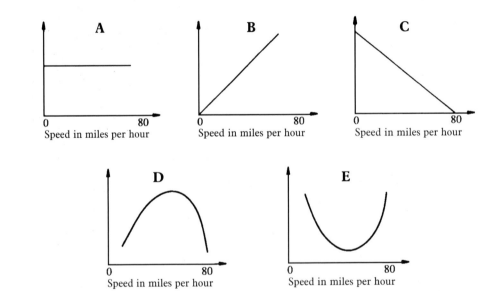

The diagrams show the shapes of five graphs A, B, C, D, and E.

The vertical axes have not been labelled.

On one of the graphs, the missing label is "Speed in km per hour".

(a) Write down the letter of this graph.

On one of the graphs the missing label is "Petrol consumption in miles per gallon".
It shows that the car travels furthest on 1 gallon of petrol when it is travelling at 56 miles per hour.

(b) Write down the letter of this graph.   **ULEAC**

270

9.

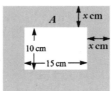

A photograph measuring 15cm by 10cm is mounted on card to leave a border $x$cm wide all the way round.

(a) Show that the area of the border, A cm^2, is given by
$$A = 4x^2 + 50x.$$

(b) (i) Complete the table of values below.

x	1	2	3	4	5	6	7	8
A		116		264		444		656

(ii) Draw the graph of A against x on the grid below.

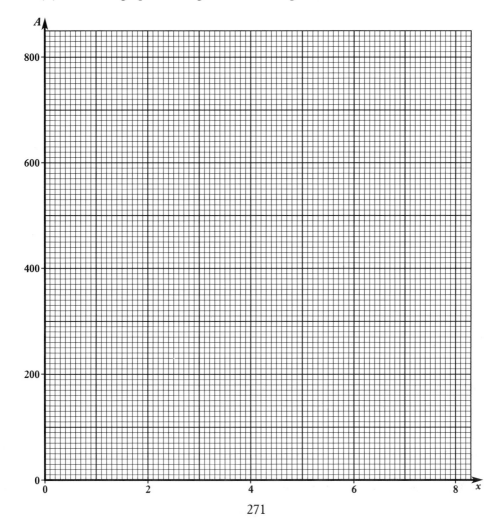

(c) The area of the border is twice the area of the photograph.
Use your graph to find the width of the border.

NEAB

10. Sketch and label the functions $y = x^3$ and $y = x^3 + 2$ on the axes below.

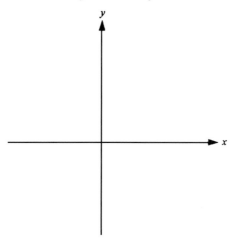

SEG

1. The gradient of a road is shown.

   (a) Write this gradient as a fraction.

   (b) How high does the road rise for every 200 metres horizontally?

2. Multiply out   (a) $3(a-b)$ (b) $a(2a-5)$ (c) $mn(m-n)$

3.
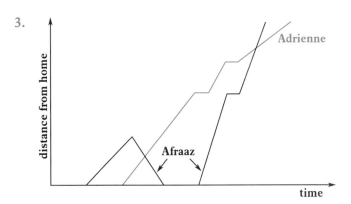

   Adrienne and her brother Afraaz set off from their home in separate cars to go to a disco.

   Afraaz left home before Adrienne. What else can you tell from the graph?

4. (a) Make P the subject of the formula $k = PVT$.

   (b) $A = 2\pi rh + \pi r^2$. Make h the subject of this formula.

   (c) $S = \frac{1}{2}(a+b+c)$. Express b in terms of S, a and c.

5. At Christmas time, a shop wraps small gifts and places them in boxes. These boxes are made from cardboard and are shaped as shown.

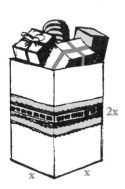

   (a) Show that the area of cardboard needed for one of these boxes is given by $A = 9x^2$.

   (b) Draw the graph of $A = 9x^2$ for values of x between 1 and 10.

   (c) One of these boxes is made from 780cm² of cardboard. Use your graph to find the approximate length of this box.

6. **(i)** Rearrange these line equations into the form $y = mx + c$.

    (a) $5x + y = 7$ **(b)** $x + 2y - 6 = 0$ **(c)** $3x - y = 1$

  (ii) Write down the gradient of each of the lines.

  (iii) Where does each line cross the y-axis?

7. The volume of a cone is given by $V = \frac{1}{3}\pi r^2 h$, where r is the radius of the base and h is the height.

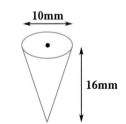

  (a) Find the volume of the sketched cone.

  (b) Find the radius of the cone for which $V = 150 \text{cm}^3$ and $h = 20 \text{cm}$.

8.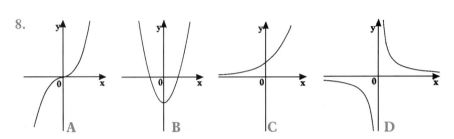

Which of the above could be the graph of $y = x^2 - 2$? Explain your choice.

9. Expand and simplify   **(a)** $2(3 - 2x) + 5x$ **(b)** $3a - 2 + a(2a - 5)$

                         (c) $5n - 2(2n - 1)$ **(d)** $3(2n - 3) - 2(n + 3)$.

10.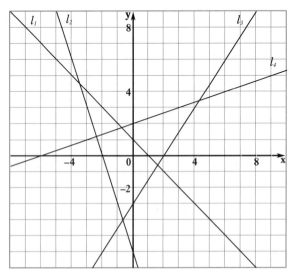

  (a) Find the gradient of each of these lines.

  (b) Use the line equation $y = mx + c$ to write down the equations of these lines.

11. One way of estimating the adult height, in metres, to which a baby is expected to grow is by using one of the formulae:

$$g = \frac{m + f - 0.13}{2} \qquad\qquad b = \frac{m + f + 0.13}{2}$$

In these formulae, g is the adult height of a baby girl, b is the adult height of a baby boy, m is the mother's height and f is the father's height.

Rearrange the formula $g = \dfrac{m + f - 0.13}{2}$ to make f the subject.

12. Draw graphs to show the region in which each of these inequalities is true. (Draw a separate graph for each.)

(a) $y \geq 0$ (b) $x < 2$ (c) $y \geq 2x - 1$ (d) $x - 2y > 2$

13. Factorise.   (a) $6 - 8n$ (b) $2a + 3a^2$ (c) $16x - 10x^2$

             (d) $\pi r^2 h + 2\pi r$ (e) $x^2 y - xy^2$

14. Draw a set of axes. Number both the x and y-axes from –5 to 5.
On this set of axes draw the following lines.

(a) $y = 2x$ (b) $y = 2$ (c) $x + 4 = 0$ (d) $x + 2y = 6$ (e) $3x - y = 4$

15. Match the graphs with the equations.

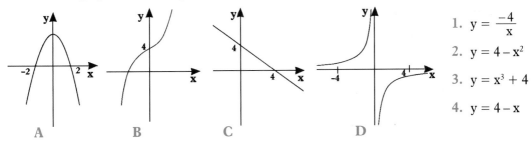

1. $y = \dfrac{-4}{x}$

2. $y = 4 - x^2$

3. $y = x^3 + 4$

4. $y = 4 - x$

16. (a) $C = \frac{5}{9}(F - 32)$ is a formula to convert temperatures given in degrees Celsius to degrees Fahrenheit. Rearrange this formula to make F the subject.

(b) The volume of a cylinder is given by $V = \pi r^2 h$.
Express r in terms of V and h.

(c) The time, T, for a pendulum to make one complete swing to and fro is given by

$T = 2\pi \sqrt{\dfrac{l}{g}}$ where l is the length of the pendulum and g is the acceleration due to gravity. Make l the subject of this formula.

17. Draw a diagram to show where both of the following inequalities are true.
$$y < x, \quad 2x + 3y \geq 6$$

18. In a kite-flying competition, all kites must have an area of 4m^2. If **a** and **b** are the lengths of the diagonals of the kites, the relationship between **a** and **b** is $a = \dfrac{8}{b}$.

    (a) Copy and complete this table.

b	1	2	3	4	5	6	7	8
a			2·7				1·1	

    (b) Draw the graph of **a** against **b**.

    (c) Use your graph to estimate the value of **a** when $b = 4\cdot5$.

19. (i) Rashid used this diagram to help expand $(3n + 2)(n + 5)$.
    How should Rashid fill in the second row?

    (ii) Use Rashid's method or some other method to expand and simplify the following.

    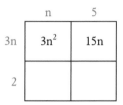

    (a) $(3n + 2)(n + 5)$ (b) $(2n - 5)(3n - 2)$

    (c) $(4x + y)(x - 2y)$ (d) $(a + bx)(c + dx)$

20. Sketch these lines, showing where they meet the x and y axes. Do not use graph paper.

    (a) $y = 3 - x$ (b) $3x - 5y = 15$ (c) $x + 2y + 7 = 0$

21. Peter was prepared to spend up to £20 buying CDs and Tapes in this sale.
    $2x + 5y \leq 20$ is an inequality which could be used to describe the amount of money Peter spent.

    (a) What does x stand for? What does y stand for?

    (b) Can x have a negative value? Can y have a negative value?

    (c) Draw a graph to show the region which contains all the possible numbers of CDs and Tapes that Peter could have bought.

22. (i) $f(x) = 3 + 2x^2$.   Find   (a) $f(1)$ (b) $f(3)$ (c) $f(-3)$ (d) $f(\tfrac{1}{2})$.

    (ii) $g(a) = \dfrac{2a + 3}{a + 1}$.   (a) For what value of **a** is $g(a) = -3$?

             (b) For what value of **a** does $g(a)$ have no answer?

23. **(i)** Factorise   (a) $x^2 + 4x + 3$ (b) $x^2 - 8x + 7$ (c) $x^2 - 13x - 30$.

   (ii) Solve the quadratic equation $x^2 + 5x - 24 = 0$.

24.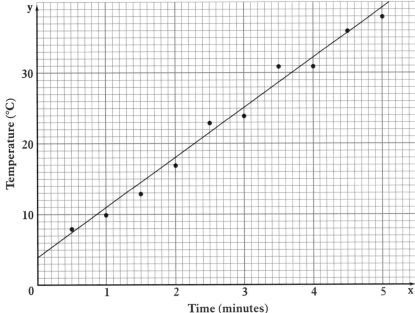

Yasmin heated a liquid for 5 minutes. Every 30 seconds she took the temperature.
Yasmin drew this scatter diagram to illustrate her results.
Find the equation of the line of best fit that Yasmin drew.

25. Sketch these graphs, showing the coordinates of just one point. Do not use graph paper.

   (a) $y = 5x^3$ (b) $y = \dfrac{4}{x}$ (c) $y = -2x^2$

26. What can you say about p if

   (a) $p^2 \le 25$ (b) $3p^2 + 5 > 17$?

27. The equations of the three sides of a triangle are
shown. (The diagram is not drawn to scale.)
The line PQ, which has equation $y = 2x - 4$, is
parallel to one of the sides of this triangle.
Which one?

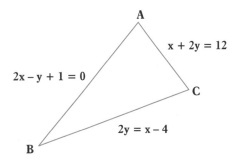

28.

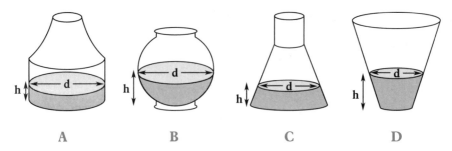

A   B   C   D

These containers are being filled with a liquid at the rate of 200m*l* per second.

(a) These graphs show how the height of the liquid is increasing with time.
Match the containers with the graphs.

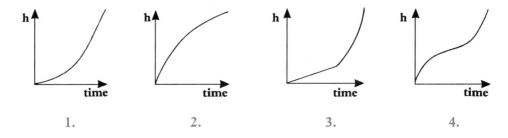

1.   2.   3.   4.

(b) These graphs show how the diameter of the surface of the liquid changes as the height increases.
Match the containers with the graphs.

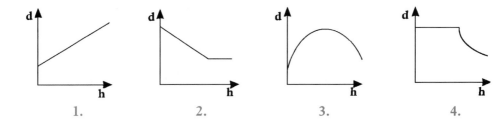

1.   2.   3.   4.

29. The formula $\dfrac{1}{u} + \dfrac{1}{v} = \dfrac{1}{f}$ is used in a Physics experiment on light.

(a) Find the value of f if $u = 6{\cdot}2$ and $v = 10$.

(b) Find the value of u if $f = 4{\cdot}6$ and $v = 8{\cdot}2$.

30. The formula for the area of a circle is $A = \pi r^2$.
The relationship between the radius and the diameter is $d = 2r$.
Express A in terms of d and π. Give your answer in its simplest form.

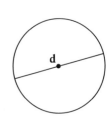

31. The product of two consecutive integers is 182.

    (a) Zara wrote the equation $n(n + 1) = 182$.
        What does n stand for? What does $n + 1$ stand for?

    (b) Show that $n(n + 1) = 182$ can be rewritten as $n^2 + n - 182 = 0$.

    (c) Solve $n^2 + n - 182 = 0$ to find the two integers.

32.

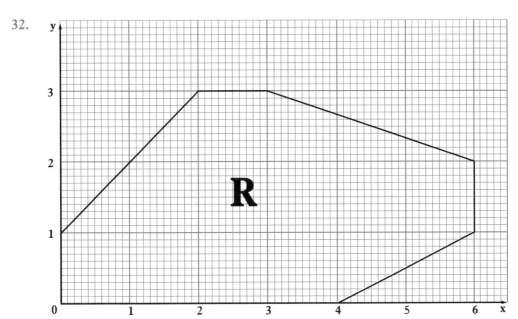

The region R is defined by seven inequalities, three of which are $y \geq 0$, $x - 2y \leq 4$, $x \leq 6$. Find the other four inequalities.

33. A DJ can control the sound level of the records he plays at a disco. The sketch graph below is a graph of the sound level against the time whilst one record was played.

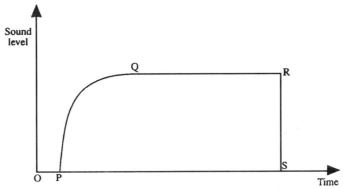

    (a) Describe how the sound level changed between P and Q on the graph whilst the record was being played.

    (b) Give one possible reason for the third part, RS, of the sketch graph.   **ULEAC**

34. The volume of a sphere is given by the formula $V = \frac{4}{3}\pi r^3$.

(a) Rearrange the formula to give r, in terms of V.

(b) Find the value of r when $V = 75$.   **SEG**

35. (a) Given $y = x^2 + 2$, complete the Table of values below.

x	-2	-1.5	-1	-0.5	0	0.5	1	1.5	2
y	6	4.25	3	2.25			3		

(b) Using the axes below, draw the graph of $y = x^2 + 2$, for values of x from –2 to 2.

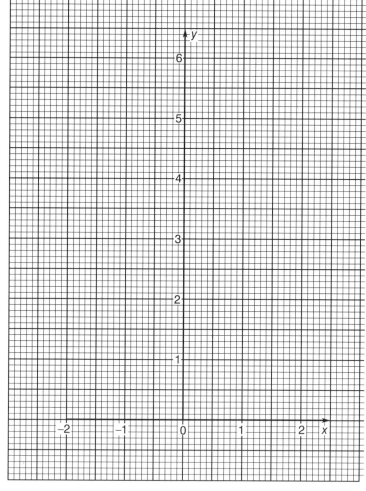

(c) Read from your graph the two values of x for which $y = 5$.   **MEG**

36. Factorise

(a) $3d + 6e$ (b) $4x^2 + 8xy$ **NICCEA**

37. (a) Solve these inequalities.

    (i) $2x + 1 \le 5$ **(ii)** $x^2 > 25$ **(iii)** $7x + 3 > 13x + 15$

  (b) Label with the letter R, the single region which satisfies all of these inequalities.

$$y < \tfrac{1}{2}x + 1, \quad x > 6, \quad y > 3$$

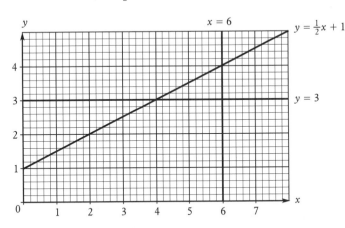

                                                               SEG

38.

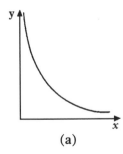 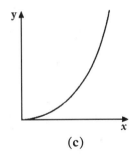

      (a)   **(b)**   **(c)**

For each graph, select the one equation which the graph could represent (for positive x).

    (i) $y = x + 3$ **(ii)** $y = x - 3$ **(iii)** $y = 3x$

    (iv) $y = 3x^2$ **(v)** $y = -3x^2$ **(vi)** $y = \dfrac{3}{x}$ **NICCEA**

39. (a) Expand $(2x + 1)(x + 4)$.

  (b) Factorise completely $4x^2 - 6x$.   **ULEAC**

40. Water in a fountain comes out of a nozzle at a speed of v m/s. The height of the water fountain, h centimetres is calculated using the formula $h = 5v^2$.

  (a) Complete the table

v	10	12	14	16	18	20
h						

  (b) Plot the values of v and h and draw the graph on the graph paper on the next page.

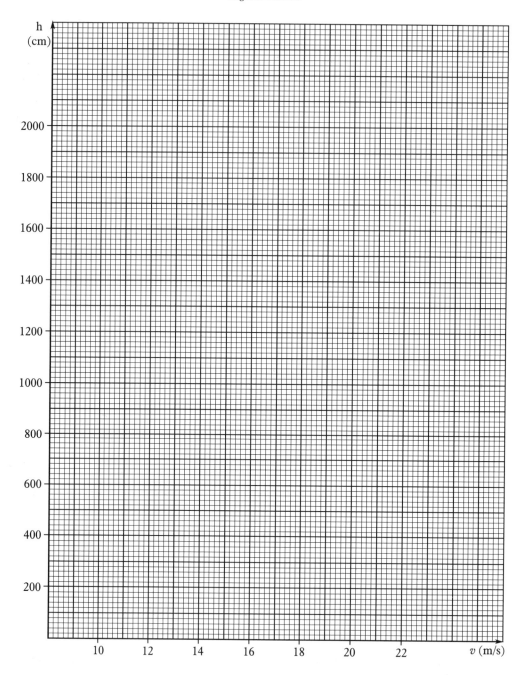

(c) Use your graph, showing its use clearly, to find

    (i) the height when water comes out at a speed of 15.5 m/s,

    (ii) the speed needed to give a height of 1750 cm.

(d) Rearrange the formula $h = 5v^2$ to give v in terms of h.

NICCEA

41. **(a)** Liquid is poured at a steady rate into the bottle shown in the diagram.
As the bottle is being filled the height, h, of the liquid in the bottle changes.
Which of the five graphs shown below shows this change?
Give a reason for your choice.

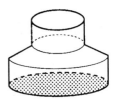

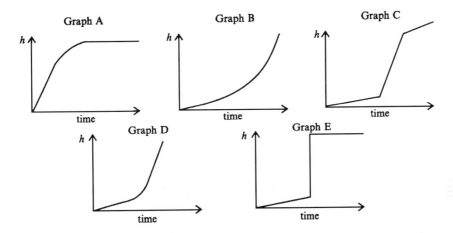

(b) Liquid is poured at a steady rate into another container. The graph on the right shows how the height, h, of the liquid in this container changes.
Sketch a picture of this container.

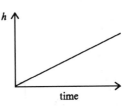

NEAB

42. In the construction of a hotel, 2400m² of floor space are available for single and double bedrooms.

A single bedroom occupies 20m² of floor space.
A double bedroom occupies 30m² of floor space.

(a) If x single bedrooms and y double bedrooms are to be constructed, show that
$$2x + 3y \leq 240.$$

(b) The owners of the hotel decided that there should be at least 60 bedrooms. Write down an inequality in x and y which represents this condition.

(c) The number of single bedrooms will be, at most, one-third of the total number of bedrooms.
Show that $$y \geq 2x.$$

(d) There are to be at least 10 single bedrooms.
Write down an inequality which represents this condition.

(e) Illustrate the above four inequalities by a suitable diagram on the graph paper on the next page. Identify the region containing the set of points (x, y) satisfying all four inequalities.

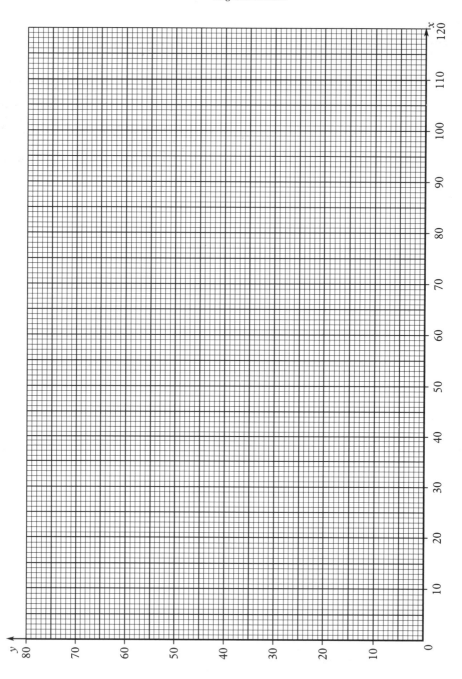

43. (a) Multiply out and simplify

$$(3x - 1)(2x + 3).$$

(b) Show how you could use your answer to **(a)** to work out 29×23.

NEAB

NICCEA

44. This formula can be used to calculate the percentage volume of carbon dioxide in the flue gases from a boiler:

$$V = k\left(1 - \frac{x}{21}\right).$$

V is the percentage volume of carbon dioxide,
x is the percentage volume of oxygen,
k is a constant for the type of fuel.

(a) Find V when $x = 4\cdot6$, $k = 11\cdot9$.

(b) Show how you would check that your answer is about the right size.

(c) Rearrange the formula to give x in terms of V.   **MEG**

45. The numbers 4, 6 and 9 are all factors of 36.

(a) Explain why 5 is not a factor of 36.

(b) (i) Complete these pairs of whole numbers which multiply to give 36.

$(2, \ldots)$, $(3, \ldots)$, $(4, \quad 9)$,

$(6, \quad 6)$, $(9, \quad 4)$, $(12, \ldots)$

(ii) Plot these six pairs of whole numbers as points on the grid and join them with a smooth curve.

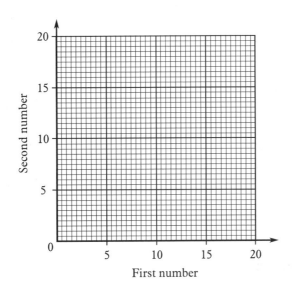

(iii) By drawing lines on your graph show how to find the number which multiplied by 5 gives 36.   **SEG**

46.

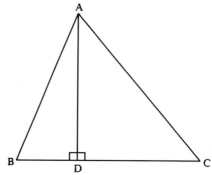

In the triangle ABC, AD is perpendicular to BC, AD is 1 unit less than AB and BD is 8 units less than AB.

(a) Letting AB = x units, show that $x^2 - 18x + 65 = 0$.

(b) Solve the equation $x^2 - 18x + 65 = 0$.

(c) State the length of AB, giving the reason why the other solution for x is not acceptable for AB.

NICCEA

47. These diagrams represent the first three square numbers.

First   Second   Third

1 dot   4 dots   9 dots

So the 3rd square number is **9** because **9** dots can be arranged as **a square** with 3 rows and 3 columns.

(a) Write down an expression for the nth square number.

(b) Test your expression for a suitable value of n.

(c) Explain whether or not 441 is a square number.

(d) Explain whether or not 1007 is a square number.

(e) Write down an expression for the $(n + 1)$th square number.

(f) Write down an expression for the difference between the $(n + 1)$th square number and the nth square number.

(g) Simplify the expression in part (f) above.

(h) Show that the difference between the $(n + 2)$th square number and the nth square number is a multiple of 4.

(i) Show that the difference between the $(n + p)$th square number and the nth square number is a multiple of p.

ULEAC

SHAPE, SPACE and MEASURES

Shape, Space and Measures Revision

2-D SHAPES

A 3-sided polygon is a triangle. A 4-sided polygon is a quadrilateral.
A 5-sided polygon is a pentagon. A 6-sided polygon is a hexagon.
A 7-sided polygon is a heptagon. An 8-sided polygon is an octagon.
A 9-sided polygon is a nonagon. A 10-sided polygon is a decagon.

A regular polygon has all its sides equal and all its angles equal.

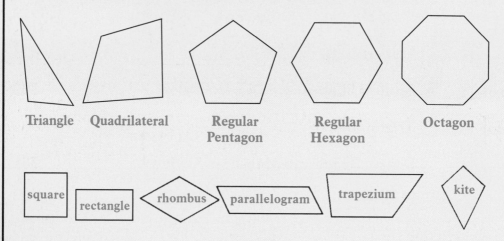

Triangle   Quadrilateral   Regular Pentagon   Regular Hexagon   Octagon

square   rectangle   rhombus   parallelogram   trapezium   kite

Some of the properties of these special quadrilaterals are shown in the following table.

	Square	Rhombus	Rectangle	Parallelogram	Kite	Trapezium
one pair of opposite sides parallel	√	√	√	√		√
two pairs of opposite sides parallel	√	√	√	√		
all sides equal	√	√				
opposite sides equal	√	√	√	√		
all angles equal	√		√			
opposite angles equal	√	√	√	√		
diagonals equal	√		√			
diagonals bisect each other	√	√	√	√		
diagonals perpendicular	√	√			√	
diagonals bisect the angles	√	√				

continued . . .

. . . from previous page

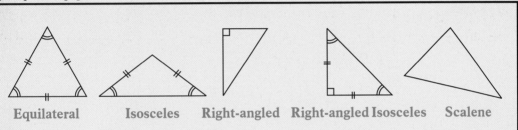

Equilateral   Isosceles   Right-angled   Right-angled Isosceles   Scalene

ANGLES

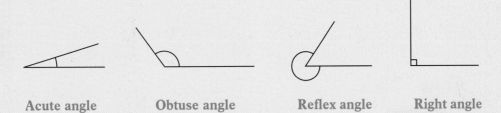

Acute angle   Obtuse angle   Reflex angle   Right angle

Angles made with Intersecting Lines

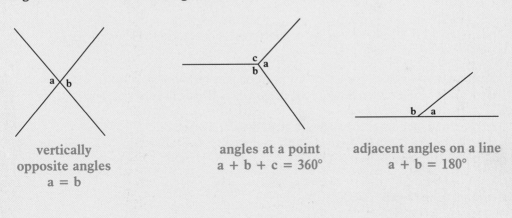

vertically
opposite angles
a = b

angles at a point
a + b + c = 360°

adjacent angles on a line
a + b = 180°

Angles made with Parallel Lines

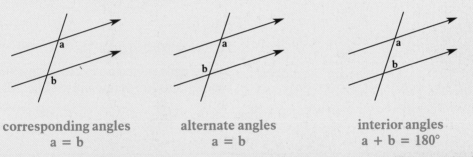

corresponding angles
a = b

alternate angles
a = b

interior angles
a + b = 180°

continued . . .

. . . *from previous page*

Triangles

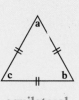

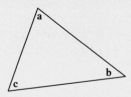
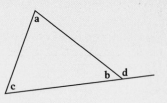

equilateral
a = b = c

isosceles
b = c

interior angles
a + b + c = 180°

exterior angle
d = a + c

Angles of a Polygon

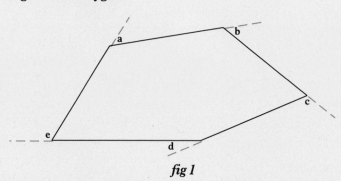

fig 1

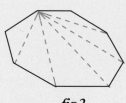

fig 2

The sum of the **exterior angles** of any polygon is equal to 360°. Hence in *fig 1*
a + b + c + d + e = 360°.

The sum of the **interior angles** of any polygon may be found as follows.

Step 1 From one vertex, draw all the diagonals to divide the polygon into triangles – see *fig 2*.

Step 2 Find the sum of the angles in all of these triangles.

For instance, *fig 2* can be divided into 6 triangles. Hence the sum of the interior angles of this 8-sided polygon is 6 × 180° = 1080°.

Bearings from North

Bearings from North are always given as 3 digits.
To find the bearing of A from B proceed as follows.

Step 1 Join AB.

Step 2 Draw a North line from B.

Step 3 Measure the angle (in a *clockwise* direction) between this North line and the line AB.

In this diagram, the bearing of A from B is 342°.

continued . . .

CONGRUENCE

Congruent shapes are the same size and the same shape. Corresponding lengths are equal; corresponding angles are equal. In congruent 3-D shapes, corresponding faces are identical.

SYMMETRY

A line of symmetry (**axis of symmetry**) divides a 2-D shape into two congruent shapes.
A plane of symmetry divides a 3-D shape into two congruent shapes.
A shape has reflective symmetry if it has a line or a plane of symmetry.
A shape has rotational symmetry if it coincides with itself more than once when it is rotated a complete turn about some point. The point about which it is rotated is called the centre of rotational symmetry. The number of times the shape coincides with itself during one complete turn is called the order of rotational symmetry.

The total order of symmetry of a shape is the sum of the order of rotational symmetry and the number of axes of symmetry.

TRANSFORMATIONS

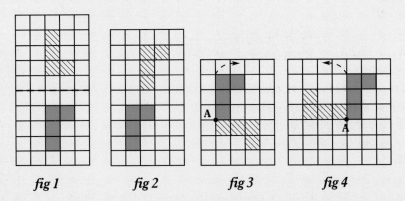

fig 1   *fig 2*   *fig 3*   *fig 4*

fig 1 illustrates a reflection (or **flip movement**). The red shape has been reflected in the dotted line to the shaded shape. The dotted line is called the mirror line.

fig 2 illustrates a translation (or **straight movement**). The red shape has been translated 1 square to the right and 4 squares up to the shaded shape. This translation is described by the vector $\begin{pmatrix} 1 \\ 4 \end{pmatrix}$

fig 3 and *fig 4* illustrate rotation (or **turning movement**). In *fig 3* the red shape has been rotated clockwise about A, through $\frac{1}{4}$ turn or 1 right angle. In *fig 4* the red shape has been rotated anticlockwise about A, through $\frac{1}{4}$ turn.

continued . . .

. . . from previous page

A shape is **tessellated,** if, when it is translated or reflected or rotated, it completely fills a space leaving no gaps.

The **scale factor** of an **enlargement** can be found by taking the ratio of the length of a side on the image shape to the length of the corresponding side on the original shape.

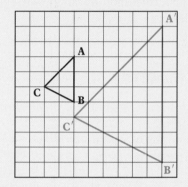

For instance, in the diagram, ABC has been enlarged to $A'B'C'$. Scale factor = $\dfrac{\text{length of } A'B'}{\text{length of } AB}$ = 3.

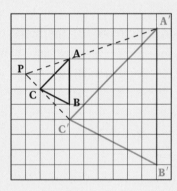

This diagram shows how the **centre of enlargement** can be found. The steps needed to find the centre of enlargement in this case are:

Step 1 Join A' and A.

Step 2 Join C' and C.

Step 3 Extend the lines $A'A$ and $C'C$. The point P, where these lines meet, is the centre of enlargement.

This diagram shows how to draw an enlargement of the triangle PQR, scale factor 2, centre of enlargement C. Beginning with just the point C and the triangle PQR we proceed as follows:

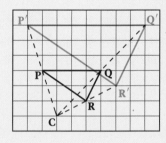

Step 1 Join C to P, C to Q and C to R.

Step 2 Extend the line CP to P' so that the length of CP' = twice the length of CP.

Step 3 Extend the line CQ to Q' so that the length of CQ' = twice the length of CQ.

Step 4 Extend the line CR to R' so that the length of CR' = twice the length of CR.

Step 5 Join P', Q' and R' to form the image triangle $P'Q'R'$.

continued . . .

. . . from previous page

If the scale factor is greater than 1, the image is larger than the original.

If the scale factor is between 0 and 1, the image is smaller than the original — see the diagram below where ABC has been enlarged, centre P, scale factor $\frac{1}{2}$.

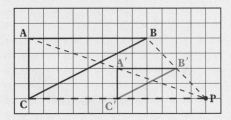

PYTHAGORAS' THEOREM

In a right-angled triangle, the longest side (the side opposite the right angle) is called the **hypotenuse.**

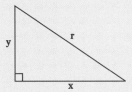

Pythagoras' Theorem: $r^2 = x^2 + y^2$ (In a right-angled triangle, the square on the hypotenuse equals the sum of the squares on the other two sides.)

MEASURES

Metric Measures

length	km	hm	Dm	**m**	dm	cm	mm
capacity	k*l*	h*l*	D*l*	*l*	d*l*	c*l*	m*l*
mass	kg	hg	Dg	**g**	dg	cg	mg

Each unit on the table is 10 times as large as the unit immediately to its right. The relationships between the metric units in common use are as follows.

continued . . .

. . . from previous page

Length	**Capacity**	**Mass**
1km = 1000m	1l = 1000ml	1kg = 1000g
1m = 1000mm	1ml = 1cm³ (1c.c.)	1g = 1000mg
1m = 100cm		1 tonne = 1000kg
1cm = 10mm		

Imperial Measure and Metric Measure

Some imperial units still in common use and the relationships between these units are as follows.

Length	**Capacity**	**Mass**
1 mile = 1760 yards	1 gallon = 8 pints	1 ton = 160 stone
1 yard = 3 feet		1 stone = 14 lb
1 foot = 12 inches		1 lb = 16oz

Rough approximations between imperial and metric units are:

1kg is about $2\frac{1}{4}$ lb, 1 litre is about $1\frac{3}{4}$ pints, 1 inch is about $2\frac{1}{2}$ cm,

5 miles is about 8km, 1m is a little longer than 3 feet.

Compound Measures

average speed = $\dfrac{\text{distance travelled}}{\text{time taken}}$ $\left(v = \dfrac{s}{t}\right)$ Units for speed are km/h, m/s, mph.

density = $\dfrac{\text{mass}}{\text{volume}}$ $\left(d = \dfrac{m}{v}\right)$ Units for density are g/cm³, kg/m³.

On a distance/time graph, distance is on the vertical axis, time is on the horizontal axis.
The slope of the graph gives the speed.
The steeper the slope of the graph, the greater the speed.

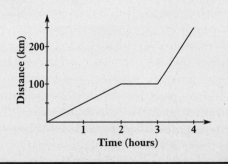

continued . . .

. . . *from previous page*

Possible Error in a Measurement

The maximum possible error in a measurement is half a unit. That is, a measurement given to the nearest mm has a possible error of 0·5mm, a measurement given to the nearest tenth of a second has a possible error of half of one-tenth of a second i.e. 0·05sec. For instance, a distance given as 289km to the nearest km could be between 288·5km and 289·5km.

AREA, PERIMETER, VOLUME

The formulae for the area of some common shapes are given below.

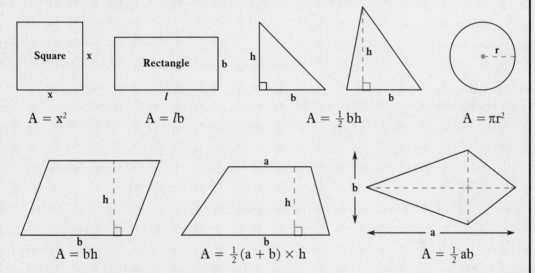

$$A = x^2 \qquad A = l\text{b} \qquad A = \tfrac{1}{2}\,\text{bh} \qquad A = \pi r^2$$

$$A = \text{bh} \qquad A = \tfrac{1}{2}(a + b) \times h \qquad A = \tfrac{1}{2}\,\text{ab}$$

Common metric units for land area are the hectare (ha) and square kilometre (km²). The hectare is derived from the unit of land measure, the are.

Some small land areas, such as building plots, are measured in m².

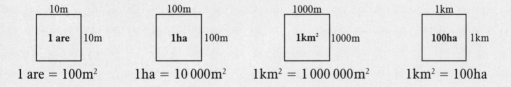

1 are = 100m²   1ha = 10 000m²   1km² = 1 000 000m²   1km² = 100ha

The acre is an imperial unit used for land areas. The approximate relationship between acres and hectares is **1ha = 2·5 acres.**

The perimeter is the distance right around the outside. The perimeter of a circle is called the circumference. The formula for the circumference of a circle is $C = 2\pi r$ or $C = \pi d$; r is the radius and d is the diameter of the circle, the value of π to 3 d.p. is 3·142.

continued . . .

. . . *from previous page*

The formulae for the **volume** of some common shapes are given below.

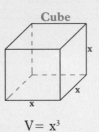

Cube

$V = x^3$

Cuboid

$V = l bh$

Cylinder

$V = \pi r^2 h$

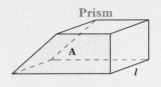

Prism

$V = Al$ where A is the area of a cross-section

LOCUS

The **locus** of an object is the set of all possible positions that this object can occupy. The path of an object, moving according to some rule, is the locus of the object. Some well known loci are shown below.

1. The locus of a point which is a constant distance from a fixed point is a circle.

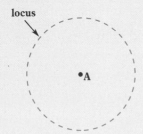

2. The locus of a point which is a constant distance from a fixed line is a pair of parallel lines.

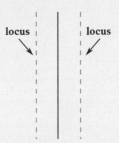

3. The locus of a point which is equidistant from two fixed points is the mediator (perpendicular bisector) of the line joining the fixed points.

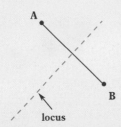

4. The locus of a point which is equidistant from two intersecting lines is the pair of lines which bisect the angles between the fixed lines.

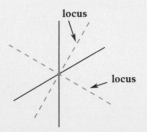

continued . . .

. . . *from previous page*

Compass Constructions

The following diagrams show **the construction of the bisector of the line BC.**

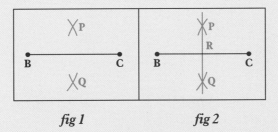

fig 1   *fig 2*

Step 1   Open out the compass so the length on the compass is a little more than half the length of the line BC. Keep this length on the compass throughout.

Step 2   With compass point firstly on B and then on C, draw arcs to meet at P and Q – see **fig 1.**

Step 3   Draw the line through P and Q – see **fig 2.** This line is the required bisector of the line BC.

Note   The point R, where PQ meets BC, is the **mid-point** of the line BC.

The following diagrams show **the construction of the line through A that is perpendicular to the line BC.**

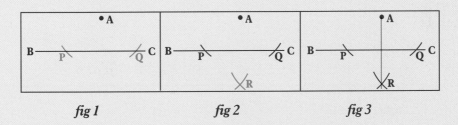

fig 1   *fig 2*   *fig 3*

Step 1   Open out the compass to any reasonable length. This length should be such that when the compass point is placed at A two arcs can be drawn that will cross BC. Keep this length on the compass throughout.

Step 2   With compass point on A, draw two arcs to meet BC at P and Q – see **fig 1.**

Step 3   With compass point firstly on P, then on Q, draw two arcs to meet at R – see **fig 2.**

Step 4   Join AR – see **fig 3.** AR is the required line.

continued . . .

. . . from previous page

The following diagrams show the construction of the line through A that is parallel to the line BC.

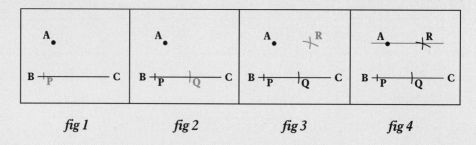

| *fig 1* | *fig 2* | *fig 3* | *fig 4* |

Step 1   Mark any point P on BC – see *fig 1*.

Step 2   Open out the compass to the length AP. Keep this length on the compass throughout.

Step 3   With compass point on P, draw an arc to meet BC at Q – see *fig 2*.

Step 4   With compass point firstly on Q and then on A, draw two arcs to meet at R – see *fig 3*.

Step 5   Draw the line through A and R – see *fig 4*. This is the required line.

The following diagrams show the construction of the bisector of the angle P.

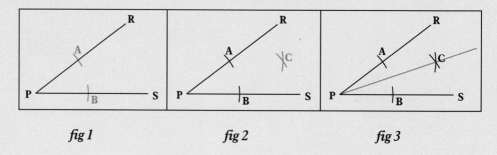

| *fig 1* | *fig 2* | *fig 3* |

Step 1   Open out the compass to any reasonable length. This length should be less than the length of either arm (PR or PS) of the angle P. Keep this length on the compass throughout.

Step 2   With compass point on P, draw arcs to meet PR and PS at A and B – see *fig 1*.

Step 3   With compass point firstly on A and then on B, draw two arcs to meet at C – see *fig 2*.

Step 4   Draw the line from P through C – see *fig 3*. This line is the required bisector of the angle P.

REVISION EXERCISE

1. Find the missing numbers.

    (a) 384mm = ... cm   (b) 2·4km = ... m   (c) 1·74*l* = ... m*l*

    (d) 194m = ... km   (e) 0·7t = ... kg   (f) 2825g = ... kg

2. (a) Trace this diagram into your book.

    (b) Through E, construct the line that is parallel to BC. Label
         as G the point where this line meets DC.
         Through F, construct the line that is perpendicular to
         DC. Label as H the point where this line meets AB.
         Colour, or shade heavily, the rectangle EGFH so that
         none of the original sloping lines can be seen in this
         rectangle.

    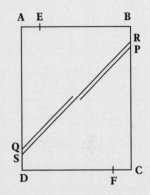

    (c) Does P appear to be on the same line as S?

    (d) Is P on the same line as S?

3. Melanie is doing a survey on oak trees. She measures the circumference of the trunk of one
    tree as 66·2cm. If Melanie's measurement is correct to the nearest tenth of a centimetre find

    (a) the greatest possible circumference

    (b) the least possible circumference of this tree.

4. Copy this diagram.

    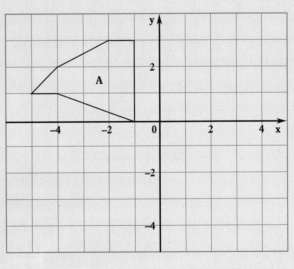

    (a) A is reflected in the x-axis to B.
         Draw B on your diagram. Write
         down the coordinates of the
         vertices of B.

    (b) A is rotated about the point
         (−1, 0), through a $\frac{1}{4}$ turn
         clockwise, to C. Draw C on
         your diagram. Write down the
         coordinates of the vertices of C.

    (c) B is reflected in the line
         x = −1 to D. Draw D on your
         diagram. Write down the
         coordinates of the vertices of D.

    (d) Describe the transformation which would map A onto D.

5. (a) Find the value of x.

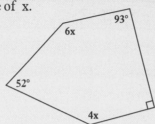

    (b) Each exterior angle of a regular polygon is equal to 36°. How many sides does this polygon have?

6. Annabel jogs from A to B, across the centre of a park. B is on a bearing of 146° from A.
    From B, Annabel jogs due West for 2km, then due North for 3km. She is then back at A.

    (a) Use Pythagoras' Theorem to find the distance AB.

    (b) Find the size of angle B in the triangle.

    (c) What is the bearing of A from B?

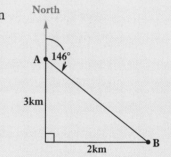

7. (i) This shape is drawn on "square dot" paper.

    (a) What is the name of this shape?

    (b) What is the size of angle A (the marked angle)?

    (c) What other angles are equal to angle A?

    (d) Is this a regular shape? Explain your answer.

    (e) What is the order of rotational symmetry of this shape?

    (ii)

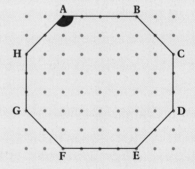

    If the length of AB is 8cm, find

    (a) the lengths of the diagonals of the kite DERQ

    (b) the area of the kite DERQ

    (c) the area of the parallelogram ABPH.

    (iii) Two triangles can be drawn by joining B, P, Q and C, D, Q. Are these triangles congruent? Explain your answer.

8.

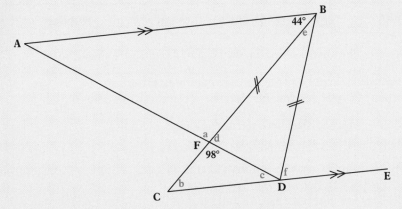

The lines AB and CE are parallel; BF = BD.
Find the size of the angles marked a, b, c, d, e and f.

9.

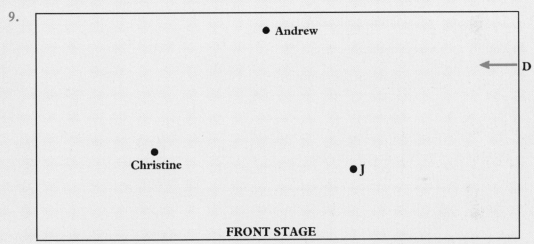

Scale 1cm represents 2m

This diagram represents an outdoor stage. Andrew and Christine are standing on the stage when John comes onto the stage at D.
John walks in the direction shown by the arrow. He walks until he is the same distance from Andrew and the chair at J. He then stops.

(a) Use your compass and ruler to construct the set of points which are the same distance from Andrew and the chair at J. Hence mark the point where John stops. Label this point as P.

(b) From P, John walks in a straight line to the chair at J. How far is it from P to J?

(c) Andrew now walks towards the front of the stage in such a way that he is always the same distance from Christine and John. Use your compass and ruler to construct the path Andrew takes.

(d) Andrew stops when he is 6m from Christine.
Use your compass to construct the set of points that are 6m from Christine. Hence mark the point where Andrew stops. How far has Andrew walked?

10.

| **12** | 74 miles | **13** | 51 miles | **14** | 45 miles | **15** |

The distances between motorway service areas 12, 13, 14 and 15 are shown.

(a) Roger stops at service area 13 and again at service area 15.
About how many kilometres does he travel between these two stops?

(b) Anne took 36 minutes to travel between service areas 14 and 15.
In mph, what was Anne's average speed?

(c) The capacity of the petrol tank of Sandhya's car is 60 litres. The petrol consumption
rate of this car is 17km/*l*. Petrol costs 51p per litre.
Sandhya fills her tank at service area 12 and again at service area 15. How much does it
cost her for the petrol she buys at service area 15?

11. The diagonals of a rhombus measure 10cm and 24cm.

Find (a) the area of the rhombus

(b) the perimeter of the rhombus.

12.

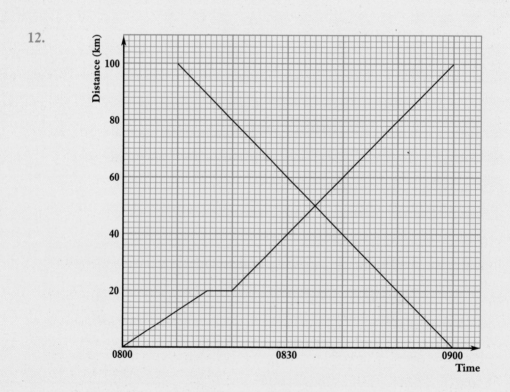

302

A train leaves Alton at 0800 hours and travels to Wayfield.
Another train leaves Wayfield arriving at Alton at 0900.

(a) At what time did the train from Wayfield leave?

(b) How far is it from Alton to Wayfield?

(c) At what time do these trains pass?

(d) How far from Wayfield do they pass?

(e) How many times did the train from Alton stop?

(f) What was the average speed of the train from Wayfield?

(g) What was the average speed of the train from Alton?

13.

(a) Find the area of the base of this cylindrical soup tin.

(b) If this tin is filled to the top, how many ml of soup does it hold? (Answer to the nearest 10ml.)

(c) The soup is poured into a microwave container, shaped as shown. Estimate the depth of soup in this container.

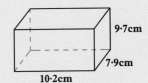

(d) Calculate the depth of soup in the microwave container. (Answer to the nearest mm.) Use your estimate as a check.

14. Aaron's average speed for a road race was 15 km/h. Peter's average speed for this race was 5 m/sec.
Who finished first, Aaron or Peter?

15.

A picnic party is translated from the mainland to Meg Island.
(i) If the boat leaves from P, find the vector of translation if it lands at
    (a) A (b) C (c) D
    (d) B.
(ii) On the return journey the picnic party lands at P. Where did they leave from if the vector of the translation is $\binom{2}{-3}$?

16. Copy this diagram.

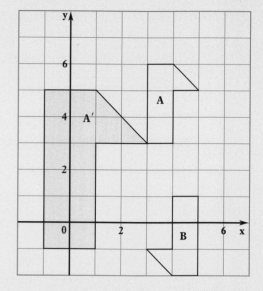

(a) A′ is an enlargement of A.
What is the scale factor of this enlargement?
What are the coordinates of the centre of this enlargement?

(b) A′ is enlarged, centre (–1, 3), scale factor $\frac{1}{2}$ to A″.
Draw A″ on your diagram.
Write down the coordinates of the vertices of A″.

(c) B is a rotation of A. The angle of this rotation is:

A. 90°   B. 360°   C. 180°   D. 270°

17.

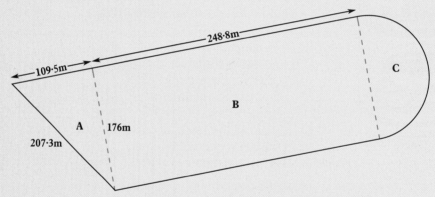

This sketch shows the shape and dimensions of Helford Common. C is a semicircle, A is a right-angled triangle and B is a rectangle.

(a) Susie estimates the area of A as follows: $\frac{1}{2} \times 100 \times 200 = 10000$m².
Estimate the area of B and the area of C.

(b) Calculate the area of Helford Common, to the nearest 10m². Use your estimate as a check.

(c) Susie wrote the area of Helford Common in hectares, to 2 d.p. What answer should she have written?

(d) About how many acres is Helford Common? (Answer to the nearest acre.)

(e) Each day, Susie jogs around Helford Common twice. About how many kilometres does she jog each day?

18. Shirdia wanted to find the surface area of a circular ice-skating rink. She decided she could do this if she measured the circumference.
Explain how Shirdia could then calculate the area.

19. Deborah's car uses oil at the rate of 1 litre per 1600km.

    (a) How much oil does this car use on an 80km journey? (Answer in m*l*.)

    (b) About how many pints is 1000m*l*?

    (c) About how many miles is 1600km?

    (d) To the nearest half of a pint, how many pints of oil will Deborah's car use in 5000 miles of motoring?

    (e) What does 1 litre of oil weigh if its density is $1 \cdot 8g/cm^3$?

20.

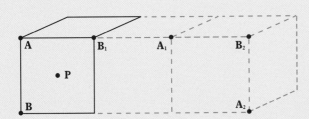

Jack moves a wool bale by rolling it along the ground, as shown by the dotted lines. The wool bale is a cube. A_1, B_1 give the positions of A and B after it has been rolled once; A_2, B_2 give the positions after it has been rolled twice.

Sketch the locus of

(a) P, the midpoint of the front face

(b) the point B.

21. (a) Make a sketch of this isosceles triangle.
    On your sketch, draw the axis of symmetry.

    (b) Use your sketch to calculate the area of the triangle.
    (**Hint:** You will need to use Pythagoras' Theorem.)

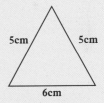

    (c)

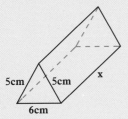

The volume of this chocolate packet is $120cm^3$.
What is the length of the packet? (x in the diagram.)

    (d) The net for the packet in (c) is cut from a piece of rectangular cardboard as shown in this sketch.
    Show that $104cm^2$ of this cardboard is wasted.

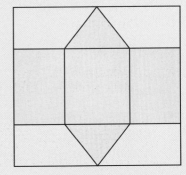

22.

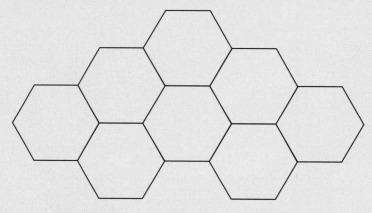

These shapes are built from 4 cubes. On isometric paper, draw another three shapes which could be built from 4 cubes. Each shape must *not* be a rotation or reflection of any of the other shapes.

23. Rebecca and Kylie are making patchwork quilts. They know they could make them by cutting material in the shape of regular hexagons. They draw the following sketch.

(a) They decide to experiment with different shapes. The first shape they experiment with is an octagon. They decide that octagons won't tessellate. Are they correct?

(b) They then decide to use octagons with another shape as a "filler". Could they use a square as a "filler"?

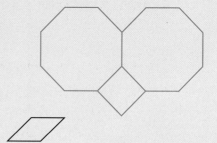

(c) Could they use a combination of octagons, and the rhombus shown?

(d) Could they use a square as a "filler" with the hexagons? If not, what shape could they use as a "filler"?

24. The distance from Carmarthen to Swansea is approximately 30 miles.
8 kilometres is approximately 5 miles.
Use this information to calculate the distance from Carmarthen to Swansea in kilometres.

WJEC

25. Peter needs 18.6m of electrical cable. Fermats store sells the cable for £1·17 per metre.

(a) How much will Peter have to pay for the cable?

Paul has a shorter piece of cable.
The diagram shows how Paul measured its length.

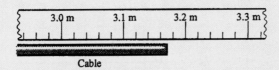

Cable

(b) How long is Paul's piece of cable?
   Give your answer to 2 decimal places.

Paul needs only 2.74m of this cable.
He cuts 2.74m from his piece of cable.

(c) How long is the remaining piece?   **SEG**

26. *In this question take* $\pi = 3\cdot14$ *or use the*
   π *button on your calculator.*

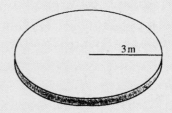

The top of a conference table is a circle
with radius 3 metres.

(a) Calculate the area of the top of the table.

(b) The edge of the table is bound by a strip of stainless steel.
   Calculate the length of the strip.   **WJEC**

27. Draw four more shapes to continue the tessellation.

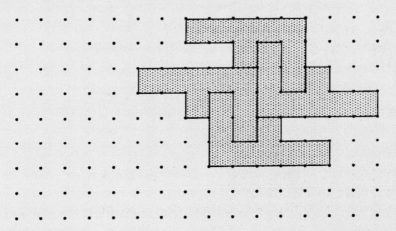

SEG

28. Complete this table. The names of the quadrilaterals may be chosen from the following list: square, parallelogram, rhombus, kite and trapezium.

Name of quadrilateral	Diagonals always cut at right angles	Number of axes of symmetry	Order of rotational symmetry
RECTANGLE			
	YES		2
		0	2
	YES	1	
			4

NICCEA

29. ABC is an equilateral triangle.
ACD is an isosceles triangle.
Angle BCD = 40°.

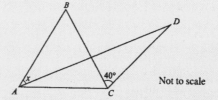

Not to scale

Work out the size of angle *x* giving a reason for your answer.

SEG

30. (a) Pauline has made part of her garden into a lawn. The lawn has parallel sides measuring 15m and 27m. These parallel sides are 9m apart. What is the area of the lawn?

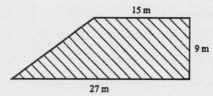

(b) Pauline is building a greenhouse. The base, *PQRS* of the greenhouse should be a rectangle measuring 2.6m by 1.4m.

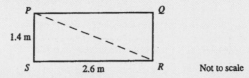

Not to scale

To check the base is rectangular Pauline has to measure the diagonal *PR*.

(i) Calculate the length of *PR* when the base is rectangular. You **must** show all your working.

(ii) When building the greenhouse Pauline finds angle *PSR* >90°. She measures *PR*. Which of the following statements is **true**?

X: *PR* is greater than it should be.
Y: *PR* is less than it should be.
Z: *PR* is the right length.

SEG

31. The travel graph illustrates the journeys of a bus and a cyclist.

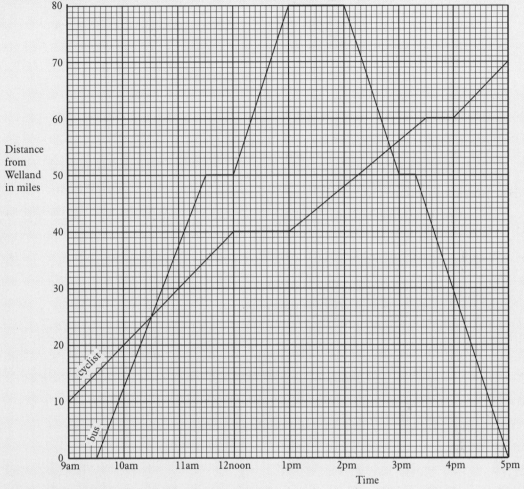

(a) When does the bus overtake the cyclist?

(b) How far does the cyclist travel?

(c) What is the average speed of the cyclist between 1 p.m. and 3.30 p.m.?

(d) When are the bus and the cyclist 50 miles apart? **MEG**

32. In each diagram shade one square to leave a net of a cube unshaded.

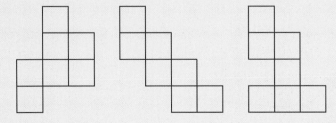

NICCEA

33. In the diagram, triangle ABC is mapped onto triangle $A'B'C'$.

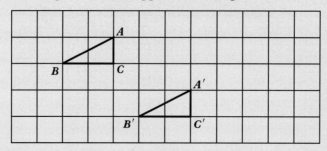

Describe fully the single transformation that maps ABC directly onto $A'B'C'$?　　**SEG**

34. Sandtown council wants to build a pavilion on a playing field.

They decided to site it at an equal distance from both gates and not more than 250m from the toilet block.

On the scale drawing below, make suitable constructions to locate the site.

Leave in your construction lines.

Show clearly where the pavilion can be built.

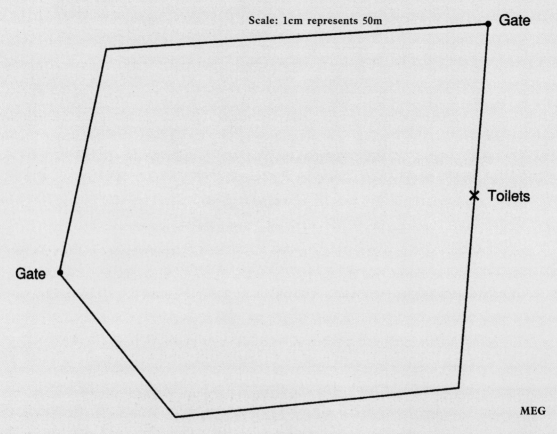

MEG

35. Here are some diagrams.
Put a tick (√) by any of these diagrams which have rotation symmetry or a cross (×) by any which do not have rotation symmetry.

   (a)   **(b)**   **(c)**   **(d)**

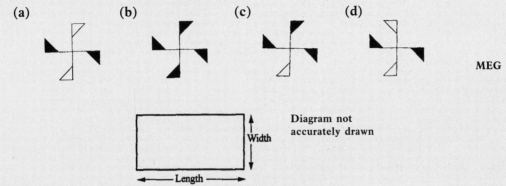

MEG

36.

Width

Length

Diagram not accurately drawn

Ceri wants to plant a rectangular lawn with area 40m².

The length of the lawn must be twice the width.

Ceri is trying to find the width by trial and improvement.

She records her results in a table.

Width (m)	Length = 2 × width (m)	area = length × width (m²)
4	8	32
5		

(a) Complete the second row of the table.

(b) Complete the table in order to find two closer estimates of the required width. ULEAC

37. During October, a central heating boiler was used, on average, for 4.5 hours per day.
During November, the same boiler was used, on average, for 5.8 hours per day.

(a) Calculate the total time for which the boiler was used during October and November.

(b) While it is being used the boiler uses 2.44 litres of oil per hour.
Calculate the amount of oil used during the two months, correct to the nearest litre.

(c) 900 litres of heating oil cost £173. Calculate:
    (i) the total cost of the oil used for the two months correct to the nearest pound,
    (ii) the mean (average) daily cost of oil used over the two months correct to the nearest penny.

(d) Show that the average daily cost in November was approximately 29% higher than the average daily cost in October. NICCEA

38. (a) The diagram shows a pair of parallel lines.
The lines marked with the arrows are parallel.
Work out the size of the angles marked $e°$, $f°$ and $g°$.

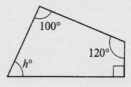

Diagram NOT
accurately drawn

(b) Work out the size of the angle marked $h°$.

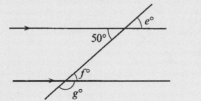

Diagram NOT
accurately drawn

ULEAC

39. A map of an island is shown.
At **H** there is a hotel and at **A** an airport.

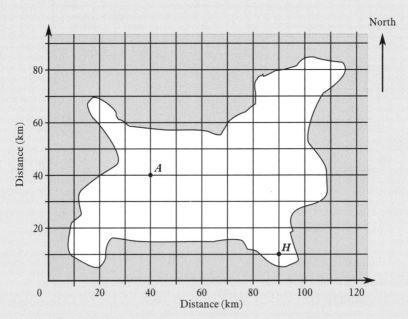

(a) A town, **T**, is due north of the hotel and on a bearing of 070° from the airport.
Mark the position of **T** on the map.

(b) Measure and write down the 3-figure bearing of **A** from **H**.

(c) Use Pythagoras' theorem to calculate the distance from **A** to **H**.
You must show your working.

SEG

312

40. This is a drawing of a crazy paving path. *PS* and *QR* are straight lines. The sides of the path are parallel, but the drawing is not to scale. Find the angles marked *a, b, c, d* and *e*. Show all your working and give a reason for each answer. The first one has already been done for you.

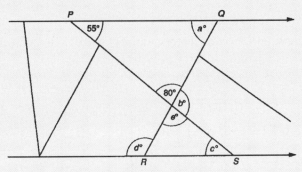

$a = 45$ because the angles of a triangle add up to $180°$.

$b = \ldots$ $c = \ldots$

because   because

$d = \ldots$ $e = \ldots$

because   because   **MEG**

41.

These diagrams show two views of a cube. Its faces have the letters **A, B, C, D, E, F** on them.

(a) Which letter is on the face opposite **A**?   **(b)** Which letter is on the face opposite **B**?

                                                            WJEC

42.

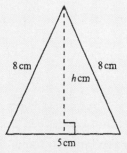

An isosceles triangle has sides 8cm, 8cm and 5cm. Use Pythagoras' Theorem to calculate the length of the height marked *h* on the diagram.   **NEAB**

43. A plan of a rectangular playing field is drawn using a scale of 1:2500.
The width of the field on the plan is 5cm.

(a) (i) Work out the real width of the field in centimetres.

(ii) Change your answer to metres.

The area of the field on the plan is 31·5cm².

(b) (i) Work out the length, in centimetres, of the playing field on the plan.

(ii) Work out the real length, in metres, of the playing field.

(iii) Work out the real area, in square metres, of the playing field.

ULEAC

44.

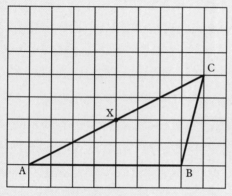

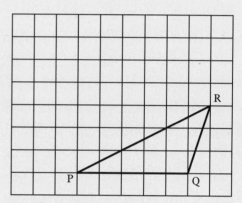

(a) In the diagram above, X is the mid-point of AC.

(i) Triangle ABC is rotated through 180° about X to give triangle CDA. Draw triangle CDA.

(ii) What name is given to all quadrilaterals of the type ABCD?

(b) Triangle PQR is reflected in PR to give triangle PSR. Draw triangle PSR.

(ii) What name is given to all quadrilaterals of the type PQRS?

MEG

45.

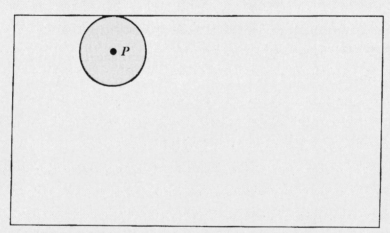

This diagram shows a wheel, centre *P*, inside a rectangular frame. The wheel rolls around the inside of the frame so that it is always touching the frame.

Draw the locus of the point *P*.

WJEC

46. The diagram represents a chocolate box in the shape of a pyramid.

The box has a square base and four triangular faces.

The net of the chocolate box is shown below.

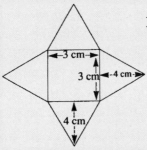

Diagram NOT accurately drawn

(a) Work out

(i) the area of the base,

(ii) the area of a triangular face,

(iii) the total surface area of the box.

Each net is cut from a square card of area 121 cm². Any card not used for the box is thrown away. *n* boxes are made.

(b) Write down a formula for the total area, A cm², of card which is thrown away.

(c) Draw an accurate net for the box.   **ULEAC**

47. A ball bearing has mass 0·44 pounds.

1 kg = 2·2 pounds.

(a) (i) Calculate the mass of the ball bearing in kilograms.

$$\text{Density} = \frac{\text{mass}}{\text{volume}}$$

(ii) When the mass of the ball bearing is measured in kg and the volume is measured in cm³, what are the units of the density?

(b) The volume of a container is given by the formula

$$V = 4L\,(3 - L)^2.$$

Using **Mass = Volume × Density** calculate the mass of the container when $L = 1·40$ cm, and 1 cm³ of the material has a mass of 0·160 kg.   **SEG**

48. The diagram shows a quadrilateral *ABCD*.
Lengths *AB* and *AD* are each 5m.
Lengths *CB* and *CD* are each 10m.
Angle *DAB* = 60°. Angle *ADC* = 136°.

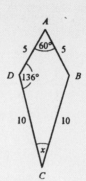

(a) Write down the length of *BD*.

(b) What is the mathematical name for this
quadrilateral?

(c) Calculate the value of angle *x*.   **SEG**

Not to scale

49.

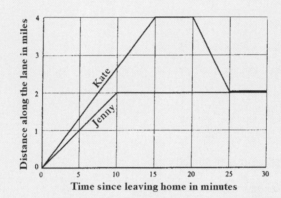

Two friends, Jenny and Kate, go for a bicycle ride down a long country lane. The graph
shows what happens in the first 30 minutes. Jenny's bicycle has a puncture after two miles.
Write an account of *Kate's* journey. Your account should include times, distances and
speeds.   **NEAB**

50.

The world long jump record was held by Bob Beamon for twenty years.
It stood at 8·90 metres.

$$\boxed{\begin{array}{l} 2\text{·}54\text{cm} = 1 \text{ inch,} \\ 12 \text{ inches} = 1 \text{ foot} \end{array}}$$

Convert 8·90 metres to feet and inches. Give your answer to the nearest half inch.   **MEG**

51. When you add a cube to the shaded place on the top of this solid ...

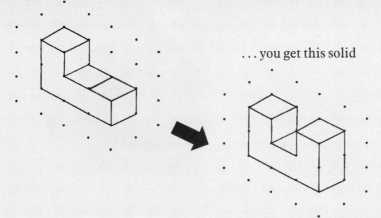

... you get this solid

Draw the solid you would get when you add a cube to **both** shaded places on this solid.

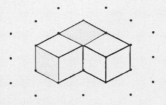

SEG

52. The parallelogram *ABCD* has vertices at (6, 3), (9, 3), (12, 9) and (9, 9) respectively.

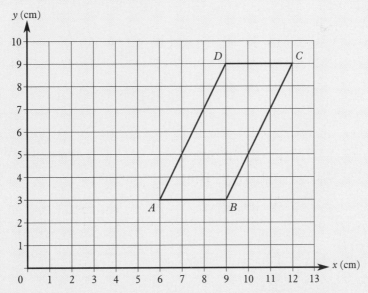

An enlargement scale factor $\frac{1}{3}$ and centre (0, 0) transforms parallelogram *ABCD* onto parallelogram *A'B'C'D'*.

(a) Draw the parallelogram *A'B'C'D'*.

(b) Calculate the area of the parallelogram *A'B'C'D'*.   **SEG**

53.

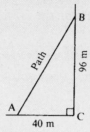

A and B are posts near to C, the corner of a park.

(a) Calculate the length of the straight path connecting A and B.

The triangle ACB is one lap. Gail starts at post A and jogs round and round the triangular lap ACB in an anti-clockwise direction.

(b) When Gail has jogged for 1 kilometre,

    (i) which lap will she be on?

    (ii) where will she be at that moment?

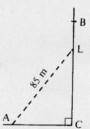

A litter bin, L, is attached to the park railings between B and C; it is 85m from A.

(c) Calculate the distance of the litter bin L from the post B.   **NICCEA**

54.

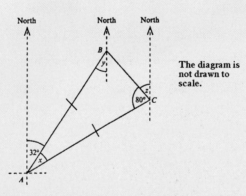

The diagram is not drawn to scale.

The diagram shows the positions of three places *A*, *B* and *C*. *AB* is the same length as *AC*.

(a) (i) Calculate the size of the angle marked *x*.

    (ii) Explain why the angle marked *y* is equal to 32°.

    (iii) Calculate the size of the angle marked *z*.

(b) Use your answers to **(a)** to calculate the bearing of

    (i) *C* from *A*,   **(ii)** *A* from *B*,   **(iii)** *B* from *C*.   **NEAB**

55.

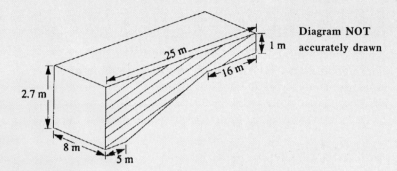

The diagram represents a swimming pool. The pool has vertical sides. The pool is 8m wide.

(a) Calculate the area of the shaded cross section.

The swimming pool is completely filled with water.

(b) Calculate the volume of water in the pool.

64m³ of water leaks out of the pool.

(c) Calculate the distance by which the water level falls. **ULEAC**

56.

Coffee Consumption
Kilograms per person, 1989

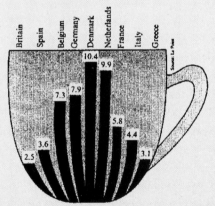

The diagram shows the average amount of coffee used in 1989 by people in various European countries.

(a) France has a population of 56.5 million. Calculate, in tonnes, the amount of coffee used in France in 1989. Give your answer correct to the nearest thousand tonnes.

(b) Hans lives alone in Denmark and in 1989 just happened to use the national average amount of coffee. Hans buys his coffee in 200g jars. Estimate how long such a jar lasted Hans in that year. **NICCEA**

57. At 0730 hours, a military aircraft flies over a beacon. It is 200km behind a civilian aircraft which is flying on the same heading but at a different height.

The military aircraft is flying at a fixed speed of 1200km/h.

The civilian aircraft is flying at a fixed speed of 800km/h.

Both aircraft are flying at constant heights.

On the grid below, draw distance/time graphs for each aircraft and use them to find the time at which the military aircraft overtakes the civilian aircraft.

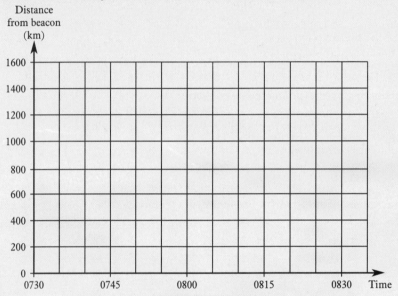

ULEAC

58.

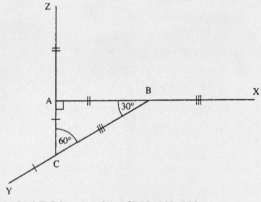

In the figure, the triangle ABC has angles of 30°, 60°, 90°.

Side AB is produced to X, making BX = BC.

Side BC is produced to Y, making CY = CA.

Side CA is produced to Z, making AZ = AB.

(i) B, A, Z are consecutive vertices of a regular figure. Name the figure.

(ii) A, C, Y are consecutive vertices of a regular figure. Name the figure.

(iii) C, B, X are consecutive vertices of a regular figure. How many sides has the figure?

NICCEA

59. This loaf of bread is cut into 30 slices, as shown.

Each slice is approximately the shape of a cuboid of width 10cm, length 11cm and depth 8mm.

(a) Calculate the volume of the loaf in cubic centimetres.

The same volume of bread is used to make a round loaf of length 24cm.

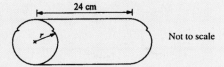

(b) What is the radius of the round loaf? Take π to be 3·14 or use the π key on your calculator.

SEG

60.

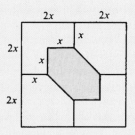

The diagram shows a square tile in which the pattern is symmetrical about both diagonals. Find the area of the *unshaded* part of the tile in terms of x.

NICCEA

Emmy Noether

Emmy Noether was born in Germany in 1882 and died in the USA in 1935.

Emmy was the only girl in her family. Her father was a professor of Mathematics. When Emmy was young, he recognised her mathematical ability and encouraged her to study mathematics.

In 1907, Emmy gained a Ph.D. from the University of Erlangen. She wished to teach at a University but had difficulty getting a job. At the beginning of this century, it was not acceptable for a woman to teach mathematics at this level. From 1913 to 1915 she occasionally taught her father's students. From 1915 to 1919 she lectured, on a casual basis, at the University of Göttingen. Some of the other mathematicians, who recognised her mathematical and teaching ability, strongly supported her application to become a permanent member of the staff. The university authorities were concerned. It is said that one of them voiced this concern as *"What will our soldiers think when they return from the war and find they are expected to learn at the feet of a woman?"* In 1919 she overcame this opposition and was made a permanent lecturer. However her salary was low compared with that of the male mathematicians.

Emmy Noether was a Jew. Because of this, she was forced by the Nazis to leave the University of Göttingen in 1933. She went to the USA to become a professor of mathematics at Bryn Mawr College. She also conducted research at the Institute for Advanced Study at Princeton. Her talents as a mathematician and a teacher were fully appreciated in the USA. She had been in the USA for less than 2 years when she died after an operation for cancer.

Emmy Noether specialised in algebra and became known as one of the most creative mathematicians of her time. She developed mathematics which is used in modern physics; in particular, in the theory of relativity. Much of her work was on non-commutative algebra. In this algebra, the order in which numbers are added or multiplied affects the answer. She published 37 papers on mathematics.

Many of Emmy Noether's colleagues and students developed important mathematical theories from ideas of hers. She was an enthusiastic and lively teacher. It has been reported that her hair, which she wore up, often fell down when she became excited during her lecturing.

After her death, the *New York Times* published a tribute to her. In this, Einstein wrote, *"In the judgement of the most competent living mathematicians, Fraulein Noether was the most significant mathematical genius thus far produced since the higher education of women began"*.

based on an article from the book "Women Sum It Up" – Hazard Press

Dimensions

DIMENSIONS for LENGTH, AREA, VOLUME

The perimeter of this rectangle is 16m. The unit of measurement used is metres (m).
The area of this rectangle is 15m². The unit of measurement used is square metres (m²).

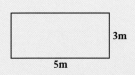

The volume of this cuboid is 60m³. The unit of measurement used is cubic metres (m³).

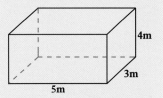

That is, for perimeter the unit used is m
        for area the unit used is m²
        for volume the unit used is m³.
These units are all related. They all refer to the unit of length, m.

We say, the dimension of perimeter is length (L)
        the dimension of area is length × length (L²)
        the dimension of volume is length × length × length (L³)

DISCUSSION EXERCISE 13:1

- The formula for the area of a circle is $A = \pi r^2$.
  If r is measured in metres, what unit of measurement is used for A?
  What is the dimension of r? What is the dimension of A?

  Consider πr^2. This is a number (π) × a length (r) × a length (r). What can you say about the dimension of π? Discuss.

- Consider the formula for the circumference of a circle, $C = 2\pi r$.
  What is the dimension of r? What is the dimension of C? What can you say about the dimension of the number 2? Discuss.

We can use dimensions to check whether a formula is reasonable.

Example   Garth cannot remember if the formula for the area of a circle is $A = 2\pi r$ or $A = \pi d$ or $A = \pi^2 r$ or $A = \pi r^2$. He checks the dimensions of these formulae as follows.

$2\pi r$	number × number × length	Dimension is L
πd	number × length	Dimension is L
$\pi^2 r$	number × number × length	Dimension is L
πr^2	number × length × length	Dimension is L²

Garth then decides that the area formula must be $A = \pi r^2$ since the dimension of area is L^2.

Worked Example   This diagram represents a piece of cheese. Which of the following expressions could be an expression for

(a) the surface area   (b) the volume?

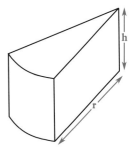

$\frac{1}{4}\pi rh + rh^2$ $\frac{1}{8}\pi r + 2h$

$\frac{1}{8}\pi r^2 h$ $\frac{1}{8}\pi r^2 h + \frac{1}{4}\pi rh$

$2rh + \frac{1}{4}\pi r$ $\frac{1}{4}\pi r^2 + 2rh + \frac{1}{4}\pi rh$

Answer   Dimension of $\frac{1}{4}\pi rh + rh^2$ is $L^2 + L^3$.

Dimension of $\frac{1}{8}\pi r + 2h$ is $L + L$; i.e. L.

Dimension of $\frac{1}{8}\pi r^2 h$ is L^3. This could be the expression for the volume.

Dimension of $\frac{1}{8}\pi r^2 h + \frac{1}{4}\pi rh$ is $L^3 + L^2$.

Dimension of $2rh + \frac{1}{4}\pi r$ is $L^2 + L$.

Dimension of $\frac{1}{4}\pi r^2 + 2rh + \frac{1}{4}\pi rh$ is $L^2 + L^2 + L^2$; i.e. L^2. This could be an expression for the surface area.

The answers are then   (a) $\frac{1}{4}\pi r^2 + 2rh + \frac{1}{4}\pi rh$ (b) $\frac{1}{8}\pi r^2 h$.

EXERCISE 13:2

1. Tariq worked out that the volume of this shape was given by $V = \frac{7}{3}\pi r^2 l^2$.

   Use dimensions to show that this formula cannot be correct.

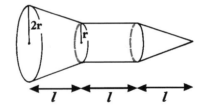

2. Angela wrote down the formula $A = \frac{4}{3}\pi r^3$ for the surface area of a sphere. Use dimensions to explain why this formula cannot be correct.

3. This diagram represents a running track. Which of the following could be an expression for
   (a) the perimeter   (b) the area?

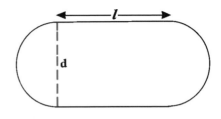

   $2l + \pi dl$ $dl + \frac{1}{4}\pi d^2$ $2\pi d^2 l + 2l^2 d$

   $2l + \pi d$ $\frac{1}{4}\pi d^2 + d^2 l$

4. Which of the following could be a formula for the volume of this glass?

   $V = \frac{26}{27}\pi^2 rh$ $V = \frac{26}{27}\pi r^2 h$

   $V = \frac{1}{9}\pi r^2 h - \frac{1}{27}\pi rh$ $V = \frac{26}{27}\pi rh$

   $V = \frac{1}{3}\pi^2 rh + \frac{1}{27}\pi r^2 h$

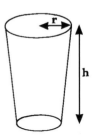

5.

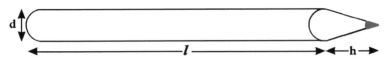

   Which of the following could be a formula for the volume of this pencil?

   $V = \frac{1}{4}\pi dl + \frac{1}{12}\pi d^2 h$ $V = \pi^2 dl^2 + \frac{1}{12}\pi d^2 l^2$

   $V = \frac{1}{4}\pi d^2 l + \frac{1}{12}\pi dh$ $V = \frac{1}{4}\pi^2 d^2 l + \pi dh$

   $V = \frac{1}{4}\pi d^2 l + \frac{1}{12}\pi^2 dh$ $V = \frac{1}{4}\pi d^2 l + \frac{1}{12}\pi d^2 h$

6.

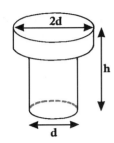

A piece of equipment in a workshop is shaped like this. Which of the following could be an expression for

(a) the surface area

(b) the volume?

$\frac{1}{4}\pi(8d + 5h)$ $\frac{1}{4}\pi d(8d + 5h)$ $\frac{1}{4}\pi dh(5\pi + 8d)$ $\frac{7}{16}\pi d^2 h^2$

$\frac{7}{16}\pi d + 5\pi dh$ $\frac{7}{16}\pi d^2 h$ $\frac{7}{16}\pi dh + \pi d$

7.

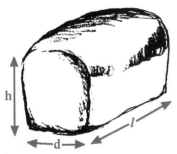

$V = \frac{1}{2}dl(2h - d) + \frac{1}{8}\pi d^2 l$

$V = \frac{1}{2}d(l + h) + \frac{1}{8}\pi dl$

$V = \frac{1}{2}l(2h - d) + \frac{1}{8}\pi d^2 l$

$V = \frac{1}{2}dl(2h - d) + \frac{1}{8}\pi d^2 l^2$

A bakery bakes bread of this shape. Which of the formulae in the list could be a formula for the volume of this bread? Is there more than one possible formula in this list?

8. This drawing represents a rubbish tin. Which of the following could be an expression for

(a) the surface area   (b) the volume?

$6ah + \frac{3}{2}\sqrt{3}\,a$ $\frac{3}{2}\sqrt{3}\,a$ $\frac{3}{2}\sqrt{3}\,a^2 h^2$

$\frac{3}{2}\sqrt{3}\,a^2 h^2 + 6a$ $\frac{3}{2}\sqrt{3}\,a^2 h$ $6ah + \frac{3}{2}\sqrt{3}\,a^2$

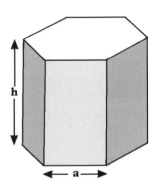

9. Which of the following expressions could be for (a) perimeter

(b) area

(c) volume?

$\pi r + \frac{1}{2}r$ $4\pi r^2 h$ πrl $\frac{1}{4}\pi d^2$ $\frac{1}{3}\pi r^2 h$

$\pi r(r + l)$ $r(\pi + 3)$ $\frac{4}{3}\pi r^3$ $\frac{1}{3}\pi r$ $\frac{4}{3}\pi r^2$

$\pi r + 4l$ $4\pi rl$ $4l^2 h$ $3lh^2$ $\frac{1}{3}\pi rh$

Review 1 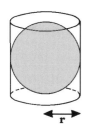 A ball is placed in a hollow cylinder, as shown in this diagram. Michael worked out a formula for the space not occupied by the ball. His formula was $V = \frac{2}{3}\pi r^2$.

Use dimensions to explain why Michael's formula cannot be correct.

Review 2 This diagram represents a test-tube.
Which of the following expressions could be for
  (a) the volume   **(b)** the surface area?

$\frac{2}{3}\pi r^3 r + \pi r^2 h$ $2\pi r (h + r)$ $\frac{2}{3}\pi r^2 + \pi r^2 h$

$2\pi r (h + \pi)$ $\frac{2}{3}\pi r^3 + \pi r^2 h$ $2\pi^2 (h + r)$

CHAPTER 13   REVIEW

1. The expressions shown in the table below can be used to calculate lengths, areas or volumes of various shapes.

    π, 2, 4 and $\frac{1}{2}$ are numbers which have no dimensions. The letters r, l, b and h represent lengths.

    Put a tick in the box underneath those expressions that can be used to calculate a volume.

$2\pi r$	$4\pi r^2$	$\pi r^2 h$	πr^2	lbh	$\frac{1}{2}$bh

                                                  ULEAC

2. By considering dimensions decide whether the following expression could be a formula for perimeter, area, volume, or none of these.

$$\frac{2}{3}\pi a^3 + \pi a^2 b$$

where *a*, *b* and *c* are all lengths.   **SEG**

3. In this question r, L and h are all lengths.
For each of these expressions state whether it is a length, an area, a volume or none of these.

(a) $2\pi r\,(r + h)$ (b) $\pi r^2 + \frac{4}{3}\pi r^3$ (c) $\pi r + 2L$ (d) $\pi r\,(2r + L)$

(e) $\pi r^2 (2r + h)$ **MEG**

4. In the following list of expressions only the letters a, b, h, r and R are lengths.

$$\pi\,(R^2 - r^2), \qquad abh, \qquad 4\,(a + b + h), \qquad b^2 - 2a^2,$$

$$a^2b, \qquad 3\pi r^2, \qquad 2\,(2b + a)$$

(a) Using only expressions from the list, write down those which might represent volume.

(b) Use dimensions to explain why the expression

$$2\pi\,(R - r)$$

could not represent area.   **SEG**

5.

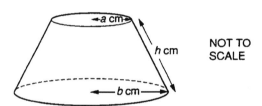

One of the formulae in the list below can be used to calculate the area of material needed to make the curved surface of the lampshade in the diagram.

(i) $\pi h\,(a + b)^2$ (ii) $\pi h^2(a + b)$ (iii) $\pi h\,(a + b)$ (iv) $\pi h^2(a + b)^2$

State which formula is correct. Give a reason for your answer.   **MEG**

6. A pressure washer is a section from a hemisphere of diameter Dcm with a cylindrical hole of diameter $d$cm in it. It is $h$cm high.

Which of these could be the formula for its curved surface area? Give a reason for your answer.

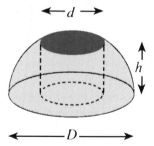

$A = \pi h\,(D + d)$ $A = 0{\cdot}25\pi h\,(D^2 + d^2)$ $A = 0{\cdot}25\pi Ddh$ $A = 0{\cdot}5\pi\,(D + d + h)$

                                                                  WJEC

7.

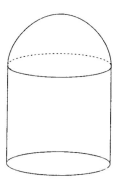

A hemisphere of radius r cm fits exactly on top of a cylinder of height $h$cm to form the solid shown above.

Tony worked out a formula for the volume, Vcm³, of the solid.

His formula was $V = \frac{2}{3}\pi r^2 + \pi rh$.

Explain why Tony's formula cannot be correct.   **ULEAC**

8.   Steven has found this diagram and expressions in an old book:

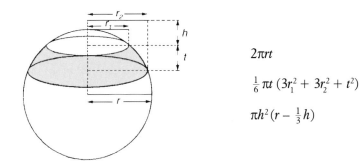

$$2\pi rt$$

$$\tfrac{1}{6}\pi t\,(3r_1^2 + 3r_2^2 + t^2)$$

$$\pi h^2\,(r - \tfrac{1}{3}h)$$

Which expression could be for the area shaded on the diagram?
Explain your choice and why the other two could not be.   **MEG**

9. x and y are lengths.
State whether each of the following could be an expression for a length, an area, a volume or none of these.

(a) $(x + 2y)(3x - y)$ **(b)** $x^2 - 3xy$ **(c)** $x + xy + 2y^3$

(d) $\dfrac{x(x + 3y)(x - y)}{(x - 2y)^2}$ **(e)** $\dfrac{x^2(x + y)(x + 2y)}{(2x - y)}$ **NEAB**

10. Kate wants to know how much chocolate will be needed for different sized eggs. Some will be solid and some will be hollow. She cannot quite remember the formulae for finding the volume and surface area.

(a) One of these formulae gives the volume of an egg.

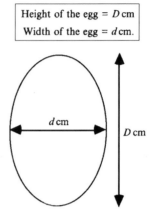

Height of the egg = D cm
Width of the egg = d cm.

Formula A: $\frac{1}{6}\pi D^2 d^2$

Formula B: $\frac{1}{6}\pi D d^2$

Formula C: $\frac{1}{6}\pi D d$

Which formula is correct?   Describe how you can tell.

(b) One of these formulae gives the surface area of an egg.

Formula D: $\frac{\pi}{\sqrt{2}} d \sqrt{d + D}$

Formula E: $\frac{\pi}{\sqrt{2}} d \sqrt{d^2 + D^2}$

Formula F: $\frac{\pi}{\sqrt{2}} d^2 \sqrt{d^2 + D^2}$

Which formula is correct?   Describe how you can tell.   **NEAB**

Carl Friedrich Gauss

Carl Gauss was born in 1777 at Brunswick and died in 1855 at Göttingen. He never left Germany, not even for a visit. He was the greatest mathematician of his time, perhaps of all time. Someone once described him as the last mathematician to know everything in his subject.

Carl's father was a labourer and contractor, as was his father before him. He did not approve of Carl becoming educated. He had hoped his son would join him in his work. Carl's mother who, as her husband, was uneducated, encouraged Carl in his studies and was always very proud of her son's achievements. She lived to see many of them, not dying until she was 97.

Carl was a child prodigy. When he was 3, he corrected the wages account his father was working on, much to his father's astonishment. He went to the local school and at 10, knew a great deal of maths. A teacher once asked Carl's class to add all the integers from 1 to 100, and was most surprised when Carl produced the correct answer immediately, with no written working.

When he was 14, one of Carl's teachers arranged a meeting with the Duke of Brunswick. The Duke was impressed with Carl and sponsored his education from then on. At 15, he went to a college in Brunswick; then at 18 he went to Göttingen University.

Just before his 19th birthday, Carl discovered how to construct, using compass and ruler only, a regular polygon of 17 sides. He then began to keep a diary, recording in this all his mathematical discoveries. Although this diary is only 19 pages long, it is one of the most valued mathematics documents of all time. Another entry in the diary, made when Carl was 19, was the discovery that every integer is the sum of three, or fewer, triangular numbers.

In 1798, Gauss received a doctorate from the University of Helmstädt. In his thesis for this doctorate he proved that every equation has a solution.

Gauss did a great deal of work on prime numbers and made many discoveries. He once said *"Mathematics is the queen of the sciences and number theory the queen of mathematics"*.

In the early 19th century, Gauss began to concentrate on subjects such as astronomy and physics. He later regretted having taken his attention away from number theory.

In 1807 he was made Director of the Göttingen Observatory and a Professor of Astronomy. He had been offered positions as Professor of Mathematics, both at Göttingen University and at St. Petersburg Academy. He did not accept these offers as he hated teaching. In a letter to a friend, he once wrote *"This winter, I am giving two courses of lectures to three students, of which one is only moderately prepared, the other less than moderately, and the third lacks both preparation and ability. Such are the onera of a mathematical profession."*

He remained at the Göttingen Observatory for the rest of his life. His health was good and his mind active, right up until the time he died.

Gauss is known as the founder of modern German mathematics. Some of his work, on mathematical applications, laid the groundwork for Einstein's theory of relativity and worldwide communications. He is said to have been frightened by the idea of international communications. His methods for calculating the orbits of heavenly bodies are still in use today.

Similar Shapes

RECOGNISING SIMILAR SHAPES

Shapes that are identical in every way are called
congruent shapes.
These shapes are congruent.

Shapes that are the same shape but different
sizes are called similar shapes.
These shapes are similar.

DISCUSSION EXERCISE 14:1

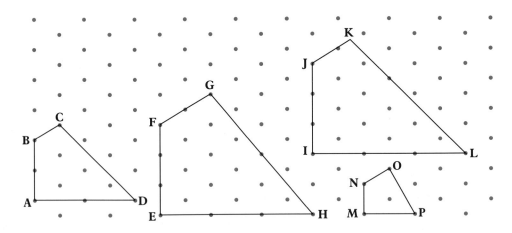

If a shape is enlarged, do we get similar shapes?
Which of the shapes above are similar shapes? Discuss.

What can you say about the angles B and J?
Which angles are equal to angle C? Which angles are equal to angle D?
What other equal angles can you find? Discuss.

Make a statement about the angles of two similar shapes.
Discuss your statement.

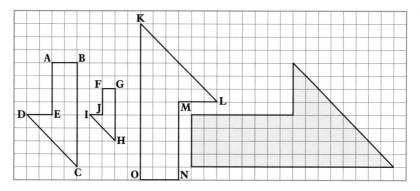

The shapes ABCDE and FGHIJ are similar. $\dfrac{\text{Length BC}}{\text{Length GH}} = \dfrac{8}{4} = 2.$

Make a statement about the ratio of the lengths of the sides in similar shapes.
Discuss your statement.

Is the shape KLMNO similar to shape ABCDE? Find the ratio of the lengths of the shortest sides of these two shapes. Make and test a statement about the ratios of the lengths of other sides on these two shapes. **Discuss**.

Choose a shape that is similar to the pink shape.
Which sides are in the same ratio? **Discuss**.

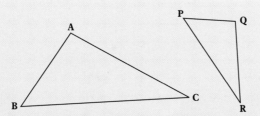

In similar shapes, the angles that are equal are called **corresponding angles**.
For instance, in these similar shapes, the corresponding angles are A and Q, C and R, B and P.

In similar shapes, the sides that are in corresponding positions are called **corresponding sides**. In similar triangles, the corresponding sides are opposite the corresponding angles. For instance, in the similar triangles above, sides BC and PR are corresponding sides since these are opposite the corresponding angles A and Q. Sides AB and PQ are also corresponding sides as are the sides AC and QR.

In the similar quadrilaterals shown here, AB and SP are corresponding sides as they both lie between the 100° and 105° angles. The other corresponding sides are BC and PQ, CD and QR, DA and RS.

EXERCISE 14:2

1. Name the similar shapes.

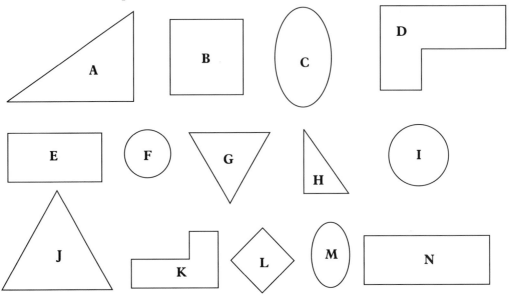

2. Which of the diagrams are similar?

    (a)   (b)

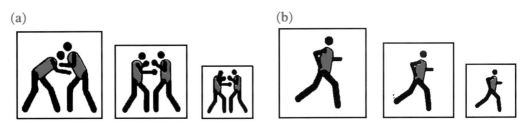

3. The following pairs of shapes are similar.
    Name the angle which corresponds to angle B.

    (a)   (b)

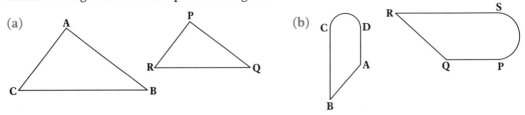

4. In the diagrams in **question 3,** name the side which corresponds to the side AB.

5. In this diagram there are two similar triangles.
    One is ΔPTS.

    (a) Name the other similar triangle.

    (b) Which angle corresponds to ∠PRQ?

    (c) Which side corresponds to PS?

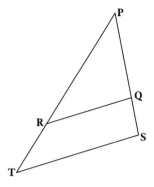

6.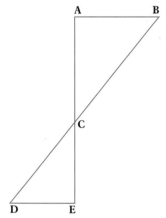

    In this diagram there are two similar triangles.

    (a) Name these similar triangles.

    (b) Which angle corresponds to angle B?

    (c) Which angle corresponds to ∠DCE?

    (d) Which side corresponds to AB?

    (e) Which side corresponds to EC?

7. Are the following pairs of triangles similar? (The triangles are NOT drawn to scale.)

    (a)

    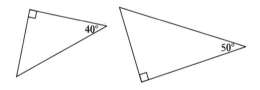

    (b)

    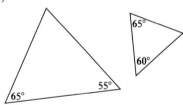

8. Which word, **always** or **sometimes**, is missing in these statements?

    (a) A guitar in a photo and the guitar in the negative of the photo are . . . similar shapes.

    (b) A building and its shadow are . . . similar shapes.

    (c) A slide and its image on a screen are . . . similar shapes.

    (d) The floor plan of a house and the floor itself are . . . similar shapes.

    (e) A photo of the front view of a racing car and the front view of the racing car itself are . . . similar shapes.

    (f) An oil painting of a daisy and the daisy itself are . . . similar shapes.

Review 1

Wayne went into the "Hall of Mirrors" at a fairground. This is how he saw himself at the first set of mirrors.
Are any of these images similar? If so, which ones?

Review 2   These two quadrilaterals are similar.

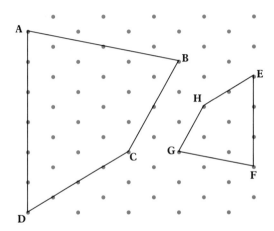

(a) Which angle corresponds to angle B?

(b) Which angle corresponds to angle F?

(c) Which side corresponds to DC?

(d) Which side corresponds to HG?

Review 3   Are the following pairs of triangles similar? (The triangles are NOT drawn to scale.)

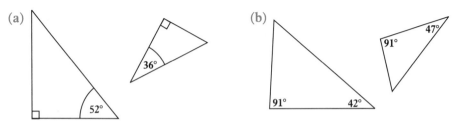

(a)

(b)

PRACTICAL EXERCISE 14:3

Enlarge a picture or a photograph from a book or brochure or magazine or newspaper using the following technique. (This is an enlargement technique used by artists.)

Step 1   Either draw a grid of 5mm squares over your selected picture or firmly attach a transparent grid (drawn up in 5mm squares) over your picture.

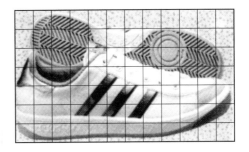

Step 2   In pencil, draw up a grid of 1cm squares. On each square of this grid, draw that part of the picture that is in the corresponding square on the original picture. Use pen for this drawing. Rub out the pencilled grid when you have finished.

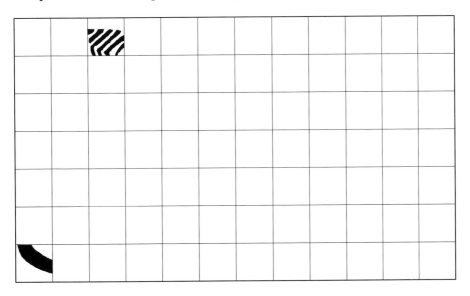

Notes   ● You could make your drawing larger by using a grid of 2cm squares or 5cm squares or . . . .

●   If you want to make a very large picture, you could cut down sheets of A4 paper so they are square; then use one of these for each grid square. If you do this, you could work on this as a group with each student enlarging part of the picture.

FINDING UNKNOWN LENGTHS

If two shapes are similar then   1.   corresponding angles are equal
                                 2.   corresponding sides are in the same ratio.

We use the fact that corresponding sides are in the same ratio to find unknown lengths.

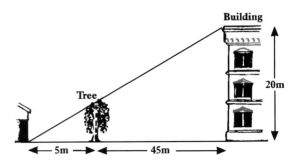

Worked Example When Jayne planted a tree 5m from a window the tree just blocked from view a building 50m away. If the building was 20m tall, how tall was the tree?

Answer

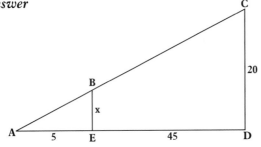

Label the diagram as shown. Let x be the height of the tree. Since ΔABE is similar to ΔACD

then $\dfrac{BE}{CD} = \dfrac{AE}{AD}$

$\dfrac{x}{20} = \dfrac{5}{50}$

$x = 20 \times \dfrac{5}{50}$

$x = 2$

That is, the tree was 2m tall.

Worked Example A light, 3·4 metres above the floor, produces a circular patch of light on the floor. The radius of this patch of light is 1·8 metres.

A table, which is 1·2m high, is placed directly under the light. What is the radius of the patch of light on the table?

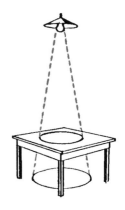

Answer The problem can be represented by the following diagrams.

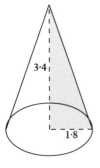
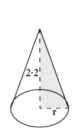

Since the shaded triangles are similar,

$\dfrac{r}{1\cdot8} = \dfrac{2\cdot2}{3\cdot4}$

$r = 1\cdot8 \times \dfrac{2\cdot2}{3\cdot4}$

$= 1\cdot2$ to 1 d.p.

That is, the radius of the patch of light on the table is 1·2m, to the nearest tenth of a metre.

Worked Example The triangles ABE and CBD are similar.
Find the length of BD and AB.

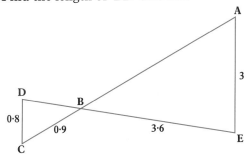

Answer Corresponding angles are A and C, E and D, ∠ABE and ∠CBD.
Corresponding sides are BE and BD, AB and CB, AE and CD.

$$\frac{BD}{BE} = \frac{CD}{AE}$$
$$\frac{BD}{3\cdot 6} = \frac{0\cdot 8}{3}$$
$$BD = 3\cdot 6 \times \frac{0\cdot 8}{3}$$
$$= 0\cdot 96$$

$$\frac{AB}{CB} = \frac{AE}{CD}$$
$$\frac{AB}{0\cdot 9} = \frac{3}{0\cdot 8}$$
$$AB = 0\cdot 9 \times \frac{3}{0\cdot 8}$$
$$= 3\cdot 375$$

EXERCISE 14:4

1. Beth, who is 1·53m tall, gets her friend Jill to help her find the height of a building.
Jill measures Beth's shadow as 2·42m.
Beth measures the shadow of the building as 19·24m. Beth then used similar triangles
to find the height of the building. What answer should she get?

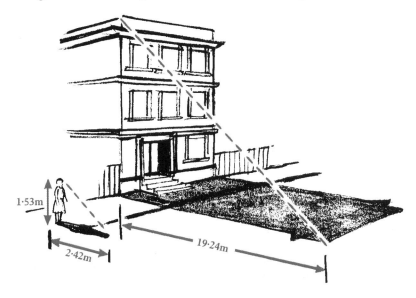

2. Find the length marked as x.

(a)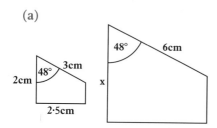

(b)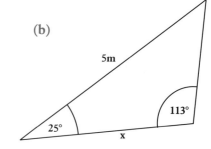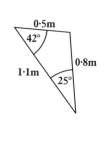

3. Find the value of *l*.

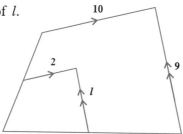

4.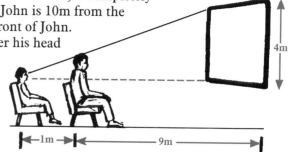

Sally is making a scale drawing of the front of a house. She is 12m from the house.

When she holds a transparent ruler vertically in front of her, she measures the door as being 4cm high.

Find the actual height of this door if Sally held the ruler 20cm from her.

5. A tall man, who is sitting up straight in his seat, is completely blocking John's view at the cinema. John is 10m from the 4m high screen. The man is 1m in front of John. How far would the man need to lower his head and shoulders if John is to be able to see all of the screen?

340

6.

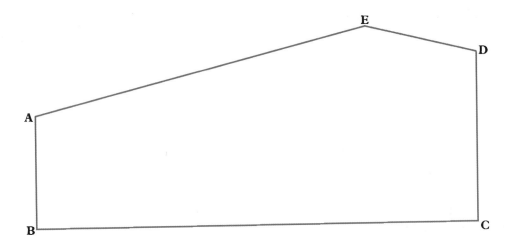

A magazine gave a pattern for a shirt. The instructions stated that each pattern piece needed to be enlarged. The diagram shows one of the pattern pieces.
Measure the length of DC and AB on this pattern piece.

When Amanda enlarged this pattern piece she made DC 36cm long. Use similar shapes to find the length Amanda made AB on her pattern.

7. Hamish was doing an experiment on light. This is one of the diagrams he drew.

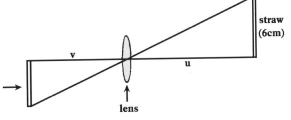

When u was 18cm the image of the straw was 5cm high. What was the distance v?

8.

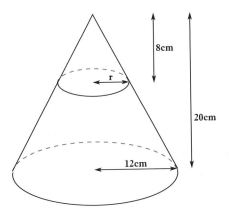

A cone is cut parallel to its base to form a smaller cone. Find the radius of this smaller cone.

9. A light is shone onto a screen, through a hole in a piece of cardboard.
   The hole is 4cm wide. The spot of light on the screen has a diameter of 10cm.
   If the cardboard is 5cm from the light, show that the screen is 12·5cm from the light.

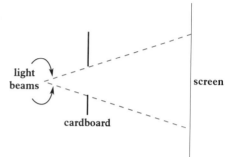

10.

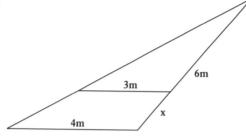

The two triangles in this diagram are similar. Find the value of x.

11.

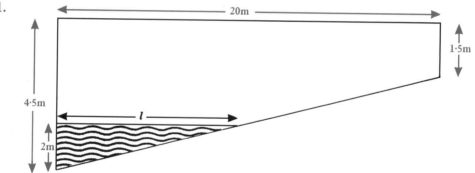

A swimming pool is being filled.
Find the length, *l*, of the surface of the water when the pool has been filled to a depth of 2m.

Review 1 Sarah found the height of a tree by placing a 30cm ruler upright in the shadow of the tree. She placed the ruler so that the end of its shadow was at the same place as the end of the shadow of the tree.
How high was this tree?

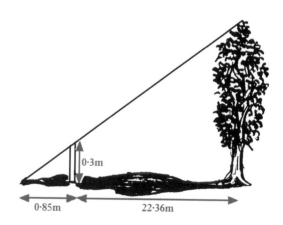

Review 2

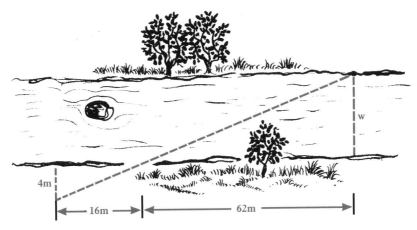

Zeke calculated the width, w, of a river by taking the measurements shown, then using similar triangles.
What answer should Zeke get for the width?

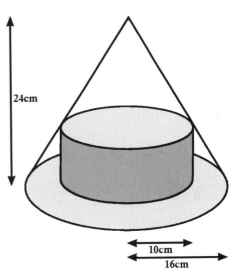

Review 3   A cylinder of radius 10cm just fits inside a hollow cone of height 24cm, as shown in the diagram. If the radius of the cone is 16cm, how tall is the cylinder?

PRACTICAL EXERCISE 14:5

1.   Use similar shapes to find the height of a tree (or a building) or the width of a road (or a stream).

2.   Choose a business. Design a suitable logo for this business.
   Adapt your logo for various uses such as: letterhead, newspaper advertisement, advertisement on the London Underground, sign outside the business premises, business cards.

   Instead of designing a logo for a business you could design a logo for a sports team or an organization such as a charity.

INVESTIGATION 14:6

SIMILAR TRIANGLES

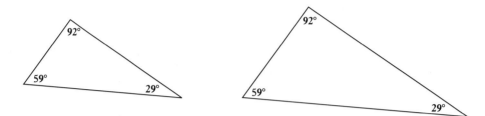

These triangles are similar since the angles of one triangle are the same as the angles of the other.

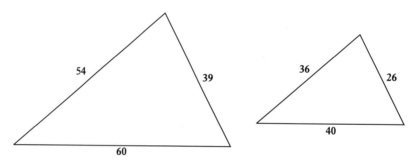

These triangles are similar since corresponding sides are in the same ratio.

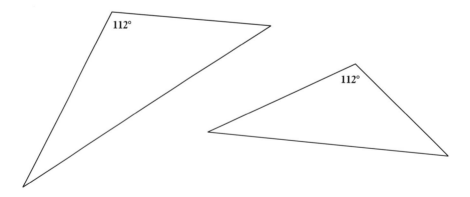

Suppose we are given just one pair of equal angles, as shown in these triangles. What is the least amount of information you need to be given about the sides to be sure the triangles are similar? **Investigate.**

CHAPTER 14   REVIEW

1.

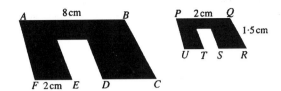

These diagrams are not drawn to scale. They show a company logo used on delivery boxes and a smaller, **similar** one used on letter headings.
Some of the measurements of the logos are shown on the diagrams.

(a) Calculate the length of *UT*.

(b) Calculate the length of *BC*.

(c) Angle *QRS* is 72°. What is the size of angle *BCD*?   **WJEC**

2.   Pet food is sold in three sizes: Small, Regular and Giant.

(a) The width and height of a Giant size packet of pet food are 30cm and 20cm.

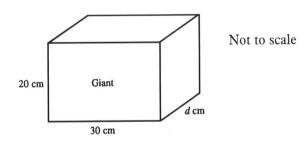

Not to scale

The volume is 16 800cm³.
Calculate the depth, *d* cm.

(b) The Regular size is an enlargement of the Small size.
The width and depth of the Small size are 9cm and 4·2cm.

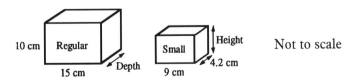

Not to scale

(i)   Calculate the height of the Small size packet.

(ii) Calculate the depth of the Regular size packet.   **SEG**

3. The diagram represents a stepladder made of two sections *AB* and *BC*.

A bar *PQ*, parallel to *AC*, is used to stabilise the ladder.

AB = 2·5 metres, *PQ* = 1·2 metres and *AC* = 1·7 metres.

Calculate the length of *BP*.

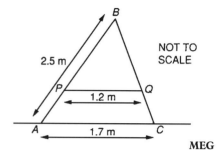

NOT TO SCALE

2.5 m

1.2 m

1.7 m

MEG

4.

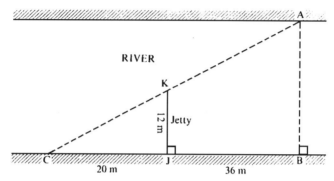

RIVER

K

12 m Jetty

C   20 m   J   36 m   B

JK is a jetty projecting into a river from one bank. A is an ash-tree on the other bank directly opposite Bob who is fishing at point B. Colin, sitting at point C, is in line with both K and A.

From the measurements given, calculate the width of the river.

NICCEA

5.

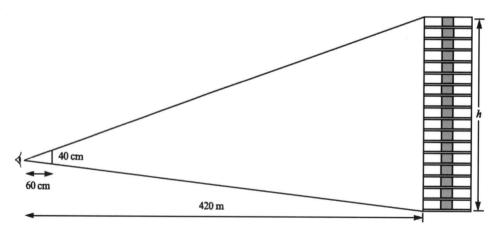

40 cm

60 cm

420 m

h

I stood 420m away from the OUB Centre, the tallest building in Singapore.
I held a piece of wood 40cm long at arms length, 60cm away from my eye.
The piece of wood, held vertically, just blocked the building from my view.
Use similar triangles to calculate the height, *h* metres, of the building.

NEAB

6.

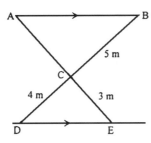

In the diagram CD = 4 metres, CE = 3 metres and BC = 5 metres. AB is parallel to DE. ACE and BCD are straight lines.

(a) Explain why triangle ABC is similar to triangle EDC.

(b) Calculate the length of AC.   **ULEAC**

7. State whether or not the triangles *ABC* and *XYZ* below are similar. Show working to support your answer.

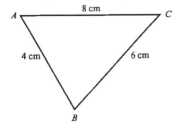 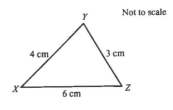

SEG

8.

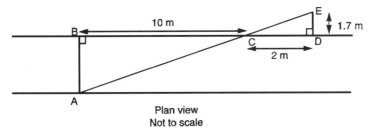

Plan view
Not to scale

Craig used the following method to find the width of a straight canal.

He placed a stake at B directly opposite a tree A on the opposite bank of the canal.
He walked 10 metres along the canal to point C where he placed another stake.
He walked another 2 metres to point D.
He then walked at right angles to the canal until he reached a point E directly in line with A and C.

(a) Explain clearly why triangle ABC is similar to triangle EDC.

(b) Given that the distance DE = 1·7 metres, find the width AB of the canal.   **MEG**

9.

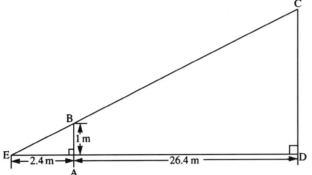

Diagram NOT accurately drawn

Using the measurements shown in the diagram, calculate the length of CD.   **ULEAC**

10.

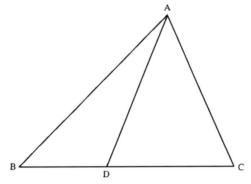

In the triangular framework shown, which is not drawn to scale, BA = BC and AC = AD.

(a) Explain why **(i)** angle ADC = angle BAC.

(ii) triangles ABC and DAC are similar.

(b) BD = 0·7m and DC = 0·9m.

Use the similar triangles to find the length of AC.   **NICCEA**

11.

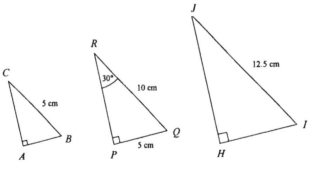

Not to scale

Triangles *ABC*, *PQR* and *HIJ* are all similar.

(a) Calculate the length of *AB*.

(b) What is the size of angle *B*?

(c) Calculate the length of *HJ*.   **SEG**

348

Tycho Brahe

Tycho Brahe was born in 1546 at Knudstrup, in what was Denmark but is now Sweden. He died in 1601 at Prague.

Tycho was born into a noble family. When very young, he was abducted by a wealthy uncle who had no children of his own. After some time, his parents gave the uncle permission to continue to raise Tycho. Tycho spent his early childhood at his uncle's castle in Tostrup. At the age of 13, he was sent to the University of Copenhagen to study law. Tycho spent 3 years at this University then another 3 years at the University of Leipzig. He was more interested in astronomy than law. He spent the daytime attending law lectures, to satisfy his uncle, and the night-time watching the stars. At the University of Copenhagen, the professor of mathematics and other maths. lecturers helped Tycho with his astronomy.

It is said that Tycho became fascinated with astronomy in 1560. A total eclipse of the Sun was predicted for August 21st of that year. When the eclipse occurred on that day Tycho was most impressed by the accuracy of the prediction. When, in 1563, another solar event was less accurately predicted Tycho decided to devote his life to gathering accurate information on the position and movement of the planets and other heavenly bodies. He needed this information to rewrite the existing inaccurate tables of data.

Considering that Brahe lived so long ago, he made an outstanding contribution to astronomy. The accuracy of his measurements is apparent from the fact that his calculation for the length of a year was only a few seconds less than its actual value.

The illustration shows Brahe with one of the very large instruments he built and used. The one shown is called a quadrant and was used to measure the angle of elevation of a heavenly body. This instrument was much more accurate than any of those used by previous astronomers. It could be used to measure angles to an accuracy of about one-tenth of a degree.

The system of movements of the planets which Brahe worked out is known as the Tychonic System. It was later shown that this system was based on incorrect assumptions. However, Brahe's work laid the foundation for Kepler and later astronomers.

After leaving University in 1565, Brahe travelled widely throughout Europe. He studied at various places and also acquired many mathematical and astronomical instruments. About 1571, Brahe built his first observatory. By this time his father and uncle had died and Brahe inherited both estates. In 1576, he planned to leave Denmark and establish an observatory in Germany. The King of Denmark, Frederick II, gave Brahe an island and financial support to persuade him to stay. The new observatory built on this island became the centre of European astronomical research. However, in 1597 Brahe did leave Denmark after he had fallen out with the King, the church and the nobility. He settled in Prague in 1599 under the patronage of Emperor Rudolf II. Brahe died in 1601. Johannes Kepler, who was Brahe's pupil and assistant, continued with his work.

As did many of the astronomers of his time, Brahe believed in astrology. That is, he believed in the power of the stars to influence human behaviour. He also believed, quite unreasonably considering his measurements, that the Earth was the centre of the Universe, and that the Sun revolved round it. He claimed that to believe otherwise was irreligious.

At times, Brahe was a quarrelsome man. He once got into a bitter argument over a geometry problem. This led to a duel in which the end of his nose was cut off with a sword.

INTRODUCTION

INVESTIGATION AND DISCUSSION EXERCISE 15:1

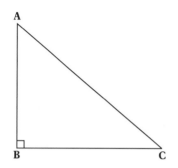

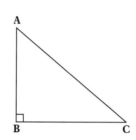

In each of these right-angled triangles, use a protractor to find the size of angle C.

In each triangle, measure the lengths of AB and BC; then calculate the ratio $\dfrac{\text{length of AB}}{\text{length of BC}}$ to two decimal places. **Discuss** your answers.

What if you had found the ratio $\dfrac{\text{length of AB}}{\text{length of AC}}$ or $\dfrac{\text{length of BC}}{\text{length of AC}}$?

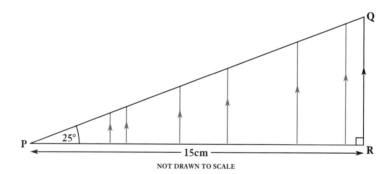

NOT DRAWN TO SCALE

Use a ruler and protractor to accurately draw the right-angled triangle PQR. Draw lines parallel to QR to form a number of triangles.

Do you expect the ratio $\dfrac{\text{length of shortest side}}{\text{length of longest side}}$ to be the same for each triangle formed?
Discuss. As part of your discussion find this ratio for each triangle.
Draw other diagrams, similar to that shown.
On one diagram make angle P equal to 30°, on another 35°, on another 40° and so on.

Is there a relationship between the ratio $\dfrac{\text{length of shortest side}}{\text{length of longest side}}$ and the size of the angle P? **Investigate.**

What if you considered the ratio of two other sides?

NAMING SIDES of a TRIANGLE

It is convenient to give "names" to the sides of a right-angled triangle.
From previous work on Pythagoras' theorem, we know that the side opposite the right angle is called the **hypotenuse**.

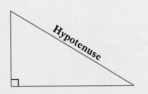

The "names" of the other two sides are **opposite side** and **adjacent side**. These "names" depend on the angle we consider.

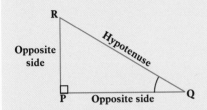

Consider the angle Q.
Since the side opposite angle Q is PR then, **for angle Q, PR is called the opposite side.**
There are two sides next to angle Q, the hypotenuse and PQ. **For angle Q, PQ is called the adjacent side.**

Consider the angle R.
Since the side opposite angle R is PQ then, **for angle R, PQ is called the opposite side.**
The side next to angle R, that is not the hypotenuse, is PR. **For angle R, PR is called the adjacent side.**

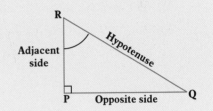

Example

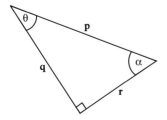

In this triangle, the hypotenuse is s. For the marked angle, the opposite side is p and the adjacent side is m.

Greek letters are often used to name angles. Greek letters commonly used for angles are α (alpha), β (beta), θ (theta).

Example

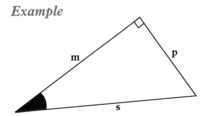

For θ, the opposite side is r and the adjacent side is q.

For α, the opposite side is q and the adjacent side is r.

EXERCISE 15:2

1. Name the hypotenuse in each of these triangles.

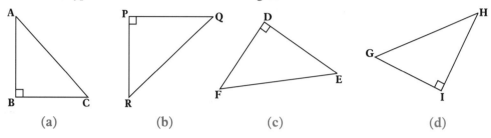

(a)　　　　　(b)　　　　　(c)　　　　　(d)

2. Refer to the triangles in **question 1.**
   (a) For angle A, name the opposite side.
   (b) For angle Q, name the adjacent side.
   (c) For angle F, name the opposite side.
   (d) For angle G, name the adjacent side.

3. Which side completes the statement for the marked angle?

   (a)　　　　　　　　　(b)　　　　　　　　　(c)

   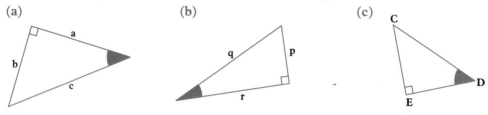

   The opposite side is . . .　　　The adjacent side is . . .　　　The adjacent side is . . .

4.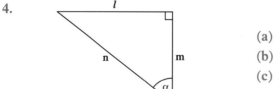

   (a) Name the hypotenuse in this triangle.
   (b) For α, name the adjacent side.
   (c) For α, name the opposite side.

Review

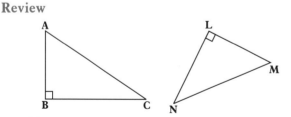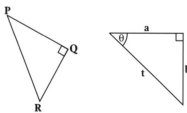

(a) Name the hypotenuse in Δ PQR.
(b) For angle N, name the opposite side.
(c) For angle A, name the adjacent side.
(d) For angle R, name the opposite side.
(e) For θ, name the adjacent side.

The ratios SINE, COSINE, TANGENT

The hypotenuse, opposite side and adjacent side have been labelled on these triangles for the 40° angle.

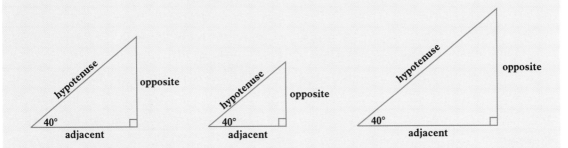

In Investigation 15:1, you found that the ratio $\dfrac{\text{shortest side}}{\text{longest side}}$ i.e. $\dfrac{\text{opposite}}{\text{hypotenuse}}$ is the same for each of these triangles.

This ratio $\dfrac{\text{opposite}}{\text{hypotenuse}}$ is given a special name. It is called the sine of 40° or **sine 40°**.

The ratio $\dfrac{\text{adjacent}}{\text{hypotenuse}}$ is called **cosine 40°**. The ratio $\dfrac{\text{opposite}}{\text{adjacent}}$ is called **tangent 40°**.

The abbreviations sin, cos, tan are used for sine, cosine, tangent.
The ratios sin A, cos A, tan A are called **trigonometrical ratios,** or **trig. ratios.**

DISCUSSION EXERCISE 15:3

● To find the value of sin 72° we could begin by accurately drawing a right-angled triangle in which one of the angles is 72°.
Does it matter how large or small we make the triangle? How could we continue?
Discuss.

The calculator can be used to find the value of sin 72°. The calculator value of sin 72° is 0·9511 to 4 decimal places. Which keys do you press to find this? Discuss.

● Discuss how to use the calculator to find the cosine or tangent of an angle.
Choose some angles. Draw right-angled triangles to work out the value of the cosine of some of your chosen angles, the tangent of some of the others and the sine of the rest.
Compare your values with the calculator values.

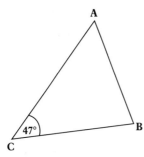

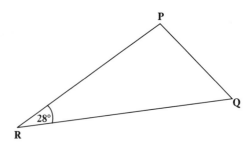

Could you use triangles, such as those shown, to work out the value of sin 47° or cos 28°? **Discuss.**

- $$\sin \theta = \frac{\text{opposite}}{\text{hypotenuse}}$$

  $$\cos \theta = \frac{\text{adjacent}}{\text{hypotenuse}}$$

  $$\tan \theta = \frac{\text{opposite}}{\text{adjacent}}$$

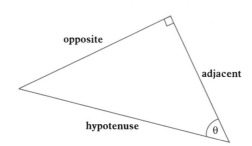

One way of remembering these trig. ratios is by using SOHCAHTOA. How can this be used to help you remember these ratios? **Discuss.**

Make up a mnemonic to help remember SOHCAHTOA. Your mnemonic could begin "**S**cience **O**r **H**istory . . ." or "**S**ome **O**ld **H**orses **C**an . . .". **Discuss** your mnemonic.

Worked Example Write, as a fraction

        (a) sin A   (b) cos A

        (c) tan C   (d) sin C.

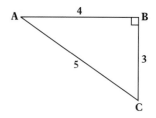

Answer

For angle A,   AC is the hypotenuse   (a) $\sin A = \frac{3}{5}$ (using $\sin A = \frac{\text{opposite}}{\text{hypotenuse}}$)
                BC is the opposite side
                AB is the adjacent side   (b) $\cos A = \frac{4}{5}$ (using $\cos A = \frac{\text{adjacent}}{\text{hypotenuse}}$)

For angle C,   AC is the hypotenuse   (c) $\tan C = \frac{4}{3}$ (using $\tan C = \frac{\text{opposite}}{\text{adjacent}}$)
                AB is the opposite side
                BC is the adjacent side   (d) $\sin C = \frac{4}{5}$ (using $\sin C = \frac{\text{opposite}}{\text{hypotenuse}}$)

Worked Example 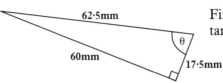 Find the values of sin θ, cos θ, tan θ giving the answers to 2 d.p.

Answer $\sin \theta = \dfrac{60}{62\cdot5}$ $\cos \theta = \dfrac{17\cdot5}{62\cdot5}$ $\tan \theta = \dfrac{60}{17\cdot5}$

$= 0\cdot96$ $= 0\cdot28$ $= 3\cdot43$ (2 d.p.)

EXERCISE 15:4

1. What is the missing side in each of the following?

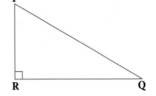

   (a) $\sin Q = \dfrac{PR}{\cdots}$ (b) $\cos Q = \dfrac{\cdots}{PQ}$ (c) $\tan Q = \dfrac{\cdots}{QR}$

   (d) $\tan P = \dfrac{QR}{\cdots}$ (e) $\cos P = \dfrac{\cdots}{PQ}$ (f) $\sin P = \dfrac{\cdots}{PQ}$

2. Write sin θ, as a fraction.

 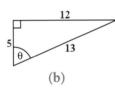 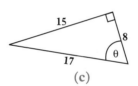 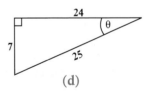

   (a)   (b)   (c)   (d)

3. For the triangles in **question 2**, write tan θ as a fraction.

4. For the triangles in **question 2**, write cos θ as a fraction.

5. Complete each trig. ratio giving the answers as decimals. Round to 2 d.p. if rounding is necessary.

   (a)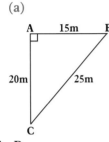

   (b)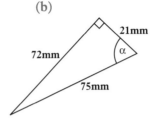

   (c)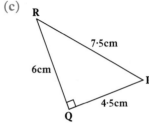

   sin B = · · ·   cos α = · · ·   tan R = · · ·
   cos C = · · ·   tan α = · · ·   sin P = · · ·
   tan B = · · ·   sin α = · · ·   cos R = · · ·
   sin C = · · ·   tan P = · · ·

Review Copy and complete.

(a) $\cos M = \dfrac{\cdots}{MP}$

(b) $\tan P = \dfrac{30}{\cdots}$

(c) $\sin M = \cdots$ (to 2 d.p.)

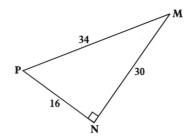

Calculator keying sequences to find the values of sin 14°, cos 14°, tan 14° are as follows.

For sin 14°:   Key $\boxed{14}$ $\boxed{\text{sin}}$ to get answer of 0·2419 to 4 d.p.

For cos 14°:   Key $\boxed{14}$ $\boxed{\text{cos}}$ to get answer of 0·9703 to 4 d.p.

For tan 14°:   Key $\boxed{14}$ $\boxed{\text{tan}}$ to get answer of 0·2493 to 4 d.p.

Note   Make sure your calculator is operating in Degree Mode.
This is MODE 4. You do not need to remember Mode 4 is Degree mode as 4 is
written beside DEG on the calculator.

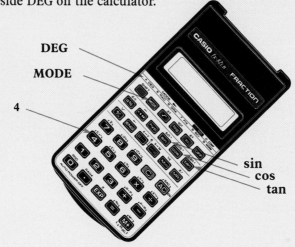

EXERCISE 15:5

**Use the calculator to find the value of the following trig. ratios, giving each answer
to 3 d.p.**

1. cos 70°   2. sin 13°   3. tan 54°   4. tan 18°   5. sin 84°

6. sin 60·7°   7. cos 24·1°   8. cos 82·7°   9. tan 58·7°   10. tan 45°

11. sin 15°   12. sin 35°   13. sin 55°   14. sin 75°   15. sin 90°

16. cos 10°   17. cos 60°   18. cos 90°   19. tan 2°   20. tan 89·9°

Review 1   tan 34°   Review 2   sin 72°   Review 3   cos 40·3°

DISCUSSION EXERCISE 15:6

Referring to the angle θ, which of x, y or r is the hypotenuse, which is the opposite side, which is the adjacent side?

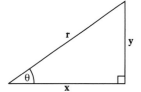

Discuss how the ratios sin θ, cos θ, tan θ may be written in terms of x, y and r.

To find the length x, we may use the formula $x = r \cos \theta$.
What formula could be used to find y? Is there more than one possible formula? **Discuss**.

Make a summary of your discussion.

FINDING the length of a SIDE

In a right-angled triangle, if we are given the length of one side and the size of an angle (other than the right angle) we can use one of the trig. ratios to find the length of one of the other sides.

Worked Example

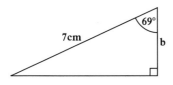

Find the length of the side marked as b.

Answer $\cos 69° = \dfrac{b}{7}$ or $\dfrac{b}{7} = \cos 69°$

$\qquad\qquad\qquad\qquad b = 7 \times \cos 69°$ (multiplying both sides by 7)
$\qquad\qquad\qquad\qquad b = 2 \cdot 5 \text{cm}$ (1 d.p.)

Keying $\boxed{7}\ \boxed{\times}\ \boxed{69}\ \boxed{\cos}\ \boxed{=}$

Note Just as $x \times y$ is usually written as xy so is $7 \times \cos 69°$ usually written as $7 \cos 69°$.

Worked Example (a)

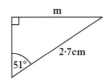

Find m.

(b)

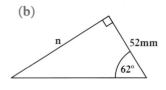

Find n.

Answer   (a) $\sin 51° = \dfrac{m}{2\cdot7}$ or $\dfrac{m}{2\cdot7} = \sin 51°$

$m = 2\cdot7 \sin 51°$ (multiplying both sides by $2\cdot7$)

$m = 2\cdot1$cm (1 d.p.)

Keying   2·7 × 51 sin =

(b) $\tan 62° = \dfrac{n}{52}$ or $\dfrac{n}{52} = \tan 62°$

$n = 52 \tan 62°$ (multiplying both sides by 52)

$n = 98$mm (to the nearest mm)

Keying   52 × 62 tan =

Worked Example   Find the length of the side marked as t.

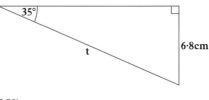

Answer $\sin 35° = \dfrac{6\cdot8}{t}$

$t \sin 35° = 6\cdot8$ (multiplying both sides by t)

$t = \dfrac{6\cdot8}{\sin 35°}$ (dividing both sides by $\sin 35°$)

$t = 11\cdot9$cm (1 d.p.)

Keying   6·8 ÷ 35 sin =

The previous worked examples show the steps to be taken to find an unknown side. These steps are:

Step 1   Write down a trig. ratio for the given angle. This ratio must involve the unknown side and a known side.

If these sides are the hypotenuse and the opposite side the trig. ratio used is sine.

If these sides are the hypotenuse and the adjacent side the trig. ratio used is cosine.

If these sides are the opposite and the adjacent sides the trig. ratio used is tangent.

Step 2   Solve the equation formed to find the unknown side.

EXERCISE 15:7

1. Which trig. ratio (sin, cos or tan) would you use to find d?

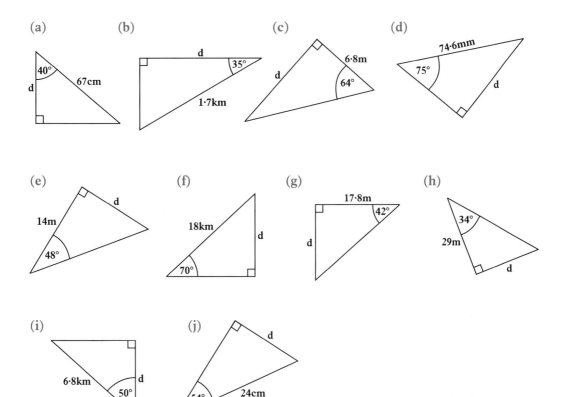

(a)

(b)

(c)

(d)

(e)

(f)

(g)

(h)

(i)

(j)

2. For each of the triangles in **question 1**, find d. Round your answers sensibly.

3. A 5·2 metre ladder leans against a wall as shown.
   How far is the bottom of this ladder from the wall?

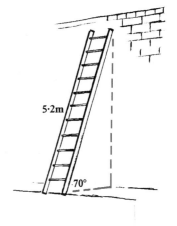

4.

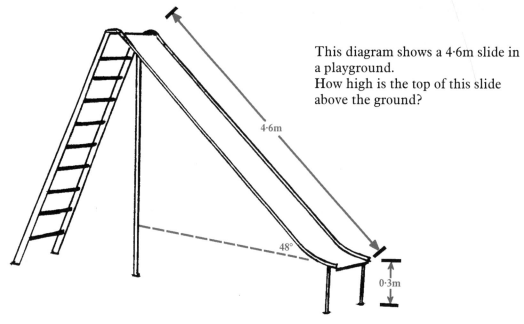

This diagram shows a 4·6m slide in a playground.
How high is the top of this slide above the ground?

5. The diagram represents the side view of the loft of a barn.
The loft is symmetrical.
What is the height h?

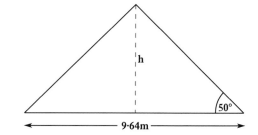

6. Find the length of **a**.

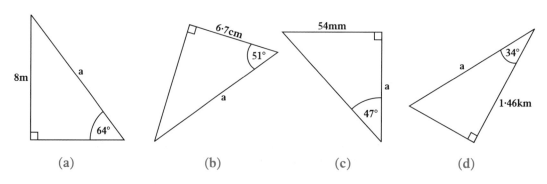

(a)　　　　　　　　(b)　　　　　　　　(c)　　　　　　　　(d)

7. When an aeroplane is at a height of 1000 metres, it is picked up on radar.
The diagram represents this situation.
How far is the aeroplane from the radar?

8.

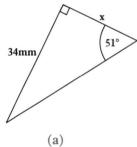

(a)   (b)   (c)   (d)

Find the length of x.

Review 1

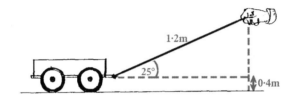

Bob is pulling a trolley along the ground, as shown in this diagram.
Find the height of Bob's hand above the ground.

Review 2   Find d in each of these triangles.

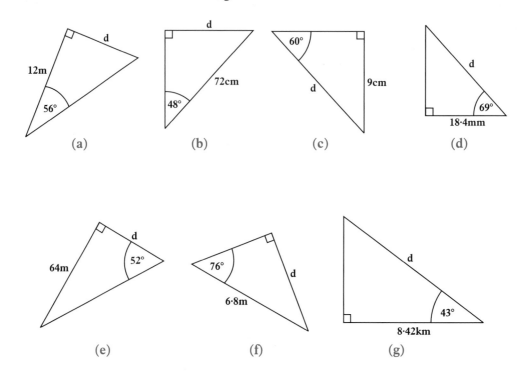

| (a) | (b) | (c) | (d) |

| (e) | (f) | (g) |

FINDING the size of an ANGLE

DISCUSSION EXERCISE 15:8

- If sin θ = 0·89, then θ = 62·9° to one decimal place.
  What keying sequence on the calculator gives this answer for θ? **Discuss.**

- The angle α could be found as follows.

  $\tan \alpha = \dfrac{4\cdot 6}{5\cdot 9}$

  $\alpha = 37\cdot 9°$ (1 d.p.), using the

  keying sequence $\boxed{4\cdot6}\ \boxed{\div}\ \boxed{5\cdot9}\ \boxed{=}\ \boxed{\text{SHIFT}}\ \boxed{\tan^{-1}}$

  Discuss each part of this keying sequence.

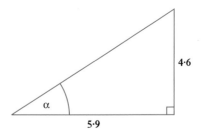

If we are given the lengths of two of the sides of a right-angled triangle we can use a trig. ratio (sin, cos or tan) to find the size of an unknown angle.
We use tan if we are given the lengths of the opposite and adjacent sides.
We use cos if we are given the lengths of the adjacent side and the hypotenuse.
We use sin if we are given the lengths of the opposite side and the hypotenuse.

Worked Example Find the size of θ if (a) $\tan \theta = 1.5$ (b) $\cos \theta = 0.6$
(c) $\sin \theta = 0.2834$

Answer (a) $\tan \theta = 1.5$
$\theta = 56.3°$ (1 d.p.)   **Keying** $\boxed{1.5}$ $\boxed{\text{SHIFT}}$ $\boxed{\tan^{-1}}$

(b) $\cos \theta = 0.6$
$\theta = 53.1°$ (1 d.p.)   **Keying** $\boxed{0.6}$ $\boxed{\text{SHIFT}}$ $\boxed{\cos^{-1}}$

(c) $\sin \theta = 0.2834$
$\theta = 16.5°$ (1 d.p.)   **Keying** $\boxed{0.2834}$ $\boxed{\text{SHIFT}}$ $\boxed{\sin^{-1}}$

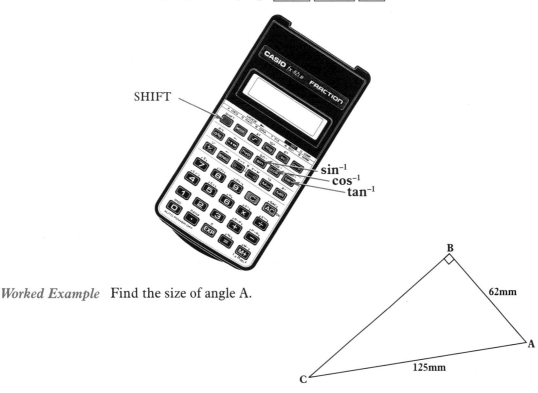

SHIFT

$\sin^{-1}$
$\cos^{-1}$
$\tan^{-1}$

Worked Example Find the size of angle A.

Answer The given lengths are AB and AC. For angle A, AC is the hypotenuse and AB is the adjacent side. Hence we use cos A to find angle A.
$$\cos A = \frac{62}{125}$$
$A = 60.3°$ (1 d.p.)   **Keying** $\boxed{62}$ $\boxed{\div}$ $\boxed{125}$ $\boxed{=}$ $\boxed{\text{SHIFT}}$ $\boxed{\cos^{-1}}$

EXERCISE 15:9

1. Find, to one decimal place, the size of angle P if:

   (a) $\sin P = 0.83$ (b) $\cos P = 0.462$ (c) $\tan P = 0.945$ (d) $\tan P = 14.6$

   (e) $\sin P = 0.345$ (f) $\cos P = 0.8236$ (g) $\tan P = 56$ (h) $\cos P = 0.125$

   (i) $\tan P = 0.82$ (j) $\sin P = \frac{1}{4}$ (k) $\tan P = \frac{2}{5}$ (l) $\cos P = \frac{2}{3}$

   (m) $\tan P = \frac{14}{9}$ (n) $\sin P = \frac{8}{11}$

2. Which of sin, cos, tan would you use to find θ ?

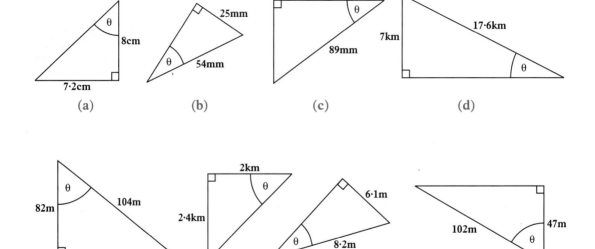

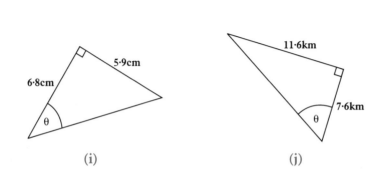

3. For the triangles drawn in **question 2**, find the size of θ. Give your answers to the nearest degree.

4. Judy was abseiling down a building.
   When she was a vertical distance of 10m
   from where she began, her hips were 1m
   from the side of the building.
   What angle did Judy's rope make with
   the building?

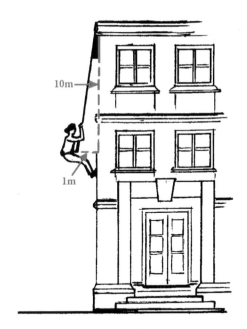

5.

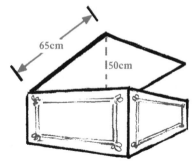

The play "Pandora's Box" was being produced
by Highfield School Drama Club.
The lid of the box they were using was 65cm
wide. It was decided to prop this lid open so
there was a 50cm wide gap.
At what angle was the lid propped open?

6. Drainage pipes were being
   laid along the diagonal of a
   rectangular field, as shown in
   this diagram.
   At what angle, to the shorter
   sides of this field, were the
   pipes laid?

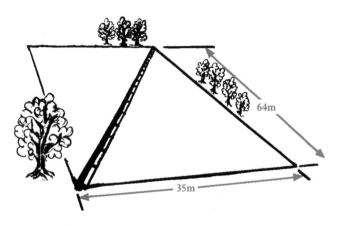

Review 1 Find, to the nearest degree, the size of α if

(a) $\cos \alpha = 0\cdot687$ (b) $\tan \alpha = 2\cdot7$ (c) $\sin \alpha = 0\cdot8$ (d) $\sin \alpha = \frac{2}{7}$

(e) $\tan \alpha = \frac{14}{5}$ (f) $\cos \alpha = \frac{3}{8}$.

Review 2

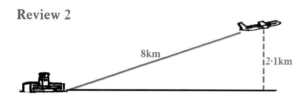

A plane, which took off from Manchester Airport, had gained an altitude of 2·1km after it had travelled 8km.
At what angle was this plane climbing?

APPLICATIONS to NAVIGATION

Navigation problems involve bearings.
Pythagoras' theorem as well as trigonometry is often needed to solve these.

Worked Example A ship travels due East from A to B, a distance of 74km. It then travels due South to C. C is 47km from B.

(a) What is the bearing of C from A?

(b) Use Pythagoras' theorem to find the distance from A to C.

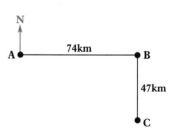

Answer (a) The required bearing is given by the angle θ. $\theta = 90° +$ angle BAC.

$\tan \text{BAC} = \frac{47}{74}$

angle BAC $= 32°$ (to the nearest degree).

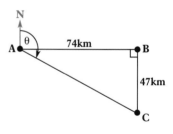

Keying $\boxed{47}$ $\boxed{\div}$ $\boxed{74}$ $\boxed{=}$ $\boxed{\text{SHIFT}}$ $\boxed{\tan^{-1}}$

Then $\theta = 122°$. The bearing of C from A is 122°.

(b) $\text{AC}^2 = \text{BC}^2 + \text{AB}^2$ (Pythagoras' theorem)

$\qquad = 47^2 + 74^2$

$\text{AC} = 88\text{km}$ (to the nearest kilometre)

Keying $\boxed{47}$ $\boxed{\text{SHIFT}}$ $\boxed{x^2}$ $\boxed{+}$ $\boxed{74}$ $\boxed{\text{SHIFT}}$ $\boxed{x^2}$ $\boxed{=}$ $\boxed{\sqrt{\ }}$

Worked Example   A yacht sails from Wicklow on a bearing of 055°. By the end of the first day the yacht has travelled 39km.
How far East of Wicklow is the yacht at the end of this day?

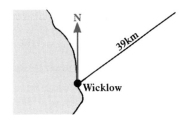

Answer   We need to find d in this diagram.

$$\theta = 90° - 55°$$
$$= 35°$$
$$\frac{d}{39} = \cos 35°$$
$$d = 39\ \cos 35° \text{ (multiplying both sides by 39)}$$
$$d = 32\text{km (to the nearest km)}$$

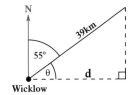

DISCUSSION EXERCISE 15:10

In both of the previous worked examples, we found a length in a right-angled triangle. We used Pythagoras' theorem to find the length in the first example and trigonometry to find the length in the second example.
Could we have used Pythagoras' theorem both times? Could we have used trigonometry both times? **Discuss.**

EXERCISE 15:11

1.   B is 10km East of A and 8km North of C.

 (a) Use trigonometry to find the size of angle BCA.

 (b) What is the bearing of A from C?

 (c) Use Pythagoras' theorem to find the distance from A to C.

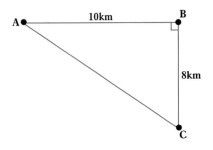

2.

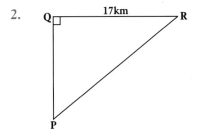

A car begins its journey at R. It travels due West to Q, a distance of 17km; then due South to P.
The bearing of R from P is 048°.

 (a) Which angle in this diagram is 48°?

 (b) What total distance did the car travel?

3. A plane flies from P to Q on a bearing of 146°.
   Q is 229km from P.

   (a) What is the size of angle RPQ?

   (b) Use trigonometry to find how far further
   East Q is than P.

   (c) Use Pythagoras' theorem to find how far
   further South Q is than P.

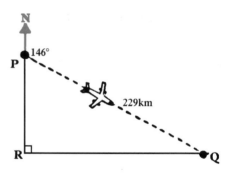

4. 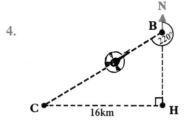 A helicopter leaves its base (B) and flies on a bearing
   of 220° to pick up an injured climber at C. It then flies
   the climber 16km to the nearest hospital (H). The
   hospital is due South of B and due East of C, as shown
   in the diagram.

   (a) What is the size of angle CBH?

   (b) Use trigonometry to find how far the hospital is from B.

   (c) Use Pythagoras' theorem to find how far the injured climber was from the
   helicopter base.

5.

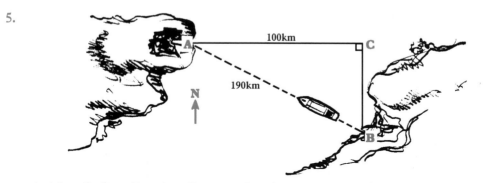

A ship sails from B to A, a distance of 190km. A is 100km further West than B.

   (a) Use Pythagoras' theorem to find how far further North A is than B.

   (b) Find the size of angle ABC. Hence find the bearing on which the ship sailed.

Review A North Sea oil pipeline runs from
W to R.
R is 84km South and 48km West of W.

   (a) Use Pythagoras' theorem to find
   the length of this pipeline.

   (b) Use trigonometry to find the size of
   angle WRA.

   (c) What is the bearing of W from R?

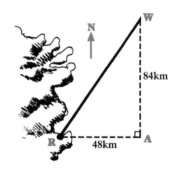

368

APPLICATIONS to SURVEYING

In surveying, distances which are difficult to measure are calculated by measuring angles, then using trigonometry.

Worked Example A surveyor, on top of a mountain, measures the angle below the horizontal to another mountain as 15°. It is known that the two mountains are 1800m apart and that the lower mountain is 1050m high. How high is the higher mountain?

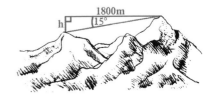

Answer The height of the higher mountain = 1050 + h.

$$\frac{h}{1800} = \tan 15°$$

$\qquad$ h = 1800 tan 15° (multiplying both sides by 1800)

$\qquad$ h = 482m (to the nearest metre)

Hence, the height of the higher mountain = 1050 + 482

$$= 1532m.$$

When we look **up** at something, the angle between the horizontal and the direction in which we are looking is called the **angle of elevation**. In this diagram, θ is the angle of elevation.

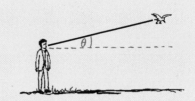

When we look **down** at something, the angle between the horizontal and the direction in which we are looking is called the **angle of depression**. In this diagram, θ is the angle of depression.

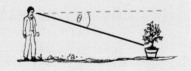

Trigonometry

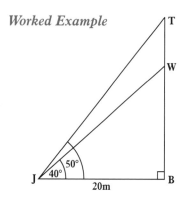

Jill found the distance of a windowsill from the top of a building as follows.

From a point 20m from the base of the building, she measured the angle of elevation of the windowsill to be 40° and the angle of elevation of the top of the building to be 50°. She drew this sketch then used trigonometry to calculate TB and WB.

(a) What further calculation did Jill need to make?

(b) How far is the windowsill from the top of the building?

Answer (a) Once TB and WB are calculated, the only further calculation to be made is subtracting WB from TB.

(b)

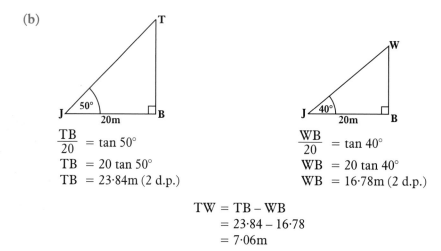

$$\frac{TB}{20} = \tan 50°$$
$$TB = 20 \tan 50°$$
$$TB = 23\cdot84m \ (2 \ d.p.)$$

$$\frac{WB}{20} = \tan 40°$$
$$WB = 20 \tan 40°$$
$$WB = 16\cdot78m \ (2 \ d.p.)$$

$$TW = TB - WB$$
$$= 23\cdot84 - 16\cdot78$$
$$= 7\cdot06m$$

Hence, to the nearest metre, the windowsill is 7m from the top of the building.

EXERCISE 15:12

1. Anita used the following method to find the width of a street. She walked along the street until she found two houses (P and Q) that were directly opposite each other. She walked a further 20m to R, then measured the angle PRQ as 37°. From these measurements she calculated w, the width of the street. What answer should Anita get?

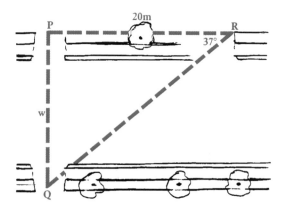

370

2.

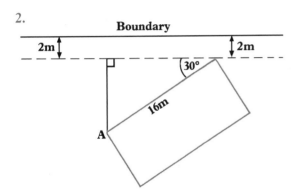

A surveyor has been asked to set out the four corners of a rectangular house at 30° to the front boundary. The surveyor starts by marking a line 2 metres from the boundary. One corner of the house is to be on this line, as shown in the diagram. How far from the boundary is the corner of the house marked as A?

3. At a distance of 80m from a church tower, Donald measured the angle of elevation of the top of the tower as 24°.

How high is this church tower?

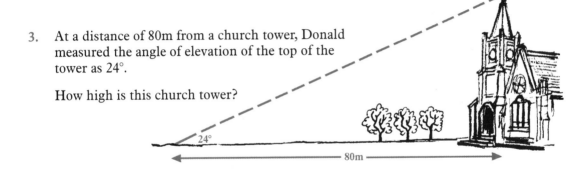

4.

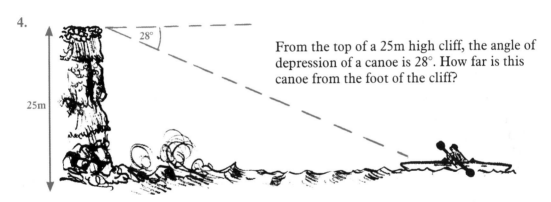

From the top of a 25m high cliff, the angle of depression of a canoe is 28°. How far is this canoe from the foot of the cliff?

5. At the edge of a beach, which is 8m wide, there is a 6m high wall. From the top of this wall, Simon measures the angle of depression of a swimmer as 16°.
How far out to sea is the swimmer?

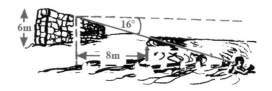

6.

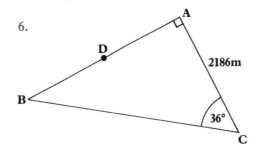

There is a trig. station at each of A, B and C.
The distance AC = 2186m.
A surveyor measures the angle ACB to be 36° and the angle CAB to be 90°.

(a) Use trigonometry to find how far B is from C.

(b) Use Pythagoras' theorem to find how far A is from B.

(c) D is a point halfway between A and B.
The surveyor measures the angle between AC and CD. What answer should the surveyor get?

7. A flagpole is on the top of a building. From the point D, 4m from the base of the building, Joanne measures the angles of elevation of the top, A, and the bottom, B, of the flagpole. Her measurements are shown on the diagram.

(a) Find the length AC.

(b) Find the length BC. Hence find the height of the flagpole.

8.

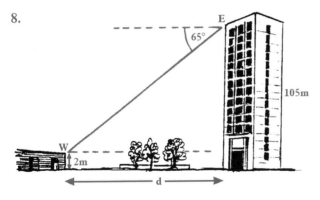

From the top of a 105m high building Ellen measures the angle of depression of the top of a 2m high wall as 65°. Ellen then calculates the distance of the wall from the building.

(a) List the steps Ellen needs to take.

(b) What answer should Ellen get?

Review 1 A rock ledge overhangs a path. Dianne stood directly under the end of this ledge, then walked back towards the rock face for 2m. At this point she measured the angle of elevation of the end of the ledge as 74°. What is the height of the end of the ledge above the path?

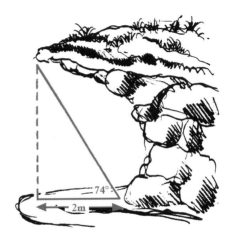

Review 2

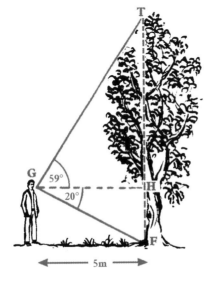

Gareth stood 5m from the foot of a tree. He measured the angle of elevation of the top of the tree as 59° and the angle of depression of the foot of the tree as 20°.

(a) What is the length of GH?

(b) Use trigonometry to find TH.

(c) What other calculations need to be made to find the height of the tree?

(d) What is the height of the tree?

Review 3 Minami finds the distance between two houseboats, P and R, on the other side of the river as follows. She begins at A, opposite houseboat P. From A she walks to B, a distance of 54m. She measures the angle ABP as 42° and angle CBR as 47°. From these measurements she is able to find the distance PR, between the two houseboats.

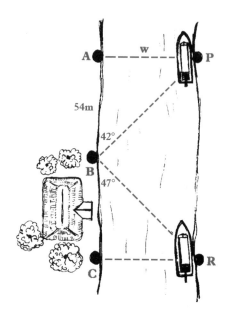

(a) Calculate w, the width of the river, using the triangle APB.

(b) Using triangle CBR, calculate the distance BC. Hence find the distance between the houseboats.

PRACTICAL EXERCISE 15:13

Use trigonometry to find the height of an object or the distance of an object from an observation point.

You could base your work on one of the examples given in the previous exercise.
Use a trundle wheel or long measuring tape to measure distances. Use a theodolite or clinometer to measure angles.

CHAPTER 15 REVIEW

1. A wire 18m long runs from the top of a pole to the ground as shown in the diagram. The wire makes an angle of 35° with the ground.

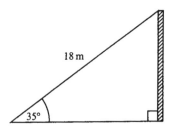

Calculate the height of the pole.
Give your answer to a suitable degree of accuracy.

NEAB

2.

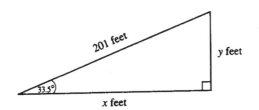

Diagram NOT
accurately drawn

The diagram represents the Bridgnorth Castle Hill Railway, which is the steepest in Great Britain.

It has 201 feet of straight track. The inclination to the horizontal is 33·5°.

(a) Calculate the value of *x*.

(b) Calculate the value of *y*.   **ULEAC**

3. Ajit stands 30m from the base of a tree.
From ground level he measures the angle of elevation of the top of the tree.
He finds that this angle is 25°.

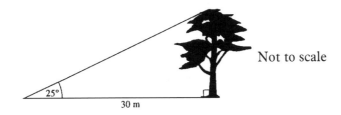

Not to scale

Calculate the height of the tree.   **SEG**

4.

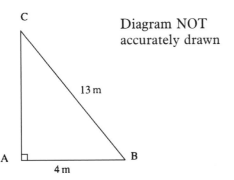

Diagram NOT
accurately drawn

ABC is a right angled triangle.
AB is of length 4m and BC is of length 13m.

(a) Calculate the length of AC.

(b) Calculate the size of angle ABC.   **ULEAC**

5. An aircraft takes off from one end, A, of a runway and it passes over the other end of the runway, B, at a height of 317 metres.
    The angle of elevation of the aircraft from end A of the runway is 5°.

    (a) Calculate the length of the runway AB.

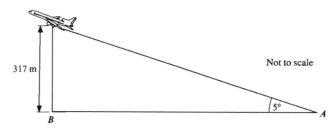

317 m   Not to scale   5°   A   B

Another aircraft, using the same runway, passes over point B at a height of 250 metres.

    (b) Calculate the angle of elevation of this aircraft from end A of the runway.   **SEG**

6.

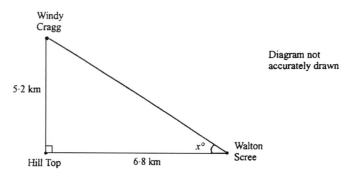

Windy Cragg   Diagram not accurately drawn   5·2 km   Hill Top   6·8 km $x°$ Walton Scree

The diagram shows three places, which are on the same horizontal plane.
Windy Cragg is 5·2km due North of Hill Top.
Walton Scree is 6·8km due East of Hill Top.

    (a) Calculate the distance from Walton Scree to Windy Cragg. Give your answer correct to 1 decimal place.

    (b) Calculate the size of the angle marked $x°$ in the diagram. Give your answer correct to 1 decimal place.

The distance of 5·2 km has been rounded to 1 decimal place.

    (c) Write down the minimum distance it could be.   **ULEAC**

7.

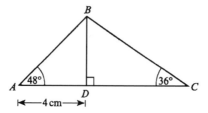

B   48°   36°   C   A   D |←—4 cm—→|

In the figure shown, calculate

    (a) the length of BD,   (b) the length of BC.   **NEAB**

8. Two ships at B and C are both due east of a point A at the base of a vertical cliff. The cliff is 130m high.
The ship at C is 350m from the bottom of the cliff.

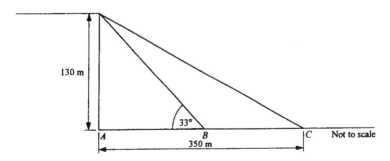

(a) (i) Calculate the distance from the top of the cliff to the ship at C.

(ii) Calculate the angle of depression from the top of the cliff to the ship at C.

(b) The angle of elevation of the top of the cliff from the ship at B is 33°.
Calculate the distance AB.   **SEG**

9.

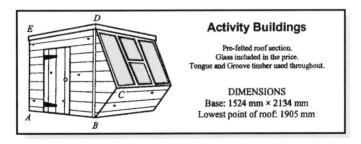

A diagram of the side view of the Activity Building is shown.

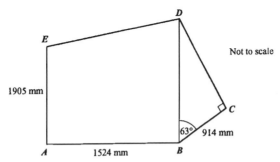

Angle $BCD = 90°$, angle $DBC = 63°$, $BC = 914$ mm.
BD and AE are vertical. AB is horizontal.

(a) Calculate the height of D above AB.

(b) Calculate the angle at which the roof ED slopes to the horizontal.   **SEG**

10. Bunting is fixed across the entrance to the sports field as shown in the diagram.

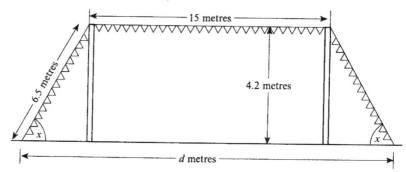

(a) Calculate the size of angle x.

(b) Pat used the Theorem of Pythagoras to find the distance d metres.
She worked out that $d = 24.9$.
Use trigonometry to check this value.

NEAB

11.

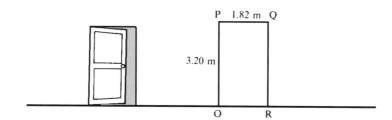

OPQR is a rectangular piece of scenery standing upright on a stage. OP = 3·20m and
PQ = 1·82m. In order to take this piece of scenery through a door, the rectangle will
have to be lowered by turning it about the corner O.

Give all answers correct to 3 significant figures.

(a) The rectangle has reached the position in
which OQ is vertical. Find the angle
which OP makes with the floor.

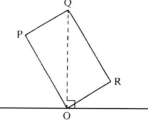

(b) In this new position, A and B are points
on the floor directly below P and R.

OA = 2·10m.

Calculate

(i) the size of angle AOP,

(ii) RB, the distance of R from the floor.

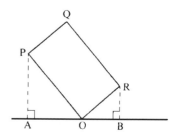

NICCEA

12. When an aeroplane takes off, its ascent is in two stages. These two stages are shown in the diagram below as *AB* and *BC*.

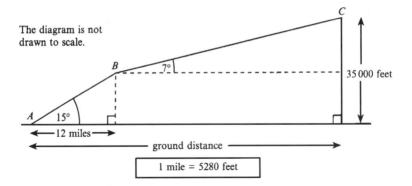

The diagram is not drawn to scale.

35 000 feet

←—12 miles—→

←——— ground distance ———→

1 mile = 5280 feet

(a) In the first stage the aeroplane climbs at an angle of 15° to the horizontal. Calculate the height it has reached when it has covered a ground distance of 12 miles. Give your answer correct to the nearest thousand feet.

(b) In the second stage the aeroplane climbs at an angle of 7° to the horizontal. At the end of its ascent it has reached a height of 35 000 feet above the ground. Calculate the total ground distance it has covered. Give your answer in miles to a reasonable degree of accuracy. **NEAB**

13.

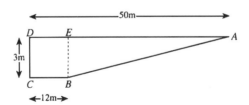

This diagram is not drawn to scale. It shows the cross-section of a swimming pool 50m long. It is 3m deep at the deep end. The deepest part of the pool is 12m long.

(a) Calculate the length of the sloping bottom of the pool *AB*.

(b) What angle does the sloping bottom *AB* make with the horizontal?

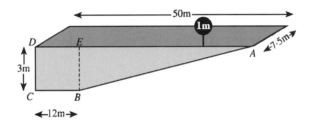

(c) There is a marker on the horizontal top *AED* to show where the pool is 1 metre deep. How far from *A* is the marker?

(d) The pool is 7·5m wide. What is its volume? **WJEC**

14.

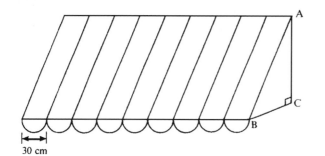

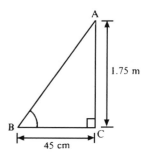

30 cm

45 cm

A sun canopy, as shown, extends 45cm from the base of a vertical rod AC 1·75m long.

(a) Calculate the angle ABC which the canopy makes with the horizontal extension arm BC.

(b) The canopy breadth (AB in diagram) is 1·81m. What is the total area of canvas in the canopy, including the semi-circles, each of diameter 30cm, across the bottom? (You may take π as 3·14) **NICCEA**

15. From a point P, on level ground, a surveyor measures the angle of elevation of R, the top of a building, as 32°.
He walks 12 metres towards the building to point Q and measures the angle of elevation of R as 57°.
X is the point on PR such that angle PXQ = 90°.

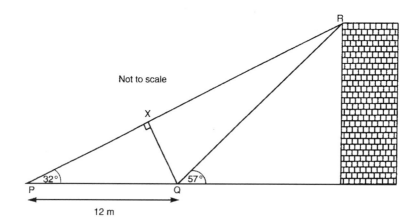

Not to scale

(a) Show that QX = 6·36m

(b) **(i)** Explain why angle PRQ is 25°

(ii) hence find the length of QR.

(c) Calculate the height of the building. **MEG**

380

1. **(i)** Find, to two decimal places, the values of

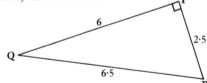

    (a) sin R

    (b) tan Q

    (c) cos Q.

  (ii) Use the calculator to find the size of the angle θ (to the nearest tenth of a degree) if

    (a) cos $\theta = 0\cdot26$

    (b) tan $\theta = 5$

    (c) sin $\theta = \frac{2}{5}$.

2.

Are any of these diagrams similar? If so, which ones?

3. A ladder makes an angle of 70° with the ground.
The foot of the ladder is 1·2m from the wall.
How long is this ladder?

4. (a)

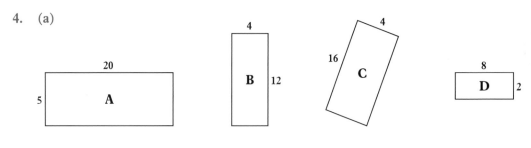

Not Drawn to Scale

One of the rectangles is not similar to the other three. Which one is not similar?

(b)

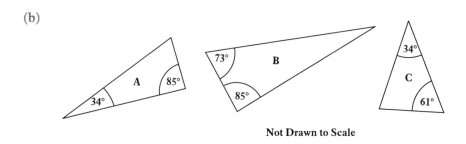

Not Drawn to Scale

Two of these triangles are similar. Which ones are these?

5. Marie used the formula $A = \frac{1}{3}\pi r^2 h$ for the surface area of a cone of radius r and height h. Use dimensions to explain why this formula cannot be correct.

6.

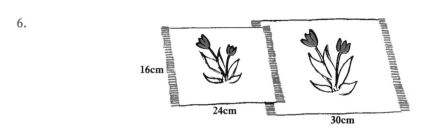

Hilary is making rectangular tablemats in two sizes. The small size measures 24cm by 16cm. The large size is 30cm long.
If Hilary's tablemats are similar shapes, find the width of a large mat.

7.

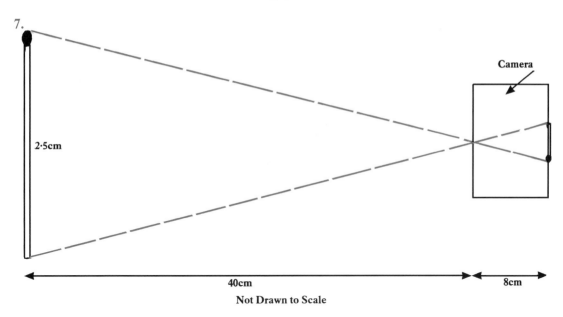

40cm

8cm

Not Drawn to Scale

This diagram represents a match and its image on the screen of a pinhole camera. The match, which is 2·5cm tall, is placed 40cm from the pinhole. If the pinhole is 8cm from the screen, how high is the image of the match?

8. It is believed that the Leaning Tower of Pisa will collapse once its top is more than 5·23 metres from the vertical. The Tower is 54·56 metres tall. Find the greatest angle the Tower can make with the vertical.

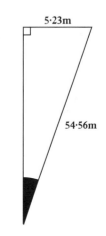

9. Ahmed stands at A, directly under the end of a crane. From A, he walks 10m to B. At B, he measures the angle of elevation of the end of the crane as 73°. How high is the end of the crane?

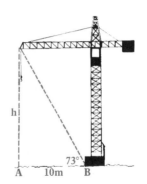

10. Anne was making a scale drawing of a school building.
    The first thing Anne did was to find the actual height of this building. At a distance of 20 metres from the building, Anne's friend held a 1 metre ruler upright. When Anne lay on the ground 3·42 metres from this ruler she could just see the top of the building. Anne then drew the following sketch and used similar shapes to calculate the height of the building.
    What answer should she get?

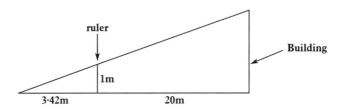

11.

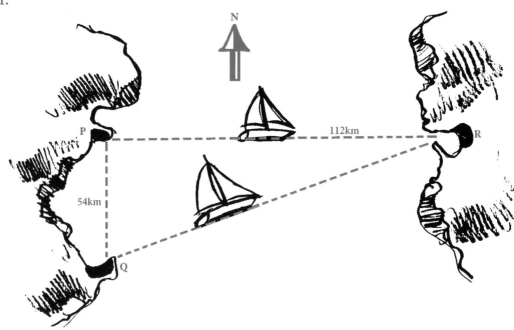

Two yachts sail into the harbour at R.
One yacht sails from P, which is 112km due West of R. The other sails from Q, which is 54km due South of P.

(a) Use Pythagoras' theorem to find the distance from Q to R.

(b) Which angle in the diagram gives the bearing of R from Q?
    Use trigonometry to find the size of this angle and hence the bearing of R from Q.

12.

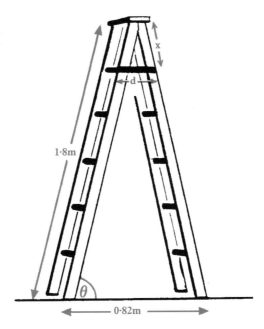

1·8m

0·82m

A symmetrical stepladder has five equally spaced steps as shown in the diagram. When the stepladder is being used it is kept stable with a bar connecting the top steps.

(a) Find the distance between each step (x in the diagram).

(b) Use similar shapes to find the length of the connecting bar (d in the diagram).

(c) Use trigonometry to find the angle each side of the stepladder makes with the ground (θ in the diagram).

13.

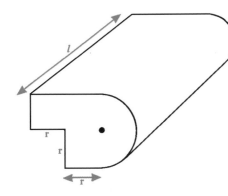

This diagram represents a brick of an unusual shape.
Which of the following expressions could be for

(a) the volume

(b) the surface area of the front face

(c) the perimeter of the front face?

$3rl + \frac{1}{2}\pi r^2 l$ $6\pi r^2 + \pi r$ $6r + \pi r$ $6r^2 + \pi r$ $3r^2 l + \frac{1}{2}\pi l$

$3r^2 l + \frac{1}{2}\pi r^2 l$ $3r^2 + \frac{1}{2}\pi r$ $3r^2 + \frac{1}{2}\pi r^2$ $3r + \frac{1}{2}\pi r^2$ $3r^2 l^2 + \frac{1}{2}\pi rl$

14. A helicopter is flying at a height of 120 metres. From this helicopter, the angle of depression of a liferaft is measured as 42°. At the same time, the angle of depression of another liferaft is measured as 31°.

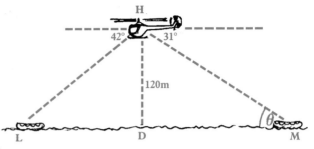

(a) What is the size of the angle θ?

(b) Use trigonometry to find the distance DM.

(c) How far apart are the two liferafts?

15.

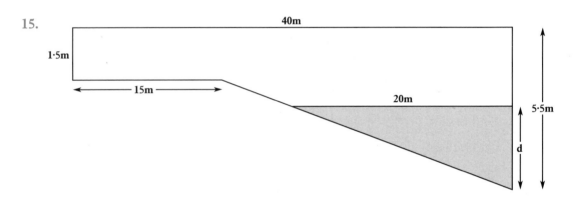

This sketch represents a swimming pool which is being emptied.
How deep is the water in this pool when the length of the surface of the water is 20m?

16. Sally is trying to estimate the height of her school. She measures the angle of elevation of the highest point as 35°. She measures the distance from the bottom of the wall along level ground as 12·6m.

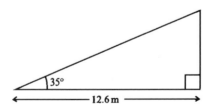

(a) Calculate the height of the school.

(b) To what degree of accuracy should Sally give her answer?
Give a reason for your answer.

NEAB

17. This quadrilateral is made from two right angled triangles.

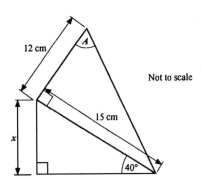

Not to scale

12 cm

15 cm

40°

(a) Calculate the length x.

(b) Calculate the angle A.

SEG

18.

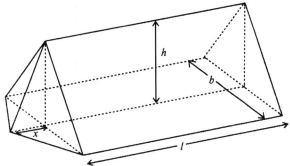

One of these formulae gives the volume of the tent.

$$V = \tfrac{1}{6}\, bh\, (3l + x^2) \qquad\qquad V = \tfrac{1}{6}\, b^2 h\, (3l + x) \qquad\qquad V = \tfrac{1}{6}\, bh\, (3l + x)$$

Look at the formulae and cross out the two that could not be correct.
Explain why each of these cannot be correct.

NEAB

19.

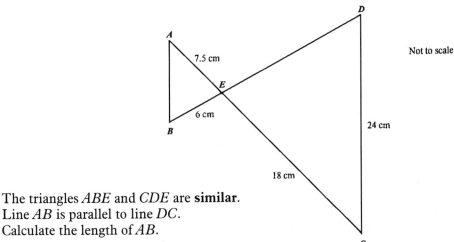

7.5 cm

6 cm

24 cm

18 cm

Not to scale

The triangles ABE and CDE are **similar**.
Line AB is parallel to line DC.
Calculate the length of AB.

SEG

20.

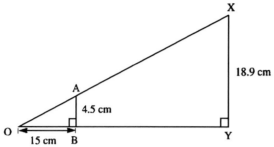

Diagram NOT accurately drawn.

18.9 cm

4.5 cm

15 cm

(a) Calculate the length of OY.

(b) Calculate the size of angle XOY.

ULEAC

21. This diagram is made from three right-angled triangles.

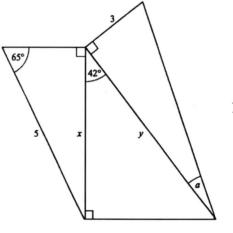

Not to scale

Calculate

(a) length *x*,　　**(b)** length *y*,　　**(c)** angle *a*.

SEG

22. The diagram shows a child's play brick in the shape of a prism.

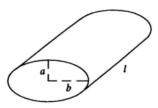

The following formulae represent certain quantities connected with this prism.

$$\pi ab, \ \pi(a + b), \ \pi abl, \ \pi(a + b)l$$

Which of these formulae represent areas?

SEG

23.

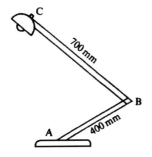

A desk lamp of the type shown in the diagram can be positioned by varying the directions of the hinged rods AB and BC which lie in a vertical plane.

Give all answers correct to 3 significant figures.

(a) The lamp is positioned with AB vertical and C situated 850mm above the level of A.

Calculate the angle which BC makes with the vertical.

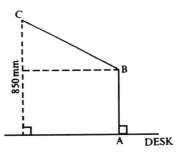

(b) The lamp is repositioned with angle ABC = 90° and C directly above A.

Calculate the angle between AB and the desk.

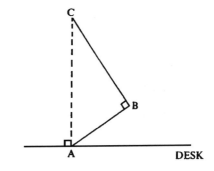

(c) The lamp is repositioned with C directly above A and AB inclined at 33° to the desk.

Calculate:

(i) the height of B above the desk,

(ii) the distance of B from AC,

(iii) the distance AC.

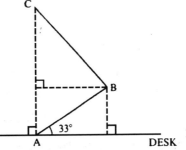

NICCEA

24.

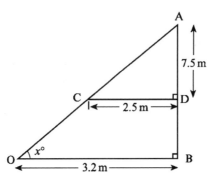

Diagram NOT accurately drawn

(a) Using the measurements shown in the diagram, calculate the length of the line AB.

Angle AOB = $x°$.
(b) Write down the value of tan $x°$.

ULEAC

25. In the diagram BC is parallel to AE.

Angle ABC = angle ADE = 90°.

AB = 5cm, BC = 9cm, DE = 3cm.

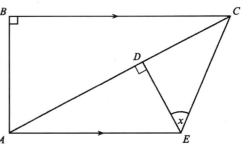

(a) Use Pythagoras' theorem to calculate the length of AC.

(b) Explain why triangles ABC and EDA are similar.

(c) Use this fact to calculate the length of AD.

(d) Calculate the angle marked x in the diagram.

NEAB

26. On a clear day, if you stand at Nefyn in North Wales (sea level) and look towards Snowdon, another mountain, Garnedd-goch, blocks the view.

From the map, the distance from Nefyn to Garnedd-goch is 21km and from Garnedd-goch to Snowdon is 11km.

The height of Snowdon is given as 1085m.

What is the lowest the height of Garnedd-goch could be?

MEG

27. The letters a, b, h, l and r represent lengths.
Which of the following formulae represent area?

$$ab, \quad \tfrac{2}{3}\pi r^3, \quad \sqrt{(a^2 + b^2)}, \quad \pi r, \quad 4\pi rl, \quad \frac{\pi r^2 h}{3}$$

SEG

28.

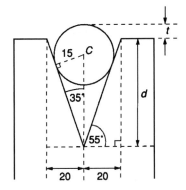

The diagram is a cross section of the edge of a door.

The circle is a seal fitted into a V-shaped groove in the door. The centre of the circle is at C. All lengths are in millimetres.

(a) Find the depth (d) of the groove.

(b) Calculate the distance (t) the seal sticks out beyond the edge of the door. **MEG**

29.

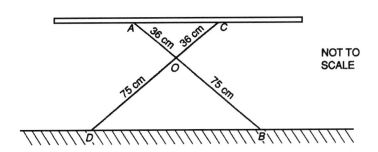

NOT TO SCALE

The diagram shows how an ironing board is supported by two legs AOB and COD. The legs are hinged at O, and C is hinged to the ironing board.

The distance between A and C can be varied.

(a) **(i)** When angle $BOD = 80°$, work out the size of angle OBD.

   (ii) What facts about angles did you use?

(b) The ironing board is placed on a horizontal floor and adjusted so that $BD = 92$cm.

   (i) Use Pythagoras' theorem to calculate the height of O above the floor.

   (ii) Use similar triangles to calculate the distance AC.

   (iii) Calculate the size of angle OBD.

(c) The ironing board is adjusted again so that AC is 90cm above the floor. Calculate the height of O above the floor. **MEG**

HANDLING DATA

Handling Data Revision

REVISION

TYPES of DATA

Discrete data can take only particular values, usually whole numbers.
Continuous data can take any value within a given range.
For instance, size of shoes is discrete data; length of shoes is continuous data.

TABLES. CHARTS. GRAPHS

27 29 28 28 30 29 27 27 29 28 29 27 30 29 28 27 28 29 29 27
This data, which gives the number of biscuits in each of 20 packets, is summarized on
the tally chart below and graphed on a bar-line graph. Since the tally chart includes
a column for frequency, it is a combined tally chart and frequency table.

Biscuits Tally Chart

Number	Tally	Frequency
27	ⅢⅠ	6
28	Ⅲ	5
29	ⅢⅡ	7
30	ⅠⅠ	2

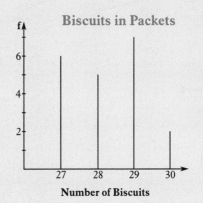

Biscuits in Packets

A bar graph may be drawn for the biscuits data.
The bar graph is similar to the bar-line graph
with the lines becoming bars.
On a bar graph the bars are not joined.

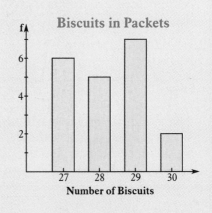

Biscuits in Packets

continued . . .

. . . from previous page

The following figures give the number of times the letter e appears in each sentence on the last page of "The Clan of the Cave Bear".

1 2 2 1 6 10 2 8 3 3 5 5 3 1 6 7 3 9 3 4 5 2 4 9 11 15 0 8

This discrete data has been **grouped** into 6 categories on the combined tally chart and frequency table, shown below.

Notice that each category is the same **width**. The first column on the table (Number of e's) could also be labelled **"class interval"**. When we group data, we should have between 6 and 15 class intervals.

The information on the tally chart is graphed as a **frequency diagram**. On a frequency diagram the bars are joined.

e's Frequency Table

Number of e's	Tally	Frequency
0–2	卌 ‖‖	8
3–5	卌 卌	10
6–8	卌	5
9–11	‖‖‖	4
12–14		0
15–17	‖	1

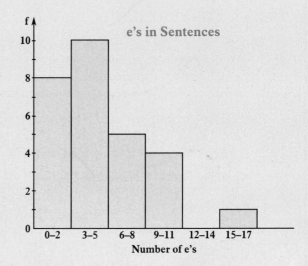

Pie Charts are circle graphs.
The circle is divided into sections.
The number of degrees in the angle at the centre of each section represents the frequency.

Hockey Matches

Won   3
Lost   15
Drawn   6

The continuous data from this table is shown graphed, on the next page, as a **frequency diagram** and as a **frequency polygon**.

Handspan of Students	
Class interval (mm)	Frequency
$170 \leq l < 180$	2
$180 \leq l < 190$	3
$190 \leq l < 200$	5
$200 \leq l < 210$	4
$210 \leq l < 220$	4

continued . . .

. . . from previous page

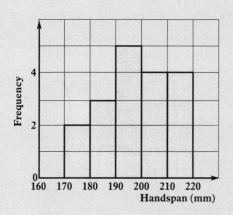

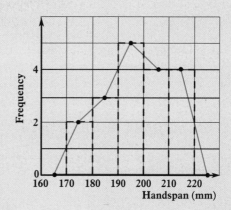

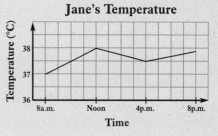

Jane's Temperature

During Jane's first 12 hours in hospital her temperature was taken at 4-hourly intervals.

At 8a.m. it was 37°C, at Noon it was 38°C, at 4p.m. it was 37·5°C and at 8p.m. it was 37·8°C.

This **line graph** shows these temperatures. It was drawn by plotting the temperatures at 8a.m., Noon, 4p.m., 8p.m. and joining the points with straight lines.

A **scatter graph** displays two aspects of data. For instance, both the length and weight of dogs could be displayed on a scatter graph. A scatter graph is sometimes called a **scatter diagram** or a **scattergram**.

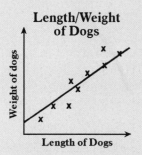

Length/Weight of Dogs

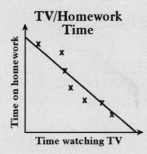

TV/Homework Time

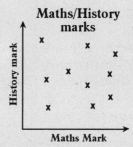

Maths/History marks

The word **correlation** is used to describe the relationship between the variables on a scatter graph. If the data shows some correlation, we can draw a line of best fit.

For **positive correlation** the points must be clustered around a line that has positive gradient. The scatter graph for Length/Weight of dogs shows positive correlation.

continued . . .

. . . *from previous page*

For **negative correlation** the points must be clustered around a line that has negative gradient. The scatter graph for TV/Homework time shows negative correlation.
If there is neither positive nor negative correlation, as in the scatter graph for Maths/History marks, we say there is **no correlation**.

MEAN. MEDIAN. MODE. RANGE

The **range** of a set of data is the difference between the largest and smallest data values. For instance, the range of 3, 2, 6, 2, 2, 3, 7 is $7 - 2 = 5$.

$$\text{Mean} = \frac{\text{Sum of all data values}}{\text{No. of items of data}}$$ For instance, the mean of 3, 2, 6, 2, 2, 3, 7 is

$$\frac{3 + 2 + 6 + 2 + 2 + 3 + 7}{7} = 3 \cdot 6 \text{ to 1 d.p.}$$

If the data is given as a **frequency distribution**, mean $= \frac{\Sigma(fx)}{\Sigma f}$

For instance
x	3	4	5	6
f	2	3	0	5
; mean $= \dfrac{2 \times 3 + 3 \times 4 + 0 \times 5 + 5 \times 6}{2 + 3 + 0 + 5} = 4 \cdot 8$.

If the data is **grouped,** we can find an approximate value for the mean by assuming that all the items of data in a given class interval have the value of the mid-point of that interval.
For instance,

Test mark	1–20	21–40	41–60	61–80	81–100
Mid-point	10·5	30·5	50·5	70·5	90·5
Frequency	2	5	7	10	1

$$\text{mean} = \frac{2 \times 10 \cdot 5 + 5 \times 30 \cdot 5 + 7 \times 50 \cdot 5 + 10 \times 70 \cdot 5 + 1 \times 90 \cdot 5}{2 + 5 + 7 + 10 + 1} = 52 \cdot 9$$

The **mode** is the value that occurs most often. For instance, the mode of 3, 2, 6, 2, 2, 3, 7 is 2. A set of data may have more than one mode or no mode. If the data is grouped we may talk about the **modal class** which is the class interval that contains more data values than any other. For instance, the modal class for the Test Marks shown above is the interval 61–80.

The **median** is the middle value of a set of data which is arranged in order. For instance, arranged in order 3, 2, 6, 2, 2, 3, 7 is 2, 2, 2, 3, 3, 6, 7. The median is the 4th value which is 3. If there is an even number of values, the median is the mean of the middle two values. If the data is grouped we can talk about the class interval which contains the median. For instance, for the previous Test Marks, the class interval which contains the median is 41–60 since the middle value (the 13th value) lies in this interval. We can calculate an **approximate value for the median.**

continued . . .

. . . from previous page

For instance, for the test marks on the previous page, the median is the 13th value. An approximate value is $41 + \frac{6}{7} \times 19 = 57 \cdot 3$ to 1 d.p.

PROBABILITY

The probability of an event that is certain to happen is 1.
The probability of an event that will never happen is 0.
The probability of any other event is between 0 and 1.

Choosing at **random** means every item has the same chance of being chosen.
Equally likely outcomes are outcomes which have the same probability of occurring.
For instance, when a coin is tossed the outcomes "a head", "a tail" are equally likely; each of these outcomes has probability of $\frac{1}{2}$.

The probability of an event may be calculated if all the possible outcomes are equally likely.

For equally likely outcomes, $\quad \boxed{P(\text{an event occurring}) = \dfrac{\text{Number of favourable outcomes}}{\text{Number of possible outcomes}}}$

For instance, the probability of getting a prime number when a die is tossed is calculated as follows.
Possible equally likely outcomes are 1, 2, 3, 4, 5, 6. Number of possible outcomes = 6.
Favourable outcomes are 2, 3, 5. Number of favourable outcomes = 3.
$P(\text{prime number}) = \frac{3}{6}$ or $\frac{1}{2}$.

Outcomes may be given as a **list,** in a **table** or in a **diagram.** For instance, the possible equally likely outcomes when two coins are tossed could be shown in any of the ways below.

HH HT TH TT

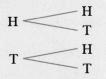

The **probability of an event not happening** is equal to $1 - P(A)$, where $P(A)$ is the probability of the event happening. For instance, when a card is chosen at random from a pack, the probability of getting the Jack of spades $= \frac{1}{52}$; the probability of not getting the Jack of spades $= \frac{51}{52}$.

Exhaustive events account for all possible outcomes. If events are exhaustive, it is certain that one of them will happen. For instance, when a die is thrown the events "an odd number", "an even number" are exhaustive events.

continued . . .

. . . from previous page

Events which cannot happen at the same time are called mutually exclusive events. For instance, if a die is tossed the events "a four", "a prime number" are mutually exclusive since both of these events cannot happen together.

Probability may be estimated from experiments. The frequency of an event is the number of times that event occurs in a number of trials. The relative frequency of an event compares the frequency with the number of trials. It is the proportion of times the event occurs in a number of trials.

$$\text{Relative frequency of an event} = \frac{\text{Number of times the event occurs}}{\text{Number of trials}}$$

If an experiment is repeated a great number of times, the relative frequency of an event occurring can be used as an estimate of the probability of that event occurring. The more often the experiment is repeated, the better the estimate will be. For instance, if in 1000 tosses of an unfair die, a "six" came up 620 times, we can estimate the probability of getting a "six" the next time we toss this die as $\frac{620}{1000}$ or 0·62.

The expected number of times an event will occur is equal to the product of the number of trials and the probability of the event occurring in any one trial. For instance, if we toss the unfair die, mentioned above, 200 times we expect to get a "six" $0·62 \times 200$ or 124 times.

SURVEYS. QUESTIONNAIRES. HYPOTHESES

The steps taken to conduct a survey are:

Step 1 **Decide** on the purpose of the survey.
Step 2 **Design** an observation sheet or a questionnaire.
Step 3 **Collect** the data. If necessary, collate the data.
Step 4 **Organise** the data onto tables and graphs or into a computer database.
Step 5 **Analyse** the data i.e. make some conclusions.

Some guidelines for designing a questionnaire are:

- Decide how the collected data is to be collated and analysed.
- Allow for *all* possible answers.
- Give clear instructions on how the questions are to be answered.
- Do not ask for information that is not needed.
- Avoid questions which people may not be willing to answer.
- Make the questions clear and concise.
- If your questions are asking for opinions, word them so that *your* opinion is not evident.
- Keep the questionnaire as short as possible.

continued . . .

. . . *from previous page*

Some useful responses to questions are:

Yes	No	
Agree	Neither Agree nor Disagree	Disagree
Always	Usually	Sometimes	Seldom	Never

Responses must be consistent with the wording of a question and should be balanced with an equal number of positive and negative responses.

One way of **analysing a list of items** which have been ranked in order of preference is by adding the products of the rank and the number of times the item was given this rank.

For instance, the order of colour preference of 100 students shown on the table below can be analysed as follows:

Blue: $\quad 1 \times 14 + 2 \times 28 + 3 \times 21 + 4 \times 19 + 5 \times 18 = 299$
Green: $\quad 1 \times 18 + 2 \times 10 + 3 \times 2 + 4 \times 32 + 5 \times 38 = 362$
Red: $\quad 1 \times 23 + 2 \times 19 + 3 \times 21 + 4 \times 23 + 5 \times 14 = 286$
White: $\quad 1 \times 11 + 2 \times 28 + 3 \times 17 + 4 \times 20 + 5 \times 24 = 318$
Black: $\quad 1 \times 34 + 2 \times 15 + 3 \times 39 + 4 \times 6 + 5 \times 6 = 235$

Since Black has the lowest total, Black is the most popular.

Rank \ Colour	Blue	Green	Red	White	Black
1	14	18	23	11	34
2	28	10	19	28	15
3	21	2	21	17	39
4	19	32	23	20	6
5	18	38	14	24	6

An **hypothesis** is a statement of one person's opinion about an issue. For instance, the statement "most students do not eat breakfast" is an hypothesis. A survey could be conducted to test this hypothesis; that is, to find whether the hypothesis is true or false. There are usually four steps in making and testing an hypothesis.

Step 1   State the hypothesis.
Step 2   Collect data related to this hypothesis.
Step 3   Collate and analyse the data.
Step 4   Use the analysis to test the hypothesis.

Experiments which involve several variables should be carefully planned. With the exception of the variable being changed, all other conditions should remain the same throughout the experiment.

Planning should consist of: Deciding which conditions to vary.
                                       Deciding what data to collect.
                                       Deciding how and when the data will be collected.
                                       Deciding how the data will be collated and displayed.
                                       Deciding how the data will be analysed.

REVISION EXERCISE

1. An unfair die is tossed many times. The results are shown on the table.

Number on die	1	2	3	4	5	6
Frequency	72	69	82	221	203	353

(a) What is the relative frequency of tossing a 6?

(b) Estimate the probability of getting an even number the next time this die is tossed.

2. (a) As part of Dean and Joanne's survey on traffic, Dean decided to display this data on a bar graph.
Draw this bar graph.

(b) Joanne decided to display the data on a pie chart.
What angle should Joanne have for each of the 5 categories?
Draw the pie chart.

Vehicle	Frequency
Lorry	5
Bus	3
Car	28
Motorbike	7
Bicycle	17

3. Mehmet was going to do a survey to test the hypothesis "people who wear glasses or contact lenses read more books than those who don't."

Write two questions, with possible responses, that Mehmet should include in his questionnaire.

4.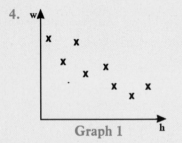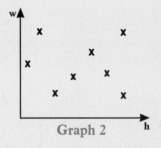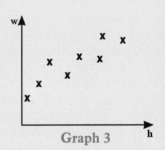

Graph 1　　　　　Graph 2　　　　　Graph 3

(a) Which of these graphs shows positive correlation between the variables h and w?

(b) Which shows negative correlation?

(c) Which shows no correlation?

5. Three coins are tossed together.

(a) Copy and complete this list of possible outcomes: HHH, HHT, HTH, . . .

(b) What is the probability of getting at least two heads?

6. Adrian made this spinner as part of a game he designed. When this spinner is spun find the probability of it stopping in the following sections.

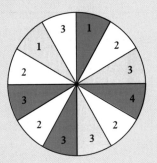

(a) Red   (b) 3

(c) Red 3   (d) prime number

(e) number less than 5   (f) number greater than 4

(g) either Red or Grey

7. As part of the comparison of the marks of her class on two tests, Ms Hassell drew the frequency polygons on the same set of axes.
The frequency diagram and frequency polygon for Test A are shown.

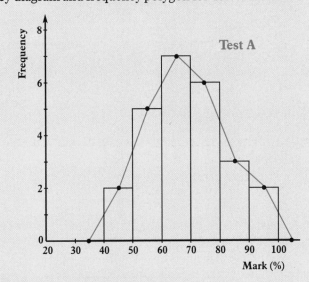

(a) Copy the frequency polygon for Test A.

(b) The marks in Test B are given in the table.

Mark Range	40 – 49	50 – 59	60 – 69	70 – 79	80 – 89	90 – 99
Frequency	3	4	3	6	8	1

On the same set of axes used in (a), draw the frequency polygon for Test B.

(c) Comment on any similarities or differences between the two frequency polygons.

8. Alison believes that students have better calculator skills than teachers.
Design an experiment to test whether this is true. Include how you propose to collect the data and how you would analyse it.

9. These line graphs show
   the midday temperatures
   at Carlisle and Calais for
   one week in June.
   Compare these
   temperatures. In your
   comparison, refer to the
   ranges and the means.

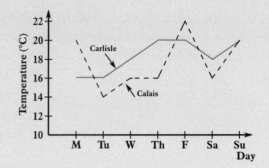

10. Bowenhill Council are proposing to allow a fun-fair to rent space in Bowenhill Park.
    Design a questionnaire to survey the opinion of people about this. Write your questions
    and responses so they are not biased.
    Explain how you would collect, organise and analyse the data. Include the following in
    your explanation.

    ● how you would take account of bias in your choice of people to complete your
      questionnaire

    ● how you might collate the data

    ● what tables and graphs you might use

    ● whether or not you might use the computer to help in your analysis of the data

11. These four discs are placed in a bag. The discs are all the same
    shape and size. Melanie chooses two of these discs at random.
    She replaces the first disc before choosing the second.
    What is the probability that the two discs she chooses, total less
    than 30p?

12. Would you expect there to be positive correlation, negative correlation or no correlation
    between the following:

    (a) the weight of suitcases filled with clothes and the volume of the suitcases

    (b) the distance cars travel on 10 litres of petrol and the weight of the cars

    (c) the time students take to run 100m and the time they take to run 200m

    (d) the time students take to run 100m and the time they take to swim 100m

    (e) the height of the oldest child in a family and the height of the youngest child?

13. Julian's family own an apple orchard. Julian conducted a survey for his family.

(i) Julian counted the number of trees in each row. His results are shown on this frequency table.

Number of trees	15	16	17	18	19	20	21	22	23
Frequency	1	0	1	3	1	3	0	1	1

    (a) How many rows of trees are there on this orchard?

    (b) How many trees are there?

    (c) What is the mean number of trees per row? (Answer to 1 d.p.)

    (d) What is the mode?

    (e) Find the median number of trees per row.

    (f) Find the range.

(ii) Julian collected data on the number of apples produced last season by each of the trees. He organised this data onto the following frequency table.

Apples produced	600 – 799	800 – 999	1000 – 1199	1200 – 1399	1400 –1599	1600 –1799
Frequency	8	14	10	34	68	76

Julian then displayed this data on a frequency diagram. Draw this graph.

Height (m)	Tally
1 –	Ⅳ I
2 –	Ⅳ Ⅳ Ⅳ Ⅳ III
3 –	Ⅳ Ⅳ Ⅳ Ⅳ Ⅳ Ⅳ Ⅳ Ⅳ Ⅳ Ⅳ Ⅳ Ⅳ Ⅳ Ⅳ Ⅳ Ⅳ IIII
4 –	Ⅳ Ⅳ Ⅳ Ⅳ Ⅳ Ⅳ Ⅳ Ⅳ Ⅳ Ⅳ Ⅳ Ⅳ Ⅳ Ⅳ Ⅳ Ⅳ II
5 – 6	Ⅳ IIII

(iii) Julian estimated the height of each tree. He entered the height of each tree on this observation sheet.
Julian then wrote up the frequency table shown below.

Class interval	1m –	2m –	3m –	4m –	5m – 6m
Mid-point	1·5m				
Frequency	6	24			

    (a) Copy and complete this frequency table.

    (b) Calculate an approximate value for the mean height.

    (c) Which class interval contains the median?

    (d) What is the modal class?

    (e) Calculate an approximate value for the median.

14. The data in the table gives the height of some 16-year old boys and their height as 3-year olds.

	Jon	Ian	Tim	Evan	Adam	Luke	Brett	Ryan	Mark	Rob
Height at 16 (m)	1·85	1·72	1·74	1·88	1·77	1·79	1·63	1·80	1·61	1·73
Height at 3 (m)	1·03	0·93	0·94	1·04	0·96	0·99	0·85	0·95	0·84	0·93

   (a) Plot this data on a scatter diagram. (Have height at 16 on the horizontal axis and height at 3 on the vertical axis.)

   (b) Draw the line of best fit.

   (c) At 16, Matthew is 1·68m tall. Estimate how tall Matthew was at 3.

   (d) When Ian's younger brother was 3, he was 1·01m tall. Estimate his height at 16.

15. In a bag there are caramel and peppermint chocolates. One of these chocolates is chosen at random.
    Sue claims that the events "choosing a caramel chocolate", "choosing a peppermint chocolate" are mutually exclusive.
    Nigel claims that these events are exhaustive.
    Who is correct, Sue or Nigel? Explain your answer.

16. Before a new disco was opened, some teenagers were surveyed. One of the questions is given below.

    ☐ *Lights*   ☐ *Music*   ☐ *Decoration*   ☐ *Service*

    Rank these from 1 to 4, putting 1 beside the one you think is most important down to 4 beside the one you think is least important.

    The responses to this question are shown collated below.

Ranking	Lights	Music	Decoration	Service
1	38	33	15	15
2	27	32	19	23
3	31	36	9	25
4	5	0	58	38

    Make some conclusions from this data.

17. As part of her Communication Studies coursework, Sarah has carried out a survey into telephone usage. She asked 30 people to keep a record of the number of long distance telephone calls that they made in one week. The results were as follows.

10	8	17	3	29	6	3	12	8	1
8	12	4	2	2	1	6	3	7	14
0	9	0	0	18	13	17	0	1	9

(a) Use tally marks to complete the frequency table.

Number of calls	Tally	Frequency
0 – 4		
5 – 9		
10 – 14		
15 – 19		
20 – 24		
25 – 29		

(b) Comment on any unusual feature of the results.   **SEG**

18.

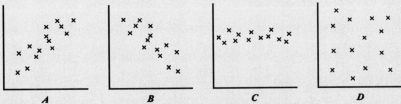

Which of the above scatter graphs *A*, *B*, *C*, or *D*, would best describe the following situations.

(a) The size of feet **compared with** the marks in a maths test.

(b) The age of adults **compared with** the height of adults.   **SEG**

19. The Table shows the best height cleared by 17 competitors in a high jump competition. Three competitors failed to clear any height at all.

Height (metres)	0	1·89	1·92	1·95	1·98	2·01	2·04
Frequency	3	3	3	2	1	4	1

(a) One of the seventeen competitors is selected at random.
Find the probability that this competitor jumped more than 2 metres.

(b) Write down the modal height.

(c) Find the median height.

(d) Find the mean height.   **MEG**

20. Lorraine is writing a questionnaire for a survey about her local Superstore.

She thinks that local people visit the store more often than people from further away. She also thinks that local people spend less money per visit.

Write three questions which would help her to test these ideas.

Each question should include at least three responses from which people choose one.   **SEG**

21. The following table is taken from a holiday brochure for the Greek island of Kos. It shows the mean midday temperature (in °F) for each of the months from April to October for Kos and for London.

	Apr.	May	Jun.	Jul.	Aug.	Sep.	Oct.
KOS	69	74	80	86	86	80	75
LONDON	55	62	70	71	71	65	59

(a) Mary says that the range of temperatures given for London is greater than the range of the temperatures given for Kos.

Is she correct? Show your working.

(b) On the following grid the line graph of the mean midday temperatures in London, from April to October, has been drawn.

Using the same grid draw a line graph showing the mean midday temperatures in Kos from April to October.

MEAN MIDDAY TEMPERATURES

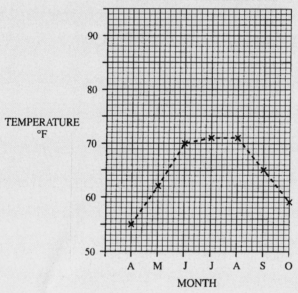

(c) (i) The midday temperatures (in °F) recorded in Kos for one week during the month of October are given below.

Sun	Mon	Tues	Wed	Thur	Fri	Sat
82	85	79	85	83	86	88

Calculate the mean midday temperatures for this week.

(ii) John is surprised at the answer to (i) as he thinks that the mean for the week should be the same as the mean for the month of October shown in the table.

Give a reason why this is not so.

WJEC

22. Boxes of eggs containing broken eggs cannot be sold in shops.
The table shows how many boxes of Grade *A* eggs and Grade *B* eggs could not be sold in a week at one shop.

Grade	Mon	Tue	Wed	Thur	Fri
A	14	16	16	14	16
B	14	12	9	11	15

(a) For the Grade *A* eggs calculate:

(i) the range; **(ii)** the mean.

(b) For the Grade *B* eggs the range is 6 boxes and the mean is 12·2 boxes.
Use this information to compare the two Grades.
Which Grade would you recommend the shopkeeper to stock?
Give a reason. **NEAB**

23. The pie-chart compares the areas of four oceans.
The total area of these four oceans is 129·6 million square miles.

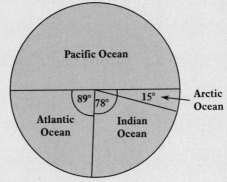

(i) Show that the area of the Pacific Ocean is twice the area of the Atlantic Ocean.

(ii) Calculate the area of the Arctic Ocean. **NEAB**

24. The table gives information about the age and value of a number of cars of the same type.

Age (years)	1	3	$4\frac{1}{2}$	6	3	5	2	$5\frac{1}{2}$	4	7
Value (£)	8200	5900	4900	3800	6200	4500	7600	2200	5200	3200

(a) Use this information to draw a scatter graph.

(b) What does the graph tell you about the value of these cars as they get older?

(c) The information is correct but the age and value of one of these cars looks out of place.
Give a possible reason for this.

(d) Draw a line of best fit.

(e) John has a car of this type which is $3\frac{1}{2}$ years old and is in average condition. Use the graph to estimate its value. **SEG**

25.

Height h (cm)	Frequency
$120 \leq h < 125$	2
$125 \leq h < 130$	5
$130 \leq h < 135$	8
$135 \leq h < 140$	14
$140 \leq h < 145$	11
$145 \leq h < 150$	9
$150 \leq h < 155$	3
$155 \leq h < 160$	1

Height h (cm)	Frequency
$120 \leq h < 130$	
$130 \leq h < 140$	
$140 \leq h < 150$	
$150 \leq h < 160$	

The height of some pupils is recorded on the table on the left.
Ann records the data using class intervals of 10cm.

(a) Complete Ann's table shown on the right.

Ann draws a frequency diagram of her data.

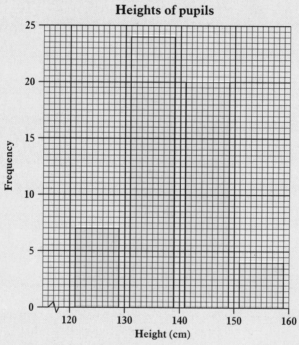

Heights of pupils

Ann has made two mistakes in drawing her diagram.
(b) What are the two mistakes?

Another pupil is included.
The pupil has a height of 150 cm.

(c) Into which of Ann's class intervals should the pupil be placed?

SEG

26.

Monthly rainfall (millimetres)

	Jan	Feb	Mar	Apr	May	June	July	Aug	Sept	Oct	Nov	Dec
Great Britain	74	44	40	48	50	29	48	37	61	75	84	70
The Gambia	0	0	0	0	1	2	84	352	185	81	27	0

(a) The mean rainfall per month in Great Britain is 55mm. Calculate the mean rainfall per month in The Gambia.

(b) Find the range of the monthly rainfall

   (i) in The Gambia,   **(ii)** in Great Britain.

(c) In which of these two countries are water shortages more likely?

(d) Explain your answer to part **(c)**, using the means **and** the ranges.

(e)

Monthly rainfall (millimetres)

	Jan	Feb	Mar	Apr	May	June	July	Aug	Sept	Oct	Nov	Dec
Geneva	48	46	56	64	76	79	74	91	90	71	79	

The table above shows the monthly rainfall figures for Geneva. The figure for December is missing. The diagram below represents the figures for all 12 months. According to this diagram, in which class interval does the December rainfall lie?

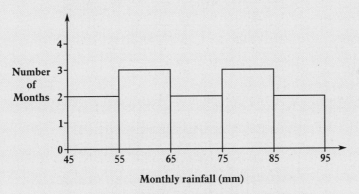

MEG

27.

CHARITIES
Income from voluntary donations in one year

Charity	Income £ (millions)
Help the Aged	30
R.S.P.C.A.	25
National Trust	50
Oxfam	35
Save the Children Fund	40

Re-present the information in an appropriate diagram.

MEG

28. A manufacturer tests electric motors by running them until they fail. The running times for fifty motors are shown in the table.

Running Time (Hours)	Midpoint	No. of Motors
0 –	0·5	10
1 –	1·5	0
2 –	2·5	0
3 –	3·5	0
4 –	4·5	2
5 –	5·5	17
6 –	6·5	20
7 – 8	7·5	1

(a) Calculate the mean running time.

(b) Find the median running time.

(c) The manufacturer uses the average running time in an advertisement.

    (i) Give a reason why he should **not** use the mean.

    (ii) Give a reason for using the mode.   **SEG**

29. The height of each of 60 plants of type *A* was measured and recorded.

Height of plant (cm)	8 –	10 –	12 –	14 –	16 –	18 –	20 – 22
Number of plants	0	2	3	18	19	18	0

(a) Draw the frequency polygon of these results.

The frequency polygon of 60 plants of type *B* is drawn below.

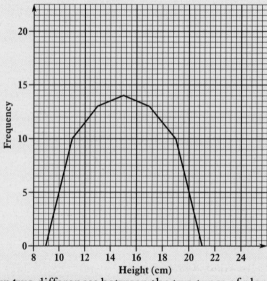

(b) Write down **two** differences between the two types of plant shown by the frequency polygons.   **SEG**

30. Phillip and Elizabeth collected information about the heights and weights of their friends. They calculated the mean, median and mode of their results.

	Mean	Median	Mode
Phillip's friends	Height 180cm	Height 175cm	Height 177cm
	Weight 50kg	Weight 45kg	Weight 40kg
Elizabeth's friends	Height 175cm	Height 175cm	Height 172cm
	Weight 45kg	Weight 50kg	Weight 50kg

Phillip says that most of his friends do not weigh as much as most of Elizabeth's friends.

(a) Explain why this may not be true.

Elizabeth says that all Phillip's friends are taller than her friends.

(b) Explain why this may not be true.   **ULEAC**

31. The students at Loovilla College decided to have a biscuit eating competition.
A random sample of 25 students was taken.
The table shows the numbers of students eating different numbers of biscuits in four minutes.

Number of Biscuits eaten in 4 minutes	Mid-point	Frequency (Number of students)	
1 – 5		2	
6 – 10		8	
11 – 15		7	
16 – 20		5	
21 – 25		2	
26 – 30		1	
		25	

(a) Calculate an estimate of the mean number of biscuits eaten in 4 minutes.

(b) Write down the modal class interval.

(c) 250 students entered the competition.
Estimate how many of them will eat more than 20 biscuits in the four minutes.

                                                                             ULEAC

32. In a survey to investigate people's newspaper reading habits, the following two questions are asked:

(a) 'Do you agree that this town's daily paper is a complete waste of money?'

(b) 'If you take a newspaper, state which one and whether you take it daily or only at weekends and if not, how you normally keep up with political news – radio? television?'

Explain, in each case, why the question is unsatisfactory and give a better question, or series of questions, to replace it.   **MEG**

33. Sheila found the mode, median and mean of sets of five numbers.
Her results are shown in the Table.

numbers	mode	median	mean
1 1 2 3 4	1	2	2·2
1 2 3 4 4	4	3	2·8
1 3 4 5 5	5	4	3·6
1 2 2 3 4	2	2	2·4
2 2 4 6 7	2	4	4·2

Sheila said 'the mean can never be between the mode and the median'.
Investigate whether she is correct by considering other sets of five numbers.   **MEG**

Sofya Kovalevskaya

Sofya Kovalevskaya was born in Moscow in 1850 and died in Stockholm in 1891. She was the daughter of a Russian general who disciplined his troops but not his daughter!

Sofya was first exposed to mathematics by an uncle who talked to her about maths. when she was quite young; too young to understand. Her father encouraged her when she showed interest in the subject and provided maths. tutors for her.

Sofya married at 18 and she and her husband went to study in Germany. Women, at that time, were not allowed to study at Russian Universities. Some claim that Sofya married in order to be able to travel abroad to continue her studies. It was not acceptable for Russian women to travel if they were not married. The situation regarding women studying at Universities in Germany was similar to that in Russia. However, Sofya had private lessons in Berlin with a famous mathematician who recognised her remarkable ability.

At the age of 24, she gained a Doctorate in Mathematics from the University of Göttingen. Sofya hadn't studied there; she was granted her degree "in absentia." Her thesis was on differential equations, an important area of mathematics. Throughout her life she continued to work in this area and made valuable contributions to the theory of differential equations.

In 1884 she was appointed to the University of Stockholm as a lecturer. Shortly after this she became the editor of the important international journal "Acta Mathematica." In 1889, she became Professor of Mathematics at Stockholm University.

In 1888 she won a prestigious prize, the Prix Borodin awarded by the French Académie des Sciences. Her entry, on the rotation of a solid body about a fixed point, impressed the judges so much that they raised the prize money from 3000 francs to 5000 francs.

In 1889, she was elected to the Russian Imperial Academy of Sciences; a great honour. She was the first woman to be elected.

Sofya had talents other than mathematical talents. She was a well known writer. Her most famous novel was "Vera Vorontzoff", published in 1893. This novel, and others she wrote, were based on her early life in Russia. She also wrote plays and poetry.

Sofya was a political activist; often taking a radical point of view and always a champion of women's rights. She was particularly outspoken about the role of women in Russian society and their limited educational opportunities.

In the past, Sofya's achievements have often been ignored by historians. In recent times, the opposite has been true – many feminist writers have made exaggerated claims about her achievements. This is a shame since her achievements were quite remarkable and do not need any exaggeration. She was the first woman mathematician to achieve international fame; the first woman to gain a Doctorate in mathematics; the first woman Professor of Mathematics and the first woman to be the editor of a major mathematical journal.

At the age of 41, Sofya died from pneumonia, a complication arising after having had influenza.

based on an article from the book "Women Sum It Up" – Hazard Press

ANALYSING DATA: quartiles, interquartile range

We may use the statistical measures, **mean, median, mode** and **range** to analyse data. Other statistical measures we may use are the **quartiles** and the **interquartile range.**

For a set of data arranged in order, the median is the middle value, the lower quartile is the middle value of the lower half of the data and the upper quartile is the middle value of the upper half of the data.

The interquartile range is the difference between the upper and lower quartiles.

That is, | **interquartile range = upper quartile – lower quartile**

Examples 1.

| 1·4 | 2 | 3·2 | 5·1 | 5·4 | 6 | 7·8 |

lower quartile = 2

median = 5·1

upper quartile = 6

$$\text{interquartile range} = 6 - 2$$
$$= 4$$

2.

| 8 | 8 | 9 | 10 | 12 | 13 | 14 | 16 | 17 | 17 |

lower quartile = 9

median = 12·5

upper quartile = 16

$$\text{interquartile range} = 16 - 9$$
$$= 7$$

3.

| 8 | 11 | 12 | 13 | 15 | 15 | 18 | 19 |

lower quartile = 11·5

median = 14

upper quartile = 16·5

$$\text{interquartile range} = 16·5 - 11·5$$
$$= 5$$

DISCUSSION EXERCISE 17:1

- 16 17 18 20 24 25 28 31 33 34 35 39 40

  This data gives the marks of 13 students for a history assignment. The median is 28, the lower quartile is 19, the upper quartile is 34·5, the interquartile range is 15·5, the range is 24.

  1 4 17 21 27 27 28 28 28 30 39 50 70

  This data gives the marks of the same 13 students for a science assignment. The median, the lower quartile, the upper quartile and the interquartile range are the same as for the history assignment; the range is 69.

  Do you think the interquartile range describes the spread of these sets of data well? Discuss.

- Discuss the advantages and disadvantages of using the interquartile range as one of the measures to describe a set of data. As part of your discussion write down several sets of data, some of which have the same interquartile range but different quartiles, some of which have the same range but different interquartile ranges, some of which have the same quartiles but different medians and so on.

-

Number of children	1	2	3	4	5	6	7	8
Frequency	16	21	18	9	5	4	0	1

  This frequency distribution shows the number of children in the families of the members of a youth club.
  How could you find the quartiles for this data? Discuss.

- Discuss how the following statements could be completed.

  "The median divides a set of data in . . . "
  "The quartiles divide a set of data into . . . "

  "One half of the data values lie below the . . . "
  "One-quarter of the data values lie below the . . . "
  "Three-quarters of the data values lie below the . . . "
  "The interquartile range is the range of the central . . . of the data".

Worked Example Margaret gathered data on the ages of the people in her modern dance class. Her data was:

12 15 15 14 13 15 15 16 17 11 17 14 16 14 12 16

What is the interquartile range for this data?

415

Answer In order, the data is:

11   12   12   13   14   14   14   15   15   15   15   16   16   16   17   17

$\uparrow$ lower quartile = 13·5 $\uparrow$ median = 15 $\uparrow$ upper quartile = 16

Interquartile range = upper quartile – lower quartile
$$= 16 - 13·5$$
$$= 2·5$$

EXERCISE 17:2

1. Find the lower quartile and the upper quartile for the following sets of data.

    (a) 12 14 14 16 18 24 27

    (b) 3   5   6   6   7   8   9   11 12 13 15 19 24 24 25

    (c) 1   1   2   3   5   7   10 10 11 14

    (d) 28 34 25 27 14 18 25 27 13 14 26 29 20

    (e) 12 10 3   7   9   5   2   11 8   4   1   15 14 16

    (f) 3   9   4   5   1   2   9   6   8   3   2   4   9   4   3   2   5   8   7   2

2. Find the interquartile range for the sets of data given in **question 1.**

3. The following data gives the marks obtained, by the students in two classes, for a maths. test.
    Mr Benzoni's class:
    14 7   12 17 18 8   9   11 13 10 15 9   18 6   19 18 7   13 20 15 16 9
    Ms Patel's class:
    8   11 13 12 14 10 15 12 12 16 13 9   12 10 9   15 8   11 14
    Find the range, median, lower quartile, upper quartile and interquartile range for each class.
    Write a sentence or two comparing the marks.

4. Jane gathered data on the number of videos the students in her class watched during one week. This data is shown in the frequency table below.

No. of videos watched	0	1	2	3	4	5	6	7	8
Frequency	7	9	3	4	1	1	0	0	1

    As part of Jane's analysis of this data she found the median, the lower quartile, the upper quartile, the interquartile range and the range.
    What answers should Jane get for these?

Review 1 Find the lower and upper quartiles and the interquartile range.

(a) 5 5 7 8 9 10 10 11 13 14 14 15 16 17 18 20

(b) 5 4 1 3 2 4 3 5 6 5

Review 2 As part of a project on school attendance, Hari wrote up the following frequency tables.

Girls' absences during June

No. of days absent	0	1	2	3	4	5	6	7	8	9	10	11	12	13
Frequency	14	5	7	1	0	4	3	0	1	4	0	0	0	1

Boys' absences during June

No. of days absent	0	1	2	3	4	5	6	7	8	9	10	11
Frequency	8	12	3	5	0	4	0	1	4	3	3	2

Hari compared the data for girls with the data for boys. As part of his comparison, he found the lower quartiles, the upper quartiles, the interquartile ranges, the medians and the ranges. What values should he get for these? Write a few sentences comparing the data.

CUMULATIVE FREQUENCY GRAPHS

This frequency distribution shows the time taken, by the 26 students in a class, to correctly answer a trigonometry problem.

It is difficult to find the median, the lower quartile or the upper quartile from this table. However, we can find these easily by drawing a **cumulative frequency graph**.

Time (sec)	Frequency
10 –	1
20 –	0
30 –	2
40 –	5
50 –	6
60 –	7
70 –	3
80 – 90	2

To draw a cumulative frequency graph we firstly write a **cumulative frequency table**. In this table we add up the frequencies as we go along; that is, the cumulative frequency table gives a "running total" of the frequencies.

Frequency Table			Cumulative Frequency Table	
Time (sec)	**Frequency**		**Time (sec)**	**Cumulative Frequency**
10 –	1		less than 20	1
20 –	0		less than 30	1
30 –	2		less than 40	3
40 –	5		less than 50	8
50 –	6		less than 60	14
60 –	7		less than 70	21
70 –	3		less than 80	24
80 – 90	2		less than 90	26

The first three cumulative frequencies are found as follows.

Total number of students who took less than 20 sec = 1.

Total number who took less than 30 sec = number who took less than 20 + number who took less than 30 = 1 + 0 = 1.

Total number who took less than 40 sec = number who took less than 20 + number who took less than 30 + number who took less than 40 = 1 + 0 + 2 = 3.

The other cumulative frequencies are found in a similar way.

To draw the cumulative frequency graph we plot the points (20, 1), (30, 1), (40, 3), (50, 8), (60, 14), (70, 21), (80, 24), (90, 26). That is, we **plot the cumulative frequency against the upper boundary of each class interval.**

Since 0 students took less than 10 sec., another point on the cumulative frequency graph is (10, 0). We plot this point along with the others. **We always begin a cumulative frequency graph on the horizontal axis.**

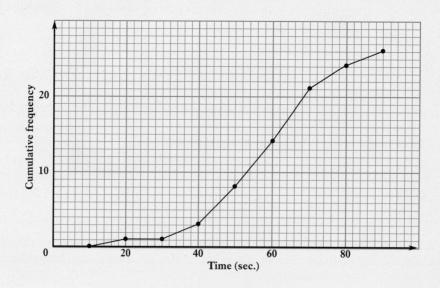

The points on a **cumulative frequency graph** are joined with a smooth curve or with straight lines.

We can find the median, the lower quartile and upper quartile from the cumulative frequency graph, as shown below.

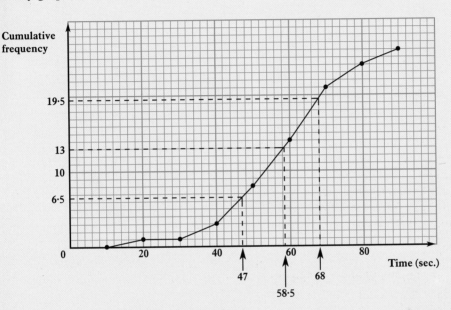

To find the median:	Since $\frac{1}{2}$ of 26 = 13, 13 students have times less than the median time. Reading from the graph, 13 students have times less than 58·5 sec. The median time is 58·5 sec.

To find the lower quartile:	Since $\frac{1}{4}$ of 26 = 6·5, 6·5 students have times less than the lower quartile. Reading from the graph, 6·5 students have times less than 47 sec. The lower quartile is 47 sec.

To find the upper quartile:	Since $\frac{3}{4}$ of 26 = 19·5, 19·5 students have times less than the upper quartile. Reading from the graph, 19·5 students have times less than 68 sec. The upper quartile is 68 sec.

EXERCISE 17:3

1.

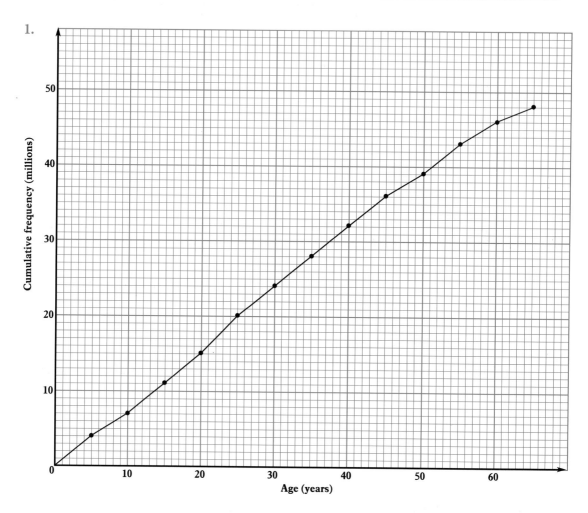

This graph is the cumulative frequency graph for the ages of people in the United Kingdom who are under the age of 65.

(a) What is the median age of these people?

(b) Find the lower and upper quartiles.

(c) What is the interquartile range?

(d) How many people are aged under 20?

(e) How many people are aged under 15?

(f) How many people are aged between 15 and 20?

(g) How many people are aged between 60 and 65?

2.

Temperature (°C)	Frequency
12 –	3
14 –	5
16 –	15
18 –	9
20 –	16
22 –	9
24 –	3
26 – 28	1

Temperature (°C)	Cumulative Frequency
below 14	3
below 16	8
below 18	23
below 20	32
below 22	48
below 24	57
below 26	60
below 28	61

During June and July, Susan kept a record of the maximum daily temperature. She organised the data as shown in the tables. Susan then drew the cumulative frequency graph.

(a) Three of the points Susan plotted for the cumulative frequency graph were (12, 0), (14, 3), (16, 8).
What other points should Susan plot?

(b) Draw the cumulative frequency graph.

(c) Use the cumulative frequency graph to find the median, the lower quartile, the upper quartile and the interquartile range.

3. Copy and complete the cumulative frequency table.

(a)

Time Spent on Leisure	Frequency
$10 \leq t < 15$	1
$15 \leq t < 20$	4
$20 \leq t < 25$	7
$25 \leq t < 30$	15
$30 \leq t < 35$	13
$35 \leq t < 40$	5
$40 \leq t < 45$	3
$45 \leq t < 50$	2

Time Spent on Leisure	Cumulative Frequency
< 15	1
< 20	5
< 25	12
< 30	
< 35	
< 40	
< 45	
< 50	

(b)

Weight of fruit (kg)	0·5 –	1·0 –	1·5 –	2·0 –	2·5 –	3·0 –	3·5 –	4·0 – 4·5
Frequency	6	5	8	7	14	18	27	12

Weight of fruit (kg)	<1·0	<1·5	<2·0	<2·5	<3·0	<3·5	<4·0	<4·5
Cumulative frequency								

(c)

Handspan (mm) at least	below	Frequency
160	170	2
170	180	0
180	190	4
190	200	10
200	210	7
210	220	3
220	230	1
230	240	1

Handspan (mm) less than	Cumulative Frequency
170	
180	
190	
200	
210	
220	
230	
240	

4. Plot the cumulative frequency graphs for the data given in **question 3.**
   Find the median, lower quartile, upper quartile and interquartile range for each set of data.

5. In the spring, Mrs. Eade fertilized one of her two rhubarb plants. Two months later, she measured the length of each stick of rhubarb on these plants. The lengths are given in the following tables.

Length of Rhubarb on Unfertilized Plant (cm)	25 –	30 –	35 –	40 –	45 –	50 – 55
Frequency	2	5	8	7	5	3

Length of Rhubarb on Fertilized Plant (cm)	25 –	30 –	35 –	40 –	45 –	50 – 55
Frequency	4	2	6	6	9	1

(a) Write cumulative frequency tables for each plant.

(b) On the same set of axes, draw both cumulative frequency graphs.

(c) Find the median length, the lower and upper quartiles and the interquartile range for each.

(d) Write a sentence or two comparing the length of the sticks of rhubarb on these plants. Use the median, quartiles and interquartile range in your comparison.

6.

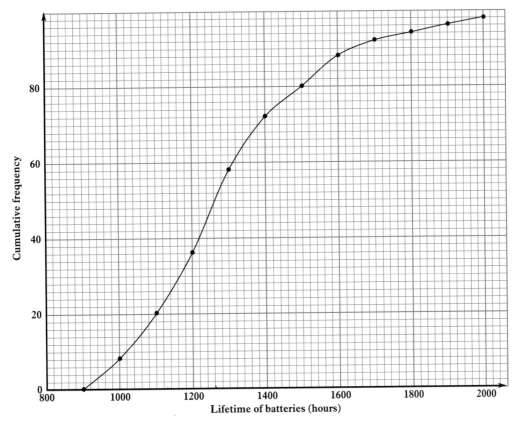

(i) Testing was carried out on a new type of calculator battery. One hundred of these batteries were tested. The time these batteries worked for (the lifetime) is shown on this cumulative frequency graph.

   (a) How can you tell from this graph that 2 of the batteries were still working after 2000 hours of use?

   (b) What is the median lifetime of the 100 batteries tested?

   (c) What is the interquartile range?

(ii) One hundred calculator batteries of another type were also tested. The results are shown in the table below.

Lifetime (hours)	1000 –	1100 –	1200 –	1300 –	1400 –	1500 –	1600 –	1700 – 1800
Frequency	3	5	9	21	33	16	7	6

   (a) Draw the cumulative frequency graph for this data.

   (b) Use the cumulative frequency graph to find the median, the quartiles and the interquartile range.

(iii) Write a sentence or two comparing the two different types of calculator batteries.

7.

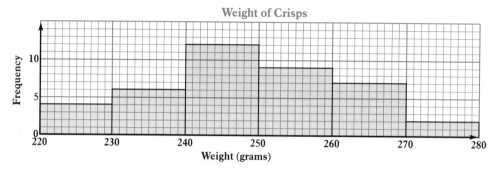

Weight of Crisps

Pamela weighed a number of packets of crisps. She drew this frequency diagram and then a cumulative frequency graph. From the cumulative frequency graph she found the median and quartiles.

(a) Two of the points Pamela plotted on the cumulative frequency graph were (220, 0) and (230, 4). What other points should Pamela plot?

(b) Draw the cumulative frequency graph.

(c) What is the median weight of these packets of crisps?

(d) What is the interquartile range?

Review 1 Kate weighed the ripe tomatoes from two different varieties of tomato plants. The weights are shown in the following tables.

Variety: Top Tom

Weight (grams)	Frequency
50 –	4
70 –	6
90 –	10
110 –	12
130 –	24
150 –	25
170 – 190	2

Variety: Goliath

Weight (grams)	Frequency
50 –	4
70 –	8
90 –	13
110 –	9
130 –	24
150 –	15
170 –	11
190 – 210	4

(a) Write cumulative frequency tables for each variety.

(b) Draw the cumulative frequency graphs.

(c) Find the median, lower quartile, upper quartile and interquartile range for both varieties of tomatoes.

(d) Write a sentence or two comparing the Top Tom tomatoes with the Goliath tomatoes.

Review 2

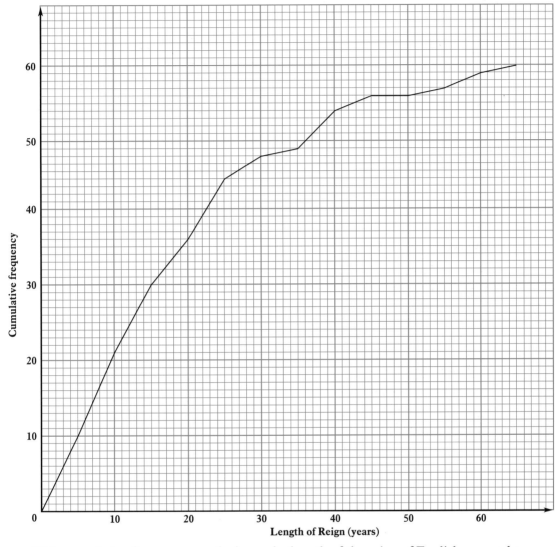

This cumulative frequency graph shows the length of the reign of English monarchs.

(a) How many monarchs reigned for less than 5 years?

(b) How many monarchs reigned for less than 10 years?

(c) How many monarchs reigned for between 5 and 10 years?

(d) How many monarchs has England had?

(e) What is the median length of reign?

(f) Find the lower and upper quartiles.

(g) What is the interquartile range?

DISCUSSION EXERCISE 17:4

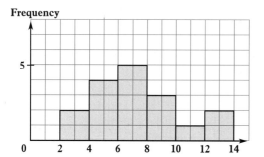

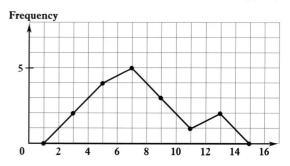

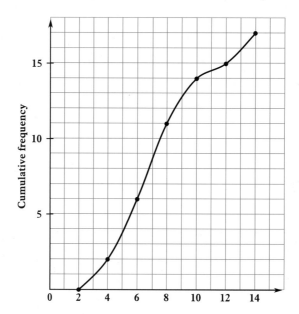

The frequency diagram, frequency polygon and cumulative frequency graph, above, all display the same data.

"Which graphs are drawn depends on the way in which we are going to analyse the data". Discuss this statement.

"The frequency polygon has greater visual impact than either the frequency diagram or the cumulative frequency graph". Discuss this statement.

Is it sensible to draw all three of the above graphs to display a set of data? Is one of these graphs more useful than the others? Discuss. As part of your discussion, you could refer to data given in the previous exercise.

The cumulative frequency graphs drawn so far in this chapter have all been for continuous data.

Cumulative frequency curves are also drawn for **grouped discrete data.**

For **continuous data,** the cumulative frequency values are the number of data values that are **less than** the upper boundaries of each class interval.

For **discrete data,** the cumulative frequency values are the number of data values that are **less than or equal to** the upper boundaries of each class interval.

Example Melanie threw a dart 30 times. The following frequency table shows Melanie's scores.

Score	Frequency
1 – 5	2
6 – 10	7
11 – 15	8
16 – 20	11
21 – 25	2

Score	Cumulative Frequency
≤ 5	2
≤ 10	9
≤ 15	17
≤ 20	28
≤ 25	30

The cumulative frequency graph is shown below. The points plotted are (5, 2), (10, 9), (15, 17), (20, 28), (25, 30) and (0, 0).

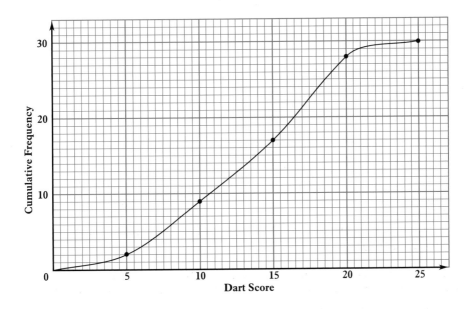

EXERCISE 17:5

1. The following table gives the prices of 35 different types of computers.

Price range (£)	1–200	201–400	401–600	601–800	801–1000	1001–1200	1201–1400	1401–1600
Frequency	1	2	6	8	7	4	5	2

(a) Copy and complete the following cumulative frequency table for these computers.

Price (£)	≤ 200	≤ 400	≤ 600	≤ 800	≤ 1000	≤ 1200	≤ 1400	≤ 1600
Cumulative Frequency	1	3	9					

(b) Draw the cumulative frequency graph.

(c) Use your graph to find the median price and the interquartile range.

2.

Claim (£)	Number of claims
1 to 100	15
101 to 200	62
201 to 300	89
301 to 400	54
401 to 500	28

Claim (£)	Cumulative Frequency
≤ 100	
≤ 200	
≤ 300	
≤ 400	
≤ 500	

This table shows the insurance claims made during one week.

(a) Copy the table and fill in the cumulative frequency column.

(b) Draw the cumulative frequency graph.

(c) Find the median insurance claim.

(d) Find the interquartile range.

(e) Use your graph to estimate the number of claims under £340.

3. Two maths. tests were trialled with 200 students. The results are shown below.

Mark range	1–10	11–20	21–30	31–40	41–50	51–60	61–70	71–80	81–90	91–100
Test A frequency	4	9	15	27	28	32	45	23	11	6
Test B frequency	7	10	24	29	34	38	31	18	7	2

(a) Copy and complete the cumulative frequency table.

Mark range	≤ 10	≤ 20	≤ 30	≤ 40	≤ 50	≤ 60	≤ 70	≤ 80	≤ 90	≤ 100
Test A cumulative frequency	4	13	28							
Test B cumulative frequency	7									

(b) Draw the cumulative frequency graphs for both tests on the same set of axes.

(c) Use the graphs to find the median, quartiles and interquartile range for each test.

(d) Write a few sentences comparing these tests.

Review Delwyn was doing a project on school netball. As part of this project she compared the number of goals scored, in the games of one season, by two schools. The following frequency table shows this information.

Goals Scored	1–10	11–20	21–30	31–40	41–50	51–60
Number of Games: School A	0	2	5	9	4	0
Number of Games: School B	1	3	4	5	5	1

(a) The cumulative frequency graph for the goals scored by school B is shown below. Use this graph to find the median, lower quartile, upper quartile and interquartile range.

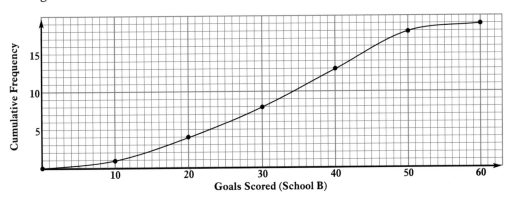

(b) Copy and complete the cumulative frequency table for school A.

Goals Scored	≤ 10	≤ 20	≤ 30	≤ 40	≤ 50
Cumulative frequency: School A					

(c) Draw the cumulative frequency graph for school A.

(d) Compare the goals scored by the two schools. In your comparison, use the medians, the quartiles and the interquartile ranges.

PRACTICAL EXERCISE 17:6

Gather some data. Some suggestions follow.
You could conduct a survey or an experiment or you could gather your data from reference books.
Draw graphs to display your data. Include cumulative frequency graphs.
Analyse your data. Include the median, quartiles and interquartile range as part of your analysis.

Suggestions: *Prices of cars advertised for sale.*
Wrist measurements of students.
Comparison of ages of male and female employees in a factory or office.
Comparison of time spent playing sport by the students in two different year groups.
Comparison of pulse rates of 10-year olds and 20-year olds.
Comparison of weekly wages earned by the workers in two industries.

If you wish, you could work as a group. If you do this, choose a theme such as sport.
Gather, display and analyse data on many aspects of this theme.

CHAPTER 17   REVIEW

1.   The speeds, in miles per hour (mph), of 200 cars travelling on the A320 road were measured. The results are shown in the table.

Speed (mph)	Cumulative Frequency
not exceeding 20	1
not exceeding 25	5
not exceeding 30	14
not exceeding 35	28
not exceeding 40	66
not exceeding 45	113
not exceeding 50	164
not exceeding 55	196
not exceeding 60	200
TOTAL	200

(a) On the grid opposite draw a cumulative frequency graph to show these figures.

(b) Use your graph to find an estimate for

(i) the median speed (in mph),   (ii) the interquartile range (in mph).

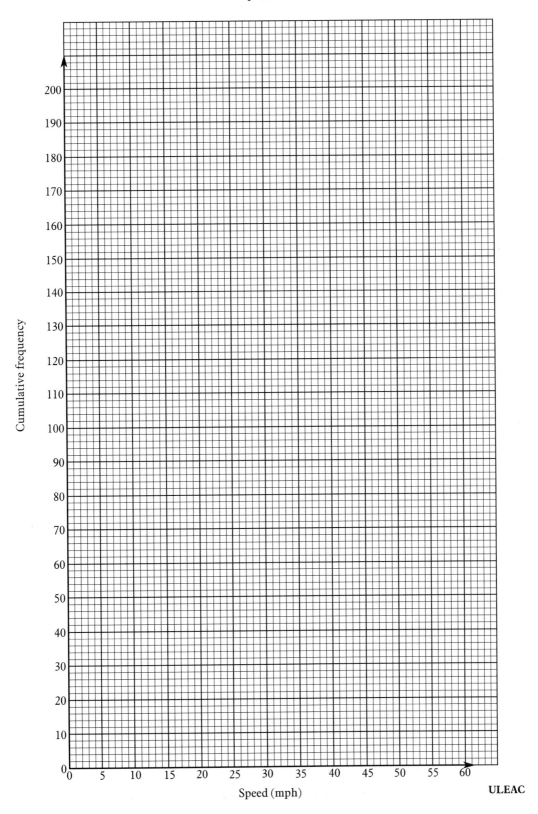

Speed (mph)

Cumulative frequency

ULEAC

2. Ahmed recorded how long it had taken him to finish each of his last 100 homeworks then constructed a cumulative frequency curve to show the results.

   Use the graph to answer the following questions.

   (a) How many homeworks took 20 minutes or less?

   (b) Estimate the median time taken to finish a homework.

   (c) Estimate the upper quartile time.

   (d) Estimate the lower quartile time.

   (e) Calculate the interquartile time.

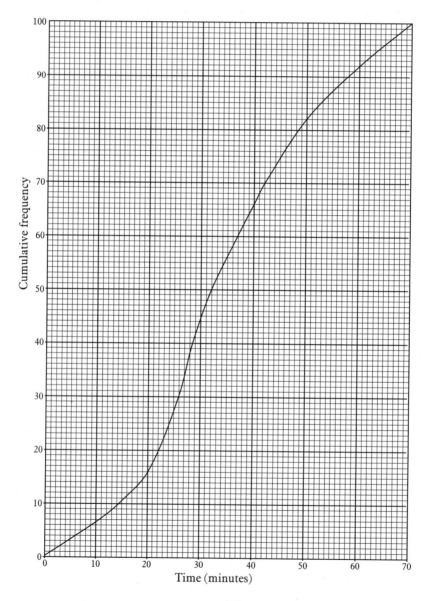

Time (minutes)

ULEAC

3. There were 360 people who took part in an 8 mile sponsored run.
The range of finishing time is shown on the following cumulative frequency curve.

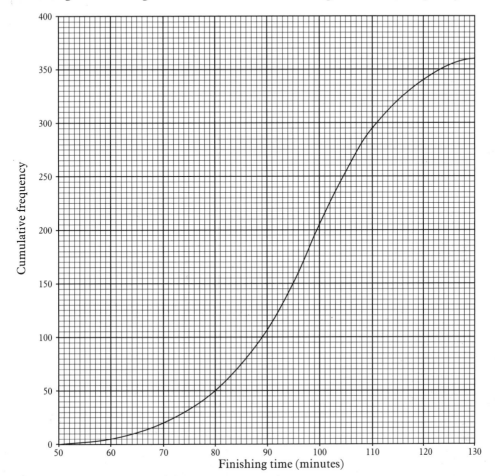

Finishing time (minutes)

(a) Use the curve to estimate the median finishing time.

(b) By drawing lines on the graph, estimate the interquartile range.

(c) How many runners beat last year's winning time of 75 minutes?   **SEG**

4.

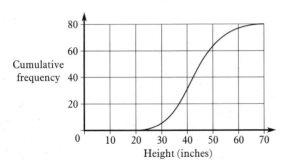

Which height is the lower quartile?

SEG

5. The cumulative frequency graph below gives information on house prices in 1992. The cumulative frequency is given as a percentage of all houses in England.

   (a) Use the graph to find the percentage of properties valued at less than £60,000.

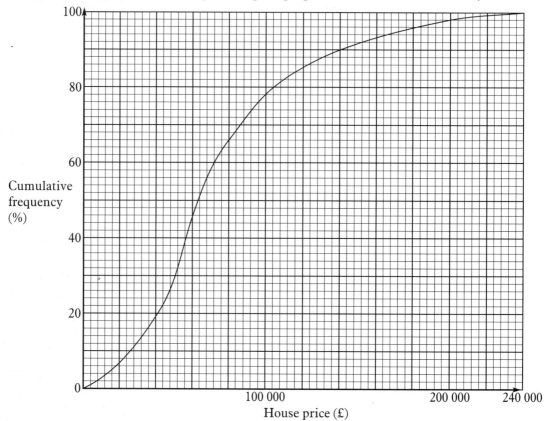

House price (£)

   (b) This grouped frequency table below gives the percentage distribution of house prices (*p*) in England in 1993. Complete the cumulative frequency table.

House prices (*p*) in pounds 1993	Percentage of houses in this class interval
$0 \leqslant p < 40\,000$	26
$40\,000 \leqslant p < 52\,000$	19
$52\,000 \leqslant p < 68\,000$	22
$68\,000 \leqslant p < 88\,000$	15
$88\,000 \leqslant p < 120\,000$	9
$120\,000 \leqslant p < 160\,000$	5
$160\,000 \leqslant p < 220\,000$	4

House prices (*p*) in pounds 1993	Cumulative frequency (%)
$0 \leqslant p < 40\,000$	
$0 \leqslant p < 52\,000$	
$0 \leqslant p < 68\,000$	
$0 \leqslant p < 88\,000$	
$0 \leqslant p < 120\,000$	
$0 \leqslant p < 160\,000$	
$0 \leqslant p < 220\,000$	

   (c) On the same grid, construct a cumulative frequency graph for your table.

   In 1992 the price of a house was £100 000.

   (d) Use both cumulative frequency graphs to estimate the price of this house in 1993. Make your method clear.

   ULEAC

434

6. Van Winkel sells tulip bulbs.

The cumulative frequency graph shows
the sizes of the bulbs in a random sample
from his stock. (The size is the largest
circumference in centimetres.)

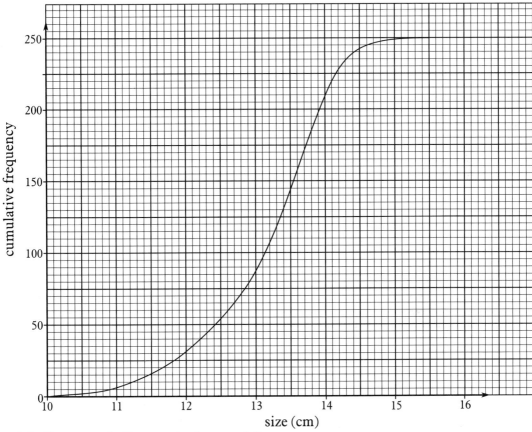

(a) How many bulbs were in the sample?

(b) Estimate **(i)** the median bulb size and **(ii)** the interquartile range.

Frans Gretel also sells tulip bulbs. This is the frequency distribution for a sample from
his stock:

Size (x cm)	Frequency	
$10 \cdot 5 \leqslant x < 11 \cdot 5$	53	
$11 \cdot 5 \leqslant x < 12 \cdot 5$	90	
$12 \cdot 5 \leqslant x < 13 \cdot 5$	57	
$13 \cdot 5 \leqslant x < 14 \cdot 5$	30	
$14 \cdot 5 \leqslant x < 15 \cdot 5$	20	

(c) Draw up a cumulative frequency table. Draw the cumulative frequency graph on
the same grid as that used for Van Winkel's bulbs.

(d) Compare the two samples.   **MEG**

7. The numbers of journeys made by a group of people using public transport in one month are summarised in the table.

Number of journeys	0–10	11–20	21–30	31–40	41–50	51–60	61–70
Number of people	4	7	8	6	3	4	0

(a) Complete the cumulative frequency table.

Number of journeys	⩽ 10	⩽ 20	⩽ 30	⩽ 40	⩽ 50	⩽ 60	⩽ 70
Cumulative frequency							

(b) (i) Draw the cumulative frequency graph.

    (ii) Use your graph to estimate the median number of journeys.

    (iii) Use your graph to estimate the number of people who made more than 44 journeys in the month.

(c) The numbers of journeys made using public transport in one month, by another group of people, are shown in the graph.

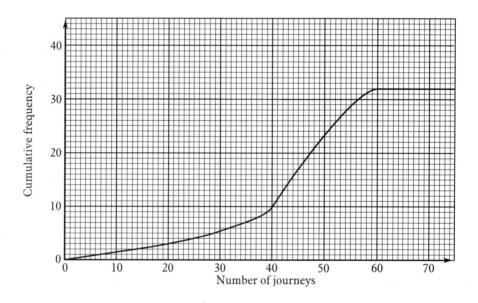

    (i) Find the inter-quartile range for this group of people. Show how you found your answer.

    (ii) Make **one** comparison between the numbers of journeys made by these two groups.

SEG

436

Niccolo Tartaglia

Niccolo Tartaglia was born in 1499 at Brescia, Italy and died in 1557 at Venice. His real name was Niccolo Fontana. He adopted the name Tartaglia, which means "stammerer" after the lower part of his face was damaged with a sabre during the French sacking of Brescia in 1512. This damage left Niccolo with a permanent stammer in his speech.

Niccolo's parents were poor and could not afford tutors for their son. Niccolo educated himself. It is claimed that since his parents could not afford to buy slate for him to write on Niccolo used tombstones as slates.

Tartaglia was one of the most important mathematicians of the 16th century. He wrote books on mathematics and military science. In the military books, he used mathematics in the study of artillery fire; the first person to do this. He also tried to find laws to describe the motion of falling bodies. Tartaglia also published translations of the early Greek mathematician's, Euclid and Archimedes. He was not always truthful and, more than once, claimed to have invented some mathematics that had been invented by someone else. It is said that he claimed to have invented the "Arithmetic Triangle" (what we know as Pascal's Triangle) although this had already been published.

Tartaglia is famous for finding a method to solve cubic equations such as $x^3 + 6x^2 + 8x = 1000$, and for the quarrel between mathematicians that followed.

He was asked by another mathematician, Cardan, to publish his solution for these equations. Tartaglia refused to do this at this time as he hoped to make his reputation by writing a book on algebra which would include this discovery. Cardan was a man of influence and he persuaded Tartaglia to show him the solution. Some say Cardan promised to introduce him to a wealthy patron; others say Cardan promised to recommend that he be appointed as artillery adviser to the Spanish Army. Tartaglia showed Cardan the solution which Cardan published. This led to a dreadful quarrel which became a public quarrel. Although Cardan did acknowledge that the solution was not his own, the solution became known as Cardan's.

Of the quarrel, a biographer many years later wrote: *"The attempt to assert exclusive right to the secret possession of a piece of information, which was the next step in the advancement of a liberal science, the refusal to add it, inscribed with his own name, to the common heap, until he had hoarded it, in hope of some day, when he was at leisure, of turning it more largely to his own advantage, could be excused in him only by the fact that he was rudely bred and self-taught, and that he was not likely to know better. Any member of a liberal profession who is miserly of knowledge, forfeits the respect of his fraternity. The promise of secrecy which Cardan had no right to make, Tartaglia had no right to demand."*

Tartaglia's best known work is a massive work of three volumes called "Treatise on Numbers and Measures." This was the best book on arithmetic that was written in Italy during the 16th century.

The ADDITION PRINCIPLE

Remember: For equally likely outcomes, P (an event occurs) = $\dfrac{\text{Number of favourable outcomes}}{\text{Number of possible outcomes}}$

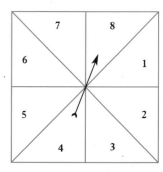

When this spinner is spun it could stop in the section marked
1 or 2 or 3 or 4 or 5 or 6 or 7 or 8. There are eight equally
likely outcomes.
The following examples refer to this spinner.

Example   Let the event "stops on an odd number" be called event A.
Let the event "stops on the 2" be called event B.

Favourable outcomes for event A are 1, 3, 5, 7.
There are four favourable outcomes.
There are eight possible outcomes. P(A) = $\frac{4}{8}$

The only favourable outcome for event B is 2.
There is one favourable outcome.
There are eight possible outcomes. P(B) = $\frac{1}{8}$

Notice that,   P(A) + P(B) $= \frac{4}{8} + \frac{1}{8}$
$= \frac{5}{8}$

The event "A *or* B" is "stops on an odd number *or* on 2."
Favourable outcomes for A *or* B are 1, 2, 3, 5, 7.
There are five favourable outcomes.
There are eight possible outcomes.

P(A *or* B) = $\frac{5}{8}$ which is the same as P(A) + P(B)

That is, in this example P(A *or* B) = P(A) + P(B).

This example illustrates the addition principle for probabilities.

Example   Let A be the event "stops on an odd number."
Let B be the event "stops on a multiple of 3."

Favourable outcomes for event A are 1, 3, 5, 7.
There are four favourable outcomes.
There are eight possible outcomes. $P(A) = \frac{4}{8}$

Favourable outcomes for event B are 3, 6.
There are two favourable outcomes.
There are eight possible outcomes. $P(B) = \frac{2}{8}$

Notice that, $P(A) + P(B) = \frac{4}{8} + \frac{2}{8}$
$= \frac{6}{8}$

The event "A *or* B" is "stops on an odd number *or* on a multiple of 3."
Favourable outcomes for "A *or* B" are 1, 3, 5, 6, 7.
There are five favourable outcomes.
There are eight possible outcomes.

$P(A \text{ } or \text{ } B) = \frac{5}{8}$ which is not the same as P(A) + P(B).

That is, in this example $P(A \text{ } or \text{ } B) \neq P(A) + P(B)$.   Why not?

The **addition principle** for probability is:

For mutually exclusive events, $P(A \text{ } or \text{ } B) = P(A) + P(B)$

Worked Example   Of 50 counters in a bag, 7 are black and 6 are white. Dana takes one counter at random. Find the probability that Dana's counter is either black or white.

Answer   The events "Black", "White" are mutually exclusive.
$P(\text{Black } or \text{ White}) = P(\text{Black}) + P(\text{White})$
$= \frac{7}{50} + \frac{6}{50}$
$= \frac{13}{50}$

Worked Example   One of the older Coxon children is to babysit for a neighbour.
$P(\text{Gavin babysits}) = 0.2$, $P(\text{Alex babysits}) = 0.35$.
Find the probability that either Gavin or Alex babysits.

Answer Since only one of the Coxon children babysits, Gavin and Alex do not babysit together. The events "Gavin babysits", "Alex babysits" are mutually exclusive.

P(Gavin *or* Alex) = P(Gavin) + P(Alex)

= 0·2 + 0·35

= 0·55

EXERCISE 18:1

1. A die is tossed.
   Find the probability of getting a 3 or an even number.

2. A card is drawn from a pack.
   Find the probability of getting an Ace or a Jack.

3. Two coins are tossed.
   Find the probability of getting two heads or two tails.

4. Two dice are thrown. Find the probability of getting a total of 7 or the same numbers on both dice.

5. The probability that Belen buys "The Mirror" is 0·2 and the probability that she buys "The Sun" is 0·25. (Belen does not buy more than one paper.)
   What is the probability that she buys either "The Mirror" or "The Sun"?

6. In a family of five, the probability that Kirstie is first home is $\frac{5}{12}$ and the probability that Bronwyn is first home is $\frac{1}{12}$.
   Find the probability that either Bronwyn or Kirstie is first home.

7. Sue drives to work in London.
   The probability that she parks on Regent Street is 0·2.
   The probability that she parks on Oxford Street is 0·18.
   What is the probability that she parks on either Regent Street or Oxford Street?

8. Six cats are fed from six different coloured feeding bowls.
   The probability that Cassius is fed from the red bowl is 0·15, the probability that Smokey is fed from the red bowl is 0·25 and the probability that McGiver is fed from the red bowl is 0·4.
   Find the probability that (a) either Cassius or Smokey is fed from the red bowl

   (b) either Smokey or McGiver is fed from the red bowl

   (c) either McGiver or Cassius is fed from the red bowl.

9. John answers the phone in his office from 9 a.m. until midday and then from 1 p.m. until 4 p.m. Ruski phones this office each day. The following table shows the probability of Ruski phoning at particular times of the day.

Time	Probability
in the morning before 9a.m.	0·15
from 9a.m. until midday	0·4
from midday until 1p.m.	0·15
in the afternoon after 4p.m.	0·05

(a) Find the probability that Ruski phones between 1p.m. and 4p.m.

(b) What is the probability that John answers Ruski's call?

10. Part of the analysis of a dentist's patients is shown on this table.

(a) Find the probability that a patient is either an adult or a school pupil.

(b) The probability that a patient is either a school pupil or female is *not* 0·3 + 0·45. Why not?

(c) What is the probability that a patient is not an adult?

(d) Find the probability of a patient having dental work other than a tooth filled.

(e) Of the next 150 patients, how many do you expect will be adults?

	Probability
Male	0·55
Female	0·45
Under school age	0·1
School pupil	0·3
Adult	0·6
Tooth filled	0·38
Reconstruction work	0·09
Tooth extract	
Teeth	

Review 1 A die is tossed.
Find the probability of getting an odd number or a six.

Review 2 The caretaker enters the school through one of three doors; the front door, the side door or the hall door. He enters through the front door with probability 0·3 and through the hall door with probability 0·05.
Find the probability that this caretaker enters the school through

(a) the side door

(b) either the front door or the hall door

(c) either the front door or the side door.

INDEPENDENT EVENTS

Event A and event B are **independent** if event A happening (or not happening) has no influence on whether event B happens. The probability of event B happening will be the same regardless of whether or not event A has happened.

Example   A coin is tossed twice. A head occurs on the first toss. This has no influence on whether or not a tail occurs on the second toss.
That is, the events "head on first toss", "tail on second toss" are independent.

Example   These counters are placed in a bag.   • • • •
Two counters are drawn at random, one after the other.   • • • •
The first counter is not replaced in the bag.
Suppose event A is "the first counter drawn is red" and event B is "the second counter drawn is red".

If event A happens, there will be 2 red counters left out of a total of 7 counters. Then $P(B) = \frac{2}{7}$.

If event A does not happen (i.e. the first counter drawn is black) there will be 3 red counters left out of a total of 7 counters. Then $P(B) = \frac{3}{7}$.

Events A and B are *not* independent.

DISCUSSION EXERCISE 18:2

● Suppose two counters are drawn with the first counter being   • • • •
replaced before the second one is drawn.   • • • •
Are the events "the first counter is red", "the second counter is red"
independent in this case? **Discuss.**

● **Discuss** whether or not the events A and B are independent in each of the following.

Sue throws two backgammon dice, one grey and the other purple.
   Event A : Sue gets a 6 on the grey die.
   Event B : Sue gets a 6 on the purple die.

Andrew uses the alarm on his clock-radio.
   Event A : There was a power failure last night.
   Event B : Andrew was late for school today.

Two babies are born on Saturday at Rochford Hospital.
  Event A : The first baby born is a girl.
  Event B : The second baby born is a boy.

Nicole and Ana are the finalists in the school tennis championship. In the final, they play a three-game match.
  Event A : Ana wins the first game of the final.
  Event B : Ana wins the second game of the final.

Femi and Oni are friends.
  Event A : Femi goes to the disco.
  Event B : Oni goes to the disco.

Jeremy and Jake sit beside each other in class.
  Event A : Jeremy catches a cold.
  Event B : Jake catches a cold.

Two cards are drawn, one after the other, from a pack of cards. The first card is not replaced before the second card is drawn.
  Event A : The first card drawn is a spade.
  Event B : The second card drawn is a spade.

Two cards are drawn, one after the other, from a pack of cards. The first card is replaced before the second card is drawn.
  Event A : The first card is the King of hearts.
  Event B : The second card is a heart.

- Event A is "it will rain on the first day of next month".
  Event B is "it will rain on the last day of next month".
  Are these events independent? Discuss.

  Suppose P(A) = 0·4 and P(B) = 0·4. Will the probability of it raining on both the first and last days of next month also be 0·4 or more than 0·4 or less than 0·4? Discuss.

- Write down some pairs of independent events and some pairs of events that are not independent. Discuss.

  For the pairs of independent events, discuss whether the probability of both events happening is less than, equal to, or more than the probability of one or other of these events happening.

- Daniel made the statement "The probability of two independent events happening is always less than the probability of one or other of these events happening". He gave an example to support this statement.
  Caitlin found a counter-example to show that Daniel's statement wasn't always correct. Think of a possible counter-example. Discuss.
  Daniel then amended his statement, so that it was always true. How might Daniel have amended his statement? Discuss.

The MULTIPLICATION PRINCIPLE

A black and a red die are tossed together.
Possible outcomes are

1, 1	1, 2	1, 3	1, 4	1, 5	1, 6
2, 1	2, 2	2, 3	2, 4	2, 5	2, 6
3, 1	3, 2	3, 3	3, 4	3, 5	3, 6
4, 1	4, 2	4, 3	4, 4	4, 5	4, 6
5, 1	5, 2	5, 3	5, 4	5, 5	5, 6
6, 1	6, 2	6, 3	6, 4	6, 5	6, 6

There are 36 possible outcomes.
The black number in each possible outcome is the number obtained on the black die, while the red number is the number obtained on the red die.

Suppose event A is "a number greater than four on the black die" and
event B is "a five on the red die".

Favourable outcomes for event A are   5, 1   5, 2   5, 3   5, 4   5, 5   5, 6   6, 1   6, 2

6, 3   6, 4   6, 5   6, 6. There are 12 favourable outcomes. $P(A) = \frac{12}{36}$ or $\frac{1}{3}$

Favourable outcomes for event B are   1, 5   2, 5   3, 5   4, 5   5, 5   6, 5.

There are 6 favourable outcomes. $P(B) = \frac{6}{36}$ or $\frac{1}{6}$

The event (A **and** B) is "a number greater than four on the black die **and** a five on the red die". Favourable outcomes for event (A **and** B) are   5, 5   6, 5.

There are 2 favourable outcomes. $P(A \ \textbf{and} \ B) = \frac{2}{36}$ or $\frac{1}{18}$

Notice that $P(A) \times P(B) = \frac{1}{3} \times \frac{1}{6}$
$$= \frac{1}{18}$$

Hence, $P(A \ \textbf{and} \ B) = P(A) \times P(B)$.   Notice that the events A and B are independent. The above example illustrates the multiplication principle for probability.

The multiplication principle for probability is:

for independent events, $P(A \ \textbf{and} \ B) = P(A) \times P(B)$

Using the multiplication principle eliminates the need to list all the possible outcomes for two events. Using the multiplication principle, the above example can be done as follows:

P(Black > 4 *and* Red 5) = P(Black > 4) × P(Red 5) since events are independent

$$= \frac{2}{6} \times \frac{1}{6}$$

$$= \frac{1}{18}$$

Worked Example **1.** Two cards are drawn from a pack, one after the other. The first card is replaced before the second card is drawn. What is the probability that both cards are Aces?

Answer We are asked to find P(both Aces). This is the same as P(Ace *and* Ace).

P(Ace *and* Ace) = P(Ace) × P(Ace) since events are independent

$$= \frac{4}{52} \times \frac{4}{52}$$

$$= \frac{1}{13} \times \frac{1}{13}$$

$$= \frac{1}{169}$$

Worked Example **2.**

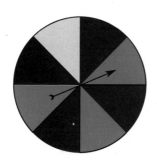

(i) The arrow on this spinner is spun once. Find the probability of the arrow stopping in

   (a) a red section

   (b) a black section.

(ii) The arrow is spun twice. What is the probability of spinning black then red?

Answer (i) (a) $\frac{3}{8}$ (b) $\frac{4}{8}$ or $\frac{1}{2}$

(ii) We want P(B *and* R) = P(B) × P(R) since events are independent

$$= \frac{1}{2} \times \frac{3}{8}$$

$$= \frac{3}{16}$$

Worked Example 3.　The probability that it will rain on any day in May is $\frac{1}{4}$.

Find the probability that

(a) it will rain on both May 1st and May 21st

(b) it will not rain on May 21st

(c) it will rain on May 1st but not on May 21st.

(Assume that raining on May 1st and raining on May 21st are independent events.)

Answer (a)　P(rain *and* rain) $= \frac{1}{4} \times \frac{1}{4}$
$$= \frac{1}{16}$$

(b)　P(not rain) $= 1 - \text{P(rain)}$
$$= 1 - \frac{1}{4}$$
$$= \frac{3}{4}$$

(c)　P(rain *and* not rain) $= \frac{1}{4} \times \frac{3}{4}$
$$= \frac{3}{16}$$

DISCUSSION EXERCISE 18:3

- Another way of finding the answer to **Worked Example 1** is by listing all the equally likely outcomes.
  Discuss this method.

- In **Worked Example 2 (ii)**, one of the outcomes is "RR".
  What are the other outcomes? Are the outcomes equally likely?
  Could the answer to this example be found by listing all the outcomes? Discuss.

- For the spinner in **Worked Example 2**, Beth said that since P(B *and* R) $= \frac{3}{16}$ then the probability of spinning black and red in any order is $2 \times \frac{3}{16}$ or $\frac{3}{8}$.
  Is Beth correct? Discuss.

EXERCISE 18:4

1. A coin is tossed twice.
   Find the probability of　(a) a head on the first toss

   (b) heads on both tosses.

2. A coin and a die are tossed.
    Find the probability of   (a) a multiple of 3 on the die

    (b) a head on the coin and a multiple of 3 on the die.

3. A die is thrown twice.
    Find the probability of a 4 and a 6 in either order.

4. A box contains 20 counters; 1 is red, 5 are blue, 10 are green and the rest are white.
    Two counters are chosen at random, the first being replaced before the second is
    chosen.
    Find the probability that (a) the first counter drawn is white

    (b) the first counter is white and the second blue

    (c) one of the counters is white and the other blue.

5. Once a month Kylie checks the oil and battery water in her car. The probability that
    the oil needs topping up is 0·3, the probability that the battery water needs topping up
    is 0·15. Find the probability that, the next time Kylie checks, both the oil and the
    battery water need topping up.

6. The probability that Irina is late for school is 0·3; the probability that Helena is late is
    0·2. What is the probability that both girls are late for school? Assume these girls do
    not know each other. Why do you need to make this assumption?

7. In one Mercedes factory, 80% of the cars manufactured are left-hand drive and the rest
    are right-hand drive. The probability that a car needs its steering adjusted before it
    leaves the factory is 0·15.
    One car is chosen at random from this factory. Find the probability that this car

    (a) is a right-hand drive

    (b) is a right-hand drive which needs its steering adjusted

    (c) is a left-hand drive which does not need its steering adjusted.

8. Of the 50 houses in Crane Close, there is always someone at home in 15 of them.

    (a) What is the probability that a house, chosen at random in Crane Close, has
         someone at home?

    (b) Alicia is conducting a survey. She chooses two houses at random, in Crane
         Close. What is the probability that Alicia finds someone at home in both of
         these houses?

9.

Brenda plays two games of patience. The probability that she gets all the cards out in any one game is $\frac{1}{5}$.

(a) Find the probability that Brenda gets all the cards out in both games.

(b) What is the probability that Brenda does not get all the cards out on the first game?

(c) Find the probability that Brenda does not get all the cards out on the first game but gets them all out on the second.

Review 1 Jamie works in a car showroom which sells British, European and Japanese cars. 65% of the cars that Jamie sells are British and 20% are Japanese.
    (a) What is the probability that Jamie sells a European car to his next customer?
    (b) Find the probability that the next two customers both buy Japanese cars. (Assume these customers do not know each other.)
    (c) Why do you need to make the assumption in **(b)**?

Review 2 This spinner is spun twice as part of a fairground game.
Find the probability of spinning

    (a) a 1 on the first spin

    (b) a 1 on both spins

    (c) a 2 on the second spin

    (d) a 3 on the first spin and a 2 on the second

    (e) a 3 and a 2, in any order, on the two spins.

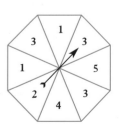

448

USING both the ADDITION and MULTIPLICATION PRINCIPLES

The first step in solving a problem concerning probability is to make a statement, in words, of the probability to be found. This statement should then be rewritten in probability language replacing **and** with ×, **or** with + where appropriate.

The addition principle $P(A \text{ or } B) = P(A) + P(B)$, for mutually exclusive events and the multiplication principle $P(A \text{ and } B) = P(A) \times P(B)$, for independent events are often used together to solve a problem. As well as this, using $P(A) = 1 - P(\text{not } A)$ often enables us to efficiently solve a problem.

Worked Example Two dice are tossed.
What is the probability of getting a six on just one of them?

Answer We require P (just one die with a 6).

$$P \text{ (just one with a 6)} = P(\text{one with a 6 } \textbf{and} \text{ the other not a 6})$$
$$= P(6 \textbf{ and } \text{not } 6 \textbf{ or } \text{not } 6 \textbf{ and } 6)$$
$$= P(6 \textbf{ and } \text{not } 6) + P(\text{not } 6 \textbf{ and } 6) \text{ events mutually exclusive}$$
$$= P(6) \times P(\text{not } 6) + P(\text{not } 6) \times P(6) \text{ events independent}$$
$$= \tfrac{1}{6} \times \tfrac{5}{6} + \tfrac{5}{6} \times \tfrac{1}{6}$$
$$= \tfrac{5}{18}$$

Worked Example Two dice are tossed.
What is the probability of getting a six on at least one of them?

Answer This problem could be solved in a similar way to the previous worked example. The solution would be fairly cumbersome. It is solved more efficiently as follows:

$$P(\text{at least one } 6) = 1 - P(\text{none with a } 6)$$
$$= 1 - P(\text{not } 6 \textbf{ and } \text{not } 6)$$
$$= 1 - \tfrac{5}{6} \times \tfrac{5}{6}$$
$$= \tfrac{11}{36}$$

The previous worked examples could have been easily solved by listing all the possible outcomes, then selecting the favourable outcomes and using

$$\text{Probability of an event} = \frac{\text{Number of favourable outcomes}}{\text{Number of possible outcomes}}.$$

This formula could have been used since all the outcomes are equally likely.

In cases where it is either not possible to list all the outcomes or it is cumbersome to do this, or the outcomes are not equally likely, the methods outlined in the previous worked examples are most useful.

Worked Example The probability that a library borrower borrows a video is 0·02. Find the probability that, of the next two borrowers, just one borrows a video.

Answer Let V be "borrows a video", NV be "not borrows a video".
We are given P(V) = 0·02.
Since P(NV) = 1 – P(V), then P(NV) = 0·98.
We require P(V *and* NV *or* NV *and* V)
= P(V *and* NV) + P(NV *and* V)   events mutually exclusive
= P(V) × P(NV) + P(NV) × P(V)   events independent
= 0·02 × 0·98 + 0·98 × 0·02
= 0·0392

EXERCISE 18:5

1. A die is tossed twice. Find the probability of getting a two on just one of these throws.

2. Two dice are tossed. Find the probability of getting the same number on both of them.

3. A black and a red die are tossed and the numbers obtained are added together. Find the probability that this sum will be 5.

4. Two coins are thrown together. Find the probability of getting

    (a) two tails   (b) no tails   (c) at least one tail

    (d) different outcomes on the coins.

5. Two dice are tossed. What is the probability of getting a six on one of them and an odd number on the other?

6. A die is tossed twice. Find the probability of getting a six on the first toss and an odd number on the second toss, or a number greater than 4 on the first toss and an even number on the second toss.

7. Two cards are chosen at random from a full 52 card pack. The first card is replaced before the second card is chosen. Find the probability that the chosen cards will be

    (a) both spades   (b) both aces   (c) the ace of spades and a diamond

    (d) the same suit   (e) different colours.

8. Of 20 counters in a bag, 8 are green, 5 are blue and the remainder are white. Two counters are drawn, one after the other, with replacement (i.e. the first counter drawn is replaced in the bag before the second counter is drawn).
   Find the probability that

    (a) at least one of the counters drawn is green

    (b) one of the counters drawn is green and the other is white

    (c) only one of the counters drawn is green

    (d) the two counters drawn are different colours.

9. There are two sets of traffic lights on Memorial Drive. The probability that the first set malfunctions is 0·02 and the probability that the second set malfunctions is 0·03. Find the probability that (a) both sets of lights malfunction

    (b) at least one of these sets of lights malfunctions

    (c) only one of these sets of lights functions correctly.

Review 1 In a box there are 4 red, 5 green and 6 yellow balls, all of the same size and weight. Darryl chooses a ball at random, replaces it then chooses another. Find the probability that Darryl chooses (a) a red then a green ball

    (b) balls of the same colour

    (c) at least one yellow ball

    (d) balls of different colours.

Review 2 The probability that an RAC car is free to respond to an emergency is 0·8. Find the probability that, of two RAC cars on duty when an emergency call comes through (a) no car is available

    (b) both cars are available

    (c) just one car is available

    (d) a car is available.

INVESTIGATION 18:6

ANALYSIS of GAMES

We can often improve our chances of winning a game that involves the throwing of dice or coins. We can do this by being aware of the probability of particular outcomes.

An analysis of "Beat the Shaker" follows.

Beat the Shaker Two players, A and B, each roll a die. A rolls first, then B. If B gets a higher number than A, then B gets 1 point. If B gets a lower number than A, or the same number, then A gets 1 point. The game continues in this manner, with A always rolling first.

Analysis

1, 1	1, 2	1, 3	1, 4	1, 5	1, 6
2, 1	2, 2	2, 3	2, 4	2, 5	2, 6
3, 1	3, 2	3, 3	3, 4	3, 5	3, 6
4, 1	4, 2	4, 3	4, 4	4, 5	4, 6
5, 1	5, 2	5, 3	5, 4	5, 5	5, 6
6, 1	6, 2	6, 3	6, 4	6, 5	6, 6

continued . . .

. . . *from previous page*

The listing on the previous page gives the possible outcomes.
A's number is listed first and B's number is listed second.
B gets a point for those outcomes in black.
A gets a point for those outcomes in red.

Since 15 of the 36 possible outcomes give B a point, then the probability of B getting a point is $\frac{15}{36}$ or $\frac{5}{12}$.

Since 21 of the 36 possible outcomes give A a point, then the probability of A getting a point is $\frac{21}{36}$ or $\frac{7}{12}$.

Then, to give yourself the best chance of winning this game, you would go first.

You should also consider the number of tosses. For example, if each player tossed the die 12 times then the expected number of points won by A is $12 \times \frac{7}{12} = 7$

and the expected number of points won by B is $12 \times \frac{5}{12} = 5$
whereas if A and B each tossed the die 60 times

then the expected number of points won by A is $60 \times \frac{7}{12} = 35$

and the expected number of points won by B is $60 \times \frac{5}{12} = 25$

There is a difference of 10 between the expected number of points after 60 tosses which is a lot more than an expected difference of 2 points after 12 tosses. So the greater the number of tosses, the safer A should feel about winning.

Choose a game you often play, that involves dice or coins. **Analyse** this game.

Invent a game that uses dice or coins. It could be based on "Beat the Shaker". **Analyse** your game. Play your game with many different opponents. If you made a good analysis you should be able to win more often than you lose.

Games of chance are those in which there is no element of skill. Examples are raffles, housie and most dice games.
Games of skill are those in which there is no element of chance (or virtually no element of chance). Examples are chess and tennis.
Many games involve both skill and chance. Examples are bridge, backgammon and football.

Some games, if analysed well, involve no element of chance. The following games are of this sort. You can always win these games. Each is a game for two players.
Play these games. Try to develop a winning (or non-losing) strategy.

GAMES 18:7

Counter Game 1: a game for 2 players.

Materials: Two piles of counters. There may be any number of counters in each pile.

The Play: Each player, in turn, removes one or more counters from just one of the piles.
The loser is the player who is forced to take the last counter.

Counter Game 2: a game for 2 players.

Materials: 15 counters set out with 7 in one row, 5 in another and 3 in the other.

The Play: Players take turns to remove any number of adjacent counters from any single row.
The winner is the player to remove the last counter.

Circle Game: a game for 2 players

Materials: The diagram shown, drawn on a piece of paper.
A blue pen for one player, a red pen for the other.

The Play: The players take it in turn to colour a circle.
The winner is the first player to have coloured three connected circles.

Grid Game: a game for 2 players.

Materials: A 4 × 4 grid.
8 counters, 4 of one colour for one player, 4 of another colour for the other player.

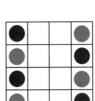

The Play: The counters are placed on the grid as shown.
Players take it in turn to move their counters.
At each turn, only one counter may be moved. Counters may be moved horizontally or vertically, one square at a time. They may not be moved diagonally.
The winner is the first player to position 3 of his or her counters beside each other, either horizontally, vertically or diagonally.

Probability

CHAPTER 18   REVIEW

1. Each week Sue borrows a book from the public library.

    She may choose a romance or a murder-mystery or a non-fiction book.

    These three actions are mutually exclusive.

    (a) Explain what 'mutually exclusive' means.

    The probability that Sue chooses a romance is 0·1 and the probability that she chooses a murder-mystery is 0·6.

    (b) What is the probability that Sue chooses a non-fiction book?

    (c) What is the probability that Sue chooses either a murder-mystery or a non-fiction book?   **SEG**

2. A pack of 52 playing cards consists of equal numbers of clubs, diamonds, hearts and spades.

    Ten cards are removed from the pack and placed face down on a table.

    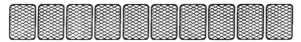

    When one of these cards is taken at random the following probabilities apply:

Type of card	Probability		Number on card	Probability
club	0·4		2	0·2
diamond	0·2		3	0·2
heart	0·1		4	0·1
spade	0·3		5	0·3
			7	0·2

    Four of the ten cards are clubs.
    They are numbered 2, 4, 5 and 7.

    One of the ten cards is taken from the table at random.

    (a) What is the probability that it is **not** a diamond?

    (b) What is the probability that it is a club or a diamond?

    (c) What is the probability that it is a club or numbered 3?

    (d) Explain why the probability that it is a club or numbered 5 is **not** 0·4 + 0·3.   **SEG**

3. In English football, a team scores 3 points if it wins, 1 point if it draws, 0 points if it loses.
The probability that my team will win their next match is 0·4. The probability that it will lose its next match is 0·25.
What is the probability that it will score at least 1 point in its next match?   **NEAB**

4. Mrs Wild drives to school each morning.
The probability that she parks her car at the front of the school is 0·6.
The probability that she parks her car at the side of the school is 0·3.

   (a) What is the probability that she will park either at the front **or** at the side of the school tomorrow morning?

   (b) In the next 200 school mornings, approximately how many times will Mrs Wild **not** park either at the front or at the side of the school?   **ULEAC**

5. The probability that Richard beats John at badminton is 0·7.
The probability that Richard beats John at squash is 0·6.
These events are independent.
Calculate, the probability that, in a week when they play one game of badminton and one game of squash

   (a) Richard wins both games,

   (b) Richard wins one game and loses the other.   **MEG**

6.

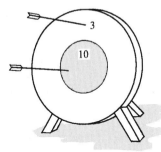

A target has a bull's-eye worth 10 points, and an outer ring worth 3 points.
Siobahn fires an arrow at the target.

The probability that she misses the target completely is $\frac{1}{9}$.

The probability that she hits the bull's eye and scores 10, is $\frac{2}{9}$.

The probability that she hits the outer ring and scores 3, is $\frac{2}{3}$.
Siobahn fires two arrows.

   (a) Calculate the probability that Siobahn fails to score with her two arrows.

   (b) Calculate the probability that she scores a total of 13 points.

   (c) Calculate the probability that she scores **either** no points **or** 6 points with her two arrows.   **SEG**

7. In the game of "Pass the Pigs", two identical toy pigs are thrown. Each pig can land in one of five positions. The five positions and the probabilities that the pig will land in each of these positions are shown in the table.

Position	Sider	Trotter	Razorback	Snouter	Leaning Jowler
	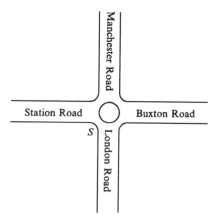				
Probability	0.57	0.2	0.2	0.02	0.01

Both pigs are thrown.

(a) Work out the probability that they will both land in the Trotter position.

10 points are scored for a "Double Trotter" when both pigs land in the Trotter position.

The only other way of scoring 10 points is when one of the toy pigs lands in the Snouter position and the other lands in the Sider position.

(b) Work out the probability that 10 points will be scored on one throw of the pigs.

ULEAC

8. The diagram shows a roundabout in a town.

The highways department wants to know how much traffic uses this roundabout.

A surveyor stands at the point marked *S*.

She counts how many of the cars from London Road turn into Station Road.

She does this at midday for four consecutive days.

Her results are shown in the table on the next page.

Number of cars counted	Number of these cars which turned into Station Road
16	9
23	11
26	14
17	9

(a) Estimate the probability that a car travelling down London Road at midday will turn into Station Road.

Give your answer to 1 decimal place.

(b) Station Road is a one-way street.

The cars that turn into Station Road can use one of three lanes as shown below.

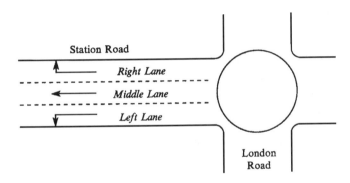

The probability that a car turning into Station Road will join the middle lane is 0·7.

The probability of a car taking the right lane equals the probability of a car joining the left lane.

Calculate an estimate of the probability that a car travelling down London Road at midday will turn left into Station Road and then take the left lane.   **NEAB**

9. The probability that an animal will give birth to a certain number of young in any one year is shown in the table below.

Number of Young	0	1	2	3
Probability	0·1	0·6	0·2	0·1

(a) Calculate the probability that the animal will give birth to either 2 or 3 young in 1995.

(b) Calculate the probability that, over a 2 year period, the animal will give birth to exactly two young.   **ULEAC**

10.

Catherine ⭕ | *ㄱ* | *S* | *Z* | ⭕ Bob

(grid with numbers)

Damien ⭕ | 4 | 3 | 2 | ⭕ Ann

In the game "HURRY HOME" players start with counters on the four blank corner squares.

An ordinary die numbered 1 to 6 is thrown by each player in turn. On each throw *all* players must move their counters to an adjoining square if the number in that square comes up on the die.

The centre square has the number 6 and the player who reaches that square first wins the game.
If two or more players reach the centre at the same time the game is declared a draw.

Examples of adjoining squares:

Ann, Bob, Catherine and Damien are ready to start a game with their counters on the corner squares.

(a) On the first throw of the die what is the probability that
    (i)   Ann must move,
    (ii) Ann, Bob and Catherine must all move,
    (iii) nobody has to move?

(b) What is the probability that Ann wins the game on the second throw of the die?

(c)

Catherine ⭕ | *ㄱ* | *S* | *Z* | ⭕ Bob

(grid with numbers)

Damien ⭕ | 4 | 3 | 2 |

Bob, Catherine and Damien start a new game with their counters on the corner squares. The first throw of the die is a 5 and the second throw is a 4.

What is the probability that Bob wins or draws on the fourth throw of the die? **NICCEA**

11. Alan, Barbara and Chris usually travel on the same bus to school.

   (a) Complete the following table by listing all the possible outcomes of Alan *(A)*, Barbara *(B)* and Chris (C) trying to catch the bus. Use a tick to indicate 'catches the bus' and a cross to indicate 'does not catch the bus'.

A✓	B✓	C✓
A✓	B✓	C✗

   (b) On any one day, the probability that Alan catches the bus is 0·8,
   the probability that Barbara catches the bus is 0·9 and
   the probability that Chris catches the bus is 0·75.

   (i) Calculate the probability that only Alan and Barbara catch the bus on any one day.

   (ii) Calculate the probability that at least two of the three pupils catch the bus on any one day. **MEG**

12. The probability that Jenny will beat Gill at tennis is $\frac{3}{5}$.

   The probability that Jenny will beat Gill at both tennis and snooker is $\frac{1}{4}$.

   What is the probability that Jenny will beat Gill at snooker? **NEAB**

Évariste Galois

Évariste Galois was born in 1811 at a village near Paris and died in 1832 at Paris.

Although his maths. writing consisted of only 60 pages, he is considered one of the greatest mathematicians of all times. He was certainly the youngest mathematician (he was 20 when he died) to make important discoveries.

Évariste's parents were well educated but had no particular talent for mathematics. His father was the mayor of the village in which the family lived. His mother was a strong-willed, unconventional woman who taught Évariste at home until he was 12.

At school, Évariste was considered to be eccentric, both by his teachers and his fellow students. He was teased by the students who regarded him with fear and anger. Évariste was so inarticulate that he was unable to make his teachers understand him. His classwork was quite poor; so poor that in one year he was demoted. During this year he became fascinated with a book on Geometry and read and understood the contents in a very short time. This book was written for mathematicians, not for school pupils.

By 16, Évariste knew he was a mathematical genius; a view not supported by his teachers. He did most of his mathematics in his head and refused to write down what he thought were obvious, trivial details. He frequently lost his temper with his teachers when they insisted that he show all his working. To Évariste, stupidity was an "unpardonable sin" – he regarded both his teachers and fellow students as stupid. It is claimed that one of his teachers said *"The mathematical madness dominates this boy. I think his parents had better let him take only mathematics. He is wasting his time here, and all he does is to torment his teachers and get into trouble"*.

Before he was 17, Évariste attempted to enter the École Polytechnique, famous for its mathematics teaching. He failed the entrance examination; the examiners did not recognise his ability because he showed so little working. The examiners suggested he prepare himself better and apply again. He did apply again but again he failed. It is claimed that during this second examination he was asked to show his working on the blackboard; he lost his temper and threw the blackboard duster at the examiner, hitting him on the head.

Just before his second attempt to enter the École Polytechnique, Évariste wrote up his maths. discoveries which he asked a famous mathematician to present at a meeting of the Académie des Sciences. The mathematician forgot to do this. To make matters worse, he also lost the article Évariste had written. Évariste became very bitter and disillusioned.

At 18, Évariste entered the École Normale where he continued his research and prepared for a career of teaching.

In 1830, he entered the Académie des Sciences mathematics competition. The secretary took Évariste's paper home to read; the secretary died and the paper was lost! It seemed that Évariste was never going to get any of his work recognised or published.

Évariste became involved in politics and was a most outspoken supporter of the 1830 revolution. Because of this, he was expelled from the École Normale. Shortly after this he was jailed for proposing a toast, at a republican meeting, that was interpreted as a threat to King Louis-Philippe. Soon after his release from jail, he was shot in a duel and left to die. Some say the duel was the result of a quarrel over a woman, others say he was challenged by those who disagreed with his political views. Évariste expected to be killed and spent the night before writing down his mathematical discoveries. These were published in 1846.

Évariste Galois is famous for developing group theory, an important branch of algebra. This theory is also important in the study of the behaviour of electrons and molecules.

DRAWING TREE DIAGRAMS

The possible outcomes of two events can be shown on a table.
A **tree diagram** is another way of showing the possible outcomes.

Example   A die is tossed twice.
Let E be the outcome "an even number" and O the
outcome "an odd number".
This table shows all the possible outcomes when the die
is tossed twice. These outcomes are EE, EO, OE, OO.

		2nd toss	
		E	O
1st toss	E	EE	EO
	O	OE	OO

The tree diagram, below, also shows all the possible outcomes.
Level 1 shows the outcomes on the first toss, level 2 shows the outcomes on the second toss.

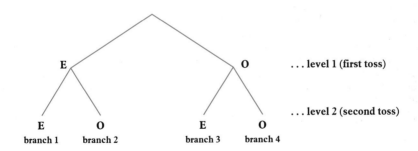

The two entries on the left-hand side of level 2 show that if the first toss
resulted in E, the second toss could result in either E or O. The two entries on
the right-hand side of level 2 show that if the first toss resulted in O, the second
toss could result in E or O.
Reading from top to bottom, down each "branch" of the tree diagram, we get
all the possible outcomes. Branch 1 gives the outcome EE, branch 2 gives the
outcome EO, branch 3 gives the outcome OE and branch 4 gives the outcome
OO.

Tree diagrams may be written horizontally instead of vertically. The information may be
written on the tree diagrams in different ways.

DISCUSSION EXERCISE 19:1

Discuss the possible outcomes shown on the following tree diagrams.

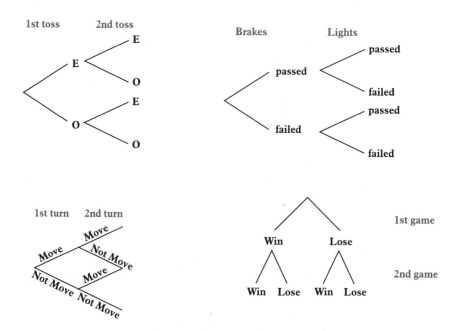

It is not necessary to have the same outcomes at each level of a tree diagram. Neither is it necessary to have the same number of outcomes at each level.

Example   A bank is going to sponsor either a sports programme (S) or quiz programme (Q) or a drama series (D) on TV. Each programme is given a rating; High (H) or Low (L). All the possible outcomes are shown on this tree diagram.

The possible outcomes are SH, SL, QH etc., where, for example, the outcome SH means the bank sponsored a sports programme and this sports programme was given a high rating.

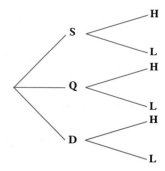

Tree diagrams for 2 events have 2 levels. Tree diagrams for 3 events have 3 levels.

Example   A family has three children. The tree diagram below shows the possible sex of these children.

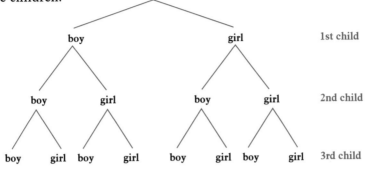

EXERCISE 19:2

1. A die is tossed twice.
    Let S be the outcome "a six", NS be the outcome "not a six".
    Draw a tree diagram to illustrate. (On each level you will have S and NS.)

2. A coin is tossed three times.
    Draw a tree diagram to show all the possible outcomes.

3. Write down all the possible outcomes for the 3 events shown.

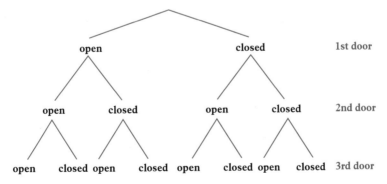

4. All the students at Deirdre's school will play sport this winter.
    They may choose from soccer, hockey or volleyball.
    They may or may not represent the school at the sport they play.
    Draw a tree diagram to illustrate.

Review   A football team may play either at home or away.
    They may win or draw or lose the game.
    Draw a tree diagram to illustrate.

USING TREE DIAGRAMS to CALCULATE PROBABILITY

Worked Example   On Rebecca's route to school there are two sets of traffic lights. The probability that Rebecca must stop at the first set is 0·7 and at the second set it is 0·4. Draw a tree diagram to illustrate.
Use the tree diagram to find the probability that Rebecca must stop at

(a) both sets of these lights

(b) just one of these sets of lights.

Answer   Firstly draw the tree diagram, see *fig 1*. Then enter the known probabilities, *fig 2*.

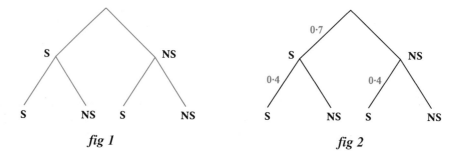

fig 1   fig 2

On the above tree diagrams S is used for stop, NS for not stop. The first level shows what happens at the first set of lights. The second level shows what happens at the second set of lights.

The next step is to fill in all the missing probabilities on *fig 2*. Since the probability of stopping at the first set of lights is 0·7, the probability of not stopping is 0·3. Since the probability of stopping at the second set of lights is 0·4, the probability of not stopping is 0·6. *fig 3* shows the completed tree diagram.

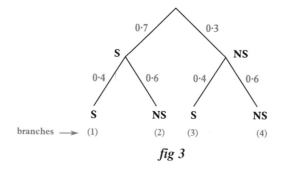

fig 3

We are now ready to answer the questions.
    (a) The event "Rebecca stops at both sets of lights" is given by branch 1.
        Probability of the outcomes on branch 1 occurring $= 0{\cdot}7 \times 0{\cdot}4$
$$= 0{\cdot}28$$
        [We multiply the probabilities written on branch 1 since
        P(S *and* S) = P(S) × P(S), using the multiplication principle.]

(b) The event "Rebecca stops at just one set of lights" is given by either branch 2 or branch 3.
Probability of the outcomes on branch 2 occurring = 0.7×0.6 or 0.42
Probability of the outcomes on branch 3 occurring = 0.3×0.4 or 0.12
Probability of the outcomes on branch 2 or branch 3 occurring = $0.42 + 0.12$
$$= 0.54$$

[We add the probabilities given by these branches since
P(branch 2 *or* branch 3) = P(branch 2) + P(branch 3) using the addition principle.]

Worked Example On Rebecca's route to school there are three sets of traffic lights.
The probability that Rebecca must stop at the first set is 0.7, at the second set it is 0.4 and at the third set it is 0.8.
Draw a tree diagram to illustrate.
Use this tree diagram to find the probability that Rebecca must stop at
(a) all three sets of lights
(b) just one of these sets of lights.

Answer There will be 3 levels in the tree diagram since there are 3 events. The first two levels are the same as in the previous worked example (shown again in *fig 1*). The completed tree diagram is shown in *fig 2*.

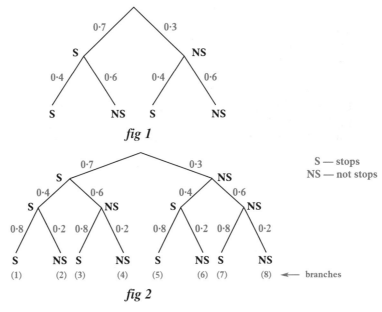

fig 1

fig 2

S — stops
NS — not stops

(a) Branch 1 gives the probability that Rebecca stops at all three sets of lights.
P(stops at all three) = $0.7 \times 0.4 \times 0.8$
$$= 0.224$$

(b) Branch 4 or branch 6 or branch 7 give the probability that Rebecca stops at just one set of lights.
P(stops at just one) = $0.7 \times 0.6 \times 0.2 + 0.3 \times 0.4 \times 0.2 + 0.3 \times 0.6 \times 0.8$
$$= 0.252$$

The previous worked examples show the steps we must take to calculate probabilities using a tree diagram.

Step 1 Draw a tree diagram for the situation.

Step 2 Write on the given probabilities.

Step 3 Work out the other probabilities and write these on.

Step 4 Decide which branches answer the question.

Step 5 Do the calculation. We do this as follows:

To find the probability of the outcomes given by any branch, we multiply the probabilities written on that branch.

To find the probability of the outcomes given by more than one branch, we calculate the probabilities on each of the branches and then add these together.

EXERCISE 19:3

1. Apprentice chefs have two exams; a theory exam. and a practical exam. 7 out of 10 apprentice chefs pass the practical exam. but only 2 out of 3 pass the theory exam.

   Copy and complete this tree diagram.

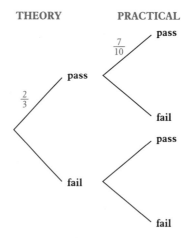

Use the tree diagram to find the probability that an apprentice chef, chosen at random

   (a) passes both the theory and practical exam.

   (b) passes the theory exam., but not the practical

   (c) passes just one of the exams.

   (d) does not pass either exam.

2. In a multiple-choice test each question has 5 possible answers.
   Robin does not know the answers to two of these questions, so he guesses.
   Copy and complete this tree diagram. (C stands for correct, NC stands for not correct.)

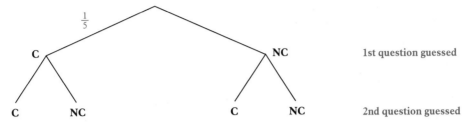

Use the tree diagram to find the probability that

    (a) Robin correctly guesses the answers to both questions

    (b) Robin correctly guesses the answer to just one of the questions

    (c) Robin correctly guesses the answer to at least one of the questions.

3. The probability that a letter posted at Shorfield Post Office is sent to a British destination is 0·9. Three letters posted at this post office are chosen at random. Copy and complete this tree diagram. (B is British destination, NB is not a British destination.)

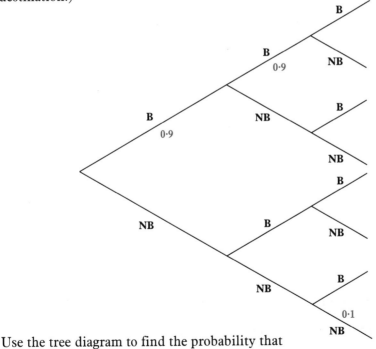

Use the tree diagram to find the probability that

    (a) all three of these letters are sent to a destination outside Britain

    (b) just two of these letters are sent to a British destination

    (c) at least one of these letters is sent to a destination in Britain.

4. **Draw tree diagrams to answer these questions.**

   (i) The probability that Kentucky Fried Chicken customers have chips with their meal is $\frac{9}{10}$; the probability of having salad with their meal is $\frac{2}{3}$.

   Find the probability that a customer will have

       (a) both chips and salad

       (b) neither chips nor salad

       (c) chips but not salad.

   (ii) One in every four calls received by a fire brigade is a false alarm. Find the probability that of the next two calls

       (a) both will be false alarms

       (b) neither will be a false alarm

       (c) one will be a false alarm.

   (iii) A cube has four red faces and two green faces. This cube is tossed twice. Find the probability that these tosses result in

       (a) both red faces

       (b) one green and one red face

       (c) at least one green face.

5. At the beginning of each netball game, the umpire tosses a coin. The captain of Yumiko's team always calls tails.
   Draw a tree diagram to show the outcome of the toss (Win or Lose) the next three times that Yumiko's captain calls.
   Use the tree diagram to find the probability that Yumiko's team

       (a) wins the toss each time   (b) wins the toss just once

       (c) wins the toss twice   (d) wins the toss at least twice.

6. The probability that everyone in Gillian's class is present on a Monday is $\frac{1}{2}$. On a Tuesday this probability is $\frac{3}{5}$ and on a Wednesday this probability is $\frac{2}{3}$.

   Draw a tree diagram to show these probabilities.
   Use the tree diagram to find the probability that during the first three days of the next school week

       (a) no one is absent from Gillian's class

       (b) all are present on two of the three days

       (c) someone is absent on each of the three days.

Review 1 A bag contains 100 discs, 70 of which are green and the rest red.
Half of the green discs and 10 of the red discs have numbers on them. A disc is chosen at random from this bag.

Copy and complete the tree diagram.

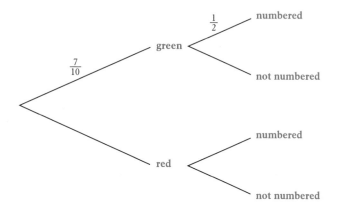

Use the tree diagram to find the probability that the disc chosen is

(a) a red disc with a number

(b) a disc with a number

(c) either a red disc with a number or a green disc without a number.

Review 2 A basketball team knows, from past experience, that it has a probability of $\frac{2}{5}$ of winning a game.
Draw a tree diagram to show the possible outcomes for the results of this team during its next two games.
Use your tree diagram to find the probability that this team wins only one of its next two games.

Review 3 Near the end of a maze there are three T junctions. (One of these is shown.)
The probability that a person turns left at each of these is: probability 0·7 at the first, 0·2 at the second and 0·4 at the third.
Use a tree diagram to find the probability that the next person to go through this maze will

    (a) turn left at all three junctions

    (b) turn left at just one of these junctions

    (c) turn right at all three junctions

    (d) turn left at more than one of these junctions.

CHAPTER 19 REVIEW

1. In a town, the probability that a family will have a freezer is $\frac{2}{3}$ and the probability that a family will have a computer is $\frac{1}{4}$.
    These probabilities are independent.

    (a) Complete the probability tree diagram below.

    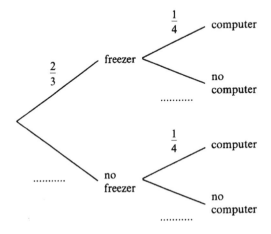

    (b) Calculate the probability that a family in the town will have a freezer but not a computer.   **ULEAC**

2. At an old people's party, the probability that Doris will win the Bingo prize is 0·05.
    The probability that she will win the raffle prize is 0·15.
    (a) Complete the tree diagram below.

    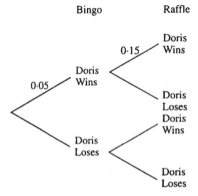

    (b) What is the probability that Doris loses both?

    (c) What is the probability that Doris wins only one of the two prizes?   **WJEC**

3. Sam often oversleeps and then arrives at College too late for the first lesson. The probability that Sam is late on any morning is 0·3.

(a) Complete and fully label the probability tree diagram below to show the possible outcomes for Monday, Tuesday and Wednesday.

MONDAY   TUESDAY   WEDNESDAY

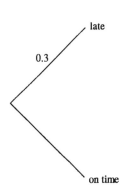

(b) What is the probability that, of these three days, Sam is on time on Tuesday only?

SEG

4. So far this season, a hockey team has scored 30 goals.
The goal scorers are given in this table.

Name	Number of goals scored
Ebun	12
Mee Ling	7
Vicky	5
Others	6
Total	30

(a) The team scores a total of 150 goals in the whole season.
Use the figures to estimate the number of goals you would **expect** Vicky to score in the whole season.

(b) The trainer has calculated the probabilities of each result for home and away games.

	win	lose	draw
Home	0.6	0.3	0.1
Away	0.35	0.45	

(i) What is the probability of a draw in an away game?

(ii) Complete the tree diagram to show all the possible outcomes for a home game followed by an away game.

Home Game   **Away Game**

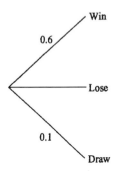

0.6 — Win

— Lose

0.1 — Draw

(iii) Calculate the probability that the team wins one game and loses the other.   **SEG**

5.

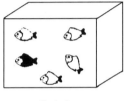 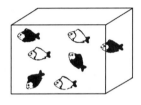

Tank A   Tank B

There are two fish tanks in a pet shop.
In tank A there are four white fish and one black fish.
In tank B there are three white fish and four black fish.

(a) Complete the tree diagram to show all the probabilities when one fish is taken out of each tank at random.

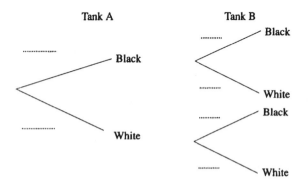

One fish is to be taken out of each tank at random.
(b) Work out the probability that

(i) the two fish will both be white,   **(ii)** the two fish will be of different colours,

(iii) the two fish will both be black.   **ULEAC**

1. Daniel gathered data on the number of students in maths. classes in his school. Daniel's data is given below.

   20   18   22   19   23   22   25   23   18   20   21   26   24   24   21   20

   As part of Daniel's analysis of this data he found the median, the range, the lower quartile, the upper quartile and the interquartile range.

   What answers should Daniel get for these?

2. Are the following pairs of events independent?
   (a) A die is tossed twice.
   > Event A : a 4 on the first throw.
   > Event B : a 4 on the second throw.

   (b) An equal number of red and blue discs are placed in a bag. Cameron chooses two of these, at random, one after the other. If the first disc chosen is blue, it is replaced in the bag. If the first disc chosen is red, it is not replaced.
   > Event P : the first disc chosen is red.
   > Event Q : the second disc chosen is blue.

3. In a cottage garden collection of flowering plants, $\frac{2}{5}$ of the plants have mottled leaves and $\frac{3}{4}$ have white flowers.

   Copy and complete this tree diagram.

   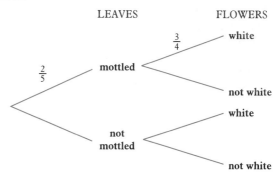

   One plant is chosen at random from this collection.
   Use your tree diagram to find the probability that this will

   (a) be a white flowered plant with mottled leaves

   (b) have neither white flowers nor mottled leaves.

4. A restaurant offers 6 choices for the main course and 4 choices for dessert.
   Two of the main courses are pasta dishes; one of the desserts is cheesecake.
   Find the probability that the next customer who has both a main course and dessert chooses both a pasta dish and cheesecake. (Assume that all choices are equally popular.)

5. Sometimes Paul drives to work, sometimes he catches the bus and the rest of the time he travels by tube.
   The probability that he takes the tube is 0·34.
   The probability that he takes the bus is 0·26.

   Find the probability that Paul

   (a) drives to work

   (b) either catches the bus or the tube

   (c) either drives or takes the bus

   (d) either drives or takes the tube.

6.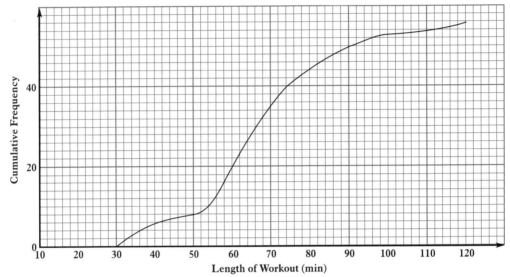

A gym. was analysing the time their members worked out for at different times of the day and on different days of the week.
The cumulative frequency graph shows the length of the workouts on a Monday of those members who arrived at the gym. before 9 a.m.

(a) How many members arrived at the gym. before 9 a.m. on this Monday?

(b) How many worked out for less than 1 hour?

(c) How many worked out for less than 90 minutes?

(d) How many worked out for between 1 hour and $1\frac{1}{2}$ hours?

(e) What is the median workout time?

(f) Find the lower and upper quartiles.

(g) What is the interquartile range?

7. During one maths. lesson, students could choose to work on an investigation or on a practical activity. They could choose to work individually or as a group.
   Draw a tree diagram to illustrate.

8.

Two cards are selected at random from these cards. The first card is replaced before the second card is chosen.

Find the probability that   (a)   the first card is a King

                                  (b)   the first card is a King and the second is a Queen

                                  (c)   both cards are red

                                  (d)   a black and a red card are chosen, in either order.

9.   (i)   Copy and complete the cumulative frequency tables.

(a)

Time (min)	Frequency
$0 \leq t < 5$	3
$5 \leq t < 10$	4
$10 \leq t < 15$	16
$15 \leq t < 20$	24
$20 \leq t < 25$	13
$25 \leq t < 30$	7

Time (min)	Cumulative Frequency
less than 5	3
less than 10	7
less than 15	23
less than 20	
less than 25	
less than 30	

(b)

Mark for Test (%)	Frequency
1–20	2
21–40	5
41–60	9
61–80	7
81–100	4

Mark (%)	Cumulative Frequency
≤ 20	
≤ 40	
≤ 60	
≤ 80	
≤ 100	27

(c)

Distance (km)	1·0 –	1·5 –	2·0 –	2·5 –	3·0 –	3·5 –	4·0 –	4·5 – 5·0
Frequency	4	4	9	12	11	17	10	6

Distance (km)	<1·5	<2·0	<2·5	<3·0	<3·5	<4·0	<4·5	<5·0
Cumulative Frequency								

(ii) Cumulative frequency graphs are to be drawn for the data in each of the tables. What points should be plotted for each?

(iii) Draw the cumulative frequency graph for (c). Use the graph to find the median and interquartile range.

10. Two faults have been discovered in Mayota cars manufactured last year. All of these cars are recalled for a check.

The probability that one of these cars has faulty seatbelts is 0·1. The probability that the steering is faulty is 0·03.

Find the probability that one of these cars has   (a) both faults

(b) neither fault

(c) just one of the faults.

11. 70% of the people who use the Tunway Library are adults, 20% are school pupils and the rest are children under school age.

60% of the adults, 40% of the school pupils and 50% of the children under school age are male.

(a) Copy and complete the tree diagram.

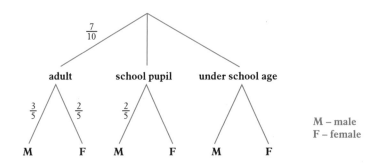

(b) One person, who uses this library, is chosen at random to complete a questionnaire. Use the tree diagram to find the probability that an adult woman is chosen.

12. (i)

House Prices (£)		
Price Range at least	below	Number of Houses
20,000	40,000	5
40,000	60,000	8
60,000	80,000	15
80,000	100,000	14
100,000	120,000	24
120,000	140,000	16
140,000	160,000	9
160,000	180,000	3
180,000	200,000	2

House Prices (£)	
Price	Cumulative Frequency
below 40,000	5
below 60,000	13
below 80,000	
below 100,000	
below 120,000	
below 140,000	
below 160,000	
below 180,000	
below 200,000	

Nathan did a survey on the prices of houses for sale in his district. The data he collected is shown above.

(a) Copy and complete the cumulative frequency table.

(b) Draw the cumulative frequency graph.
Use this graph to find the median price and the interquartile range.

(ii) Nathan's cousin, David, lives in another district. David did a survey on the prices of houses advertised for sale in his district. David drew the cumulative frequency graph shown below, for his data.
Write a few sentences comparing the prices of houses in Nathan's and David's districts.

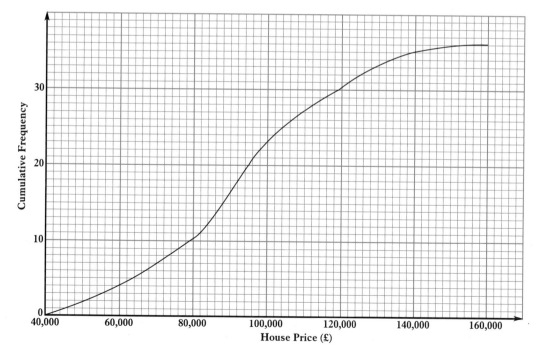

477

13. In a fairground game of chance, the probability of winning a prize is $\frac{3}{10}$. Barbara plays this game three times.

   Using a tree diagram, or otherwise, find the probability that Barbara

   (a) wins 3 prizes

   (b) wins just one prize

   (c) wins at least one prize

   (d) does not win a prize.

14. A coin and a die are tossed together. What is the probability of getting either a head or a six or both?

15. In a game of Monopoly a player rolls two fair, six-sided dice.

   The numbers on the dice are added together.

   The player then moves his counter that number of squares round the board, in a clockwise direction.

   (a) List all the possible outcomes when two dice are rolled.
   Show the total sum obtained each time.

   (b) David's counter is on the square called Fenchurch Street Station.

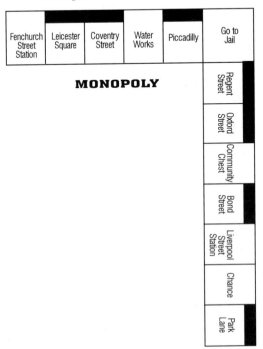

(i) Use your answer to (a) to find the most likely square he will land on next.

(ii) The probability that he will land on the square called 'Go to Jail' is $\frac{1}{9}$.
What is the probability that he will not land on this square?

(c) In this game David did land on the square called 'Go to Jail'.

The rules of the game say that a player can 'Get out of Jail' if he gets a double when he rolls the two dice.

[That is if he gets 6,6 or 5,5 or 4,4 etc.]

The probability that David will get a double on his first try is $\frac{1}{6}$.

The probability that he will not get a double first time but will get a double on his second try is $\frac{5}{36}$.

(i) Calculate the probability that David will get a double on either his first or his second roll of the dice.

(ii) Calculate the probability that David will get a double on both his first and his second roll of the dice. **NEAB**

16. In a survey 200 people were asked which of certain TV programmes they watch.

The results are in the table.

Programme	Number
Neighbours	107
Coronation Street	88
Emmerdale	76
EastEnders	94
Brookside	44
Casualty	120

Andrea and Bill were two of those asked.

(a) What is the probability that Andrea

(i) watches Neighbours?

(ii) does not watch Neighbours?

(b) 'The probability that Bill watches either Emmerdale or Casualty is $0.38 + 0.60$.'
Explain why this statement may be false. **MEG**

17. Over a period of seventy days the highest daily temperature at the resort of Puerto Rico was recorded.

The results were as follows.

Temperature (°F)	<62	62–	65–	68–	71–	74–	77–	80–83
Number of Days	0	8	9	11	15	20	6	1

Temperature (°F)	<62	<65	<68	<71	<74	<77	<80	<83
Cumulative Frequency								

(a) Complete the cumulative frequency row in the table of results.

(b) Draw the cumulative frequency curve for these data.

(c) Use the curve to estimate

    (i) the median temperature,

    (ii) the inter-quartile range.

For the same seventy day period the highest daily temperature for London was recorded.

The cumulative frequency curve obtained from the London data is drawn below.

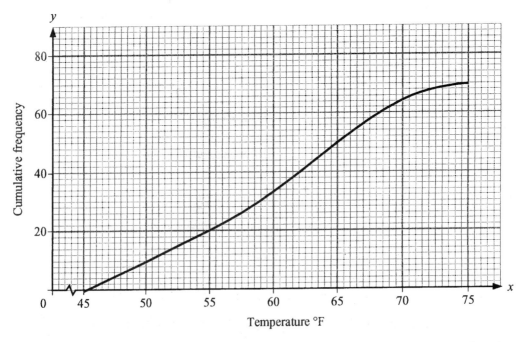

(d) What can you say about the spread of temperatures in London compared to those in Puerto Rico?

           SEG

18. A dice is biased as follows:

The probability of scoring a 6 is 0·4.

The probability of scoring a 5 is 0·2.

(a) Julia throws the dice once. Calculate the probability that the score will be 5 or 6.

(b) Jeff throws the dice twice. Calculate the probability that both scores will be 6's.

SEG

19. Ahmed and Kate play a game of tennis.

The probability that Ahmed will win is $\frac{5}{8}$.

Ahmed and Kate play a game of snooker.

The probability that Kate will win is $\frac{4}{7}$.

(a) Complete the probability tree diagram below.

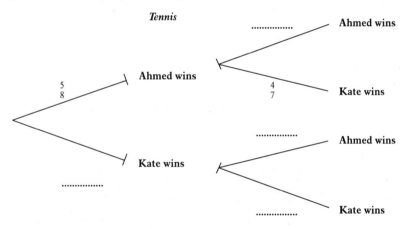

(b) Calculate the probability that Kate will win both games.

ULEAC

20. Two fair dice are thrown and the difference between the larger and smaller scores is noted every time.

(a) (i) What is the probability that the difference is zero?

    (ii) What is the probability that the difference is **greater** than 2?

(b) What is the most likely difference?

(c) When the difference is zero, the two dice are thrown a second time and the difference between the larger and smaller score is noted once more.

    (i) What is the probability of obtaining a zero difference both times?

    (ii) What is the combined probability of obtaining a difference of two or more on either the first or second throw?

SEG

21.

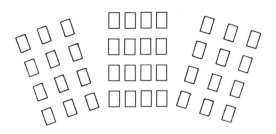

In a Paul Daniels Magic Show the seating is arranged as shown. There are 20 women and 18 men present. All the seats are numbered.

Paul randomly selects a seat number.

(a) What is the probability that the seat is empty?

(b) What is the probability that a woman is in the seat?

If instead Paul randomly selects two seat numbers, what is the probability that

(c) both seats are occupied by men,

(d) one seat is occupied by a woman and the other by a man?   **NICCEA**

22. Vicki investigated the times taken to serve 120 customers at a supermarket called Pricewell. Her results are shown below.

Time (seconds)	20–30	30–40	40–50	50–60	60–70
Number of customers	4	17	48	16	35

(a) (i) Calculate an estimate of the mean time to serve the customers.

(ii) Write down the modal class for the serving times.

Vicki decided to extend her investigation to another supermarket called Costsave. She obtained the times taken to serve 120 customers at Costsave. Her extended table is shown below.

Time (seconds)	20–30	30–40	40–50	50–60	60–70
Number of customers at Pricewell	4	17	48	16	35
Number of customers at Costsave	5	20	54	36	5

(b) Vicki correctly worked out the mean and modal class for the times at Costsave. She also worked out correctly the median of the times for each supermarket.

Use your answers to part **(a)** to complete the table below.

	Pricewell	Costsave
median	48.1	46.5
modal class		40–50
mean		46.3

Which average in this table represents the data most fairly? Give a reason for your answer.

(c)

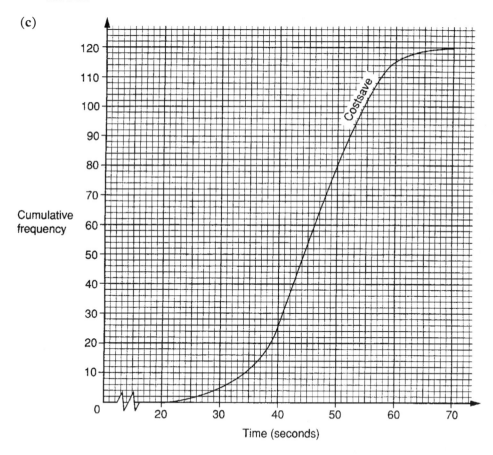

The graph shows the cumulative frequency curve for the serving times at Costsave.

(i) On the same axes, show the cumulative frequency curve for the serving times at Pricewell.

(ii) Complete the table below.

	Pricewell	Costsave
lower quartile		41
upper quartile		53
inter-quartile range		12

(iii) Use the information in the table to comment on the difference in the distributions of the serving times at Pricewell and Costsave. **MEG**

23. 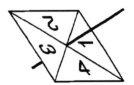 A spinner, with its edges numbered one to four, is biased.

For one spin, the probability of scoring 1 is 0·2,

the probability of scoring 3 is 0·3

and the probability of scoring 4 is 0·15.

(a) Calculate the probability of scoring 2 with one spin.

(b) The spinner is used in a board game called 'Steeplechase'. In the game, a player's counter is moved forwards at each turn by the score shown on the spinner.

If the player's counter lands on one of the two squares numbered 27 and 28 (labelled 'WATER JUMP'), the player is out of the game.

23	24	25	26	WATER JUMP 27	28	29	30	31

(i) Ann's counter is on square 26.

Find the probability that she will **not** be out of the game after one more turn.

(ii) Peter's counter is on square 25.

Find the probability that, after two more turns, his counter will be on square 29.

MEG

INDEX

NUMBER ANSWERS

Number Revision

Revision Exercise

1. (a) 100 times as large (b) 1000 times as large   2. b, c   3. (a) $\frac{2}{25}$ (b) $\frac{6}{25}$ (c) $\frac{1}{6}$ (d) $\frac{3}{10}$
(e) $\frac{7}{1000}$ 4. (b) $437 \times 82 = 35834$, $416 \div 52 = 8$ 5. Lucy pays 44p more.   6. (a) 32 (b) 13
(c) –2 (d) 2 (e) 49 (f) 180 (g) 2000 (h) 45 (i) 0·128 (j) 3·2 (k) 10 (l) –6
7. (a) $24 = 2 \times 2 \times 2 \times 3$, $45 = 3 \times 3 \times 5$ (b) 360 (c) $60 = 2 \times 2 \times 3 \times 5$ (d) 15   8. £12600
9. (a) 8m (b) 240mm   10. (a) $\boxed{(}$ needed before 18 and $\boxed{)}$ needed after 24 or $\boxed{=}$ needed after 24
(b) another $\boxed{)}$ needed after the first $\boxed{)}$ (c) the second $\boxed{\text{Min}}$ should be $\boxed{\text{MR}}$ 11. 31 bicycles
and 13 tricycles   12. –5   13. –1239   14. (a) 81 (b) 2 (c) 3   15. (a) 1658 (b) about 829
16. 2465·9km   17. (a) 50000mm = 50m (b) 1250m (c) 3km (d) 4km (e) Little Wadd Farm
18. (a) 16 (b) 2 (c) 64 (d) 8·5 (to 1d.p.) (e) 31·9 (to 1 d.p.) (f) 2   19. (a) 374 (b) 29·1%
(c) 41·5% (d) 16 more tested ; an increase of 4·5% (e) 35·3   20. (a) 20 : 9 (b) 1 : 3 (c) 3 : 8
21. (a) 95 marks (b) £34·80   22. (a) Natasha (b) One possible answer is a = 15, b = 16
23. (a) 0·17 (2 d.p.) (b) 16·7% (3 s.f.)   24. 20   25. 9·2% (1 d.p.)   26. (a) 70 (b) 50
27. (a) 0·807 (3 s.f.) (b) 0·398 (3 s.f.)   28. (i) (a) £398 (b) £648 (c) £382 (ii) £938   29. (a) 36
(c) Every square number is the sum of two consecutive triangular numbers.   30. £176·25
31. (a) A possible answer is

3	7	4
2	5	3
1	4	6

(b) Not possible since 16 + 9 + 18 is not equal to 15 + 17 + 14.   32. 10   33. A possible answer is 153.   34. Sarah's   35. (i) $72 \times 100 = 7200$ (ii) $60 \times 30 = 1800$ 36. (a) 770 (b) (i) 19 (ii) 9
37. (a) 700 miles, 70 litres (b) just under 10 miles   38. 13·7, 13·66   39. (a) Question 3
(b) Question 2   40. (a) £103·60 (b) £5·60 (c) 9 : 7   41. (a) $\frac{1}{8}$ (b) 12·5%   42. (a) $\frac{18}{25}$
(b) Spain (c) 36,000,000   43. (a) £37·59 (b) £67·13 to the nearest penny   44. (a) 20×30
(b) 600   45. –5°C   46. (a)

16	3	2	13
5	10	11	8
9	6	7	12
4	15	14	1

(b) Four possible groups are: the four numbers on each diagonal, the four corners numbers, the four numbers 10, 11, 7, 6 in the innermost square.
47. (a) £3 (b) 5%

48. (a) (i) A possible sequence is $\boxed{(}$ $\boxed{10.21}$ $\boxed{+}$ $\boxed{29.75}$ $\boxed{)}$ $\boxed{\div}$ $\boxed{(}$ $\boxed{0.2}$ $\boxed{\times}$ $\boxed{45}$ $\boxed{)}$ $\boxed{=}$
(ii) 4·44 (b) A possible estimate is $\dfrac{10 + 30}{0 \cdot 2 \times 40} = \dfrac{40}{8} = 5$ 49. (a) 580cm (b) 29cm
50. (a) (i) 4 ounces (ii) 5 ounces (b) 27   51. 1·8   52. (a) 174,000 (b) 17,000
(c) 15·4% (1 d.p.)   53. The plan should be 50mm by 80mm.   54. (a) 9°C (b) –2°C
55. (a) (i) 6·79 (3 s.f.) (ii) 3·3 (2 s.f.) (iii) 0·98 (2 s.f.) (b) A possible estimate is
$\frac{1}{4} + \frac{3}{4} = 0 \cdot 25 + 0 \cdot 75 = 1$ 56. 7000kg   57. (a) 1700 (b) A possible estimate is
$500 + 700 + 100 = 1300$ (c) The police statement is reasonable. Reduction is about 400 and
400 as a percentage of 1700 is about 23·5% (1 d.p.)   58. The English beer is better value.
It costs 0·4 pesetas per m*l* whereas the Spanish beer costs about 0·45 pesetas (2 d.p.) per m*l*.
59. £2400, £2000, £1600   60. (a) 95p (b) £10·54 (c) 9% (d) 5·2% (1 d.p.)   61. (a) 6·3
(b) Since 40 lies between the square numbers 36 and 49 then $\sqrt{40}$ lies between 6 and 7. The
difference between 36 and 49 is 13. 40 lies $\frac{4}{13}$ or about $\frac{1}{3}$ of the way between 36 and 49.
(c) 6·32

Chapter 1 Problem Solving

Discussion Exercise 1:2

● Siobhan rode Ginger ● Janine 2nd and 3rd races, Karen 4th and 5th races, Sharon 1st and
6th races

Page 38

Exercise 1:3

1. 11   2. 3   3. Eade boy   4. $3\frac{1}{2}$ hours   5. Tuesday   6. 20 along each side and 1 at each corner if the path is one slab wide. The path could be three slabs wide; the 84 slabs would then be sufficient to border a square with side the same length as 4 slabs.   7. Coopers at 17, Andersons at 19, Taylors at 21   8. A-Megan, B-Rebecca, C-Annabel, D-Heather, E-Lisa   9. at least 3   **Review 1** 60   **Review 2** Jake-collie, Paz-terrier, Churchill-labrador, Millie-spaniel

Page 40

Chapter 1 Review

1. 65   2. Tuesday

Chapter 2   Fractions

Page 42

Discussion Exercise 2:1

1. £80   2. £1600

Page 43

Exercise 2:3

1. (a) $\frac{5}{7}, \frac{2}{5}, \frac{3}{4}, \frac{8}{9}, \frac{5}{6}, \frac{3}{10}$ (b) $\frac{7}{5}, \frac{4}{3}, \frac{17}{4}, \frac{6}{5}, \frac{9}{8}, \frac{10}{3}$ 2. (a) $2\frac{3}{5}$ (b) $4\frac{1}{4}$ (c) $1\frac{2}{3}$ (d) $4\frac{1}{2}$
(e) $2\frac{1}{5}$ (f) $3\frac{1}{6}$ (g) $12\frac{1}{2}$ (h) $8\frac{1}{3}$ (i) $5\frac{1}{7}$ (j) $1\frac{5}{9}$ 3. (a) $\frac{11}{4}$ (b) $\frac{7}{5}$ (c) $\frac{12}{5}$ (d) $\frac{13}{8}$ (e) $\frac{21}{4}$
(f) $\frac{17}{6}$ (g) $\frac{43}{8}$ (h) $\frac{43}{6}$ (i) $\frac{31}{9}$ (j) $\frac{53}{10}$ **Review (i)** (a) $5\frac{3}{5}$ (b) $2\frac{5}{7}$ **(ii)** (a) $\frac{13}{4}$ (b) $\frac{17}{3}$

Page 46

Exercise 2:5

1. (a) $\frac{4}{35}$ (b) $\frac{2}{5}$ (c) $\frac{10}{27}$ (d) $\frac{8}{15}$ (e) $\frac{15}{22}$ (f) $2\frac{2}{5}$ (g) $1\frac{5}{7}$ (h) $6\frac{2}{3}$ (i) $\frac{1}{2}$ (j) $2\frac{1}{4}$ 2. (a) $7\frac{1}{2}$
(b) $4\frac{1}{3}$ (c) 6   (d) $4\frac{2}{3}$ (e) $11\frac{2}{3}$ (f) 10   (g) $3\frac{1}{4}$ (h) $13\frac{1}{3}$ 3. (a) $2\frac{1}{4}$ (b) $7\frac{1}{9}$ (c) 2   (d) $13\frac{3}{4}$
4. Yes   5. $\frac{1}{10}$ 6. 216 miles   7. $11\frac{3}{8}$ square metres   8. (b) There are many answers.
Review 1 (a) $5\frac{1}{3}$ (b) $\frac{1}{6}$ (c) 16   (d) $5\frac{1}{5}$ **Review 2** $2\frac{7}{9}$ square metres

Page 48

Exercise 2:7

1. (a) $\frac{1}{4}$ (b) $\frac{1}{5}$ (c) $\frac{9}{50}$ (d) $\frac{5}{32}$ (e) $\frac{7}{30}$ (f) 4   (g) $2\frac{1}{2}$ (h) 30   (i) 12   (j) 20   (k) $1\frac{1}{3}$ (l) $\frac{7}{8}$
(m) $1\frac{1}{5}$ (n) $1\frac{1}{4}$ 2. (a) $1\frac{2}{5}$ (b) $2\frac{1}{5}$ (c) $\frac{5}{8}$ (d) $\frac{5}{9}$ (e) $1\frac{9}{10}$ (f) 6   (g) 3   (h) $1\frac{1}{2}$ (i) 6
(j) $11\frac{1}{3}$ 3. 10   4. $1\frac{7}{9}$ 5. 8 hours   6. £1·20   7. 24   8. (b) There is more than one answer.   **Review 1** (a) $\frac{2}{3}$ (b) 9   (c) $1\frac{7}{8}$ **Review 2** 8   **Review 3** 14

Page 51

Exercise 2:9

1. (a) $\frac{2}{3}$ (b) $\frac{2}{3}$ (c) $\frac{5}{9}$ (d) $\frac{1}{3}$ (e) 1   (f) $1\frac{1}{2}$ (g) $1\frac{1}{4}$ (h) $\frac{3}{8}$ 2. (a) $\frac{7}{10}$ (b) $\frac{5}{8}$ (c) $\frac{1}{12}$
(d) $\frac{7}{12}$ (e) $1\frac{7}{12}$ (f) $\frac{17}{24}$ (g) $\frac{37}{60}$ 3. (a) $1\frac{1}{2}$ (b) $1\frac{13}{24}$ (c) $\frac{8}{15}$ (d) $\frac{1}{4}$ 4. $\frac{1}{6}$ 5. the glass
6. $\frac{1}{6}$ 7. $\frac{19}{40}$ 8. $1\frac{1}{6}$ **Review 1** (a) $\frac{8}{9}$ (b) $\frac{1}{6}$ (c) $1\frac{5}{12}$ (d) $\frac{1}{6}$ **Review 2** $\frac{1}{30}$

Page 53

Exercise 2:11

1. (a) $4\frac{1}{4}$ (b) $4\frac{11}{12}$ (c) $1\frac{3}{10}$ (d) $6\frac{1}{5}$ (e) $1\frac{7}{8}$ (f) $1\frac{8}{15}$ (g) $\frac{5}{6}$ 2. $6\frac{1}{4}$ hours   3. $3\frac{3}{8}$ pages
4. 8   5. There are many possible answers.

6. (a)

$\frac{1}{2}$	$1\frac{1}{3}$	$1\frac{1}{6}$
$1\frac{2}{3}$	1	$\frac{1}{3}$
$\frac{5}{6}$	$\frac{2}{3}$	$1\frac{1}{2}$

(b)

$2\frac{4}{5}$	$1\frac{1}{20}$	$1\frac{2}{5}$
$\frac{7}{20}$	$1\frac{3}{4}$	$3\frac{3}{20}$
$2\frac{1}{10}$	$2\frac{9}{20}$	$\frac{7}{10}$

(c)

$1\frac{7}{12}$	$5\frac{13}{24}$	$4\frac{3}{4}$
$7\frac{1}{8}$	$3\frac{23}{24}$	$\frac{19}{24}$
$3\frac{1}{6}$	$2\frac{3}{8}$	$6\frac{1}{3}$

Review 1 (a) $4\frac{19}{20}$ (b) $1\frac{5}{12}$ (c) $\frac{17}{24}$ **Review 2** (a) $20\frac{1}{20}\,l$ (b) $\frac{9}{20}\,l$

Page 54

Exercise 2:12

1. (a) ÷   (b) +   (c) ×   (d) −   2. $10\frac{1}{2}$ 3. $\frac{1}{6}$ 4. 291 km

490

5. (a)

$\frac{2}{5}$	×	$1\frac{7}{8}$	=	$\frac{3}{4}$
÷	■	÷	■	÷
$\frac{1}{2}$	×	$\frac{3}{4}$	=	$\frac{3}{8}$
=	■	=	■	=
$\frac{4}{5}$	×	$2\frac{1}{2}$	=	2

(b)

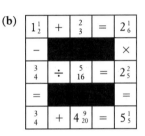

$1\frac{1}{2}$	+	$\frac{2}{3}$	=	$2\frac{1}{6}$
−	■	■	■	×
$\frac{3}{4}$	÷	$\frac{5}{16}$	=	$2\frac{2}{5}$
=	■	■	■	=
$\frac{3}{4}$	+	$4\frac{9}{20}$	=	$5\frac{1}{5}$

6. (a) $\frac{4}{15}$ **(b)** £5720   **7.** 16km   **8. (a)** 60mm (or 6cm) **(b)** $\frac{3}{4}$ **9.** $\frac{3}{16}$ **10.** 60*l*   **11.** 15
Review 1 (a) $\frac{5}{12}$ **(b)** I. M. Mahon **(c)** 1689   **Review 2** £50

Page 57   **Exercise 2:14**

1. 5   **2.** 5   **3.** 0   **4.** $3\frac{5}{14}$ **5.** $1\frac{1}{2}$ **6.** $1\frac{1}{6}$ **7.** $1\frac{5}{6}$ **8.** $1\frac{1}{8}$ **9.** $4\frac{2}{3}$ **10.** $1\frac{1}{5}$
Review 1 $\frac{7}{16}$ **Review 2** $5\frac{1}{10}$

Page 58   **Puzzle 2:15**

$\frac{1}{2} + \frac{1}{3} + \frac{1}{9}$ is not equal to 1.

Page 58   **Chapter 2 Review**

1. (a) $8\frac{1}{4}$ **(b)** $\frac{5}{6}$ **(c)** $1\frac{3}{7}$ **(d)** $\frac{11}{15}$ **(e)** $6\frac{5}{8}$ **(f)** $\frac{2}{3}$ **2. (a)** $\frac{1}{12}$ **(b)** 84   **3.** 9 square inches
4. $5\frac{1}{12}$ inches   **5.** £47·03 to the nearest penny   **6. (a)** 117·8cm³ (1 d.p.) **(b)** $34\frac{7}{8}$ cm

Chapter 3   Proportional Changes

Page 63   **Exercise 3:2**

1. £1000   **2.** £45000   **3.** 550   **4.** £1·08   **5.** 492   **6.** 16·8cm   **7.** £1750   **8.** £150   **9.** 133cm
10. £16   **11.** 1500g   **12.** Drama 53 Chess 21 Painting 69 Cricket 57 Craft 100 Athletics 49
13. £188   **14.** 54%   **Review 1** 680   **Review 2** 50cm   **Review 3** Belt £9·95 Handbag £35

Page 66   **Exercise 3:4**

1. £4   **2.** £1·50   **3.** £18·53 (to the nearest penny)   **4.** £360   **5.** 16·38cm by 21·06cm   **6.** £28
7. £1,542,593   **8.** 9541   **9.** 7·7cm   **10.** £199   **11. (a)** 1481 **(b)** 1550   **12.** 8·55%
13. £35327·50   **14.** C   **15.** £300   **Review 1** 27630   **Review 2** £15300

Page 69   **Puzzles 3:5**

1. 20%   **2.** 500   **3.** 28·57% (to 2 d.p.)   **4.** The first gets £15 and the second £36.   **5.** 33%

Page 69   **Chapter 3 Review**

1. £6348   **2.** £66   **3. (a)** £43·18 **(b)** £598·03   **4. (a)** 30p **(b)** 120g   **5. (a)** £2140 **(b)** £2805·10
6. (a) £450,000 **(b)** 4% decrease   **7. (a)** 42·5% **(b) (i)** £2662·20 **(ii)** £1725·50 **(c)** £6980

Chapter 4   Estimating Answers to Calculations

Page 76   **Exercise 4:2**

1. Possible estimates are: **(a)** about 32 **(b)** about 7 **(c)** about 140 **(d)** a little more than 100
(e) about 150 **(f)** about 2 **(g)** about 20 **(h)** about 15 **(i)** about 30 **(j)** about $\frac{1}{2}$ **(k)** about
3200   **2.** Possible answers are: **(a)** 869 (3 s.f.) **(b)** 5·1 (1 d.p.) **(c)** 9·0 (2 s.f.) **(d)** 3·31 (3 s.f.)
(e) 175 (3 s.f.) **(f)** 130 **(g)** 10·5 (3 s.f.) **(h)** 10·6 (3 s.f.) **(i)** 14 (2 s.f.) **(j)** 1280 (3 s.f.)

(k) 0·63 (2 s.f.) (l) 24·4 (1 d.p.) **3.** about 400 **4.** about 20 **5.(a)** £79·44 (to the nearest penny) **(b)** 22·43m **(c)** £881·95 **(d)** £18·01 (to the nearest penny) **(e)** 233cm² (3 s.f.) **(f)** 2240cm² (3 s.f.) **(g)** 31200mm³ (3 s.f.) **(h)** 10 hours 50 minutes **(i)** 36 **Review 1** Possible answers are: **(a)** about 200 **(b)** about 60 **(c)** about 40 **(d)** about 5 **(e)** about 50 **Review 2** Possible answers are: **(a)** 384 (3 s.f.) **(b)** 4·8 (1 d.p.) **(c)** 5·66 (3 s.f.) **(d)** 19·4 (3 s.f.) **Review 3** 2400cm³ (2 s.f.)

Page 78

Chapter 4 Review

2.(a) No **(b)(i)** 25m² **(ii)** 75·24m³ or 75m³, to the nearest cubic metre **3.(a)** y = 150 and x = 4 **(b)** 30 **4.(a)** Since 35 × 10p = £3·50 and 5 × 10p = £0·50 the answer must be a whole number of pounds. **7.(a)(i)** v = 120, u = 20, t = 5 **(ii)** 20 **(b)** Needs [=] before [÷] **8.** The answer is not about the right size. An estimate shows the answer should be about £7 or £8. **9.** The estimate is about right. **10.(a)** 8 pence per mile **(b)** 37·55 litres **(c)(i)** 28·8 miles per gallon (1 d.p.) **11.(b)** Hannah's answer is not the right order of magnitude. It should be about 100.

Chapter 5   Calculation

Page 82

Puzzle 5:1

Possible answers are $1 = \sqrt{1}$; $2 = \sqrt{4} \times 1$; $3 = 1 \times 1 + \sqrt{4}$; $4 = \sqrt{2+2} + 1 + 1$;

$5 = \sqrt{4} + 2 \times 2 - 1 \times 1$; $6 = \sqrt{4} \times 2 + 2 - 1 \times 2 + 2$; $7 = \sqrt{2 \times 2 \times 2 \times 2} + 2 + 1 \times 1$;

$8 = 1 + \sqrt{4} + 2 - 2 + 4 - 4 + 1 + 4$; $9 = \sqrt{2+2} + 4 \times 2 - 4 \times 2 + 4 + 4 - 1$;

$10 = \sqrt{2+2} + 1 \times 4 \times 2 - 1 \times 4 \times 2 + 4 + 4$

Page 84

Exercise 5:2

1.(a) 551·37 **(b)** 8·89 **(c)** 0·62 **(d)** 4·30 **2.** 28cm **3.(a)** −3 **(b)** 32 **(c)** −4 **(d)** 39 **(e)** −5 **(f)** 21 **(g)** −34 **(h)** 15 **(i)** 5 **(j)** −3 **(k)** 3·4 **(l)** 9 **(m)** 4 **(n)** 3 **(o)** 3 **(p)** 5·5 **4.(a)** 1·4 (1 d.p.) **(b)** 1·06 **(c)** 10·2 (1 d.p.) **(d)** −1·5 (1 d.p.) **(e)** 15·4 (1 d.p.) **(f)** −5·515 **(g)** −1·1 (1 d.p.) **(h)** 7·8 (1 d.p.) **(i)** −6·8 (1 d.p.) **(j)** 10·25 **(k)** 13·9 (1 d.p.) **(l)** 13·8 (1 d.p.) **(m)** 4·056 **(n)** 20·7 (1 d.p.) **Review (a)** 300·763 **(b)** 1·4 (1 d.p.) **(c)** 4·7 (1 d.p.) **(d)** −60 **(e)** −7 **(f)** −7·9 (1 d.p.) **(g)** −8·704 **(h)** −2·6 (1 d.p.) **(i)** 3·6 (1 d.p.) **(j)** 74·0 (1 d.p.)

Page 86

Exercise 5:3

1.(a) Area = 3m², Perimeter = $7\frac{1}{6}$ m **(b)** Area = $7\frac{1}{2}$m², Perimeter = $11\frac{1}{6}$ m **2.** (4, 2), (−2, 5) $(2\frac{1}{2}, 2\frac{3}{4})$, $(-3\frac{1}{2}, 5\frac{3}{4})$, $(9, -\frac{1}{2})$ **3.(a)** −7 **(b)** 5 **(c)** 4 **(d)** $-3\frac{1}{2}$ **(e)** −1 **4.(a)** $5\frac{1}{2}$ **(b)** 55 **5.(a)** −22 **(b)** 12 **(c)** $-6\frac{1}{2}$ **(d)** $-4\frac{1}{2}$ **(e)** 12 **(f)** 4 **(g)** $-15\frac{1}{2}$ **(h)** −2 **(i)** −22 **(j)** 0 **6.(a)** $3\frac{2}{3}$ **(b)** $3\frac{7}{12}$ **7.(a)** 14 **(b)** 20 **8.(a)** 212°F **(b)** 32°F **(c)** 14°F **(d)** 5°F **(e)** −40°F **9.(a)** 100 **(b)** $4\frac{1}{4}$ **10.** 240 cubic units **11.** Alison 49, Brenda $50\frac{2}{5}$, Ben $49\frac{1}{5}$ **12.(a)** £18 **(b)** £12 **13.(a)** 52·5 **(b)** −2·25 **(c)** −1·25 **(d)** −7·75 **14.(a)** 8m **(b)** 6·864m **(c)** 29·512m **15.(a)** 1·263m **(b)** 30·663m **16.** 37·5cm² **17.** $3\frac{1}{3}$ **Review 1(a)** −10°C **(b)** −20°C **Review 2(a)** −4 **(b)** −22 **(c)** 6 **(d)** 5 **(e)** 0·25 **Review 3(a)** $17\frac{1}{2}$ **(b)** 187 **Review 4(a)** 2 minutes **(b)** $1\frac{3}{5}$ minutes

Page 92

Exercise 5:6

1.(a) 5^9 **(b)** 5^7 **(c)** 5^8 **(d)** 5^{17} **(e)** 5^3 **(f)** 5^4 **(g)** 5^{12} **(h)** 5^4 **(i)** 5^6 **(j)** 5^{16} **(k)** 5^6 **2.(a)** $2^7 = 128$ **(b)** $3^5 = 243$ **(c)** $5^2 = 25$ **(d)** $2^7 = 128$ **(e)** $4^2 = 16$ **(f)** $2^4 = 16$ **(g)** $7^1 = 7$ **(h)** $5^2 = 25$ **3.** None **4.** b, c, d, e, f are all correct **5.(a)** x^9 **(b)** a^{12} **(c)** p^8 **(d)** x^{14} **(e)** b^{a+x} **(f)** b^{a+c} **(g)** a^{x-b} **(h)** a^{xy} **(i)** x^{6a} **(j)** p^{12x} **(k)** x^{2p} **(l)** b^{2a} **(m)** a^8 **(n)** x^3 **6.(a)** x^4y^6 **(b)** $a^{12}b^4$ **(c)** $x^{10}y^5z^{15}$ **(d)** $16a^8b^{12}$ **(e)** $27p^9q^{15}$ **(f)** $16a^{10}x^8$ **(g)** $32x^5y^{15}z^5$ **7.(a)** 3^2 **(b)** 5^9 **(c)** 2^2 **Review 1** d is correct **Review 2(a)** a^7 **(b)** p^{12} **(c)** a^6 **(d)** y^4 **(e)** x^{15} **(f)** $9a^8$ **(g)** $8x^9y^{12}$ **Review 3** 2^4

Page 95

Exercise 5:9

1.(a) $\frac{3}{2}$ **(b)** $\frac{4}{3}$ **(c)** $\frac{10}{3}$ **(d)** $\frac{7}{8}$ **(e)** $\frac{4}{5}$ **(f)** 6 **(g)** $\frac{1}{7}$ **(h)** $\frac{1}{8}$ **(i)** $\frac{10}{7}$ **(j)** $\frac{10}{13}$ **2.(a)** $\frac{a}{c}$

(b) $\frac{c}{a}$ **(c)** $\frac{x}{z}$ **(d)** $\frac{z}{x}$ **(e)** $\frac{x}{a}$ **(f)** $\frac{a}{x}$ **(g)** $\frac{1}{x}$ **(h)** $\frac{1}{d}$ **(i)** $\frac{1}{2z}$ **(j)** $\frac{1}{5x}$ **(k)** $\frac{4}{x}$ **(l)** $\frac{x}{2}$ 3. **(a)** 7·1
(b) 0·14 **(c)** 3·3 **(d)** 0·1 **(e)** 0·04 **(f)** 0·019   Review 1 **(a)** $\frac{4}{3}$ **(b)** $\frac{1}{9}$ **(c)** 10 **(d)** $\frac{1}{k}$ **(e)** $\frac{1}{3k}$
(f) $\frac{3k}{a}$ Review 2 **(a)** 1·67 **(b)** 0·05 **(c)** 0·86

Page 97 | **Exercise 5:11**

1. **(a)** $\frac{2}{9}$ or $0\cdot\dot{2}$ **(b)** $\frac{2}{5}$ or 0·4 **(c)** $2\cdot\dot{7}$ **(d)** 1·5 **(e)** 2 **(f)** $\frac{2}{3}$ **(g)** −0·24 **(h)** −0·2   2. **(a)** 4·8 hours
or 4 hrs 48 min **(b)** $4\cdot1\dot{6}$ hours or 4 hours 10 min **(c)** 4·4 sec **(d)** 27·5 sec   3. **(a)** 600cm³
(b) 40cm³   4. 3 min   5. 1·97 ohms (2 d.p.)   Review 1 **(a)** $\frac{3}{8}$ or 0·375 **(b)** 0·5
Review 2 5 amps

Page 98 | **Chapter 5 Review**

1. **(i) (a)** 3^{11} **(b)** 3^3 **(c)** 3^{10} **(d)** 3^9 **(ii)** b **(iii) (a)** x^6y^3 **(b)** x^{8p} **(c)** $9x^2y^8$ **(iv)** 2^6 **(v) (a)** $\frac{11}{3}$
(b) $\frac{3}{7}$ **(c)** $\frac{4}{a}$ **(d)** $\frac{1}{3}$ **(e)** $\frac{5x}{a}$ **(f)** $\frac{1}{2x}$ **(vi) (a)** 0·625 **(b)** 1   2. **(a)** 327·79cm (2 d.p.) for
calculator value of π, 327·63cm (2 d.p.) for π = 3·14 **(b)** $\boxed{=}$ $\boxed{\times}$ 3. £62·90 4. $3\frac{1}{2}$ 5. 44,900m
6. **(a)** Tony calculated 13×3^2 not $(13 \times 3)^2$ **(b)** 1521 7. 1·375 8. 28·8 (1 d.p.)
9. 2988·4cm² (1 d.p.) 10. **(a)** −15·0 (1 d.p.) **(b)** 17·2 (1 d.p.) 11. 38·9 (1 d.p.) 12. 6·12
13. **(i)** $\frac{11}{12}$ **(ii)** $\frac{2}{11}$ 14. −14°C 15. 4·02 (2 d.p.) 16. 9·6cm

Chapter 6 Standard Form

Page 103 | **Exercise 6:2**

1. 5 2. 2 3. 5 4. 8 5. −7 6. −6 7. −4 8. −10 9. 4 10. −9 11. 3 12. −3
Review 1 4 Review 2 −9

Page 106 | **Exercise 6:4**

1. a, d, g, i 2. **(a)** 340 **(b)** 8120 **(c)** 0·0625 **(d)** 0·008 **(e)** 70300 **(f)** 2·05 **(g)** 0·78
(h) 0·000101 **(i)** 370 000 **(j)** 0·000 037 **(k)** 15·2 **(l)** 3·4 **(m)** 0·00481 **(n)** 80 **(o)** 0·000 026 1
(p) 60 000 000 000 **(q)** 0·0705 **(r)** 815·4 **(s)** 0·008154 **(t)** 94·07 **(u)** 0·9407 **(v)** 60000
(w) 0·0006 3. **(a)** 1 **(b)** 2 **(c)** 0 **(d)** 1 **(e)** 3 **(f)** −1 **(g)** −2 **(h)** −1 **(i)** −3 **(j)** 0 **(k)** 1 **(l)** −2
(m) −1 **(n)** 1 **(o)** −4 4. **(a)** $6\cdot4 \times 10^1$ **(b)** $7\cdot82 \times 10^2$ **(c)** $3\cdot64 \times 10^3$ **(d)** $5\cdot52 \times 10^1$
(e) $7\cdot0 \times 10^0$ **(f)** $1\cdot0 \times 10^3$ **(g)** $3\cdot42 \times 10^1$ **(h)** $5\cdot5561 \times 10^2$ **(i)** $7\cdot24 \times 10^1$ **(j)** $8\cdot0 \times 10^{-1}$
(k) $9\cdot1 \times 10^{-1}$ **(l)** $4\cdot3 \times 10^{-3}$ **(m)** $8\cdot04 \times 10^{-1}$ **(n)** $4\cdot0 \times 10^{-2}$ **(o)** $2\cdot4 \times 10^0$ **(p)** $2\cdot4 \times 10^{-1}$
(q) $2\cdot4 \times 10^1$ **(r)** $2\cdot4 \times 10^{-3}$ **(s)** $2\cdot4 \times 10^2$ **(t)** $9\cdot0 \times 10^0$ **(u)** $9\cdot0 \times 10^1$ **(v)** $9\cdot0 \times 10^{-2}$
(w) $9\cdot0 \times 10^{-1}$ 5. $6\cdot12 \times 10^7$ 6. 18 000 000 7. 1 900 000 8. $3\cdot0 \times 10^5$ km/sec
9. 9 460 000 000 000 km 10. $1\cdot5 \times 10^{10}$ light years 11. 0·000 000 3 sec 12. 0·00005cm
13. $1\cdot0 \times 10^{-10}$mm Review 1 **(a)** 23000 **(b)** 2·3 **(c)** 0·00023 **(d)** 0·30504 **(e)** 9 010 000
(f) 0·0064 **(g)** 346·5 Review 2 **(a)** $5\cdot27 \times 10^1$ **(b)** $1\cdot6005 \times 10^4$ **(c)** $6\cdot0 \times 10^0$ **(d)** $8\cdot3 \times 10^{-1}$
(e) $1\cdot0 \times 10^{-1}$ **(f)** $2\cdot0 \times 10^{-4}$ Review 3 2 200 000 Review 4 Sun: $1\cdot6 \times 10^{-5}$ light years
Milky Way: $2\cdot6 \times 10^4$ light years

Page 108 | **Exercise 6:5**

1. **(a)** $7\cdot4 \times 10^9$ **(b)** $8\cdot5 \times 10^9$ **(c)** $7\cdot28 \times 10^7$ **(d)** $4\cdot8 \times 10^3$ **(e)** $8\cdot24 \times 10^{-8}$ **(f)** $2\cdot12 \times 10^3$
(g) $2\cdot3 \times 10^{-3}$ **(h)** $2\cdot1 \times 10^8$ **(i)** $1\cdot5 \times 10^2$ 2. **(a)** $1\cdot44 \times 10^{13}$ **(b)** $3\cdot0 \times 10^2$ **(c)** $7\cdot0 \times 10^5$
(d) $1\cdot28 \times 10^{-5}$ **(e)** $8\cdot0 \times 10^1$ **(f)** $4\cdot86 \times 10^5$ **(g)** $1\cdot17384 \times 10^{11}$ **(h)** $9\cdot1154 \times 10^{-1}$ **(i)** $1\cdot2 \times 10^{-2}$
(j) $6\cdot2548 \times 10^{-4}$ **(k)** $1\cdot9 \times 10^{-5}$ 3. $4\cdot68 \times 10^5$ mm² 4. $1\cdot35 \times 10^{-19}$ grams 5. about $1\cdot42 \times 10^7$
6. $2\cdot04 \times 10^2$ kg 7. $2\cdot5 \times 10^{-1}$ m³ 8. $2\cdot37 \times 10^2$ 9. about $4\cdot2 \times 10^1$ light-years
10. **(a)** Pluto **(b)** Jupiter **(c)** Saturn **(d)** Pluto **(e)** Neptune **(f)** 5 **(g)** 1 : 50 11. $5\cdot97 \times 10^{21}$
tonne 12. **(a)** $1\cdot0 \times 10^{18}$ **(b)** $1\cdot0 \times 10^{24}$ 13. **(a)** 10^3 **(b)** 10^{-4} Review 1 **(a)** $9\cdot6 \times 10^5$
(b) $1\cdot06 \times 10^6$ **(c)** $4\cdot2 \times 10^5$ **(d)** $5\cdot07 \times 10^{-3}$ **(e)** $5\cdot0 \times 10^{-2}$ Review 2 $1\cdot0 \times 10^3$ (1000 times larger)
Review 3 **(i) (a)** Paris **(b)** Darwin **(c)** Darwin **(d)** Paris **(ii)** 240 : 23
Review 4 **(a)** $2\cdot0 \times 10^{-1}$ km/sec **(b)** about $1\cdot08 \times 10^9$ km/h

Page 111

Exercise 6:8

1. (a) 6.95×10^3 (b) 1.88×10^5 (c) 6.104×10^2 (d) 4.15267×10^7 (e) 8.89719×10^2
(f) 7.6008541×10^2 (g) 7.34×10^{-3} (h) 3.0662×10^{-2} (i) 6.506×10^9 2. about $£1.1 \times 10^{11}$
3. about 1.528×10^5 4. about 6.717×10^5 tonne 5. about 7.963×10^5 6. about 8.514×10^9
7. about 1.238×10^5 8. 3.86×10^8 **Review 1** (a) 6.601×10^{-2} (b) -8.73×10^0
Review 2 (a) about 8.28×10^7 km^2 (b) about 2.47×10^8 km^2

Page 114

Exercise 6:10

1. 9.21×10^{20} 2. 3.7×10^{22} 3. 6.2×10^{25} 4. 5.830×10^{23} 5. 1.84 6. 89.88 7. 3.0×10^{-20}
8. 20.3 9. 6.1×10^{-19} 10. 0.444 11. 3.57×10^{14} 12. 1.62×10^{-6} **Review 1** 139
Review 2 2.59×10^{-16}

Page 115

Chapter 6 Review

1. (a) $52\,000\,000$ (b) 1.2×10^{-1} cm 2. (a) 2.7×10^{-23} (b) 1.35×10^{-14} grams
3. (a) 9.6×10^{-3} cm (b) (i) 1.188×10^8 sheets (ii) 1.14×10^6 cm 4. (a) 4.17×10^{-5} kg
(b) $0.000\,041\,7$ kg 5. (a) 2.3×10^7 (b) 2.735×10^7 kg (c) 1.2 kg (2 s.f.)
6. 2×10^{11} tonnes (1 s.f.) 7. about 27% 8. (a) 1.496×10^8 (b) 2.575×10^6 (4 s.f.)
9. (a) (i) about 4 (ii) 200 (b) 1.1×10^{21} m^3 10. (a) (i) 0.00035 g (ii) 3.5×10^{-4} g
(b) 2.9×10^3 pints (2 s.f.) 11. 8min 19sec 12. (a) 5.0×10^{101} (b) 5.0×10^{-8} (c) 10^{10}
13. (a) 365.5 (1 d.p.) (b) 3.7374×10^7 acres (c) 1 acre $= 4.047 \times 10^{-3}$ km^2 (4 s.f.)
14. 8.54×10^8 15. (a) 5.948×10^{21} tonnes (4 s.f.) (b) 2.516×10^{20} tonnes (4 s.f.)

Chapter 7 Number Review

Page 120

1. $(4, -1), (-2, -4), (-1, -3\frac{1}{2}), (1\frac{1}{2}, -2\frac{1}{4}), (-1\frac{1}{2}, -3\frac{3}{4})$ 2. (a) 8 (b) -3 3. (a) $4\frac{1}{6}$ (b) $\frac{59}{8}$
4. 5.1×10^6 5. 15 6. (a) about 20 (b) about 800 7. (a) -1 (b) -153 (c) -31 (d) -2.6
8. 1.14×10^{-4} years 9. $\frac{7}{15}$ 10. 1360 hours 11. (a) 47000 (b) 0.06 (c) 1.8
12. (a) 2.9 (2 s.f.) (b) 0.12 (2 s.f.) (c) 0.11 (2 s.f.) (d) 0.024 (2 s.f.) 13. $10\frac{2}{3}$ m^2 14. 8
15. (a) 356.3 (1 d.p.) (b) 11.3 (1 d.p.) 16. (a) 4.0×10^{-12} (b) 4.0×10^{-15} 17. (a) 3^{11} (b) 3^6
(c) 3^8 (d) 3^{10} 18. (a) about 209 people per square kilometre (b) about 99 people per square
kilometre 19. 6 20. 72kg 21. 18.6 (1 d.p.) 22. (a) No (b) about 3000 times
(c) Andromeda Galaxy (d) $1 : 6250$ (e) 9.5×10^{12} km (f) 4.2 light-years (2 s.f.) 23. 20 hours
24. (a) -2.0 (1 d.p.) (b) 5.21 (c) -12.94 (d) -5.5 25. 1053 26. Jimmy owns Jess, John owns
Julip, Justin owns Jip 27. (a) 15 (b) $\frac{5}{4}$ (c) $\frac{1}{7}$ (d) $\frac{x}{b}$ (e) $\frac{1}{2z}$ 28. £182 29. $52\frac{1}{2}$
30. (a) $\frac{1}{10}$ (b) 30 (c) $7\frac{1}{2}$ (d) $\frac{5}{6}$ (e) $1\frac{5}{7}$ (f) $\frac{7}{12}$ (g) $1\frac{13}{20}$ (h) $8\frac{4}{15}$ (i) $1\frac{5}{12}$ (j) $2\frac{9}{10}$
(k) $1\frac{3}{4}$ 31. (b) Area $= 446.16$ cm^2, Perimeter $= 98.1$ cm 32. (a) a^{x+b} (b) a^{x-b} (c) a^{xb} (d) a^{x+b-z}
(e) a^6 (f) a^6b^8 (g) $9a^8b^2$ 33. $\frac{9}{20}$ 34. C 35. (a) 33100 or 3.31×10^4 (b) 2.25×10^{-3} or 0.00225
(c) 3.56×10^{17} (3 s.f.) (d) 0.0197 (3 s.f.) 36. The last digit of 7^{107} is 3. 37. (a) 4.05×10^9
years (b) 3.15×10^8 years 38. $\frac{32}{41}$ 39. 3 40. (a) Eric has calculated $\left(4.8 + \frac{1.27}{1.2}\right)^2$
(b) A possible calculator sequence is $\boxed{(}\ \boxed{4}\ \boxed{.}\ \boxed{8}\ \boxed{+}\ \boxed{1}\ \boxed{.}\ \boxed{2}\ \boxed{7}\ \boxed{=}\ \boxed{\div}\ \boxed{1}\ \boxed{.}\ \boxed{2}\ \boxed{)}\ \boxed{x^2}$
which gives answer of 25.6 to 3 s.f. 41. 2.5125×10^{-21} grams 42. (a) £88.20 (b) £1822.50
43. (a) 4.29 (b) 4.652 (c) 50 (d) 2.5 44. (a) (i) Saturn (ii) 209 times heavier (3 s.f.)
(b) $1 : 0.11$ 45. (a) $-1\frac{5}{8}$ (b) $-\frac{5}{8}$ 46. 59.4 47. (a) £313.50 (b) 35% (c) £205 48. $8\frac{3}{8}$
49. (a) 5.76×10^7 square miles (b) 29.2% (3 s.f.) 50. (a) 2.0 (2 s.f.) 51. (a) 9.79×10^7
(b) 35.0 (3 s.f.) (c) 4.96×10^5 square miles (3 s.f.) 52. (a) -117.6 (b) 24

ALGEBRA ANSWERS

Algebra Revision

Revision Exercise

1. (a) 2, 3, 11, 19 **(b)** 8 **(c)** 2 **(d)** 4, 8, 20 **(e)** 1, 2, 4, 20   **2.** Three possible ways are 1, 2, 4, 7, 11, 16, . . . 1, 2, 4, 8, 16, 32, . . . 1, 2, 4, 5, 7, 8, 10, 11, . . .   **3.** 21 **4. (a)** 7 **(b)** 0·5 **(c)** −2·5
(d) −10   **5. (i) (a)** $n \le 3$ **(b)** $n > -4$ **(c)** $1 < n \le 5$ **(ii) (a)**

(b) −2, −1, 0, 1   **6. (a)** Jason **(b)** return journey by 5km/h   **7. (a)** 3h + 16 = 5h − 2 **(b)** 9
8. 3   **9. (a)** 25, 36, 49 **(b)** 13, 21, 34 **(c)** 13, 18, 24 **(d)** 125, 216, 343 **(e)** 2, 1, 0·5 **(f)** 13, 21, 34
The sequence in (f) is the Fibonacci sequence   **10. (a)** D **(b)** C   **11. (i) (a)** x + 2 **(b)** 4x + 4
(c) x(x + 2) **(ii)** 4·5m   **12. (a)** 4n + 3 = 2n + 12; n = 4·5 **(b)** 18cm   **13. (a)** 20 rods and 12
bolts in the 2nd size screen, 26 rods and 15 bolts in the 3rd size screen **(b)** r = 2b − 4
14. (a) a = 5, b = −2, **(b)** m = 2, n = 0·5   **15. (a)** −2n − 3a **(b)** 12 − x   **16.** −1, 0, 1, 2
17. (a) 200 + 75d = 100d **(b)** 8   **18. (a)** $\boxed{5}\;\boxed{8}\;\boxed{3}\;\boxed{2}$, $\boxed{5}\;\boxed{3}\;\boxed{2}\;\boxed{8}$, $\boxed{8}\;\boxed{3}\;\boxed{5}\;\boxed{2}$
(b) 12   **19. (a)** This is the sequence on the right. 7th term = 4374 **(b)** $t_n = 3n - 1$ **20. (a)** a is
the price each adult paid, s is the price each student paid. **(b)** 5a + 44s = 184   **(c)** Adults paid
£6 each; students paid £3·50 each.   **(d)** £84 assuming that each student paid the child's fare.
21. (a) 65 dots **(b)** 176 dots **(c)** $t_n = 3n^2 - 2n$ **(d)** 1160   **22. (a)** $n \le 5.5$ **(b)** $n < -0.4$
23. (a) and (c)

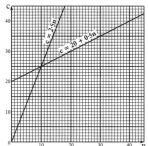

(b) C = 2·5n **(c)** 10 games   **24. (b)** 18·4m
25. (i) (a)

x	0	3	6
y	8	4	0

(b)

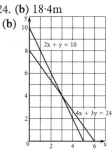

(ii) (a) 4f + 3s = 24 **(b)** 3 marks for each question in the first section; 4 marks for each question
in the second section. **(iii)** The solution for the equations in (b) can be found by finding where
the graphs drawn in (a) meet.   **26. (a)** 7 and 13 **(b)** 21   **27. (i) (a)** 1 + 3 + 5 + 7 = 16;
1 + 3 + 5 + 7 + 9 = 25 **(b)** $S_n = n^2$ **(c)** 625 **(d)** 19 **(ii) (a)** Possible examples are
1 + 3 = 4, 1 + 3 + 5 = 9, 1 + 3 + 5 + 7 = 16. **(b)** A possible example is 3 + 5 = 8.
(c) A possible correct statement is "if you add together two or more consecutive odd numbers,
beginning with 1, you always get a square number".   **28. (a)** 2(a + 2b + c) **(b)** 22   **29. (a)** 22 ;
the rule is "add 5" **(b)** 81; the rule is "multiply by 3"   **30. (a)** 3, 13, 23 **(b)** 4, 25 **(c)** 28 **(d)** 64
(e) 15   **31.** x = 2, y = 5   **32. (a)** 13, 15, 17, 19 Sum = 64 = 4^3 **(b)** Row 10 **(c)** 20^3 = 8000
(d) x + 2   **33.** −3, −2, −1, 0, 1, 2, 3,   **34. (a)** 5 **(b)** 6·25 **(c)** 7   **35.** Any of (2, 5), (3, 5), (4, 5),
(5, 5), (6, 5), (7, 5), (8, 5), (9, 5), (3, 6), (4, 6), (5, 6), (6, 6), (7, 6), (8, 6), (9, 6), (4, 7), (5, 7), (6, 7),
(7, 7), (8, 7), (9, 7)   **36. (a) (i)** − 4, −3, −2, −1, 0, 1 **(ii)** 16 **(b)** $x \ge 10, x < 20$
37. (a) (i)

House	Basement Flat	Middle Flat	Top Flat
1	1	2	3
2	4	5	6
3	7	8	9
4	10	11	12
5	13	14	15

(ii) 30 **(iii)** 22 and 28 **(b) (i)** Middle flat = 3h − 1 where h is the house number
(ii) No. When we solve the equation 94 = 3h − 1, h is not a whole number.

38. (a) 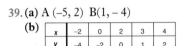 **(b)**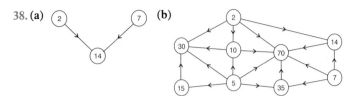

39. (a) A (–5, 2) B(1, – 4)

(b)

x	–2	0	2	3	4
y	–4	–2	0	1	2

(c) and (d)

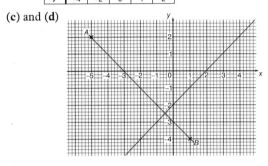

(d) (–0·5, –2·5)   **40. (a)** 4x + 20 **(b)** 9x + 5 = 4x + 20 **(c)** 3kg

41.

Sequence				next term	n^{th} term
1	4	9	16	25	n^2
5	8	11	14	17	3n + 2
$\frac{1}{5}$	$\frac{2}{6}$	$\frac{3}{7}$	$\frac{4}{8}$	$\frac{5}{9}$	$\frac{n}{n+4}$

42. (a) (i)

x	100	200	300
y	15	18	21

(ii)

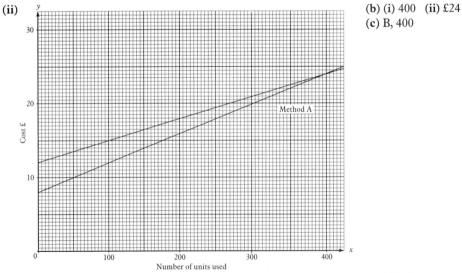

(b) (i) 400 **(ii)** £24
(c) B, 400

43. (b) (i) Number is 10^2 (or 1 + 3 + 5 + 7 + 9 + 11 + 13 + 15 + 17 + 19) **(ii)** n^2
44. (a) x + 50 **(b)** 2x + 100 **(c)** 4x + 150 **(d)** 4x + 1·50 = 6·70; x = £1·30   **45. (a)** £12·60
(b) 5   **46.** 9·5   **47.** x = 0·5, y = 2·5

48. **(a)** –28°C **(b)** 39000 feet   **49.** 8 must be changed to 7. The difference between consecutive terms is given by 1, 2, 3, 4, 5, 6, 7, . . .   **50.** **(a) (i)** 120 + 5g = 130
(ii) 2cm **(b) (i)** 20p + 2 (p – 1) **(ii)** 40   **51.** **(b)** x = y + 3 **(c)**

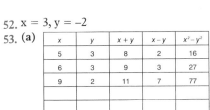

x	3	7	10
y	0	4	7

(d) longlife lasts 8·5 hours, standard life lasts 5·5 hours.

52. x = 3, y = –2
53. **(a)**

x	y	x + y	x − y	x² − y²
5	3	8	2	16
6	3	9	3	27
9	2	11	7	77

(c) The numbers in the last column can be found by multiplying those in the two previous columns.
54. **(a)** w = 2b + 1 **(b)** 45
55. **(a)** $\frac{1}{1}$, $\frac{2}{3}$, $\frac{3}{5}$, $\frac{4}{7}$, $\frac{5}{9}$ **(b)** $\frac{n}{3n-1}$
56. 15   **57.** **(a)** about £1·29

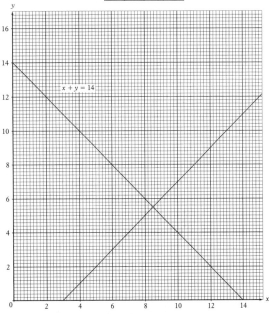

58. **(a)** 40s + 30d = 1500 **(b)** s = 18, d = 26
59. **(a) (i)** 11 × 11 × 11 = 1331
11 × 11 × 11 × 11 = 14641

(ii) Each number begins and ends with 1. The other numbers are found by adding the two numbers immediately above on the previous line.
(b) 11 × 11 × 11 × 11 × 11 = 161051. This is the same pattern if we begin at the right and "carry" digits.
60. **(a)** 2 metres **(b) (ii)** a = –5, b = 40
(c) 20·75m   **61.** x = 2·9
62. **(a)** x + 3
(b) (i) Area = x(x + 3) = x² + 3x.
If x = 8, x² + 3x = 88;
if x = 9, x² + 3x = 108 **(ii)** 8·6m

(b)

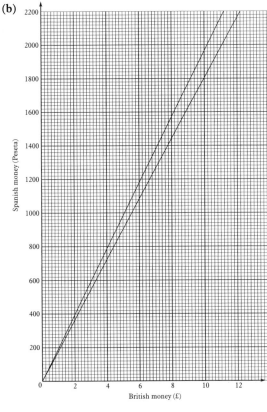

Chapter 8   Formulae. Functions. Expressions. Quadratic Expressions

Page 158

Exercise 8:2

1. (a) $h = \dfrac{2A}{b}$ (b) $h = \dfrac{2A}{a+b}$ (c) $h = \dfrac{V}{lb}$ (d) $h = \dfrac{3V}{A}$ 2. (a) $r = \dfrac{d}{2}$ (b) $r = \dfrac{c}{2\pi}$

3. (a) $l = \dfrac{A}{\pi r}$ (b) $l = \dfrac{P}{2} - w$ 4. (a) $m = \dfrac{y-c}{x}$ (b) $m = dv$ (c) $m = \dfrac{F}{a}$ 5. (a) $I = \dfrac{V}{R}$

(b) $x = \dfrac{y-2}{m} - 3$ (c) $P = \dfrac{100I}{RT}$ (d) $r = \dfrac{D-5s}{\pi}$ (e) $s = \dfrac{v^2 - u^2}{2a}$ (f) $b = \dfrac{2A}{h} - a$

(g) $R = \dfrac{100A}{P} - 100$ (h) $h = \dfrac{A}{2\pi r} - r$ **Review** (a) $y = mx$ (b) $x = \dfrac{y}{m}$ (c) $t = \dfrac{v-u}{a}$

(d) $C = \dfrac{5(F-32)}{9}$

Page 161

Exercise 8:4

1. (a) $r = \sqrt{\dfrac{A}{\pi}}$ (b) $r = \sqrt{\dfrac{3V}{\pi h}}$ 2. (a) $x = \pm\sqrt{a}$ (b) $x = \pm\sqrt{\dfrac{b}{5}}$ (c) $x = \pm\sqrt{\dfrac{2}{c}}$

(d) $x = \pm\sqrt{\dfrac{bd}{a}}$ 3. $l = \sqrt{\dfrac{3I}{m}}$ 4. $v = \pm\sqrt{\dfrac{2E}{m}}$ 5. $t = \sqrt{\dfrac{2s}{g}}$ 6. $y = \pm\sqrt{4ax}$

7. (a) $r = \sqrt[3]{V}$ (b) $r = \sqrt[3]{\dfrac{3V}{4\pi}}$ 8. (a) $l = n^2$ (b) $l = n^2 + 2$ (c) $l = \dfrac{a^2}{n^2}$ (d) $l = \dfrac{a}{n^2}$

9. $l = g\left(\dfrac{T}{2\pi}\right)^2$ **Review** (a) $d = \sqrt{\dfrac{c}{I}}$ (b) $r = \sqrt{\dfrac{A}{4\pi}}$ (c) $x = \pm\sqrt{a^2 y}$ (d) $n = \dfrac{a^2}{b^2} - 1$

Page 163

Exercise 8:6

1. (a) 9   (b) 40   (c) 3·75   (d) –5   2. (a) 900°   (b) 17   3. 1·56cm   4. (a) 58·5   (b) 2·20   (c) 12·0
5. (a) 400   (b) 17   6. (a) $x = \sqrt[3]{V}$ (b) 4·31mm   7. (a) 70·0   (b) 1·20   8. (a) 4·59
(b) 23·6, –23·6   (c) 4·0625   9. (a) 10·5   (b) 12   (c) 2·72   10. (a) 6·35   (b) 6·71   11. (a) 141
(b) 4·23   12. (a) 3·49   (b) 36   **Review 1** (a) 381·8   (b) 90   (c) 7   (d) 3   **Review 2** (a) 1·6
(b) 6, – 6

Page 166

Exercise 8:7

1. $A = \dfrac{P^2}{16}$ 2. $x = \dfrac{1}{y^2}$ 3. $s = \dfrac{v^2}{2a}$ 4. $y = 3x - 5$ **Review** $A = \dfrac{C^2}{4\pi}$

Page 167

Exercise 8:9

1. $f(1) = 3$, $f(2) = 5$, $f(-2) = -3$, $f(-5) = -9$, $f(\frac{1}{2}) = 2$, $f(-\frac{3}{4}) = -\frac{1}{2}$ 2. $f(5) = 4$, $f(1) = 2$,
$f(-3) = 0$, $f(-7) = -2$, $f(0) = 1\frac{1}{2}$, $f(\frac{2}{3}) = 1\frac{5}{6}$, $f(1\frac{1}{2}) = 2\frac{1}{4}$ 3. $f(3) = 22$, $f(2) = 7$, $f(-1) = -2$,
$f(-2) = 7$, $f(\frac{1}{3}) = -4\frac{2}{3}$, $f(-\frac{1}{2}) = -4\frac{1}{4}$ 4. $g(4) = 2\frac{3}{4}$, $g(1) = 5$, $g(0)$ has no answer, $g(-2) = \frac{1}{2}$,
$g(-\frac{1}{2}) = -4$ 5. $h(1) = 0$, $h(5) = \frac{1}{2}$, $h(0) = -\frac{1}{3}$, $h(-1) = -1$, $h(-3)$ has no answer   6. –2
7. (a) 5   (b) 1   (c) $1\frac{1}{6}$ (d) $-\frac{1}{3}$ (e) $-\frac{1}{2}$ (f) 15   (g) $-\frac{1}{8}$ 8. (a) 2, –10   (b) 3, –1   (c) 1, –5
(d) –3, –7   (e) 4, 2   9. (a) –3·1   (b) $-\frac{3}{5}$ (c) 0·7   (d) $3\frac{1}{3}$ **Review 1** $g(2) = -9$, $g(-2) = -9$,
$g(\frac{1}{2}) = 6$ **Review 2** 5, 1   **Review 3** $\frac{1}{8}$ **Review 4** –5

Page 171

Exercise 8:11

1. (a) $5x + 15$ (b) $3n - 12$ (c) $10 + 6n$ (d) $12 - 8a$ (e) $8x - 28$ (f) $15p + 5$ (g) $18 - 24n$
(h) $2 - 6n$ (i) $5n + 3n^2$ (j) $2x^2 + 3x$ (k) $3x - 2x^2$ (l) $a^2 - 5a$ (m) $6a - 2a^2$ (n) $8n^2 + 12n$
2. (a) $-3n - 6$ (b) $-6 - 8a$ (c) $-8n + 4$ (d) $-15 + 20x$ (e) $-18x - 30$ (f) $-20 + 25x$
(g) $-2p^2 - 4p$ (h) $-6a^2 - 15a$ (i) $-12x + 3x^2$ (j) $-6n - 2n^2$ (k) $-6q^2 + 15q$ 3. (a) $4x + 4b$
(b) $3x - 3a$ (c) $nx - 2ax$ (d) $4an + n^2$ (e) $12a - 15ax$ (f) $6n - 8an$ (g) $15an - 10n^2$ (h) $-6ax - 2x^2$
(i) $-4x^2 + 4ax$ (j) $-6an + 8ax$ (k) $p^2 q + pq^2$ (l) $\pi r^2 + 2\pi rh$ (m) $abh - a^2 b$ (n) $rs^2 - r^2 s$
4. (a) $13 + 6n$ (b) $1 - 3n$ (c) $5n^2 + 3n$ (d) $11n - 2n^2$ (e) $2x^2 + 4x$ (f) $14a - 2a^2 + 5$ (g) $5n + 9$
(h) $7x + 18$ (i) $16a - 8$ (j) $n^2 - 8n$ (k) $6x^2 - x$ (l) $4x + x^2 - 4$ (m) $10 + n + 2n^2$
(n) $4x^2 - 3x - 12$ **Review 1** (a) $2l + 2w$ (b) $-3 + 6a$ (c) $x^2 + 4x$ (d) $2an - 10n^2$ (e) $-12n - 9n^2$
(f) $ab^2 - a^2 b$ **Review 2** (a) $-5 + 6n$ (b) $2 - 5a - 3a^2$ (c) $10n^2 - 3n$ (d) $16 - 9x$

Exercise 8:13

1. **(a)** $3x + 6 = 3(x + 2)$ **(b)** $5a - 10 = 5(a - 2)$ **(c)** $14x + 4 = 2(7x + 2)$ **(d)** $16n - 12 = 4(4n - 3)$
(e) $4x + 4 = 4(x + 1)$ **(f)** $12n - 4 = 4(3n - 1)$ **(g)** $15d - 25 = 5(3d - 5)$ **(h)** $18 + 3n = 3(6 + n)$
(i) $6 - 3a = 3(2 - a)$ **(j)** $6 + 9x = 3(2 + 3x)$ **(k)** $15x - 10 = 5(3x - 2)$ 2. **(a)** $2(n + 1)$ **(b)** $3(1 - a)$
(c) $4(x + 3)$ **(d)** $6(1 + 2a)$ **(e)** $7(2y - 1)$ **(f)** $3(3x + 1)$ **(g)** $4(2 - 3y)$ **(h)** $5(2x + 5)$ **(i)** $4(2n + 1)$
(j) $11(1 - 2n)$ **(k)** $5(2 + 3n)$ **(l)** $3(3 - 7x)$ **(m)** $4(3n + 2)$ **(n)** $5(8 - 3n)$ **(o)** $2(x - 10)$
(p) $4(5n + 4)$ **(q)** $6(3 - a)$ **(r)** $4(3 + 4n)$ **(s)** $2(3x - 10)$ **(t)** $3(7 - 2n)$ **(u)** $8(4x - 3)$ **(v)** $6(3n + 4)$
(w) $8(2y - 3)$ **(x)** $12(2 - 3n)$ **(y)** $8(5 + 3a)$ **(z)** $9(2a - 5)$ 3. **(a)** $2n^2 + n = n(2n + 1)$
(b) $ax - a = a(x - 1)$ **(c)** $4x + 3x^2 = x(4 + 3x)$ **(d)** $6x - x^2 = x(6 - x)$ **(e)** $10n^2 + 4 = 2(5n^2 + 2)$
(f) $30n + 12n^2 = 6n(5 + 2n)$ **(g)** $6p^2q + 3p = 3p(2pq + 1)$ **(h)** $\pi r - \pi h = \pi(r - h)$
4. **(a)** $x(x + 5)$ **(b)** $a(a + 9)$ **(c)** $p(p - 3)$ **(d)** $y(5 - y)$ **(e)** $x(1 + x)$ **(f)** $y(2y - 5)$ **(g)** $a(1 + 2a)$
(h) $n(4n - 1)$ **(i)** $p(2 - 5p)$ **(j)** $a(5 + 6a)$ **(k)** $a(2 + a)$ **(l)** $a(5 - a)$ **(m)** $x(5x + 2)$ **(n)** $n(9n + 4)$
(o) $2(a^2 + 1)$ **(p)** $5(1 + n^2)$ **(q)** $4(2x^2 + 1)$ **(r)** $3(4 - y^2)$ 5. **(a)** $2x(2x + 1)$ **(b)** $3a(3a - 1)$
(c) $3b(2 + b)$ **(d)** $4n(3 - n)$ **(e)** $8a(2 - a)$ **(f)** $8n(3n + 4)$ **(g)** $6x(5 - 2x)$ **(h)** $4a(2a - n^2)$
(i) $pq(p + q)$ **(j)** $ab(b - a)$ **(k)** $6q(p^2 + 2q)$ **(l)** $4pq(2p - q)$ **(m)** $3ab(a - 2b)$ **(n)** $n^2(n + 1)$
(o) $2a^2(3 - 4a)$ **Review (a)** $5(a - 3)$ **(b)** $4(3n - 8)$ **(c)** $a(3a + 5)$ **(d)** $5n(3 - 4n)$ **(e)** $\pi r(r + h)$
(f) $4ab(3b - 2a)$

Exercise 8:15

1. **(a)** $6n^2 + 13n + 6$ **(b)** $6x^2 + 13x + 5$ **(c)** $12a^2 + 13a + 3$ **(d)** $12n^2 - 11n - 5$
(e) $2a^2 + 11a - 21$ **(f)** $2x^2 - 5x - 12$ **(g)** $10x^2 - 17x + 3$ **(h)** $n^2 - 3n - 28$ **(i)** $2x^2 + x - 15$
(j) $5n^2 - 21n + 4$ **(k)** $3x^2 + 14x - 5$ **(l)** $9a^2 + 3a - 2$ **(m)** $6x^2 - 5x - 6$ **(n)** $2n^2 - 9n + 9$
(o) $5y^2 + 8y - 4$ **(p)** $3x^2 + 4x - 4$ **(q)** $10a^2 + 29a + 10$ **(r)** $6 - 7d - 3d^2$ **(s)** $6 - 5x - 6x^2$
(t) $3 + 5n - 2n^2$ **(u)** $9x^2 - 4$ **(v)** $4 - n^2$ **(w)** $25x^2 - 16$ 2. **(a)** $a^2 + 5an + 6n^2$ **(b)** $3x^2 + 4ax + a^2$
(c) $6a^2 + 13an + 5n^2$ **(d)** $2c^2 - 5cx - 3x^2$ **(e)** $10x^2 - 3ax - a^2$ **(f)** $6x^2 - 5xy + y^2$ **(g)** $6a^2 + 19an + 10n^2$
(h) $6x^2 - nx - 2n^2$ **(i)** $15a^2 - 14an - 8n^2$ **(j)** $10n^2 - 17ny + 3y^2$ **(k)** $15a^2 + an - 6n^2$
(l) $12n^2 - 11nx + 2x^2$ **(m)** $4x^2 - n^2$ **(n)** $9n^2 - 4a^2$ **(o)** $25x^2 - 4y^2$ **(p)** $ax^2 + dx + acx + dc$
(q) $bn^2 + cn + abn + ac$ **(r)** $abn^2 + any - bnx - xy$ **(s)** $abx^2 - adx + bcx - cd$
(t) $qs - qx + psx - px^2$ **(u)** $ap + bp + aq + bq$ **(v)** $2ps + 6pt - as - 3at$
(w) $5ax - 15bx + 2an - 6bn$ 3. **(a)** $(3x - 1)(2x + 1)$ **(b)** $6x^2 + x - 1$ **Review 1 (a)** $x^2 + 7x + 10$
(b) $6n^2 - 11n + 3$ **(c)** $5 - 13a - 6a^2$ **(d)** $6y^2 - 5y - 6$ **(e)** $25x^2 - 4$ **Review 2 (a)** $2a^2 + 7ab + 3b^2$
(b) $12x^2 + 5nx - 2n^2$ **(c)** $rtx^2 - rux + stx - su$ **(d)** $3np - 6nq + ap - 2aq$

Exercise 8:17

1. **(a)** $1, 7$ **(b)** $5, -1$ **(c)** $-5, -3$ **(d)** $5, -7$ **(e)** $5, 9$ **(f)** $-6, -2$ **(g)** $6, -4$ **(h)** $-20, -10$
2. **(a)** $x^2 + 5x + 4 = (x + 4)(x + 1)$ **(b)** $p^2 + 8p + 12 = (p + 6)(p + 2)$
(c) $a^2 - 8a + 15 = (a - 5)(a - 3)$ **(d)** $x^2 - x - 20 = (x + 4)(x - 5)$
(e) $x^2 + 8x + 15 = (x + 3)(x + 5)$ **(f)** $y^2 - 5y + 4 = (y - 1)(y - 4)$ **(g)** $p^2 - 2p - 3 = (p + 1)(p - 3)$
(h) $x^2 - 7x + 12 = (x - 4)(x - 3)$ **(i)** $x^2 - 5x - 14 = (x + 2)(x - 7)$ **(j)** $p^2 + 2p - 3 = (p + 3)(p - 1)$
(k) $a^2 - 4a - 5 = (a - 5)(a + 1)$ **(l)** $a^2 + 3a - 28 = (a - 4)(a + 7)$
(m) $y^2 + 105y + 500 = (y + 100)(y + 5)$ **(n)** $x^2 + 5x - 50 = (x + 10)(x - 5)$
(o) $x^2 - 50x + 600 = (x - 20)(x - 30)$ **(p)** $a^2 - 12a - 160 = (a + 8)(a - 20)$ 3. **(a)** $(x + 2)(x + 5)$
(b) $(a + 1)(a + 7)$ **(c)** $(y + 1)(y + 5)$ **(d)** $(p + 3)(p + 1)$ **(e)** $(x - 11)(x - 1)$ **(f)** $(a - 3)(a - 1)$
(g) $(x - 5)(x - 2)$ **(h)** $(p + 7)(p - 3)$ **(i)** $(x - 5)(x + 2)$ **(j)** $(a + 5)(a - 3)$ **(k)** $(x + 4)(x + 3)$
(l) $(x - 6)(x - 2)$ **(m)** $(x - 4)(x + 3)$ **(n)** $(a + 4)(a - 3)$ **(o)** $(p + 10)(p - 1)$ **(p)** $(p - 8)(p - 2)$
(q) $(x - 6)(x + 4)$ **(r)** $(a + 8)(a + 3)$ **(s)** $(a - 24)(a - 1)$ **(t)** $(p + 8)(p - 3)$ **(u)** $(x - 10)(x - 3)$
(v) $(x + 6)(x - 5)$ **(w)** $(a - 9)(a + 4)$ **(x)** $(x - 18)(x - 2)$ **(y)** $(x - 3)(x - 3)$ 4. **(a)** $(a - 7)(a + 3)$
(b) $(x + 10)(x + 5)$ **(c)** $(p - 5)(p - 5)$ **(d)** $(x - 9)(x - 3)$ **(e)** $(a + 7)(a - 6)$ **(f)** $(x - 7)(x - 5)$
(g) $(a + 12)(a - 4)$ **(h)** $(p - 10)(p + 7)$ **(i)** $(p + 6)(p - 20)$ **(j)** $(x + 15)(x + 4)$ **(k)** $(x + 20)(x - 12)$
Review (a) $(a + 9)(a + 1)$ **(b)** $(x - 2)(x + 1)$ **(c)** $(p - 1)(p - 11)$ **(d)** $(x + 5)(x - 4)$
(e) $(a - 2)(a - 4)$ **(f)** $(y + 5)(y - 3)$ **(g)** $(p - 9)(p + 4)$ **(h)** $(x - 12)(x + 3)$ **(i)** $(a - 4)(a - 3)$
(j) $(y + 6)(y - 1)$ **(k)** $(a + 5)(a - 3)$ **(l)** $(x + 14)(x + 3)$ **(m)** $(a - 8)(a - 6)$
(n) $(x + 15)(x - 4)$ **(o)** $(p + 100)(p - 2)$ **(p)** $(n + 12)(n + 12)$ **(q)** $(x - 24)(x - 15)$

Exercise 8:19

1. (a) 2 or 7 (b) 1 or 3 (c) –3 or 2 (d) –4 or –5 (e) 2 or –1 (f) –5 or 2 (g) 3 or 8 (h) 4 or –5
(i) 6 or 7 (j) –3 or 5 (k) –5 or –9 (l) 15 or –1 (m) –17 or 7 (n) 5 or –12 (o) –24 or –30
(p) –18 or –50 (q) –20 or 100 (r) –28 or –34 (s) 78 or –78 (t) 8 2. (a) –1, –4 (b) –2, –8
(c) –3, 2 (d) 3, –2 (e) 1, 5 (f) 3, 5 (g) –2, –5 (h) –12, 1 (i) –5, 3 (j) –4, 3 (k) 6, –1 (l) 4, 3
(m) 8, –3 (n) 8, 3 (o) –8, 3 (p) –8, –3 (q) –6, 4 (r) 4, 6 (s) 12, 2 (t) 1, –24 (u) 6, –4
(v) 24, –1 3. (a) 0 or 5 (b) 0 or –3 (c) 0 or –5 (d) 0 or 6 (e) 0 or –24 4. (a) $a^2 + 4a - 12 = 0$;
2 or –6 (b) $x^2 + x - 12 = 0$; –4 or 3 (c) $n^2 - 3n - 10 = 0$; 5 or –2 (d) $x^2 - 7x - 8 = 0$; 8 or –1
(e) $n^2 - 2n - 8 = 0$; 4 or –2 (f) $n^2 + 11n + 24 = 0$; –3 or –8 (g) $a^2 + 5a - 14 = 0$; –7 or 2
(h) $a^2 - 4a - 5 = 0$; 5 or –1 (i) $y^2 - 7y + 6 = 0$; 1 or 6 (j) $x^2 - 3x + 2 = 0$; 1 or 2
Review 1 (a) –8 or 7 (b) –5 or –3 (c) 3 or –5 (d) –8 or 3 (e) 0 or –10 Review 2 (a) 1 or 3
(b) –1 or –13 (c) 8 or –5 (d) 1 or –6 (e) 1 or 9 (f) 9 or –2 (g) –5 (h) 3 or 6 (i) 0 or 9
(j) 12 or –2 (k) 0 or –12 (l) –8 or 5 Review 3 (a) 6, –1 (b) 2, 5 (c) 3, –7 (d) 1 or –6

Exercise 8:20

1. 6 seconds 2. $t^2 + 3t = 130$ or $t^2 + 3t - 130 = 0$. It took Amanda 10 seconds.
3. (a) $n^2 + n - 42 = 0$ (b) –7 or 6 4. (a) $(n + 5)(n - 3) = 48$ (c) –9 or 7 (d) length = 12cm,
width = 4cm 5. 5 hours 6. (b) 11 sides 7. 10 is the only possible answer
8. (a) $a^2 - a - 210 = 0$ (b) 15 9. (a) 2n + 2 (d) – 8 or 7 (e) 14 and 16 Review 1 6, –5
Review 2 6 seconds Review 3 (b) – 7 or 4 (c) If n = –7 the triangle would have a negative
value for the base and the height. This is not possible.

Chapter 8 Review

1. (a) x (4x + 5) (b) (x + 2)(x + 3) (c) (x – 5)(x + 4) 2. –11 or 6 3. (a) £76 (b) $d = \frac{C - 22}{3}$
4. (a) $2x^2 + 5x - 12$ 5. 3x(2x + 3) 6. (a) 6x(6 + x) (b) $x = \frac{y - 3}{5}$ 7. (a) $6x^2 + 5x - 6$
(b) 3x(x – 5) 8. (a) $\pi r(2r + h)$ (b) $h = \frac{A - 2\pi r^2}{\pi r}$ 9. (a) $2x^2 - 5x - 12$ (b) 5x(2x – 1)
10. (a) 18 – 3x (b) 3x(2x + y) 11. (a) 3pq(4p – 5q) (b) $2x^2 + 7x - 15$ (c) $n = \frac{C - 120}{40}$
12. $L = \frac{10T^2}{4\pi^2}$ or $L = \frac{5T^2}{2\pi^2}$ 13. 20, 30 14. (a) $0.7 \times 100 = 70, 70 \times 6 = 420$
(b) a(x + y) (c) $0.7(470 + 130) = 0.7 \times 600 = 420$ 15. (a) 3.325 (b) $h = \frac{40W - (r + 1)^2}{2r}$
(c) 8·6 (1d.p.) 16. (a) (i) $4x^2 + 12x$ (ii) $4x^2 + 12x + 9$ (b) 9 17. (a) 10x + 10y
(b) 100x + 10(x + y) + y = 100x + 10x + 10y + y = 110x + 11y (c) 11(10x + y) which is divisible
by 11 18. (a) $K = 8.04357 \times 10^{23}$ (b) $T = \sqrt{\frac{R^3}{K}}$ (c) 0·61 years (2 s.f.) 19. (a) (i) 1 (ii) 1·8
(iii) 1·5 (b) $y = \frac{x^2}{2} + 1$

Chapter 9 Straight-Line Graphs: y = mx + c

Exercise 9:3

1. (a) l_4, l_5, l_6, l_7, l_8, (b) l_1, l_2, l_3, l_9 (c) l_4, and l_8, ; l_3 and l_9 2. AB : 2, CD : $\frac{1}{4}$, EF : $\frac{1}{2}$, GH : 1,
IJ : $\frac{3}{4}$, KL : 3, MN : 1 3. AB : –1, CD : $-\frac{1}{5}$, EF : $-\frac{2}{3}$, GH : $-\frac{2}{5}$, IJ : –2, KL : –5, MN : – 4
4. $l_1 : -\frac{1}{2}, l_2 : -1, l_3 : \frac{1}{4}, l_4 : 1, l_5 : -3, l_6 : 2, l_7 : \frac{2}{5}$ 5. PQ : –2, QR : 1, PR : $-\frac{1}{5}$ 6. (a) $\frac{1}{5}$ (b) 20
7. AB : 20%, BC : 15%, CD : 20%, DE : 0%, EF : 35% 8. (a) $\frac{1}{12}$ (b) 4·6m Review 1 $l_1 : -\frac{1}{5}$,
$l_2 : -1, l_3 : \frac{1}{4}, l_4 : 3, l_5 : \frac{5}{2}, l_6 : -\frac{3}{2}$ Review 2 4 Review 3 $\frac{1}{5}$ and – 3

Page 200

Exercise 9:5

1. (a) 2 (b) $\frac{1}{3}$ (c) 1 (d) –3 (e) $-\frac{1}{2}$ (f) 3 (g) –1 (h) 5 (i) –5 (j) $\frac{2}{3}$ (k) $-\frac{3}{5}$ 2. (a) 5 (b) 0
(c) –2 (d) 2 (e) 6 (f) 2 (g) 4 (h) 3 (i) 3 (j) –7 (k) 0

3. 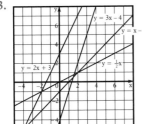   4. 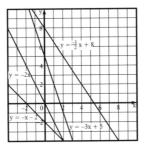   5.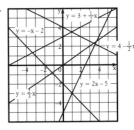

6. (a) (2, 3) (b) (3, 0) (c) (–2, 1) (d) (–1, –3) (e) (0, –2) (f) ($\frac{1}{2}$, 2) (g) (–2, $\frac{1}{2}$)
7. (3, 4), (6, 1), (1, – 4), (–2, –1)   **Review 1** (a) –2 (b) $\frac{2}{3}$ (c) 3 (d) –1   **Review 2** (a) 7 (b) 0
(c) –8 (d) 4   **Review 3** (a) (2, –2) (b) (–3, –1) (c) (2, 2)

Page 203

Exercise 9:7

1. (a) $y = -x + 3$ (b) $y = -x + 6$ (c) $y = -x - 7$ (d) $y = \frac{2}{3}x + 2$ (e) $y = \frac{1}{2}x - 2$
(f) $y = \frac{3}{2}x + 2$ (g) $y = -\frac{1}{2}x + 1$ (h) $y = -\frac{1}{3}x - 1$ (i) $y = -x + \frac{1}{2}$ (j) $y = -\frac{3}{2}x - 2$
(k) $y = -\frac{1}{2}x + \frac{1}{2}$ (l) $y = -2x - 1$ 2. (a) $y = x - 4$ (b) $y = x + 1$ (c) $y = 3x - 6$
(d) $y = 2x + 2$ (e) $y = \frac{2}{3}x - 4$ (f) $y = \frac{3}{2}x + 3$ (g) $y = \frac{1}{4}x - 1$ (h) $y = \frac{2}{5}x - 2$ (i) $y = x - 6$
(j) $y = 2x + \frac{1}{2}$ (k) $y = \frac{3}{4}x - 3$

3. 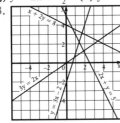   4. 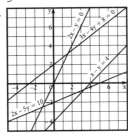   Review 2 (a)

5. (a) (–3, 2) (b) (3, –2) (c) (1, 1) (d) (3, –5) (e) (–2, 1)
6. (–1, 3), (6, – 4), (–3, –1)   **Review 1** (a) $y = -x - 2$ (b) $y = \frac{1}{3}x - 2$ (c) $y = -\frac{1}{2}x + 4$
(d) $y = -2x + \frac{2}{3}$ (e) $y = x - 7$ (f) $y = \frac{2}{3}x + 6$ (g) $y = -x + 4$ **Review 2** (b) (–2, – 4)

Page 207

Exercise 9:10

1. (a) $x + y = 0$ (b) $x + 2y = 3$ (c) $3x + y = 1$ (d) $y + 4 = 0$ (e) $x + 3 = 0$
(f) $x + 2y + 3 = 0$ (g) $2x + y + 3 = 0$ (h) $2y = x + 2$ (i) $2x + 3y = 12$ (j) $5y = 2x$
(k) $2y = 6x - 1$ (l) $5x + 5y = 2$ (m) $x + 2y = 6$ or $2y = 6 - x$ 2. (a) $l_1 : y + 6 = 0$,
$l_2 : 2y = x - 4$, $l_3 : 3y = x + 6$, $l_4 : 2x + 3y = 12$, $l_5 : 3x + 4y = 24$ (b) $l_1 : 2y = 3x + 10$,
$l_2 : x + 2y + 6 = 0$, $l_3 : x + 4y = 12$, $l_4 : 4x + 3y = 0$, $l_5 : x + 2 = 0$ 3. AB : $x + 2y = 8$,
BC : $2y = x$, CA : $x + 4y = 18$ 4. (a) C (b) $y = 5x + 10$ 5. $5y = x + 30$
Review 1 (a) $2x + 3y = 0$ (b) $4y = 3x - 8$ (c) $x + 2y + 1 = 0$ (d) $x + 4 = 0$
Review 2 $l_1 : x + 5 = 0$, $l_2 : y = 2x + 5$, $l_3 : x = 13$, $l_4 : 3y = 2x - 6$, $l_5 : 5y = 2x$, $l_6 : y = 7$,
$l_7 : x + 3y = 6$, $l_8 : x + 2y = 6$.

Page 209

Chapter 9   Review

1. (a) B (b) D (c) C (d) A   2. (b) (i) –2   (ii)
3. (a) see graph at top of next page
(b) $l = w + 5$ 4. (a) $y = 3x + 2$, $y = 5x + 2$
(b) $y = 3x + 2$, $y = 3x - 3$ 5. (a) (i) $\frac{1}{2}$
(ii) charge in £ per minute   (b) $C = \frac{1}{2}t + 10$
(c) 148 minutes

501

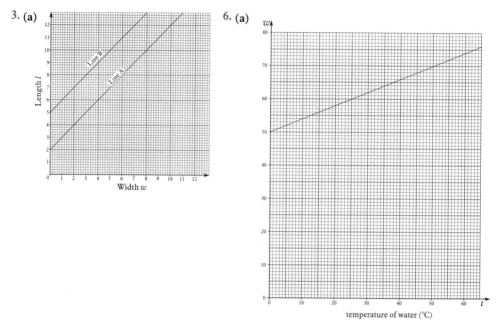

3. (a)

6. (a)

temperature of water (°C)

6. **(b) (i)** 32·5°C   **(ii)** about 67·5 grams   **(c) (i)** $a = \frac{2}{5}$, $b = 50$ **(ii)** 88 grams

Chapter 10   Inequalities

Exercise 10:2

1. (a)   (b)   (c)   (d)   (e)

(f)   (g)   (h)   (i)   (j)

(k)   Review (a)   (b)   (c)   (d)

2. (a) A
   (b) C
   (c) B

Page 219   **Exercise 10:4**

In these answers, just the required region is shown shaded.

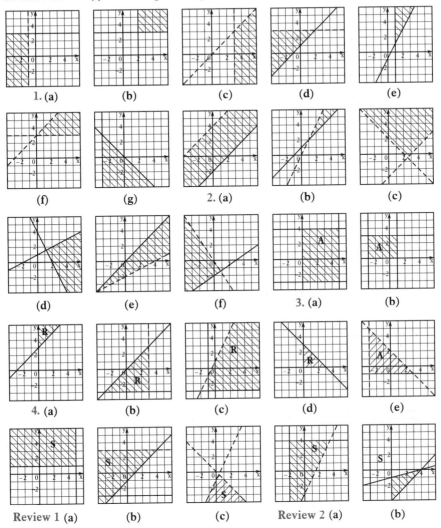

1. (a)   (b)   (c)   (d)   (e)

(f)   (g)   2. (a)   (b)   (c)

(d)   (e)   (f)   3. (a)   (b)

4. (a)   (b)   (c)   (d)   (e)

Review 1 (a)   (b)   (c)   Review 2 (a)   (b)

Page 220   **Exercise 10:5**

1. (a) x is the number of £5 cards;   2. (a) x is the number of   3. (a) **No**
                                              £2 books;

   y is the number of £10 cards.   y is the number of   (b)
                                              £1 books.

   (b) No   (b) No
   (c)   (c)
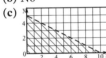

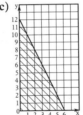
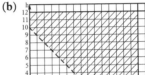

503

4. (a) No. $h \geq 0$, $s \geq 0$
   (b) $h \leq 3$, $s \leq 3$
   (c)

Review (a) No
   (b) $w \geq 0$, $m \geq 3$, $w \leq 6$
   (c)

Page 222

Exercise 10:6

1. (a) $y \leq 3$, $y \geq x - 2$, $x + y \geq -2$, $y \leq x$ (b) $y \leq 3$, $y \geq 2x - 2$, $x \geq 0$, $y + 3x \geq 0$
2. $y \leq 2$, $2y \geq x$, $x + 3y \geq 3$ 3. $y \geq 0$, $x \geq 0$, $y \leq 2x + 1$, $y \leq 3$, $x + 3y \leq 12$, $x \leq 6$
4. $x + y \geq 2$, $y \geq 1$, $2y \leq x + 4$ 5. $x \geq 2$, $y \leq 6$, $x + 2y \geq 6$
Review $y \geq 0$, $x + y \geq 0$, $3y \leq x + 12$, $x \leq 3$

Page 226

Exercise 10:7

1. (a) $x \geq 3$ or $x \leq -3$ (b) $x > 2$ or $x < -2$ (c) $n > 6$ or $n < -6$ (d) $n \geq 10$ or $n \leq -10$
   (e) $-5 < a < 5$ (f) $-10 < a < 10$ (g) $-7 \leq x \leq 7$ (h) $x > 8$ or $x < -8$ (i) $x > 9$ or $x < -9$
   (j) $-2 \leq n \leq 2$ 2. (a) $x \geq 2$ or $x \leq -2$ (b) $x \geq 4$ or $x \leq -4$ (c) $-2 < x < 2$ (d) $-7 < x < 7$
   (e) $x > 5$ or $x < -5$ (f) $-8 \leq x \leq 8$ (g) $-3 < x < 3$ (h) $-6 \leq x \leq 6$ (i) $-5 < x < 5$
   (j) $x > 1$ or $x < -1$ 3. (a) $-5, -4, -3, -2, -1, 0, 1, 2, 3, 4, 5$ (b) $-2, -1, 0, 1, 2$
   (c) $-3, -2, -1, 0, 1, 2, 3$ (d) $-1, 0, 1$ (e) $\ldots, -4, -3, -2, 2, 3, 4, \ldots$ (f) $\ldots, -4, -3, -2, 2, 3, 4, \ldots$
   4. (a) p is greater than 4 or less than -4.   (b) p is between -7 and 7.   Review (a) $n > 5$ or $n < -5$
   (b) $a \geq 8$ or $a \leq -8$ (b) $-2 \leq x \leq 2$

Page 227

Chapter 10   Review

1.

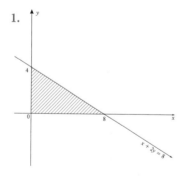

2. (a)

x	-2	-1	0	1	2	3
y	-5	-3	-1	1	3	5

(b) and (d)

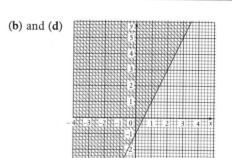

(c) $0{\cdot}75$

3.

4.

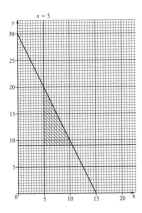

7. **(a) (i)** $x < 4 \cdot 5$ **(ii)** to 2 d.p. $x \le -4 \cdot 36$ or $x \ge 4 \cdot 36$

   (b)

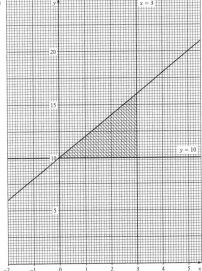

5. **(a)** $x < 2$ **(b)** $-1 < x < 1$

6. **(a) (i)** -5 **(ii)** 1 **(b) (i)** $x \ge 2$
   (ii) $x > 3$ **(iii)** $-5 < x < 5$

8. **(b)**

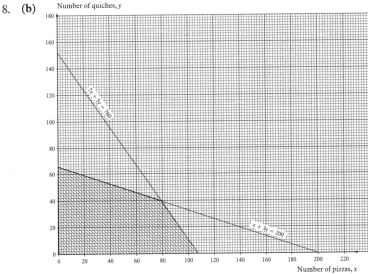

9. **(a)** $x < 6$ **(b)** $x \le -4$ or $x \ge 4$ 10. **(b)** $x \le 20,\ 25x + 40y \le 750$ or $5x + 8y \le 150$

   (c)

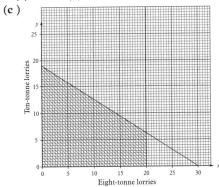

11. (a) (i) x ≥ 6
(b)

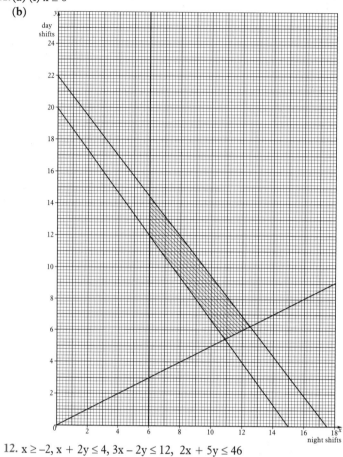

12. x ≥ −2, x + 2y ≤ 4, 3x − 2y ≤ 12, 2x + 5y ≤ 46

Chapter 11   Graphs of some Special Functions and Real-Life Situations

Page 241   **Exercise 11:4**

1. (a) D   (b) B   (c) D   (d) A   (e) A

2. (a)

x	−3	−2	−1	0	1	2	3
y	−13·5	−4	−0·5	0	0·5	4	13·5

(b)

x	−4	−3	−2	−1	0	1	2	3	4
y	11	4	−1	−4	−5	−4	−1	4	11

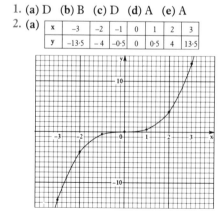

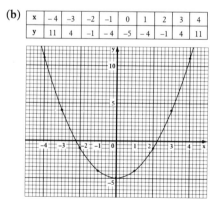

(c)

x	−3	−2	−1	0	1	2	3
y	−9	4	5	0	−5	−4	9

(d)

x	−5	−4	−3	−2	−1	−½	0	½	1	2	3	4	5
y	2	2½	3⅓	5	10	20	no value	−20	−10	−5	−3⅓	−2½	−2

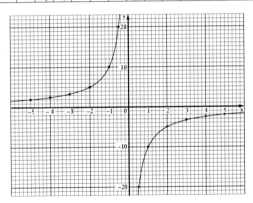

3. (a) A-2, B-1, C-4, D-3 **(b)** A-4, B-2, C-3, D-1 **(c)** A-3, B-4, C-1, D-2

4. (b)

x	5	10	15	20	25	30
y	12	6	4	3	2·4	2

(c)

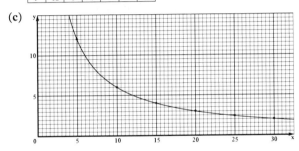

(d) 8cm

5. (i) (b)

x	5	10	15	20	25
V	250	2000	6750	16000	31250

(c)

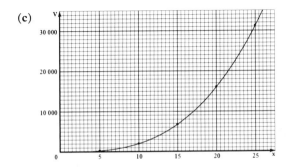

(d) about 21·5cm

507

5. (ii) (b)

x	5	10	15	20	25
A	200	800	1800	3200	5000

Review 1 D   Review 2 (a) B (b) C (d) A

Review 3 (b)

x	4	8	12	16	20
A	144	576	1296	2304	3600

(c)

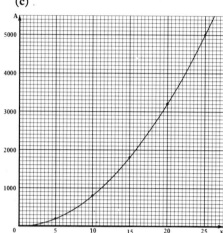

(c)

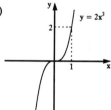

(d) about 2000cm²

(e) about 18cm

(d) about 17·7cm

Page 250   **Exercise 11:7**

1. (a)

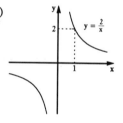

(b)

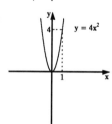

(c)

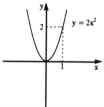

(d)

(e)

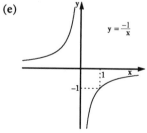

(f)

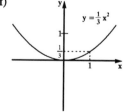

508

(g)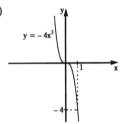

(h)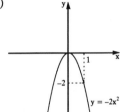

(i)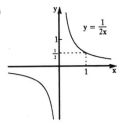

(j)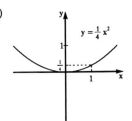

(k)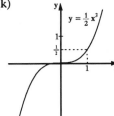

(l)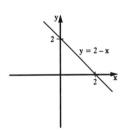

2. **(a)**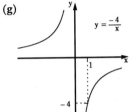

(b)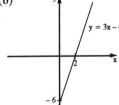

(c)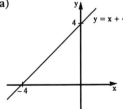

(d)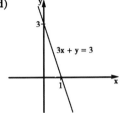

(e)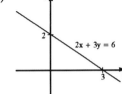

(f)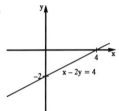

(g)

2x − 5y = 10

(h)

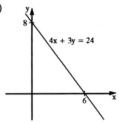

4x + 3y = 24

(i)

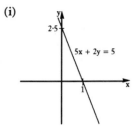

5x + 2y = 5

(j)

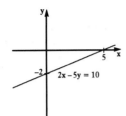

4x − 2y = 6

(k)

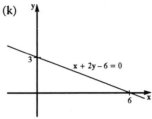

x + 2y − 6 = 0

(l)

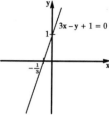

3x − y + 1 = 0

(m)

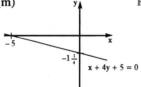

x + 4y + 5 = 0

Review 1 **(a)**

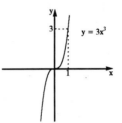

$y = 3x^3$

(b)

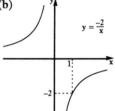

$y = \dfrac{-2}{x}$

(c)

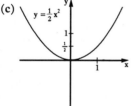

$y = \dfrac{1}{2}x^2$

Review 2 **(a)**

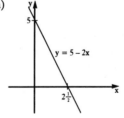

y = 5 − 2x

(b)

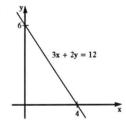

3x + 2y = 12

(c)

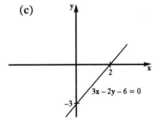

3x − 2y − 6 = 0

(d)

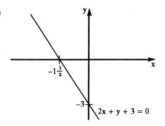

2x + y + 3 = 0

Exercise 11:10

1. **(a)** £10   **(b)** the second cheapest   **(c)** Ann bought the second cheapest, Aaron bought the cheapest.   **2. (a)** March 7th   **(b)** 9 times   **(c)** Yes   **3. (a)** June   **(b)** July and August
(c) £3000   **(d)** £51,000   **(f)** £4000   **4. (a)** No   **(b)** Jess   **(c)** Jasper   **(d)** 1 minute   **(e)** hot
(f) cold   **Review (a)** 30l **(b)** 1200km   **(c)** twice   **(d)** 60l **(e)** $\frac{1}{2}$ **(f)** 80l **(g)** yes   **(h)** 15km/l
(i) 6·7 litres per 100km

Exercise 11:14

2. **(a)** At about 26 seconds and 53 seconds.   **(b)** Karen finished before Susan.   **(c)** Karen
(d) Susan was about 15m ahead.   **3. (a)** The bookshop sold out of these books. **(b)** The bookshop got in a new supply of these books.   **(c)** They sold more in this week than any other week. There may have been an advertising programme since sales increased rapidly.   **5.** C or D
6. **(a)** 30mm   **(b)** none   **7.** A and 2, B and 3, C and 1, D and 4   **8.** A and 4, B and 3,
C and 2, D and 1   **Review 1** A and 3, B and 4, C and 2, D and 1

Chapter 11 Review

1. **(a)** £320   **(b)**

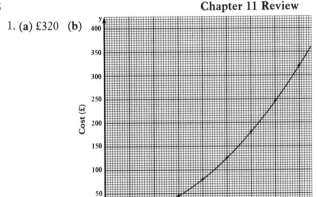

(c) about 5·5m   **2. (a)** Jane is jumping in the air off the platform. At B, she is at the greatest height and begins to dive down.   **(b)** Between B and C Jane goes from the greatest height in the air (at B) to the surface of the water (at C). Her speed increases as she goes from B to C.   **(c)** At C Jane hits the water. Her speed decreases while she is diving into the water and coming back to the surface again (at D).   **(d)** Jane's speed increases as she begins to swim.   **(e)** Jane is swimming at a steady rate to the edge of the pool (at F)   **(f)** Jane's speed decreases as she stops at the edge of the pool.

3. **(i)** (−0·5, 0)   **(ii)**

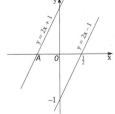

(iii) The graphs $y = 2x + 1$ and $y = 2x − 1$ are parallel. They do not meet.

4. (a) $3 \to 9$, $2 \to 4$, $-2 \to 4$, $-3 \to 9$

5. A

6. (a)

x	-3	-2	-1	0	1	2	3
$y = x^2 - 3$	6	1	-2	-3	-2	1	6

(b)

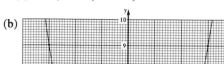

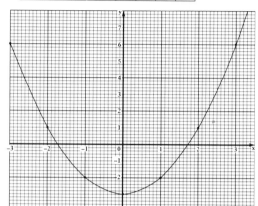

(b) about $-2\cdot45$ and $2\cdot45$ **7. (i)** c   **(ii)** d

8. (a) B   **(b)** D

(c) about $2\cdot55$ **(d)** about $2\cdot25$

9. (b) (i)

x	1	2	3	4	5	6	7	8
A	54	116	186	264	350	444	546	656

10.

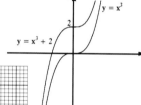

(ii)

(c) about $4\cdot4$cm

Chapter 12   Algebra Review

1. (a) $\frac{3}{20}$ (b) 30 metres   2. (a) $3a - 3b$ (b) $2a^2 - 5a$ (c) $m^2n - mn^2$ 4. (a) $P = \frac{K}{VT}$

(b) $h = \frac{A - \pi r^2}{2\pi r}$ (c) $b = 2S - a - c$

5. (b)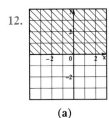

(c) about 9·3cm   6. (i) (a) $y = -5x + 7$ (b) $y = -\frac{1}{2}x + 3$
(c) $y = 3x - 1$ (ii) (a) -5 (b) $-\frac{1}{2}$ (c) 3 (iii) (a) 7 (b) 3
(c) -1 7. (a) 420mm^2 (2 s.f.) (b) 2·7cm (2 s.f.)   8. B since
this is the only parabola.   9. (a) $6 + x$ (b) $2a^2 - 2a - 2$
(c) $n + 2$ (d) $4n - 15$ 10. (a) l_1 has gradient -1, l_2 has
gradient -3, l_3 has gradient $\frac{3}{2}$, l_4 has gradient $\frac{1}{3}$ (b) l_1 is
$x + y = 1$, l_2 is $3x + y + 6 = 0$, l_3 is $2y = 3x - 6$ or
$3x - 2y = 6$, l_4 is $3y = x + 6$ or $x - 3y + 6 = 0$
11. $f = 2g - m + 0·13$

12.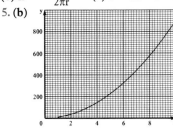

    (a)   (b)   (c)   (d)

13. (a) $2(3 - 4n)$ (b) $a(2 + 3a)$ (c) $2x(8 - 5x)$ (d) $\pi r(rh + 2)$ (e) $xy(x - y)$
14. 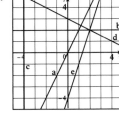   15. A-2, B-3, C-4, D-1   16. (a) $F = \frac{9}{5}C + 32$ (b) $r = \sqrt{\frac{V}{\pi h}}$

(c) $l = \frac{gT^2}{4\pi^2}$ 17.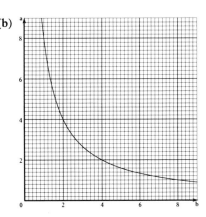

18. (a)

b	1	2	3	4	5	6	7	8
a	8	4	2·7	2	1·6	1·3	1·1	1

(b)

(c) 1·8

19. (i) 2 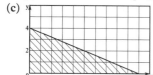   **(ii) (a)** $3n^2 + 17n + 10$ **(b)** $6n^2 - 19n + 10$ **(c)** $4x^2 - 7xy - 2y^2$
(d) $ac + bcx + adx + bdx^2$

20. (a)
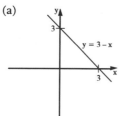

(b)
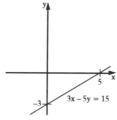

(c)
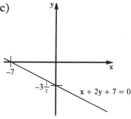

21. (a) x is the number of tapes, y is the number of CDs. **(b)** Neither x nor y can have a negative value.
(c)

22. (i) (a) 5 **(b)** 21 **(c)** 21 **(d)** $3\frac{1}{2}$ **(ii) (a)** –1·2 **(b)** –1
23. (i) (a) $(x + 3)(x + 1)$ **(b)** $(x - 7)(x - 1)$ **(c)** $(x - 15)(x + 2)$
(ii) –8 or 3   **24.** $y = 7x + 4$
25. (a)
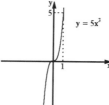

(b)
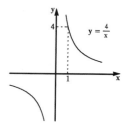

(c)
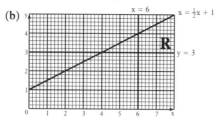

26. (a) $-5 \le p \le 5$ **(b)** $p < -2$ or $p > 2$ **27.** AB   **28. (a)** A-3,
B-4, C-1, D-2 **(b)** A-4, B-3, C-2, D-1   **29. (a)** 3·8 (2 s.f.)
(b) 10·5 (3 s.f.)   **30.** $A = \frac{\pi d^2}{4}$ **31. (a)** n stands for one of the
integers, n + 1 stands for the other. **(c)** –14 and –13 or 13 and 14.
32. $x \ge 0, y \le x + 1, y \le 3, x + 3y \le 12$ **33. (a)** The sound level
increased very quickly, then quite slowly, then it stayed at the
same level. **(b)** A possible reason is that the record finished.
34. (a) $r = \sqrt[3]{\frac{3V}{4\pi}}$ **(b)** 2·6 (2 s.f.)

35. (a)

x	-2	-1·5	-1	-0·5	0	0·5	1	1·5	2
y	6	4·25	3	2·25	0	2·25	3	4·25	6

(b)
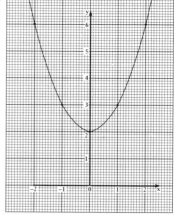

(c) about –1·7 and 1·7   **36. (a)** 3 (d + 2e)
(b) 4x (x + 2y)   **37. (a) (i)** $x \le 2$
(ii) $x < -5$ or $x > 5$ **(iii)** $x < -2$
(b)
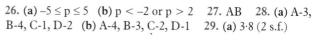

38. a could have equation vi, b could have equation i, c could have equation iv
39. (a) $2x^2 + 9x + 4$ **(b)** $2x (2x - 3)$
40. (a)

v	10	12	14	16	18	20
h	500	720	980	1280	1620	2000

(b)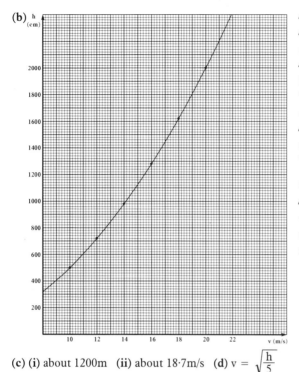

(c) (i) about 1200m **(ii)** about 18·7m/s **(d)** $v = \sqrt{\dfrac{h}{5}}$

41. **(a)** D **(b)** a cylinder
42. **(b)** $x + y \geq 60$ **(d)** $x \geq 10$
(e) see graph at bottom of page
43. **(a)** $6x^2 + 7x - 3$ **(b)** If x is replaced
by 10 then $(3x - 1)(2x + 3) = 29 \times 23$.
The answer to 29×23 is then
$6 \times 10^2 + 7 \times 10 - 3 = 667$
44. **(a)** 9·3 (2 s.f.) **(b)** A possible
estimation is
$V = 10(1 - \frac{5}{20}) = 10 \times \frac{3}{4} = 7.5$
(c) $x = 21 - \frac{21V}{k}$ or $x = 21(1 - \frac{V}{k})$
45. **(a)** 5 does not divide into 36
without a remainder. **(b) (i)** (2, 18),
(3, 12), (12, 3)
(ii) and (iii)

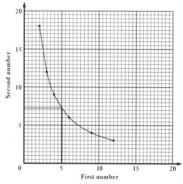

46. **(b)** 5 or 13 **(c)** 13 units. 5 is not acceptable since this would give –3 for BD which is
impossible. 47. **(a)** n^2 **(c)** 441 is a square number **(d)** 1007 is not a square number **(e)** $(n + 1)^2$
(f) $(n + 1)^2 - n^2$ **(g)** $2n + 1$ **(h)** difference is $(n + 2)^2 - n^2$ which simplifies to $4(n + 1)$
(i) difference is $(n + p)^2 - n^2$ which simplifes to $p(2n + 1)$

42. **(e)**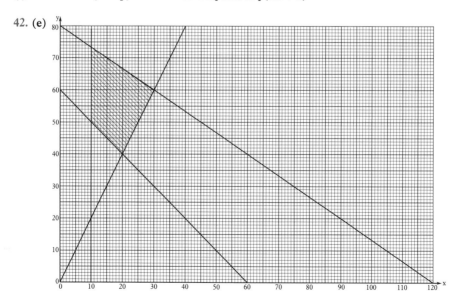

SHAPE, SPACE and MEASURES ANSWERS

Shape, Space and Measures Revision

Page 299   **Revision Exercise**

1. (a) 38·4 (b) 2400 (c) 1740 (d) 0·194 (e) 700 (f) 2·825   3. (a) 66·25cm (b) 66·15cm
4. (a) (–1, 0), (–4, –1), (–5, –1), (–4, –2), (–2, –3), (–1, –3) (b) (–1, 0), (2, 0), (2, 1), (1, 3), (0, 4), (0, 3)
(c) (–1, 0), (–1, –3), (0, –3), (2, –2), (3, –1), (2, –1) (d) Rotation about (–1, 0) through 180°
5. (a) 30·5 (b) 10   6. (a) 3·6km (2 s.f.) (b) 56° (c) 326°   7. (i) (a) octagon (b) 135°
(c) All the interior angles of this octagon. (d) No. The sides are not equal. (e) 2
(ii) (a) 12cm and 8cm (b) 48cm² (c) 32cm² (iii) Yes. One possible explanation is:
corresponding sides are equal.   8. a = 98°, b = 44°, c = 38°, d = 82°, e = 16°, f = 60°
9. (b) 5·4m (d) 4·3m   10. (a) 153·6km (b) 75mph (c) £8·16   11. (a) 120cm² (b) 52cm
12. (a) 0810 (b) 100km (c) 0835 (d) 50km (e) once (f) 120km/h (g) 100km/h
13. (a) 45·4cm² (3 s.f.) (b) 500m*l* (d) 6·2cm   14. Peter 15. (i) (a) $\binom{-2}{3}$ (b) $\binom{-5}{6}$ (c) $\binom{2}{3}$
(d) $\binom{6}{3}$ (ii) A   16. (a) scale factor = 2, centre of enlargement is (7, 7) (b) (–1, 1), (–1, 4), (0, 4),
(1, 3), (0, 3), (0, 1) (c) C   17. (b) 65590m² (c) 6·56ha (d) 16 acres (e) about 2km
18. Shirdia could use C = 2πr to find the radius, then A = πr² to find the surface area
19. (a) 50m*l* (b) about 1¾ pints (c) about 1000 (d) about 9 pints (e) 1800 grams
20. (a) 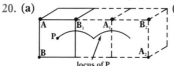 (b) 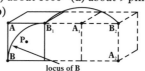   21. (a)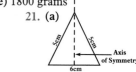

locus of P   locus of B

(b) 12cm² (c) 10cm   22.

23. (a) Yes (b) Yes (c) No (d) A square cannot be used. An equilateral triangle could be.
24. 48km 25. (a) £21·76 (b) 3·17m (c) 0·43m   26. (a) 28·26m² (2 d.p.) using π = 3·14 or
28·27m² using the π button on your calculator. (b) 18·85m (2 d.p.)
27. 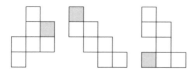   28.

Name of quadrilateral	Diagonals always cut at right angles	Number of axes of symmetry	Order of rotational symmetry
RECTANGLE	NO	2	2
RHOMBUS	YES	2	2
PARALLELOGRAM	NO	0	2
KITE	YES	1	1
SQUARE	YES	4	4

29. 20° (∠s in isosceles and equilateral ∆s)
30. (a) 189m² (b) 2·95m (3 s.f.) (c) X
31. (a) 10·30 am (b) 60 miles (c) 8 mph (d) 4·30pm
32. Possible answers are:

34.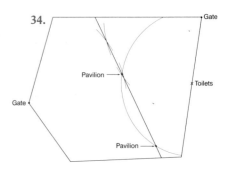

33. Translation. The vector of this translation is $\binom{3}{-2}$

35. (a) √ **(b)** √ **(c)** × **(d)** × **36. (a)** 5, 10, 50
(b) Possible answers are: 3rd row 4·5, 9, 40·5;
4th row 4·48, 8·96, 40·1408 **37. (a)** 313·5
hours **(b)** 765 litres **(c) (i)** £147
(ii) £2·41 **38. (a)** 7680cm³
(b) (i) 50·3cm (3 s.f.) **(ii)** 2011cm³ (4 s.f.)
40. b = 100° (adjacent angles on line add to
180°), c = 55° (angles of △ add to 180° *or*
exterior angle of △ *or* alt ∠s // lines are equal),
d = 135° (interior angles // lines add to 180°),
e = 80° (vertically opposite angles equal *or*
adjacent angles on line add to 180° *or* exterior
∠ of △) **41. (a)** D **(b)** E
42. 7·6cm (2 s.f.) **43. (a) (i)** 12500cm
(ii) 125m **(b) (i)** 6·3cm **(ii)** 157·5m
(iii) 19687·5m²

39. (a)

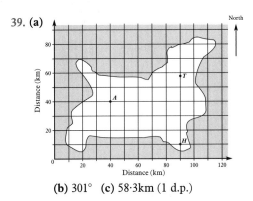

(b) 301° **(c)** 58·3km (1 d.p.)

44. (a)
(i)

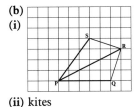

(ii) parallelograms

(b)
(i)

(ii) kites

45.

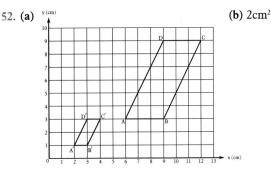

46. (a) (i) 9cm² **(ii)** 6cm² **(iii)** 33cm² **(b)** A = 88n **47. (a) (i)** 0·2kg **(ii)** kg per cm³
(b) 2·29kg (3 s.f.) **48. (a)** 5m **(b)** kite **(c)** 28° **49.** The account could be as follows. In the
first 15 minutes, Kate cycled steadily at 16mph. She covered 4 miles in this time. She then
rested for 5 minutes. She then cycled 2 miles back along the lane until she met Jenny. She was
cycling steadily at 24mph for 5 minutes. Kate stopped and talked with Jenny for 5 minutes.
50. 29 feet 2½ inches.

51.

52. (a)

(b) 2cm²

53. (a) 104m **(b) (i)** 5th **(ii)** C **(c)** 21m
54. (a) (i) 20° **(ii)** alt. ∠s // lines are equal
(iii) 48° **(b) (i)** 052° **(ii)** 212° **(iii)** 312°
55. (a) 36·9m² **(b)** 295·2m³ **(c)** 0·32m
56. (a) 328,000 tonnes **(b)** 1 week **58. (i)** square
(ii) hexagon **(iii)** 12 **59. (a)** 2640cm³
(b) 5·9cm (2 s.f.) **60.** 13x²

57.

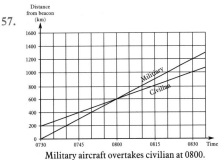

Military aircraft overtakes civilian at 0800.

Chapter 13   Dimensions

Exercise 13:2

1. Dimension for volume must be L³. Dimension for $\frac{7}{3}\pi r^2 l^2$ is L⁴.   **2.** Dimension for area must be L². Dimension for $\frac{4}{3}\pi r^3$ is L³.   **3. (a)** $2l + \pi d$ **(b)** $dl + \frac{1}{4}\pi d^2$ **4.** $V = \frac{26}{27}\pi r^2 h$
5. $V = \frac{1}{4}\pi d^2 l + \frac{1}{12}\pi d^2 h$ **6. (a)** $\frac{1}{4}\pi d\,(8d + 5h)$ **(b)** $\frac{7}{16}\pi d^2 h$ **7.** $V = \frac{1}{2}dl\,(2h - d) + \frac{1}{8}\pi d^2 l$;
No   **8. (a)** $6ah + \frac{3}{2}\sqrt{3}a^2$ **(b)** $\frac{3}{2}\sqrt{3}a^2 h$ **9. (a)** $\pi r + \frac{1}{2}r$, $r(\pi + 3)$, $\frac{1}{3}\pi r$, $\pi r + 4l$
(b) $\pi r l$, $\frac{1}{4}\pi d^2$, $\pi r\,(r + l)$, $\frac{4}{3}\pi r^2$, $4\pi r l$, $\frac{1}{3}\pi r h$ **(c)** $4\pi r^2 h$, $\frac{1}{3}\pi r^2 h$, $\frac{4}{3}\pi r^3$, $4l^2 h$, $3lh^2$
Review 1 Dimension for volume must be L³. Dimension of $\frac{2}{3}\pi r^2$ is L².
Review 2 (a) $\frac{2}{3}\pi r^3 + \pi r^2 h$ **(b)** $2\pi r\,(h + r)$

Chapter 13 Review

1. √ underneath $\pi r^2 h$ and lbh **2.** volume   **3. (a)** area   **(b)** none   **(c)** length   **(d)** area   **(e)** volume
4. (a) abh, a²b   **(b)** 2 and π have no dimension, R and r have dimension length. Hence
$2\pi\,(R - r)$ has dimension length not (length)² which is the dimension for area.
5. (iii) since dimension is (length)²   **6.** $A = \pi h\,(D + d)$ since this is the only formula which has dimension (length)².   **7.** This formula has dimension (length)² not (length)³ which is the dimension for volume.   **8.** $2\pi rt$ The other two formulae do not have dimension (length)².
9. (a) area   **(b)** area   **(c)** none   **(d)** length   **(e)** volume   **10. (a)** Formula B since it has dimension (length)³ which is the dimension for volume   **(b)** Formula E. The dimension of $\sqrt{d^2 + D^2}$ is $\sqrt{(length)^2}$ = length. Hence the dimension of $\frac{\pi}{\sqrt{2}}d\sqrt{d^2 + D^2}$ is length × length which is the dimension for area.

Chapter 14   Similar Shapes

Exercise 14:2

1. A and H, B and L, C and M, D and K, F and I, G and J   **2. (a)** the last two   **(b)** all three
3. (a) Q   **(b)** R   **4. (a)** PQ   **(b)** QR   **5. (a)** ΔPRQ   **(b)** ∠PTS   **(c)** PQ   **6. (a)** ΔACB, ΔECD
(b) D   **(c)** ∠BCA   **(d)** ED   **(e)** AC   **7. (a)** Yes   **(b)** Yes   **8. (a)** always   **(b)** sometimes
(c) sometimes   **(d)** always   **(e)** always   **(f)** sometimes   **Review 1** Yes; the image on the left and the image third from the left are similar.   **Review 2 (a)** G   **(b)** A   **(c)** EH   **(d)** CB
Review 3 (a) No   **(b)** Yes

Exercise 14:4

1. 12·16m (2 d.p.)   **2. (a)** 4cm   **(b)** 3·6m (1 d.p.)   **3.** 1·8   **4.** 2·4m   **5.** 40cm   **6.** 24cm
7. 15cm   **8.** 4·8cm   **10.** 2m   **11.** 13·3m (1 d.p.)   **Review 1** 8·19m (2 d.p.)   **Review 2** 15·5m
Review 3 9cm

Chapter 14 Review

1. (a) 0·5cm   **(b)** 6cm   **(c)** 72°   **2. (a)** 28cm   **(b) (i)** 6cm   **(ii)** 7cm   **3.** 1·76m (2 d.p.)   **4.** 33·6m
5. 280m   **6. (a)** The triangles are equiangular since ∠A = ∠E (alt. ∠s // lines), ∠B = ∠D
(alt. ∠s // lines), ∠ACB = ∠ECD (3rd ∠ of triangles). **(b)** 3·75m   **7.** They are not similar since lengths of sides are not in the same ratio.   **8. (a)** The triangles are equiangular since ∠B = ∠D
(both 90°), ∠BCA = ∠ECD (vert. opp. ∠s), ∠BAC = ∠DEC (3rd ∠ of triangles).   **(b)** 8·5m
9. 12m   **10. (a) (i)** base ∠s isosc. Δ   **(ii)** The triangles are equiangular since ∠BAC = ∠ACB
(base ∠s isosc. ΔABC), ∠ACB = ∠ADC (base ∠s isosc. ΔADC), ∠ADC = ∠BAC (3rd ∠ of triangles)   **(b)** 1·2m   **11. (a)** 2·5cm   **(b)** 60°   **(c)** 10·8cm (1 d.p.)

Chapter 15   Trigonometry

Page 352   **Exercise 15:2**

1. (a) AC (b) QR (c) EF (d) GH   2. (a) BC (b) PQ (c) DE (d) GI   3. (a) b (b) r (c) DE
4. (a) n (b) m (c) *l*   Review (a) PR (b) LM (c) AB (d) PQ (e) a

Page 355   **Exercise 15:4**

1. (a) PQ (b) QR (c) PR (d) PR (e) PR (f) QR   2. (a) $\frac{4}{5}$ (b) $\frac{12}{13}$ (c) $\frac{15}{17}$ (d) $\frac{7}{25}$
3. (a) $\frac{4}{3}$ (b) $\frac{12}{5}$ (c) $\frac{15}{8}$ (d) $\frac{7}{24}$ 4. (a) $\frac{3}{5}$ (b) $\frac{5}{13}$ (c) $\frac{8}{17}$ (d) $\frac{24}{25}$ 5. (a) sin B = 0·8,
cos C = 0·8, tan B = 1·33 (2 d.p.), sin C = 0·6 (b) cos α = 0·28, tan α = 3·43 (2 d.p.),
sin α = 0·96 (c) tan R = 0·75, sin P = 0·8, cos R = 0·8, tan P = 1·33 (2 d.p.)
Review (a) MN (b) 16 (c) 0·47

Page 356   **Exercise 15:5**

1. 0·342   2. 0·225   3. 1·376   4. 0·325   5. 0·995   6. 0·872   7. 0·913   8. 0·127   9. 1·645
10. 1   11. 0·259   12. 0·574   13. 0·819   14. 0·966   15. 1   16. 0·985   17. 0·5   18. 0
19. 0·035   20. 572·957   Review 1 0·675   Review 2 0·951   Review 3 0·763

Page 359   **Exercise 15:7**

1. (a) cos (b) cos (c) tan (d) sin (e) tan (f) sin (g) tan (h) tan (i) cos (j) sin
2. (a) 51cm (2 s.f.) (b) 1·4km (2 s.f.) (c) 14m (2 s.f.) (d) 72·1mm (3 s.f.) (e) 16m (2 s.f.)
(f) 17km (2 s.f.) (g) 16·0 (3 s.f.) (h) 20m (2 s.f.) (i) 4·4km (2 s.f.) (j) 19cm (2 s.f.)
3. 1·8m (2 s.f.)   4. 3·7m (2 s.f.)   5. 5·74m (2 d.p.)   6. (a) 8·9m (2 s.f.) (b) 10·6cm (1 d.p.)
(c) 50·4mm (1 d.p.) (d) 1·76km (3 s.f.)   7. 2366m (to the nearest metre)   8. (a) 28mm (2 s.f.)
(b) 4·35m (3 s.f.) (c) 3·1cm (2 s.f.) (d) 8·2cm (2 s.f.)   Review 1 0·91m (2 s.f.)
Review 2 (a) 18m (2 s.f.) (b) 54cm (2 s.f.) (c) 10cm (2 s.f.) (d) 51·3mm (3 s.f.) (e) 50m (2 s.f.)
(f) 6·6m (2 s.f.) (g) 11·5km (3 s.f.)

Page 364   **Exercise 15:9**

1. (a) 56·1° (b) 62·5° (c) 43·4° (d) 86·1° (e) 20·2° (f) 34·6° (g) 89·0° (h) 82·8° (i) 39·4°
(j) 14·5° (k) 21·8° (l) 48·2° (m) 57·3° (n) 46·7°   2. (a) tan (b) sin (c) cos (d) sin (e) cos
(f) tan (g) sin (h) cos (i) tan (j) tan   3. (a) 42° (b) 28° (c) 44° (d) 23° (e) 38° (f) 50°
(g) 48° (h) 63° (i) 41° (j) 57°   4. 5·7° (1 d.p.)   5. 50·3° (1 d.p.)   6. 61·3° (1 d.p.)
Review 1 (a) 47° (b) 70° (c) 53° (d) 17° (e) 70° (f) 68°   Review 2 15° (to the nearest degree)

Page 367   **Exercise 15:11**

1. (a) 51° (to the nearest degree) (b) 309° (c) 13km (to the nearest km)   2. (a) P (b) 32km
(to the nearest km)   3. (a) 34° (b) 128km (to the nearest km) (c) 190km (to the nearest km)
4. (a) 40° (b) 19km (to the nearest km) (c) 25km (to the nearest km)   5. (a) 162km (to the
nearest km) (b) 32° (to the nearest degree); the bearing is 328°   Review (a) 97km (to the
nearest km) (b) 60° (to the nearest degree) (c) 030°

Answers

Exercise 15:12

1. 15m (to the nearest metre)   2. 10m   3. 36m (to the nearest metre)   4. 47m (to the nearest metre)   5. 13m (to the nearest metre)   6. (a) 2702m (to the nearest metre)   (b) 1588m (to the nearest metre)   (c) 20° (to the nearest degree)   7. (a) 13·1m (to the nearest metre)
(b) BC = 9·9m (to the nearest metre); height of flagpole = 3·2m   8. (a) **Step 1:** find angle WET.
Step 2: find ET. **Step 3:** Use trigonometry to find WT.   (b) 48m (to the nearest metre)
Review 1 7 metres (to the nearest metre)   **Review 2** (a) 5m   (b) 8m (to the nearest metre)
(c) HF needs to be calculated. TH and HF need to be added.   (d) 10m (to the nearest metre)
Review 3 (a) 48·62m (2 d.p.)   (b) BC = 45m (to the nearest metre). Distance between the houseboats = 99m (to the nearest metre).

Chapter 15 Review

1. 10m (2 s.f.)   2. (a) 168 feet (3 s.f.)   (b) 111 feet (3 s.f.)   3. 14m (2 s.f.)   4. (a) 12·4m (1 d.p.)
(b) 72° (to nearest degree)   5. (a) 3623m (4 s.f.)   (b) 4° (to the nearest degree)   6. (a) 8·6 km
(b) 37·4°   (c) 5·15km   7. (a) 4·44cm (3 s.f.)   (b) 7·6cm (2 s.f.)   8. (a) (i) 373·4m (1 d.p.)   (ii) 20°
(to the nearest degree)   (b) 200m (3 s.f.)   9. (a) 2013m (4 s.f.)   (b) 4° (to the nearest degree)
10. (a) 40·3° (1 d.p.)   11. (a) 60·4°   (b) (i) 49·0°   (ii) 1·19m   12. (a) 17,000 feet   (b) 40 miles
(2 s.f.)   13. (a) 38·1m (1 d.p.)   (b) 4·5° (1 d.p.)   (c) 12·7m (1 d.p.)   (d) 697·5m^3
14. (a) 75·6° (3 s.f.)   (b) 5·21m^2 (3 s.f.)   15. (b) (i) $\angle$PRQ + 32° = 57° (ext. $\angle$ of Δ)
(ii) 15·0m (3 s.f.)   (c) 12·6m (3 s.f.)

Chapter 16   Shape, Space and Measures Review

1. (i) (a) 0·92   (b) 0·42   (c) 0·92   (ii) (a) 74·9°   (b) 78·7°   (c) 23·6°   2. The largest and smallest
diagrams are similar.   3. 3·5m (1 d.p.)   4. (a) B   (b) A and C   5. Dimension for area must be
L^2. Dimension for $\frac{1}{3}\pi r^2 h$ is L^3.   6. 20cm   7. 0·5cm   8. 5·5° (1 d.p.)   9. 32·7m
10. 6·85m (2 d.p.)   11. (a) 124km (to the nearest kilometre)   (b) angle PQR; 064°   12. (a) 0·3m
(b) 0·14m (2 d.p.)   (c) 76·8° (1 d.p.)   13. (a) $3r^2 l + \frac{1}{2}\pi r^2 l$ (b) $3r^2 + \frac{1}{2}\pi r^2$ (c) $6r + \pi r$
14. (a) 31°   (b) 200m (to the nearest metre)   (c) 333m (to the nearest metre)   15. 3·2m
16. (a) 8·8m (2 s.f.)   (b) 2 s.f. since one of the measurements given is just to 2 s.f.
17. (a) 9·6cm (2 s.f.)   (b) 51° (to nearest degree)18. V = $\frac{1}{6}$bh $(3l + x^2)$ cannot be correct since $3l$,
dimension length, cannot be added to x^2, dimension (length)^2. V = $\frac{1}{6}$b^{2}h $(3l + x)$ cannot be
correct since this has dimension (length)^4.   19. 10cm   20. (a) 63cm   (b) 17° (to nearest
degree)   21. (a) 4·5m (2 s.f.)   (b) 6·1m (2 s.f.)   (c) 26° (to the nearest degree)   22. $\pi(a + b)l$ and
πab   23. (a) 50·0°   (b) 29·7°   (c) (i) 218mm   (ii) 335mm   (iii) 833mm   24. (a) 9·6m   (b) 3
25. (a) 10·3cm (1 d.p.)   (c) 5·4cm   (d) 58·5° (1 d.p.)   26. 712m (to nearest metre)   27. ab and
$4\pi r l$ 28. (a) 28·6mm (1 d.p.)   (b) 12·6mm (1 d.p.)   29. (a) (i) 50°
(ii) $\angle$ sum of Δ, $\angle$s in isosc. Δ (b) (i) 59·2cm (1 d.p.)   (ii) 44·16cm   (iii) 52° (to nearest degree)
(c) 60·8cm (1 d.p.)

HANDLING DATA ANSWERS

Handling Data Revision

Revision Exercise

1. (a) $\frac{353}{1000}$ (b) $\frac{643}{1000}$

2. (a)

(b) Lorry 30°, Bus 18°, Car 168°, Motorbike 42°, Bicycle 102°

3. Possible questions are:

Do you wear glasses or contact lenses to read?

Always ☐   Sometimes ☐   Never ☐

How many books did you read last month?

More than 4 ☐ 4 ☐ 3 ☐ 2 ☐ 1 ☐ 0 ☐

4. (a) Graph 3 (b) Graph 1 (c) Graph 2 5. (a) HHH, HHT, HTH, THH, HTT, THT, TTH,

TTT (b) $\frac{1}{2}$ 6. (a) $\frac{1}{3}$ (b) $\frac{5}{12}$ (c) $\frac{1}{6}$ (d) $\frac{3}{4}$ (e) 1 (f) 0 (g) $\frac{7}{12}$

7.

9. Calais: mean midday temperature = 17·7°C (1 d.p.), range = 8°C   Carlisle: mean = 18·3°C (1 d.p.),

range = 4°C   11. $\frac{3}{8}$ 12. (a) positive correlation

(b) negative correlation (c) positive correlation

(d) no correlation (e) no correlation 13. (i) (a) 11

(b) 210 (c) 19·1 trees (1 d.p.) (d) 18 and 20

(e) 19 trees (f) 8 trees

13. (ii)

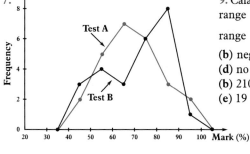

(iii) (a)

Class interval	1m -	2m -	3m -	4m -	5m - 6m
Mid-point	1·5m	2·5m	3·5m	4·5m	5·5m
Frequency	6	24	84	87	9

(b) 3·8m (1 d.p.) (c) 3m–4m

(d) 4m–5m (e) 3·9m (1 d.p.)

14. (a)
(b)

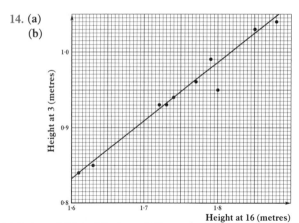

(c) about 0·89m (d) about 1·83m   15. Both are correct. The events are exhaustive since one of them must happen. The events are mutually exclusive since they cannot happen together.
16. Conclusions such as the following could be made: It seems that both the lights and the music are of equal importance since the same number ranked lights as 1 or 2 as ranked music 1 or 2. The lights and the music seem to be of much greater importance than the decoration or service since only about 34% ranked decoration as 1 or 2 and only about 38% ranked service as 1 or 2.

17. (a)

Number of calls	Tally	Frequency
0 – 4	ЖЖ ЖЖ |||	13
5 – 9	ЖЖ |||	8
10 – 14	ЖЖ	5
15 – 19	|||	3
20 – 24		
25 – 29			1

(b) A possible answer is – only one person made more than 19 calls and this person made 29.   18. (a) D (b) C

19. (a) $\frac{5}{17}$ (b) 2·01m (c) 1·92m (d) 1·61m (2 d.p.)

20. Possible questions and responses are:

How far from the Superstore do you live?
   less than 1 km ☐   between 1 and 2 km ☐   more than 2 km ☐

How often have you visited the Superstore in the last week?
   1 ☐   2 ☐   3 ☐   4 ☐   5 ☐   more than 5 ☐

How much did you spend today?
   less than £10 ☐   between £10 and £20 ☐   more than £20 ☐

21. (a) No. Range for London is 16, range for Kos is 17.
(b)

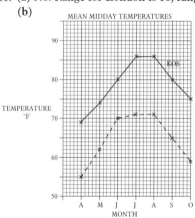

(c) (i) 84°F (ii) There is no reason why the mean for any 7 days should be the same as the mean for 31 days. 22. (a) (i) 2 (ii) 15·2 (b) Grade B since the average number of boxes not sold is less than for Grade A. 23. (i) Angle for Pacific Ocean is 178° since 360° − 15° − 78° − 89° = 178°. 178° is twice 89°.
(ii) 5·4 million square miles.

24. (a)
(d)

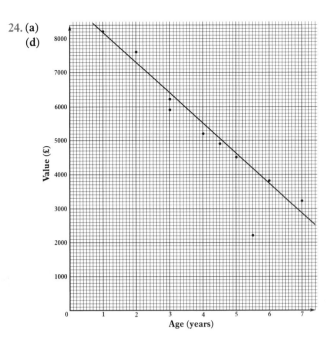

Age (years)

(b) As they get older they decrease in value. **(c)** This car could have been in very poor condition for its age. **(d)** In drawing the line of best fit, the point for the car in poor condition has been ignored. **(e)** about £5900

25. (a)

Height *h* (cm)	Frequency
120 ≤ *h* < 130	7
130 ≤ *h* < 140	22
140 ≤ *h* < 150	20
150 ≤ *h* < 160	4

(b) The "bars" of the graph should be joined. The height of the bar for 130 ≤ *h* < 140 is incorrect. **(c)** the last class interval

26. (a) 61mm **(b) (i)** 352mm **(ii)** 55mm **(c)** the Gambia **(d)** the means are similar but the range in the Gambia is many times that of Great Britain **(e)** 55–65   **27.** Suitable graphs would be a pie graph, a pictogram, a bar chart.   **28. (a)** 4·9 hours **(b)** 5·8 hours (1 d.p.) **(c) (i)** The 10 which failed in less than 1 hour bring the mean down. **(ii)** The mode of 6–7 hours is higher than the mean.   **29. (a)**

Frequency

Height (cm)

(b) There is less variation in the heights of Type A plants. Type A plants tend to be taller than Type B.

30. (a) The mean weight of Phillip's friends is greater than that of Elizabeth's friends.
(b) Elizabeth may have shorter friends on average than Phillip's but she could still have the tallest friend.   **31. (a)** 13 **(b)** 6–10 **(c)** 30   **32. (a)** The question is biased. A better question could be: "The daily paper is value for money." Strongly Agree ☐   Agree ☐   Not Sure ☐
Disagree ☐   Strongly Disagree ☐

(b) The question is too long. Better questions could be:
 1. "Do you take a newspaper?" Yes ☐   No ☐
If your answer to question 1. was Yes, please answer question 2.
If your answer to question 1. was No, please answer question 3.

 2. "When do you take a newspaper?"   Daily ☐   Weekends Only ☐

 3. "How do you keep up with political news?" Radio ☐   TV ☐   Other ☐

33. She is incorrect. For instance, the numbers 1, 1, 8, 9, 10 have mode 1, median 8, mean 5·8.

Chapter 17   Cumulative Frequency

Exercise 17:2

1. **(a)** lower quartile = 14, upper quartile = 24   **(b)** lower quartile = 6, upper quartile = 19
(c) lower quartile = 2, upper quartile = 10   **(d)** lower quartile = 16, upper quartile = 27·5
(e) lower quartile = 4, upper quartile = 12   **(f)** lower quartile = 2·5, upper quartile = 7·5
2. **(a)** 10   **(b)** 13   **(c)** 8   **(d)** 11·5   **(e)** 8   **(f)** 5   3. Mr Benzoni's class: range = 14, median = 13,
lower quartile = 9, upper quartile = 17, interquartile range = 8; Ms Patel's class: range = 8,
median = 12, lower quartile = 10, upper quartile = 14, interquartile range = 4   4. median = 1,
lower quartile = 0, upper quartile = 3, interquartile range = 3, range = 8
Review 1 (a) lower quartile = 8·5, upper quartile = 15·5, interquartile range = 7
(b) lower quartile = 3, upper quartile = 5, interquartile range = 2
Review 2 Girls: lower quartile = 0, upper quartile = 5, interquartile range = 5, median = 2,
range = 13; Boys: lower quartile = 1, upper quartile = 8, interquartile range = 7, median = 2,
range = 11

Exercise 17:3

The answers read from the graphs are approximate answers.

1. **(a)** 30   **(b)** lower quartile = 16, upper quartile = 45   **(c)** 29   **(d)** 15 million   **(e)** 11 million
(f) 4 million   **(g)** 2 million   2. **(a)** (18, 23), (20, 32), (22, 48), (24, 57), (26, 60), (28, 61)
2. **(b)**

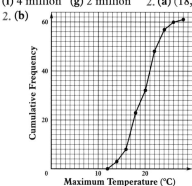

(c) median = 19·5°
lower quartile = 17°
upper quartile = 21·5°
interquartile range = 4·5°

3. **(a)**

Time Spent on Leisure	Cumulative Frequency
< 15	1
< 20	5
< 25	12
< 30	27
< 35	40
< 40	45
< 45	48
< 50	50

(c)

Handspan (mm) less than	Cumulative Frequency
170	2
180	2
190	6
200	16
210	23
220	26
230	27
240	28

3. **(b)**

Weight of fruit (kg)	< 1·0	< 1·5	< 2·0	< 2·5	< 3·0	< 3·5	< 4·0	< 4·5
Cumulative Frequency	6	11	19	26	40	58	85	97

4.(a)

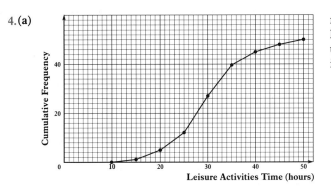

median = 29·5 hours
lower quartile = 25·5 hours
upper quartile = 33·5 hours
interquartile range = 8 hours

(b)

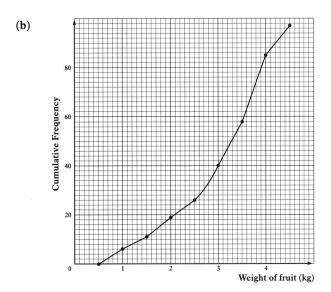

median = 3·25kg
lower quartile = 2·4kg
upper quartile = 3·8kg
interquartile range = 1·4kg

(c)

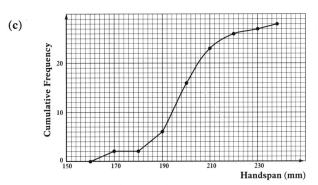

median = 198mm
lower quartile = 191mm
upper quartile = 206mm
interquartile range = 15mm

5.(a)

Length of Rhubarb on Unfertilized Plant (cm)	< 30	< 35	< 40	< 45	< 50	<55
Cumulative Frequency	2	7	15	22	27	30

Length of Rhubarb on Fertilized Plant (cm)	< 30	< 35	< 40	< 45	< 50	<55
Cumulative Frequency	4	6	12	18	27	28

(b)

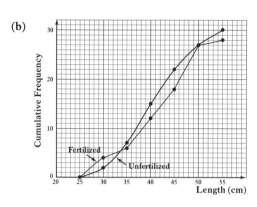

(c) Unfertilized: median = 40cm
  lower quartile = 35·5cm
  upper quartile = 45·5cm
  interquartile range = 10cm
Fertilised: median = 41·5cm
  lower quartile = 36cm
  upper quartile = 46·5cm
  interquartile range = 10·5cm

6. **(i) (a)** Since 98 have lifetimes less than 2000 hours then 2 are still working after 2000 hours of use. **(b)** 1260 hours **(c)** 300 hours **(ii) (a)**
(b) median = 1430 hours
  lower quartile = 1350 hours
  upper quartile = 1520 hours
  interquartile range = 170 hours

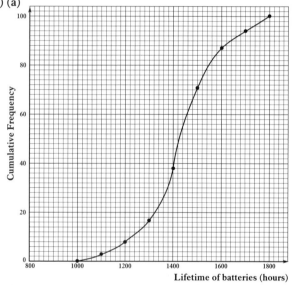

7. **(a)** (240, 10), (250, 22), (260, 31), (270, 38), (280, 40)
(b)

(c) 248 grams **(d)** 19 grams

Review 1 (a)

Variety: Top Tom

Weight (grams)	Cumulative Frequency
< 70	4
< 90	10
< 110	20
< 130	32
< 150	56
< 170	81
< 190	83

Variety: Goliath

Weight (grams)	Cumulative Frequency
< 70	4
< 90	12
< 110	25
< 130	34
< 150	58
< 170	73
< 190	84
< 210	88

(b)

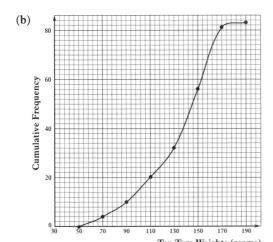

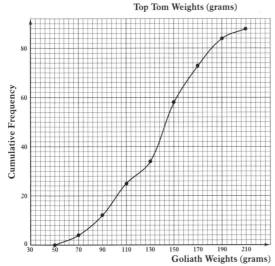

(c) Top Tom: median = 140g
lower quartile = 112g
upper quartile = 153g
interquartile range = 41g
Goliath: median = 140g
lower quartile = 106g
upper quartile = 159g
interquartile range = 53g

Review 2 (a) 10 **(b)** 21 **(c)** 11 **(d)** 60
(e) 15 years **(f)** lower quartile = 7·5 years,
upper quartile = 26·5 years **(g)** 19 years

Page 428

Exercise 17:5

1. (a)

Price (£)	≤ 200	≤ 400	≤ 600	≤ 800	≤ 1000	≤ 1200	≤ 1400	≤ 1600
Cumulative Frequency	1	3	9	17	24	28	33	35

(b)

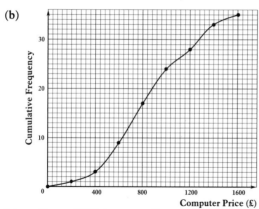

(c) median = £820, interquartile range = £530

2. (a)

Claim (£)	Cumulative Frequency
≤ 100	15
≤ 200	77
≤ 300	166
≤ 400	220
≤ 500	248

(b)

(c) median = £250 **(d)** £150 **(e)** 190

3. (a)

Mark range	≤ 10	≤ 20	≤ 30	≤ 40	≤ 50	≤ 60	≤ 70	≤ 80	≤ 90	≤ 100
Test A cumulative frequency	4	13	28	55	83	115	160	183	194	200
Test B cumulative frequency	7	17	41	70	104	142	173	191	198	200

(b)

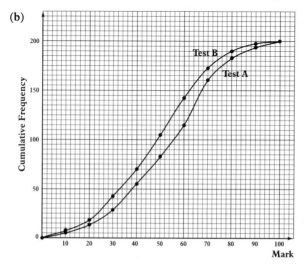

(c) Test A: median = 56, lower quartile = 39, upper quartile = 67, interquartile range = 28
Test B: median = 49, lower quartile = 33, upper quartile = 62, interquartile range = 29

528

Review (a) median = 33, lower quartile = 22, upper quartile = 42, interquartile range = 20

(b)

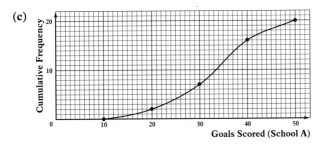

Goals Scored	≤ 10	≤ 20	≤ 30	≤ 40	≤ 50
Cumulative frequency: School A	0	2	7	16	20

(c)

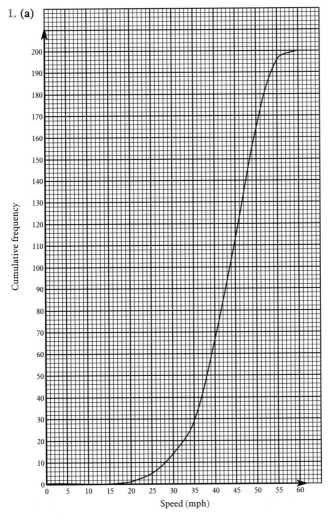

Page 430

CHAPTER 17   REVIEW

Some of your answers may differ slightly from those given.

1. (a)

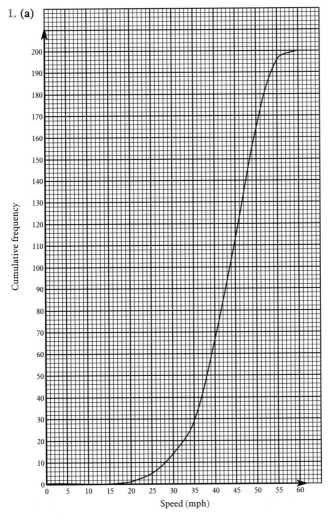

(b) (i) about 44mph
(ii) about 11mph
2. **(a)** 16   **(b)** 32 min
(c) 45 min **(d)** about 24 min
(e) about 21 min
3. **(a)** about $97\frac{1}{2}$ min
(b) about 19 min   **(c)** about 32
4. about 37 inches

529

5. (a) about 45%

(b)

House prices (*p*) in pounds 1993	Cumulative frequency (%)
$0 \leq p < 40\,000$	26
$0 \leq p < 52\,000$	45
$0 \leq p < 68\,000$	67
$0 \leq p < 88\,000$	82
$0 \leq p < 120\,000$	91
$0 \leq p < 160\,000$	96
$0 \leq p < 220\,000$	100

(c)

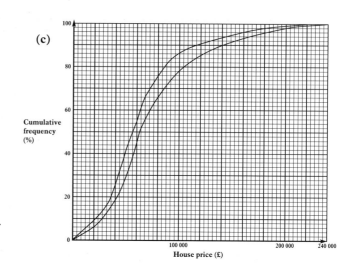

(d) about £82,000. In 1992, 78% were below £100,000; in 1993 78% were below £82,000.

6. (a) 250 **(b) (i)** about 13·35cm **(c)**
(ii) about 1·2cm

(c)

Size (*x* cm)	Frequency
< 11·5	53
< 12·5	143
< 13·5	200
< 14·5	230
< 15·5	250

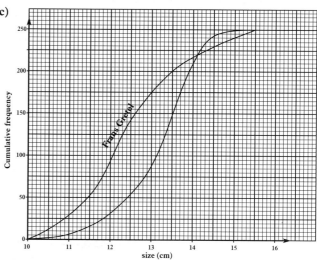

(d) A possible comparison is: Frans Gretel has more smaller bulbs and fewer large bulbs than Van Winkel.

7. (a)

Number of journeys	≤10	≤20	≤30	≤40	≤50	≤60	≤70
Cumulative frequency	4	11	19	25	28	32	32

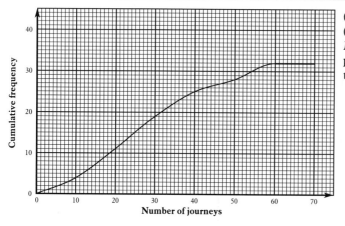

(b) (ii) 26 **(iii)** 5 **(c) (i)** 13
(ii) A possible comparison is –
More of the second group of people made fewer journeys than those in the first group.

Chapter 18   Probability

Exercise 18:1

1. $\frac{2}{3}$ 2. $\frac{2}{13}$ 3. $\frac{1}{2}$ 4. $\frac{1}{3}$ 5. 0·45   6. $\frac{1}{2}$ 7. 0·38   8. (a) 0·4   (b) 0·65   (c) 0·55

9. (a) 0·25   (b) 0·65   10. (a) 0·9   (b) because some patients are both female and school pupils; that is, these are not mutually exclusive   (c) 0·4   (d) 0·62   (e) 90   Review 1 $\frac{2}{3}$

Review 2 (a) 0·65   (b) 0·35   (c) 0·95

Exercise 18:4

1. (a) $\frac{1}{2}$ (b) $\frac{1}{4}$ 2. (a) $\frac{1}{3}$ (b) $\frac{1}{6}$ 3. $\frac{1}{18}$ 4. (a) $\frac{1}{5}$ (b) $\frac{1}{20}$ (c) $\frac{1}{10}$ 5. 0·045   6. 0·06 If they know each other the events are not independent and the probabilities cannot be multiplied.   7. (a) 0·2   (b) 0·03   (c) 0·68   8. (a) $\frac{3}{10}$ (b) $\frac{9}{100}$ 9. (a) $\frac{1}{25}$ (b) $\frac{4}{5}$ (c) $\frac{4}{25}$

Review 1 (a) 0·15   (b) 0·04   If they know each other the events are not independent and the probabilities cannot be multiplied.   Review 2 (a) $\frac{1}{4}$ (b) $\frac{1}{16}$ (c) $\frac{1}{8}$ (d) $\frac{3}{64}$ (e) $\frac{3}{32}$

Exercise 18:5

1. $\frac{5}{18}$ 2. $\frac{1}{6}$ 3. $\frac{1}{9}$ 4. (a) $\frac{1}{4}$ (b) $\frac{1}{4}$ (c) $\frac{3}{4}$ (d) $\frac{1}{2}$ 5. $\frac{1}{6}$ 6. $\frac{1}{4}$ 7. (a) $\frac{1}{16}$ (b) $\frac{1}{169}$

(c) $\frac{1}{104}$ (d) $\frac{1}{4}$ (e) $\frac{1}{2}$ 8. (a) $\frac{16}{25}$ (b) $\frac{7}{25}$ (c) $\frac{12}{25}$ (d) $\frac{131}{200}$ 9. (a) 0·0006   (b) 0·0494

(c) 0·0488   Review 1 (a) $\frac{4}{45}$ (b) $\frac{77}{225}$ (c) $\frac{16}{25}$ (d) $\frac{148}{225}$ Review 2 (a) 0·04   (b) 0·64   (c) 0·32

(d) 0·96

CHAPTER 18   REVIEW

1. (a) No two of these actions can occur at the same time.   (b) 0·3   (c) 0·9   2. (a) 0·8   (b) 0·6 (c) 0·6   (d) because taking a club and taking a 5 are not mutually exclusive   3. 0·75   4. (a) 0·9

(b) 20   5. (a) 0·42   (b) 0·46   6. (a) $\frac{1}{81}$ (b) $\frac{8}{27}$ (c) $\frac{37}{81}$ 7. (a) 0·04   (b) 0·514   8. (a) 0·5

(b) 0·08 (1 s.f.)   9. (a) 0·3   (b) 0·4   10. (a) (i) $\frac{1}{2}$ (ii) $\frac{1}{6}$ (iii) $\frac{1}{3}$ (b) $\frac{1}{36}$ (c) $\frac{1}{18}$

11. (a)

A ✓	B ✓	C ✓
A ✓	B ✓	C ✗
A ✓	B ✗	C ✓
A ✓	B ✗	C ✗
A ✗	B ✓	C ✓
A ✗	B ✗	C ✓
A ✗	B ✓	C ✗
A ✗	B ✗	C ✗

(b) (i) 0·18   (ii) 0·915

12. $\frac{5}{12}$

Chapter 19 Tree Diagrams

Page 463   **Exercise 19:2**

1.
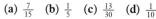

2.
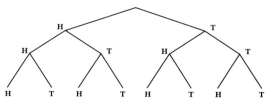

3. If O stands for open, C stands for closed, the possible outcomes are: OOO, OOC, OCO, OCC, COO, COC, CCO, CCC.

4.
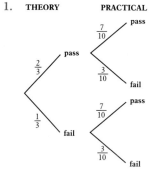

S – soccer H – hockey
V – volleyball R – represents school
NR – doesn't represent school

Review
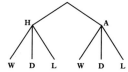

H – home A – away
W – win D – draw
L – lose

Page 466   **Exercise 19:3**

1. THEORY   PRACTICAL
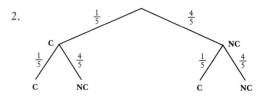

(a) $\frac{7}{15}$ (b) $\frac{1}{5}$ (c) $\frac{13}{30}$ (d) $\frac{1}{10}$

3.
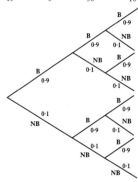

2.

(a) $\frac{1}{25}$ (b) $\frac{8}{25}$ (c) $\frac{9}{25}$

(a) 0·001 (b) 0·243 (c) 0·999

4. (i)

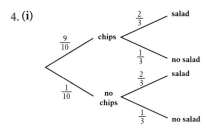

(ii)

1st call   2nd call

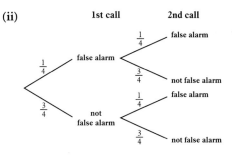

(a) $\frac{3}{5}$ **(b)** $\frac{1}{30}$ **(c)** $\frac{3}{10}$

(a) $\frac{1}{16}$ **(b)** $\frac{9}{16}$ **(c)** $\frac{3}{8}$

(iii)

1st toss 2nd toss

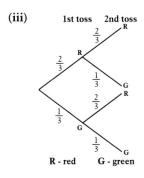

R - red   G - green

(a) $\frac{4}{9}$ **(b)** $\frac{4}{9}$ **(c)** $\frac{5}{9}$

5.

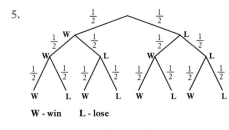

W - win   L - lose

(a) $\frac{1}{8}$ **(b)** $\frac{3}{8}$ **(c)** $\frac{3}{8}$ **(d)** $\frac{1}{2}$

6.

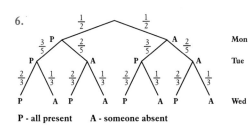

P - all present   A - someone absent

(a) $\frac{1}{5}$ **(b)** $\frac{13}{30}$ **(c)** $\frac{1}{15}$

Review 1

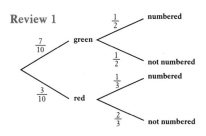

(a) $\frac{1}{10}$ **(b)** $\frac{9}{20}$ **(c)** $\frac{9}{20}$

Review 2

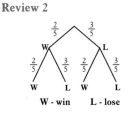

W - win   L - lose

P(wins only 1 game) = $\frac{12}{25}$

Review 3

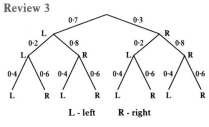

L - left   R - right

(a) 0·056 **(b)** 0·468 **(c)** 0·144 **(d)** 0·388

CHAPTER 19   REVIEW

1. (a)

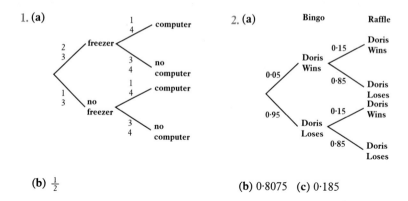

(b) $\frac{1}{2}$

2. (a)

(b) 0·8075   (c) 0·185

3. (a)   **MONDAY**   **TUESDAY**   **WEDNESDAY**   (b) 0·063

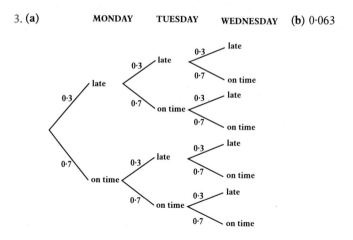

4. (a) 25   (b) (i) 0·2

(ii)

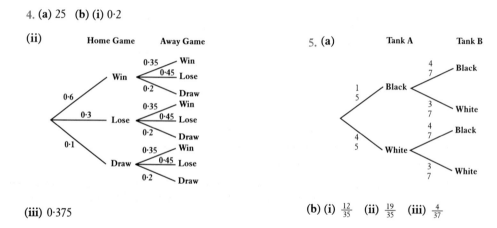

5. (a)

(iii) 0·375

(b) (i) $\frac{12}{35}$ (ii) $\frac{19}{35}$ (iii) $\frac{4}{37}$

Answers

Chapter 20   Handling Data Review

Page 473

1. median = 21·5, range = 8, lower quartile = 20, upper quartile = 23·5, interquartile range = 3·5   2. (a) Yes (b) No

3.

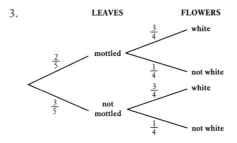

(a) $\frac{3}{10}$ (b) $\frac{3}{20}$ 4. $\frac{1}{12}$ 5. (a) 0·4 (b) 0·6 (c) 0·66 (d) 0·74   6. (a) 56 (b) 20 (c) 50 (d) 30
(e) 65 min (f) lower quartile = 57 min, upper quartile = 77 min (g) 20 min   7. a possible tree diagram is:

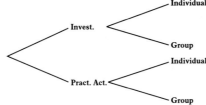

8. (a) $\frac{1}{5}$ (b) $\frac{2}{25}$ (c) $\frac{9}{25}$ (d) $\frac{12}{25}$

9. (i) (a)

Time (min)	Cumulative Frequency
less than 5	3
less than 10	7
less than 15	23
less than 20	47
less than 25	60
less than 30	67

(b)

Mark (%)	Cumulative Frequency
≤ 20	2
≤ 40	7
≤ 60	16
≤ 80	23
≤ 100	27

(c)

Distance (km)	< 1·5	< 2·0	< 2·5	< 3·0	< 3·5	< 4·0	< 4·5	< 5·0
Cumulative Frequency	4	8	17	29	40	57	67	73

(ii) (a) (0, 0), (5, 3), (10, 7), (15, 23), (20, 47), (25, 60), (30, 67) (b) (0, 0), (20, 2), (40, 7), (60, 16), (80, 23), (100, 27) (c) (1·0, 0), (1·5, 4), (2·0, 8), (2·5, 17), (3·0, 29), (3·5, 40), (4·0, 57), (4·5, 67), (5·0, 73)

(iii)

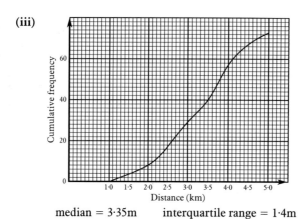

median = 3·35m   interquartile range = 1·4m

10. (a) 0·003 **(b)** 0·873 **(c)** 0·124

11. (a)

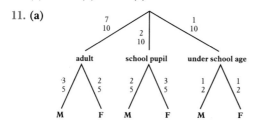

(b) $\frac{7}{25}$ **12. (i) (a)**

House Prices (£)	
Price	Cumulative Frequency
below 40,000	5
below 60,000	13
below 80,000	28
below 100,000	42
below 120,000	66
below 140,000	82
below 160,000	91
below 180,000	94
below 200,000	96

(b)

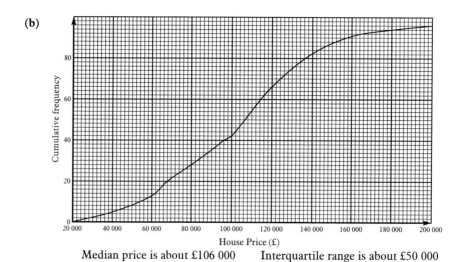

Median price is about £106 000   Interquartile range is about £50 000

(ii) In David's district, median is about £92 000, lower quartile is about £76 000, upper quartile is about £110 000, interquartile range is about £34 000. These figures should be included in the comparison.

13. (a) $\frac{27}{1000}$ **(b)** $\frac{441}{1000}$ **(c)** $\frac{657}{1000}$ **(d)** $\frac{343}{1000}$ **14.** $\frac{7}{12}$

15. (a)

1, 1 Sum 2	1, 2 Sum 3	1, 3 Sum 4	1, 4 Sum 5	1, 5 Sum 6	1, 6 Sum 7
2, 1 Sum 3	2, 2 Sum 4	2, 3 Sum 5	2, 4 Sum 6	2, 5 Sum 7	2, 6 Sum 8
3, 1 Sum 4	3, 2 Sum 5	3, 3 Sum 6	3, 4 Sum 7	3, 5 Sum 8	3, 6 Sum 9
4, 1 Sum 5	4, 2 Sum 6	4, 3 Sum 7	4, 4 Sum 8	4, 5 Sum 9	4, 6 Sum 10
5, 1 Sum 6	5, 2 Sum 7	5, 3 Sum 8	5, 4 Sum 9	5, 5 Sum 10	5, 6 Sum 11
6, 1 Sum 7	6, 2 Sum 8	6, 3 Sum 9	6, 4 Sum 10	6, 5 Sum 11	6, 6 Sum 12

(b) (i) Oxford Street **(ii)** $\frac{8}{9}$ **(c) (i)** $\frac{11}{36}$ **(ii)** $\frac{1}{36}$ **16. (a) (i)** $\frac{107}{200}$ **(ii)** $\frac{93}{200}$ **(iii)** The events "watches Emmerdale", "watches Casualty" are not mutually exclusive; i.e. Bill could watch both.

17. (a)

Temperature (°F)	<62	<65	<68	<71	<74	<77	<80	<83
Cumulative Frequency	0	8	17	28	43	63	69	70

(b)

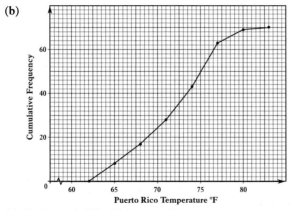

(c) (i) about 72·5°F **(ii)** about 7·5°F
(d) The spread of temperatures in London is greater than in Puerto Rico.
18. (a) 0·6 **(b)** 0·16

19. (a)

Tennis	Snooker

$\frac{5}{8}$ Ahmed wins
$\frac{3}{7}$ Ahmed wins
$\frac{4}{7}$ Kate wins
$\frac{3}{8}$ Kate wins
$\frac{3}{7}$ Ahmed wins
$\frac{4}{7}$ Kate wins

(b) $\frac{3}{14}$ **20. (a) (i)** $\frac{1}{6}$ **(ii)** $\frac{1}{3}$ **(b)** 1 **(c) (i)** $\frac{1}{36}$ **(ii)** $\frac{35}{54}$ **21. (a)** $\frac{1}{20}$ **(b)** $\frac{1}{2}$ **(c)** $\frac{81}{400}$ **(d)** $\frac{9}{20}$

22. (a) (i) 50·1 sec (1 d.p.)   **(ii)** 40 – 50

(b)

	Pricewell	Costsave
median	48·1	46·5
modal class	40 – 50	40 – 50
mean	50·1	46·3

The mean represents the data most fairly. This takes into account the large number of Pricewell customers who took 60 – 70 seconds to serve.

(c) (i)

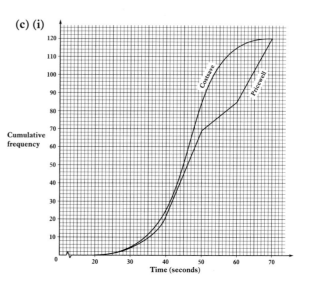

(c) (ii)

	Pricewell	Costsave
lower quartile	42	41
upper quartile	61·5	53
inter-quartile range	19·5	12

(iii) Since the inter-quartile range is greater at Pricewell than Costsave more customers at Pricewell take a longer time to serve.

23. (a) 0·35   **(b) (i)** 0·45   **(ii)** 0·06